BROTHERS IN BLOOD

BROTHERS IN BLOOD

THE INTERNATIONAL TERRORIST NETWORK

OVID DEMARIS

CHARLES SCRIBNER'S SONS · NEW YORK

IN MEMORY OF MY FATHER
ERNEST JOSEPH DESMARAIS

Library of Congress Cataloging in Publication Data
Demaris, Ovid.
  Brothers in blood.
  Includes index.
  1. Terrorism. 2. Terrorists. I. Title.
HV6431.D45   364.1   77–9872
ISBN 0–684–15192–8

1 3 5 7 9 11 13 15 17 19 H/C 20 18 16 14 12 10 8 6 4 2

PRINTED IN THE UNITED STATES OF AMERICA

CONTENTS

BOOK ONE   1

CARLOS

BOOK TWO   65

GENESIS

BOOK THREE   215

THE PEOPLE'S WAR
OF ULRIKE MEINHOF

BOOK FOUR   265

A TERRIBLE BEAUTY

BOOK FIVE   375

APOCALYPSE

INDEX   425

BOOK ONE

CARLOS

Only seconds before the terrorists struck, Vienna's Inspector Anton Tichler was telling Inspector Josef Janda about his retirement plans for an extended Middle Eastern holiday. As a lifelong student of that region's history, Tichler had mastered Arabic and Persian, a specialty that was not overlooked by his superiors. When the Shah of Iran came to Austria for his yearly medical checkup, Tichler was detailed to provide security and liaison. And when the Organization of Petroleum Exporting Countries (OPEC) had selected Vienna as the site for its biannual conference, Tichler had been the first to be assigned to the security detail. For a man of sixty, he appeared to be in splendid physical condition. By comparison, Janda, a burly man with a ready smile, looked more like a successful farmer than a policeman.

The OPEC headquarters were located in a modest seven-story structure at Dr. Karl Lueger-Ring 10, one of the busiest boulevards in Vienna. Known as the Texaco Building because of that company's large electric sign over the door, it was also occupied by a branch of the Vienna Municipality Administration, the Canadian embassy, the offices of two private firms, and a private apartment. Access to all floors was provided by three self-service elevators and two staircases equipped with heavy steel doors, in compliance with Austrian fire regulations.

The first thing a visitor saw upon entering the anteroom to OPEC's quarters on the second floor was a floor-to-ceiling wall of glass bricks and a sliding glass door leading to the reception area. Once inside reception, the visitor was greeted by Edith Heller, the tall, ash-blond receptionist. Corridors to the right and left of her desk led to staff offices, the communications room, and the conference chamber.

Sunday, December 21, 1975, was bitterly cold in Vienna. The city lay under a thick mantle of snow. Beginning on Friday that week, there had been an exodus to ski resorts for the Christmas holiday. Even Tichler, who was working his last shift that morning before his retirement, was planning on taking his wife to Switzerland when he came off duty at one o'clock.

Eleven oil ministers and their delegations had convened at 10:50 A.M. with an agenda that included questions concerning the fixing of a new oil price. A group of journalists had assembled in the lobby downstairs to await developments. Just outside the front door, a uniformed policeman stood talking to a correspondent for an American publication.

At about 11:40 A.M., five young men and a woman, all carrying Adidas

3

sports bags, came to the door and asked the correspondent if the conference was still in progress. Although he had no reason for suspicion, the correspondent watched them wend their way across the small lobby to the far flight of stairs. The one who had addressed the correspondent appeared to be the leader. He wore a Basque beret and an open white trench coat over a brown leather jacket. He was above average height and had long, curly hair, with wide sideburns down to his jawline, a moustache, and just the beginning of a goatee. As he turned sideways to wait for the others, his silhouette reminded the reporter of Che Guevara. The woman, who seemed barely out of her teens and very petite, had pulled a gray woolen ski cap so tightly over her head that it completely covered her hair. The last man to disappear behind the red steel door was small and dark, with a moustache and long black hair that curled up on his neck. He wore a big fur hat. It occurred to the correspondent that they were an unlikely group for OPEC people, but it was only a passing thought, certainly not anything worth repeating to the policeman.

What he did not know, of course, was that the young man in the beret was Ilich Ramírez Sánchez, who at that moment was the most famous—and most wanted—terrorist in the world. Known universally by the pseudonym of Carlos Martínez Torres, the world press, in imitation of British journalists, had taken to calling him "The Jackal," after the main character in Frederick Forsyth's thriller *The Day of the Jackal.* If anyone truly epitomized the mobility and diversity of international terrorism it was this twenty-six-year-old multilingual Venezuelan. His escapades, as we shall see, revealed connections between terrorist groups in Asia, the Middle East, Africa, Europe, and South America. Among his known exploits were the bombing of Le Drugstore in Paris, the firing of RPG-7 missiles at an El Al airliner at Orly Airport, the murder of two French intelligence officers and the Lebanese informer who had brought them to his Latin Quarter apartment, and the plotting of some of the most bizarre terrorist ventures in recent years. As a good luck charm that day, he wore a light blue roll-neck shirt, a gift from Dr. George Habash, his mentor and leader of the Popular Front for the Liberation of Palestine (PFLP), one of the most radical of the terrorist groups constituting the Arab Rejection Front, which has sworn never to negotiate with Israel.

The girl in the ski cap was Gabriele Kroecher-Tiedemann, a twenty-three-year-old member of West Germany's Baader-Meinhof gang, whose terroristic activities had begun at an early age. Identified in a Berlin bank robbery in February 1972, she was apprehended fifteen months later after a gun battle with police. She was sentenced to eight years in prison, but on March 3, 1975, she and four other prisoners were flown to Aden, the capital of South Yemen, as part of the ransom paid by the government for the release of Peter Lorenz, the leader of West Berlin's Christian Democratic party, who had been kidnapped by the Second of June Movement, a younger offshoot of the Baader-Meinhof gang. Her presence in Vienna marked her first public appearance since receiving asylum in Aden.

Upstairs on the second floor, at precisely that moment, Tichler was telling Janda about his retirement plans. Both men were in plain clothes and each was armed with a lightweight Walther PPK automatic in a quick-draw holster. They were standing in the anteroom near the sliding glass door, in animated conversation, while inside the reception room Edith Heller was struggling to stay awake in a room with a dozen people smoking and chatting all around her.

There was a buzz and she turned to the small telephone switchboard to the right of her desk. "Good morning, OPEC," she said in English. Tichler chose that moment to walk toward the elevators. When Heller looked up from her switchboard, men with guns were swarming through the place. Tichler, she noticed through the open glass door, was standing by the elevators with his hands up, and a young man in a Basque beret, whom she would later describe as "a tall, handsome man with curly brownish-blond hair," was pointing a Beretta machine pistol at his midsection. Then all hell broke loose.

Shots were fired and people in the reception room scrambled behind chairs and a black leather couch. Someone motioned for Heller to drop behind her desk, which she did, taking the telephone with her. There is no record at the Federal Police Directorate of her call, but people crouching on the floor beside her marveled at her courage when she screamed into the phone, "This is OPEC! They're shooting all over the place! OPEC! OPEC! This is OPEC!" Then she saw a pistol only inches away, and before she could see the face of the terrorist leaning over the desk, the gun went off and a bullet passed straight through the telephone into the floor. Two more shots destroyed the switchboard. Ears ringing from the shots, Edith Heller could not believe she was still alive.

Anton Tichler was not that fortunate. As a young policeman, he had been taught a special judo hold to disarm a man holding a weapon at close range. Under the best of conditions, it was a risky maneuver. It required great speed and strength, not to mention courage. For those who knew Tichler, there was no doubt that he was a proud and brave man. Yet Janda was shocked when he saw Tichler seize the barrel of the Beretta machine pistol. For a moment it looked like the old man might succeed in wresting the weapon out of the surprised terrorist's hands. But the thickset young man recovered quickly. Now both men were fighting for their lives. Tichler held on as long as he could, but it was an unequal contest. With a violent twisting motion, Carlos wrenched the weapon out of Tichler's hands, the movement sending both men staggering in opposite directions like contestants letting go in a tug-of-war.

As the momentum carried Carlos into the reception room, Tichler stumbled toward one of the elevators just as the doors were opening. What happened next was witnessed by the coffee-trolley lady standing in the elevator facing Tichler. From the expressions on their faces, both were terrified. There was no question that Tichler knew he was in serious trouble. Just as he was stepping into the elevator, Gabriele came up behind him and asked in English, "Are you a policeman?"

"Yes," said Tichler, as he began to raise his hands over his head without turning to face the girl, who at that moment was taking careful aim at the back of his neck. The bullet entered just below the hairline, and Tichler dropped at her feet, dying. With a motion of her gun, she sent the terrified coffee-trolley lady screaming into the reception room, to hide under Edith Heller's desk. Gabriele then pulled Tichler's body into the elevator and with a perverse theatrical touch, she sent it down to the ground floor. A Lenin axiom: "The product of terror is terror." Tichler's pistol was still in its fast-draw holster, unfired, when he was found.

Ala Hassan Saeed al-Khafari, the Iraqi oil minister's bodyguard, was also a proud man. It did not take this tall, slender young man long to decide on a course of action. Just as Gabriele turned away from the elevator, Hassan grabbed her right arm and tried to twist the gun out of her hand. For Janda, who had passively witnessed Tichler's fate, there was no question that Hassan was stronger and quicker than Tichler and that the girl was weaker than Carlos, but it was still a futile gamble. As soon as Gabriele realized that he might get the best of her, she reached inside her clothing with her left hand, pulled out a second pistol, and shot Hassan in the face.

At that moment, Carlos grabbed Janda by the arm and ran him down the corridor leading to the conference room, firing shots into the ceiling as they went until bullets hit the wiring, extinguishing the corridor lights. Carlos pushed Janda into a staff office and closed the door. Making his way cautiously down the darkened corridor, lit only by dim emergency lights, he stopped to investigate another office only to come face to face with Yousef Ismirli, a member of the Libyan delegation.

There was madness in the air that morning. Ismirli's first impulse when he saw Carlos was to yank at his machine pistol so fiercely that it came out of his grasp. Only the shoulder strap prevented Ismirli from gaining complete control of the weapon. But again it was a hopeless gesture. Carlos pulled a pistol from his waistband and in a fit of rage fired five times—one of the bullets passing through Ismirli's body struck the right arm of a member of the Kuwaiti delegation.

The first thing Janda did was to hide his pistol and holster in a desk drawer. Then he telephoned for assistance. The taped emergency call was timed at 11:45 A.M. and the shots that killed Ismirli can be heard on the recording.

The first terrorist to reach the conference room was Yusef, the one in the big fur hat. He pointed his submachine gun at the ceiling and fired several rounds. Everybody hit the floor simultaneously, including Sheik Ahmed Zaki Yamani, the oil minister for Saudi Arabia.

"Suddenly there were shots fired inside the conference hall," Yamani later recalled. "I turned toward the door and saw two gunmen with masked faces. Together with my colleagues I dropped under the conference table, hoping it would protect us from flying bullets. First I thought that our attackers were Europeans dissatisfied with the rise in oil prices, who had resolved to take their revenge on those believed responsible for the rise. I was sure that I was destined to die.

"I heard a terrorist say in Arabic with a foreign accent, 'Yusef, put the explosive there on the table!' " Charges of explosive plastique, primed and wired for detonation, were set in the middle of the large conference table. A Trotsky axiom: "Intimidation is a useful tool."

"Another one," said Yamani, "was asking in English, 'Have you found Yamani?' The Gabonese oil minister looked at me with pity when one of the terrorists began to examine our faces. When his eyes met mine, he saluted me sarcastically and went to inform his colleagues." This terrorist, whose name was Khaled, was the second in command.

Yamani stayed under the table while other hostages were herded into the room and instructed to "get down, *down.*"

"The two terrorists in the room left when two others entered," Yamani said. "One was a girl in her early twenties. She said to her boss, and she was smiling, 'I have killed two,' to which he laughed and replied, 'Right, so I have killed one myself.' Then he pointed at me and declared in Arabic with a foreign accent that they were Palestinian commandos on a mission to enforce certain demands. Their operation, he said, was directed against Iran and the kingdom of Saudi Arabia, and he asked for the cooperation of all in their very own interest."

When he first saw Carlos, Yamani became convinced that the terrorists were actually Israeli secret agents, members of the Israeli counterterrorist Ha Mossad assassin squads, who were waging a secret and deadly war against Palestinian terrorists in streets and alleys all over the world. When later told of this, Carlos would comment, "It's not my fault that I have the face of a Jew."

It took the police a flat five minutes to respond to Janda's call. A squad of the Einsatz Kommandos (SWAT team), in steel helmets and flak jackets and armed with Israeli Uzi submachine guns, surrounded the building while three Kommandos stormed one of the staircases in an attempt to gain access to the second floor. Within an hour, there were five hundred armed men in the area.

A fire-fight broke out between Hans-Joachim Klein, another Baader-Meinhof terrorist, and Kommando Kurt Leopolder, a Wehrmacht veteran, who got as far as the body of Hassan, which was lying in the anteroom a few feet from the sliding glass door. As Leopolder turned him over to see if he were still alive, Klein opened fire from the conference room corridor. Leopolder rolled away and squeezed off a full magazine in Klein's direction. One of Leopolder's bullets ricocheted off the wall, impacted against Klein's machine pistol, and fragmented into his stomach. There was a cry and the firing stopped. A moment later the firing started again and Leopolder was hit in the buttocks. Then, to his amazement, a grenade exploded in the corridor, followed by Klein's warning, in English, "Get out or everybody will be killed." Leopolder painfully crawled back to the staircase and the attack was abandoned. By 12:02 P.M. all seventy-one hostages were firmly in the hands of the terrorists.

While Sheik Yamani "kept silent, reading verses of the Koran suited to this occasion," Carlos began what would eventually consist of twenty hours of negotiations with the Austrian government. As his first courier, he singled out Grizelda Carey, the English secretary to the OPEC secretary-general. She was asked to copy a handwritten note addressed to Austrian authorities demanding that a six-page propaganda communiqué be broadcast over the Austrian radio network (ORF) every two hours and that a bus, with its windows curtained, be outside at seven the next morning to transport them and the hostages to the Vienna airport where a DC-9 airliner should be ready for departure. In the event of any delay the hostages would be shot at intervals of fifteen minutes. It was signed "The Arm of the Arab Revolution."

The communiqué, which was in French, was typical of the revolutionary rhetoric expounded by the various factions of the Arab Rejection Front, whose goal is nothing less than the total dismantling of Israel. There was, according to the front, a "powerful plot" aimed at "bringing about the capitulation of the Arab Peoples to Zionism." The plot was twofold: to break the Palestinian liberation movement's resistance and to promote "the splitting up of Arab unity by means of including, among other activities, the staging of religious conflicts, as in Lebanon."

The structure of the Palestine Liberation Organization will be gone into later in this book, but suffice it to say at this point that although all the Palestinian guerrilla groups are officially members of the PLO—it is an umbrella organization—a militant faction withdrew in 1974 from the PLO Executive Committee to form the Arab Rejection Front, which opposes Yasir Arafat's diplomatic efforts to create an embryonic Palestinian state that would coexist with Israel. Arafat's forgotten battle cry of driving the Israelis into the sea remains the goal of the Rejection Front.

Participants in this plot, according to Carlos's communiqué, included not only "American imperialism" and "Zionist aggressors" but also "several Arab governments who are prepared to capitulate." The latter—with particular reference to Egypt's president, Anwar el-Sadat, and the regime in Iran—were "traitors to both the Arab and the Palestinian cause, while the governments of Syria and Iraq, the most progressive of Arab regimes, are acting in support of the Arab peoples."

The communiqué then went on to enumerate familiar demands:

The Arm of the Arab Revolution demands renewed confirmation of observance of the three principles laid down at the Arab summit of Khartoum: "No negotiations, no treaty, and no recognition to be granted to the Zionist aggressor state!" . . . [We refuse to] recognize any compromise or plan for the achievement of peaceful solutions to the Middle East conflict. We denounce the opening of the Suez Canal to Israeli ships. We demand the renewal of the triumphal advance of the heroic Egyptian army in the framework of a war for total liberation. We demand that oil resources in the Arab world be nationalized, and that economic support be given to the peoples of the Third World allied in friendship, but on the condition that priority be given to Palestinian resistance.

All political elements and forces close to the Peoples' efforts as well as all governments are invited to act speedily and frankly in taking a stand on these serious questions, on which depend both the future destiny of the loyal camp and the fate of the camp of national treason.

In conclusion, The Arm of the Arab Revolution apologizes for the difficulties which our action has caused to the peace-loving Austrian people, and we ask them to understand the earnest and noble motives of this action. The Arm of the Arab Revolution is a movement uniting the fighting elements in all Arab countries which, expressing the rise of national consciousness and carried by the deep understanding of the Arab Peoples' fate and future, has resolved on counteracting the imperialist-Zionist plot, striking down its supporters, and applying the sanctions of revolution to all personalities and parties involved in this plot.

After Grizelda Carey was dispatched on her mission, Carlos turned his attention to Klein, who was stretched out on a chair with his shirt rolled up to reveal a small black hole just below his naval. Klein seemed quite surprised that there was no blood. Carlos patted him affectionately on the side of the head. Klein seemed a neophyte. A check of his background revealed that he had previously worked in Stuttgart as a messenger for Klaus Croissant, who was Andreas Baader's attorney until the court disqualified him. Klein's big moment was in 1974. He got to chauffeur Jean-Paul Sartre around Stuttgart when the French philosopher went to visit members of the Baader-Meinhof gang in their prison block at Stammheim, a prison built especially to house them at a cost of $6 million. Klein, who had been born in Frankfurt on December 21, 1947, had a police record that included charges of aggravated robbery, attempted arson, attempted housebreaking, and consorting with criminals.

"We've got to get you to a hospital," Carlos said. "That wound needs looking after." Klein jumped up and started walking around the room as if to show he was fine, but the effort immediately exhausted him. He sat down again and suddenly pulled off the balaclava mask he had put on before entering the conference room. His face was pale and his hair soaked in perspiration. "Don't worry," Carlos said, "you'll be on the plane with us when we leave."

Edith Heller was sent to make arrangements for Klein's hospitalization. Getting back to the business at hand, Carlos's first choice for a mediator in his negotiations with Austrian authorities was the Libyan ambassador. To voice his request to the police waiting in the lobby, Carlos sent Algerian Oil Minister Belaid Abdesselam with instructions that he return promptly after delivering his message. When it was discovered that the Libyan ambassador was in Prague, the Iraqi chargé d'affaires, Riyadh al-Azzawi, offered his services.

Bearing in mind the radical politics of Iraq, it occurred to some that al-Azzawi's presence in the OPEC lobby was a little too convenient for comfort. But one only has to meet this young diplomat to know that it was not a conspiracy but a genuine desire to help that immediately took him to the scene when he heard of the attack. His selection as mediator was beneficial to both sides.

The first thing al-Azzawi saw when he came down the dimly lit corridor leading to the conference room were two men with submachine guns and pistols. Abdesselam was escorted back into the conference room, and al-Azzawi was taken into one of the staff offices and searched for weapons.

Carlos spoke in English. "I am the leader of this operation," he said and went on to repeat the earlier written demands submitted through Grizelda Carey. "I want you to tell the Austrian authorities that if they don't do everything I ask, I will kill all the people we have, Austrians and Arabs."

Al-Azzawi's normally pleasant, round face—with features that are more puckish than handsome—grew suddenly determined. "I can't do that," he said, trying to maintain a level of dignity in his voice. "I don't know you. I have to know who I'm dealing with, where you're from—what do you want from this?"

Instead of getting angry, Carlos said, "We are revolutionaries, not criminals. We work for the Arab revolution all over the world."

"But you're not an Arab," al-Azzawi countered.

"That is of no importance. Many people believe in the revolution."

Al-Azzawi looked closely at this man with the aquiline features, who spoke English with a Spanish accent. It was all very strange. "But we have many Arab people who can do everything the revolution needs."

Carlos thoughtfully stroked his scraggly goatee as he studied al-Azzawi. "Not all Arabs are good revolutionaries," he said, "but I have much admiration for the Iraqi people. They are good liberals."

Al-Azzawi, who is given to nervous smiles, could not suppress one now. "How can you be a revolutionary when you kill innocent people?"

Carlos refrained from reminding al-Azzawi of another revolutionary axiom: There are no innocent people—one is either part of the solution, or part of the problem. Instead he said, "We were defending ourselves. We had to attack OPEC and they tried to stop us."

Al-Azzawi knew about the death of the policeman Tichler, but he had no idea what had transpired in the conference room. "As the chargé d'affaires of Iraq, I have to know if our delegation is alive. I want to speak to my delegation." Al-Azzawi knew he was speaking bluntly. He wished he could have tempered his words, but English was such a poor diplomatic language.

He was surprised then when Carlos apologized, saying that the girl who killed Hassan had had no recourse, because he had tried to disarm her. Then Carlos left and came back with the Iraqi oil minister, who explained in rapid Arabic about the two Arabs killed and went on to urge extreme caution, pointing out that the terrorists were extremely dangerous. As he saw it, they had no choice but to comply with their every demand.

After the oil minister left, Carlos repeated his instructions for the Austrian authorities, and before al-Azzawi departed, he said, "Tell them I'm from Venezuela and my name is Carlos. Tell them I'm the famous Carlos. They know me."

This was the beginning of a busy nineteen hours for al-Azzawi, who was to make countless trips between OPEC and the chancellery, where Austrian Chancellor Bruno Kreisky agonized over every minute detail of every decision. Kreisky had been burned before: terrorists had forced him to close the Schoenau transit camp for Jews leaving Russia, and the resulting publicity had left its psychological scars.

All the ambassadors from the OPEC nations, without exception, wanted him to grant every request. The Iranian ambassador was particularly insistent. Once his police had briefed him on Carlos, Kreisky needed no further coaching. Since Vienna promoted itself as an international conference center, it would not do to lose all the ministers from the world's oil kingdoms in one wild bloodbath.

"This Carlos is very dangerous," Kreisky said, looking around the table at the ambassadors nervously awaiting his decision. "We have heard much about him and his ruthless methods. In my opinion, we have to go along with him." The ambassadors were so relieved that they applauded. "The fact that they have already killed members from delegations of countries that are allied to the Palestinians convinces me that they would not hesitate to kill all the hostages if we frustrated their plan." Kreisky turned to al-Azzawi: "How did they look to you? Did they seem nervous or frightened?"

"My minister told me they were laughing about killing the people," he replied. "They looked very calm and determined."

This seemed to distress Kreisky, who on occasion could wax quite philosophical on terrorism. "There is a very deep brutality, I would say partly a very artificial brutality about these people," he said in an interview a few weeks later. "I think some of them may not be brutal in private life. They've made up their mind to accept this brutality. It's part of a system and this makes it so terrible. This is an intellectual process. I'm afraid we live in a very bad world. We must try to find ways and means to stop terrorism but I'm very pessimistic. It's like trying to stop wars. We have the wrong system of education. There are so many social diseases. We are guilty for many things because we have a society that is not so well organized as conservative people usually believe.

"There are two ways to fight terrorism. First, we must try to solve the problems behind terrorism, the problems in the background, which are terribly complicated and leave me very skeptical about finding any solution; barring that, we must build up as much security as possible, learning as we go along, but that is very costly and restrictive, and not all that successful. We must always remember that our society is built on law, and that it is better to liquidate oppression than people. Liquidation of oppression stops terrorism. What I'm saying is that we must solve the problems behind terrorism. It would be better to build new societies than new security systems. I know this makes me very unpopular in some countries and among some people, but this is my conviction, and I am here to say what I believe."

On that Sunday, however, Bruno Kreisky did not express those thoughts to al-Azzawi and the ambassadors. Before making his decision, he talked with opposition leaders as well as leaders in his own party. Then he requested that the captive oil ministers express their wishes in writing, a request approved by Carlos, and the result was unanimous that Kreisky comply with all demands.

Al-Azzawi was a busy man. The chancellor agreed to cooperate with Carlos on one condition. He had to release all Austrian people and foreign employees who were not members of oil-country delegations. Carlos's response was "I am the commander here, I command Kreisky and everybody else. Nobody can tell me what to do. I shall decide who I take with me and who I leave behind."

"We talk about it a long time," al-Azzawi said, "and I say to him, 'The chancellor has a right to decide about the Austrian people. He must do what is right for his people.' He thought about this and said, 'Well, I didn't intend to take them with me anyway, but I don't want anybody telling me what I can and cannot do. This is my operation.' He thought some more and gave me a very stern look. 'I will promise, but they have to return our wounded comrade to us, and if they don't agree, I will shoot and I will start with the Austrian people.'

"So I told the chancellor and he said, 'I can't accept that. Go back and tell him that the wounded one has to stay behind because the doctors say he will die if they take him from the hospital.'

"I went back to Carlos, and he was very nervous. He said, 'No, the chancellor has to stop these things. Tell him that I know all the tricks. He must do what I say or I will start shooting the people in a half an hour.'

"There was a doctor with the chancellor and he tried to explain to me how dangerous it was to take the wounded one from the hospital. He wanted to come with me to explain this to Carlos, but before leaving the chancellery I had to tell the ambassadors what was happening.

"The doctor waited downstairs and when I told Carlos that he wanted to see him, he said, 'No, I don't want anybody to explain anything. Tell Kreisky that we are not cowards, we don't leave our comrade in a battle. We are in a war and we don't leave prisoners for the other side. We take him with us even if he dies.'

"I came back to Kreisky and after much discussion he agreed to have the wounded one waiting in the airplane. But they had to release the people before they went to the airport. When I told Carlos, he said, 'Good, I will accept that as Kreisky's word of honor. He will bring our friend to the airplane and I will release the people here.' "

Earlier in the evening, al-Azzawi had asked Carlos "to please allow me to bring some food to the people." The police delivered sandwiches and fruit, but Carlos was not satisfied. "What is that?" he asked, pointing to the food in disgust. "Don't they know that most of these people are Muslims and can't eat this food?" Having heard that a buffet luncheon had been prepared by the Hilton Hotel for an OPEC reception, Carlos asked for that food to be brought in. When it arrived, he had it placed on the large conference table and told everyone to have a party. "Look," he told al-Azzawi, "I treat them very well. They feel like they are in a party at the Hilton."

In reflecting on his role as mediator, al-Azzawi said he was too busy to worry about his own safety. He felt he had to hide his emotions. "When I heard that Hassan was killed, I was very angry, but I didn't let them see that because it was important to be friendly with them so that they could trust me and speak with me in a trusting way. If they knew how angry I was, they wouldn't speak to me. Later our oil minister told me that Carlos came to him in the airplane and said that the Iraqi chargé d'affaires is a very brave man."

Meanwhile, as the negotiations proceeded, Sheik Yamani was oppressed by a sense of doom. "The news that the leader's name was Carlos came as a big shock to me," he said. "Last summer the French police found among some of his papers a detailed plan for my assassination, which showed that he was completely informed about my movements and places of contacts in the town they had chosen to carry out their plan." When the Saudi secret service learned that Carlos was living in a villa in Tripoli that was guarded by Libyan security men, they sent Maj. Mohammed Ali el-Sohaily and Maj. Fahad el-Ghannam to ask President Muammar Qaddafi of Libya to hand Carlos over to Yasir Arafat's moderate faction of the PLO. Qaddafi denied all knowledge of Carlos's existence.

Carlos asked Yamani to accompany him to one of the staff offices, and Yamani was "convinced that he was going to kill me. It is the terrorist's usual practice to take a victim off to an isolated place, away from the other hostages, when they plan an execution. I sat in a dark room with Carlos, resigned to my fate, then he started talking to me in a polite and quiet manner, and even assured me of his esteem. I was listening to his words which were so incredible to me. But soon afterwards I was to be confronted with the bitter reality of truth when he said, 'Despite our respect for you we are compelled to kill you.' This action, he added, was intended as an expression of protest against the policy of my government. Unless the Austrian government responded to his demands to broadcast their political statement by six o'clock that evening, I would be the first executed. Carlos continued by saying that it was his desire that I should not harbor any hatred or bitterness against them for their intention to kill me, and that, indeed, he expected a man of my intelligence to understand their noble aims and purposes.

"First I thought he was maneuvering to frighten me with this strange talk, and to extort from me compliance with certain things by psychological pressure. I replied, 'How can you inform me of your intention to kill me and then ask me not to feel any bitterness against you? Undoubtedly, you are exerting pressure on me so as to compel me to do something.' With a sardonic laugh, he said, 'After all, who are you that I could use you as a means for me to apply pressure? I am exercising pressure on the Austrian government just to get out of this place.' "

When the deadline passed without the communiqué being broadcast, Carlos came to remind Yamani of the terms prescribed. "The ways of the human soul are strange," Yamani observed. "After Carlos left, my feelings changed and my anguish abated. I started to think not of myself, but of my family, children, and relatives, and those to whom I was responsible. I began to write a farewell letter containing directives on what I wanted them to do, and I asked my colleague, Khader Harazallah, to have it delivered. How greatly relieved was I when finally the Vienna radio carried the statement a few minutes later, and when the Austrian government agreed to provide an aircraft to take us with them wherever they wanted to go."

Al-Azzawi had brought Carlos his own radio and everyone listened to the communiqué, delivered in atrocious French, but the terrorists seemed more concerned with their request being granted than in the fractured delivery. Why a French message in a German-speaking country? Why a manifesto at all? In an age of instant communication, propaganda is now a *sine qua non* of terrorism. In this operation, it may well have been a knee-jerk reaction. Middle East analysts would say that the communiqué echoed many of the thoughts expressed elsewhere by President Qaddafi. Whatever language the terrorists chose was immaterial. It was not long before the world's mass media had focused on Vienna and the drama received lavish coverage.

Carlos was visibly relaxed, almost euphoric, as he strolled around the room, answering all questions, a small smile playing at the corners of his mouth. He told Yamani and Jamshid Amouzegar, the Iranian oil minister, that he had personally trained forty commandos and promised to lead other raids in the future.

When one of the male hostages asked Carlos to release the women, Carlos put his arm around Gabriele. "Don't you think she's scared?" he asked.

"Scared?" said the hostage. "You tell me she's scared and she's just killed two men. She chose this work. These women didn't."

Carlos laughed and moved on, the subject plainly closed. It was a long, sleepless night for all concerned.

As the regular physician for many OPEC employees, Dr. Wiriya Rawenduzy felt obliged morally to render any assistance he could to the hostages. Although his offer was refused out of hand by the terrorists, he remained in the OPEC lobby throughout the day and night on the off chance that he might be needed.

At five o'clock on Monday morning, Kreisky sent an emissary to ask Rawenduzy if he would accompany Klein on the flight, and he accepted without hesitation. He was already on the plane with his patient lying on a stretcher placed across some seats when the terrorists and hostages arrived. A few minutes after takeoff, Abdesselam introduced Rawenduzy to Carlos.

"I understand you're from Iraq," Carlos said.

"Please, Mr. Carlos, I am from Iraq Kurdistan and I came to help not only your wounded fellow, but the other passengers when they need me." Rawenduzy, who is a tall, handsome man, a polished version of a hill tribesman, took a deep breath before continuing. "I don't want anybody to smoke during the flight."

Later recalling this conversation, Rawenduzy said, "I think he was surprised because it is not normal to make demands of armed people. Everybody is happy to shut his mouth and to do everything he's told. But he was very thankful that I was ready to sacrifice my time to help them. I told him it was a great mistake to oblige his friend to fly after such a severe operation. I would do my best to keep him alive, but I could not be responsible if he died.

"He was polite and courteous and assured me that everything was all right, that I had nothing to worry about. Still I didn't want anything to happen during the trip. I was very careful to do everything possible for this patient, who was in great pain and very weak from loss of blood. I wanted him to land alive, but I didn't know where we were going."

Nor did Capt. Manfred Pollak, the pilot of the DC-9, know the destination when he left Vienna. But that was not what worried him at that moment. Seated directly behind him was a fellow in a big fur hat, who brandished a submachine gun and carried two pistols in his waistband. When Austrian Airlines first contacted Pollak, he was told that the terrorists would leave their weapons behind when they boarded the plane. "The terrorists refused to go unarmed and they said they would give the destination after we were airborne," Pollak recalled. "So we took off with an uncertain destination, but I did have landing clearance for Algiers. The understanding was that all hostages would be freed after landing in Algiers. So I set my course and after a half an hour Carlos came to confirm that destination."

Captain Pollak took that opportunity to point out what could happen if a bullet penetrated the walls of the cabin at high altitude. The differential pressure could cause the cabin to implode. Carlos shrugged, smiled, and walked away. Although maintaining his professional "cool," as he put it, Pollak found it hard to dismiss the foreboding of disaster that nipped at the edges of his mind everytime he looked at the submachine gun pointed at the instrument panel.

"It was a quiet trip," Rawenduzy said. "The girl, Gabriele, was with Klein most of the time. She whispered to him and wiped his brow. I think she encouraged him. You could see that they were close, that their relationship was more than casual.

"Carlos spent most of his time talking with the Algerian oil minister. During the flight I asked Carlos three or four times when we were going to land, because the oxygen bomb I had for Klein was good for three and a half hours. Carlos came every time I asked for him, and the first time, he told me we would be landing in two hours and later in one and a half hours, but I could see that the negotiations between him and Mr. Abdesselam was not all right. I asked him where we were going to land, and he said perhaps in Baghdad. I said this man will be dead long before we get there. We must land within the hour.

" 'Don't worry about it,' he told me. 'I promise we will land in Algiers the next hour.'

" 'Will you please check with the pilot to see if that time is accurate. And will you ask the pilot to radio ahead for an ambulance and surgical equipment, and for a physician and oxygen.' He left and when he came back he was smiling. 'You can stop worrying,' he said. 'Everything is going to be all right.' "

"When the plane departed Vienna and became airborne, a feeling of relief appeared on Carlos's face," Yamani said. Earlier Carlos had told him that he would take the oil ministers on a triumphant tour of the Middle East, to display them like prized game. "After I learned of the destination, I asked him, 'Why did you choose Algiers as your first destination?'

" 'Algeria is a revolutionary country,' he said, 'and I could not decline their invitation. Despite the fact that I am not in cooperation with the Algerians, they cannot obstruct my plan.'

" 'Will our stopover in Algiers be long?' I asked.

" 'Not more than two hours during which I will release some ministers whom I had previously decided to set free in Libya.'

" 'Where will we be staying tonight?'

" 'Do not ask too many questions,' he said."

As he watched Carlos and the other terrorists move around the plane, chatting with the hostages, giving autographs, laughing good-naturedly, Dr. Rawenduzy was struck by the paradox of the situation. They were polite, friendly, actually jovial at times, and yet in the flicker of an eyelash they could become killers, crazy people who would shoot not just one or two people but everybody. To a man who had dedicated himself to preserving life, such irrational behavior was incomprehensible. He could not understand total dedication to a cause—any cause—which made it possible to kill without hesitation.

He asked Gabriele about it, not knowing that she had killed Tichler and Hassan, because it bothered him. "This policeman was admired by the whole Arabic diplomatic corps," he said. "At the same time, he was a good man and close to his retirement. Why did you people kill him?"

"We had orders not to shoot anyone," Gabriele answered, "but he opposed us and we were obliged to do this." Then she showed the doctor where Hassan had torn her gray, fur-lined jacket down the right side. "I'm sorry, but they gave us no choice," she said.

Carlos stopped to give his autograph to the Nigerian minister, writing, "Flight Vienna to Algeria, 22.12.75, Carlos."

"He acted like a movie star," says Valentin Hernández Acosta, the Venezuelan oil minister. "He boasted of his deeds, handed out autographs, and told us the OPEC attack was a completely new operation developed by himself to secure existence of a Palestinian state."

Carlos had sought out Hernández in the OPEC conference room to tell him that he was a countryman and that his real name was Ilich Ramírez Sánchez. "He didn't talk in the same manner immediately after the violence as he did later when he had calmed down. We spent twenty-six hours together. At first he was keen to tell me he was Venezuelan. We talked in Vienna, in the plane, everywhere. It was clear that he wished to establish contact with us."

Asked later if the police would arrest Carlos if he returned to Venezuela, Hernández replied, "How do you know that he hasn't already been back several times?" He went on to explain that the police had never questioned him because he had never "officially" returned to Venezuela, but there were rumors he had entered the country via the Colombian border.

In the course of their conversation, Carlos asked Hernández to deliver a handwritten letter addressed to his mother, Doña Elba Sánchez Ramírez, in Caracas, and later, when the French police asked to see the letter, Hernández refused, saying its contents were confidential. He did, however, permit them to photocopy the envelope. (Photographs of Carlos taken at Algiers airport, along with analysis of his handwriting, positively identified him as the same person known as Ilich Ramírez Sánchez who was wanted by French, British, and West German police.)

The flight to Algiers took two hours and twenty minutes. For most of the hostages, it was a pleasant enough journey, under the circumstances. However, for Yamani and Amouzegar, who were seated together, there was the ominous presence of Khaled, who kept making threatening gestures in their direction.

As the plane came in for a landing, all the curtains were drawn. Carlos stationed himself by the rear door, his Beretta machine pistol at the ready, while the others, assuming strategic positions, kept their weapons pointed at the hostages. The Algerian foreign minister, Abdelaziz Bouteflika, came on board, accompanied by a physician and medical assistants. No one else was allowed to enter.

"So my mission had come to an end," Rawenduzy recalled. "I explained the medical situation to the Algerian physician. While they were preparing to take Klein to the hospital, Carlos invited me to leave the airplane with him and the foreign minister. We were the only ones permitted to leave. So I say to Carlos that now I must return to Vienna, and he joked with me at first before saying it was all right, doctor, and thank you very much. He patted my shoulder and said, 'I will send you back in a private airplane.' I said, 'No, thank you, it is enough to choose a normal airplane.' He laughed and we shook hands, and that was the last time I talked to Carlos."

To Captain Pollak, it seemed like hours before Carlos came to the cockpit. By then most of the hostages had been released, including all the oil ministers from non-Arab states. Although he had been released, Abdesselam returned to act as mediator. When Pollak finally got his chance to ask Carlos if he could return to Vienna, Carlos said, "Not yet, maybe tomorrow. First we have to go to Tripoli and to Baghdad."

"This news left me a little dismayed," Pollak said. "This was the twenty-second of December and I could see myself somewhere in the desert on Christmas Eve. I said, 'Okay, we can make Tripoli very easily, but Baghdad is too long a leg for a DC-9. I will have to make an intermediate landing for refueling in Damascus or maybe Beirut.'

"I could tell he was a little frustrated by this, and the impression I got was that he wasn't very keen about landing in either of those places. Then he started negotiating for a bigger airplane, one that could go directly from Tripoli to Baghdad, but he was told there was none available. So we left for Tripoli."

"When the airplane took off, the terrorists showed the first signs of exhaustion," Yamani said. "The weather outside was rainy and stormy, and even Carlos was nervous. Their faces showed how tired they were. The girl went forward and burst into tears.

"Carlos sat next to me and tried to hide his worries by talking about himself, his childhood, his studies, his friends, his adventures, his love affairs."

As they approached Tripoli, Yamani asked if that was the last stop.

"I told you before, you ask too many questions," Carlos said.

"Are you expecting difficulties in Libya?"

Carlos looked at him in a "strangely astonished way" and said, "On the contrary, the President [Qaddafi] will be there to receive us, and a Boeing plane will be ready to take us to Baghdad."

"Will the plane land in Damascus?"

"I gave you my opinion regarding the Syrians. They have become deviationists and grown dangerous," Carlos said, ignoring the fact that the communiqué had praised them. "I will not set foot on their land."

He almost did not set foot in Tripoli. The plane had to hold for an hour, until, in fact, Pollak radioed that he was running short on fuel. Then he had to stop the airplane immediately after leaving the runway. Carlos came into the cockpit to ask why they were stopped, and Pollak said the control tower would not allow him to taxi to the apron. Carlos wanted him to taxi to the place reserved for Qaddafi, but the tower refused permission.

Carlos was angry now. He looked at Pollak and shook his head. "I worked for a month preparing this commando action and now we won't get the proper honor from the Libyan government. God! How can I work for these people? They are so inefficient."

Later, on the way back to Algiers, Carlos would tell Yamani, "These people [Libyans] are not disciplined. One cannot work with them."

Upon their arrival in Tripoli, Abdesselam and Khaled had gone to the control tower to negotiate with Libyan officials who were in telephonic contact with Qaddafi's representative, Premier Abdul Salem Jalloud. The real negotiations for the release of the oil ministers were taking place in Tripoli. Gathered there with Jalloud for the occasion were the Algerian ambassador to Libya and the leaders of the Arab Rejection Front—George Habash and Ahmed Jibril of the PFLP and Nayef Hawatmeh, leader of the Popular Democratic Front for the Liberation of Palestine. It was hours before the terms they proposed for the release of Yamani and Amouzegar—Saudi Arabia and Iran were the real targets—were accepted by King Khalid and the Shah.

By two o'clock that morning, Carlos was fed up with waiting. The Boeing would not be available until eight in the morning, and after getting approval from Habash, he released all the hostages except Yamani and Amouzegar and gave Pollak instructions to fly back to Algiers.

"As he left the plane in Tripoli," Yamani recalled, "one of my Saudi colleagues said to Carlos, 'For God's sake, don't do anything to Zaki Yamani.' Carlos replied, laughing, 'I have here in Libya received instructions from my bosses that neither Yamani or Amouzegar should be harmed. I can now promise that they are safe.' "

But Yamani was not completely convinced. There was still Khaled to worry about, but the return flight to Algiers was uneventful. More negotiations followed in Algiers, until finally an agreement was reached and Algerian security men came on board to disarm the terrorists. It was then that Khaled made his move.

"Khaled asked if he could speak to us, and the security men agreed," Yamani said. "But as he began to speak, Khaled looked here and there, and rubbed his right hand nervously over his chest."

At this point, Bouteflika thrust a glass of orange juice into Khaled's hand and security men closed in, searched him, and discovered a pistol hidden under his arm. Khaled was furious. "I came to carry out the agreed execution of these criminals," he said. "Now you have made the realization of my goal impossible."

"When I left the airplane, Carlos thanked me and apologized for the inconvenience," Pollak said. "Then he gave me two big cigars that he said were presents to him from Fidel Castro."

An hour later, Carlos and Maria Teresa Lara, a Venezuelan journalist and intellectual Marxist he had met in Paris, were relaxing in room 505 at the Edwardier Hotel in Algiers. All the terrorists had been granted political asylum, with the added guarantee that they could not be extradited. Algeria explained its position by saying the decision was reached on the advice of a dozen states: "These demands were essentially political and no government of the Organization of Petroleum Exporting Countries was unaware that the liberation of the hostages was reached by agreeing to the demands which included the release of the guerrillas, which took place after the whole operation was completed." It denounced what it termed a "violent and tendentious campaign in the Western press aimed at tarnishing Algeria's image over its handling of the affair."

The argument was academic. No government was clamoring to extradite the terrorists. Austria made an informal request, but West Germany completely ignored the episode. What would France give to get its hands on the man who had murdered two agents of its counterintelligence organization, the

Direction de la Surveillance de Territoire (DST), not to mention the bombing mutilations of a few of its citizens? Not very much. No extradition request was made to the Algerian government. In fact, no one in the Western European intelligence community wanted to apprehend Carlos. The countries directly involved in his crimes—England, France, West Germany, and Austria—were more afraid of the consequences of Carlos's capture than of his freedom. Intelligence decisions on Carlos in these countries were being made at the governmental level: the policy was to protect possible targets defensively and not to seek out Carlos offensively. It was the type of policy, according to the Israelis, that only encourages global terrorism.

The OPEC incident quickly became just another episode for the history books. It had hit with a great splash of ink that covered the world. Terrorism has no equal in capturing the public's imagination. It is fascinating theater. That is why it is aimed as much at the audience as the victims. Alexander Solzhenitsyn sees parallels between the Russia of the nineteenth century and the West today: there is the same "universal adulation of revolutionaries, . . . if not as a cult of terror in society, then as a fierce defense of the terrorists."

Although the "propaganda of the deed," as terrorism is called by some media experts, was an important element of the OPEC raid, giving the terrorist their worldwide forum, it was not the main objective, which became the subject of endless speculation, all of it impossible to confirm. There were rumors in Beirut that Yamani and Amouzegar were ransomed for $1 million each, paid into a bank in Aden and earmarked for the Arab Rejection Front. Egyptian reports said that Qaddafi paid Carlos $2 million and Klein $200,000 as compensation for his wound, from which he ultimately recovered. When a Swedish journalist asked Qaddafi if he was behind the OPEC raid, he replied, "It's a rumor that has no basis. It's addressed against Libya because we fight for freedom. They have no proof." French sources said Carlos received 5 million francs from Algerian President Houari Boumedienne. And so it went.

On a more distinctly political level, it was believed that Habash received an agreement from Saudi Arabia to give up its support of Egyptian President el-Sadat and to stop interfering with affairs in Lebanon, referring specifically to the support of the right-wing forces then in conflict with the liberals and Palestinians. The OPEC raid was promoted as a major victory by the Rejection Front in its opposition to the "deviationist" policies of Egypt, Syria, Jordan, and the Yasir Arafat faction of the PLO, who were willing to settle for a mini-Palestinian state consisting of the West Bank and Gaza.

Arafat denounced the OPEC raid as an imperialist maneuver to discredit Palestinians before a meeting of the UN Security Council the following month. Arafat felt that the raid, coming as it did at a time when he was trying to put his best diplomatic foot forward, was intended as an embarrassment to him. It was not the first time the Rejection Front had plotted to upset his diplomatic cart. In October 1974 it had plotted to assassinate Arab leaders attending an Arab summit in Rabat, Morocco. The conspiracy was exposed when Moroccan authorities seized a truck loaded with weapons that were to be used to kill

Arafat as well as kings Hussein of Jordan, Hassan of Morocco, and Faisal of Saudi Arabia. The organizer of the mission was Salah Khalaf, the founder of the Black September terrorist band (the name derives from the bloody Jordanian civil war of September 1970 when Hussein purged his country of the PLO).

In response to Arafat's criticism, the Arm of the Arab Revolution released to Beirut newspapers a communiqué that said: "We weren't surprised by criticism of the operation from Egypt and Persian Gulf countries. But we were surprised by the Palestine Liberation Organization's slide toward the camp of distortion and its striking out at a group of heroic Arab strugglers who pledged their blood to save the Palestinian cause and, through it, the cause of Arab destiny from plots of liquidation and destruction."

Ha Mossad L'Tafkidim Meyubadim, or the Institution for Special Tasks, Israel's ultrasecret counterterrorist organization, known also as the Wrath of God, is responsible for planning and executing Israel's intelligence operations on a worldwide basis. It has spies and informers throughout the Middle East and North Africa. Its agents are secretly trained at hidden Israeli military installations, and their expertise runs the gamut from information-gathering to assassination by "hit teams" dispatched to any part of the world. Its information pipeline in the Arab world is second to none.

Here is Ha Mossad's secret assessment of the OPEC raid: The Algerian government commissioned Carlos for the raid because of Arab League support for Moroccan and Mauritanian plans to take over the el-Aaiun regime of Spanish Sahara from the Madrid government and with it control of the phosphate-rich area of Northwest Africa. Loss of the Algerian claim to "independence"—and hence of a left-wing regime in the new territory backed by the local guerrillas (Polisarios) and supported, financed, trained, and equipped by the Algerians—would mean Moroccan control of the world phosphate market and a sort of economic control of Algeria by the Moroccans. It was Algeria's hope to pressure the oil-rich Arab states to drop their backing of the Moroccan claim to the Sahara and thereby help Algeria to become a phosphate-rich nation.

Ha Mossad believes that because of the OPEC raid, Carlos has affected changes in the power alignment of the Arab world. The Saudi government had stopped paying the PLO its regular stipend because of its backing of the Saudi prince responsible for King Faisal's death. Payments were to be resumed to the PLO's liberal factions. Even Soviet intelligence was strengthened in the Middle East because the OPEC raid gave the Russians new ideas on ways of weakening rightist regimes and strengthening leftist ones through the use of mixed groups of global terrorists that could not be linked to the KGB's Department V, the Soviet's most ultrasecret foreign intelligence operation. Its mission is to immobilize Western nations by creating chaos during international crises. Called "wet affairs" *(mokrie dela),* because of its bloody history, Department V carries out political murders, kidnappings, and sabotage.

Before getting too deeply enmeshed in the convolutions of Middle East politics, let us first take a closer look at Ilich Ramírez Sánchez, alias Carlos Martínez Torres, the man behind the headlines. If anyone can be called the first international terrorist, it is this twenty-six-year-old Venezuelan, who speaks fluent Spanish, English, and Russian and passable French, Arabic, and German. Among his connections in the terror network were the Soviet KGB and the Cuban Dirección General de Inteligencia (DGI), an espionage agency completely controlled by the KGB. Besides working with various Palestinian and North African terrorist groups, Carlos established connections with the Japanese United Red Army; the Irish Republican Army; the last remnants of the Uruguayan Tupamaros and the South American terrorists; the Baader-Meinhof gang; the Eritrean Liberation Front; the Turkish Popular Liberation Front; Basque, Breton, and Corsican separatist movements; and, no doubt, others not yet discovered.

The French, who were the first to begin piecing together the Carlos jigsaw puzzle, were shocked by what they discovered. The unveiling of Carlos's Paris activities was described by Interior Minister Michel Poniatowski as "one of the most important cases of international terrorism to come to the attention of any Western police force in recent years." Considering what they had learned, it was a modest assessment even for the conservative French.

Carlos became an intriguing mystery. That old chestnut about one man's terrorist being another man's patriot was reroasted to a fine flavor in Third World countries. Even the right-wing daily *El Nacional* in Carlos's hometown of Caracas was comparing him to Simón Bolívar, the George Washington of South American independence. However, these questions remained: Who was Carlos and how serious was the threat of international terrorism?

When he heard that his son had directed the OPEC operation, Dr. José Altagracia Ramírez Navas could not suppress his pride. "My son has turned out to be a general," he told the London *Observer*. He went on to explain that the change from a capitalist to a socialist system was only possible through armed struggle. "So philosophically and politically I am in total agreement with my son, Ilich," he said, "although we may diverge a little on strategic matters."

Born on a ranch in the Venezuelan Andes near San Cristóbal, Dr. Ramírez studied for the priesthood two years before deciding on a legal career. He was studying law in Bogotá, Colombia, when war broke out in Europe, and it was then that he came under the influence of populist Jorge Eliecer Gaitan, later murdered, and Gustavo Machado, a leader of the then outlawed Venezuelan Communist party.

"I was pro-Soviet up to the time of Khrushchev," he said, "but now I think that the Communist parties have become conservative. Today, my sympathies are with the extreme Left. Perhaps I'm more drawn toward Peking, but I don't understand, for example, how Mao's revolutionary China maintains relations with Pinochet and the other butchers in Chile."

Dr. Ramírez so admired Lenin that he gave each of his three sons one of his hero's names—Ilich, born on October 12, 1949; Lenin, in 1951; and Vladimir, in 1958. However, his devotion to Lenin did not prevent him from amassing a fortune in real estate holdings. Nor did it stop him from providing his family with bourgeois comforts. From an early age, Ilich and his brothers traveled almost continuously with their mother around South America and the Caribbean. Accompanied by tutors, they studied the mores and languages of the countries visited—English in Jamaica and Miami, Portuguese in Brazil, and various dialects and customs in Mexico and Cuba.

At the age of fourteen, Ilich began his formal education at the Colegio Fermin Toro. That was in 1963, shortly after the dictator Marcos Pérez Jiménez was overthrown and the new liberal government of Rómulo Betancourt came under attack from the Right as well as from the Communist party, which had been banned for its support of anti-Betancourt guerrillas. Many of the students, including Ilich, demonstrated in support of the Communists.

Upon Ilich's graduation in 1966, Dr. Ramírez decided that his eldest son was ready to begin his political education. The school selected was Camp Mantanzas in Havana, Cuba, which specialized in political indoctrination and the art of subversion. The school, which was operated by Fidel Castro's secret service, was under the direction of the notorious Col. Victor Simonov, of the KGB, who became the operational boss of Cuba's DGI. The instructor in charge of guerrilla training was Antonio Dages Bouvier, an Ecuadorian, who would later share a London flat with Ilich.

One of the tactics taught for survival in the field encouraged the students to "get girls as helpers. Make friends with these seemingly harmless creatures for they are useful in providing refuge and in avoiding suspicion." This was one lesson that Ilich took to heart.

He studied for two years before his baptism of fire. His first mission was to land secretly on the Venezuelan coast and make contact. Something went wrong. He was picked up almost immediately by the police. He was questioned and turned loose. He went back to Cuba only to return a few weeks later to help stir up student unrest at the University of Caracas. He fared no better. Picked up by the police, this time he was grilled for twelve hours and was not released until his father intervened.

Dr. Ramírez decided it was time for a change. Ilich had studied Russian in Cuba and now he was enrolled as a sociology student at the Patrice Lumumba University in Moscow, which is operated by the KGB as a training center for young revolutionaries from Third World nations. They are given an upper university education, along with political indoctrination. Promising students receive training in terrorism, sabotage, and guerrilla war techniques at camps in Odessa, Baku, Simferopol, and Tashkent. Similar courses are provided for members of Moscow-controlled Communist parties, but in a separate program, through the Lenin Institute in Moscow, an appendage of the central committee of the Soviet party. Ilich received extensive training in firearms, explosives, the use of aliases, the forging of passports, clandestine communications, and safe houses.

There is no evidence that he objected to any of this. His father provided him with a generous allowance, enough to earn him quite a reputation as a "swinger." He loved poker, girls, music, conversation, good food, wine, and rum (not necessarily in that order) and was generous with his friends.

There is no available record of what actually happened in Moscow the two years Ilich was there. It is known that during the first year he was involved in an elaborately staged "spontaneous" demonstration outside of the Lebanese embassy, which had refused to renew the passports of its young nationals studying at Lumumba. He was seized for throwing a stone through a window, became involved in a scuffle with a Russian policeman, and was arrested.

At the start of his second year, he developed a stomach ulcer and went to join his mother in London, where he received treatment at a hospital for several months. His mother, who was then separated from his father, resided at the fashionable Phillimore Court, a five-story block in the heart of the Kensington shopping center. Señora Sánchez decorated her flat with beautiful antiques and objets d'art. These luxuries were made possible by a monthly allowance of $3,000 that she received from her estranged husband.

Captain Carlos Porras, naval attaché at the Venezuelan embassy in London, described Ilich's mother as "a charming and lovely woman who was invited to many social gatherings in London. Often all her three sons would come along with her. The last time I remember seeing Ilich was at a party in September or October of last year [1974]. He seemed to do nothing except travel a great deal. He was always coming back from somewhere or off to somewhere else. He gave the impression of a wealthy young man. He was always very fashionably dressed when I saw him.

"I don't think his mother knew what he was doing. I have a feeling he may have told her lies, but I can't say why. He and I said very little to each other—mostly just pleasantries. The last time we talked about his educational stay in Moscow. I didn't want to discuss politics with him, so I believe I changed the subject."

It is doubtful that anyone will ever really know what happened when Ilich returned to Moscow to complete his studies. It was reported that he spent so much time pursuing girls and bourgeois pleasures, habits his teachers characterized as debauchery, that he was expelled from the Soviet Union for "disrepute morals" and "provocative activities."

Needless to say, Western intelligence services were immediately alerted. Expulsion is an old trick used by the KGB to whitewash agents they plan on using in foreign countries. The machinations of the intelligence business being what they are, spies thrive on doublethink; and before long the thinking had come full circle, and Ilich was written off. With the benefit of hindsight, however, it is rather difficult, if not impossible, to believe that the Cubans and the Russians, who had Ilich under a microscope for nearly four years, could have failed to appreciate his potential.

Upon leaving the Soviet Union, Ilich traveled to East Berlin, where he was briefed on the leaders of the Baader-Meinhof gang, which had launched a terror campaign—bombings, murders, burnings, bank robberies—that years later West German chancellor Helmut Schmidt would call "the most serious challenge in the twenty-six-year history of our democracy."

Members of the Baader-Meinhof gang, as well as student terrorists, were constantly supported by the KGB-controlled East German secret police with houses in East Berlin, false papers and identity cards, money, arms and ammunition, and terrorist training. Transportation was provided from East Berlin to the Middle East, where they were placed in contact with the PFLP and other guerrilla groups. Among the first members of the Baader-Meinhof gang to receive guerrilla training at Palestinian camps were Andreas Baader, Ulrike Meinhof, Horst Mahler, Gudrun Ensslin, and Ingrid Siepmann.

When Ilich crossed over to West Berlin, he knew precisely whom to contact. The relationships he established on that first visit with Baader-Meinhof leaders were lasting ones. From there he traveled the "terror route" to Beirut, where he met Habash and his operational chief, Dr. Wadi Haddad, who was in charge of guerrilla training camps in Lebanon, Jordan, and South Yemen. This was Ilich's first involvement with the Palestinians, and it too would become a lasting one. Whatever credentials Ilich brought with him to Beirut, they were good enough to get him immediately into a leadership position. One of the significant contacts Ilich had made at Lumumba was his friendship with Mohammed Boudia, an Algerian classmate who became director of the PFLP's European network. It was an interesting relationship because they had a remarkable physical resemblance. This would later confuse Ha Mossad assassins who dogged Boudia's footsteps nearly two years before they got him—if they did.

Ha Mossad credits Boudia with initiating much of what they call the "global terror network." It also believes that Boudia served two functions in Europe: he recruited, organized, and designed many anti-Israeli actions for the PFLP, and as a KGB operative, he worked to unite various terrorist groups into an international network. His boss was Yuri Kotov, who was an expert in Middle East affairs and was listed as a Soviet foreign ministry attaché when he served as a KGB station officer in Israel. In 1967, with the break in diplomatic relations between the two countries, Kotov moved on to the Russian embassy in Beirut, where his reputation as a *bon vivant* followed him. Yet he made little effort to hide his true responsibilities.

Kotov followed Boudia to Paris, becoming chief of the KGB's Western European division. It was Kotov, Ha Mossad believes, who brought Ilich into the KGB structure. He contrived the expulsion from Lumumba as a smoke screen to confuse intelligence services.

It was not until February 1971 that Ilich returned to London, but instead of moving in with his mother and brothers, he shared two "safe" apartments with Bouvier, his old guerrilla training instructor from Camp Mantanzas. Middle-aged and of medium height, with short straight gray hair and a gray moustache, Bouvier, who wore horn-rimmed glasses and preferred conservative business suits, looked rather more like a banker than a terrorist. Although Ilich was receiving a monthly allowance of about $800 from his father, he had unlimited access to an account opened by Bouvier in his middle name, Dages.

As part of his cover, Ilich enrolled at the London School of Economics and joined his mother on the diplomatic cocktail circuit. To the people he met, he was just another wealthy Latin American playboy. Dressed in smartly tailored suits, with his beautiful mother on one arm and a lovely girl on the other, he cut quite a figure along Embassy Row. But that was his bourgeois front. A few embassy parties go a long way in establishing a young man's social credentials in a foreign capital. The impression he created was one of being bright and articulate, but seldom controversial. There were times when he expressed approval of the terrorist strategies of the Provisional Irish Republican Army (IRA). He would compare the Irish problem to that of the Palestinians, whose hostility toward Israel he supported. But that was as far as he would go, and then only in the heat of an argument others endorsed. What his wealthy acquaintances did not realize, of course, was that he was the liaison between the PFLP and the IRA, his first assignment in England.

Before long Ilich was frequenting the racially mixed Bayswater area, spending less time with his mother and on his studies, and more making friends with Latin Americans, Basques, Africans, Arabs, and Japanese living in that polyglot ghetto. He met girls who were not as lovely as the ones he introduced to his mother but who were far more helpful in his work.

Ilich began making frequent flights to Europe and the Middle East, using a string of aliases and false passports to cover his tracks. Among the identities assumed were Cenon Clarke and Glenn Gebhard of New York; Adolfo José Muller Bernal of Chile; Carlos Andres Martínez Torres, a Peruvian economist; Hector Hugo DuPont, an Anglo-Frenchman; and Hector Hipodikon.

Ilich-Carlos met regularly with Boudia in Paris, and when Boudia was summoned to Beirut in May 1972 for a conference with Habash, Carlos was left in charge of the European operation. Upon his return to Paris, Boudia had exciting news. Habash had introduced him to Fusako Shigenobu, a pretty little nurse who had been working in a refugee hospital since arriving in Lebanon early in 1972. She had also masterminded some of the most bizarre atrocities perpetrated by the Rengo Sekigun, or United Red Army (URA).

The URA was founded as a coalition of the Red Army and the United Tokyo-Yokohama Struggle Council Against the U.S.-Japan Security Treaty. The two groups were the most radical on the far Left that came out of the turbulent Japanese student movement of the late 1960s. The student movement, Zengakuren, reached its peak in 1969 and then gradually died away. By then Japanese Communists were firmly set on their path to parliamentary government. Of the many antiimperialist factions into which the students were divided, only a few—none with a membership greater than three hundred—held to their belief in violent revolution.

Forsaking Japan because it was "unripe for revolution," Fusako and a small band of URA members (including students, nurses, doctors, and engineers, a cross section of young upper-class Japan) were enticed to the Middle East because it appeared to be exactly what they were looking for: an organization committed to international guerrilla warfare and different from the revolutionary movements in China, Latin America, and Indochina. The PFLP offered "ideological purity."

In memoirs written for a Japanese magazine to make money for the movement and to publicize it, Fusako revealed the URA's impulse for action: "We don't trust talk, only actions." She quoted Mao Tse-tung as saying, "Without a people's army, the people have nothing." And "Only with guns can the whole world be transformed." It was a dedication to action, not ideology.

The Japanese student movement was inspired by a violent revolutionary Marxism, and the URA was the distillation of the most extreme elements of that movement. It was the search for an international revolutionary base that brought the members of the movement to Lebanon. Faith in the virtue of violence by small revolutionary groups is well known in Japanese history. It is a tradition that brings extreme loyalty to an idea rather than to a leader—until the leader becomes the personification of that idea. The radical's sense of isolation is intensified in Japan by the nation's concept of the group society in which individualism is suspect, even feared. An old Japanese proverb says that "The peg that stands up is the one that is hammered down."

Captured URA members have talked vaguely about revolutionary Marxism, but few seem to have any grasp of Marxist theories. Happy as they may appear to be with their affiliation with the PFLP, it is merely part of a larger strategy of organizing a worldwide uprising of workers. Beneath their revolutionary fervor lies a streak of national romanticism, springing from the tradition of samurai warriors. Few countries could provide revolutionaries so dedicated to nihilistic violence and self-sacrifice. The idea of violence is strong in the Japanese mind, particularly when the violence proceeds from a sense of duty. Japan, as a country, has no philosophy of life, only a philosophy of death.

For the disgruntled college student who is offered nothing more from life than becoming an anonymous cog in a world dominated by the gross national product, the URA appears to offer the attraction of something worth dying for. Whatever the older generation may believe, there is a greater degree of moral support for the URA in Japan than is generally admitted.

Fusako Shigenobu's faction of the URA, the traveling "elite," is viewed by young liberals as a rare example of ideological commitment in a bleak spiritual landscape, for Japan is a nation without religious foundation. The URA appears an oasis of nonmaterialism in the postwar generation's allegiance to industrialization and pollution. It is a ray of idealistic sunshine.

Fusako is well aware of this political consciousness. In her memoirs, she wrote: "We intend to recruit young people who have lost hope in living—lost hope in their families, in society. We want to get their explosive energy."

Be that as it may, the sheer irrational brutality of Japanese fanatics knows no bound. Shortly before Fusako and her followers left for the Middle East in late 1971, thirty URA members fled to caves and primitive huts in the snow-covered slopes of Mt. Haruna in Gumma County, on the edge of the central Japanese Alps. Following the example of one of their heroes, Chairman Mao, they had fled into the mountains not only to escape from a police crackdown in Tokyo but to plot no less the armed overthrow of the Japanese government. The police had so frustrated the group's need for action that it had disintegrated to the point where it had lost all sense of reality. They were so frustrated that they turned the violence in on themselves.

The group was dominated by Tsuneo Mori, the son of a hotel owner, and Hiroko Nagata, the daughter of a respectable businessman. Both were twenty-seven and college dropouts. Records indicate that most URA members are from middle- or upper-middle-class families.

It was not long before ideology gave way to violence. It began when some members questioned Mori's thesis that the time was ripe for the violent overthrow of the Japanese government. This opposition was interpreted by Mori and Nagata as an example of "bourgeois revisionism." At first they argued the merits of immediate urban guerrilla warfare and armed retaliation against the police; but as they fled from hideout to hideout in the bitter cold of the mountain range, the rancor intensified and Mori launched a series of mock trials, bringing into play a process of logic called *sokatsu*. This is an obscure word, and the closest English translation is "colligation" or "synthesis," which is defined as "a process of logic bringing together isolated facts, especially with a view to forming one conception or general principle."

There is no evidence as to how exhaustive a *sokatsu* Mori conducted, but what emerged from the testimony of those who later confessed to the police was that Mori used this dubious exercise as an excuse to persecute those who opposed him. Ritualized mock trials and *sokatsu* were started to determine the guilt of the accused. "Once the process of *sokatsu* starts," one survivor recalled, "only death awaits you."

Nagata, who suffered from a hyperthyroid condition that made her eyes bulge in an unattractive manner, became the prosecutor. Her interest was not in the pursuit of logic. She concentrated on sexual behavior. The charges leading to mock trials ranged from wearing lipstick and earrings (despicable bourgeois habits), to displaying sexual attraction, to hampering the movement by marrying and becoming pregnant. Those were the political crimes of the women. The men were charged with having sex with the girls, or with "failure to maintain a revolutionary attitude." There were heated discussions on the definition of a "pure revolution." One of the most puerile arguments centered on the question of whether guns alone or both guns and bombs were necessary to carry out a revolution.

The ritual followed a pattern. As the members sat around during the evening, Mori or Nagata would start picking on one of them. "We didn't ask you to bring a baby back from Tokyo," Nagata screamed at Tunichi

Yamamoto. "But you did come back with the baby and your wife. You also washed diapers, didn't you?" With those words, Yamamoto's death was sealed. He was beaten and tortured until he confessed. The sentence in all cases was death. The procedure varied little. The victims were stripped, gagged, beaten, tortured, stabbed, strangled, and then tied outdoors in subfreezing temperatures and abandoned. After two days and nights of pleading for mercy, Yamamoto died.

Yoshitaka Kato, age twenty-one, was tortured and beaten, and then his two teen-age brothers were ordered to grasp a knife jointly and plunge it into his heart. When they flinched on their first effort, Mori ordered them to do it again.

Those sentenced to death were beaten and tortured for several days before being killed or left outside to freeze to death. A girl eight months pregnant was first whipped with wire, and then, when pressure on her abdomen failed to abort the child, she was tied to a tree and left to freeze to death. One girl was left bound and gagged under the floor of the hut for three days before dying, where she could hear the others above cooking food and gossiping. One young man bled to death after biting off his tongue.

Nagata was particularly active in the torture of women, and she particularly enjoyed shaving their heads as they lay helpless on the ground. Fourteen members died in a period of a few weeks. This grisly orgy shocked the public, which resorted to the Confucian ethic of blaming the parents. One father hanged himself, and another resigned from his headmaster's job.

Psychologists conjectured that the primitive mountain conditions had driven the group to a primeval state. Popular opinion in Japan was understandably reluctant to blame its own society and the pressures it exerts on young people to conform to a philosophy of materialism, but left-wing intellectuals believed that rampant hedonism had increasingly isolated a small group of frustrated idealists, driving them further and further into extreme positions. Before leaving for their mountain refuge, the group had circulated this statement: "Armed revolution is the only means conceivable for an anguished rebirth of a new Japan in which all corrupt politics will be eliminated."

Of the sixteen jailed for the killings, six were women. About a third of the URA members who followed Fusako Shigenobu to the Middle East were women. Some Japanese argue that the URA and other radical factions provide an extreme outlet for women's frustrations in a society where they are still very much second-class citizens.

Fusako has been described as a pretty but "generally rather sexless" woman whose "one great love is the Red Army." She is attractive enough— with long, shiny black hair, sparkling eyes, and a brilliant smile—to appeal to most Japanese men. She certainly did to Tsuyoshi Okudaira, whom she married shortly before going to Lebanon. It is not known if Okudaira ever dreamed of marital bliss; if he did, it was short-lived. Fusako consented to be his wife for the sole purpose of using his name to get to Lebanon on her "honeymoon": the marriage was never consummated. Once in Beirut, she set up what she called "the first headquarters of the Japanese revolution abroad."

Fusako could not be more suited for her role as the "Queen of the Red Army" if she were a character in a Japanese novel. Her father was a member of the Blood Oath League, a notorious right-wing student group of the 1930s that planned assassinations of Japanese business and political leaders. She comes naturally to her chosen profession. "I am an optimist," she said in her memoirs, "and I never get disheartened. I have never thought of giving up the struggle."

Upon his return to Paris, Boudia explained the mission planned by Habash and Fusako. Carlos was impressed. His job was to deliver the necessary weapons to Fusako's husband in Rome. On that assignment, Carlos traveled as Hector Hipodikon.

Air France Flight No. 132 landed at Tel Aviv's Lod International Airport shortly after ten o'clock on the evening of May 30, 1972. It was a lovely evening, and the passengers, many of whom were pilgrims from Puerto Rico, were excited about their visit to the Holy Land. Tsuyoshi Okudaira and two companions moved casually along with the other passengers as they passed through the passport control section on their way to the baggage conveyor belt. Having been the last to board the flight in Rome, they knew their luggage would be among the first to arrive.

They removed their jackets and quietly exchanged last-minute instructions. When their luggage reached them, they were ready to spring into action. In a matter of seconds, they had pulled out three Czech-made VZ58 lightweight submachine guns and half a dozen grenades. Standing back to back so that they formed a circle and with legs spread apart, they began firing from the hip into the crowd of waiting passengers, sweeping their weapons from side to side. Then they raised them and started shooting at the spectators waiting behind a glass partition, shattering several of the heavy glass panels. Their first magazines emptied, they lobbed grenades into the crowd. People were blown apart by the exploding shrapnel, which had a lethal range of fifty-eight feet. Several were decapitated and others were later found without limbs.

They reversed the magazines in their guns and began firing again. In the bedlam and confusion that followed, one of the terrorists was killed by a companion who swung his gun too far. Then the other two raced from the building onto the airplane parking apron, firing bursts into passengers just stepping off an arriving El Al airliner. This had been their original target. Their instructions had been not to fire on the Air France passengers but to wait for the El Al flight because then most of the victims would be Israelis or people with direct loyalties to Israel. However, the PFLP, which took credit for the massacre, later observed that it did not regard tourists visiting Israel as innocent civilians: "The mere choice of our occupied territory as a place for tourism is in itself a bias in favor of the enemy."

The two terrorists finally ran out of ammunition. Okudaira pulled the pin from his last grenade and clutched it to his body. The explosion decapitated him. The remaining terrorist, Kozo Okamoto, was captured by an El Al employee as he tried to escape into the darkness.

When it was all over, twenty-seven people were dead and seventy-eight others were wounded. At his trial five weeks later, Okamoto gloried in his actions. "Revolutionary warfare is a war of justice," he told the court. "And so I admit very frankly what I have done." As for the revolution, he insisted it would go on: "In Washington and New York, the houses of simple folk must be destroyed. That is how they will be able to feel the sweeping torrent of world revolution. The slaughter of human beings is inevitable. . . . We know it will become more severe than battles between nations." All three terrorists had vowed to commit suicide. "We soldiers after we die want to become the three stars of Orion," he said. "The revolution will go on and there will be many more stars." In return for his confession, he was promised a pistol and one bullet "for his own personal use." "I want to follow them," he had said repeatedly of his two companions, but the promise was not kept. For his crime he was sentenced to life imprisonment.

Kozo Okamoto's brother, Takeshi Okamoto, was one of the first heroes of the URA. On March 30, 1970, Takeshi and eight other URA members brandishing samurai swords hijacked a Japan Air Lines jet on a domestic flight with 137 passengers aboard and ordered it flown to P'yongyang, North Korea. The nine hijackers were taken into custody and were not heard from until three years later, when the government noted that they had confessed their errors and had become "good workers."

Kozo, a third-year agricultural student at Kagoshima University, had promised his father, a retired welfare officer, that he would not follow in Takeshi's footsteps. His second brother was an assistant professor at Tokyo University. Kozo told Israeli police that he was recruited in Japan by Bassim, a representative of the PFLP and husband of Leila Khalad, the Arabs' most famous female terrorist. Bassim showed him a film made jointly by Fusako and the PFLP entitled *Declaration of World War by the Red Army and the PFLP*. He was given an airplane ticket to Beirut and, with his two companions, was instructed in handling explosives and machine guns at a training camp in Lebanon.

In the pocket of one of the Lod terrorists police found this excerpt from Rimbaud's *A Season in Hell:*

> To whom shall I hire myself out? What beast should I adore? What holy image attack? What hearts break? What lies uphold? In what blood tread?
> Rather steer clear of the law. The hard life, simple brutishness, to lift with withered fist the coffin's lid, to sit, to suffocate. And thus no old age, no dangers.

In retracing the steps of the terrorists, police learned that two weeks before the massacre, the three Japanese youths had appeared in Rome behaving like tourists—with cameras slung over shoulders they had visited the Spanish Steps, the Trevi Fountain, and other historical attractions. The waiter at a *pensione* recalled that they had difficulty eating spaghetti and left no tips. A young Oriental woman was said to have visited them, but there was nothing at all suspicious in their behavior. It was not until much later that Okamoto revealed that the single Arab contact they had in Rome was Hector Hipodikon, the man who delivered the weapons and familiarized them in their use. Three years later London police would find this false passport hidden among weapons and explosives in a suitcase Carlos had left at a girlfriend's flat.

In many ways, Carlos's revolutionary thinking was similar to Fusako's. One of his favorite sayings was "You do things with bullets—bullets are real." He told Claude Meier, a Baader-Meinhof follower, that he was committed to world revolution. Like Fusako, he found that the Palestinians were limited in their approach. Their obsession with the destruction of Israel limited their focus to the point where they had no interest in what happened elsewhere in the world unless it had a bearing on the Middle East. He worked with the Arabs because they provided him with the revolutionary infrastructure he needed for his international operation.

During the fall and winter of 1972, following Black September's assault on the Olympic Village in Munich and the murder of eleven Israeli athletes, Mohammed Boudia became extremely jumpy. Ha Mossad assassination squads were sweeping across Europe methodically liquidating Arab terrorists. Wadal Adel Zwaiter, the Black September boss in Italy, was the first to be killed. Black September retaliated by murdering five Jordanian agents in West Germany suspected of passing information to the Israelis.

A clandestine war had been declared. Carlos's assignment was to kill Khader Kano, a Syrian journalist and double agent who was passing on information to the Israeli consulate in Belgium. Carlos followed him to a Paris apartment and pumped three bullets into his heart.

A Ha Mossad squad retaliated by killing Boudia's deputy, Dr. Mahmoud Hamshari, with a sophisticated explosive device. A powerful plastique bomb was planted under his telephone table, and to make sure they had the right man, the caller asked, "Is this really Dr. Hamshari?" "Lui-même," he replied. A split second later the bomb was triggered by a high-pitch tone transmitted on the line.

With Hamshari dead, Boudia appointed Carlos as his deputy. The tempo accelerated on both sides. There were a score of murders in Nicosia, Madrid, Khartoum, Rome, Beirut, and Paris. By June 28, 1973, Boudia's number had come up. He was blown up in his Renault sedan early one morning as he was leaving the Paris apartment of one of his many mistresses.

Not only was Carlos appointed by the PFLP to succeed Boudia (the assumption being that a Latin American was less likely to attract Ha Mossad's attention), but Kotov made him the KGB's European coordinator of terrorism. (The Russians are always anxious to demonstrate the weakness of democratic societies.) Yet Carlos remained a free agent and could initiate his own operations for the PFLP, or he could free-lance contract work for good revolutionaries like Qaddafi and Boumedienne.

Carlos's first request to Habash was that he be permitted to revere Boudia's memory by setting up a special group of Arab commandos to be named after him. Habash agreed, but suggested that Carlos finance the Commando Boudia cell himself. For the necessary financing, Carlos turned to Qaddafi, who was already a staunch Black September supporter. Their main arms depot in Europe was located in the basement of the Libyan embassy in Bonn. As one terrorist observed, if someone had dropped a match in the place, half of the West German capital would have gone up in smoke.

It was at this time that Carlos began working with Michel Wahab Moukarbel, who was a Beirut interior decorator and Habash's paymaster and liaison in Europe. Posing as an art student at the Sorbonne, Moukarbel had a fetish for keeping meticulous records of all disbursements, however incriminating, incurred in the planning and execution of terrorist acts.

For his base of operation, Carlos selected a villa in Villiers sur Marne, just outside Paris, which was being used by a Turkish-Palestinian network. The place was equipped with a vast arsenal of weapons and explosives and a powerful radio set beamed on Beirut. As always, Carlos maintained his heavy traveling schedule, continuing his contacts with other terrorist groups and recruiting new members; in London and Paris, he stepped up his campaign of seducing Latin American girls who could provide him with safe houses.

Also during this period he was busy compiling an assassination list of public figures who were either Jewish or in sympathy with Israel. Some would receive letter bombs, but others, like J. Edward Sieff, who was honorary vice-president of the Zionist Federation of Great Britain, would merit a personal visit.

At seven o'clock on the evening of December 30, 1973, a hooded Carlos knocked at the door of Sieff's St. John's Wood home. When the butler answered, Carlos pointed his pistol and said, "I want to see Mr. Sieff." The terrified butler led Carlos to a bathroom on the first-floor landing and opened the door. Sieff, who was fully dressed, turned to face the two men, a surprised look on his face. Without a word, Carlos shot him in the mouth from a distance of about four feet. Sieff fell to the floor and Carlos ran from the house. Sieff miraculously survived because of remarkably strong teeth, which deflected the heavy 9-mm bullet to an angle that lodged it in his spine instead of his brain. Carlos was not linked with the shooting until the gun he used was found with other weapons and passports belonging to him.

In the summer of 1973, Carlos helped Takahashi Taketomo set up the URA's Paris cell. A former professor at Rikkyo University and an expert on eighteenth-century French literature, Taketomo was in charge of the URA's European network. His orders came directly from Fusako Shigenobu in Lebanon.

In an attempt to broaden the base of the URA's operation, Fusako had stepped up the recruiting program. She not only concentrated on the growing bands of young Japanese turning to hippie-style lives in various European capitals but saw to it that leaflets were smuggled into Japan and distributed on university campuses. All a prospective recruit had to do, the leaflets promised, was to make his intentions known. "Within a month, we will contact you. We have that kind of network everywhere." However, becoming an accepted member of the URA was not just a question of signing up with the nearest recruiting officer. It was not quite that simple, as Yun Nishikawa would discover.

On May 21, 1973, as the *Grigori Ordshonikidse,* two days out of Yokohama, made ready to dock in Nochodka, the Soviet border patrol took up positions on the gangway. Nochodka is the civilian port of the military reservation of Vladivostok and the eastern terminus of the Trans-Siberian railroad.

In Russian and in English, the passengers were asked to have their passports, visas, and tickets ready. One of the passengers was Yun Nishikawa, who was traveling a prescribed route to Europe. This included the Green Express of the Trans-Siberian, which is the longest railroad line in the world: some fifty-eight hundred miles separate Nochodka from Moscow, the transfer station for Nishikawa's continuing journey to the West.

Nishikawa had received some indoctrination before departing on his odyssey. He knew that the aim of the URA was, as stated in its writings, "the realization of the simultaneous world revolution by means of revolutionary struggle." Its global function was to support the "united armed struggle of the populations of all countries." Its four enemies were world imperialism, Israeli Zionism, the anti-Arab movement, and revisionism in the Soviet Union. Nishikawa was told that the URA had built up a widely diversified organization outside of Japan. This included retreats in Beirut and Baghdad, a training camp in the hinterlands of Aden, a network of cells in Europe, and confidants in West Germany. The URA used Arabic organizational names, and the manner of giving orders was absolute. Members received only tactical explanations. They were guided and supported by a completely centralized authority. The introduction of new soldiers into the organization happened in an airtight manner. The newcomer remained on his own until shortly before the moment of decisive action. Only then did he become part of the group.

Nishikawa's odyssey was to prepare him for his entry into the URA. From Moscow, he journeyed to Helsinki, where he had been announced by the central agency and a confidant put him up for two nights. From there it was on to Stockholm and then Hamburg, where he took a room in a hotel near the main railroad station and familiarized himself with the layout of the city. Continuing with his travels, he visited Bonn, Brussels, Paris, Barcelona, Valencia, and Madrid.

It was in Madrid that he received his first trial assignment. He was instructed to assume a secondary role of support during the hijacking of a Japan Air Lines 747 jumbo jet on July 20, 1973, shortly after it had left Amsterdam. The goals of the mission were the release of URA prisoners in Japan and the recovery of the $6 million that Japan had paid in compensation to the victims of the Lod massacre. But the Japanese and three Arab terrorists became confused when their leader, a Latin American woman, was killed by the accidental explosion of a grenade she was carrying in her handbag. Instead of negotiating, they landed in Benghazi, Libya, where they released the passengers and proceeded to destroy the aircraft with explosives. A statement later issued by the Organization of the Sons of Occupied Territories said the act was in retaliation for the payment made by Japan in the Lod incident.

At the end of July, Nishikawa traveled to Rabat, Tunis, and Cairo, leisurely sightseeing as he went; he finally arrived in Beirut early in September. It was here in Beirut that the preliminary test for his acceptance into the URA took place.

During the oath-taking the recruit was asked ceremonially, "Are you determined to act like a soldier?"

Nishikawa replied, "I am determined."

"Are you determined to die, are you determined to do this absolutely?"

Again Nishikawa vowed, "I am determined, absolutely."

With the ceremony over, Nishikawa moved in the direction of Europe. During the next three months he visited Damascus, Amman, Baghdad, Istanbul, Athens, Rome, Geneva, and Zurich. At the beginning of 1974, he arrived in Paris, staying a few days, before continuing to London and Scotland, returning to London at the end of February. He spent two weeks going back and forth between East and West Berlin. He noticed that he could get from West to East Berlin by elevated train or subway without being checked by the authorities. Travel time from the last station of West Berlin to the first station of the eastern sector was no more than two and a half minutes. This was the kind of information that interested him as a prospective terrorist.

In mid-March, Nishikawa returned to Beirut. The time had come for him to receive military guerrilla training. The camp was situated in the People's Democratic Republic of South Yemen in the rocky backcountry of Aden. The Arab instructors were supported by soldiers of the Yemenite army. Nishikawa, together with five other Japanese recruits, was instructed in the use of automatic weapons, bombs, and TNT explosives. They had access to semiautomatic weapons, submachine guns, pistols, and bazookas of Soviet origin. His training as a future bomber consisted of practice with hand grenades, explosives, detonators, plastic bombs, mines, time fuses, and fuses. He studied attack formations, reconnaissance activities, conspiratorial behavior, reactions of the enemy, and one-man attacks. He practiced attacking tanks, armored cars, and bullet-proof limousines.

Commands were given in a mixture of Arabic and pidgin English that sounded like it was copied from a John Wayne film: "All right, you guys, up, up, march, march!" or "Run, double time, march, stop! Lie down! Stand up! Lie down!" The day was from 5 A.M. to 10 P.M. It went on seven days a week for two and a half months. Then it was on to Baghdad to attend a course on "strategy of translation." This code phrase designated the abduction of well-known personalities within the Japanese economy with the aim of extorting large sums of money for the support of the URA in foreign countries. The specific plan was to abduct representatives of the Mitsubishi and Marubeni companies located in Düsseldorf. This plan was the creation of Professor Taketomo and Fusako Shigenobu.

Nishikawa's next trip was to Paris, but this time he traveled with the bosses. Once in Paris, Nishikawa, Fusako, and Taketomo met with others in the apartment of Yoko Hidakas, a student at the Sorbonne. Recognizing the extreme difficulties inherent in the enterprise, Fusako decided to send Taketomo, Nishikawa, and a reconnaissance group to Düsseldorf to study the situation. For further reinforcement, Fusako later assigned Yutaka Furaya to the reconnaissance group. Furaya arrived in Düsseldorf with authorization placing him in charge of the undertaking. This created a rift in the group, and Furaya was recalled to Beirut.

This time the Beirut police were alerted. It was rumored that a Mossad undercover agent had whispered in their ear, and they in turn had tipped off the French when Furaya boarded a flight for Orly Airport on July 28. Of course, the Israelis, the Lebanese, and the French all strongly denied this, insisting that Furaya was already a known terrorist.

In January 1974, Furaya, a Japanese companion, and two PFLP members had unsuccessfully tried to blow up the Shell Oil refinery in Singapore. After setting a small fire, they seized eight hostages aboard a ferryboat and demanded safe passage to an Arab country. As the negotiations dragged on, five PFLP terrorists seized the Japanese embassy in Kuwait, holding the ambassador and eleven hostages until their four comrades were flown from Singapore to Kuwait. The hostages were released, and all nine terrorists flew to Aden and freedom.

On his flight to Orly, Furaya was traveling as a student under the alias of Koji Susuki. From the way he behaved, he certainly did not expect any trouble. He jauntily waved his passport in the air as he went through customs. But they were waiting for him.

A customs officer asked him to open his bag. "Mon Dieu," said he, plucking three false passports lying on top of Furaya's neatly packed clothes, "what have we here?" Furaya was hustled to a private office and his bag was carefully taken apart, revealing a false bottom with $10,000 in bogus traveler's checks and coded messages exposing the URA's current "battle plan." Although there were no specific dates or places, the decoded orders revealed a general plan for attacks on Japanese embassies, businesses, and prominent Japanese industrialists in Europe. There were instructions for five Palestinian "commandos" to meet at a "certain" place in Europe for strategy talks preliminary to joint operations by the URA and PFLP. Fusako Shigenobu had sent orders for Japanese leaders in Paris to contact her through an unidentified Japanese staying at a "building" or an "apartment" in Beirut. Police conjectured that the raid was going to be against athletes at the Seventh Asian Games soon to open in Teheran.

Of even greater importance, the papers revealed Furaya's Paris contact to be Mariko Yamamoto, an employee in an elegant Japanese gift shop called

Mitsukoshi, on the Avenue de l'Opéra, in the center of the wealthiest part of Paris. It specialized in selling the big names of Paris, such as Yves St. Laurent and Dior, to wealthy Japanese tourists who wanted to buy souvenirs from someone who spoke Japanese.

It was a perfect cover, for no one would suspect a messenger amid the thousands of Japanese visiting the shop every week. And Mariko was the ideal contact, a young, well-groomed, middle-class girl, a graduate of Tokyo Women's Christian College. The store management, then unaware of her activities, would later describe her as a "quiet, moon-faced girl, always smiling —a good worker."

She had been there just over a year, and during that time all messages from Japan and Beirut for the URA's Paris base were channeled through her. She was a strong-willed, determined woman: when her cover was finally broken, she told the French police absolutely nothing. However, before picking her up, the police had watched her flat and the flats of her visitors until they felt they had cracked the URA's Paris operation—discovering at the same time how little they and other European security forces knew about it. Despite warnings from the Israelis after the Lod massacre that Japanese terrorists were branching out to Europe, the French had not the foggiest notion of what was going on until the Israelis tipped them off to Furaya.

Surveillance of Mariko's flat led them to Takahashi Taketomo; raids on other flats resulted in the arrest of six more Japanese, but only temporarily. In French law, intention alone cannot be punished. Furaya was held on charges of carrying counterfeit checks and forged passports, but the other eight were expelled to countries of their choice. Taketomo chose to go to Amsterdam, giving Poland as his eventual destination. Mariko chose Rome; from there she went to Switzerland and on to Beirut, where she assumed leadership of a new group named VZ58 in memory of the weapons used at Lod. Two went to Sweden, and two more to Japan, where they were questioned by police and released. The destination of the other two is unknown.

So the French were left with Furaya, who proved to be more than they could handle.

Meanwhile, the Düsseldorf raid was called off, but Mitsubishi did not entirely escape. At the end of August, a massive explosion at Mitsubishi's Tokyo headquarters, in the heart of the busy Marunouchi business district, killed eight persons and injured more than three hundred others. A few weeks later, a time bomb in the Mitsui Trading House injured sixteen persons.

As for Yun Nishikawa, who had been brought in on the planning of the now abandoned Düsseldorf operation, he had remained at the ready as an instant "active reserve." Between June and the beginning of August, he reappeared in Düsseldorf, Cologne, Frankfurt, Vienna, and Berlin. The news of Furaya's arrest reached him on August 10, at which time he received orders to return to Baghdad via East Berlin, Sofia, and Belgrade. Upon his arrival in Baghdad on September 6, he was told that he must be ready to engage "in the struggle for the liberation" of his compatriot Furaya. Twenty-four hours later, Nishikawa was once again in Vienna, where he was contacted by a liaison officer from Stockholm and told to proceed to Switzerland to meet with other URA members.

It was in Zurich that Nishikawa first met Carlos and Moukarbel. The task of devising a tactical plan to liberate Furaya was assigned to Carlos's Commando Boudia. Among Moukarbel's meticulous bookkeeping records found in the Paris flat of Ampara Silva Masmela after his death were notations choreographing his and Carlos's movements on behalf of the Japanese. They showed that the two traveled to The Hague, Zurich, and Amsterdam several times in August and September. A note dated September 3 told of a meeting in Zurich "with the Japanese" in which final plans were worked out for the attack on the French embassy at The Hague. The cost of the operation was 4,000 Swiss francs.

On September 12, Carlos, Nishikawa, and the two other URA soldiers designated for the attack took the train to Amsterdam. There Nishikawa was told that other URA members had already completed the preliminary work for the hostage action. The attack was set for the next day. The URA soldier Kuzuo Tohira was to stand at the ready as a reservist. Nishikawa's moment of glory had arrived. The next day he would finally go into action.

Armed with pistols and grenades supplied by Carlos, the three Japanese strode into the French embassy in The Hague, rode the elevator to the fourth floor, and seized eleven hostages, including the French ambassador, Count Jacques Senard. The scenario had a familiar ring: unless Furaya was released by three the next morning, they would begin killing the hostages, one by one. The French did not lose any time in responding. Furaya was hustled on a French air force jet and flown to The Hague.

But the French lost control of the situation when Premier Joop den Uyl of the Netherlands tried to resist the terrorists' demands. The negotiations became deadlocked. At one point, the Japanese refused to communicate with government officials. However, they were using the telephones to contact URA leaders throughout Europe, and the calls were recorded and filed for future reference. One of the interesting revelations was the respect paid to Fusako Shigenobu, who was referred to as the "Queen of the Red Army."

Since it was his operation, Carlos decided to do something to get it unstuck. On Sunday, September 15, a terrorist hurled a grenade into a crowd of young people gathered at the popular Le Drugstore on St. Germain-des-Près on the Left Bank. Two were killed and thirty-four injured. At first it was thought that the attack had been directed at the owner, a French Jew named Bleustein-Blanchet, but later a man speaking French with a strong Spanish accent telephoned two news agencies, Agence France Presse and Reuter's, to say that the attack was a warning to the French and Dutch to grant the demands of the Japanese commandos at The Hague. "Otherwise we shall attack a cinema next."

An important piece of evidence came to light when detectives sifting through the debris found the grenade's detonator. It was identified as a USM26 that had come from a batch of seventy-five stolen in 1972 during an armed raid by the Baader-Meinhof gang on an American depot at Miesau, West Germany. (Grenades left behind at The Hague by the Japanese would later be identified as coming from the same stolen batch. Following Moukarbel's murder, police would find more of the stolen grenades hidden in suitcases belonging to Carlos. And Flex-U, a powerful plastics explosive, also stolen from Miesau, was used by Carlos for car bombs that went off in front of the right-wing newspaper *L'Aurore,* the Jewish magazine *L'Arche,* and the right-wing magazine *Minute.*)

The Dutch and French capitulated the very next day. The terrorists and Furaya were flown to Damascus. "Operation gone smoothly according to plan," Nishikawa reported to Beirut headquarters. "All participants are well."

Back in Beirut, Fusako Shigenobu initiated a critique of the maneuver. Nishikawa and the other soldiers joined with Shigenobu in analyzing the elements that had made The Hague a success and Düsseldorf a failure.

A month later Nishikawa and two others traveled to Copenhagen, with stops in Athens and Vienna. Their assignment was to plan a commando action against the Lebanese consulate in the Danish capital. Discouraged by various obstacles, they decided to switch to the Lebanese embassy in Stockholm. Still not pleased with the situation, they went to inspect the ambassador's home. But it was not to be. They were identified, arrested, and quickly deported to Japan, where police awaited them. Nishikawa, who had been determined to die, confessed it all during interrogation.

Wilfried Boese was twenty-five when he first met Carlos in 1974. He was described by his father as an "idealist on the wrong track" who was "still struggling with his religion of Marx and Mao and so forth." As a teen-ager, Boese had been a follower of Daniel Cohn-Bendit, the professional revolutionary and hero of the student movement of the late 1960s. Boese, his friends said, was an "unequivocal enemy of force."

Brigitte Kuhlmann, whom Boese later married, was a student of pedagogy from Hannover who wrote poetry and cared for spastic patients in order to "alleviate suffering through action." This full-bosomed daughter of Lower Saxony was known on the anarchist scene as an "extremely sensible type." Her creed was "Whoever is not for the RAF [the Red Army Faction was the designation of the Baader-Meinhof gang before the press began popularizing its two leaders, Andreas Baader and Ulrike Meinhof] is for Genscher." Hans Dietrich Genscher was federal minister of the interior and hence head of all West German police agencies.

Wilfried and Brigitte met in the offices of Red Star, a Frankfurt left-wing book publishing house that police suspected of being a central meeting place and school for terrorists. Two of their associates at Red Star were Hans-Joachim Klein, who would later participate in the OPEC raid, and Johannes Weinrich, a twenty-seven-year-old executive with the publishing firm. Boese and Weinrich lived in the same apartment building at Hohenstrasse 26.

All four, along with Klein's mistress, Hanna Elisa Krabbe, were members of the Second of June Movement then under the leadership of Ralf Reinders. Founded by Reinders in 1971, it was considered the most violent of the RAF splinter groups. The name commemorates the date of the death of Benno Ohnesorge, who was shot during a student demonstration against the Shah of Iran's visit to Berlin on June 2, 1967. Its symbol was a Soviet star with a submachine gun. It was Reinders, with the help of Carlos, who plotted the kidnapping of Peter Lorenz, which resulted in the release of five prisoners, including Gabriele Kroecher-Tiedemann. And it was Reinders who volunteered the services of Weinrich and Boese when Carlos was asked by Habash to launch a rocket attack on an El Al plane at Orly Airport. The target was not just any ordinary El Al plane: it would be carrying Israeli Foreign Minister Yigal Allon.

Toward the end of 1974, a three-man PFLP team arrived in Paris with Russia's most sophisticated antitank-grenade launcher, the RPG-7, a recoilless launcher firing fin-stabilized hollow-charge grenades that can penetrate 250 millimeters of armor. Weighing only 5 kilos, the launcher has an effective range of 300 meters.

While waiting for the date and flight number to be supplied by Beirut, Carlos, Moukarbel, Weinrich, and Boese carefully surveyed the airport. In Moukarbel's detailed records, police later found the disbursement of 2 francs for an entry ticket to Orly's public viewing deck.

One of Weinrich's tasks was to rent the two cars to be used by the terrorists. The false identification papers he used for this had been stolen by Ulrike Meinhof back in 1970 during a raid on the mayor's office in Lang-Gons, near Giessen.

The Orly attack took place around noon on January 13, 1975. Whether Allon, who was on his way to Washington for a round of talks with Secretary of State Henry Kissinger, was on that plane is not known. In any event, the attack itself was a total bust. Two rockets were fired at the Israeli airliner, a Boeing 707 carrying 136 passengers, as it was taxiing slowly toward a takeoff for New York. Both rockets, fired from a distance of thirty-five yards, missed the plane. The first round plowed into an airport catering building, and the second crashed through a parked Yugoslav DC-9 without exploding, tearing a hole under its right wing.

A Swissair official who saw the attack said, "I saw two men standing by a car aiming what looked like a bazooka at two planes. A big, tall, dark man aged about thirty carried the bazooka on his shoulder. The second explosion was much stronger. I saw the man with his bazooka recoil with the backfire and smash his car windshield."

The attack was made from a public-access road leading from Orly West to the terminal at Orly South. In their rush to escape, the terrorists dropped a 7.65-mm pistol of East European make marked with a star, and police later found the escape car, a white Peugeot, abandoned a few miles away near a suburban cemetery. Two RPG-7 launchers and an unexploded shell were in the back seat.

That evening an anonymous caller told Reuter's that the attack was the work of an Arab guerrilla group named the Mohammed Boudia Commandos. The attack failed, but the message did not fail to strike terror in the hearts of passengers and security forces. At London's Heathrow Airport, troops with light tanks staged a "security exercise." Security measures were tightened all over Western Europe.

A few days later the PFLP team decided to hit Orly again. Carlos advised against it, but when the Palestinian faction in his group insisted on carrying it out, he refused to assume responsibility. They were on their own.

This time they were spotted before they could fire a single rocket. A security officer guarding an El Al aircraft watched incredulously as a hooded man on the observation deck carefully leveled a bazooka in his direction. He promptly fired his submachine gun at the man. Another hooded man threw a grenade back. In the running gunfight that followed, three terrorists captured ten hostages and held them in a lavatory until French authorities agreed to place a Boeing 707 at their disposal. But once in the sky over the Middle East, the terrorists discovered that all Arab airports were closed to them. It was not until their plane was nearly out of fuel that Baghdad gave them permission to land.

The abduction of Peter Lorenz by the Second of June Movement in February 1975 had been such a success that Ralf Reinders again turned to Carlos for help when he received a two-word message smuggled from Ulrike Meinhof's prison cell: "Attack consulates."

Just after noon on April 24, seven terrorists burst into the West German embassy in Stockholm and seized the ambassador and eleven other hostages. They demanded the release of twenty-six Baader-Meinhof prisoners, including the eponymous leaders, whose trial had been set for May 21. They wanted $20,000 for each prisoner, access to lawyers, and a Boeing 707 waiting at Frankfurt to take the released prisoners to a destination of their choice. Unless their demands were met by ten o'clock that evening, one of the hostages would die every hour. In the event of an attack by the police, they would blow up the embassy. To show they meant business, they killed the military attaché when the police failed to pull back from the embassy building as directed. Police dressed only in underclothes were allowed to collect the body.

The Bonn government rejected their demands. Chancellor Helmut Schmidt told the Swedish prime minister, Olof Palme, that responsibility for operations would be left to the Swedish government. When informed of the decision, the terrorists refused to believe it. Nothing had changed, they said, and they marched Dr. Heinz Hillegaart, the economic counselor, to an open window so that police and television cameras could witness their determination.

"Hello, listen to me," Hillegaart yelled from the window. "Hello, listen to me." He repeated this several times. Then came three rapid shots from a machine gun, which killed him instantly.

The hostages looked at each other, wondering who was next. Their fears mounted when the terrorists began laying wires to 15 kilos of dynamite in the next room. The explosion came just before midnight. "A tremendous bang, a terrible pressure wave, walls collapsed, fragments of walls and furniture hit us," a hostage recalled.

The top floor burst into flames just as the terrorists came charging from the building, firing their submachine guns. All were captured after a furious battle except Ulrich Wessel, who ran back into the blazing building to avoid capture and then shot himself. One of those captured was Klein's mistress, Hanna Elisa Krabbe.

Not only was the attack a disaster for the terrorists involved, but the tough stand taken by the Germans and Swedes would serve as encouragement to other governments to follow suit. It was all the more frustrating for Reinders, who had rejected Carlos's suggestion to abduct the West German ambassador in Rome, Herman Meyer-Lindenberg; a sudden reinforcement of the guards had deterred Reinders.

One week later, in retaliation, Reinders and Carlos took out their frustrations by bombing the nuclear power plant at Fessenheim in Alsace, on the Rhine, which was still under construction. The bombing caused damages into the millions of dollars. Two charges destroyed the area planned for the reactor. Responsibility for the attack was claimed by a group calling itself Ulrike Meinhof–Puig Antich. A Spanish anarchist, Antich was executed in 1974. Police, however, would find scientific evidence linking the explosives found in Carlos's Paris flat with that used at Fessenheim.

While in Germany on this last trip, Carlos went to Frankfurt to visit Wilfried Boese and Brigitte Kuhlmann. He came unannounced to their apartment, on Hohenstrasse 26, and while they were pleased to see him, they were more than a little surprised when they opened the door. Boese would later tell the police that Carlos acted as though there were nothing unusual about his appearance. He said "comrades" had given him the address but volunteered no further explanation.

But this was not a social visit. Carlos, Boese said, wanted him to undertake a secret mission to Spain. Boese was supposed to gather "information about arrests, convictions, and political circumstances" that would be supportive of the Basque separatist movement. Before leaving that day, Carlos instructed Boese to meet him at the café Hôtel de Ville in Paris on June 24 for a more detailed discussion of the project.

Barry Woodhams had a nodding acquaintance with Carlos for about a year before being formally introduced. He would see him at various clubs in the Bayswater area, places where a young man could enjoy a pint or two in a convivial atmosphere without being swindled or rushed. Carlos appeared to be a pleasant enough sort, always elegantly attired, conveying the impression of someone with money in his pocket. And he seemed to be a real charmer with the ladies, his taste running to young dark-eyed señoritas, rather plump but always well groomed.

This was something Barry could appreciate. His latest girlfriend, Angela Otaola, fitted that description. She was Basque and worked as a waitress in a Bayswater restaurant. Not that she was the waitress type; at least, she was from a class different from that of the type of English girl who went in for that sort of work. She had left Spain, where she was a university student, because she did not like Franco's politics. Performing menial work was the quickest way of getting an entry visa. After seven years she would become naturalized, which meant she would be free to pursue any line of work.

After dating for a few weeks, Barry moved into Angela's flat. She had taken three separate rooms, each with its own lock, on the third floor of a sleazy, foul-smelling building that had given Barry pause for reconsideration the first night she brought him home. The building's entrance was on Hereford Road, between a laundry and an Indian restaurant. A narrow alleyway led to a small, very grubby courtyard, from which one went up a dark, filthy staircase. Halfway up the steps, the odor was so overpowering that Barry nearly turned back. But once he reached the top landing, everything was suddenly clean and pleasant. All three rooms were nicely furnished—nothing expensive but tasteful and comfortable.

It was about a week after Barry had moved in that Angela introduced him to Carlos. She had known Carlos for nearly two years, having dated him when she was a waitress at the Ducks and Drakes in Bayswater. She had been serious about Carlos at first, but he was away so much of the time and had so many other interests that her ardor had cooled down. They had drifted gradually into a platonic friendship they both seemed to enjoy. She found him to be an attractive, cultivated gentleman, a man of the world, and yet he was relaxed with all kinds of people.

Except for an occasional twinge of jealousy, Barry liked having Carlos around. He was not quite sure what Angela's relationship had been, but he was egotistical enough to believe that she would never be unfaithful as long as she had him in her bed. As for Carlos, he never gave any indication in his words or deeds to suggest anything other than friendship. In fact, whenever he was alone with Barry, Carlos enjoyed talking about his many girlfriends scattered across Europe. One time he said that his London girlfriend, Maria Romero, looked after him more efficiently than Angela looked after Barry.

"He was overwhelming in some ways," Barry recalled. "He was intensely intelligent and could speak on a wide variety of topics. All conversations with him would sooner or later turn into a kind of debate. He was hardheaded about getting his way. And there was this aura of affluence around him, that he was slightly more high-class, better situated than the rest of us.

"Yet he talked a great deal about money. He wanted to be rich. One time the American Express office got robbed and the gang made a clean getaway with about a quarter-million pounds, and Carlos said, 'I'd like to organize a bank raid like that and make a lot of money.' Then he looked at me and said, 'I want to be rich.' I said I'd join him if he could organize a perfect raid where nobody got caught."

Barry became suspicious of Carlos long before his deeds became public. "For a rich boy brought up in a big city, he knew too much about guns. Guns were something I had been brought up with in Zambia—my father was with the Colonial Service—and I started playing with guns when I was seven. We lived on a large plantation and I learned to hunt game with all sorts of weapons. I told him I could get nineteen out of twenty on the range with a .22 rifle. He said he could do it with a handgun. When I told him I used to shoot game from a kneeling position, with my elbow resting on my knee, he said that this was dangerous when shooting people. I was presenting too much of a target. 'But I wasn't shooting at people,' I said. He smiled and said, 'You should learn to shoot from a prone position, it's safer.'

"On another occasion, however, Carlos said he favored the death penalty in certain circumstances. Two criminals had just been guillotined in France for murder, and Carlos went on to say that it was a case of really brutal murder. 'Men who kill for money and not for political reasons,' Carlos said, 'deserve to die themselves.' "

Barry and Angela were socialists, and their political views, they felt, were more militant than Carlos's. He never discussed the Middle East or international politics, but he would on occasion criticize British politics. He could not understand why the extreme Left was not as active as the extreme Right.

"He said he was a Peruvian economist representing a Peruvian company in Europe. He was always talking about business and contacts and traveling all over the place. Every time he came back from a trip to Europe, he brought us a couple hundred duty-free Marlboro cigarettes and a great big bottle of Bacardi rum. He always dropped in unannounced, and if we had others in for dinner, he wouldn't stay. We'd say, 'Come on, you can join us, sit down.' 'Oh, no, no, no.' We'd give him a glass of wine and he'd say, 'I'll be gone in a minute.' The next time I turned around he was gone.

"He never wanted to intrude. He was a very relaxed guy. He'd walk in, take off his jacket, sit back in one of the chairs, and start talking about anything and everything under the sun. He loved to talk and argue, all very friendly, but he had to get the best of you. He had a fantastic command of the English language, but he spoke very fast, clipping off the words in such a way that it sounded like they were all joined together. He didn't have an American or British accent, it was all his own. It was the same when he spoke Spanish. He talked so fast even Angela couldn't follow him at times.

"He used to invite us out quite often. He'd say, 'Come on, come on, come to Churchills with me.' But his idea of going out was around midnight or one in the morning. I had to be at work in the morning. [Barry was a research technician in biochemistry with the Chemical Warfare Defense Establishment.] So we used to sit around the flat and drink. He was quite a poker player. He bragged that he used to play every night of the week, and for big money.

He frequented all the smart gambling places in London.

"He never talked about his mother, but he used to make fun of his brother who was dark skinned whereas he was light skinned. He always called his brother the 'nigger.' He'd say, 'My nigger brother.' He liked to brag about the people he knew, about drinking Napoleon brandy at some rich friend's house, trying to impress us with his social life. He played tennis at Queen Elizabeth College, which is about two hundred yards from Phillimore Court, where his mother lived.

"One night we got going on security systems at airports. I told him about seeing a television program on how they had increased security precautions at airports, but he just shrugged it off: 'They're a waste of time because they won't work for someone who knows what he's doing.' Then he went on to tell me about Charles de Gaulle Airport in Paris. He explained about the all-glass tunnels with the moving walks that took people to their planes. There were two security guards at the head of the tunnel and one up on top looking down. 'If you have three or four people who are well organized,' Carlos said, 'and who are absolutely determined, all you have to do is shoot the two guards on the gate and run like hell down the tunnel. You can forget about the guard on top. The tunnel is crowded with people and with the distortion in the glass, we'll be on the plane before he gets a shot off. We might lose one man, but no more than that.'

"He wasn't giving it as a hypothetical situation. He was saying, 'I've been there lots and lots of times and I know what can be done.' When I mentioned the new devices that check your luggage and sniff for explosives, his answer was the same: 'It's easy if you're absolutely determined. You can get anything through.' "

But Carlos would not elaborate. It was then that Barry got suspicious enough to open a black plastic holdall Carlos had left with Angela almost a year before Barry had moved in with her. Carlos had asked her to look after the bag because he traveled a lot and hated to leave valuables unprotected in a hotel room. In the event something happened and he could not reenter Britain, she was to give the holdall to Maria Romero. Maria Nydia Romero de Tobon was a thirty-nine-year-old lawyer with the Colombian Trades Union in London. She was known professionally as Nydia Tobon. Carlos had given Angela a telephone number where Maria could be reached.

"I didn't look in the bag," Angela said. "Spanish people who are asked to look after something would never touch it." From time to time, Carlos would take the bag into another room and go through it. The bag, which was extremely heavy, was kept in the living room, next to the record player, and Barry had bumped it a couple times, wondering each time why it was so heavy.

The day after the conversation about de Gaulle Airport and while Angela was at work, Barry carefully picked the lock and opened the bag. The first thing he saw was a Czech Vzor 7.65-mm automatic pistol with a twelve-inch silencer, ammunition, and two empty magazines. There was a 9-mm Browning pistol and a 7.65 Mauser pistol, both with ammunition; three M26 grenades;

several black rubber coshes; about two pounds of gelignite wrapped in an orange polythene bag from a Paris children's shop; a brown paper bag containing puttylike explosive; a Chilean passport in the name of Adolfo José Muller Bernal, with a picture of Carlos in it; three rubber stamps for forging British entry visas, one of which had Arabic script on the back; a Kuwaiti driver's license and passport details in the name of Hector Hugo DuPont; and sheaves of newspaper clippings from the London Jewish *Chronicle* of prominent people and organizations involved in the Zionist movement.

There was a list of some five hundred names written in red ink on exercise-book paper and in a black address book. This list was obviously culled from the contacts book of someone with connections in show business, industry, and politics—it included private addresses, unlisted telephone numbers, nicknames, photographs, diagrams of streets near the homes, references to favorite leisure and daily activities, and roads frequently traveled. The names ranged all the way from J. Edward Sieff to playwright John Osborne and his wife, actress Jill Bennett, to Lady Elliott of Harewood and Lord Drogheda, to conductor Norman Del Mar.

In a locked cash box at the bottom of the holdall, Barry found a pen-size gas-disseminating pistol that could also fire bullets, a Russian hand grenade, and a passport belonging to Michel Moukarbel.

That evening Barry told Angela about the contents of the holdall. They discussed it a long time before deciding that the safest move was to put it back by the record player and not say anything about it. Barry made sure that everything was back in its proper place. "If we had decided to tell him I had looked in the bag," Barry said, "I would have wanted one of those guns in my hand at the time. It was like opening Pandora's Box. We were damned if we went to the police, and damned if we didn't. That's what you get for being nosy. And I might add, that's what you get for being nice like Angela and doing a friend a favor." Barry was referring to what later happened to Angela when the police learned of the arms cache. But that is getting ahead of the story.

There was another Angela in Paris, Angela Armstrong, but this one was an observer, a friend of Carlos's mistress, Nancy Sanchez, a Venezuelan girl whose small second-story flat at 9, rue Toullier, in the heart of the Latin Quarter, would become the vehicle for Carlos's dramatic debut onto the stage of international terrorism.

Far from being a Spanish beauty, Nancy was a rather plain-looking girl, with dark Indian features and black hair styled in a bushy Afro. She was a sociology student, and her flat was about a stone's throw from the Sorbonne. The building at 9, rue Toullier was typical of the area—a little run-down but kind of colorful, standard Left Bank architecture, a square structure with a square courtyard, with outdoor winding staircase and narrow flying bridge across the courtyard.

Nancy shared the flat, which was one large room with a small kitchenette and bathroom, with Maria Teresa Lara, a psychology student at the Sorbonne who was also a Venezuelan journalist and a dedicated Marxist. After Carlos moved in with Nancy, they hung a curtain to separate their bed from the rest of the room.

It was the perfect address for Carlos. Whatever the place lacked in appointments was made up for in conveniences. The area was populated by thousands of students, again a polyglot-hippie ambiance, where landlords collected their rents and asked no questions. Carlos was just another face in the crowd, a chameleon blending with the terrain. Around one corner was the Sorbonne and around the other was the post office, with its banks of telephone booths from which he could make international calls.

Angela Armstrong was a secretary at the Collège de France, one of the great institutions of higher learning in Paris. Although a British girl born in South Africa, she spoke flawless French. In her own quiet, reserved way, she was attractive; she was the mother of a small girl, born soon after the student unrest of May 1968, whom she was bringing up alone. She was totally devoted to her daughter, spending every moment away from work with her. Consequently, her only social contacts were the moments she spent at Nancy's flat during her lunch hour. She would walk the three blocks to 9, rue Toullier and there join with students who also brought their lunch in a paper bag. They would sit around, play the guitar, and sing Spanish songs.

"The first time I met Carlos was at Nancy's place in late December of 1974," Angela recalled. "I came in the room and he was sitting in Nancy's big chair. He's fairly well built and he sort of filled it. He seemed very much at home, very sure of himself. He was better dressed then most of the students, more classic clothes—not blue jeans, T-shirt, or long hair, just neatly dressed, well-groomed.

"He spoke to everybody as if this was his flat. Nancy seemed very taken with him. She said that he was Peruvian and that he worked for some international company as a commercial correspondent traveling a lot and making a great deal of money.

"I remember saying something in French, and Nancy telling me that Carlos didn't speak French, but spoke very good English, and he, just to show that he did, said something to me in English, and he did speak excellent English."

Since Carlos could speak passable French, this prompts some interesting speculation. Either he was more comfortable in languages in which he was fluent, or he wanted to eavesdrop on people who thought they were speaking a language he could not understand. Of course, there are other explanations.

Angela found it surprising that he would pose as a Peruvian, because "Peruvians know other Peruvians; that's how it works with the Latin Americans in Paris. All Venezuelans, for example, seem to stick together. The students who came to Nancy's flat were mostly Venezuelans.

"There were always a lot of young people there. Students who lived in rooms with no water came to have a shower, some came to do their wash, others came to borrow books or just to sit for a half an hour before a class. There was a constant flow of people. You'd meet someone once and you might never see them again. It was just a very casual atmosphere.

"Nancy was always a very happy girl, but a month later she was rather depressed. She said Carlos was in Geneva and she hadn't seen him in two weeks. It was very serious between them, she said, and when he came back, she was thinking of sharing the room with him. From then on, every time she talked to me about Carlos, it was always about how fantastic he was. This wasn't the Nancy I knew, not the carefree, independent girl, who had lots of boyfriends and who was very serious about her studies. Now she was prepared to give up a lot of things for him, and it was obvious that he dominated her.

"I couldn't understand it. The more she talked to me about him, the more it didn't fit with the girl I knew. Nancy was the kind of girl who brought happiness when she came into a room. People would be sitting around, talking quietly, and she'd come and things started to move. She would pick up her small Spanish guitar, which had its own particular sound, and she would play and sing. My favorite song was *Gracias a la vida,* which means "Give Thanks for Life," and was written by a woman who committed suicide, which was a kind of contradiction. Everyone would sing along with Nancy. She brought life into a room. It was always like this until Carlos came along.

"I remember all the times I came across that little bridge and heard the music. I knew it was Nancy playing. The green drapes would be open and I'd knock on the door and go right in, saying, 'Cómo está?' and there was a certain liveliness that makes me feel sad now when I think about it.

"Then one day the green drapes were drawn and the door was locked. Carlos had installed a little peep hole in the door. Now you had to knock and wait while somebody came to look at you. There was a pause and then the door would open. That changed the whole atmosphere.

"And there was the problem of Maria Teresa Lara, who was withdrawn but very sure of what she was doing. You felt that she had tremendous control over herself and that unlike most of the Latin Americans who were there to have a good time, to drink and sing, she had plans for the future, she went to the library, she did certain things. Tremendous determination. She was the leader of conversations on political matters. A complete opposite of happy-go-lucky Nancy.

"Maria fell for Carlos. I came in there one day, and they weren't speaking to each other and it was because of Carlos. Nancy explained to me that when you have a bed on either side of a curtain, it's awkward. The feeling of tension grew, and it was because they both wanted Carlos. The atmosphere in the room became even more strained, but this didn't seem to bother Carlos.

"The last time I saw Nancy with Carlos was on the afternoon of June 27, 1975, just a few hours before the murders. I was at the post office, waiting for a call to be put through to my mother in London, when he came and sat beside me.

"He said, 'Oh, what a nuisance. I can't get England on the phone.' He was trying to get it direct himself. [Angela Otaola would later tell police that Carlos had called her from Paris on that day: "He phoned to say he was in Paris and did I want anything special brought back for my birthday."] Nancy was leaving for Venezuela that evening, going home for the summer holiday, and she had gone to the Sorbonne to arrange for her fall classes.

"He said he didn't like the university, that being a student was a waste of time, that it annoyed and bored him, and that he didn't like that kind of scene. From that I deduced he had been an unhappy student. I sat there on this bench in front of the telephone booth, and I didn't have anything to say to him. I saw his reflection in the glass, and I wondered what Nancy saw in him. It was just intuition, something I can't explain, but there was something I didn't like about him. It's hard to explain, because he was naturally friendly, and he was someone in whom you could very easily have confidence. In spite of the way I felt about him, I thought he was someone I could talk to very naturally if I had a problem.

"Then I took my call, and when I finished, Nancy was back. She was completely demoralized. Her face was chalk white and she looked awful. I wanted to say something, but Carlos was right there, and I disliked him even more then. His attitude toward her was so superior. Later, when I learned the kind of a man he was, I wondered if Nancy had found out about him. Perhaps that was why she was so downhearted.

"At one point he pinched her cheek and said, 'Hey, Negrita, cheer up, everything is all right.' I didn't like that at all. It was very demeaning, and I was surprised she accepted that kind of treatment.

"She seemed to pull herself together then. She told me she was leaving for Caracas that evening, and I said, 'Bon voyage, see you in September,' and she said, 'We're having a few drinks at about five or six, and we'd love to have you come.' I thanked her and said I had to go home to look after my daughter. If I had gone I might not be here today."

There should have been more on Carlos's mind that day than a farewell party for a girlfriend. There was the problem of Michel Moukarbel. Carlos had not heard from him in seven days. He had called him at the safe house in London only to learn from Antonio Bouvier that Moukarbel had not arrived as scheduled.

Carlos first became aware of the problem on June 13 when he met with Moukarbel at a prearranged rendezvous near the Seine River. Moukarbel had just returned from Beirut and was carrying coded instructions from George Habash and 10,000 French francs, which he handed to Carlos in a sealed envelope. With their business concluded, Moukarbel gave him the bad news. Lebanese police, he said, picked him up in Beirut on June 9 and interrogated him for twenty-four hours. They roughed him up some, but he swore he told them nothing but lies. A foreigner, who looked like a CIA agent, had quietly sat through the interrogation.

Carlos was furious. Why had Moukarbel kept his rendezvous with him?

Didn't he realize that the CIA collaborated with the Israelis and the French DST, who were probably watching him at this very moment in the hope that he would lead them to other members of the group. Moukarbel must cut all contacts and lead the police on a wild-goose chase for one week. Then he should fly to London, where he would receive further instructions from Bouvier.

Assuming that he was himself under surveillance, Carlos returned to 9, rue Toullier by a circuitous route that involved the Métro, taxis, and buses that no surveillance could follow. But there was something Moukarbel had not had the heart to tell Carlos: Lebanese police had confiscated a notebook with code names and code addresses.

Once they had allowed "the bird" to fly to Paris, the DST had monitored his telephone conversations with Beirut, during which the name of Carlos had come up several times. Upon his arrival at Charles de Gaulle Airport, a surveillance detail followed him to the banks of the Seine and took pictures of both men and of the envelope being exchanged. They lost the other man (Carlos) in the Métro, and surveillance of Moukarbel proved extremely difficult. He seemed to run around Paris without rhyme or reason.

On June 20 the communications center of the French secret service sent a coded message to all police agencies and services of the Federal Republic of Germany, England, and other West European countries. The topic: counterintelligence. The subject: Moukarbel, Michel, Wahab, born June 13, 1941, in Askele, Lebanese citizen, decorator, living in Beirut. Works in the service of the PFLP. His task: the establishing of preoperative relationships with people who are supposed to undertake terrorist activities at the request of the PFLP.

Moukarbel, the report said, had left Paris on a flight to London. The danger existed that he would travel via the British airport into another country and elude surveillance. British police acted at once. They arrested Moukarbel during the passport check at Heathrow and deported him to France on the next flight out. This time the DST awaited him in an official capacity.

At five o'clock on the afternoon of Sunday, June 22, the DST began its interrogation. The agent in charge of the investigation was Commissaire Principal Jean Herranz. Assisting him were Raymond Dous and Jean Donatini. At first Moukarbel refused to answer any questions. A search of his luggage seemed to verify Herranz's assumption that he was a terrorist. Secreted in his suitcase was a barrel filled with ten kilos of potash chloride, a chemical used in the manufacture of incendiary and explosive devices, and a metal object that could be used as a firing pin. Realizing he had to offer a defense, Moukarbel said he bought the potash to get rid of weeds. A likely story, said Herranz as he settled down for a long and brutally exhaustive session, the kind the DST excels in.

On June 24, surveillance of an address found on Moukarbel paid off. When Wilfried Boese knocked at the door of Moukarbel's Latin Quarter flat, he was greeted by armed DST agents, who immediately took him to Herranz at the Ministry of the Interior. Boese first identified himself as Axel Klaudius, residing in Wennenden, near Stuttgart. When the passport was exposed as a forgery, Boese decided to tell part of the story.

The man who gave him this passport, he said, had appeared at his Frankfurt apartment one day without any notification. All Boese knew about him was that he called himself Carlos and he was a South American. He had presented his "plans" in a few words. He was concerned about Spain. That country, according to Carlos, was a "powder keg," and German comrades would be supplied with work. Carlos wanted Boese to travel to Spain to collect information about the political situation, above all about arrests and trials in Madrid, Barcelona, and Seville. The trip, Carlos assured him, would be without danger because among the millions of German-speaking tourists, Boese would not appear conspicuous. The details of this assignment were to be discussed at great length during their meeting in Paris.

Boese admitted he had met with Carlos at the café Hôtel de Ville just prior to going to Moukarbel's flat. At that meeting, Carlos had given money, the false Klaudius passport, and, as a contact point in Paris, Moukarbel's flat at 26, Avenue Claude Vellefaux in the Tenth District. And that, said Boese, was the full story of his adventure with this so-called terrorist.

After two days of interrogation Boese was delivered to West German authorities at Sarreguemines and later released on bail by an unsuspecting judge in Saarbrücken. The last time Boese was reported seen in West Germany was on September 20, 1975, when he and his bride, Brigitte Kuhlmann, appeared in Ober Olm bei Mainz to attend a party for the "freakwork" commune. A few days later, the couple took down their self-made wooden bed in their two-room apartment at Hohenstrasse 26 and vanished into the terrorist underworld. But Boese was not finished with Carlos. A year later he would surface as the leader of the group that skyjacked the Air France jetliner to Entebbe, Uganda.

Confronted with Boese's statement and with pictures taken of him with Carlos, Moukarbel began to waver. By now he was exhausted to the point of collapse. The interrogation had been going on for five days. The method used by the DST is for the agents to take notes and later dictate them to the interrogee, who takes down in longhand what they think he told them. By the fifth day, Moukarbel's handwriting was completely illegible. The last page of his confession was signed with an X.

A French prison, or any prison for that matter, is not a happy prospect to contemplate. So when Herranz finally promised Moukarbel exoneration in exchange for "cooperation and information," he agreed to take his captors to an apartment where they possibly could receive information on the whereabouts of this Carlos they seemed so interested in finding.

What Moukarbel did not understand, of course, was that he would not have been jailed. The last thing the French wanted was a confrontation with terrorists. It had been a hard year. The catalog of events included the two bazooka attacks at Orly; a doubleheader at The Hague and Le Drugstore; the kidnapping of the French ambassador to Somali; the gunning down near Etoile of Ramon Tradal, the Uruguayan military attaché, who previously had been head of his country's military intelligence during the Tupamaros' repression; and, on top of this, the confirmation by Libya that a squadron of French-made Mirage fighters fought for the Egyptians during the October 1973 Arab-Israeli war, in flagrant violation of the sales contract. Finally, the Middle East was a vital source of precious oil and a rich market for defense contracts.

It was a delicate situation. Paris was getting a reputation as a switching station for world terrorism. The French solution was to penetrate the terrorist network to the point where they could present their proposition to the leaders. They would tell them to do what they wished, but not in France or in French territories. So if the terrorists would quietly remove themselves to a neighboring country, the French would bid them farewell with no hard feelings. It was the kind of *quid pro quo,* they felt, the terrorists could not refuse. The French approach to terrorism had grown soft. The policy, as enunciated by William Studer, a high Interior Ministry official, was "no rough stuff, no reprisals for obvious reasons."

But Moukarbel and Carlos were not aware of this policy. In his confused state, Moukarbel may have convinced himself that Carlos would not be at 9, rue Toullier that evening. After all, he was seldom in one place for long. This way the students could warn him of the police's interest. Even if Carlos was there, what the police would see was a young South American playboy living with a couple of hippie college girls. Surely, the French, of all people, would not find anything sinister in *l'amour.*

On the other hand, Herranz and his two assistants, Dous and Donatini, had absolutely no intention of arresting anyone or taking anyone into custody —even of a preventive type, as in Moukarbel's case. They were not going to harass or threaten anyone. They had come for a little chat, to see what this Carlos had to say for himself. Perhaps they could win one more terrorist contact to their side. If they did, it would take them one step closer to the leaders they were trying to reach. They felt they were still nibbling at the edges of the network. They came unarmed because they were in complete ignorance of the nature of the situation they were about to face.

The last thing Herranz expected as he stood before the entrance to 9, rue Toullier was violence. It was about 9:30 on a muggy Friday evening, and the rabbit-warren streets of the Latin Quarter were crowded with young people out for an evening's entertainment. Herranz gazed absently at the Chinese artifacts in the window of an antique shop while Moukarbel scanned the names on the mail boxes, continuing his charade that he had never personally visited this address. All he knew, as he had explained, was that Carlos had mentioned that his girlfriend, Nancy Sanchez, lived here.

They climbed the winding iron staircase and crossed the little bridge. The door and drapes were closed, but they could hear music and singing coming from the flat. Leaving Moukarbel outside with Dous, Herranz knocked at the door several times before it was opened by Carlos. He was wearing tinted glasses and held a bottle in his hand. After Herranz and Donatini had identified themselves, they were invited inside and introduced to the three students there with him: Lema Palomares Duque, Edgar José Marino Muller, and Luis Angel Urdaneta Urbina.

Herranz accepted a drink, and the two men sat down at Carlos's invitation. Herranz asked about Nancy, and Carlos said she had left earlier that evening for Caracas. They had given her a farewell party, which explained the wine and music. Gradually, Herranz began questioning Carlos about his activities and relationships, and Carlos, sitting in Nancy's big chair, talked at great length about his business career. When Herranz brought up the name of Wilfried Boese, Carlos blandly denied knowing him. It must be another Carlos, he suggested, pointing out that it was a popular name. After a half hour of pleasant but unproductive conversation, Herranz motioned to Donatini, who excused himself and went outside to get Moukarbel.

Carlos remained seated, but his eyes behind the tinted glasses hardened when Moukarbel came into the room. Moukarbel tried to say something in Arabic, but Herranz silenced him. What Herranz wanted to know from Carlos was whether he recognized Moukarbel. Since Herranz was in possession of a photograph showing the two of them together, he already knew the answer to his question. What really interested him was how accomplished a liar he was dealing with. This could work to Herranz's advantage. Liars could be useful, especially when they got themselves out on a limb that Herranz could saw off.

Carlos looked directly at Moukarbel and denied knowing him. Herranz played his trump, handing Carlos the photograph and at the same time asking to see his passport. Carlos went behind the curtain to get it, and when he came out again, there was a 7.65-mm Russian automatic in his hand. Before anyone knew what was happening, he squeezed off five shots that instantly killed Moukarbel, Dous, and Donatini and critically wounded Herranz. All four men were down on the floor as Carlos quickly stepped toward Moukarbel, leaned forward, and fired another bullet into his head. He straightened up, looked at the students who were screaming hysterically, and ran out the door. It had taken less than ten seconds. A neighbor saw Carlos dash across the bridge and take the stairs four at a time. A moment later he had vanished into the Paris night.

Herranz, who recovered from his wound, would later say that he had never thought Carlos to be anything but another middleman. He had been shocked to see him come out shooting. Such behavior, he felt, was incomprehensible. What Herranz failed to understand was that he had come into contact with a trained terrorist, a man who killed not from passion but from a conditioned reflex. The question of whether or not to kill was not something Carlos agonized over. It was a decision that already had been made for him; he was ready at all times to kill to protect his cause. Carlos probably made his decision to kill all four the moment he suspected that Moukarbel had betrayed him. At that moment his years of training took over, and the only question remaining was one of strategy: how to kill and escape. Consequently, he was probably already on the street before anyone realized what had happened.

The three students were arrested, and the room was searched. On the table near the big chair, Marx's *Das Kapital* lay open. The students said Carlos was in charge of a circle of students who were taking a self-study course in dialectic materialism prescribed by the Soviet Union for prospective party members. They described Carlos as a man of great self-assurance and a somewhat imperial presence.

From the scene of the shooting, Carlos went directly to 11, rue Amélie, taking refuge in the flat of another girlfriend, Ampara Silva Masmela, a twenty-four-year-old Colombian who worked in a Paris bank. Taking pen in hand, Carlos wrote three letters that evening. The content of his letter to Scotland Yard has not been disclosed, but in the one to the DST, he charged that six DST agents, whom he named, had collaborated with the CIA and Israeli intelligence in the assassinations of Mahmoud Hamshari and Dr. Basil Koubaissi, an Iraqi PFLP member.

In a letter to Angela Otaola in London, he wrote:

Dear Angela,

As you know things were very serious here and I've taken off.

I did not ring you because I had to tear up your postcard. I'm sending you this letter in duplicate to the bistro [where Angela worked] and to your house because if anything happens to me and I've got the address wrong, one of them will reach you.

Don't ring my girlfriend [Maria Romero] yet. I'm going on a trip for an undetermined time. But I hope I won't be long in returning.

As for the *"Chiquitin"* [little baby] I've sent him to a better life for his treachery.

Kisses,
Carlos

Back at 9, rue Toullier, police found some interesting notations in Carlos's handwriting. One note said, "R. A. Jap contact Paris *cité.*" Another one referred to the South American House on Boulevard Jourdan, Paris, which was being used by second and third stringers of the Baader-Meinhof gang. On the same piece of paper Carlos wrote, "Germans without leadership, contact Frankfurt." They were to find their leader in Carlos, who already had jotted down the names of Gabriele Kroecher-Tiedemann and Hans-Joachim Klein —they would later help him storm OPEC—and next to their names was the notation "Our battle group Arm of the Arab Revolution." This shows that Carlos had already selected some members and the group's designation at least six months before the date of the operation. It is this ability to plan ahead that has earned him the respect of leaders like Habash, Haddad, and Qaddafi.

That Saturday morning, while the police were combing Paris for Carlos, Angela Armstrong, unaware of the commotion, had gone to Les Invalides air terminal to buy a ticket and fill out the necessary papers to send her daughter alone on a flight to London. School was out for the summer, and Angela's mother, a widow, was looking forward to spending some time with her granddaughter.

"We were waiting in this long line when I turned around and saw Carlos in the doorway. I was glad there was someone to talk to—it would break the monotony of waiting. I called to him, and he very casually sauntered over and put his arm on my shoulder in a friendly manner and walked me toward the exit. It meant that I would lose my place in line, but there was not much I could do about it. I said, 'This is my daughter, Nina.' He nodded and said, 'No problem.' I said, 'Oh, really.' I didn't know what to say. He said, 'I'm not from Peru. No, no, no—sorry, I'm not Peruvian.' I thought, well, that's strange. Then he said, 'Did you hear about me in the news?' I told him I didn't know what news he was talking about, and then he started speaking Spanish very fast, and I said, 'Look, it's no good. I can't understand you. It's too fast.' He nodded again and said, 'I've killed three men. It's not my habit to kill, but that dirty Arab betrayed me. I kill all those who betray me.'

"I was dumbfounded. I couldn't say anything. 'Oh, listen,' he said, 'write to Nancy and tell her to stay in Venezuela.' In the same breath, he mentioned something about three students having witnessed the shooting, naming them, and said, 'No problem, they're okay. Now I'm off to the Middle East.' His last words were about having to redo papers and what a nuisance it was. He said good-bye and sauntered out. I quickly went back to the line and I thought, 'He's not drunk and he seems quite sane; what on earth was that all about?' It wasn't until I bought a newspaper at the kiosk near my Métro station that I learned what had happened at Nancy's flat. That's when my panic started. I thought, My God, I'm going to be killed.

"It was terrifying to think that this person I had just talked to in complete confidence was a dangerous man. My reactions became irrational. The next morning I put my daughter on the plane and I went to talk with Venezuelan friends of Nancy's. I told them what had happened, and I was hoping they would tell me what to do, but all they were thinking about was how to get out of France. They were really scared. They said Maria Teresa Lara was in Marseilles and had telephoned to ask for money to get to Algiers.

"For two days I went around asking people for advice. I was positive I was being followed. I was running around in blind panic until the DST arrested me. I thought, okay, the decision has been made for me. I've got nothing to hide. I haven't done anything wrong. Perhaps they will be a little annoyed with me for not going straightaway to them, that would be something against me, but I never imagined that I would be brought before the special State Security Court and charged with 'collusion with agents from a foreign power likely to prejudice France's diplomatic situation.'

"All the arresting officers said to me was 'Don't worry, keep calm.' I was brought to the Ministry of the Interior, and I tried to explain to the two officers there that I would have come in on my own. I said, 'I know you want me because I saw Carlos at Les Invalides. I'll tell you exactly how it happened.'

Then I realized they didn't know anything about it. At this point six more men came rushing into the room, and from the furor, it was obvious they thought they had caught someone important. The atmosphere completely changed.

"The interrogation went on for four days and four nights—I can't remember exactly what happened. They tried every form of psychology: the hard line, the standing up, the being manacled to a cupboard, leaving me alone, walking around me and slapping me with a ruler. I got to the point where I wasn't physically able to talk any more.

"Whatever I said, they yelled that it wasn't true, that I was telling lies. All eight men stood there shouting at me. At one point, the door opened, a man came in and said something I never heard because he slapped me so hard I fell down. I got up, and he slapped me down again. He went out and I never saw him again. But I haven't forgotten his face.

"For the first fortnight in prison my heart was beating so hard, my blood pressure was so high that I couldn't think. They took me to the reception area one day and put me in a little cubicle with a double pane of glass, and a few minutes later my mother walked in. The expression on her face, the pain in her eyes told me what she had gone through, and I became hysterical. They nearly dragged me out. I kept crying, 'Well, it's my mother; I have a right to see my mother.' I told her all the charges against me and that I was innocent. I tried to tell her how it happened, but I was in such a state, I couldn't be rational.

"She brought me three flowers, which probably sounds silly, but it meant a lot, because normally you're not allowed to receive flowers. That evening they gave me the three flowers. I had such a feeling of pain. I would never wish to be the cause of the anguish I saw on my mother's face. She believed me, but she was a victim of the press same as I was. When you see articles saying these other girls had arms in their flat but the real spy is Angela Armstrong, the typical English girl but who speaks three languages. I was the perfect front. They compared me to Ulrike Meinhof. Even the stories that tried to be fair were slightly deformed, and sometimes I feel their injustice is even greater.

"After twenty-one days, I was told that I was leaving. I couldn't believe it, but it was true. I was released but on the condition that I sign in three times a week, that I stay in the apartment I live in now, and my passport was taken away of course. My lawyer thinks it will be at least two years before the case is cleared. He hopes, and I hope, that there will be no charge and the case will be dropped. I am learning to live with it. There is nothing you can do; you feel injustice, you feel each time you see the way old friends react to you, you want to explain, this is how it happened, not what you read in the newspapers, but it's impossible, you realize you just have to live with it. What else can you do?"

After completing their search at 9, rue Toullier, a police surveillance detail arrested and interrogated all visitors. Even after the story had appeared on the front pages of every major European newspaper, there was still a brisk traffic to the door of Nancy Sanchez's flat. Ulrike Schaz, a German national, was held for her support of the Palestinians; Jean-Mariel Leleu, a Frenchman from Lille, was found to be an acquaintance of Certania Menezes, a Brazilian with connections to the revolutionary Argentinian People's Liberation Army; and Luis Gonzales Duque, a Venezuelan medical student, belonged to MIR, his country's revolutionary Left.

During the interrogation of Gonzales, it came out that he, along with Carlos and some of the girls who frequented the flat, had close contacts with three Cuban DGI agents—Paul Rodriguez Sainz, Ernesto Reyes Herrera, and Pedro Larra Zamora—who were posing as cultural attachés at the Cuban embassy in Paris. Sainz was found to be the DGI's deputy head in France, and Larra was the one who provided funds disguised as study grants. The Cubans used a travel agency, Voyages pour les Jeunes, as a cover. Lema Palomares Duque, who had witnessed the shooting, and Albaida Salazar, both close friends of Carlos, along with thirty-two French students, had visited Cuba on "study grants" the previous summer to participate in an international brigade. Nancy Sanchez had contacts with Larra; and Maria Nydia Romero de Tobon, said the French, had direct links with Angel Dalmau, the second secretary to the Cuban embassy in London.

Whitehall dismissed the allegation as untrue. "The French were being a bit naughty, weren't they?" a spokesman remarked. It was true, he said, that Cuba had close links with the PLO and that Arafat had been an honored guest in Cuba the previous November, after his appearance before the UN General Assembly, but the PLO had announced it had no connection with Carlos nor his Middle Eastern contacts.

That was a little too naïve for the French to swallow. There was no question that the Cubans were actively engaged in funneling money and instructions to Carlos. But the KGB involvement placed President Valéry Giscard d'Estaing in a difficult diplomatic position. Alerted by Interior Minister Poniatowski of the Cuban DGI's involvement, the president sanctioned the expulsion of the three Cubans but stipulated that no mention was to be made of the KGB. This directive was followed during the on-the-record press conference, but off the record, the ministry's spokesman observed that the DGI had always worked for the KGB.

In his official statement to the press, Giscard said, "We believe that the Cubans have been turned by the Communist bloc into the main center of hostile activities in the French capital." What he wanted to say was that the Cubans have been increasingly used by the KGB as its agents for undercover work in Europe, the Middle East, and the Mediterranean and Persian Gulf nations. He went on to say, "The Carlos case, which until now constituted a striking demonstration of the unity of action among terrorist groups, has now been enriched with important elements, showing the assistance given to international terrorism by certain states. Today's development of the case confirms the close link between terrorist networks and the espionage service of certain states." Also expelled were Lema Palomares Duque, Albaida Salazar, and Maria Teresa Lara, who was already in Algiers and would later meet Carlos at the Edwardier Hotel.

It was not until Monday evening that police arrived at 11, rue Amélie. Going through Moukarbel's effects after his death, DST agents had discovered Ampara Silva Masmela's name on a check stub, dated June 13, in the amount of 2,500 francs. Tracing a series of endorsement signatures on it, they finally got her address from a jeweler.

Ampara quickly admitted that she had been Carlos's mistress for a year and that he had spent Friday night with her. Both Carlos and Moukarbel had left suitcases with her for safekeeping. The arsenal in Carlos's suitcase at this address was even more impressive than the one he had left with Angela Otaola. It contained ten automatic pistols; two Czech Scorpion submachine guns, with folding butt and silencer, a weapon designed for assassination work; eighteen hand grenades, with seven USM-26s from the same batch stolen at Meisau, while others were of Bulgarian make similar to those found in a suitcase abandoned by Japanese URA terrorists in Paris; twenty kilos of Flex-U high-powered plastics explosive; thirty-one pyrotechnical detonators and eighteen delaying releases; hundreds of rounds of ammunition in cartons, clips, and magazines; transistors identical to those found by French police in a 1973 raid on a Turkish terrorist cell that was planning attacks on Israelis living in Geneva (the thirty members were delivered to the frontier of their choice); textbooks on explosives and "the setting of traps"; sophisticated equipment and material to manufacture false passports and other identity documents, and forged passport stamps from various countries; four false passports in names earlier mentioned, plus Carlos's legal passport made out to Ilich Ramírez Sánchez; maps of bombed buildings; and another long list of assassination prospects that included, besides prominent Jews and French officials such as Poniatowski and Jacques Soustelle, some distinguished Middle Eastern names. Topping the list were Ali Aref, prime minister of the French Territory of the Afars and Issas (formerly French Somaliland); Mrs. Gihane el-Sadat, wife of the Egyptian president; and Sheik Yamani, whose name pointed the way to Carlos's next major operation, the OPEC raid.

Even more revealing were the contents of Moukarbel's suitcase. His astounding record-keeping was the key to the unraveling of Carlos's Paris network. Hotel bills, airline tickets, bills from travel and car rental agencies, checkbooks, documents dealing with the cell's coding system, and three note-books loaded with operational details. It was the kind of bonanza police usually only dream about.

By piecing it together, they were able to reconstruct Carlos's and Mou-karbel's movements for the preparation and execution of terrorist acts in Paris, Amsterdam, The Hague, London, Frankfurt, Zurich, and other places; the dates, as mentioned before, corresponded at all times with the specific time the acts were committed. For example, detailed plans of the offices of *L'Arche,*

L'Aurore, and *Minute* were found along with the dates of the bombings. There were studies concerning proposed attacks on the homes of "politicians of various tendencies, journalists, and intellectuals," police said.

And there were plans that had been abandoned for one reason or another:

- The abduction or murder of Mihdi el-Jabber, ambassador of the Arabian Emirate in London, planned for August or September 1974.
- Michael Archamides Doxi, a Greek member of Carlos's Commando Boudia, was ordered in 1973 to plant a bomb at Tel Aviv's Lod Airport. He refused and applied for asylum in Sweden.
- An "Action Israel," not described in any closer detail, called for eight terrorists to travel through several countries. This group, police theorized, may have been responsible for the attack on Tel Aviv's Savoy Hotel, in which eighteen persons lost their lives on March 5, 1975.
- A plan to assassinate Asher Ben-Nathan, Israeli ambassador in Paris, showed that the Israeli embassy was under observation from September 1974 to January 1975. Information collected included a list of buildings belonging to the embassy, the number of embassy limousines, as well as the license numbers of cars used by other embassy members. During her interrogation, Ampara Silva Masmela revealed that Carlos told her the ambassador was to have been attacked in his car. Set for January or February of 1975, technical difficulties caused the operation to be canceled.
- A plan for placing a bomb on a ship passing through the Suez Canal, timed to sink it at a point that would block the canal.

Despite the revelations in rue Amélie, the police dragnet failed to snare Carlos. At least now they knew that the man they hunted had turned Paris into an international clearinghouse for liberation movements dedicated to world revolution. Paris, with its half-million Arab refugees and thousands of foreign students, was the ideal recruiting place for terror organizations.

On Tuesday the British press ran a picture of Carlos, and Barry Woodhams knew it was time to act. Without consulting Angela, he first contacted the *Guardian,* a London newspaper, because, as he said, "I knew if I'd just gone to the police, I'm certain I would have sat in that bloody jail for four or five weeks, and nobody would have known where I was. I'd have just disappeared. I wanted someone in authority on my side." As it was, Barry spent one week in a "bloody grubby little cell" before the police convinced him that he should be a prosecution witness against Angela.

"The police had to charge somebody," Woodhams explained. "Theoretically, it was her flat—I was staying with her, but I had my own flat around the corner. I was the one who told the police about it, so that made me a police witness. But they only charged her with possession of the guns and ammunition. It would have been much worse if they had charged her with the whole lot. As it was, she served eight months and was deported to Spain."

The next one caught in the Carlos web was Maria Nydia Romero de Tobon. She was charged with possessing a false passport, one belonging to Antonio Dages Bouvier, which was found in her apartment. It contained the same forged entry visa stamp for Britain that appeared on other forged passports belonging to Carlos.

Maria was born in Colombia of an eminently respectable family. Her grandfather was one of the founders of the ruling Liberal party. A doctor of law and a student at the London School of Economics, Maria was a member of the Secretariat of the Colombian Communist party and her former husband was involved with the World Federation of Democratic Youth, a Communist-front organization. Her work as a trades union lawyer in London so impressed Colombian President Alphonso Lopez Michelsen that while on a visit to England he offered her a position in his administration. She turned it down; she wanted to stay in London because she wished to complete her studies and because the older of her two sons was in trouble with the British police for drug and theft offenses.

Acquaintances described her as a woman of charm and intelligence. Police saw her as something else. They saw a Communist, one who made frequent trips to Europe, including East Germany, and they saw a woman who seemed to lead two lives, one as a socialite and leader in the South American community and the other as a consort of hippie Left Bank types.

Maria met Carlos at the Colombian Center, where she worked. Because of her poor English, she was starved for a normal intellectual relationship. In Carlos she found an intellectual equal. They were both Maoists, she said, who thought Russia was too bourgeois.

At the time of their meeting, she was also close to a nervous breakdown because of worry over her son. One day Carlos gave her a stolen Italian identity card and told her to send her son out of the country and never see him again. She gratefully accepted it "because he was thinking of me and my son" but determined not to use it. She realized she acted stupidly, but "I was thinking as a mother, not a lawyer."

At her trial, on charges of possessing a stolen identity card and of using a false passport, evidence was introduced that she acted as a banker for Carlos, that she also helped Antonio Bouvier find a safe house by posing as his wife for the rental agent, and that she had met another of Carlos's associates, Michel Moukarbel, whom she knew as André. In fact, on Saturday morning, the day after the rue Toullier murders, she received a cryptic telephone message from Carlos: "Tell Maria that André was killed in a vehicle accident." On June 23, one day after Moukarbel was picked up by the DST, she had gone to France to meet him. When he failed to appear, she met Carlos instead.

She received regular monthly payments of 500 French francs from Carlos, which were posted to her from France. Once he asked her to bank £1,000 for him, and she later returned nine-tenths of it to him. She looked after documents for him and for Bouvier. She began to worry about the false passport Bouvier had left with her when she realized he had gone abroad without it. Police found in her flat two other identity documents that belonged to former boyfriends.

She testified that she had no idea Carlos was a terrorist. She thought he was working for political exiles, which explained the need for secrecy and the use of false names. As for Bouvier, she had been told he was being followed and needed a secluded house. Like Angela Otaola, whom she once met, she was jailed for one year and ordered deported upon completion of her sentence.

London police found that Carlos and Bouvier had taken joint tenancy of at least two flats in West London, but it was impossible to determine if they had lived in the flats or simply set them up as bases. Outside of a general description and the assumption that he and Carlos were leading a "continuing campaign of terrorism that has as its object Jewish persons not only in this country, but elsewhere in Europe," the police knew next to nothing about Antonio Bouvier. He vanished from England without a trace. Like Wilfried Boese and Gabriele Kroecher-Tiedemann, he would resurface in Entebbe a year later.

As well as can be determined, Carlos fled to Madrid on Sunday and was met by a PFLP contact, a former Chilean consul, who helped him travel to Algiers. He spent seven weeks in the Algerian capital before going to Tripoli, where he lived in a villa protected by Libyan security forces. It was there that he completed the plan for the OPEC raid, guided, of course, by Wadi Haddad, the PFLP's chief of operations, whom he met in Baghdad at the end of November. From there he flew to Madrid and on to Frankfurt where he collected his two German comrades and three Palestinians. They arrived in Vienna on December 19, two days before the attack.

Shortly after Carlos had escaped from Paris, Bassam Abu Sherif, a PFLP leader, said that Carlos was "a long-standing member" of the PFLP and his guerrilla network extended from Europe through the Middle East to Asia and South America. It was a "revolutionary organization which has done its best to support the Palestinian struggle to liberate Palestine by working against imperialism and Zionism."

Abu Sherif boasted that Carlos "is outside of the grasp of the police forces which are after him. You can tell all that Carlos will make his presence felt in the months to come. He will prove our point." Then after the OPEC raid, Abu Sherif described Carlos as "the most brilliant agent and our chief international operative." Carlos was recruited to the PFLP "about five years ago," he said, and underwent "orientation" in the Arab Rejection Front's training and indoctrination camps in the Jordan Valley, then under virtual control of the Palestinians. But Carlos was just one of a large number of European, Latin American, Asian, and African guerrillas who formed a "terror bank" from which specific people or groups could be drawn for operations planned by various revolutionary leaders. As an example, Abu Sherif said that Carlos recruited the terrorists for at least six of its major operations in Europe during the past eighteen months. "In our business," said Abu Sherif, "people like Carlos are indispensable, and we have people like him everywhere."

However many people like him they may have had, Carlos himself seemed to be everywhere. Early in January 1976, Ha Mossad reported that he was seen in Beirut. Three months later the Uruguayan army said that he was in Montevideo. He had come with his gang to assassinate Chilean dictator Augusto Pinochet, who was scheduled at that time to pay an official visit to the Uruguayan capital. In July he was sighted at the Olympic Village in Montreal.

The one operation not credited to him was the skyjacking of the Air France jetliner to Entebbe, Uganda. No one connected him to Wilfried Boese, the leader of that operation, and Gabriele Kroecher-Tiedemann, both killed by Israeli commandos. Nor did they connect him with Antonio Bouvier, who managed to escape during the Israeli attack. Although his name was not linked with this mission, it would be strange indeed if he had not had a hand in it.

He was seen in London, Paris, and Bonn. In fact, the most popular expression with security police everywhere was "Carlos was here!"

He became such a phantomlike figure that the idea caught on that Carlos was not a real person. The French believed he had been killed by other terrorists; the Germans said that he was no more than a code word for an international terror organization; and the Israelis, who hate for their enemies to become legends, advanced the theory that there were four different Carloses.

As his persona grew more mysterious, his image seemed to fade on police photographs. He was tall, he was short; he was fat, he was thin; his features were soft, they were sharp; he looked like Fidel, like Che, like a Jew, like a Palestinian, and sometimes, of course, like a South American. He was cruel, humane, vain, gentle, cold-blooded, generous, vicious, pleasant, petulant, intelligent, reckless, thoughtful, and fanatic. He was a Soviet agent, a Cuban spy, a Maoist, a Marxist, a Trotskyite, a playboy, a gangster—he was anything anybody wanted him to be.

One of the most perplexing aspects of terrorism for many people is motivation. What is the motivation behind Palestinian terrorism? What is the Palestinians' moral imperative? Their justification for this murderous global conspiracy? How does this burning hatred for the Israelis, this war to the death, justify the slaughter of innocent people in the airports and cities of the rest of the world?

For example, what was the justification for the attack at Rome's Leonardo da Vinci Airport a week before Christmas in 1973? What was the objective of the five Palestinians who indiscriminately firebombed one plane of holiday travelers, machine-gunned others, and escaped by hijacking another plane? Thirty-one persons died and countless others were injured, many permanently disfigured by the flames that nearly took their lives. The only ransom demanded was the release of two Black September terrorists who had been captured after killing three people and wounding fifty-five others in a machine-gun attack at the Athens airport earlier that same year. When the two released Black Septembrists refused to board the skyjacked airplane, they flew away without them. The goal could not have been the release of their comrades.

The objective was simply one more act of terror. Nothing is more terrifying than senseless brutality. People all over the world were repulsed by it, and many, no doubt, became duly terrified of airports. People who had no interest in the Palestinian problem, who could not have cared less about the whole Middle East unless it involved higher prices at their local gas station, were suddenly awakened by their sense of outrage. They listened to the six o'clock news, and one more tiny input registered somewhere in their unconsciousness. Others, of course, read everything they could find on it.

Much of what they read and felt was expressed in a *New York Times* editorial. In part it said, "This latest crime against humanity does not even have the political excuse sometimes advanced in defense of terrorism. To shoot up innocent bystanders in any airport lounge, to toss incendiary bombs into a passenger plane, then to hijack another plane and murder innocent 'hostages' in cold blood is savage barbarism. . . ."

J. Bowyer Bell took exception to the *Times*'s reasoning in his book *Transnational Terror:*

> This *Times* editorial reflects the usual Western response to political terrorism: outraged moral indignation coupled with a demand for swift justice by sanctioned means. There could be no political "excuse" for the murder of innocents, only prompt and appropriate punishment.
>
> Not all observers were able to judge so unequivocally, although many found it hard to accept the Black September argument that anyone traveling to Israel, no matter what his nationality, is an enemy of Palestine and that anyone aboard an American airliner could be a legitimate Palestinian target. Still, some drew swift parallels to the death of innocents at American hands in Hiroshima and Nagasaki. Others asked if the more recent use of American B-52s over Hanoi was an appropriate military exercise, while the Palestinian use of incendiary grenades in Rome was not. And, it was asked, given Palestinian objectives, could the Rome incident really be called senseless when those meeting in Geneva [arranged by Kissinger, to seek a Middle East accommodation] would do so under a Palestinian shadow? Proponents of this view argued that to brand the Rome massacre a "crime against humanity" would be the first step by the comfortable and powerful towards limiting the weapons available to those rebels everywhere who wage unconventional war for the weak against institutionalized injustice or repressive regimes.

As the five Rome terrorists came down the ramp of the Lufthansa plane that had taken them to Kuwait and freedom, they raised their hands high in the air, making the V-for-victory sign, and proclaimed that the massacre, which they called Operation Hilton, had been a great victory for justice.

"We are Palestinian Arabs, proud of what we did. We are not criminals. The criminals are those who bomb Palestinian refugee camps in Lebanon."

Behind their words of pride in the cold-blooded murder of unknown strangers is the story of an interminable struggle. Even to begin to understand it, one must look at the history of that biblical land and its people.

BOOK TWO

GENESIS

srael has no boundaries, only cease-fire lines. On the other side of those lines are beaten, humiliated enemy populations that outnumber Israel's thirty to one. Those enemies live for the day when a magic combination of aid from the Soviet Union, faltering American support, and the lowering of Israel's guard will enable them to drive their hated neighbor into the sea. Until that dreamed-of day, they nurture, supply, and finance the terrorists who unceasingly harass the Middle East's only democratic state.

It takes only ninety minutes to drive by car across Israel from the Mediterranean to the Jordan Valley. It would probably take an armored column about three times as long to cut this small nation in half, if the column could advance unopposed. The history of Israel tells us this is not likely to happen.

The Israelis trace their history back more than thirty-five centuries. The Old Testament of the Bible is the record of the first thousand years, its basic authenticity borne out by other sources. Like the Arabs, the Jews are a Semitic people with roots in the ancient country of Mesopotamia, which lay between the Tigris and Euphrates rivers, in what is today Iraq. The patriarchs—Abraham, Isaac, and Jacob—were the leaders at different periods of this group of nomadic shepherds. It was Abraham who led them into the fertile crescent of land bordering the Mediterranean that is now known as Israel. The name *Israel* was originally conferred by God on Jacob, whose twelve sons were the founders of the twelve tribes of Israel.

The Jews were already a monotheistic people when they trickled into the land that the Bible says was promised to them by Jehovah. Even in those days the area was a crossroads for trade and travel and inhabited by a mixture of peoples with whom the Hebrews struggled for living space.

The Canaanites, the Phoenicians, the Philistines, and the Aramaeans all laid claim to parts or all of the land between the desert and the sea. It was the Romans who later named it Palestine after the Philistines.

In 63 B.C., at the time Pompey's legions breached the walls of Jerusalem and made Judea a client state of Rome, there were 3 million Jews in Palestine. In the next hundred years, Jerusalem became one of the most important cities in the Middle East and its population grew to 200,000. This was also the period when Jesus of Nazareth lived.

The Jews, however, refused to be assimilated and rose time after time in rebellion against their Roman masters. In the year 70 they made another attempt to reestablish an autonomous state and the Roman legions led by Titus stormed Jerusalem, burning the Second Temple and killing 600,000 Jews, according to Titus's own estimate. Judea was devastated, Jerusalem renamed Aelia Capitolina and made into a Roman colony from which Jews were barred.

The Diaspora, the scattering of the Jews throughout the world, is usually dated from the fall of the Second Temple, but there were still enough Jews in Palestine in 135 to rise again under Simon Bar Kochba. This revolt was ruthlessly put down and the survivors massacred or sold into slavery. When the Roman Empire was divided in 395, Palestine became part of the Eastern, or Byzantine, Empire.

During the fifth and sixth centuries there were small, scattered Jewish settlements among the largely Christian population in Palestine. Centuries of separation from the homeland never totally eliminated the dream of someday returning. The saying among Jews that they would meet "next year in Jerusalem" had an inner meaning to those who spoke it, a significance that went deeper than mere symbolism, one that went back to the Babylonian captivity.

Following the death of the Prophet Mohammed, the desert peoples known as Arabs set forth to conquer a great empire and to spread their religion, their culture, and their language. While Europe slept through the Dark Ages, Islam subdued half the known world. Under the caliphate of Omar, successor to the Prophet, they became rulers of Palestine.

The Mosque of Omar, called the Dome of the Rock, had been erected in the city of Jerusalem in 691 near the spot where Mohammed was believed to have ascended to heaven. It was also close to the place where Solomon had built the First Temple in the tenth century before Christ. Jerusalem had now become the third most sacred city in Islam, following only Mecca and Medina. This one city was thus holy to the adherents of three of the world's great religions—Judaism, Christianity, and Islam. The seeds had been sown for endless bloodshed.

The Seljuk Turks, the Greeks, and the Crusaders all had their moment in Palestine. The Ottoman Turks toppled the Mamluk Empire in the sixteenth century, and their rule lasted until 1917. During this long period, Arab power was pushed back into the southern parts of what is today Saudi Arabia. The Arab population was badly thinned out by famine and oppression. Marauding Bedouin tribes and Turkish misrule had turned what had once been a "land of milk and honey" into a barren land of goat herders and shepherds interspersed among small waterless agricultural areas, sleepy villages, and moribund towns. At the turn of the twentieth century, there were little more than a quarter of a million Muslims, Christians, and Jews in Palestine.

The First Zionist Congress, convened in 1897 in response to the proposals of Leon Pinsker, a Russian Jew, and Theodor Herzl, an Austrian Jewish journalist, created a renewed interest in returning to Palestine and reviving Jewish national life. Only in a country of their own would the Jews be free of the insecurity, persecution, expulsion, and outright massacre they suffered in exile. With the skills the Jews brought with them to Palestine, there was a recovery, and since Jewish immigration took place almost simultaneously with an increase in the Arab population, there were nearly 700,000 people in the country west of the Jordan by the outbreak of World War I.

Called the Sick Man of Europe, the Turkish empire had been staggering along for a century, being nibbled at by its neighbors and subjected to numerous successful rebellions of its misruled provinces. Then it made the final, fatal mistake of fighting on the wrong side in the Great War.

Armed conflict between England and Turkey presented both Jews and Arabs with an opportunity. Arab nationalists, who dreamed of an Arab state, accepted Sharif Hussein as their representative in dealing with the British. Later called the Damascus Protocol, they demanded an independent Arab state to be set up in an "area bounded on the north by a line from Mersin-Adana to the Persian frontier, on the east by Persia and the Persian Gulf, on the south by the Indian Ocean, and on the west by the Red and Mediterranean seas." In a series of ten letters between Sharif and Sir Henry McMahon, the British high commissioner in Egypt, these demands were renegotiated to provide certain exceptions, among them Aden, the "districts of Mersin and Alexandretta and portions of Syria lying to the west of the districts of Damascus, Homs, Hama, and Aleppo." If the British intended to exclude Palestine from the Arab state it was not made clear to the Arabs, but since Arab nationalist sentiment in that area was slight, it was also agreed to see that the "future government of those territories should be based upon the principles of the consent of the governed."

Assuming they had been promised all that they wanted, the Arabs began their revolt on June 5, 1916. Bedouin horsemen rode out of the Arabian desert led by a romantic young Englishman, T. E. Lawrence, and Sharif Hussein of the Hedjaz. Although Arab fighting forces played little part in the major campaigns, and Palestinian Arabs no part, the desert warriors did serve to tie down a number of Turkish regiments and to cover the flanks of the British advance into Palestine.

The British, in the meantime, made a separate deal with various British Zionists, which came to be known as the Balfour Declaration. The declaration was in the nature of an official letter sent by British Foreign Secretary Arthur Balfour to a private British subject, Lord Lionel Walter Rothschild. The government had carefully worked out the text of the Balfour Declaration, several different versions having been prepared before the final draft was produced. The statement "Palestine shall be reconstituted as the National Home of the Jewish people" had originally been approved and then withdrawn. The wording finally chosen was softened to "the establishment in Palestine of a National Home for the Jewish people" with the further qualification that "nothing shall be done which may prejudice the civic and religious rights of the existing non-Jewish communities or the rights and political status enjoyed by Jews in any other country." This last stipulation was considered necessary because many English Jews opposed the idea of Zionism, claiming that establishing a Jewish national home might prejudice the position of Jews in other countries.

Much of the argument and claims that have been and continue to be made concerning the rights of Arab and Jew in Palestine are based on these two seemingly conflicting promises made by British politicians. When Arab complaints became particularly loud, Balfour reminded them that it was Great Britain and not they who had liberated the territory in contention; with all they had gained they should not begrudge the Jews the "small notch" of territory in Palestine.

The Balfour Declaration was publicly endorsed by President Wilson and by the French and Italian governments. It had the support of the Russian government until it was overthrown by the Bolsheviks. More importantly, it was recognized by the League of Nations and became a central part of the League mandate granted to the United Kingdom in July 1922. This is significant because theoretically England was not the ruler in Palestine, but was acting under a mandate issued by the League which called on the British to place "the country under such political, administrative and economic conditions as well as secure the establishment of the Jewish National Home." This, of course, was easier said than done.

It was not until the late 1920s that the heavy flow of Jews into Palestine created Arab-Jewish disagreements that led to bloodshed. There had been local Arab hostility against Jews which broke out in violent disturbances on April 4, 1920, at the Muslim festival of Nebi Musa. This was followed by a massacre of Jews in Jaffa during the Jewish celebration of May Day 1921. But the real beginning of actual conflict between Israeli and Arab is generally assumed to have been the so-called Wailing Wall incident.

The Wailing Wall is all that remains of the Second Temple, destroyed by Titus in the year A.D. 70. The wall formed part of the western exterior of the temple, and the custom from early in the Diaspora for Jews living in Palestine or those journeying there as pilgrims was to pray before the wall. (One of the memorable events of the Six-Day War was the way thousands of Jews hurried to the Wailing Wall to pray after Jerusalem fell to Israeli forces.) The wall is the most sacred structure in the Jewish religion. Unfortunately, it is also part of the Haram al-Sharif, in which was kept the rock from which Mohammed was said to have ascended to heaven on his horse, leaving a hoof print behind. This is one of the most sacred spots in Islam, and resentment grew among the Arabs because the Jews were allowed to pray there.

Arab nationalism and anti-Jewish sentiment continued to grow over the years, fanned by the Arab-language press and by the circulation of such anti-Semitic propaganda as *The Protocols of the Learned Elders of Zion.* Although originally written by Russian propagandists during the period of the czars, it was a favorite tool of Hitler's. It still turns up from time to time in the United States and elsewhere in the hands of bigots who declare it to be a verbatim account of Zionist plans to take over control of the world.

Trouble began at the wall on Yom Kippur (the Day of Atonement), September 24, 1928. The day before, Arab leaders had complained to the

British that a screen used in the Jewish worship had been bolted to the pavement in front of the wall and that additional gasoline lamps and mats had been placed there. Through a misunderstanding, the Jews failed to remove the offending objects, and when the police removed them, there was a scuffle in which a few Jews were injured. The incident was blown out of all proportion by both sides, but Arab opinion was deliberately inflamed.

The Arab press and agents of Haj Amin el-Husseini, the Grand Mufti of Jerusalem, spread rumors that the Jews intended to take over the Mosque of El Aksa, starting with the western wall, the Wailing Wall. The Jews denied they had any such intention, but the Supreme Muslim Council, set up by the British to manage Muslim religious affairs, which was under the presidency of the Mufti, issued demands that "seats, lamps, objects of worship or reading" be forbidden the Jews in the area around the wall.

Almost a year passed, during which rancor and hostility continued to grow, until on August 15, 1929, a couple of hundred young Jews marched on the wall with the permission of the British. A Zionist flag was unfurled, and the Zionist anthem "Hatikvah" was sung. The youths shouted slogans such as "The wall is ours!" and "Shame on those who profane our holy place!" There was no violence during the demonstration, and the police did not interfere.

The next day, however, some two thousand enraged Arabs appeared at the wall and listened while one of the sheikhs of the mosque harangued them, declaiming against the Jews for profaning Muslim holy places. The only Jewish objects in sight were partitions used to separate men from women during the service and a table used by the shammes, or Jewish sexton. The angry mob smashed the table to pieces, tore down the partitions, and burned some prayer books and prayer sheets. The shammes was roughed up and his clothes torn. Short of both troops and police, the government made no move against the demonstrators.

The number of British troops in Palestine had been steadily reduced over the years on the assumption that as "relations between the Arab and Jewish communities continued to improve," there would be no need for them. And so when the Wailing Wall incident escalated into violence, in all of Palestine there was only a single armored-car section and some base details, a total of 6 officers and 70 men. These troops were stationed at Ramla, about twenty miles from Jerusalem on the Jaffa road. The only immediately available reinforcements were some 33 officers and 551 men of the frontier force in Transjordan.

The police force consisted of 1,376 men, but only 31 officers and 142 men were British; the rest were Arabs, most of them worse than useless in a situation where Arabs were fighting Jews.

If the small force at Ramla had been moved into Jerusalem, the presence of armored cars might have had a restraining effect, but they were not brought to the scene and no attempt was made to summon the reinforcements from Transjordan. An almost total failure of intelligence services can probably be blamed for the fact that the British administration remained blissfully unaware that a large part of the Muslim population, urged on to violence by its religious and lay leaders, was about to explode.

At dawn on August 23, large numbers of Arab men and boys began moving into the city through the open gates of Jerusalem. The police officer in charge, Kingsley Heath, noticing that most of the new arrivals were carrying heavy sticks and clubs, ordered his men at the gates either to confiscate the weapons or to turn the Arabs back. Heath's immediate superior, a Major Saunders, countermanded this sensible order and then hurried off to consult the Grand Mufti.

"Your Eminence," Saunders began, "it has come to the attention of the administration that large numbers of young people are pouring into the city from outlying districts. Can you explain this movement?"

A short, slender man with an open, pleasant face and neatly trimmed beard, Haj Amin el-Husseini was the most virulent enemy the Jews had in the Arab world, but now he smiled beatifically and made a deprecating gesture. "My people are simply coming for morning worship at the mosque," he said. "It is Friday, and as you know, it is the custom of the peasants to come for midday prayer."

"Of course, Your Eminence," Saunders replied, "but I was not aware that clubs and heavy sticks were part of your worship."

"Those are for self-defense," the Grand Mufti replied. "My people are afraid that due to strained relations between them and the others, they might be attacked by the unbelievers during their prayers."

Either Saunders was extraordinarily naïve and believed the Mufti or he felt that attempting to disarm the thousands of Arabs streaming through the gates might precipitate the very violence the government sought to avoid. It was another in a series of administrative blunders that cost hundreds of lives.

As Saunders was leaving the Grand Mufti's palace, the Arab leader called after him, "The administration can rest assured that I am doing everything in my power to restrain my people, and there will be no trouble unless they are provoked." Three hours later he was addressing a gathering of twenty thousand Arabs. His address was not recorded, but there can be no doubt that it was the spark that set off the explosion of Arab hatred.

Following his harangue, the mob divided into two parts, one moving out of the Damascus gate and the other along the Jaffa road. Armed now with swords and knives as well as sticks and clubs, the group on the road to Jaffa came upon an elderly Jewish man returning from market with a basket over his arm. Without a word the leaders fell on the man and hacked him to pieces. As though that had been a signal for the massacre to begin, the Arabs split up into bands and began to hunt down and kill the Jews in the city.

The police, armed only with batons and with their Arab members hanging back, were totally unable to control the mobs. A telephone call to Ramla turned out the troops there plus two sections of armored cars—a total of ten —and some hastily gathered reinforcements, mainly clerks, storekeepers, and mechanics.

Violence spread rapidly over Jerusalem and into outlying areas as more and more Arabs surged into the city armed with rifles and pistols. Snipers opened fire on the Jewish quarters, and fires were soon raging in numerous areas. The troops arriving from Ramla came under fire also; but the machine guns of the armored cars dispersed the snipers, and the column pushed into the Old City, restoring order as it went.

Out of sight of the grossly inadequate military forces, however, the massacre went on. Jewish settlements were attacked, and buildings burned; rioting continued in the New City; and the Jews started to defend themselves as well as they could.

The now thoroughly alarmed acting high commissioner was desperately calling for reinforcements from every possible source. Earlier in the afternoon he had radioed Malta for naval assistance and the landing of marines. He had cabled the colonial officer for a battalion of troops to be dispatched at once. The next day he telegraphed the high commissioner for Egypt to send all available troops. Traveling by rail through Sinai and Gaza, the troops from Egypt arrived fairly quickly. If they had been requested a day or two earlier, they might have been able to prevent the slaughter.

The Arabs were launching murderous attacks on Jewish quarters and settlements all over the countryside. In Hebron sixty Jews were killed, mainly women and children, and over fifty were wounded. The synagogue was desecrated, and the Jewish hospital ransacked. In other areas, especially those where Jews were a small minority, whole settlements were totally destroyed.

Before the troops succeeded in putting an end to the city rioting, it had resulted in 472 Jewish deaths. In addition, 268 Arabs were killed, mostly when soldiers were forced to fire on rampaging mobs. Attacks on scattered Jewish settlements by marauding Arab desert tribes continued long after a semblance of peace had been forced on the urban areas.

The incident was investigated by the Shaw Commission, a British-appointed committee, which did its utmost to avoid offending the Arabs. It reported that the violence had not been premeditated and exonerated the Grand Mufti and the Arab Executive, an all-embracing political and roof organization, from responsibility. The League of Nations Commission on Mandated Territories, however, rejected the commission's exoneration of the Arab leadership and criticized the British because "such inadequate forces had been maintained in the country as to jeopardize the security of persons and property."

Zionists also criticized the Shaw report because it suggested the slowing of Jewish immigration as one solution to the problems of Palestine. It was hoped that if immigration was kept at a low level, a gradual absorption of Jews into the population would mean peaceful coexistence between the two groups.

As it happened, the rise of Hitler in Germany caused the tide of immigration to rise beyond even the wildest dreams of the Zionists. Arab anger rose again to fever pitch, and through the next few years there was talk in Arab cafés of a new *jihad* (holy war) and a gathering of arms for a renewed effort to drive out the Jews. It was only the appointment of Sir Arthur Wauchope, an able general, excellent administrator, and student of Middle Eastern affairs, as high commissioner that kept open warfare from breaking out sooner than it did.

At this point a new complication arose. The leadership of Chaim Weizmann came under attack in the Zionist Congress by revisionists under the direction of Vladimir Jabotinsky. Rejecting Weizmann's gradualism and his acceptance of an Arab presence on the east bank of the Jordan, the revisionists were maximalists who wanted not only all of Palestine but all territory that had been part of King David's kingdom at its height. And they were ready to use violence to gain their ends.

Jewish paramilitary organizations were not new. There had been Jewish self-defense forces in Europe for years. In Russia the Hashomer (Watchmen) and in Poland the Betar had attempted to defend the people against the savage pogroms instituted there, and they were the forerunners of the Hagana and the Irgun Zevai Leumi in Palestine.

The growth of Arab guerrilla forces paralleled, and in some cases preceded, that of the Jewish forces. There was sporadic violence through the 1930s. The Arab Executive complained about the increased Jewish immigration from Germany, declaring that "the general tendency of Jews to take possession of the lands of this holy country and their streaming into it by hundreds and thousands through illegal means has terrified the country."

While the Arab Executive, and especially the Grand Mufti, were to blame for most of the violence that ensued, the Zionist revisionists with their extreme demands and guerrilla tactics must share the blame.

The British had granted the Jewish Agency the right to organize self-defense forces, and over the years these had been gradually increased. The Hagana was the military arm of the Jewish Agency in Palestine. As early as 1920 it had taken part in defending settlements against Arab attack, and although illegal, it was not only tolerated by the British but sometimes encouraged. By 1936 this paramilitary group had approximately ten thousand members, two thousand of whom were in the Palmah, its spearhead force of full-time troops.

As Arab terror increased, more Zionists began switching from the Hagana to the more aggressive Irgun. Jabotinsky, they knew, was a fighter. He had cooperated with the British during World War I and was instrumental in the formation of the Jewish legion in Egypt to fight against the Central Powers. He was involved in Arab-Jewish rioting in 1920 and was sentenced by a mandate court to fifteen years in prison. The sentence was thrown out by higher authority because Jabotinsky had seemingly only engaged in organizing the Jewish quarter of Jerusalem to defend itself.

Elected to the Zionist Executive in 1921, Jabotinsky almost from the beginning was bitterly opposed to the more moderate policies of Dr. Weizmann. He advocated a Jewish state that also incorporated Jordan and resigned in 1923 in protest over the Executive's acceptance of the white paper of that year that separated Transjordan from Palestine. He set up the World Union of Zionist Revisionists, which demanded a Jewish state with boundaries equal to, or larger than, the ones of the Jewish kingdom of David and Solomon. In 1929 he left Palestine to attend the Zionist Congress in Zurich and the British took the opportunity to ban him from the country. When the Congress refused to support an immediate demand for a Jewish state in 1935, he led a revisionist walkout and set up the New Zionist Organization with himself as president.

That same year he began to form his followers into armed units. The Irgun grew out of these units, and defectors from the Hagana swelled their ranks. Under the leadership of David Raziel it later became one of the more active terrorist groups in Palestine. It and the more fanatic Stern Gang were organized as urban rather than backcountry guerrillas. The Irgun and the Stern Gang may, in fact, be considered the forerunners of a brand of urban guerrilla warfare that has plagued so many countries during the second half of the twentieth century.

Chaim Weizmann, in his book *Trial and Error,* attacked "the tragic, futile, un-Jewish resort to terrorism."

That the British encouraged self-defense and perhaps counterattack by the Jews is evidenced by the formation of the Special Night Squads under a British officer, Capt. Orde Charles Wingate, who proved his brilliance as a leader of commandos again in Burma after he became General Wingate. The squads he trained in Palestine were intended for antiguerrilla raids during the most extensive period of Arab terrorism, and many of the Jewish guerrillas who were later to bedevil the British received their knowledge of the tactics of irregular warfare from him.

The history of the Middle East would be entirely different if the British in 1938, after having crushed another Arab rebellion, had not then decided to compromise with the Arabs. Faced with a rapidly approaching major war and apprehensive about what action the Arab nations might take, Britain decided to meet Arab demands to curtail Jewish immigration to Palestine.

At a round-table conference called in London, the Arabs refused to sit down with the Jews. Each group had to be negotiated with separately. When a white paper was issued May 17, 1939, following the conference, it became clear that rather than take a chance of driving millions of Arabs into the ranks of Hitler's friends, the British had settled on appeasement.

The government proposed to establish within ten years an independent Palestine. During the transition period, the people of the country would have an increasing participation in government. In order to facilitate this gradual takeover, Arab and Jewish representatives were to be appointed heads of various departments in proportion to their respective populations. Then came the restrictions placed on immigration, and this was the worst part of the white paper from the Jewish point of view. At a time when a refuge was desperately needed for millions of Jews fleeing from persecution in Europe, immigration to Palestine was frozen and restrictions placed on the sale of Arab land to Jews. For five years, only seventy-five thousand Jews were to be permitted entry, and after that, immigration would be permitted only with agreement of the Arabs.

Zionists all over the world condemned the white paper. It was a clear breach of faith and a surrender to Arab terrorism. A statement by the Jewish Agency proclaimed it a violation of the League of Nations mandate that had set up the Jewish national home. It ended with this declaration: "The historic bond between the people and the land of Israel cannot be broken, and the Jews will never accept the closing to them of the gates of Palestine, nor let their national home be converted into a ghetto."

In a speech before the House of Commons on May 23, 1939, Winston Churchill attacked the white paper as destroying the whole concept of a Jewish national home, which as colonial secretary he had set forth in his memorandum of 1922. What sort of national home was it for the Jews when the government intended in five years that "the door of that home is to be shut and barred in their faces?"

He urged his colleagues to vote against acceptance of the white paper despite the fact that his own Conservative party had proposed it:

> It is strange indeed that we should turn away from our task in Palestine at the moment when, as the Secretary of State told us yesterday, the local disorders have been largely mastered. It is stranger still that we should turn away when the great experiment and bright dream, the historic dream, has proved its power to succeed. Yesterday the Minister responsible decanted eloquently in glowing passages upon the magnificent work which the Jewish colonists have done. They have made the desert bloom. They have started a score of thriving industries. . . . They have founded a great city on the barren shore. They have harnessed the Jordan and spread its electricity throughout the land. So far from being persecuted, the Arabs crowded into the country and multiplied till their population has increased more than even all world Jewry could lift up the Jewish population. . . .
>
> We are asked to submit—and this is what rankles most with me—to an agitation which is fed with foreign money, and ceaselessly inflamed by Nazi and by Fascist propaganda.

With his usual prescience Churchill had struck the heart of the matter. In the fruitless hope of winning extensive Arab aid in the war against Hitlerism, the British government was appeasing those who had turned to terrorism and punishing those who had not.

The lesson was not lost on either Arab or Jew.

The League of Nations, which had suffered from impotence most of its life and was headed toward oblivion, had enough courage left to point out that there was no provision in the mandate for consultation with the rulers of the Arab states. To do so would have implied they had some rights in the matter. "Whence had they derived such a right?" the League asked. "Was not consent to the establishment of a Jewish national home in Palestine the very moderate price which the Arabs had agreed to pay for the liberation of lands extending from the Red Sea to the borders of Cilicia on one hand, and Iran and the Mediterranean on the other, for the independence they were then winning, or had already won, and which they would never have gained by their own efforts, and for all of which they had to thank the Allied Powers and, particularly, the British forces in the Near East?"

The British government, however, was not listening to Churchill or the last words of the League of Nations. They were following the advice of so-called Arabists, a network of civil servants, scholars, and well-placed journalists who admired Arab culture and believed that British interests lay with the Arabs. Because of their influence, the government went even further toward stopping immigration than the white paper had set forth. On July 12, it suspended Jewish entry into Palestine for six months, beginning October 1.

The Arabs surprised the British completely by rejecting the white paper, which granted them more than they had asked. They now demanded total independence, no more Jewish immigration, and a perpetual minority position for the Jews already in the country. They also continued their flirtation with Germany and Italy.

The Twenty-first Zionist Congress met in Geneva with the specter of World War II looming over it and the reality of the white paper staring it in the face. It unanimously rejected the white paper, of course, but then fell into extended debate over what attitude to take toward Great Britain.

The Jewish State party, headed by Meir Grossman, advocated civil disobedience and a refusal of all cooperation. A larger group under the leadership of David Ben-Gurion took a more moderate stance but pointed out that noncooperation with the mandatory power would be justified, since the League mandate commission had condemned the white paper. Dr. Weizmann stated that given the fact of Hitlerism, Jews would have to cooperate with the British in the coming war.

It soon became obvious to every rational Jew that Weizmann was right. The Jews indeed had no choice but to support the Allies. There were less rational elements among them, however, who refused to see the inevitability of their choice. Most of them were to be found in the Irgun, which turned its guns mainly on the British. With some cooperation from the Hagana, or at least its secret radio station, the Irgun began sabotage and other activities against the mandate government.

The Hagana devoted itself chiefly to self-defense but with the added element of smuggling in so-called illegal immigrants. The plight of Jews fleeing from Nazi atrocities in Europe was desperate. Large numbers of them, especially from the Balkans, found themselves stranded in southeastern Europe with advancing German armies behind them and the closed border of Palestine ahead of them.

Between 1939 and 1943, the Hagana smuggled in large quantities of arms as well as twenty thousand Jews. These were in addition to the nineteen thousand legal immigrants, and new villages had to be set up hurriedly in sections of the country that had previously had few, if any, Jewish residents. This enraged the Arabs, who accused the British of complicity because many of the young men smuggled in were directed into the British army by the Jewish Agency with the idea of training them for the Israeli army Zionists already envisioned.

Far more immigrants were turned back, however, than were smuggled in. Faced with returning to within reach of the Germans, many committed suicide.

Ships carrying refugees were turned back. One of the first tragic incidents involved the small cattle boat *Struma,* which arrived with 769 refugees on board and was refused permission to enter a Palestinian port. Sent to sea again after a stay in Istanbul, the ship blew up, perhaps because it struck a mine or because its own weak boilers exploded, and sank near the Bosporus with the loss of all on board.

There was an outbreak of Irgun terrorism following this incident, but later, in 1939, faced with making a choice between fascism and British rule, the Irgun declared a peace in Palestine. This did not sit well with a Polish Jew named Abraham Stern, who lived in Italy during Mussolini's rule. Since Italian fascism, unlike German fascism, was not particularly anti-Semitic, Stern had become something of an admirer of Il Duce. He had also become violently anti-British. He saw England as a greater danger to Jews than the Axis states. Outraged by the Irgun's proclamation of a truce, Stern broke with the group and founded Lohamei Herut Yisrael (Fighters for the Freedom of Israel), commonly called the Stern Gang. Most of those who joined were recent arrivals, many Polish Jews who had suffered under Nazi occupation. Yet there was a distinctive fascist turn to their thinking.

Stern's first act was to try to get aid from Mussolini. Under his theory that any enemy of Great Britain must be a friend of the Jews, he even considered dealing with Hitler. This was before the whole truth about the holocaust going on in Germany was generally known, but enough was known to discourage such a move. Of all the leaders of terror groups, Stern was not only the most fanatic but the most stupid as well. Although the Stern Gang never consisted of more than three hundred young men and women, its ceaseless sabotage and terrorist activities (even when Rommel's panzers were advancing toward Palestine) must have been of some help to the Nazi cause.

Pro-Axis sentiment was high in the Arab world. The Grand Mufti, Haj Amin el-Husseini, who had been forced to flee to Syria after the revolt of 1938, later joined forces in Iraq with Rashid Ali al-Kilani and other pro-Nazi army officers in an unsuccessful attempt to overthrow the government. Forced to resume his travels, he visited Italy and Germany. Photographs show him in earnest conversation with Hitler, and he became a close friend of Adolf Eichmann and Heinrich Himmler.

All through the war years, el-Husseini exerted every effort to advance the Nazi cause. He conducted a pro-Axis propaganda campaign among Muslim prisoners of war, he helped organize an SS division of Bosnian Muslims, and he enthusiastically endorsed Hitler's plans for the extermination of European Jewry. He made propaganda broadcasts aimed at the Arab world, trying to convince his coreligionists to rise against the Allies.

His influence was so strong in Egypt that the British, engaged in a life-and-death struggle with Rommel's forces, had to be constantly on guard against being stabbed in the back. He organized Muslims into units called Black Legions, which were responsible for the worst atrocities perpetuated in Yugoslavia, and he promoted pro-Nazi groups in Greece, Java, India, Africa, and Indonesia.

When it seemed as though Rommel's panzers were going to push on through Egypt, cut the Suez Canal, and take Palestine, the Grand Mufti was delighted. He asked Himmler to provide him after the war with a "special adviser" from Eichmann's department to help him solve the Jewish question in the Middle East. His plans to enter Jerusalem at the head of Axis troops were shelved after Rommel was sent reeling back from El Alamein. After the war, el-Husseini found that his activities in the Nazi cause had not lost him prestige in the Arab world. Given asylum in Egypt, he was awarded the presidency of the Arab Higher Committee of Palestine, an inclusive roof organization that replaced the Arab Executive, but had to exercise his office from abroad because a hangman's noose awaited him in Palestine.

As the tide of Axis power receded from North Africa, the activities of the Stern Gang became more violent. Even though there were forty thousand or more Palestinian Jews serving in the British forces in the Middle East, the gang never gave up its terror campaign. Stern himself was captured during one raid and then killed while trying to escape. As victory became more sure for the Allied cause, the gang redoubled its effort to drive the British out of Palestine.

The slogan of the official world Zionist organization had been, "We shall fight the white paper as if there were no war, and we shall fight the war as if there were no white paper." The Stern Gang adopted the Arab saying "The enemy of my enemy is my friend."

On August 7, 1944, the gang's gunmen attempted to assassinate Sir Harold MacMichael, the high commissioner. The attempt was foiled, but Sir Harold and two of his escorts were wounded. Then in Cairo, on November 6, two young Stern Gang gunmen assassinated Lord Moyne, British minister of state in the Middle East and a personal friend of Winston Churchill. The crime had a shattering effect on the British.

An attempt has been made by some American writers to picture the killers as heroes and martyrs (they were hanged) to the cause of Israel. A better case can be made for the view that they immeasurably harmed the cause of Israeli independence, much more than, say, the Grand Mufti had with all his machinations and hatred. The assassination turned British public opinion from its mainly pro-Zionist sympathy to one that was, if not pro-Arab, at least a "plague on both your houses" attitude.

Churchill himself expressed that sentiment in an angry statement to the House of Commons. "This shameful crime has shocked the world and has affected none more strongly than those like myself who, in the past, have been consistent friends of the Jews and constant architects of their future. If our dreams for Zionism are to end in the smoke of an assassin's pistol, and the labours for its future produce a new set of gangsters worthy of Nazi Germany, many like myself will have to reconsider the position we have maintained so consistently and so long in the past."

Rational Jews and Zionists were also shocked by the act, and the *Palestine Post* said of Churchill's speech, "There is no one from whom the bitter word could have come with better grace and greater sincerity, or been received with greater understanding."

The Stern Gang was not in the least inhibited by the outcry from moderate Zionists. Their campaign of terror continued. The National Council of Jews in Palestine issued a statement calling on the Jewish population to condemn terrorism, but the plea had no effect. Government offices were damaged by incendiary bombs, and two British police officers were murdered in the Jewish quarter of Haifa. In another incident, two police cars were blown up and several British police inspectors narrowly escaped injury. The Stern Gang's specialty was shooting British police in the back, and on one day in Tel Aviv six policemen were murdered in broad daylight while shoppers looked the other way. Explosions destroyed police stations in Jerusalem and Jaffa.

The Irgun was also now back in the business of terror. In January 1944, it had issued a statement ending its self-declared truce. "There is no longer any armistice between the Jewish people and the British administration. . . . This, then, is our demand: Immediate transfer of power in Eretz Israel [Land Israel] to a Provisional Hebrew Government."

Like the Grand Mufti, the Irgun was motivated at least in part by religious fervor, as was made clear by a declaration by its leader Menahem Begin: "We shall fight, every Jew in the Homeland will fight. The God of Israel, the Lord of Hosts, will aid us."

Born in 1913 in a part of Russia that became Poland after World War I, Begin assumed leadership in 1939 of the Polish branch of Betar, the youth movement of the Zionist revisionist group headed by Jabotinsky. The Russian invasion trapped him in Russian-held territory, but he went on with his activity on behalf of Zionism. Arrested by Soviet authorities, he managed to win his freedom, joining the Polish army-in-exile and reaching Israel with a contingent of it.

When David Raziel, the founder of the Irgun, was killed in 1943 while on a secret mission in Iraq, Begin took over its leadership. Following Irgun's dissolution in 1948, he founded Herut, a political party of the far Right. If any

Israeli political group can be said to have fascist overtones, it is Herut, but it is also based on extremely conservative religious beliefs and extreme nationalism.

By 1942 news about Hitler's slaughter of the Jews was beginning to leak out of Germany. In May of that year a conference was called by the American Emergency Committee for Zionist Affairs. Held at the Biltmore Hotel in New York City, it produced a document that openly asked for the establishment of a Jewish state in Israel. In conclusion it said, "The Conference declares that the new world order that will follow victory cannot be established on foundations of peace, justice, and equality, unless the problem of Jewish homelessness is finally solved. The Conference urges that the gates of Palestine be opened; that the Jewish Agency be vested with control of immigration into Palestine and with the necessary authority for upbuilding the country, including the development of its unoccupied and uncultivated lands; and that Palestine be established as a Jewish Commonwealth integrated in the structure of the new democratic world. Then and only then will the age-old wrong to the Jewish people be righted."

Called the Biltmore Program, it was so popular within Palestine that support of it by David Ben-Gurion and his Mapai party during the 1944 elections got him 66 percent of the vote.

As the war came to an end, the Jewish Agency, the Zionist Congress, and their military wing, the Hagana, had to decide whether or not to support the Irgun and the Stern Gang. It was expected that when the British Labour party came into power in 1945, it would at least move to increase immigration into Palestine. When it was learned that the 1939 white paper, with a few modifications, was to stand, the decision was made to engage in civil disobedience, to attack some British installations, but for the most part to refrain from assassination and murder.

The first Hagana raids were carried out in October and November by its active service units, the Palmah. They were aimed at the Palestinian railway system, blowing it up in 153 places and completely disrupting all traffic. A number of police launches were destroyed in Haifa and Jaffa, and an attempt was made to blow up the Haifa oil refinery. Cooperating with the Hagana, the Irgun attacked the railroad station and yards at Lod, damaging three locomotives, blowing up a boxcar, and burning down an engine shed.

The British charged that the Jewish Agency was involved, and this was confirmed when a series of telegrams came to light. One of these, exchanged between the agency leaders and the Hagana, read in part: "It has also been suggested that we cause one serious incident. We would then publish a declaration to the effect that it is only a warning and an indication of much more serious incidents that would threaten the safety of all British interests in the country should the Government decide against us. . . . the Stern Group have expressed their willingness to join us completely on the basis of our programs of activity. Wire your views on the question of the Union."

When Irgun gunmen raided two police stations and an arms dump, killing nine British soldiers and policemen, Ben-Gurion informed the new high commissioner, Sir Alan Cunningham, that the Zionist movement disassociated itself from these crimes. The British had reason to doubt him.

Everything the British did now seemed wrong. Any move taken to appease the Arabs outraged the Jews and vice versa. In January 1946, the British navy turned back a ship carrying nine hundred illegal immigrants. This angered the Jews, and later the same month, the Arabs became incensed when Cunningham announced that the legal limit of fifteen hundred immigrants a month would continue.

On January 28 the high commissioner announced new Emergency Regulations that called for the death penalty for acts of terror and in some cases even for membership in a terrorist group.

The British made another mistake in January when they permitted the Grand Mufti's cousin, Jamal el-Husseini, to return to Palestine in the hope that this might prove a sop to Arab opinion. That any Husseini would be moderate was a naïve assumption. Jamal was acting for the Grand Mufti, who was issuing orders from Egypt. Both had but one thought, that of driving the Jews and British out of Palestine.

The Irgun and the Stern Gang launched a series of raids aimed chiefly at British facilities used to prohibit free immigration. They struck police posts, the Mount Carmel radar station, and three British airfields of reconnaissance planes used to spot incoming immigrant ships. Fifteen planes were destroyed, but four Palmah men were killed. Half of Tel Aviv defiantly turned out to honor them at their funeral.

The British retaliated with roadblocks, searches, passport checks, and raids on suspected terrorist safe houses. The Jews resisted violently when the search was for Hagana men but usually submitted passively if Irgun or Stern Gang members were being sought. Never, however, was there cooperation in finding even the worst killers.

In a raid on the British Airborne Division's car park in Tel Aviv, Stern gunmen killed seven guards as they lay sleeping. The British were enraged at this "premeditated and unprovoked murder of innocent, helpless men." The gang replied that a state of war existed and that their gunmen were soldiers acting under orders. British troops reacted by rioting in the Jewish towns of Natanya and Be'er Tuveyah, smashing windows and breaking up furniture. In retaliation, the Palmah struck all over the mandated territory. Various units hit rail and bridge crossings along the Palestine border.

With evidence in their possession of the Jewish Agency's collaboration in some instances of terror, the British moved directly against that group. On June 29 they seized all the agency's papers and arrested four members of the Jewish Executive in their homes. The British had made a nearly clean sweep of Jewish leaders, missing only David Ben-Gurion, who was in Paris at the time. They also carried out extensive sweeps of Jewish settlements, arresting twenty-seven hundred Jews, including other leaders, most of whom were taken to the detention camp at Latrun to broil under the summer sun. The raids were made in accordance with regulations that placed limits on the civil liberties of persons not arrested.

The next day, Israel Galili, the commander of the Hagana, abandoning all restraint, agreed to allow the Irgun to activate Operation Chick, the bombing of the King David Hotel in Jerusalem. At the same time, the Stern Gang was to carry out an operation against the David Brothers Building. British security was very tight around the hotel because the southwest wing had been taken over for British military headquarters and other offices housed the mandate secretariat. The David Brothers Building housed the British Military Police and its Special Investigations Branch. There was a defensive line of barbed wire around the entire area and nets to prevent hand grenades from being thrown through the windows. The doors were of steel and sandbag emplacements had been set up at strategic points. A previous attempt to attack the hotel with homemade rockets had failed, but Irgun spies had since discovered a glaring weakness in the building's defense—the basement, which was unprotected and extended under the whole building.

The Regence Café occupied part of the hotel, and it was into its part of the basement that on July 12 a dozen men in flowing Arab robes carried milk cans as though making a delivery. Arab kitchen workers in the basement were overpowered, and the milk cans were moved to the British wing of the hotel. The cans, labeled MINES—DO NOT TOUCH, contained a powerful mixture of TNT and gelignite concocted by the Irgun's explosive expert, whose code name was Gideon. While the terrorists were planting the mines, a British officer and policeman entering the area were murdered. When the mines were in place, the Arab kitchen help was freed and threatened with death if they did not run for their lives.

A claim that a telephone warning to the hotel switchboard was made in time to evacuate the hotel was never verified. What is known is that within minutes after the terrorists fled, a monstrous explosion shook the whole city. The entire southwest wing, as well as other parts of the building, collapsed, burying over a hundred men, women, and children. After the survivors had been dug out, over eighty bodies were found. The victims were Arabs, British clerks, and Jewish guests who happened to be in the hotel at 12:37 P.M. that day.

Jewish leaders tried desperately to avoid responsibility. Galili telephoned Begin and urged him to announce that his group was solely responsible. Ben-Gurion told a reporter in Paris, "The Irgun is the enemy of the Jewish people."

The British military commander drew up orders for his men to boycott and ostracize all the Jews in Palestine. This action and those that followed were to have far-reaching effects during the British withdrawal from Palestine and later when the Israelis themselves became the targets for savage terror raids.

The British on July 24 issued a white paper implicating the Jewish Agency and the Hagana in the explosion. Extensive searches in Tel Aviv and elsewhere by 20,000 paratroopers failed to locate the killers, although 110,000 Jews were questioned in four days and 787 were detained and interned at Rafa.

Dr. Weizmann believed that the terrorists were compromising the position of Jews all over the world. The reaction to their crime posed a grave danger to the very future of Israel. Today's headlines show that he was right. Terror breeds more terror—especially successful terror.

In another effort to solve the problem, the British proposed a compromise scheme that would have divided Palestine into separate Jewish and Arab provinces with Jerusalem and the Negev as neutral districts. Neither the Jews nor the Arabs were interested.

The dilemma remained and the conflict went on. Illegal refugees were placed in detention camps on Cyprus; this alienated the Jews still more, and so their raids continued. Finally, the British tried to appease both sides. Five of the Grand Mufti's exiled partisans were permitted to return to Palestine and Jewish Agency leaders were released from internment. The Hagana responded by condemning terrorism and breaking its ties with the Irgun and the Stern Gang. Again neither Arabs nor Jews lessened their demands.

The Arabs had been watching the struggle between the Jews and the British from the sidelines while preparing for a final showdown. Despite the Grand Mufti's efforts to unite all Arab resistance forces under his banner, there were splits. The old feud between the followers of the Husseini and the Nashashibi families for political control was still active; each clan had raised its own private army, but neither would combine with the other to form a single army like the Hagana. But like the Jews, the Arabs were stockpiling arms for the day of reckoning. That day was to come much sooner than either side expected.

The British introduced flogging as a punishment for terrorism in December, when violence escalated again. On December 27, a young Irgun gunman named Kimchi was given eighteen lashes. The Irgun kidnapped a British major and three noncommissioned officers and flogged each eighteen times. On the night of December 29, a British patrol opened fire on a speeding carload of terrorists, killing one and capturing four others, who were tried under the Emergency Regulations, convicted, and sentenced to death.

The British seemed determined to crush terrorism once and for all. Eighty thousand troops and sixteen thousand police, plus the Transjordanian Arab Legion, had been concentrated in Palestine. Most British civilians had been evacuated, and sixty huge concrete police bunkers called Taggart forts were built in strategic places. All fraternization with Jews was prohibited, and warships were moved to the coast. Everything appeared to be ready for a massive campaign on a scale that had destroyed the Arab rebellion of 1936–38. However, the burden of crushing the Jewish terrorist network appeared too costly in bad publicity and in actual money. Besides, the British were plagued with problems around the world and at home. Palestine had become such an intolerable burden that they decided to get out from under by handing the whole problem over to the United Nations.

Meeting in special session, the United Nations established an eleven-nation group, the United Nations Special Committee on Palestine (UNSCOP). Composed of delegates from Australia, Canada, Czechoslovakia, Guatemala, India, Iran, the Netherlands, Peru, Sweden, Uruguay, and Yugoslavia, the committee was presumably neutral. However, the delegates from Guatemala and Uruguay were said to be "embarrassingly pro-Zionist." The Indian and Iranian delegates were almost as pro-Arab. The rest were more or less open to persuasion. Justice Emil Sandstrom of Sweden chaired the committee, and Dr. Ralph Bunche, director-general of the Trusteeship Council, went to Palestine with the delegates as an adviser.

Although none of the three groups under study in Palestine—Britons, Arabs, Jews—had much confidence in the ability of UNSCOP to solve their problems, all but the Palestinian Arabs eventually agreed to cooperate. The Arab nations and British administrators were willing to meet with the committee and so was the Jewish leadership, but the Arab Higher Committee, headed by the Grand Mufti, refused to even talk to the UN delegates, a position that tended to compromise their cause from the beginning.

The committee opened its hearing in Palestine on June 16, just as the situation was reaching crisis stage. An Irgun attack group had carried out a daring raid against the old castle at Acre, a prison where the British were holding many terrorists as well as other prisoners. Blasting open the walls of the prison with dynamite, the terrorists had freed 250 prisoners, but five of their members had been captured. Found guilty of terrorist crimes, three of the five were handed death sentences on the day UNSCOP began its hearings.

Members of UNSCOP were, of course, impressed with the remarkable things the Jews had done to make the desert bloom, especially in the Negev. At times, however, they were propagandized by clever Zionist ploys and elaborate subterfuge.

One dramatically staged incident in 1947 made headlines around the world. It involved the refugee ship *Exodus,* an unseaworthy former excursion ship that was purchased in America, sailed to France, and packed by Hagana agents with forty-five hundred illegal immigrants in space originally designed to hold seven hundred passengers. The ship was then sent forth, its arrival on the Palestinian coast timed for the period of the UNSCOP hearings.

When the British cruiser *Ajax* came alongside, the British had to fight their way on board. They were confronted by "a maze of barbed wire, wooden fencing and other obstacles." The other obstacles included a jet of live steam from a pipe hooked up to the boiler and hundreds of cans of food hurled at them by the refugees. During the wild battle that followed, three Jews were killed and over a hundred injured.

Resentful of the way they had been tricked into displaying excessive force, the British shipped the refugees back to displaced-persons camps in Germany instead of to Cyprus, the usual procedure. Skilled Zionist propagandists turned it into a cause célèbre.

The British claimed that the refugees had opened fire on them and had used tear gas, iron pipes, and clubs. Hagana supporters admitted to UNSCOP that the British could not have gained control of the *Exodus* without the use of force. Whatever the truth of the *Exodus* affair, it had certainly been carried out with perfect timing to make the maximum impression on the UNSCOP members.

The Hagana, which had supposedly broken its ties with the Stern Gang and the Irgun, was the agency chiefly responsible for transporting illegal immigrants to Palestine. The constant arrival of immigrants served not only to heat up the quarrel between Arab and Jew but also provided a reservoir of manpower for the Hagana. The Arabs complained bitterly that the British were looking the other way while Palestine was being flooded with their enemies. At the time of the UNSCOP investigation, the Hagana had a membership of about fifty-five thousand on an active footing and another thirty-five thousand in reserve.

Although not a terrorist group by any standards, the Hagana itself was capable of some highly irresponsible actions at times, In his book *Strictly Illegal,* Munya Mardor, a Hagana officer, tells of having placed a bomb on board the ship *Patria,* which was taking illegal immigrants away from Palestine to internment in Mauritius. The ship sank in Haifa Harbor, drowning 240 of the 1,900 refugees aboard.

Unlike the terrorists, the Hagana was willing to accept partition, a solution toward which UNSCOP was increasingly inclined. The committee was told, "If partition involving a viable state should be offered, it would be accepted." But if the amount of land offered the Jews was insufficient, Hagana would fight.

The Arabs had sworn to fight if there was any partition whatsoever, and Hagana was asked if it could deal with such a situation on its own. The leaders felt that they could repulse any attack from the Arab population of Palestine and could hold their own even if the Arab states sent help. Their confidence was based on their belief that their forces were better trained and would ultimately be better armed because they had their own small-scale munitions industry. They also were confident that Jews abroad would help and that the Arab nations would not dare commit their total forces to a war for Palestine. All the Hagana asked from UNSCOP was that the Jews be given ". . . a legal basis for arming and defending themselves."

Hagana leaders admitted that the illegal immigrant program was used to bring in fighting men to defend the Jewish position: "The basic consideration is the building of Palestine as a whole, but all such illegal immigrants immediately join the ranks of Hagana. Because the method of transportation of illegal immigrants is difficult and involves much hardship, it is not possible to bring many old or infirm persons."

On the subject of terrorism, UN representatives were told, "Terror is a very grave thing and cannot be suppressed by the British Government. Terroristic activities are an evidence of Jews giving vent to their strong feelings. Hagana believes that it can cope with terroristic activity only if immigration and settlement are freely permitted in Palestine."

UNSCOP members also met with Irgun leaders, who, like the Grand Mufti, were willing to settle for nothing less than everything. They wanted not only all of Palestine but Transjordan as well, claiming that it had been illegally separated from Palestine by the British.

"Is it possible that the nations of the world don't see the justice of our cause? Don't they understand that this is our land, that we are returning to it and will continue to return to it, and that no one and nothing can halt this irresistible tide?" one Jewish terrorist leader asked.

The terrorists rejected the idea of partition. "We could consider that to be a death penalty. We will fight against it. We must have immigration of more than one million Jews from Europe to Palestine within the next two years."

When the Irgun was told it was unlikely that the United Nations would hand over all of Palestine to a people who were a minority there, the reply was "Remember, if the European Jews are considered to be what they really are —Palestinian citizens in exile—we would have a Jewish majority in Palestine now!"

Menahem Begin proclaimed that "not only the Jews but also the Arabs want independence from the British, both peoples want freedom and want the invader banished from this land." He did not indicate how he became a spokesman for the Arabs, but he did make it clear what he thought of partition: "What a Jewish state! A ghetto! A state unable to handle Jewish immigration. That will be the Jewish state!" He wanted nothing less than restitution of all land held by the Biblical Jewish kingdom at its height.

Finding Begin not open to reason on the plan for the future, UNSCOP members tried to win his agreement to a cease-fire until they could make a decision. He stated flatly that this would be possible only if the British agreed to unlimited immigration: the mandate government had to halt its "violence" first.

Unable to make headway with Begin on that subject, committee members tried to at least prevent the murder of two British sergeants who had been kidnapped in retaliation for the arrest of terrorists. Again they ran into a stone wall. "Three of our soldiers have been unjustly condemned to death by an illegal military court," Begin said. "We are holding the sergeants as a guarantee against the hanging of our men. The British military courts have no right to function in Palestine. They are the courts of an army of occupation. To counteract these unlawful courts, we establish courts of our own. And we never execute a man without judging him first."

There was an explicitly totalitarian kind of doublethink in many of Begin's statements that should have been obvious to the UN representatives. Unilaterally he and his small band of fanatics declared established courts illegal and set up their own, and his declaration that he spoke for Arab and Jew in demanding British withdrawal had a familiar ring to it. Begin and the Grand Mufti were alike in more than just their fanaticism.

His final word on the British sergeants was, "They are soldiers of an army invading our soil. Britain must suffer the consequences if she refuses to respect the laws of war and executes our soldiers when they are prisoners of war."

During their stay in Palestine, UNSCOP members received many complaints about mistreatment of terrorists at the hands of authorities. The matter was taken up with Sir Henry Gurney, chief secretary of the Palestine mandatory government. Some members of the UN delegation were concerned about the number of persons being held under the Palestine Emergency Regulations (similar to the preventive-detention laws used by the British in Northern Ireland), under which those suspected of terrorism could be interned for an indefinite period without a trial. Sir Henry said there were 291 Jewish prisoners interned in Kenya and another 515 in Palestine. Asked why they had never been brought to trial, he explained that it was impossible to get people to testify against terrorists, either because they sympathized with them or feared reprisal.

Because the absent Grand Mufti refused to recognize the presence of the United Nations, Palestinian Arabs declined to cooperate in any way. Presenting their case therefore fell to representatives from the Arab states. As spokesmen for a "democratic" Palestine, these leaders were singularly unfitted, since not one of their own countries had ever come close to developing a truly democratic nation. Some of the points they made, however, did have validity.

The Arabs had a two-to-one majority in Palestine, they pointed out, and consequently should rule by popular sovereignty. They also had a natural right to the country because of their continuous connection with it over the centuries. The term *Arab* in relation to Palestine, they claimed, referred not to the seventh-century invaders from the Arabian peninsula, but to "the indigenous population which intermarried with the invaders and became permanently Arabicized." And they further claimed they had been promised Palestine in the McMahon letters. Their one invalid claim was that the mandate for Palestine from the League of Nations was illegal. Great Britain had acquired Palestine the same way all its previous rulers had—by conquest. Since it had chosen to legitimatize that acquisition through the international organization, it had every right to dispose of the land as it saw fit. After all, it was Britain who asked the United Nations to step in, giving it the right to make any decision it thought equitable for the area.

UNSCOP members were convinced by now that the mandate should come to an end, and the majority leaned toward partition as the only solution. Their talks with the leaders of Lebanon, Syria, and Jordan convinced them that were an Arab state to be set up, almost half the Jews in Palestine would be driven out. True or not, most of the delegates believed that was what Hamid Franjyeh, foreign minister of Lebanon, was telling them when he said that all Jews who had entered Palestine since the Balfour Declaration of 1917 would be considered illegal immigrants. The committee interpreted this to mean that some 400,000 of the approximately 700,000 Jews would be expelled. They also had to keep in mind that the government of an Arab Palestine would be headed by the Grand Mufti. That made it difficult to believe that the remaining 300,000 Jews would be safe for very long.

UNSCOP was told that in addition to Jews being expelled, "Arabic would be compulsory in all schools; government control would prevent subversive teaching; and the constitution would provide that religious bodies and other societies could maintain private schools and universities."

"Let us suppose that Palestine becomes an Arab state," the Guatemalan delegate said to his colleagues. "There is documentation, unfortunately, to show that during the war, many of the present members of the Arab Higher Committee were supporters of Nazism. From what I have seen in Palestine, the Arab Committee would most likely come into power if all Palestine is converted into an Arab state."

The Arab leaders denied, of course, that the Arab Higher Committee contained ex-Nazis or that the Jews would be persecuted. This was hardly persuasive in view of the fact that the Grand Mufti's chief aide was Jamal el-Husseini, vice-chairman of the Arab Higher Committee, who had vowed to drench the soil of Palestine in blood rather than give up an inch of it to Jews. Also close to the Grand Mufti were Musa Bey Alami, chief disseminator of anti-British and anti-Jewish propaganda during the war; Emile al-Ghouri, his press officer and secretary of the Palestine Arab party; and Fauzi ed-Din el-Kauwakji, former terrorist leader and later commander of the Arab Liberation Army (ALA).

Asked what they would accept in compromise, the Arab leaders stated they would accept nothing. This was also the stand of the Irgun and the Stern Gang, but they were not official Jewish spokesmen. The majority of Jews were willing to accept partition. This flexibility, contrasted with Arab intransigence, weighed heavily with UNSCOP.

High Commissioner Cunningham had a final word for the delegates: "No solution can be found which gives absolute justice to everyone. It is clear, too, that no solution can be found which will be wholly agreed to by everyone. Therefore, it seems that to a greater or lesser degree whatever solution you find must be imposed. There must be a solution, however. Time has shown a constantly accelerated deterioration of conditions in this country. The sands are running out. The only answer is an early political solution."

UNSCOP left Palestine for Geneva to work out its recommendations. The visit of a subcommittee to displaced-persons camps in Germany and Austria produced more disturbing information, which also was taken into consideration as it drew up a plan it hoped would set Palestine on the path to peace and stability.

A majority of committee members—Canada, Czechoslovakia, Guatemala, the Netherlands, Peru, Sweden, and Uruguay—voted for a partition that would give the Arabs western Galilee, the coastal plain in the far north and south, plus the major part of central Palestine. The Jews were to have the central coastal plain from a point south of Acre to one just north of Isdud, plus the barren and nearly uninhabited Negev stretching down to the

Gulf of 'Aqaba. An area around Jerusalem and Bethlehem would form an international zone to be administered by the United Nations. There would be a two-year period, beginning September 1, 1947, during which Great Britain would remain as administrator, either alone or with another UN member. On the all-important matter of Jewish immigration, the rate of 6,250 immigrants a month was to be maintained during the two-year period and lowered to 5,000 per month after that. There would be an economic union between the Arab and Jewish sections that would last for ten years. It was understood that the Jews, with their superior technology and economic development, would aid the Palestinian Arabs.

The remaining UNSCOP nations, headed by India and Iran with Australia abstaining, voted for a plan that more closely suited the Arabs by leaving Palestine as one nation and shutting down Jewish immigration after a period of three years.

The biggest stumbling block in the partition plan was the distribution of the populations. There would be close to 500,000 Jews in the Jewish state and an almost equal number of Arabs. The Arab state would have 725,000 Arabs and 10,000 Jews. Jerusalem would contain 100,000 Jews and 105,000 non-Jews. Later forms of the plan redistributed the population more evenly, but in the war that followed, the borders and ethnic balance of the country were totally changed from those that UNSCOP labored so hard to establish.

While the UN delegates were still deliberating, another act of terrorism occurred in Palestine, one that embittered the British against the Jews more than any previous act and has had an effect on British attitudes toward Israel down to the present day.

The Irgun had threatened to murder the two British sergeants it had kidnapped if the three Irgun gunmen captured in the terrorist attack on Acre prison were executed. When their death sentence was duly carried out, some of the terrorists hesitated to enforce the threat. Not so Amihai Faglin. It was he who had planned the mass escape from Acre Fortress and the bombing of the King David Hotel in Jerusalem.

Seething with rage, Faglin went to see Begin at a secret hideout in Tel Aviv. He found three other Irgun leaders there trying to persuade Begin to release the young sergeants. As soon as he could get Begin alone, Faglin told him, "We've got to go through with it. If we don't, there'll never be an end to the hangings and our future warnings will mean nothing."

Having intended to carry out the murders from the beginning, Begin agreed. He had only been waiting for a volunteer. Faglin drove through the darkened streets to the huge diamond factory where the two British soldiers were imprisoned in a twelve-foot-square box hidden under a floor. They had been kept there in total darkness with one blanket each and a bucket to serve as a toilet. Given very little food and water, they were already weak and ill.

"Bring one of them up," Faglin ordered. "Hurry up!"

The Irgun men on guard hauled the first victim up out of the cage. White-faced and with hollow, sunken eyes, the sergeant was unable to stand as they dragged him into the next room, where a rope had been tossed over a rafter.

"Are you going to hang me?" the English soldier asked when they placed a hood over his head and lifted him up onto a chair under the rope.

There was no answer.

"Can I leave a message?"

"We won't be able to deliver any message," Faglin said. "You must prepare to die."

The looped end of the rope was placed around his neck and the chair kicked from under him. This was not a hangman's noose, and so, the soldier, whose hands had been tied to prevent his trying to free himself, slowly strangled to death while Faglin watched, holding a pistol to shoot him in case the British should arrive in a rescue attempt.

When the first sergeant was dead, Faglin ordered the second one brought up and hanged. Both bodies were then placed in a truck and taken to an orange grove, where they were rehung from a tree. Faglin ordered a mine placed under the dangling corpses before telephoning the British authorities and telling them where to find the bodies. The mine went off as he had planned while the dead soldiers were being cut down and a British medical officer was badly injured. Faglin received a promotion for his night's work, and British public opinion once more turned against Israel.

On November 29, 1947, after considerable jockeying and delays, the United Nations, meeting at Lake Success, New York, voted on the UNSCOP resolution for the partition of Palestine. The Jews had accepted the resolution; the Arabs had vowed to oppose it, by war if necessary.

The vote, it was assumed beforehand, would be close because a two-thirds majority was needed. The votes of several small states were to prove decisive. Zionist circles in America exerted every pressure they could to persuade the U.S. government to use its influence on Liberia, Haiti, the Philippines, and Ethiopia. The State Department was swayed by its Arabists, who were determined to prevent American pressure on other countries to vote for partition. Loy Henderson, chief of the Division of Near Eastern and African Affairs, telephoned U.S. delegate Herschel Johnson and said, "Remember, Herschel, no pressure tactics. I've given my word to the Arabs."

There were other American delegates, however, like Mrs. Eleanor Roosevelt and Gen. John Hilldring, who were determined to go all out to help the Jews. Mrs. Roosevelt was naturally sympathetic to those she considered underdogs, and General Hilldring, a professional soldier, had seen the Nazi death camps and decided the Jews must have a safe home.

The Arab leaders warned the world repeatedly that Palestine would not be a safe home for the Jews. They made no bones about partition meaning war.

Azam Pasha, secretary of the Arab League, threatened "a war of extermination and a momentous massacre which will be spoken of like the Mongolian massacres and those of the Crusades."

"The partition line will be nothing but a line of fire and blood!" warned Jamal el-Husseini, then acting president of the Arab Higher Committee.

Without American pressure on wavering states, the Zionists were afraid that they could not get the necessary two-thirds vote. They were desperate but not to the point of resorting to a plan proposed by Jewish underworld figures who offered to kidnap antipartition delegates and hold them until after the vote was taken. Instead they decided to appeal directly to President Harry Truman through his old Jewish business partner, Eddie Jacobson.

Herschel Johnson received another telephone call, this one from the White House. "Herschel, the President wants the delegation to exert every possible influence on other delegations to support partition."

"But the State Department . . ."

"Never mind the State Department! This is an order from the President!"

Shortly thereafter, Mrs. Roosevelt and other American delegates began to move from delegation to delegation, saying, "The President of the United States has asked me to seek your support for the partition plan."

The final vote was thirty-three for, thirteen against, and ten abstentions. The United States, the Soviet Union, France, and most South American and European countries voted yes. The Arab countries, India, and others voted no. The United Kingdom abstained. Cheers broke out in the balcony as the vote was announced, and they were echoed in Tel Aviv and Jerusalem as Jews heard the news on shortwave radio and rushed into the streets to celebrate.

But in the Arab quarters in Palestine the shout of "Kill the Jews!" resounded and was taken up in places as far away as Aden and Algiers.

In Cairo, Haj Amin el-Husseini was summoned to the telephone. The call was from Emile al-Ghouri, now head of the political department of the Arab Higher Committee.

"What is happening in Jerusalem?" the Grand Mufti asked.

"Everyone is furious at the news."

"What do you suggest we should do?"

"We suggest a general strike."

"There might be violence," the Grand Mufti said, "and we're not ready for that yet."

"We can't hold the people back," al-Ghouri said. "We have no choice."

"Well, do as you see fit."

The general strike called by the Arab Higher Committee developed into rioting just as the Grand Mufti had predicted, and on December 2, 1947, the Arabs began to attack Jewish homes and businesses. Unarmed British police stood by helplessly while whole areas were burned down. British troops were finally turned out to disperse the mobs, but that was only the beginning.

The Arab Higher Committee had met in Lebanon in October to plan for the formation of local and national committees in all Arab towns and some 275 villages to raise guerrilla fighters. Arms had been promised by the Arab states and an Arab liberation army was planned in Syria that would advance into Palestine.

By December 11, the Arabs had begun to attack Jews throughout the country, their immediate objectives being to cut communication lines, isolate outlying villages, and convince the world they would never accept partition.

On December 12, a busload of BOAC employees traveling from Lod to Jerusalem was halted by Arab terrorists and the thirteen passengers ordered to get out. They were divided into two groups, British and Arabs in one, and the four Jews in the other. A burst of gunfire cut the Jews down, and the bus was then allowed to continue on its way.

In the Jewish quarter of the Old City, there were 1,700 Jews. They were defended by perhaps 150 Hagana men and surrounded by more than 20,000 Arabs. Sniping now became almost constant, and two Jews were stabbed to death. Finally when an Arab mob tried to smash its way into the synagogue where hundreds of Jews were being sheltered, British troops were rushed to the scene. Fired upon by rioters, they had to disperse the mob with gunfire.

A massive attack by Arab guerrillas was launched on the Etzion bloc of settlements atop the Hebron hills on January 14, 1948. Jewish settlements in this area had been wiped out in 1929 and 1936. Now a thousand Arabs shouting, "Jihad! Jihad!" rushed the Jewish barbed-wire and sandbag defenses. Hebron was to go to the Arabs under the partition plan, but despite British warnings that there were not sufficient troops to watch over every isolated area, the Jews were determined to hang on until the last. Now the Arabs were trying to sweep them away in one determined rush, but they failed to reckon with the fact that the settlement had a machine gun. They were cut down and thrown back, leaving a 150 dead on the hillsides.

At this point the Hagana made a serious mistake. Several convoys trying to reach the Hebron Jews with supplies had been attacked and a number of men killed, so the Hagana decided to send out a patrol of forty fighters, mostly Hebrew University students. They moved out in makeshift armored cars and were accompanied by the girlfriend of one young man. When they arrived at Hartug, thirty-five of the student warriors left the armored cars and pushed on toward the Hebron hills. They were spotted by Arab guerrillas and surrounded. Greatly outnumbered, the Jews fought on all night, but at dawn the Arabs closed in. The three youths who still remained on their feet committed suicide by exploding a hand grenade. The girl and two wounded men were found in a cave and killed on the spot.

Alerted by the sounds of heavy gunfire, British police called in military reinforcements and hurried to the scene of the fighting. What they found and brought into Kfar Etzion was so grisly that they requested that all the women go inside and the lights be dimmed.

When the British removed the tarpaulins from the three trucks, the men of Kfar Etzion stared in horror. "Hunks of mutilated flesh—testicles stuffed into eye sockets, penises into mouths—lay piled in the truck in a pool of blood," Dan Kurzman wrote in *Genesis 1948*. The slaughter of the "Thirty-five" was to set the pattern for later fighting and to account for the fact that neither side in Palestine tended to take prisoners.

The several thousand Arabs who had assaulted Kfar Etzion and butchered the student patrol were Arab Higher Committee forces, commanded by Abd el-Kader el-Husseini, a cousin of the Grand Mufti, a journalist by profession with a long history of stirring up Arab hatred of the Jews. He had been a leader of terrorist groups as far back as 1936, when he had been wounded in a fight with a British patrol and taken prisoner. He escaped and returned to the field only to be wounded again. In 1941, he escaped to Iraq, where he helped the Grand Mufti plot the pro-Nazi coup and led a Palestinian contingent in the fighting that followed with the British and the Arab Legion. Captured again by the British, he was locked up for three years. At the end of the war he was released and immediately formed the Sacred Fighters, the military arm of the Arab Higher Committee, which he was now leading into action.

In late January Abd el-Kader el-Husseini was at his headquarters in Beir Zeit, a village near Rammallah, plotting another terrorist attack. His reason for this was twofold. The first was to take revenge for the bombing of the Damascus Gate and the dynamiting of Arab buildings in Jaffa. Most Jews had followed a policy of defending themselves against Arab attack but not counterattacking unless it became absolutely necessary. The Jewish leaders, wanting to prove to the world that they could hang on, had decided not to give up a single one of their settlements, no matter how isolated. This made it necessary to spread their fighting men thinly and precluded any aggressive action. They also felt that if they did no more than defend themselves, the moderate Arabs might stay neutral. As usual the fanatics of the Stern Gang and the Irgun did not agree with this policy and had carried out several acts of terrorism, including the Damascus Gate and Jaffa incidents.

Before taking over command of the Sacred Fighters, Abd el-Kader had been in Cairo with the Grand Mufti trying desperately to acquire weapons from the Arab nations only to find that most of those available were going to Syria to arm the new ALA, under the command of Fauzi ed-Din el-Kauwakji, another of the Arab terrorist commanders in the 1936–39 period.

This was Abd el-Kader's second reason for wanting to stage a brilliant piece of terrorism. If he could excite admiration among the Arab nations, it might result in having the bulk of the arms given to the Grand Mufti's forces rather than to the outsiders in the ALA. Although the slaughter of the Thirty-five had been portrayed as a dazzling Arab victory, it had tended more to enrage the Jews than to enthrall the Arabs outside of Palestine. Something else was needed, and Abd el-Kader thought he knew what it was and who could carry it out for him.

Among the Arab terrorists were several British deserters who had become so infuriated at Jewish terrorism that they had left the army to seek revenge on their own. One of these was Eddie Brown, a former corporal whose brother had been murdered by Irgun gunmen. A tall, blond young man, he was willing to do anything to get back at the Jews, and it was he who was chosen to lead the attack Abd el-Kader planned.

On February 1, two stolen British vehicles—a car in which sat two obviously Western men in British army uniforms and a five-ton truck driven by an Arab in police uniform—were stopped by British sentries at the Nablus Gate of Jerusalem. Brown showed his identity card, and the two vehicles were allowed to pass through into the Jewish New City. A few minutes later, the convoy was stopped at a Hagana checkpoint and passed on just as easily.

The car and truck drew up in front of the building that housed the Jewish-operated *Palestine Post.* In the back of the truck were two barrels of TNT to accomplish the mission—the destruction of the newspaper. The driver of the truck crawled into the back, lit a long fuse, and then walked over and got in the car with the two Englishmen. The car passed back through both the Hagana and British checkpoints and disappeared into the Old City.

The resulting blast wrecked the building, killed a linotype operator, and wounded more than twenty other people, mostly in the composing room. Fire cut off those upstairs, but they escaped with the aid of several American newsmen who rushed to the scene from a nearby bar.

A few hours later an abbreviated edition of the *Palestine Post* was on the streets, having been turned out in a neighboring printshop. An editorial on the front page proclaimed, "The truth is louder than TNT and burns brighter than the flames of arson."

Pleased with his success, Abd el-Kader made further plans. He now had six British deserters in the Sacred Fighters and decided to use them to strike an even heavier blow against the Jews in the New City.

This time three trucks were used, escorted by a stolen British armored car with a young blond man in police uniform standing in the turret. The trucks had no trouble passing either British or Hagana checkpoints and drove to the Atlantic Hotel on Ben Yehuda Street. A nightwatchman from the nearby Palestine Discount Bank hurried over to investigate when they pulled up in front of the hotel. He was killed, the fuses to the dynamite in the trucks were lit, and the terrorists all piled into the armored car and drove off. The explosion destroyed the hotel and adjacent buildings and heavily damaged the bank; 46 Jews were killed and approximately 130 were injured.

The next attack was even more daring and was carried out by a single Christian Arab named Abu Yussef, a chauffeur of the U.S. consulate-general in Jerusalem. Because he drove an official American car, it was easy for him to gain entry to the compound of the Jewish Agency, where the Zionist leadership had its offices. Abd el-Kader supplied the explosives, and Abu Yussef did the rest. The car was moved just before the explosion occurred, saving the lives of Ben-Gurion and other leaders, but thirteen officials of the Jewish Foundation Fund were killed and forty other people injured.

A tip on the movement of a Jewish convoy afforded the Sacred Fighters another opportunity. Nineteen makeshift Hagana armored cars and thirty-three trucks and buses loaded with some two hundred Jewish fighters were cut off and surrounded on March 27 on the Kfar Etzion road. Halted by a roadblock, the cars and trucks were attacked by swarms of Arabs. A few cars managed to turn around on the narrow road and escape back to Kfar Etzion, but the rest were forced to take refuge in a nearby building, where they were trapped and soon running out of ammunition. Alerted by radio, Jewish officials rushed to the nearest British post to plead for help.

But the British were reluctant to act, partly because they were still reacting to the Jewish terror campaign and partly because they were under strict orders from the new Labour government in London to carry out their evacuation of the mandate without becoming involved in actions against either Jews or Arabs. They were willing to rescue women and children but not armed Hagana fighters. It was explained there were women with the convoy and a compromise was struck between Jewish leaders and British commanders. The British would extricate the Jews if they were willing to leave their arms and convoy behind. Reluctantly this was agreed to, and British armored cars and half-tracks arrived in time to save most of the trapped Jews, who refused to leave until they were persuaded to do so by Dr. Jacques de Reynier, a Red Cross representative who had accompanied the British column.

The terrorist acts in the New City, the destruction of the Kfar Etzion convoy, and the fact that the United States seemed to be backing off from its propartition stand convinced the Jewish leadership that they must take the offensive.

A new factor had also appeared on the scene with the arrival of the first guerrilla units of the ALA. They had begun showing up as early as January 20, and as their numbers increased, Fauzi ed-Din el-Kauwakji took over command. The first impulse of the British forces was to run this motley crew of imported terrorists out of the country, and since at that time there were still almost fifty thousand British troops left in Palestine, it would have been little more than an afternoon's work.

In the ALA's first action, an attack on the Jewish settlements of Dan and Kfar Szold, Gen. Sir Gordon MacMillan had sent a troop of armored cars to each kibbutz to help the defenders, and their machine guns had scattered the attackers very quickly. In another action, the ALA mistakenly ambushed a convoy of Irish Guards. Despite the advantage of surprise and superior numbers, the Arabs were badly beaten, suffering numerous casualties and having eight of their men taken prisoner. Interrogation by Irish Guard officers revealed the eight to be regulars from the Syrian army. After another clash, an Arab attack on the kibbutz at Tirat Zvi, during which the British rescue column laid down a heavy mortar barrage to force the Arabs back, el-Kauwakji agreed to an armistice, promising he would not attack the Jews until after the May deadline for the British withdrawal. Unknown to the British, he had already made an agreement with Jewish agents not to attack them for the time being, to stand aside while they battled with the Sacred Fighters and other groups supporting the Grand Mufti. A representative of the Arab League, el-Kauwakji was quite willing to see the Grand Mufti's forces mauled before he intervened.

The British commanding officer in Palestine felt it was his duty to get rid of the ALA. It was one thing to stand by, as ordered by London, while Palestinian Arabs and Jews killed each other; it was something else altogether to permit the mandate to be invaded before the British were gone. Sir Gordon MacMillan therefore radioed Sir John Crocker, the British Middle East commander in the Suez Canal zone, for orders and received a three-word reply: "Drive them out!"

Before he could act, however, he received an urgent message from London reinforcing the previous order not to become involved in any fighting unless it interfered with British withdrawal.

Throughout the period of 1947–48, the British government policy was to have no policy. This left the men on the scene in both civil and military branches with more responsibility than they cared to assume and led to constant changes in direction that confused both Jews and Arabs as to British intentions.

Then Abd el-Kader el-Husseini was killed in an attack on a Jewish village, and thereafter the Sacred Fighters were less effective. His death had another aftereffect, however, that was of incalculable importance to the fighting in Palestine and to the future of Israel as well. On hearing of Abd el-Kader's death, most of the Arabs who had been warring with the Jews in and around the villages of Kastel and Deir Yassin in the early part of April 1948 headed for Jerusalem to attend the funeral. This left the Arab villages almost defenseless. It was an opportunity the Stern Gang and Irgun soldiers could not resist. Without the knowledge of Jewish leaders they decided to attack Deir Yassin.

In *Armageddon in the Middle East,* Dana Adams Schmidt, an American newsman, tells of receiving a tip that a "rather special story on the Jewish side" would be available if he was willing to leave Jerusalem for the suburbs where the fighting had been heavy. That night members of the Irgun took Schmidt and other journalists to Deir Yassin.

The terrorists claimed they had been forced to attack the village because Arab snipers had been firing on them from it. At first the villagers had raised a white flag but then had opened fire again. "Unfortunately there were a good many civilian casualties. We had to throw hand grenades into some of the houses," Schmidt was told. Later a spokesman for the Arab Higher Committee told him that at least two hundred men, women, and children had been killed and their bodies thrown into a well. It was, he said, not a battle but "a systematic act of terrorism, clinical, calculated, methodical, and designed to reinforce the panic of the Palestinian Arabs already set in motion by the dynamiting of their villages."

In another interview with an Irgun leader, the newsman was told that they did not want to act as they had at Deir Yassin but that "it is the only way. We have no other weapons that will move the British and frighten the Arabs. But, believe me, it is not out of hatred for them—only out of love for our own people."

The attack was led by Mordechai Raanan, the Irgun commander in

Jerusalem, and Yehoshua Zetler, the Sternist chief in the same city. Raanan, a twenty-five-year-old veteran of terrorist campaigns, hated the local Hagana commander, David Shaltiel, a former French Foreign Legion officer, and constantly disobeyed orders he received from other Hagana leaders. The capture of Deir Yassin presented him with a chance to get the jump on the more conservative group and win credit for his own organization.

Stern and Irgun terrorists attacked the village from two directions at 4:30 in the morning and found it almost defenseless. The people of Deir Yassin had always tried to maintain good relations with their Jewish neighbors who surrounded them on all sides and bought most of the fruit the town's orchards produced. Some days before the attack four strangers had fired at Jews from the village; the *mukhtar,* the Arab mayor, had apologized and assured the Jews there would be no repetition of the act. The town's leaders had also met with those from nearby Jewish towns and agreed with them to keep the peace no matter what happened in other areas.

The terrorists swept into the village shooting and lobbing hand grenades in all directions. An armored car with a loudspeaker that was supposedly intended to broadcast warnings to Arab civilians to evacuate had, according to the Irgun, fallen into a ditch and was inoperable. The startled Arabs grabbed what weapons they could find and started shooting back. That infuriated the invaders, and the slaughter began in earnest.

Going from house to house, they tossed hand grenades through windows and then stood in the doorways and sprayed the interiors with automatic-weapon fire. It made no difference that most of the Arabs were unarmed and that nearly all of the occupants were women and children.

As more and more of the Arabs found guns and returned the fire, the attackers called for dynamite to blast them out of their houses. The terrorists were experts with dynamite, and as house after house was blasted, resistance slackened. That did not abate the fury of the attack, however. Stern and Irgun gunmen continued killing indiscriminately, shooting down anyone they found regardless of age or sex. Later both gangs would try to blame the massacre on the "lunatic fringe" of the other group, but while it was going on, they appeared to be trying to outdo each other in their fanatic urge to kill.

When all the houses in the village had been destroyed except that of the *mukhtar,* which stood on a hill, the Jews burst into it and killed the mayor's wife and grandson. The other women were herded out by gunmen who said they had just received orders from their commanders not to kill any more women and children.

The surviving inhabitants were taken out into the village square where the men were separated from the women and children. The men were shot, and the others loaded into trucks to be driven through Jewish Jerusalem. There, instead of the cheering they expected, the killers were greeted by shocked silence.

At 5:30 that evening, David Shaltiel, the Hagana commander, drove out to Deir Yassin. The tough ex-Legionnaire was horrified by what he saw.

"What have you done here?" he roared at Raanan.

"The place is completely under our control," Raanan said. "Send some men to take over for us."

"We're not going to take responsibility for your murders!" Shaltiel told him. "You must bury the dead and hold the village yourself."

When a Hagana patrol reached the town the next morning, there was a mountain of bodies piled in a quarry, some half charred because the terrorists had attempted to burn them when they began to smell.

Since the gang members had refused to bury the dead, saying, "We're fighters, not pallbearers! We're leaving," a Hagana-led party of Jewish schoolboys was brought in to perform the grisly task. Weeping and vomiting, they dug the graves and buried the murdered Arabs. How many they buried is not known exactly. Some say the death toll was around 250, others claim it may have been as high as 1,000.

What is known is the effect the massacre had on events that followed. It sent a wave of terror through the Arabs of Palestine, and it was used as propaganda by both sides. More important, it and other Jewish acts of terror set a pattern for terrorism in the Middle East that continues to this day.

At the time most Jews recognized the true nature of the action and denounced it.

"For a full day, Irgun and Stern soldiers stood and slaughtered men, women, and children, not in the course of the operation, but in a premeditated act which had as its intention slaughter and murder only. They also took spoils, and when they finished their work, they fled," David Shaltiel said in his official dispatch to a horrified Ben-Gurion.

Although Nathan Friedman-Yellin, head of the Sternists, was bitter about what his field forces had done, Menahem Begin defended the action then and continues to do so to this day. "The massacre was not only justified, but there would not have been a state of Israel without the victory of Deir Yassin," he has said.

News of the massacre was spread by word of mouth from Arab village to Arab village and also by means of both Jewish and Arab radio stations. In fact, Arab broadcasts exaggerated the number killed so much that Glubb Pasha, the British commander of the Arab Legion, was convinced that thousands of Arabs had been killed.

The effect on the Arab population was soon obvious. Whole towns were evacuated by their defenders at the approach of small Jewish patrols. Deir Yassin had a similar effect on the city of Haifa, although it should be noted that nearly twenty thousand Arabs had left the city before the April massacre.

The roughly equal Jewish and Arab forces massed for battle in Haifa after Maj. Gen. Hugh Stockwell, commander of northern Palestine, informed both sides that he had been ordered to withdraw all troops from the city proper in order to protect the port facilities from which British soldiers were shipped out of Palestine. The Arabs in Haifa were almost leaderless when the crisis struck. Not only had most of the well-to-do fled but so had the lawyers, the scholars, and other natural leaders. Even the commander of the fighting forces had left, obstensibly to bring reinforcements from Syria. The man in charge in his absence was killed during a Jewish ambush and command then fell to a worker in the city sanitation department.

The fighting was over in less than twenty-four hours. The Jews were victorious after inflicting three hundred casualties on the Arabs. General Stockwell then asked the Jewish leaders if they were willing to offer terms to their defeated opponents; they agreed to do so.

A delegation that called itself the Arab National Committee for Haifa appeared at Stockwell's headquarters to ask that the Jews be driven out of the city. Stockwell pointed out that his orders were not to involve British troops except to protect their lines of communications. He could not take sides against the Jews, but he would be glad to arrange an armistice between the two sides. The delegation, composed of two Muslims, Farid Saad and Sheikh Abdul Rahman Murad, and four Christians, Elias Koussa, Victor Khayat, Anis Nasr, and George Muammar, agreed to meet with Jewish leaders.

At four in the afternoon on April 22, 1948, representatives of the two groups met at the Haifa town hall. They greeted each other warmly and some embraced, since they had known each other for years. They settled down to have coffee while they waited for the British commander to appear. When Stockwell entered and assumed the chair of the meeting, Shabetai Levy, the Jewish mayor of Haifa, was the first to speak.

He told the Arabs that he was aware that many of their people were fleeing the city and that there was panic in the Arab quarters. He said the Jews did not want a single Arab to leave and urged his old friends to remain and live in peace with the Jews as they had for forty years in the past.

Stockwell then explained the terms of the armistice. The Hagana was to have control of the city, the Arabs were to give up their arms, and a curfew was to be instituted in the Arab quarters. In return the Jews promised that all inhabitants would have equal rights and duties. The general concluded his explanation with the remark that he considered the terms "reasonable and moderate."

The Arab delegation then requested a break in negotiations so that they could consult with the "Arab States" for advice, but when the Christian members returned without their Muslim colleagues, it was clear that something had happened. The atmosphere was no longer warm and friendly. The Arabs said they would not sign such a document under any circumstances, nor would they sign anything. They asked that the Arabs be allowed to leave the city and that the British facilitate their evacuation. "We do not recognize you and we shall return when you are no longer here," one Arab leader told the Jews.

Stockwell asked the four Arabs if they had lost their senses. "You have made a foolish decision. Think it over, as you'll regret it afterwards. You must accept the condition of the Jews. They are fair enough. After all, it was you who began the fighting and the Jews have won."

Levy pleaded with the Arabs, and there were tears in his eyes as he spoke. "We do not want a single Arab to leave. Arabs and Jews can once more live together in peace as we have in the past. You will remain equal citizens in every way."

The Arabs remained adamant. They could not sign an armistice that they considered "degrading." They would be branded "traitors" by their people if they accepted it.

It is not known exactly what happened during the three hours the Arab delegates were absent from the negotiating table. Was the decision made in Haifa by the Arab National Committee for that city, or was it made by the Arab Higher Committee through Damascus? It is not clear in any of the eyewitness accounts. Hagana officers talked about having seen an intercepted telegram sent by the Grand Mufti to the Haifa Arabs ordering the evacuation, but no copy of the telegram has ever been produced. Neutral witnesses present at the time are almost unanimous in saying that the Jews did everything in their power to prevent the evacuation but that it was ordered by the Grand Mufti.

There is no doubt there was panic among the Arab populace, but many had begun to leave as early as December 1947. By March 1948, twenty-five thousand had left, and this was before Deir Yassin and before there had been any serious fighting. Another twenty thousand left in the first half of April, after the arrival of the ALA in Palestine, and persistent rumors circulated in the Arab community that people should leave so that the air forces of the Arab states would feel free to bomb the city. Thousands more were fleeing toward the port area and along the road to Acre even as Koussa and his colleagues were leaving the town hall to seek advice.

The question as to why the Arabs left is still being argued. The Jews say they left voluntarily; the Arabs, their supporters in the United Nations, and the New Left in America say they were driven out by the Jews. Haifa, because of the large number of neutral observers on hand to record what they saw and heard, has become a pivotal part of the argument.

The Jews claim the Arabs received orders to leave from their leaders, especially the Arab Higher Committee; that the orders were conveyed by radio; and that the rationale behind them was to clear the way for invading Arab armies. The Arabs claim the Jews deliberately used physical and psychological terror to drive the Arabs out. Since the Palestinian refugees are the very eye of the storm of terrorism, not only in the Middle East but worldwide, it is important to examine both contentions carefully.

The British chief of police in Haifa, A. J. Bridmead, referred in his official reports to Jewish efforts to curb the panic of their Arab neighbors. "The situation in Haifa remains unchanged. Every effort is being made by the Jews to persuade the Arab populace to stay and carry on their normal lives, to get their shops and businesses open, to be assured that their lives and interests will be safe."

That the appeal was not having the desired effect was made clear in another Bridmead report: "An appeal has been made to the Arabs by the Jews to reopen their shops and businesses in order to relieve the difficulties of feeding the Arab population. Evacuation was still going on yesterday and several trips were made by Z-craft to Acre. Roads, too, were crowded. Arab leaders reiterated their determination to evacuate the entire Arab population and they have been given the loan of 10 three-ton military trucks as of this morning to assist the evacuation."

Two days later he reported, "The Jews are still making every effort to persuade the Arab population to remain and settle back into their normal lives in the town."

The Jewish Workers Council appealed to fellow workers to remain:

> For years we have lived together in our city, Haifa, in security and in mutual understanding and brotherhood. Thanks to this, our city flourished and developed for the good of both Jewish and Arab residents, and thus did Haifa serve as an example to other cities in Palestine. . . . At this junction we believe it necessary to state in the frankest terms: We are a peace-loving people! There is no cause for the fear which others try to instill in you. There is no hatred in our hearts nor evil in our intentions towards peace-loving residents who, like us, are bent upon work and creative effort.
>
> Do not fear! Do not destroy your homes with your own hands; do not block off your sources of livelihood and do not bring upon yourself tragedy by unnecessary evacuation and self-imposed burdens. By moving out you will be overtaken by poverty and humiliation. But in this city, yours and ours, Haifa, the gates are open for work, for life, and for peace, for you and your families. . . . We are ready to come to your help, in restoring normal conditions, to assist you in obtaining food supplies, and to open up job opportunities. . . .

An article in the London *Economist* (October 2, 1948) by a British correspondent in Haifa said:

> During the subsequent days the Israeli authorities who were now in complete control of Haifa . . . urged all Arabs to remain in Haifa, and guaranteed them protection and security. So far as I know, most of the British civilian residents whose advice was asked by Arab friends told the latter they would be wise to stay. Various factors influenced their decision to seek safety in flight. There is but little doubt that by far the most potent of these factors was the announcements made over the air by the Arab Higher Executive urging all Arabs in Haifa to quit. The reason given was that upon the final withdrawal of the British, combined armies of the Arab States would invade Palestine and drive the Jews into the sea, and it was clearly intimated that those Arabs who remained in Haifa and accepted Jewish protection would be regarded as renegades.

Henry C. Stebbens, a member of the mandatory government of Palestine in 1947–48, also witnessed what happened in Haifa. In answer to a pro-Arab letter published in the *Evening Standard* of London, he wrote about his experience. The Palestinians were not, as had been claimed, "kicked out of their homes by the Israelis." He said that out of his Arab staff of two hundred and his labor force of eighteen hundred, all but a few had fled between January and April 1948 despite his strenuous efforts to prevail upon them to stay. He listed the reasons they had given for leaving:

1. The Arab terrorism engendered by the November 1947 UN partition resolution frightened them to the depth of their imaginative souls and they feared Jewish reprisal.

2. Propagandist promises of a bloodbath as soon as the mandate ended in which the streets of the cities would run with blood.

3. The promised invasion by the foreign Arab armies . . . was preceded by extensive broadcasts from Cairo, Damascus, Amman, and Beirut to the effect that any Arabs who stayed would be hanged as collaborators with the Jews.

Stebbens said the Arabs were the victims of their own propaganda. Many of his Arab friends from those days whom he has seen since told him of their regret that they had not listened to him and remained in their homes.

The Arab National Committee of Haifa sent a memorandum to the governments of the Arab League states on April 27, 1948, explaining their decision to order evacuation. "The signing of a truce would be a disgrace to the Arab population of Haifa. . . . Our delegation proudly refused to sign the truce and asked that the evacuation of the population and their transfer to the neighboring Arab countries be facilitated. . . . The military and civil authorities and the Jewish representatives expressed their profound regret at this grave decision. The Mayor adjourned the meeting with a passionate appeal to the [Arab] population to reconsider its decision."

At the time that message was sent forty thousand Arabs were already in the act of fleeing the city. They crowded onto the docks and swarmed aboard every craft they could find, no matter how unseaworthy. They drove out in cars or loaded into British army tanks; some of them walked. Among those who left in style was Leila Khaled, who later became a terrorist hijacker. Contrary to her story of having been driven from her home by Jews, her mother simply called a taxi and, against the express wishes of Leila's father, had the family taken out of town during his absence.

Of the entire population of Haifa, all but five or six thousand Arabs fled, most leaving behind everything they owned. The panic was so great that rumors reached Foreign Minister Ernest Bevin that twenty-three thousand Arabs had been massacred while the British army had stood by and done nothing. Bevin demanded that Stockwell turn out his troops to protect the remaining Arabs and was informed that there had been no massacre and that Arab casualties had been light in the brief period of fighting.

The situation in Haifa seems fairly clear-cut. In other areas what happened is less clear. Marie Syrkin, a professor at Brandeis University, was in Israel six weeks after the proclamation of nationhood in June 1948 and was able to speak to eyewitnesses of the mass flight at a time when "there were no documents and no studies. All that was available in those days was the fresh reactions of Jews and Arabs—as yet undoctored by policy."

She spoke to Arabs who had not fled and to the clergy of various faiths who had watched their flocks virtually disappear overnight. Those who stayed said those who had fled could just as easily have stayed but instead had "listened to the Mufti." Christian clergy told of the unreasoning fear among their people, which they could do nothing to ease or dispel. The mother superior of one nunnery said she had urged the Arabs who lived nearby to remain, telling them, "Don't be afraid; I'll protect you!" But they would not listen. "They ran!" she said.

The Jews, according to Syrkin, were as bewildered by what had happened as were the Muslims and Christians, and they had many opinions as to why the mass exodus had taken place. Some said Arab leaders had ordered it, others felt it was the fault of the British. There were Jews who blamed it on the Irgun massacre at Deir Yassin and Jews who said the Grand Mufti's "atrocity propaganda had backfired."

Syrkin found that many Arabs had fled before the massacre, however, as had so many in Haifa. The Sharon area, for one, was almost empty of Arabs because so many of them had headed for the Arab-held hills before Deir Yassin was destroyed.

In Tiberias the Jews literally woke up one morning and found all their Arab neighbors gone. They issued a statement that said: "We did not dispossess them; they themselves chose this course. But the day will come when the Arabs will return to their homes and property in this town. In the meantime, let no citizen touch their property."

Syrkin points out in her *Commentary* article "Israel, the Arabs and the Middle East" that after months of bloody fighting, the Jews were less willing to be so generous and there were cases where Jews did drive Arabs out of their villages, particularly along the Tel Aviv–Jerusalem highway, which the Hagana was waging a desperate fight to keep open against considerable odds.

In the case of Jaffa, which was an Irgun operation, the Jews may have been the aggressors. We have it on General Stockwell's testimony that in Haifa it was the Arabs who attacked first, and the Haifa affair preceded the one in Jaffa by over a week. It should be remembered that the Jews in Jerusalem and other cities had been attacked by Arab mobs almost immediately after the UN decision and that terrorist attacks on communications had begun about the same time. In addition, scattered Jewish settlements such as Kfar Etzion had come under attack shortly thereafter.

In an account that tilts toward the Arab side, Colin Smith in *The Palestinians* presents the contentions of the Institute for Palestine Studies in Beirut, which claims that the Palestinians were panicked by the use of "clever psychological warfare tactics." The Jews allegedly spread rumors that Iraqi and Syrian invading armies were carrying contagious diseases such as smallpox and cholera. The institute says that the Jews resorted to a concentrated psychological offensive before every attack on an Arab locality and that Hagana radio would broadcast warnings to the people to leave before 5:15 A.M.: "Take pity on your wives and children and get out of this bloodbath. Get out by the Jericho Road; that is still open to you. If you stay, you invite disaster."

At the time, there were Arabs who recognized that their own leadership was at least partially to blame for the flight of the Palestinians, and they said so. "The fact that there are these refugees is the direct consequence of the act of the Arab states in opposing partition and the Jewish State," Emile al-Ghouri said in an interview on September 6, 1948.

The Jordanian daily *Palestine* on February 19, 1949, blamed the Arab leaders. "The Arab States, which had encouraged the Palestine Arabs to leave their homes temporarily in order to be out of the way of the Arab invasion armies, have failed to keep their promises to help these refugees."

The Cairo daily *Al-Akhbar* spoke of the reason for the refugee problem: "May 15, 1948 arrived [and] on that very day the Mufti of Jerusalem appealed to the Arabs of Palestine to leave the country, because the Arab armies were about to enter and fight in their stead. . . ."

If it is an Israeli "myth," as writer I. F. Stone once suggested, that the Palestinians fled on their own, one must conclude that it is a myth the Arabs also believe.

As British withdrawal accelerated, instances of terrorism increased. One of these was the Arab attack on a Jewish hospital convoy on its way from Jerusalem to the Hadassah Hospital on Mount Scopus. Two of the late Abd el-Kader el-Husseini's lieutenants, Mohammed Abdel Najar and Adil Abd Latif, decided to revenge Deir Yassin so that "our people will find new spirit." The convoy consisted of two armor-plated ambulances, two buses, three trucks, and two homemade armored cars. There were 105 people in the various vehicles, mostly doctors, nurses, and other medical personnel. The ambulances were painted red and white and bore the Jewish equivalent of the Red Cross, the red Star of David. Shortly after passing the last British army post on the approach to Mount Scopus, the leading armored car was blasted by an electrically detonated mine. In trying to go on past the damaged car or turn around while under fire from Sacred Fighter gunmen, the convoy vehicles slid into ditches and became hopelessly trapped.

Najar had only forty guerrillas with him armed with grenades, Molotov cocktails, and small arms, but the Jews were mostly noncombatants unable to move or defend themselves. All the Arab leader had to do was finish them off before the British intervened. Najar gave his orders and his men closed in around the helpless convoy, whose only guns were in the first and last armored cars.

In the New City section of Jerusalem, Jewish leaders heard the sound of gunfire and realized that the convoy was under attack. Unable to contact the commanding officer of the British troops, four Hagana armored cars tried to push through to the convoy but were ambushed by Arabs and had to retreat.

By now hundreds of local Arabs had rushed to join the original forty; but to a British convoy passing along on the nearby Nablus road that crossed the one to Scopus, it looked as though the Jews were holding the ambushers at bay, and so it continued on its way without interfering.

The British finally arrived in force and opened fire on the Arab positions, sweeping the hills with machine-gun and mortar fire. Arab casualties were heavy, and Najar was wounded. The Arabs retreated, and the British moved on to the convoy.

They found only twenty-eight survivors. Seventy-six charred or bullet-riddled corpses—doctors, nurses, and staff workers of the hospital—were loaded into trucks. The living were transferred to British armored cars and taken back to town. The bitter seed sown at Deir Yassin was coming to harvest.

Egyptian terrorists also entered the struggle in Palestine. Gamal Abdel Nasser, then a young captain, tried to form regular Egyptian army troops into guerrilla units but found that even the Grand Mufti was not enthusiastic about his offer. Nasser had hated the British since he was a member of the ultranationalist, green-shirted Young Egypt party during World War II. He had been among those who urged King Farouk to welcome the Nazis into Egypt and was jubilant when the king, thinking Rommel's tanks were on the way, had dismissed his pro-British government. His joy was short-lived. The British brought tanks into Cairo, knocked down the gates of the palace, and took Farouk prisoner, refusing to release him until he appointed another pro-British premier. "Overwhelmed with shame and rage," Nasser formed what he called the Free Officers, a secret society, and began to plot to seize power in Egypt.

Nasser's efforts to send terrorists against the Jews failed, but the more powerful Muslim Brotherhood, an ultra-right-wing political and religious organization, did send in its gunmen. In an attack on the kibbutz at Kfar Darom, the Muslim Brothers showed fanatical courage before they were beaten off and withdrew, leaving their dead behind. The Jews found that every one of the slain brothers wore a parchment about twelve by eighteen inches long, covered with Arabic script proclaiming the wearer "a true Muslim fighting the Jihad, who is therefore immune to all manner of lead and steel." In the pockets of each dead man were a box of matches and a razor blade, the matches to burn down Jewish buildings and the razor blade to castrate Jewish prisoners.

On April 28 the British escorted one last food convoy through to the Jews besieged by Arabs in the Old City of Jerusalem. Among those who went along was Yehudit Weingarten, daughter of Rabbi A. Mordechai Weingarten, the spiritual leader of the Jews in that area. Yehudit had asked for permission to take some of the rabbi's personal possessions to him, and the British had agreed to the request. What she carried under British escort and through Arab lines was a heavy Lewis machine gun, broken down and packed in a suitcase, plus ammunition for it. The gun was vitally needed by the outnumbered Jews as it became increasingly clear that British withdrawal was imminent.

Neither the Arabs nor the Jews in Jerusalem knew the exact date when the last British troops would pull out. All that was known was that they would be gone before May 15. The side that could most accurately determine the exact time of withdrawal would have an advantage, for they could take over British police posts and appropriate any equipment left behind. Arab fighters and Hagana men kept close watch for any signs of regiment activity. Finally on May 13, a Hagana officer got the word they wanted when a short, blond British soldier approached a roadblock and said, "My name is Albert Melville. We're leaving now, but I'd like to stay here and fight with you." So the Hagana had a recruit plus the information they needed to get the jump on the Arabs.

A short time later, the British commander, Major Allen, halted his column of men in front of Rabbi Weingarten's house and handed the keys to the Zion Gate to him. "From the year A.D. 70 until today, the keys to Jerusalem have never been in the hands of Jews. This is the first time in more than eighteen centuries that you are so privileged."

Allen also handed the old man a Sten gun and several clips of ammunition before shaking hands. "Let us part as friends. I hope that you have a complete victory. Good luck and shalom."

The Union Jack had hardly fluttered down over Government House before the Republic of Israel was proclaimed. David Ben-Gurion had decided to present the United States and the world with a *fait accompli* and see what the effect would be.

A struggle had been going on in America between Arabists and Zionists, the same kind of struggle that had so often caused wobbling in British policy on Palestine—the Balfours and Churchills against the Middle East experts. Now U.S. Arabists were apparently in ascendance in the State Department and were pushing a plan for a new truce and a continuation of the mandate plus changes in the partition provisions. What would their reaction be to the announcement?

The man who played such a prominent part in bringing Israel to this moment was Ben-Gurion. Born in Plonsk, Poland, in 1886, he had arrived in Palestine in 1906 and spent several years working as a farmer. He became active in the Socialist Zionist party, Po'ale Zion, and was an early supporter of an independent state in Palestine. He founded the General Federation of Labor, the Histadrut, in 1920, and was elected chairman of the Zionist Executive and the Jewish Agency in 1935. He supported the British during World War II with the statement "Fight the war as if there was no white paper and the white paper as if there were no war." He was the leading advocate of the Biltmore Program. As the days of the mandate approached the end, he was a strong opponent of the Irgun and the Stern Gang and their terror tactics against the British, but he worked tirelessly for the creation of a Jewish defense force.

This man, who might be considered the George Washington of Israel, had now led the Jewish Agency and the Zionist Executive into establishing a Jewish state, but was he being premature? Would the Arabists in the State Department and Arab supporters in the United Nations react vigorously against this presumption? The Jewish leaders could only wait and see.

On May 14, President Truman, on the advice of Gen. George Marshall, asked Chaim Weizmann to forward a request for recognition of the new state to his desk. The Jewish representatives were almost too stunned to act. They had expected bitter opposition from the State Department and now here was the president of the United States taking the initiative. No one was even sure what to call the new state. At first they merely asked for recognition of the "Jewish State," but at the last minute they called to say it was to be the "State of Israel."

In the United Nations, the American delegation was still engaged in pushing for a new trustee plan for at least Jerusalem when a call was received from Washington and Philip Jessup rose to announce: "This government has been informed that a Jewish state has been proclaimed in Palestine, and recognition has been requested by the provisional government thereof. The United States recognizes the provisional government as the *de facto* authority of the new State of Israel."

The Arabs were enraged but probably not as incensed as were Arabists in the State Department, who were reminded once again that the president had a mind of his own.

The proclamation of the State of Israel had worked, but now the new nation was faced with a desperate war. The British were gone, and the armies of the Arab states were crossing borders just as they had threatened. The most dangerous of these was the well-trained and disciplined Arab Legion, which withdrew across the Allenby Bridge one day as a British unit had recrossed it the next as an Arab invading force. Almost immediately it succeeded in doing what none of the Palestine Arabs had done in months of fighting: it took a Jewish kibbutz. And not just a single isolated kibbutz but a whole complex of them, the so-called Etzion bloc in the Hebron hills.

After heavy fighting, the Jews, out of ammunition and suffering heavy casualties, came out carrying a white flag. To their dismay, the thirty Jewish survivors, including a girl radio operator, found themselves surrounded by a mob of local Arabs instead of Arab Legion regulars. They were ordered to sit down, then to stand up, and finally an Arab wearing a *kaffiyeh,* the symbol of the terrorists, took pictures while his companions opened fire with Sten guns.

The girl was among the few not killed, and she was dragged into the woods by two Arabs who began arguing over who would rape her first. Suddenly shots rang out and they both fell dead. A legion officer ran to her side, Sten gun still smoking, and stuffed a piece of bread into her mouth, thus invoking the old law of Arab hospitality.

"Eat this!" he ordered. "Now you are under my protection."

Pushing through a mob of irregulars, he managed to get the girl into his armored car and drove off while the local Arabs shouted after him, "Kill her! Kill her!"

The bodies of twenty other girls, mostly nurses and medical workers, were found in a cellar where they had been slaughtered. Only the radio girl and two young men who had been protected by an elderly local Arab until rescued from the mob by two legion officers survived the assault. At the other kibbutzim of the complex, the legion accepted the surrender of the Jews and hurriedly loaded them into armored cars and trucks, driving them to their command post in Hebron. The girl also was taken there and insisted on being locked up with the other prisoners, refusing the offer of her rescuer to marry her.

Inside the jail were several hundred Jewish prisoners of war and outside were thousands of Arabs shouting, "Kill them! Kill them! Give them to us!" The Arab Legion had to move its armored cars into a circle around the jail and finally was forced to open fire with machine guns to protect its prisoners from the mob that shouted throughout the night, "Give us the Jews! Give us the Jews! Remember Deir Yassin!"

The fighting, which had gone badly at first for the Jews, soon shifted in their favor with the arrival of weapons collected from all over the world. The Arab irregulars were badly beaten, and the regular armies pushed back. Even the legion was fought to a standstill in and around Jerusalem. The United Nations then intervened with a truce proposal that was accepted by both sides while they rearmed and filled up their ranks with fresh troops.

During the lull in the fighting terrorism did not die out. The Sacred Fighters attacked Jews, and Irgun gunmen found Arab targets. One of the most violent incidents, however, found Jew pitted against Jew, the Hagana against the Irgun.

The worldwide search for arms was conducted by both organizations. The Irgun discovered a willing ally in the foreign minister of France, Georges Bidault. Convinced by Irgun leaders that they would come to power after the establishment of the State of Israel, Bidault arranged for large supplies of arms, which were loaded onto a surplus LST, the *Altalena,* for the voyage to Israel. These arms were not intended to fight the Arabs but to enable the Irgun to seize power from the Hagana and impose its rightist rule on the new country. Aboard the ship were a number of Americans, including its captain, who had joined the Irgun after seeing a proterrorist play, *A Flag Is Born,* by Ben Hecht. As the arms ship approached the coast of Israel, David Ben-Gurion was warned. On board were 5,000 rifles, 300 Bren guns, 150 Spandaus, 5 caterpillar-track armored cars, 3 million rounds of ammunition, and several thousand bombs.

Ben-Gurion was well aware that if those arms were brought into the country, they would strengthen the Irgun so drastically as to leave the future of Israel in doubt. If the Irgun came to power, there would be no democratic state; there would be an ultra-right-wing, neofascist regime totally unlike the government dreamed of by Zionist leaders. To those who had struggled so hard and so long, a state ruled by terrorists was not worth having.

"Let the ship come," Ben-Gurion said, "but the arms will go to the army whatever happens."

Begin was enraged. There were enough arms on the *Altalena* to equip several battalions, and Begin was determined they would be used by his squads, not the Hagana's. He has since denied that he intended to overthrow the government once the equipment was in his hands, but his field commanders were soon to try just that.

As the LST headed in toward shore, Ben-Gurion ordered five hundred Hagana troops onto the landing site, a small pier on the shore of Kfar Vitkin where Irgun terrorists were waiting to receive the arms.

Barricades were set up to prevent Irgun trucks from reaching the dock toward which the *Altalena* was backing. As the confrontation loomed nearer, thousands of onlookers gathered on the beaches. Begin himself rushed to the scene and gathered his men around the dock, but they were quickly surrounded by Hagana troops. The shooting began when Irgun trucks loaded with terrorists tried to break through to reach their comrades on the beach. Heavy Irgun casualties resulted, and Begin and his group retreated onto the ship and pulled away from shore. Begin ordered the *Altalena* to steam south to Tel Aviv, where he intended to arouse the population against the government and seize power.

Two corvettes of the new Israeli navy tried to block the passage of the LST, but heavy machine-gun fire from the ship drove them off long enough for the American captain to steer his craft in among neutral merchant ships lying at anchor, where the warships did not dare fire. The *Altalena* headed for the beach to unload its arms but struck a submerged wreck about a hundred yards from the shore and could go no farther.

Begin had placed one of the most fanatical of all the Irgun leaders in command of the ship. Abraham Stavsky was a revisionist who in 1933 had murdered Dr. Chaim Arlosoroff of the Jewish Agency's Political Department. Stavsky was now determined to bring down the new government of Israel and replace it with one of the extreme Right.

Hundreds of Irgun terrorists were gathering in Tel Aviv under the command of Amihai Faglin and Bezael Stolnitzky. The latter suggested they fight their way through to the beach and help those on the ship get the arms ashore. Faglin was for more daring tactics: "We'll head for Ramat Gan [a suburb of Tel-Aviv] and take over the government. If they resist, we'll wipe them out."

Ben-Gurion was informed by Yigal Allon, the new commander of the combined Israeli forces, that there were few loyal troops in the city and that most of them were girls and the walking wounded. The greatest part of the men were on various fronts facing the Arabs.

"Yigal," Ben-Gurion said, "the Irgun has caught us at the right time when most of our troops are defending the border settlements or on leave. We are faced with open revolt. Not only is Tel Aviv in danger of falling to the rebels, but the very future of the state is at stake. You are to take personal command of the Tel Aviv area. Your new assignment may be the toughest one you've had so far. This time you may have to kill Jews. But I'm depending on you to do what is necessary for the state of Israel."

Gathering every man he could from outlying areas, Allon attacked the beachhead that the Irgun had established. By the time government troops had cleared the area, six of the Irgunists were dead and eighteen wounded. The army had two killed and six wounded.

A motorboat loaded with arms headed ashore from the LST and came under fire from the troops while people watched from nearby buildings and the beach. An order was given on board the *Altalena* for the Bren guns to fire, but Begin lost his nerve and went running to the loudspeaker set up on the bow. "Stop shooting!" he bellowed. "Do not kill your own brothers!"

Shortly afterward the loudspeaker was blown off its mounting. Fighting continued along the beach, and as Irgun men fell they were replaced by others, mainly deserters from the army who were in Tel Aviv and came hurrying to the waterfront. In addition, three battalions of Irgun gunmen had left their positions in the front lines against the Arabs to rush to do battle with the legitimate troops of the new nation. This permitted the enemy to take over important areas without hindrance. They finally succeeded in taking over Hagana headquarters on the shore and threatened to take over Palmah and naval headquarters as well as a good part of the city. For a short time it seemed as though the battle for democracy in Israel had been lost. Then the Third Battalion of the Yiftach Brigade was brought in and turned the tide in the government's favor.

Artillery fire from shore finally set the *Altalena* on fire, and the ammunition in the hold began to explode. The American captain hoisted a white flag and gave the order to abandon ship, but Begin screeched at the others not to surrender.

"Take it down!" the Irgun leader screamed hysterically. "It's better to die here. Then at least people will see how evil the government is."

"Throw him overboard," the captain ordered, and two crew members picked the man up and tossed him in the water, where he was picked up by a raft.

The wounded were lowered onto rafts and the ship abandoned. Among the wounded was Stavsky, who later died in the hospital. Faglin and Stolnitzky, on their way to seize the government and kill its leaders if necessary, were surrounded by Hagana armored cars and forced to surrender. Begin toyed with a plan to capture Jerusalem and set up a "Free Judaea" state but was talked out of it. Israel had survived its most serious crisis. It would be menaced by terrorists in the future but never to the degree that it was threatened by its own. Even at this time they were still too strong for Ben-Gurion to disband them as he wished; it would take one more act of senseless terror that shocked the world to bring that about.

The first truce of the War of Liberation came to an end and fresh fighting broke out between the Israelis and the Arabs. The now better-armed Israelis succeeded in driving the Arabs back until the United Nations managed to arrange a second and longer truce. Count Folke Bernadotte, a member of the Swedish royal family who had gained fame during World War II by saving the lives of thousands of Jews, arrived in Jerusalem to act as UN mediator. The Irgun and Stern Gang extremists were, of course, opposed to a truce. They envisioned an Israel that stretched from the Euphrates to the Nile and considered negotiation treason. Israel Shieb, Nathan Friedman-Yellin, and three other members of the Stern Gang's Central Committee held a meeting on September 10 to devise a "solution" to the Bernadotte problem.

"We must show the world that it is just as futile for the United Nations to interfere in our affairs as it was for the British," Shieb said.

Yitzhak Yizernitzky, another Stern leader, agreed. He believed that when "a man goes forth to kill another he does not know he must believe one thing only—that by his act he will change the course of History."

These same men had plotted the murder of Sir Harold MacMichael, the British high commissioner in Palestine, and Lord Moyne, British minister of state in the Middle East. MacMichael had been only wounded, but Moyne had died. They were determined to kill Bernadotte but did not want the Stern Gang to take the blame, and so they resorted to a tactic that would be adopted by Arab terrorists in later years: they invented a paper organization called the Fatherland Front, which, like Black September and more recently Black June, would take the blame for a crime too vicious for the parent group to admit to. Yehoshau Zetler, one of the "heroes" of Deir Yassin; Stanley Goldfoot, a South African Jew and strong supporter of apartheid; and Joshua Cohen, a sabra (Israel-born Jew), took part in the final planning of the assassination. Goldfoot, a journalist, was able to learn that Bernadotte was scheduled to cross from Arab territory to Jewish territory at the Mandelbaum Gate to meet an Israeli official. Changes in the scheduling made it necessary for the killers to pass up the chance to kill the count at the gate, but about five hundred yards along the road a jeep with four men in it set up a roadblock. Zetler and Goldfoot stood on a low hill nearby to watch because they "did not want to miss the show that was to shake the world."

As the UN cars approached the roadblock, four men in Israeli uniform moved toward the car as though to check credentials. Instead they drew their guns and a "thin, dark, clean-shaven" young man of about thirty stuck the barrel of his gun through the window and opened fire at point-blank range, killing the count and one of the officers with him. Another officer, Colonel Begley, who attempted to grapple with the killers, was badly burned by a gunflash. The murderers then shot out the tires of the UN cars and fled.

While the Stern Gang leaders celebrated their success, David Ben-

Gurion came to a decision that he would have to smash both the Irgun and Stern groups once and for all if Israel was to survive.

The Jewish leader did outlaw the terrorist gangs, but those responsible for the murder of Count Bernadotte were never punished. Some of them were arrested, among them Friedman-Yellin and Stanley Goldfoot, and sentenced to prison for terrorist activities but were soon released. Friedman-Yellin was elected to the Knesset in 1949.

The 1948 war ended in victory for Israel on all fronts except that around Jerusalem. There the Arab Legion retained control of the Old City, while the Jews held the New. However, the end of the war did not bring peace. No treaty was ever signed, and Arab states such as Egypt later based their policies on the claim that a state of war still existed. The reasons for this, although too complicated to deal with in detail, were in part the result of UN blundering.

The war also left a legacy of hate. The Arabs, who felt humiliated, determined to reverse the decision one day on new fields of battle. Even those feelings might have faded with the passage of time if there had not been a much graver and more perplexing issue between Israel and her neighbors. That issue is one that still occupies center stage today, the issue that has been responsible for a major share of terrorism in the world since the 1940s—the Palestinian refugees.

More than 60 million persons have become refugees since the beginning of World War II; 150 million have left their homes since the 1920s. Of all these, only the Palestinian refugees of 1948 and 1967 remain a problem. The others have all been resettled with the aid of host countries, usually without outside assistance.

Only the Palestinian Arabs still consider themselves refugees and have not been absorbed into the countries into which they fled. A great deal of rhetoric by Arabs and sympathizers with the Palestinian cause has been expended trying to account for the fact that many Palestinians remain homeless after thirty years. The explanation is simple: the Arab world has refused to absorb the refugees because only as long as they are refugees can they be used as a weapon against Israel. It was obvious that if they could be kept festering in miserable isolated camps long enough, they would explode. The explosion came in the form of terrorism and has brought death to hundreds of innocent people all over the world. The Arab states helped create the Palestinian refugees and have been a potent factor in maintaining them in their misery.

The Palestinians have become such an issue that even their numbers are a matter of doubt. Colin Smith, whose view is generally pro-Arab, mentions three million; Joe Alex Morris, the *Los Angeles Times* Middle East correspondent, says four million; Joseph Kraft and other liberal columnists also greatly exaggerate the total or simply accept the liberation organizations' estimates of their numbers. More careful researchers have cast serious doubts not only on the Palestinian claims but even on those put forward by the United Nations Relief and Works Agency (UNRWA) for Palestine refugees.

The last census taken of the Arab population of Palestine was during the British mandate. At that time there were 1.2 million Arabs living in the country. Of these, 450,000 lived in areas that were still in Arab hands after the 1948 war. Other estimates place the figure as high as 550,000. It is therefore evident that the highest possible number of Arabs who could have been living in parts of Palestine that became Israel could not have been higher than 750,000. Since 160,000 of these chose to remain in Israel, that leaves only 590,000 who became refugees during the 1947–48 period. The numbers quoted by Arabs and their supporters speak of there being 900,000 to 1 million refugees by the end of 1949, 1.5 million by the mid-1960s, and upward of 2 million by 1974. This of course adds up to more Palestinian refugees than there were people in the country to start with. Another 300,000 Arabs fled in the wake of the 1967 war, but a third of these were refugees from the UNRWA camps in Jordan running for a second time. Over a million Arabs in the West Bank area, which fell to Israel in 1967, chose to remain and are still there; about 15,000 of those who fled have returned, and others are in the process of returing to their homes.

The Palestinian refugees have become a constant issue in the United Nations, being used as a weapon against Israel by Arab, Communist, and Third World nations. By exaggerating the number of refugees and insisting always that they are an Israeli problem, not one for the Arab states, supporters of the Palestinian cause have been able to build up considerable world sympathy for the cause and by extension for the terrorists, who are its most active battlers. In this mythology, which dwells on the sufferings of the expelled Arabs, there is no mention of the other side, the Jews who were driven out of the Arab states during and after the 1948 war.

It has, in fact, become fashionable to say that the Arab refugees are innocent victims of a people who had been refugees themselves. I. F. Stone expressed this idea in a foreword to the autobiography of Fouz el-Asmar, an Israeli Arab. He wrote, "It was a moral tragedy that in making a home for the remnants of the Holocaust we were drawn into a war in which we had to make a kindred people homeless, a people who had done us no harm. To believe in a presiding God, one must believe him a capricious and spiteful demon to have piled that cruel necessity on his Chosen People in the wake of the human furnace of Hitler. . . . There was an Arab leader who said the war [of 1948] would be the greatest blood-letting since the Middle Ages. . . . Had the Arabs won, the guilt would lie on them; we won, so the guilt lies on us."

It is true that sometimes under enlightened rulers the Jews were treated better in Muslim countries than in Christian, but that was not generally true. In most Muslim countries during most periods of history, their treatment was no better and at times worse. The Koran, unlike the New Testament, prescribes the treatment for *dhimmi,* or "unbelievers," whether Christian or Jew. The followers of Mohammed are forbidden to have dealings with Jews and the seventh-century Covenant of Omar, which codified laws for the *dhimmi* by which they would be permitted to exist among believers, prescribed the death penalty for those who broke the laws. Jews were forced to wear distinctive clothing, a black habit with a sash and a yellow piece of cloth as a form of identification. They were not allowed to practice their religion in public nor to bury their dead with any moaning that might offend Muslims. They were forbidden to drink wine or own a horse. The law set lightly on Muslims who murdered Christians or Jews but was draconian against a Jew who raised his hand to a Muslim. The testimony in court of a Jew or Christian against a Muslim was invalid, and they had to pay a special head tax for the privilege of living.

In earlier centuries the harsh laws were sometimes enforced and sometimes not but in the twentieth century Jews living in Muslim countries were almost universally ill-treated. In Morocco in 1948 there were 300,000 Jews. On June 7 of that year, mobs in Oujda sacked the Jewish quarter, killing 4 and wounding another 30. In nearby Djerada 30 Jews were massacred by Arab mobs the same night. The new revolutionary government passed laws so severe that they drove out 300,000 Jews. With the return of the sultan in 1961, there was some relaxing of the laws; but by 1973 only 25,000 of the original 300,000 Jews remained.

There were 23,000 Jews in Tunisia in 1948. Following the revolutionary government's program of Arabization, Jews became the scapegoats, and many were arrested for "economic" crimes. By 1973 all but 9,000 Jews had been driven out.

Algeria had 150,000 Jews in 1948. Pogroms in that country had occurred in 1882, 1897, 1898, and during the 1930s when many Jews of Constantine, were massacred despite French intervention. In 1961, the Front de Libération Nationale (FLN) attacked the large cities where most of the Jews lived and 100,000 were forced to flee the country. The FLN desecrated the Great Synagogue at Algiers and the Jewish cemetery at Oran and finally succeeded in driving out all but 900 Jews by 1973.

There were 40,000 Jews living in Libya in 1948. In Tripoli in 1945, 120 Jews had been killed by mobs of Arabs. After independence most of the others were driven from the country, 17 being murdered after the Six-Day War and many arrested. In 1976 there were only about 70 Jews remaining in the country ruled by Qaddafi.

Jews have been in Egypt since biblical times, and Alexandria had once been at least partially a Jewish city. In 1945 the pro-Nazi Young Egypt group led anti-Jewish rioting in which many Jews were killed. In 1947 a new law for companies made it practically impossible for Jewish businesses to operate. Egypt had 75,000 Jews in 1948, when bombings, burnings, and looting destroyed almost $50 million worth of Jewish property. After the overthrow of King Farouk by Nasser and his Free Officers, life for Jews became intolerable in that country. After the Suez War, 3,000 Jews were arrested and imprisoned without trial. Thousands of others were presented with deportation orders forcing them to quit the country within days and leave all their property behind. By 1967 Nasser had managed to force all but 3,000 Jews out of Egypt.

The Grand Mufti had once requested the Axis powers to "acknowledge the Arab right to settle the question of Jewish elements in Palestine and other Arab countries in accordance with the national and racial interest of the Arabs and along the lines similar to those used to solve the Jewish question in Germany."

Nasser and Qaddafi came close to that target, and Anwar el-Sadat was not far behind them when he published in the 1950s an "open letter" to Hitler in which he expressed the hope that the Nazi dictator was still alive somewhere and would return some day to finish his extermination of the Jews. In 1972 he echoed the anti-Jewish instructions in the Koran with these words: "It is written that they shall be demeaned and made wretched. . . . We shall celebrate the defeat of Israeli arrogance so that they shall return and be as the Koran said of them, a people 'condemned to humiliation and misery.' " There were fewer than 500 Jews remaining in the land ruled by the "moderate" el-Sadat in 1976; the rest were driven out to find new homes, mostly in Israel.

Syria had 45,000 Jews in 1948. They had prospered under the Turks and the French, but when the Arabs took over, they at once became the target for both official and unofficial violence. Anti-Jewish legislation froze bank accounts and confiscated property. New laws forbade Jews to sell their property or move more than three miles from their homes. Special identity cards were issued to them, and they were allowed to work at only certain jobs. Government employees and military personnel were forbidden to patronize Jewish shops. Today there are fewer than 4,000 Jews in Syria, and they are under constant attack.

Iraq was the home of 125,000 Jews in 1948. Since then the revolutionary government has conducted an almost incessant campaign of terror against them. Nine Jews were hanged in public and 68 tried as Israeli spies in January 1968 while chanting mobs moved through the streets assaulting other Jews. By 1973 only 400 Jews remained in Iraq.

Yemen, where 54,000 Jews lived in 1948, had none in 1976. Hundreds were killed, and the rest found shelter on British bases until they were carried to Israel by Operation Magic Carpet. Before that it was legal to stone a Jew to death, and the law decreed that "fatherless Jewish children under thirteen be taken from their mothers and raised as Muslims."

In Aden there were 5,000 Jews in 1947, but in 1976 there were none. In December 1947 Arab mobs attacked the Jewish quarter, killing several people and burning down buildings. Between 1948 and 1967 most Aden Jews fled to Israel. The 130 who remained fled after the riots in June 1967.

Of the Jews expelled from the Arab countries, over 700,000 were absorbed into Israel between 1948 and 1976. There are fewer than 35,000 Jews still living in Arab countries. The number of Jews forced out of the Arab world is almost exactly equal to the number of Arab refugees who fled from Israel or were forced to leave. In effect, an exchange of populations had taken place. But the Arab nations, for reasons of their own, have refused to absorb the

Palestinians, while Israel, with far less territory and fewer resources, has taken in and found room for the Jews.

But the displaced Palestinians exist, and the very fact that hundreds of thousands of them have been kept in dreary and unpleasant refugee camps for as much as thirty years has bred hatred and terrorism. They deserve a closer look.

In May 1950, when the United Nations set up UNRWA, there were 957,000 "refugees" on relief rolls. The Arab countries refused to permit UNRWA to conduct any census of these people, or even to check to make sure they were genuine. There can be no doubt that at least 300,000 of the "refugees" either were local Arabs who discovered they could live better on the meager fare in the UNRWA camps or were nonexistent. Over the years 60 to 70 percent of their upkeep has been paid by the United States, with Great Britain paying around 20 percent. The Arab states have contributed almost nothing and not a penny has come from their friends among the Communist countries.

This refusal to resettle the refugees or make their lot any better is not mere miserliness on the part of Arab and Communist nations. It is based on a policy decision made shortly after the 1948 war. That policy had become set by 1956, shortly before the Suez War, when Ben H. Bagdikian, an American journalist, visited the camps.

At that time there were approximately 368,000 Palestinians living in refugee camps consisting of stone huts or tents. The camps were scattered throughout Lebanon, Syria, the Gaza Strip, and Jordan. The remaining two-thirds of those who called themselves Palestinian refugees were living outside the camps, mostly in Jordan.

"Every day I teach my daughter to hate the Jews," Bagdikian was told by an educated Palestinian who, like some ninety-seven hundred others, worked as an employee of UNRWA.

Bagdikian found this was not unusual. The camps were hotbeds of hatred for Israel and for the United States as well. Hatred was taught in the UN-sponsored schools; books paid for with American money were filled with anti-Semitism. One such book, a history text for third-year junior high school, contained a line that might well have come out of a German textbook in the 1940s: "The Jews in Europe were persecuted and despised because of their corruption, meanness, and treachery."

Everywhere the American newsman heard the same kind of talk from the refugees. "There is only one possible solution. Take back our land and push the Jews into the sea," one man said.

"I hold nothing against you as an American," another said. "I know that many Americans understand our problem. But how can we trust the American government when 84 percent of American business is controlled by Jews and 95 percent of the press is owned by Zionists?"

Radios supplied by UNRWA carried a steady flow of anti-Jewish and anti-American propaganda beamed at the camps by Arab governments. Interspersed among the hymns of hate were favorable references to the Soviet Union and other "friends" of the refugees.

"Let the United States keep its hands out of it!" the reporter was told. "We can take care of the Jews. If the Americans interfere, let it be sure of this: if it sends ten thousand troops, Russia will send a hundred thousand."

Another man asked, "What has the United States ever done for us? Look what Russia is doing."

When Bagdikian told them America was paying for most of their upkeep, they simply looked blank. The UNRWA representatives, Palestinians with Marxist orientation for the most part, had carefully kept it from the people that the hated Americans were feeding them and paying for their education in schools set up in the camps.

The longer people had been away from Israel, Bagdikian found, the grander their homes had been. They spoke of vast acreages and the fine houses they had been driven from at the point of a gun and never tired of talking about how they would someday return and drive the Jews into the sea.

At that time the Palestinians were kept in as much misery as the Arab governments could manage. Any attempt to improve their lot was rejected or destroyed. A UN plan to build up water resources and agriculture in the Jordan Valley, backed by $200 million from America, was rejected by the Arab states. Musa el-Alami, a Palestinian lawyer who had studied scientific agriculture, had set up with Ford Foundation money the Arab Development Society in the Jordan Valley. Twelve hundred refugees were working there for wages and learning new agricultural skills when a mob descended on the project. Thirty thousand refugees bearing torches smashed everything they could get their hands on. Clothing, furniture, trucks, and tractors were all burned, twenty thousand chickens were killed, and even the crops were destroyed.

"They were organized," el-Alami said. "For three days representatives from other camps gathered at this one before the attack. They were incited by demagogues to destroy this place. They told me that I was an agent of the West and that this project was a symbol of Western imperialism. . . . I was in Beirut or they would have killed me. My assistant was left for dead."

Later the leaders of the mob came to el-Alami and apologized, saying they had been misled, but he felt that given the chance, they would do the same thing all over again.

Musa el-Alami was no friend of Israel. He believed that the Arabs' land had been stolen and should be returned, but he did not think keeping his fellow refugees in misery and want would contribute to that cause. He said that the Arab governments felt that "whatever gives the refugees hope is treason."

Some former officials of the Arab states saw what their countries were doing and had the courage to speak out against it. Khaled al-Azm, Syria's prime minister following the 1948 war, wrote in his memoirs in 1972: "Since 1948 it is we who demanded the return of the refugees while at the same time it is we who made them leave. . . . We brought disaster upon one million refugees. . . . We rendered them dispossessed, unemployed. We accustomed them to begging and participated in lowering their morale. Then we exploited them in executing crimes of murder, arson, and throwing bombs at men, women, and children. All this we did in the service of political purposes in Lebanon and Jordan."

Over the years other Arab leaders have made it clear why they wish to keep the Arab refugees in a state of misery and hatred.

"Any discussion aimed at a solution of the Palestine problem which will not be based on ensuring the refugees the right to annihilate Israel will be regarded as desecration of the Arab people and an act of treason," said a resolution adopted by the Conference of Arab Refugees at Homs in Syria, July 11–12, 1957.

"If the refugees return to Israel, Israel will cease to exist," said President Nasser of Egypt in an interview with the Swiss newspaper *Neue Zuericher Zeitung* (September 1, 1960).

"The day for the realization of the Arab hope for the return of the refugees to Palestine means the liquidation of Israel," said Abdullah al-Yafi, the "moderate" prime minister of Lebanon, on April 29, 1966.

Coupled with these statements were demands that Israel accept the return of the Palestinians. To ask a country of 2 million people to accept 1 million or more returnees sworn to its destruction is asking it to commit suicide, but that is precisely what the Arab states, the Communist countries, and the so-called Third World nations have persisted in doing. It might be noted that among the countries most vociferous in their demands on Israel are India, Poland, East Germany, and Czechoslovakia. No one has suggested, however, that India accept the return of the 8 million Muslims it drove out of its territory following the end of British rule; that Poland take back the 6½ million Germans it ran out; or that Czechoslovakia repatriate the 2,068,000 driven beyond its borders. The United Nations has not demanded that East Germany make room for its 2,739,000 refugees. It has to be admitted that North Vietnam, since its conquest of South Vietnam, has taken back the 800,000 refugees who had fled south; according to the *Los Angeles Times,* more than 300,000 of them are now in concentration camps that are politically referred to as "reeducation centers."

Only Israel has been asked to accept the return of every person who was a refugee, the son or grandson of a refugee, or just anyone who claims to have once lived in Palestine.

The refugee camps were breeding places for terrorism in 1956, and when James A. Michener visited them prior to the Six-Day War in 1967, he found the conditions no different.

The camp near Jericho was a huge, sprawling collection of tents and lean-tos with no paved roads, water system, or sewage disposal. It had few medical facilities and no proper schools. All it had was an oversupply of hate.

"In two or three years we are going to march into Israel and slaughter every Jew. We shall go directly to Haifa and drive into the sea any who have escaped. Then my father will go back to the mansion he used to own, before the Jews drove him out, and Palestine will again be free." (Sir Hugh Stockwell's words to the Arab National Committee of Haifa when they said they were going to evacuate the city come to mind: "You have made a very foolish decision. Think it over. You will regret it later.")

Almost every Arab whom Michener met claimed to have lived in a fine house in Haifa before the 1948 war. A Jewish friend who had often heard this offered to take the American writer around in Haifa and let him see just how many mansions there could have been in the city in those days. Michener found very few and came to the conclusion that time and distance had magnified the grandeur of the lost homes.

Michener also discovered, as did a group of American senators who made a spot check of the refugees, that many were not Palestinians but local Arabs to whom the barely adequate UNRWA rations looked good enough for them to pretend to be refugees and have themselves entered on the rolls. This was encouraged by the Arab states, who supported anything that would exacerbate the problem of the refugees under the theory that "the worse things are, the better they are."

Egypt even sponsored a group called the Organization for Shattering Refugee Settlement Programmes, the avowed aim of which was to prevent any attempt to solve the problem of refugees in the countries that had given them sanctuary.

From the seeds of hatred so deliberately sowed in the fertile soil of Palestinian misery and frustration has come today's terrorism. And yet it goes back even further, back to the traditional life-style of the Arabs, back to the blood feuds between tribes, the very real worship of violence in Arab society.

"Violence," a Libyan cabinet minister told writer John Laffin, "is the Muslim's most positive form of prayer."

Dr. Sania Hamady, herself an Arab, has written that in Arab countries "life is a fearful test, for modern Arab society is ruthless, stern, and pitiless. It worships strength and has no compassion for weakness."

Civil strife is a permanent Arab condition, and by their very nature Arab governments are oppressive. No fewer than eighty revolts have occurred in Arab countries between 1948 and 1973, most of them bloodily violent and thirty of them successful, with a total of twenty-two leaders killed. In the last twenty-five years, more than eighty political murders have been recorded, including those of eighteen heads of state and prime ministers.

The Iraqi record of political violence is one of the worst. At least 2,423 Iraqis were murdered following the military revolution in March 1959, and in February 1963 another revolution led to the slaying of as many as 5,000.

Religious as well as political dissidents have been slaughtered in Arab countries: In January 1965, about two hundred worshippers at the Grand Mosque of Bani; in March 1970, thirty thousand members of the El Ansar sect were killed on Aba Island in the Nile by Sudanese troops.

Personal relationships among Arabs are also volatile. For example, it is a matter of honor for the men in a family to kill a woman who has "sinned."

The terrible savagery Arabs can resort to when aroused is exemplified in an incident told by Falih Hanzal in *The Secrets of the Assassination of the Royal Family of Iraq,* published in Beirut in 1971. On July 14, 1958, a military coup led by Brig. Gen. Abd-ul-Karim Qassem and his Free Officers resulted in the royal palace being surrounded by rebel troops and cadets. In response to a white flag from the palace, the royal family and Prime Minister Nuri Said were ordered to leave their basement refuge by a side door that opened into a garden. When they were all outside, an officer opened fire with a machine gun. Others followed suit and within a few minutes had slaughtered the king, his uncle, the uncle's mother and sister, and all their servants. An orphan boy, Ja'far, brought up by Princess Abdiyya, was found hiding in a corner of the palace and was dragged out and murdered also. The regent, Prince Abd al-Ilah, was turned over to the mob. Ropes were attached to his neck and armpits and tied to the back of a truck, which dragged him through the streets while the mob screeched, "Allah is great!" Knives and hatchets were used to dismember the body, and young men ran off waving the bloody limbs around their heads and screaming joyfully. At the Ministry of Defense, the mutilated trunk was hoisted up onto a balcony, where a young man on a lamppost hacked at it with a knife and stabbed it repeatedly in the back. Then, in an excess of insane rage, the knife wielder began cutting off hunks of flesh, working from the buttocks up, and tossing bloody fragments of what had once been a human being to the cheering mob below. What remained of the body was thrown into the Tigris River.

General Qassem, who had presided over this orgy, came to the same kind of fate when he was overthrown in 1963. He was executed and buried in a secret grave, but dogs dug up his corpse and started to eat it. A group of peasants tried to put the body in a coffin, but the secret police heard of it and dumped the body into the Tigris.

Not only is Arab society naturally violent, but it is deliberately kept violent by its leaders for their own purposes. "The hatred which we indoctrinate into the minds of our children from their birth is sacred," wrote Syria's Minister of Education Suleiman al-Knash in a letter to René Maheu, director-general of UNESCO. Parenthetically, it is interesting to note that while Israel has been banned from UNESCO as racist, Syria is still a member.

The tradition of terrorism in Arab society can be traced all the way back to the Old Man of the Mountain and his Assassins. Even the term used by Arab terrorists during the 1950s, *fedayeen,* meaning "one who sacrifices or goes on a suicidal mission," goes back to this Ismailitic sect, which produced the Assassins of the eleventh, twelfth, and thirteenth centuries. This group was an offshoot of Shiite Islam, recognizing Ismail, who died in 755, as the seventh Imam and deriving its name from him. Its main doctrines are based on esoteric interpretation of the Koran and on adaptations of Neoplatonic philosophies. Legend has it that the term *Assassin* comes from *Hashishin,* which is derived from *hashish.* The actual cult of the Assassins, or hashish smokers, was founded by Hasan ibn-al-Sabbah near the end of the eleventh century. It was active from then on until crushed in Persia by the Mongols under Hulagu and by the Mamluk Baybars in Syria.

Hasan was a native of Khorāsān and a Shiite who developed his own modification of the Ismailitic doctrine that called for assassination of enemies of the faith. He attracted a considerable following and formed them into a secret society with headquarters in a strong mountain fortress, the Rock of Alamut, in Persia. He came to be known as *Shaykh-al-Jabal,* which is translated as "the Old Man of the Mountain." Under him were three *da'l-al-Kirbal,* or "grand princes," who ruled the three provinces over which the Old Man's power extended. Next came the *da'is,* or "priors," who were fully initiated into all the secret doctrines and had the responsibility of spreading the faith. Under these were the *rafigs,* or "initiates." Fifth were the *fida'is,* or "the devoted ones," the actual assassins from whose name we get the current *fedayeen.* The last two classes were the novices and the common people.

One of the first victims of the Assassins was a former friend of Hasan's, the Seljuk leader Nazam-al-Mulk, whose son also died at their hands. The caliphs Mustarshid and Rashid fell victims to the secret murderers, and during the Crusades the Assassins slew Count Raymond of Toulouse and Conrad of Montferrat.

Although their numerous murders made them the dread of their neighbors, the Ismailis were less successful in regular military operations, and many of their castles were taken from them. They did acquire another stronghold in Syria, and it is this branch of the sect that we know the most about.

It was under Mohammed I, the third *Shaykh-al-Jabal,* that the fortress Maşyāf became their chief headquarters. It was there that the Old Man set up a miniature paradise for his followers, particularly for the *fida'is.* The enclosed valley was turned into a beautiful garden that held every imaginable delight. It had elegant palaces and pavilions covered with marvelous paintings and gilded. Every known fruit grew in the garden and runnels ran through it filled with wine, milk, honey, and water. The loveliest women in the world sang and played music and danced seductively for the young men. The Old Man wanted his Assassins to believe this actually was the Paradise of the Koran and added to the illusion by having them smoke hashish. They were permitted to indulge in every pleasure until the Old Man decided on a target and summoned one of them to him.

"Whence did you come?" the *fida'i* would be asked.

"From Paradise," the youth would answer sincerely.

"Go then and slay the man I shall name," he would be commanded. "When you return, my angels shall bear thee again to Paradise. And should you die, nevertheless they will carry you to Paradise."

Naturally the chosen youth would do anything his master asked, to get back to the delights of Paradise.

The chief enemy of the Ismailis was the established Sunni branch of Islam. Murders were planned and carried out against the Sunni to terrorize and weaken their hold so that eventually they could be overthrown.

"To kill these people is no more unlawful than rainwater," Mohammed I said. "To shed the blood of a heretic is more meritorious than to kill seventy Greek infidels."

Reportedly all a Muslim ruler could do when informed that he was on the Old Man's death list was either hurriedly to make amends in some way or to make out his will. Ubayd Allal al-Khatib, a chieftain of the city of Isfahan, was an enemy of the Old Man. Although he took every precaution, surrounded himself with bodyguards, and wore mail under his robes, he was still struck down while at prayer in a mosque.

Even the great Saladin feared the Assassins after discovering that two of his most trusted Mamluk bodyguards would kill him if ordered to do so by the Old Man. It took newcomers to the Middle East, the Mongols, to destroy the Assassins. Hulagu, brother of Mangu Khan, captured their strongholds and took their last *Shaykh* prisoner. The Old Man was executed along with twelve thousand of his followers. The sect continued to exist for some years longer in Syria, until the Mamluk sultan Baybars I ravaged the country and killed nearly all of the sect's members. Supposedly there are still some devotees of the cult lingering in the Syrian mountains, and the Ismaili sect has a fairly large membership.

The Aga Khan is a descendant of the leaders of the Assassins. The Ismailis to some extent merged with the Sufi sect of mystics, and the Sufis were an influence on the founders of the Muslim Brotherhood, which in turn influenced both General Nasser and the founders of al-Fatah.

The 1948 war was not followed by peace in the Middle East, only a change in the form of warfare. Egypt in particular maintained that a state of war still existed and instituted a blockade of Israel, not only shutting down its borders but closing the Suez Canal and the Gulf of 'Aqaba to Israeli shipping and to all ships that traded with the Jewish state or carried Israeli goods. Even if the basic premise that a state of war still existed were accepted, the closing of the Suez Canal was illegal under international law and so was the blockade of the gulf. Israel protested to the United Nations but with the usual lack of results.

The Egyptian economic blockade was the most damaging to the Israeli economy, but the actions of the other Arab states were also harmful and irritating. Their borders were totally closed to the Jewish state. Israeli citizens were not permitted to cross them and neither were other travelers with an Israeli visa stamp on their passports. Airlines that landed at Israeli airports were not permitted to use Arab fields. A blacklist of firms that did business with Israel was set up (which only recently was declared illegal in this country) and even a blacklist of firms with Jewish executives was tried, although without much success.

That the Israeli economy was badly damaged by these seemingly petulant tactics there can be no doubt, but through hard work and excellent social planning, Israel began to prosper. It was unbearable to the Arabs that the nation that had defeated them and, in their opinion, had stolen their land should continue to exist, much less prosper while they stagnated.

The first sporadic attacks against Israel were unorganized, launched from Jordan, from Syria, or from the Gaza Strip, where 125,000 Palestinian refugees were kept by Egypt in the worst possible living conditions. These early attacks usually consisted of sheep-stealing or an occasional sniping incident. They were not sponsored or encouraged by the Arab states but were permitted with the excuse given, "We are not the Jews' policemen."

The only Arab state that attempted to make peace with Israel during this period was King Abdullah's Jordan. A peace agreement setting up definite borders was actually reached in March 1950, but the uproar it caused forced Abdullah to back down; he was denounced and threatened in Egypt, Syria, Saudi Arabia, and Iraq as a traitor to Islam. He did not give up his determination to settle with Israel—and incidentally establish his claim to the area still held by his Arab Legion in Palestine—and probably would have eventually signed the treaty if the hand of the terrorist had not once again changed the history of the Middle East. On July 20, 1951, Abdullah was visiting the Mosque of Omar in Jerusalem when he was struck down by an assassin. The evidence all pointed to the Grand Mufti as the instigator, and several of his relatives were definitely implicated.

Terrorism in the Arab world increased during the early 1950s and became more highly organized. Following the rise to power of Nasser in 1952 and the shift of Soviet support from Israel to Egypt, such acts came to have the official backing of the Egyptian government. Coupled with the deterioration of UN supervision of the border areas, this left Israel with only its own resources to meet a growing menace.

While the Egyptians were organizing and training terror units, who were already calling themselves *fedayeen,* the Syrian army was engaged in a campaign of terror against Israeli front-line villages and farms. Guns placed in the Golan Heights commanded a large part of Galilee and regularly shelled Israeli targets. Small bands of terrorists also crossed the border to attack villages or isolated farms. Finally, on April 5, 1951, when seven policemen were murdered by terrorists, the Israeli air force went into action and bombed Syrian positions on the Golan Heights for an hour. Syria went to the United Nations with its complaint, and while the Security Council was considering the problem, heavy fighting broke out in the demilitarized zone north of the Sea of Galilee, which lasted twelve days. The pattern of terrorist attack followed by a conventional Israeli response had thus been set, a pattern, like so many others in the Middle East, that continues until the present.

Attacks by Syrian raiders on Israeli fishermen on the Sea of Galilee resulted in further Israeli attacks against Syrian positions, including one in December 1955 that caused fifty Syrian deaths. In January of the next year, the United Nations set a precedent, which has also continued down through the years, of condemning Israel for responding to attacks on its borders.

Not only were the Syrians by then supporting raids into Israel, but they had agreed to accept on their territory terrorists who had been trained in commando tactics in Egypt. Difficult as the situation along the Syrian border had become for Israel, that along the much longer Jordan border was worse. On the upper levels of government, Jordanians took no part in encouraging guerrilla attacks and even occasionally tried to prevent them, but among the lower echelons it was customary to look the other way and pretend ignorance.

From June 1949 until October 1954, Israel reported 1,612 violations of its border from Jordanian terrorists. During this period, there had been 124 Israelis killed, and in retaliation Israeli forces had killed 266 terrorists. In March 1953, for instance, 11 Israelis were killed in a single raid in the eastern Negev. A raid was launched against the Jordanian village of Nahhaleen in reprisal, and on October 14, half a battalion of troops was sent across the border to attack the terrorist center in Qibiya. By striking at night, the Israelis achieved total surprise and destroyed 41 houses and a school with bazookas and hand grenades. They left 42 dead, including women and children. The Arabs raised such an outcry that world opinion was swayed against Israel despite the extreme provocation it had suffered. It was later pointed out in Israel's defense, however, that 57 Israelis had been killed along the border in 1953 but that the death rate had dropped to 34 in 1954 and 11 in 1955. To some degree, at least, instant retaliation seemed justified by these results.

The typical terrorist of this period was probably similar to the young man killed by an Israeli police patrol near Tuklarm. One of a band of infiltrators who had been detected and ambushed, he was the only casualty, his companions having escaped back across the border. On his clothing was found a paper with a message in Arabic: "To whom it may concern: The holder of this document, Mahmud Suleiman, of Nablus, is on active service." It was signed "Second Lieutenant [signature illegible], on behalf of the Intelligence Officer of the Western Area."

The existence of such a document would indicate there was some organization but no formalized group, certainly not an ideological one, for striking at the Israelis.

In the Gaza Strip the situation was much the same except that by the middle of the 1950s the attacks were being carefully arranged by Egypt, and Nasser had begun training Palestinians in commando tactics for raids deep into Israel. Late in February 1955, a *fedayeen* foray was launched from the Gaza Strip that penetrated all the way to the environs of Tel Aviv. Israel struck back February 28, sending two platoons into the Gaza Strip, killing 38 and wounding 31 Egyptian troopers. Nasser said later that this raid was the turning point, that it made him go to the Soviets for arms. While that statement is open to question, the Egyptian attacks and Israeli reprisals were certainly part of the buildup to the Suez War of 1956, which for a brief time seemed to threaten escalation into a confrontation between the major powers. During the period of "peace" between 1948 and 1956, Israel had lost 1,176 citizens killed by terrorists. Open warfare was to prove far less costly.

An arms embargo was placed on the Middle East by the United States, the United Kingdom, and France. Nasser turned to the Soviets for weapons and on September 27 announced that large shipments of arms would begin to come from Czechoslovakia.

Israel was faced with a terrible dilemma. Its arms supplies were largely cut off by the embargo and if it waited until Egypt was completely armed with Czech weapons, its position could become untenable very quickly. At that point, plans for a preventive war against Egypt appeared on the desks of Israeli officials.

It was then that Israel discovered it was not friendless. A socialist government was in power in France and many of its leaders looked with favor on a small democratic socialist state in the Middle East that was surrounded by Arab dictatorships and autocracies. Others in the French government of Guy Mollet had fought beside some of the Israeli leaders in the resistance movement during World War II. It was more important motives, however, that moved the French to begin secret talks with Israel concerning the supplying of arms. Egypt had been one of the chief backers of the Algerian rebels in the long war that was still going on against the French in that country, so revenge as well as economic reasons contributed to the decision to help Israel.

The economic factor came from the problem of the Suez Canal. After years of negotiating and considerable guerrilla activity by the Muslim Brotherhood in the canal zone, the British had agreed to withdraw their troops from the waterway with the understanding that it was to be maintained as an open passage for all nations. No sooner had they gone, however, than Nasser broke the agreement and nationalized the canal, which had been largely owned by British and French investors.

So now the Mollet government not only was ready to help Israel with arms but came up with a bolder scheme—an Israeli preventive war against Egypt coordinated with an Anglo-French move to retake the canal.

Israel was confronted with a rapidly deteriorating situation. Although the French Mystère fighters were later to prove far superior to the Russian MIGs, they were slower in arriving and much smaller in numbers than those the Czechs were sending to Egypt. The withdrawal from the canal zone of British troops, who had acted as a buffer between Israel and Egypt, and the stepped-up terrorist attacks had been followed by new Egyptian moves. Nasser forced Jordan to dismiss Glubb Pasha from command of the Arab Legion, and on October 20, Egypt and Syria signed a mutual-defense pact. To the Israelis it looked as though they were being boxed in by vastly superior forces. The French plan seemed the only possible out. The decision was made to attack in the Sinai desert and drive toward the Suez Canal. When the Israelis approached the canal, the French and British would land on the pretext that the canal must be protected.

The Israeli attack smashed the Egyptian forces in the Sinai within hours, and despite the delays in gathering troops and aircraft by the Anglo-French, they also were able to take most of their objectives. What saved Nasser from complete defeat was a worldwide outcry against the attackers. The Soviet Union threatened to bombard French and British cities with long-range rockets, which it did not have at the time. American Secretary of State John Foster Dulles, the advocate of massive retaliation, wilted before the empty Soviet threats and joined with them to force the French and British to withdraw from the canal. He then turned his attention to Israel and, with intimidation and promises of aid, plus an intimation that the United States would help to keep the Gulf of 'Aqaba open, forced the victorious nation to give up all it had gained in the brief war.

Again there was no peace, only the reestablishment of cease-fire lines and a return to the ceaseless unconventional war waged by the Arab states against Israel. The period between the Suez War and the Six-Day War also saw the growth of the Palestinian terrorist groups as we know them today. That growth is partly the story of al-Fatah and partly that of Yasir Arafat, its founder and head.

It is also, strangely enough, a continuation of the story of the Husseini family of Jerusalem and its fifty-year campaign to drive the Jews into the sea. This family, particularly Haj Amin el-Husseini, bore a large part of the responsibility for the Arab rejection of partition and the decision to go to war in 1948. The Grand Mufti fell out with the Arab governments who financed and equipped the conflict when he demanded supreme command of all the armies for his cousin Abd el-Kader and they preferred to support the ALA of Fauzi el-Kauwakji. After the 1948 defeat, the Grand Mufti tried to set up an "All-Palestine Government" in exile, but it was only a facade. He continued his campaign of hatred against the Jews, extending it to the rulers of Jordan, and finally had King Abdullah assassinated in 1951. President Nasser eventually had el-Husseini driven from Egypt because of his connections with the fanatic Muslim Brotherhood and his dabbling in Egyptian politics. El-Husseini's political influence declined after King Abdullah's murder, but he remained one of the most revered leaders of Islam in spite of his record as a disciple of Adolf Hitler. This can be readily understood when one realizes that Adolf Eichmann is considered by many Arabs to be a *shadid,* a martyr.

Haj el-Husseini died on July 5, 1974, in Beirut and was buried there. Up until the last, his Higher Arab Committee for Palestine was issuing anti-Zionist diatribes. His fall from influence and subsequent death did not, however, end Israel's troubles with the Husseini family. In *Strike Terror,* Ehud Yaari, an Israeli reporter, delved into the background of Yasir Arafat.

"Among the Palestinians themselves, numerous stories circulate about the identity of Fatah's leader," Yaari wrote. "There are many families carrying the Arafat name in Lidda, Safed, Jerusalem, Gaza, Nablus, and many legends are told about him. The people of the West Bank believed for a long time that Arafat worked for UNRWA (United Nations Relief) in Nablus, and that he, in fact, came from Acre. Several months after Israeli forces entered the Gaza Strip, a search for his relatives began and numerous members of the Arafat families were questioned. And, indeed, the answer was found in Gaza.

"The man's real name—made known here for the first time—is Abd el-Rahman Abd el-Rauf Arafat el-Qudwa el-Husseini. . . . Yasir Arafat, then, has a special reason to avoid mention of his full name for it reveals his kinship to the former Grand Mufti of Jerusalem. . . . Arafat is also related to the Husseini family through his mother, who comes from the ancient and well-known family of Abu-Su'ud from Jerusalem."

According to PLO releases, Arafat was born in Jerusalem near the Wailing Wall and grew up during the disturbances in the city. Yaari's sources indicate he was actually born in Cairo. One of Arafat's cousins told Yaari that the Jerusalem story was only to cover up the fact that he was born outside of Palestine. His parents, of course, were Palestinians and his father became a wealthy property owner in Egypt. Arafat grew up in Cairo, where he attended Egyptian schools, and his Arabic "still carries some remnants of the Egyptian dialect, which differs from the Palestinian one in many details."

Arafat's official biography says he became personal secretary to Abd el-Kader el-Husseini, the one member of the family who actually fought in the ranks of the guerrilla forces it turned loose in Palestine. Supposedly Arafat and his father had joined a Palestinian militia group called al-Jihad al-Maudaddas (the Holy Struggle), which later merged with el-Kader's Sacred Fighters. His duties at the time consisted of running arms across the border into Palestine.

Yaari casts doubt on Arafat's service with Abd el-Kader but believes it is almost certain that his older brother, Jamal Arafat, was one of the terror gang. Yasir claims to have been appointed secretary to Abd el-Kader at the age of eighteen, but Yaari was unable to locate anyone close to the guerrilla leader who remembered him. Yaari does feel, however, that there is no doubt that Abd el-Kader had a great influence on young Yasir and that many of el-Kader's ideas went into the founding of al-Fatah. His name is prominent in the first hymn of al-Fatah and its pamphlets often praise him.

After the leader of the Sacred Fighters was killed while climbing a hill alone in the battle for Qastel, a stronghold on the road between Jerusalem and the coast, the Arafats are said to have left Jerusalem and reached Gaza with thousands of other refugees. It was there that Yasir became associated with the Muslim Brotherhood and its bands of terrorists. At that time Gaza was the center of support for Brotherhood Volunteer Battalions, and although it is claimed by associates of Arafat that he never was a member, it is certain that it influenced him in the founding of his own terrorist group. During this same 1948 period, Nasser also came under the influence of the brotherhood and may even have become an active member.

In an interview in October 1968, Arafat spoke of those early days. "Since I first opened my eyes to this world, I was able to hear the sound of bullets. . . . Of course I joined the fighting of 1948 just as thousands of my brethren . . . because we believed it was a fight to defend our existence and the existence of the Arab people."

The Muslim Brotherhood was an ultraconservative religious and political organization founded in Egypt in 1929 by Hassan al-Banna. He took the title Supreme Guide from the Dervish orders and the Sufis. He also drew many of his group's organizational and missionary techniques from the same source. The purpose of the brotherhood was to make the Koran the law of every Muslim state. Islam was to be the basis of not only the religious, but also the political and social, life. The brotherhood concept of Islam was basically fundamentalist, with certain reformist tendencies. Its Pan-Islamic ambitions were combined with powerful xenophobic and Pan-Arabic feelings plus strong anti-Jewish sentiments.

At the time when Arafat and Nasser came into contact with it, membership in the Muslim Brotherhood was estimated to be between 100,000 and 1 million. Later it was said to have as many as 3 million adherents, almost all in Egypt. In the early 1950s, approximately a third of the officers in the Egyptian army and over half the students in the country were believed to be members of the brotherhood. In December 1948, King Farouk's prime minister, Nokrashy Pasha, banned the brotherhood and shortly thereafter the prime minister was murdered by a brotherhood assassin. On February 12, 1949, Farouk's "Iron Guard" (palace officers) killed Hassan al-Banna as a birthday present for the king. The group's property was confiscated and about 15,000 of its members sent off to concentration camps in the Sinai. The brotherhood went underground until 1951, when it was permitted to resume activities limited to spiritual, social, and cultural matters.

In the meantime, Nasser had been organizing his Free Officers with the avowed intention of overthrowing the corrupt and inefficient Farouk. In July 1952 the time to strike arrived. Gen. Mohammed Naguib, who was strongly supported by the brotherhood, was included in the plot, and on July 22, 1952, he became the first head of the junta that ruled Egypt in Farouk's place. At least four members of the Officers Committee, which ruled under Naguib, were said to be brotherhood members, and so the measures instituted by the Farouk government against the group were abrogated.

Naguib and Nasser almost immediately fell out. Naguib wished to return Egypt to the parliamentary system and permit the reestablishment of political parties, which had been banned when the junta came to power. The brotherhood had not been banned at the time, because it claimed to be a religious rather than a political organization. The struggle between Nasser and Naguib continued through 1953 and 1954, with the brotherhood playing a part on Naguib's side and Naguib trying to advance the cause of the brotherhood with the junta.

The official leadership of the Muslim Brotherhood was in the hands of Hassan al-Hadibi, who had been appointed Supreme Guide by King Farouk after the murder of Hassan al-Banna. Al-Hadibi apparently wanted to keep the brotherhood as a religious group only, insisting that it refrain from direct interference in politics and denying that it had ever engaged in assassination or maintained terror units. Such a denial was nonsense, of course, since everybody knew that Muslim Brotherhood volunteers had participated in terrorist raids against the Israelis in 1948 and had fought against the British in the Suez

Canal zone in 1951. Among those who served with the brotherhood forces in 1951 had been Yasir Arafat, one more proof of his connection with the extreme right-wing religious group.

While al-Hadibi was claiming that brotherhood members "are not fanatics but zealots, zealots for the basic Islamic principles of morality and social justice," the director of the brotherhood's Special Office, Saleh Eshmawy, was operating an assassination bureau.

The difference between these two approaches to Muslim Brotherhood philosophy is based on their divergent interpretations of the brotherhood's motto, *Hok, Kuwa, Huriya,* meaning "Law, Power, Freedom." Members of the group seemed to be pretty much agreed on what *hok* and *huriya* meant, but there was a fundamental disagreement on the concept of *kuwa.* The Supreme Guide insisted, *"Kuwa does not mean force, violence, or assassination. Only for national ends will we use kuwa. "*

Eshmawy, on the other hand, made it quite clear that *kuwa* did mean "force," that when translated into English "force" was nearer its meaning than "power," and it would be used in defense of Egypt's freedom. When that freedom was threatened, he said, it was not only the right of the brotherhood to strike but its duty. Thus, the assassination of Nokrashy Pasha had been an obligation that had to be met. Violence was never used, however, without giving the victim several chances to mend his ways—that is, to conform to the wishes of the Muslim Brotherhood. "Assassination occurs only after we have first advised the victim of his errors, then warned him. If he ignores our advice and warning, only then do we shoot him."

Eshmawy, as director of the Special Office, had given the orders for Nokrashy's murder and for the canal zone attack. He intended to convert the whole of the brotherhood into a nationalist movement that would one day unite all of the Arab states into one warlike empire that would destroy Israel and drive all Western influence out of the Middle East.

It was in this atmosphere of anti-Israeli, anti-Western agitation that Yasir Arafat got his training at King Faud University. His formal education was in engineering, but the real influence on his life was the political turmoil that was sweeping the campuses of Egypt at the time. He was deep into university politics from the beginning, was elected chairman of the Palestinian Student Federation in 1952, and held the position until 1956, when he became chairman of the Palestinian Alumni Federation, which linked Palestinian university graduates all over the Arab world and beyond. All during this period he was close to the Muslim Brotherhood and aligned student groups, often joining them in demonstrations and riots.

Nasser and Naguib continued their struggle for control of the junta ruling Egypt. In January 1953, Nasser established the National Liberation Organization as the only legal political organization in the country. In May of that year he was appointed deputy prime minister and minister of the interior. The struggle came to a head in February 1954, when Nasser became prime minister and tried to remove Naguib from the junta. Naguib resisted and

Nasser was deposed. Demonstrations and counterdemonstrations shook the country, pro-Nasser and pro-Naguib student riots took place, and Arafat participated on the side of the Muslim Brotherhood and Naguib. Nasser won the battle and in April 1954 again became prime minister, relegating Naguib to the post of president, a figurehead position that he was stripped of in November 1954.

Nasser next turned on the Muslim Brotherhood. An attempt to assassinate him in October 1954 gave him the excuse he needed to wipe out the organization. Thousands were arrested and al-Hadibi, Eshmawy, and five other officers were given show trials. All seven were sentenced to death, but later the Supreme Guide's sentence was commuted to life imprisonment.

Nasser continued his ruthless drive against the brotherhood, and by September 1956 the concentration camps were full of his enemies. Simax and Dakhla in the Western Desert, Kenna in Upper Egypt, and the notorious Jarum el-Sheik in the Sinai held members of the brotherhood, former officials of the old Wafd party, Communists, and alleged Communists. At least twenty professors were imprisoned and two hundred more were dismissed from Cairo University. Two professors, who supposedly admitted to being Communists, were brought to trial but were acquitted because they bore marks that could only have been caused by torture. Dr. Ismail Sabri's fingernails had been torn out, and Dr. Mahmoud Shawi had been set upon by specially trained Alsatian dogs. Nasser admitted to there being five thousand prisoners, but the figure was probably closer to thirty thousand.

It was almost certainly during this period that Arafat saw the inside of an Egyptian jail, which he has spoken of. All his father's considerable property had been confiscated and the older man had died penniless in 1954. Yasir had learned much from his association with the Muslim Brotherhood, however. He and his colleagues had learned efficient methods of organizing underground activities and been indoctrinated with belief in the justice and benefits of indiscriminate terrorism. But association with the brotherhood left a rightist stamp on him that remains to this day and sometimes makes his relationship with other terrorist groups and leftist Arab regimes difficult.

While he was at the university, Arafat met Khalil el-Wazir. The slim, moustachioed Wazir had entered the university at the age of twenty to study the humanities. Some time later he joined Arafat's group, and the pair have been inseparable ever since.

In 1956 Yasir Arafat was trained in sabotage at an Egyptian army school. He claims to have taken part in the defense of Port Said against British paratroopers and to have helped clear mines from the Sinai planted by the Israelis before their withdrawal. In 1957 Arafat left Egypt, probably at the invitation of Nasser, and joined his brother in Kuwait, where he obtained the post of highway engineer. The brother married, but Yasir never has. He does not drink or smoke and shows no interest in women.

Khalil el-Wazir failed at college and went to Saudi Arabia to teach for a while. He married and then moved to Kuwait to rejoin Arafat. There one day in the summer of 1957 a dozen men met on a deserted beach outside the town of Al-Kuwait a few hours before sunset. Their purpose in meeting was to set up a terrorist organization that would one day drive the Jews out of Palestine. Three of them were associates of Arafat's from Cairo, all more or less steeped in the philosophy of the Muslim Brotherhood. Khalil el-Wazir (Abu Jihad), Salah Khalaf (Abu Ayad), and Zuhair al-Alami had traveled with Arafat to Prague in 1956 as representatives of the General Union of Palestinian Students. It is not clear whether they were contacted during this visit by Soviet agents as were so many other student delegates to these international conferences. Perhaps because of their known association with the brotherhood, they did not seem like good prospects.

Others at the meeting on the beach near Al-Kuwait were Faruq el-Qaddumi (Abu Lutuf), Muhammed Yussif al-Najar (Abu Yussif), Khalid al-Hassan (Abu Said), and Kamal Adwan. These four, together with Arafat and his three associates from Cairo, remained the core of their organization's leadership until 1973, when al-Najar and Kamal Adwan were executed by Israeli commandos in Beirut.

Arafat was twenty-eight in 1957, a short (five feet, five inches) man with a receding chin, brown eyes that rolled excitedly, a small unkempt moustache, and a soft, chubby body. There on that Kuwaiti beach, he and his comrades proclaimed themselves the Generation of Revenge, which would pick up the torch of Palestinian statehood that had fallen from the hands of the Generation of Disaster, meaning the Grand Mufti's generation. They named their new organization Harakat al-Tahrir al-Watani al-Filistini (Palestinian National Liberation Movement) but then searched for a shorter, more dramatic name. They first tried using the initials of the longer name, but that spelled the Arabic word *hataf* and would not do at all because it meant "death from a lightning stroke." So they reversed the letters and produced the name *al-Fatah.* In later years there was much speculation about the meaning of the word and various observers tried to make something different out of it. Some members of al-Fatah assumed it came from a verse in the Koran that promises an "upcoming conquest" by Allah. Others said the word stood for the slogan "Palestine Shall Be Free." As late as 1973, *New York Times* correspondent Dana Adams Schmidt was claiming it came from the Arabic word *fath,* or "victory."

Arafat was the leader of al-Fatah and toured the Middle East and Europe, preaching "liberation" wherever large numbers of Palestinians gathered and recruiting members. He also allied himself with similar groups, established connections in Lebanon, and made preparations to transfer the secret organization's headquarters to Beirut.

At the end of 1958 a small monthly magazine, *Filastinuna Nida el-Hyal* ("Our Palestine—The Call of Life"), began publication in Beirut. The nominal publisher was Ibad el-Rahman (the Worshippers of the All-Merciful), supposedly a religious group. The editor was listed as Twfik Khuri, a wealthy merchant from Beirut. In reality, *Filastinuna* was the organ of al-Fatah, the Ibad el-Rahman being used as a front.

Arafat also allied himself with a stronger extremist religious group called the Islamic Liberation party, whose members were called Nabhanians after the family name of the founder, Sheikh Taqi el-Din el-Nabhani. These people were fanatic activists on the order of the Muslim Brotherhood. They had underground cells on the West Bank and were outlaws in Jordan and Lebanon. Arafat eventually found the Nabhanians incompatible with his aims for al-Fatah and broke with them, drawing some of their members with him. He kept up the relationship with Ibad, however, until the actual beginnings of al-Fatah's terrorist operations.

Contact was also maintained with several leaders of the Muslim Brotherhood who had fled into exile after Nasser turned on them. Among those Arafat reportedly saw frequently were Sa'id Ramdan, who had fled to Switzerland, and Kamel Isma'il el-Sherif, a member of the Muslim Brotherhood volunteers during the 1948 war. El-Sherif later joined the Jordanian diplomatic service and became ambassador to West Germany, where it is said he was very helpful to Arafat in organizing large numbers of Palestinian students attending universities there. If this is true, he was the first of a long line of Arab diplomats to become involved in terrorist activities in Europe and other parts of the world.

While Arafat was involved in transferring his quarters from Kuwait to Beirut because the latter was much closer to Israel and the centers of communication of the Arab world, Nasser decided to take up the cause of what he called the "Palestinian entity." The Egyptian dictator believed that if he could awaken the aspirations of the Palestinians, he could use them to further his own dream of a Pan-Arabic empire with himself at its head. Iraq also grabbed hold of the "Palestinian entity" idea, and General Qassem engaged in a struggle with Nasser to see who could more effectively exploit the concept.

King Hussein of Jordan was strongly opposed to such manipulating of the Palestinians and considered himself their protector. Over 50 percent of the population of his small kingdom was Palestinian, and his was the only country that had made some attempt to bring them into the life of the nation. Jordan was the only Arab state that automatically granted citizenship to the refugees within its borders and even brought them into the government. Egypt had refused to permit the majority of them to enter the country proper, keeping them penned up in the Gaza Strip under the worst conditions of any Arab state.

In spite of his cynical exploitation of them, it was Nasser who was the most popular figure among the Palestinians, the one they looked to for aid that seldom, if ever, materialized. Even when he was honest with them—as in 1962 when he slapped his empty trouser pockets at a meeting in Gaza and declared, "I have no plan for the liberation of Palestine"—they still believed in him.

His real indifference to their welfare and hopes for returning to Palestine were masked under the vitriolic rhetoric he permitted Radio Cairo to beam at the rest of the Arab world: "The Arab people will pronounce the death sentence against criminal Israel—namely, disappearance. Israel is the cancer, the malignant wound in the body of Arabism, for which there is no cure but eradication. There is no need to emphasize that the liquidation of Israel and the restoration of the plundered Palestine Arab land are at the head of our national objectives."

As so often happens in the Arab world, words proved more important than actions, and Nasser's picture appeared in the huts of peasants all over the area and went up on the walls in refugee camps as the savior of the Palestinian people.

This period also saw a proliferation of Palestinian "resistance" groups. The Arab Front of the Liberation of Palestine was formed when three other organizations combined: the National Front of the Liberation of Palestine, the Palestinian Revolutionary Movement, and the General Command of Palestinian Self-Organization. Societies calling themselves the Red Hand and the Black Hand came into being and were followed by the Palestinian Military Organization and the Arab Palestinian Fedayeen. Many of these groups formed and issued a ringing proclamation one day and went out of business the next; others existed on paper only, and some were just fronts for extorting money from well-to-do Palestinians. The Palestinian Rebels Front of Mohammed Abu Sakhila; the Palestinian Liberation Front; and, most notable, the Arab Nationalist Movement (ANM), which merged with the Palestinian Liberation Front to form the PFLP, still exist today. The PFLP is headed by George Habash, who studied medicine at the American University of Beirut, the chief breeding ground of Middle Eastern terrorism. Habash (born in 1925) is somewhat older than most terrorists and was at first opposed to such violent methods, preferring Marxist agitation, but later became one of the most fanatically violent of all.

The Arab world was filled with excitement at the victory of the Algerian rebels over the French when President Charles de Gaulle surrendered the province to them. The Palestinians in particular were thrilled by the outcome of the Algerian conflict because they viewed it as a forerunner of their own eventual victory over Israel. They failed to take into consideration the real reason for the Algerian victory, which was a failure of French nerve on the home front produced by an extensive propaganda drive by leftist French intellectuals who favored the Marxist guerrillas. De Gaulle's surrender to the rebels actually came, in fact, after the French army had succeeded in all but crushing them in battle. There was no way in the late 1950s or early 1960s in which Israeli nerve could have been destroyed by a similar campaign. France had given up a colony, not the homeland itself, which is what the Jews would have to do after such a settlement.

Arafat immediately began negotiations for Algerian aid against Israel, and in December 1962, he and Khalil el-Wazir, along with several other leaders, visited the country at the invitation of President Muhammad Ben-Bella and Chief of Staff Houari Boumedienne (Ben-Bella was later overthrown and imprisoned or murdered by Boumedienne). Ben-Bella refused to help Arafat without Nasser's consent, but Boumedienne agreed to train small groups of al-Fatah men on condition that Arafat would make the group the tool of Algeria and not of any other Arab state. As it turned out, the Algerian assistance consisted of little more than a handsome headquarters building in Algeria, where al-Fatah opened its first official office. A quarrel with Ben-Bella in 1963 resulted in Arafat's having to leave the country. Nevertheless, the ties that were set up at that time have remained, and Algeria has been one of the chief supporters of Arab terrorism, particularly of hijacking and transnational violence, ever since.

To implement further his policy of turning the Palestinians into a tool to serve his expansionist aims, Nasser had the Arab League Council call upon one Ahmed Shukeiri to "represent Palestine" and work up plans for the Palestinian entity. "The time had come," the league announced on September 5, 1963, "for the Palestinian people to take the responsibility for the solution of its problems."

Shukeiri was carefully chosen by Nasser not only because he was a consummate demagogue but also because he was totally under the control of the Egyptian dictator. Shukeiri, then fifty-one, had been born in Acre to an affluent family. His father, Sheikh Assad, was once the "Leader of the North," a mufti in the Turkish army and an influential force among the Arabs of Galilee. Ahmed Shukeiri had been an extreme nationalist during the mandate and after 1948 had become assistant secretary of the Arab League and then Saudi Arabia's delegate to the United Nations. The Saudis had fired him because of his extremist views and constant attacks on the West at a time when Saudi Arabia was closely aligned with British and American policy. Following his dismissal by the Saudis, Shukeiri had been taken in by the Egyptians because of his usefulness as a hard-working demagogue, and when Nasser needed someone to form a group to represent the Palestinians, Shukeiri was available.

In February 1964, the Arab states held a summit meeting in Cairo and approved, along with several other proposals, the Egyptian plan for setting up the PLO with Shukeiri as its head.

On May 22, 1964, Shukeiri, having traveled throughout the Arab world calling for the extinction of Israel and organizing cells, opened the first Palestinian National Congress in Jerusalem with a carefully contrived manifesto: "In the name of God, the Magnificent, the Compassionate, Believing in the right of the Palestine Arab people to its sacred homeland, Palestine, and affirming the inevitability of battle to liberate the usurped part of it, and its determination to bring out its effective revolutionary entity . . . I do hereby proclaim the establishment of the Palestine Liberation Organization as a mobilizing leadership of the forces of the Palestine Arab people to wage the battle of liberation. . . ."

He then read the covenant of the group. In view of the fact that at least one important article was kept secret by the PLO for propaganda reasons, it might be well to look at some of the more relevant ones out of a total of thirty-three:

Article 1. Palestine is the homeland of the Palestinian Arab people and an integral part of the great Arab homeland, and the people of Palestine are a part of the Arab nation.

Article 2. Palestine with boundaries that existed at the time of the British mandate is an integral regional unit.

Article 3. The Palestinian Arab people possess the legal right to their homeland, and when the liberation of their homeland is completed, they will exercise self-determination solely according to their own will and choice.

Article 4. The Palestinian personality is an innate, persistent characteristic that does not disappear, and it is transferred from fathers to sons. The Zionist occupation and the dispersal of the Palestinian Arab people as a result of the disasters that befell them do not deprive them of their Palestinian personality and affiliation and do not nullify them.

Article 6. Jews who were living permanently in Palestine until the beginning of the Zionist invasion will be considered Palestinians.

Article 9. Armed struggle is the only way to liberate Palestine and is therefore a strategy and not a tactic.

Article 10. Fedayeen action forms the nucleus of the popular Palestinian war of liberation.

Article 15. The liberation of Palestine, from an Arab viewpoint, is a national duty to drive the Zionist, imperialist invasion from the great Arab homeland and to purge the Zionist presence from Palestine. Its full responsibilities fall upon the Arab nation, people, and governments, with the Palestinian Arab people at their head.

Article 19. The partitioning of Palestine in 1947 and the establishment of Israel are fundamentally null and void, whatever time has elapsed, because they were contrary to the wish of the people of Palestine and their natural right to their homeland, and contradict the principles embodied in the Charter of the United Nations, the first of which is the right to self-determination.

Article 20. The Balfour Declaration, the mandate document, and what has been based on them are considered null and void. The claim of a historical or spiritual tie between the Jews and Palestine does not tally with historical realities or with the constituents of statehood in their true sense. Judaism, in its character as a religion or revelation, is not a nationality with an independent existence. Likewise, the Jews are not one people with an independent personality. They are rather citizens of the states to which they belong.

Article 21. The Palestinian Arab people, in expressing themselves through the armed Palestinian revolution, reject every solution that is substituted for a complete liberation of Palestine and reject all plans that aim at the settlement of the Palestine issue or its internationalization.

Article 22. Zionism is a political movement organically related to world imperialism and hostile to all movements of liberation and progress in the world. It is a racist and fanatical movement in its formation; aggressive, expansionist, and colonialist in its aims; and fascist and Nazi in its means. Israel is the tool of the Zionist movement and a human and geographical base for world imperialism. It is a concentration and jumping-off point for imperialism in the heart of the Arab homeland, to strike at the hopes of the Arab nation of liberation, unity, and progress.

It is Article 6, of course, that is most important in that it is indicative of the true designs of the PLO, which are the liquidation of Israel as a state and most likely as a people as well. It is this article that was kept secret for many years, partly with the connivance of the Western press, since it was printed in the Arab press but not picked up by the media in Europe or the United States.

"Jews who were living permanently in Palestine until the beginning of the Zionist invasion will be considered Palestinians," Article 6 reads, but it does not define when the "Zionist invasion" began. Other documents issued by the PLO and al-Fatah have dated it variously as from the creation of the State of Israel in 1948 or from the publication of the Balfour Declaration in 1917. In his speech before the United Nations on November 13, 1974, Arafat extended the date even further in the past, declaring, "The Jewish invasion of Palestine began in 1881."

By almost any of three definitions, most Jews presently living in Israel would be considered illegal immigrants in a PLO-dominated Palestine and either driven out or exterminated. Shukeiri in his heyday as head of the PLO often spoke of "driving the Jews into the sea." Later, for the same reason the article was originally kept secret, he explained that what he meant by this was that "since Jews had come to Palestine by sea, they should return to their homes the same way."

The PLO has at times, especially today, attempted to project a moderate image by talking about replacing Israel with a "democratic, secular Palestine in which Muslims, Christians, and Jews would live together equally."

The fact is that there is not one example of a democratic or secular state anywhere in the Arab or Muslim world. The lack of democracy is generally known; what is not so well known is that each and every Arab state includes in its constitution an article establishing Islam as the state religion.

In the PLO covenant, Article 2 is important mainly for its implications for Jordan. In saying that the borders of Palestine would be considered those of the British mandate, the PLO includes Jordan in the territory it proposes to liberate. Thus, the establishment of its Palestinian Arab state would bring about the elimination of both Israel and Jordan as they exist today.

Article 21 makes it clear that the PLO has no intention of attaining its objectives by any means other than violence. Article 22 labels Israel as racist, a concept later accepted by a United Nations controlled by totalitarian and authoritarian states. Despite the fact that it was the Arabs who were closely allied with Nazism and fascism during World War II, Article 22 also brands Zionism as being Nazi and fascist. It probably makes its most popular appeal in the so-called Third World countries when it accuses Israel of being a tool of imperialism.

With regard to the last accusation, precisely which are the imperialist states of today? By any objective criteria, only two states fall into that category —the Soviet Union and India, both strong supporters of the Arab, not Israeli, cause. It is ludicrous for the Soviet Union, which has seized Latvia, Estonia, Lithuania, large parts of Poland, Finland, Romania, and Mongolia; who maintains colonial domination over East Germany, Poland, and Czechoslovakia; and who exerts considerable influence over Romania, Yugoslavia, Vietnam, Cuba, and North Korea to lecture Israel on imperialism. It is equally ridiculous for India, who during the last twenty years has fought three wars of aggression against Pakistan and one against China; has seized the Kashmiri, Goa, and Sikkim; and has conducted genocidal campaigns against tribal peoples along its borders.

The fate of Israel after a PLO victory is described in a publication not intended for outside consumption. In pamphlet no. 8 in a series put out by al-Fatah called "Revolutionary Studies," a clear picture is given:

> The liberation action is not only the removal of an armed imperialist base; but, more important—it is the destruction of a society. Our armed violence will be expressed in many ways. In addition to the destruction of the military force for the Zionist occupying state, it will also be turned toward the destruction of the means of life of Zionist society in all their forms—industrial, agricultural, and financial. The armed violence must seek to destroy the military, political, economic, financial, and ideological institutions of the Zionist occupying state, so as to prevent all possibility of the growth of a new Zionist society.
>
> The aim of the Palestine Liberation War is not only to inflict a military defeat but also to destroy the Zionist character of the occupied land, whether it is human or social.
>
> If we consider all aspects of the Palestinian problem, we shall see there is a need to conciliate many sides regarding our approach to the solution of the Palestinian problem. For example: if we attach to world public opinion weight and the capacity of decision, we must supply to public opinion a solution which will satisfy it or will be acceptable to it, even marginally. When we speak about satisfying the will of world public opinion, we do not mean the character of the solution to the Palestinian problem, but the method we shall adopt in solving it.
>
> World opinion has no right to argue with us about the need to solve this problem. But it has a right to know the way of the solution, so that it will not imprint us with Fascism, anti-Semitism or other non-human labels.
>
> Catering to the satisfaction of world public opinion is an important step in obtaining the support of public opinion to the solution we propose.

The PLO is not an elected body, but an establishment set up, financed, and maintained by the Arab governments. It is the umbrella organization of the Palestinian terrorist groups. The Executive Committee of the PLO has fourteen members, seven of whom represent terrorist organizations. Two are from al-Fatah, which today has close links with Egypt and Saudi Arabia but which was formerly financed by Syria and to a certain extent Libya. Black September is a front group for al-Fatah, although this is denied by Arafat and other leaders.

One member is from al-Sa'iqa, a terrorist group of Palestinians financed and operated by Syria. It is completely under the control of the Syrian army, many of its leaders are army officers, and its terrorist acts have the approval of the army.

Another member of the Executive Committee is from the Arab Liberation Front (ALF), a rather small, inactive terrorist group set up and maintained by Iraq for the purpose of serving its own interests. Few, if any, Palestinians are in ALF, most members being Iraqis.

One representative is from the PFLP, which has financial, ideological, and operational links with Iraq. It also has financial, ideological, and operational links with Libya. There is also reason to believe it has support from the Soviet Union and China. Habash's group, as noted earlier, has the most extensive international terrorist contacts of any of the terror groups.

Another PLO Executive Committee member is from the Popular Democratic Front for the Liberation of Palestine (PDFLP), headed by Nayef Hawatmeh, an extreme leftist organization financially linked with Iraq, the Republic of South Yemen, and, at times, Syria. Another is from the PFLP—General Command (PFLP—GC) headed by Jibril, an organization linked with Libya and apparently Iraq as well.

There are seven independent members linked with one or the other of the organizations. Three of the seven are members of the National Palestinian Front, which is linked with al-Fatah. Al-Fatah, now the mainstay of the PLO, and Arafat at first viewed the establishment of an organization by the Arab states to represent the Palestinian people as an infringement on their territory. They believed that they represented the Palestinians and that al-Fatah would have to spur Arab governments to a war with Israel. As Arafat was to express it for the world press in Cairo in June 1965 at the meeting of the Palestinian National Congress set up by the PLO, "Entangle the Arab nations in a war with Israel."

Filastinuna called upon all Palestinians to leave groups under the control of Arab states and join al-Fatah to fight for the cause of Palestinian liberation rather than devote themselves to furthering the purposes of the Arab states. When Nasser refused to go to war with Israel over the diversion of water from the Jordan, Filastinuna attacked him and called upon the people to revolt against their governments. Then in a quick change of policy, it called upon the Arab states to "surround Palestine with a preventive belt of defenses and watch the battle between us and the Zionists."

The Israelis at first paid little attention to al-Fatah, since for all its rhetoric of violence it had not as yet committed a single terrorist act. The Soviet Union also viewed it dimly because it distrusted terrorist groups over which it had no control and was dedicated to the preservation of the Arab states, which it could influence.

There were Arabs who objected to al-Fatah's talk about "sacred violence," a term lifted from Franz Fanon, the psychiatrist from Martinique who helped the Algerians against the French (and whose works *Black Faces, White Masks* and *The Wretched of the Earth* were a fad among America's New Left).

Palestinian writer Naji Alush asked, "Why should we suppose that the Israeli army will stand with its hands tied in the face of *fedayeen*'s attacks? The Israeli army will destroy Arab villages and cities and may even take a decisive step and, for example, occupy the whole West Bank."

Al-Fatah was enraged by this sort of reasoning and struck back in *Filastinuna* with typical hyperbole:

> We announce to the whole world that we shall launch our revolution with sticks and knives, with old revolvers and crooked hunting rifles, in order to teach a lesson to those who suffer from nightmares about Israeli tanks and planes. Everybody says that Israel will blow up Gaza, massacre the Palestinians, invade the Arab countries. Israel. Israel. Israel. But nobody considers what we can do —how we shall burn citrus plantations, demolish factories, blow up bridges, and cut off oil communication lines. The revolution will last a year, two years and more, up to twenty or thirty years. As a matter of fact, let the Zionists conquer the West Bank, blow up Gaza, and massacre our population. Let the American Sixth Fleet make a move. The Arab people will stand as a man to help the revolution. History has never seen the failure of a popular revolution.

Defiant words, but up until then al-Fatah had not struck a single blow against Israel. Despite ten years or more of organizing and preparing, it still was not ready to make its first move until December 31, 1964.

Arafat had received the backing of the Ba'ath party, which ruled Syria, for a raid into Israel, but it was not willing to supply the military personnel for the raid. Since al-Fatah had no trained terrorists at that time, Arafat decided to go to the refugee camps in Lebanon to find men who were brave enough or desperate enough to make the attempt. At Ein el-Hilwe, one of largest of the camps, he contacted several Palestinians who had previously worked for Syrian intelligence and made a deal with them for the raid into Israel to plant a bomb along the Beit Netopha canal. It was agreed that the raiders would be paid ahead of time and that al-Fatah would supply the explosives and submachine guns.

The raiders were to have struck on New Year's Eve, but either some of them lost their nerve or Lebanese intelligence was alert, because they were all arrested before they ever left Ein el-Hilwe.

Not knowing that their hired guns had been headed off at the pass, al-Fatah men dropped unstamped envelopes containing "Military Communiqué No. 1" into the mail boxes of all Lebanese newspapers. Other al-Fatah members dashed around Beirut in a blue Volkswagen nailing up posters announcing the raid and its victorious conclusion. "The 'Storm' troops have moved towards the occupied land to open the offensive against the enemy."

The next morning the papers that had received the letters describing a brilliantly successful raid into Israel filled their pages with banner headlines and sensational stories. Two days later the Lebanese government let the word out that the so-called Storm troops had been sitting in jail during the time they were supposedly striking at Israel. Al-Fatah had set a pattern of announcing victories before winning them that would often damage its image.

Al-Fatah's second operation was a little more successful in that it actually penetrated Israeli territory. This attempt was also aimed at a canal and was led by Ahmed Musah, who had joined the group back in October 1963. Musah was somewhat atypical of al-Fatah members at that time in that he came from a poor background and had been active in anti-Jewish terrorism during the mandate period. He was born in Tiberias in 1922 and, when a young man, had spent time in a British jail for attacking Jewish settlement guards near Tiberias. After the 1948 war he moved to Nazareth and drifted into Jordan sometime later. During the years when he fathered eight children he earned his living by infiltrating Israel to steal and commit sabotage. Since al-Fatah had money and was willing to pay for experienced border-crossers, he became a member.

On January 2, 1965, Musah and two others loaded down with heavy rifles and submachine guns forded the Jordan River and, crawling through the reeds along the bank, moved through the Beisan Valley to the banks of the national-carrier water canal in the Beit Netopha Valley. The Israeli National Water Carrier was a cause célèbre for the Arabs, who claimed that the Jews were diverting water that belonged to Arabs. To strike at it had considerable symbolic if no practical value. Reaching the canal, the three terrorists unloaded ten sticks of gelignite near one of the gates and hurried back toward Jordan. They crossed the border on the morning of January 4 and promptly ran into a Jordanian army patrol. When the soldiers demanded the surrender of *fedayeen* arms, shooting broke out and Musah was killed—the first member of al-Fatah to die, as it were, in the line of duty.

In the meantime, the gelignite had been discovered by an employee of the water company. He had drawn out the inexpertly inserted charge and called for an Israeli patrol, which followed the tracks of the intruders to the border and then turned back.

The news that al-Fatah had at last struck at the enemy brought wild elation to student groups in West Germany and al-Fatah cells in Kuwait, Lebanon, and Syria. The Arab world, however, did not react at all in the way Arafat and his comrades expected.

Al-Anwar, Egypt's hired newspaper mouthpiece in Lebanon, said that "CENTO [Central Treaty Organization] agents have assigned a small group of Palestinians the task of setting up al-Fatah. . . . the organization has connections with Western agents and with Israel. . . . the aim is to offer Israel an excuse for attacking Arab states and for preventing the diversion of the River Jordan tributaries. . . ."

Other Egyptian propaganda sources called al-Fatah an "agent of imperialism playing a dangerous and provocative role." An Indian correspondent in the employ of Egypt wrote that al-Fatah was the creation of India's enemy Pakistan. Even the Soviets got into the act with a thoughtful note to the Israelis claiming that they knew al-Fatah was actually a front for the CIA.

Most Arabs knew little or nothing about al-Fatah at the time and were confused by the attacks in their own press against it. Shukeiri, whose PLO had not exactly covered itself with glory in attacking Israel, apparently was afraid that he was being upstaged by this independent rival and hastened to announce, "Only the Palestine Liberation Army [PLA] can authorize any Palestinian military operation. The PLA alone is responsible for the military enlistment of the Palestinian people for the liberation of occupied Palestine." The PLA was the five-thousand-strong military arm of the PLO, which up to that time had been as reluctant as al-Fatah to strike.

The practical result of the raid and its aftermath was that Arafat and al-Fatah agents in Lebanon were rounded up by Lebanese security forces and jailed. Arafat spent forty days in prison before being freed through Syrian influence. But since the Lebanese were still opposed to their territory being used for raids into Israel, the leader of al-Fatah moved his headquarters to Damascus in the middle of 1965.

Al-Fatah mounted ten raids during 1965, seven from Jordan and three from Gaza. Those from Gaza prompted the Egyptians to round up al-Fatah members in the Gaza Strip and forbid raids to be launched from there. Another of the raids produced al-Fatah's first media hero. He was a colorful character named Mahmud Bakr Hijazi, who was captured by the Israelis during an operation in the southern Judaea area. When placed on trial Hajazi attracted the attention of the world press and several well-known leftist lawyers rushed to Jerusalem to defend him. "One man's terrorist is another man's patriot" is a popular statement among academics of the liberal Left, but occasionally a terrorist becomes every man's patriot, at least for a little while.

Mahmud Bakr Hijazi was another such phenomenon. He was painted by al-Fatah propaganda and the Western media as a "Palestinian giant" and a member of the "generation of revenge." His contemptuous behavior in court and his frequent hunger strikes added to his glamorous image. It was not until he had been convicted and his sentence commuted to life in prison that anyone ever got around to pointing out that Hajazi was a reform-school graduate and a lifetime criminal who had taken al-Fatah money because he wanted to get married. Hajazi was a flash in the pan as a hero, even by media standards, and by February 1971, the Israelis had come to consider him so unimportant that they exchanged him for a simple nightwatchman who had been kidnapped by terrorists.

Al-Fatah's operations in Jordan were more successful than those in Gaza, although a group operating in the Mount Hebron region was arrested by the Jordanians. In other areas, despite King Hussein's strict orders, local leaders, village mayors, and some army officers tended to look the other way where terrorists were concerned. It was not until after Israel struck back at the towns of Kalkaila, Jenin, and Shuna in May of 1965 and at Kalkaila again in September, because they harbored terrorists, that the Jordanians cracked down. Under Gen. Mohammed Rasul el-Kailani, Hussein's chief of intelligence, the Jordanians forced Arafat to shift his operations back to Syria.

The headquarters in Damascus was underground, but there Arafat and his lieutenants, Khalil el-Wazir, Salah Khalaf, Bashir el-Maghribi, and Walid Arab Nasser, did not have to be afraid of arrest. At this time Arafat was in charge of field operations and Wazir took care of publicity. Al-Fatah began to publish *Sout el-Asifa* ("The Voice of the Storm") and then produced its first hymn:

> Farewell, tears and sorrow,
> Farewell, sighs and grief,
> Our people has come to loathe you;
> Welcome, blood and heroic death,
> Welcome, "El-Asifa," who brings death and ruin to our enemies.

The year 1965 was important to Yasir Arafat for another reason: he got to meet that most glamorous of all terrorist leaders—Che Guevara, the Argentine-born Cuban hero of young revolutionaries everywhere. Arafat may have received inspiration from Guevara but apparently little of practical value.

Also in June of that year al-Fatah delegates attended the Palestinian National Congress in Cairo and met the world press for the first time. It was here that they stated their intention to "entangle the Arab nations in a war with Israel."

Nasser, knowing his country's weakness, was trying to avoid war with Israel and therefore exerted every effort to prevail upon al-Fatah to go out of business and leave the terrorist field to his tame PLO, but Arafat and his comrades remained adamant.

By the end of 1965 al-Fatah had conducted thirty-five raids into Israel, twenty-five originating in Jordan because the Syrians preferred to have Hussein take the blame and the possible consequences. Most of the attacks were mere pinpricks to Israel, but as the terrorists became more expert with Syrian training, their effectiveness increased. Israel made the mistake of following a policy of nonretaliation, which seemed to encourage the attacks instead of moderating them.

John Laffin says in *Fedayeen:* "Israel gave stern warnings about retaliation and reprisal but in fact adopted a moderate policy and did not act against Syria. This encouraged Egypt as well as Syria to think that sabotage activities could be stepped up without risk of war or massive retaliation. By being moderate Israel invited Egyptian-Syrian aggression. Ironically, Nasser, constantly urged to endorse terrorism, was driven into the Syrian-Fatah camp by Israeli moderation."

In May 1966 Israel complained to the United Nations about al-Fatah's activities; but her problems were ignored, and al-Fatah received some of the publicity it hungered for. That same month, however, Arafat began having trouble when General Jedid, then Syrian head of state, who moved to take closer control of al-Fatah. Arafat refused to permit this, and the Syrians then tried terrorist tactics against the organization. When these failed to budge the leadership of al-Fatah, Syria assigned Capt. Yussuf Urabi, a Palestinian officer of the Syrian army, to take control of the group from inside. Arafat struck quickly, dispatching assassins to murder Urabi in the Yarmuk refugee camp. Syrian reaction to this was to kill Mohammed Mashma, Arafat's military assistant, and imprison Arafat and eleven other leaders.

Probably through the intervention of Defense Minister Hafiz Assad, who later became president, Arafat and his comrades were released. Assad proclaimed his dedication to the cause of Palestinian liberation: "We shall never call for nor accept peace. We shall only accept war and the restoration of the usurped land. We have resolved to drench this land with our blood to oust the aggressors and throw you into the sea for good."

Terrorist groups were now springing up like mushrooms and disappearing almost as fast. The Heroes of the Return, founded by Arab nationalists, began to launch raids into Israel. Their first mission was a total failure, with three men being killed and a fourth captured by an Israeli border patrol. Shukeiri, who had not endorsed al-Fatah, seemed to do so for the Heroes.

The Abd el-Kader Husseini Unit leaped into action by blowing up the Jerusalem railway near Batir. By January 1967 the Abd el-Latif Sharuru Unit, the Ibrahim Abu-Dia Unit, the Isma'il Ben-Ibrahim Unit of the Syrian-controlled Palestine Liberation Front (headed by Ahmed Jibril) had all appeared on the scene.

Nasser had not given up his determination either to put al-Fatah out of business or to co-opt it. The group had sent delegates to the Palestine National Congress meeting in Cairo, but neither Arafat nor el-Wazir had attended, because they knew Nasser had put a price on their heads. Finally, Nasser sent Shukeiri to Beirut to talk to Arafat and el-Wazir. If Arafat would not disband al-Fatah, would he merge it with the PLO? Arafat agreed to the merger if al-Fatah had two-thirds of the seats on the executive committee. This was not merger; it was outright absorption of the PLO by al-Fatah. Shukeiri had to give up and go back to Cairo.

On January 1, 1967, al-Fatah published another of its exaggerated claims of damage done to Israel. It claimed to have brought about the "destruction of dozens of tanks, the slaughter of hundreds of enemy soldiers, the creation of a dangerous, tension-filled atmosphere in Palestine. . . ."

Coming more and more under the control of the Syrians, Arafat was faced with the possibility of al-Fatah becoming merely the terrorist arm of the Ba'ath party. Arafat did not agree with the far-leftist attitude of Ba'ath, probably because of his early rightist background, and wanted to keep al-Fatah an organization without an ideology.

"Our ideological theory is very simple," he once explained. "Our country has been occupied. The majority of our people have been kicked out by Zionism and Imperialism from their homes. We wait and wait for the justice of the United Nations, for the justice of the world, while our people are suffering in the tents and caves. But our dispersion was realized. None of our hopes. But our dispersion was aggravated. We have believed that the only way to return to our homes and our land is the armed struggle. We believe in this theory without any complications and with complete clarity and this is our aim and our hope."

Between January and June 1967, *fedayeen* groups carried out thirty-seven raids, a marked increase over thirty-five for the whole year of 1965 and forty-one for all of 1966. Thirteen of the attacks had come from Syria, thirteen from Jordan, and eleven from Lebanon but none from the Egyptian-held Gaza Strip. Eleven Israelis had been killed and sixty-two wounded; *fedayeen* losses had come to seven killed and two captured. The increase in terrorist attacks led Israel to change its policy on retaliation, and after a mine incident in which three soldiers were killed in Judaea, a large-scale raid was launched in the Mount Hebron area that resulted in a clash with Jordanian troops.

The *fedayeen* claimed credit for the outbreak of the 1967 Israeli-Arab war, but the Arab governments prefer to lay the blame on Israel. That it was mainly the blundering of the Arab governments that brought on the June war has been conceded by most objective observers, such as Evan M. Wilson, U.S. consul-general in Jerusalem at that time: "It seems clear that Arab leaders themselves were responsible for starting the June war. They had duped themselves with their own fiery rhetoric and had become prisoners of their own propaganda. They thought they would win."

Terrorism played an important part in the events that led up to the war. Syria had not only permitted the increase in al-Fatah raids into Israel in 1967 but had also begun a campaign of harassment and bombardment of Israeli settlements from the Golan Heights. The Syrian prime minister had told a press conference in October 1966, "We are not sentinels over Israel's security and are not the leash that restrains the revolution of the displaced and persecuted Palestinian people."

On April 7, the Israelis struck back with air attacks on the battery position on the Golan Heights. Syrian MIGs scrambled to meet the incoming Israeli fighter bombers. Six MIGs were shot down, and the rest were chased all the way to the outskirts of Damascus.

Nasser, who had a mutual-defense pact with Syria, was criticized by the more radical Arab press for not responding to the Israeli counterattack. He was accused of hiding behind the UN troops that had been stationed in Sinai since the Suez War. At this point in the already unstable situation, the Soviets deliberately fed false intelligence information to Nasser; it purported to show that the Israelis had massed eighteen battalions on the Syrian border and were preparing for a preventive war against Syria. The Soviet purpose in this provocative action is not clear except that it was in keeping with that nation's policy of hoping to profit from disruption in any part of the world.

On May 14, to the accompaniment of a heavy bombardment of anti-Israeli propaganda in the Arab press, the Egyptian army was mobilized and two divisions were moved forward into Sinai. Nasser followed this with a demand on May 16 that the UN forces in the Sinai be partially withdrawn. The UN commander replied that withdrawal would have to be total, so the Egyptians demanded a complete withdrawal. The uselessness of the United Nations in a Middle Eastern situation was clearly seen at this point when Secretary-General U Thant, with no attempt at negotiation or resort to procedural delays, began the withdrawal of the buffer force between the Egyptians and the Israelis.

Nasser, apparently a captive of his own propaganda and pushed by the more radical (and more distant from Israel) Arab nations, moved his troops into all UN positions, including the vital one at Sharm al-Sheikh, which commanded the entrance to the Gulf of 'Aqaba, at the head of which was Israel's only access to the Red Sea. Since the opening on the gulf had been the only gain Israel had been permitted to keep after the Suez War, any closing of it had been declared to constitute an act of war.

The Egyptian buildup in the Sinai was rapid. On May 17 there were thirty thousand troops on the peninsula, and by May 19, forty thousand. Troops that had been operating against royalist rebels in Yemen were being transferred to the Sinai, and by May 21 it was estimated that the buildup had reached eighty thousand men.

Nasser's reasons for these provocative moves and the equally provocative rhetoric of threats that went with them have never been clear. Apparently he knew that his army was not ready to face that of Israel, and yet he threatened to attack the Jewish state and blockade its shipping at 'Aqaba. It has been conjectured that he thought the United Nations would restrain Israel or would intervene before his army could suffer a major defeat.

Israel had begun its mobilization shortly after Egypt's and had made another futile appeal to the United Nations. Then it had appealed to the maritime nations, headed by the United States and Great Britain, to open the Straits of Tiran at Sharm al-Sheikh.

The Israeli mobilization was only partial, but now the other Arab states were mobilizing. Premier Levi Eshkol of Israel was faced with a dilemma. Could Israel afford to wait for the maritime nations to do something about the straits? Could it afford to do nothing while the slower mobilization of the Arab states gained momentum? The Israeli cabinet met on May 27 to decide whether to wait to see if the United States could bring about the opening of the straits or to go to war and do it themselves. The cabinet vote ended in a tie, which Eshkol broke by voting for war. But there was a delay in translating the vote into action, since the National Religious party did not trust the judgment of anyone but Moshe Dayan and demanded that he be named minister of defense.

On May 30 King Hussein flew to Cairo to sign a treaty with Nasser and to meet with Ahmed Shukeiri. Iraq signed the treaty on June 4. By that date

Egyptian commando battalions had been flown to Jordan and were deployed on the West Bank. Israel seemed surrounded and menaced by numerically superior forces.

Nasser had welcomed Iraq to the Egypto-Jordanian alliance by proclaiming: "We are so eager for battle in order to force the enemy to awake from his dreams and meet Arab reality face to face."

Time magazine in its June 16, 1967, issue said of that moment in history, "With hostile Arab populations of 110,000,000 menacing their own of 2,700,000, the Israelis could be forgiven for feeling a fearful itch in the trigger finger."

The Cairo air-raid sirens began to wail early in the morning as the first Israeli strikes went in. Before the day was over, the air forces of the Arab states had in effect ceased to exist. Caught on the ground, the planes were destroyed by pinpoint bombing and strafing.

The Arab world reacted with its usual bombast. "Our people have been waiting for twenty years for this battle," Radio Cairo screamed. "Now we will teach Israel the lesson of death! The Arab armies have a rendezvous in Israel."

Mobs jammed the streets of Cairo, chanting, "We shall fight. We shall fight. Our beloved Nasser; we are behind you to Tel Aviv."

"Kill the Jews!" screeched Radio Baghdad.

"We shall destroy Israel in four days," a Syrian general predicted.

Moshe Dayan said over Radio Kol Israel, "Soldiers of Israel Defense Forces, on this day our hopes and security are with you."

The country was still only three-fourths mobilized, and Dayan's message was followed by the reading of a list of coded names of units being called up: "Love of Zion, Close Shave, Men of Work, Alternating Current, Open Window, Good Friends."

Throughout the country middle-aged men and beardless youths could be seen pouring into the streets, half in uniform, half in mufti, bundles and knapsacks thrown over their shoulders as they headed for the places the coded messages had indicated. Waiting for them were laundry trucks, ice-cream trucks, taxis, and private cars to rush them to their units.

In effect, though, the war had ended in the first few hours with the destruction of three hundred Egyptian planes, sixty Syrian, thirty-five Jordanian, and fifteen Iraqi. Israel had lost nineteen.

Israeli tanks followed the planes in, and the destruction of the Egyptian army in Sinai followed. Then the Israelis turned on Jordan and captured Jerusalem and the West Bank. Here they were no longer fighting the superbly trained Arab Legion but a large, less expert Jordanian army made up of more Palestinians than Bedouins. Syria's turn came in a few days; and the Golan Heights, from which Israel had been shelled for years and from which al-Fatah raids had struck so often, fell into Israeli hands.

With the Israelis at the Suez Canal and in Sharm al-Sheikh, the Arabs called on the United Nations to save them. The Soviets, who had played a large part in starting the war for their own reasons, moved quickly to rescue their friends, demanding an Israeli withdrawal to the cease-fire lines of 1948 and 1956. American vetoes blocked UN meddling in the affair, and both sides settled down to another armed truce.

The Arab defeat in the Six-Day War was followed by the acceleration of terrorist activity. The Arab world had witnessed the failure and even the disgrace of its armies. Only the terrorists seemed to offer a way of striking back at a nation whose army seemed to make it invulnerable in the foreseeable future to conventional warfare. The defeat brought new members flocking to al-Fatah and other established groups. It led to the creation of new groups and brought a change in the time and scope of terrorist attacks.

Anyone who witnessed the behavior of Arab delegates in the United Nations after the June war knows that the Arab nations were near psychological collapse. Feeling shamed and disgraced, they were willing to turn to any safety valve to relieve the emotional pressures. Al-Fatah alone seemed untouched by the debacle. Arafat proposed to take the offensive by moving the terrorist operational centers to Israeli-occupied territory, especially on the West Bank. Other members of the ten-man Central Committee opposed the move as dangerous and impractical, but Arafat had his way.

"This movement [al-Fatah]," Lebanese professor and writer Hisham Sharabi wrote, "was able after the 1967 defeat, when despair and shame engulfed the entire Arab world from Rabat to Baghdad, to raise the banner of defiance."

The Soviets were still skeptical of the value of the *fedayeen* and referred to them as the "most backward elements" of the Arab national movement. That is not to say that they were not aiding the terrorists with money, weapons, and even some training, but they were not willing to embrace them at the expense of relations with the Arab states, which they considered more useful to their policy of keeping the Middle East in a state of perpetual turmoil.

Arafat crossed over into the West Bank sometime in July 1967 under the alias of Abu Mohammed. Later he used Dr. Fauze Arafat and, daringly enough, one of his own actual names, Dr. Husseini. He was joined in Israeli-occupied territory by his deputy, Omar Abu-Leila, a graduate of Baghdad Military College who used the *nom de guerre* of Captain Muj'ahid. Also with him was Fa'iz, a former captain in the Jordanian army who had deserted to join the terrorists.

Mossad intelligence agents for once seem to have been lacking in alertness, for the easily recognized terrorist leader was able to move about openly without disguise as he established headquarters in the casbah of Nablus in Samaria and held meetings in town cafés or the New General Library.

For a period of six months Arafat remained in Samaria, contacting already established cells and recruiting new members, including an engineer from Jerusalem named Kamal Nimri, who was made al-Fatah chief in the Holy City. Arafat had at least one narrow escape during this time when he and Abu-Leila were traveling by bus from Nablus to Ramallah. Israeli police boarded the bus and began to check identity cards, but apparently because Arafat and his companion were dressed as shepherds, they were not questioned.

The theory behind Arafat's activities on the West Bank was that the Israelis would have to rule with a heavy hand over an area where there were over a million Palestinians. That harsh rule would cause resistance, which in turn would force the Jews to resort to a rule of terror that would alienate all elements of the population and at the same time result in world condemnation of the conquerors. Enough terror and counterterror would ultimately result in open resistance by the population and eventual revolution.

The Israelis, however, countered this tactic with a firm, but just, system of rule, exemplified by Moshe Dayan's statement that the ideal he would like to see in the "administrated" territories would be for an Arab to be born and grow up without ever having to see an Israeli soldier or policeman.

This did not prevent charges being made that the Israelis mistreated Arabs in the occupied area. As early as 1968, there were accusations of brutality against Israeli police and charges that captured terrorists were being tortured.

"No occupation could be worse than this one," Mayor Hamid Canaan of Nablus told a reporter in May 1968. "No one could believe in more inhumane treatment than this." The mayor was complaining about Israeli destruction of the homes of terrorist suspects. Six houses in a nearby village had been blown up after the sons of the owners had been identified as part of a gang of al-Fatah saboteurs killed in a cave hideout close to the village. "In spite of the families having lost sons, the authorities also blew up their houses," the mayor said. He also charged that Israelis tortured al-Fatah prisoners and other suspected terrorists. "There have been many cases of prisoners burned. Not every prisoner, but enough to give the population the idea. Those dogs are used for torture, not tracking."

The reporter did confirm that two Israeli border policemen had been brought to trial charged with killing two Arabs during an argument over a vehicle accident and that two others were awaiting trial for killing a terrorist suspect and wounding a second.

Mayor Canaan refused to give the names of terrorists he claimed had been tortured, nor could he offer any proof of his claims. He was intensely anti-Israeli and had just recently returned from a trip to Beirut, where he had taken part in an anti-Israeli conference. He admitted that he had been able to make the trip without any interference from Israeli authorities.

There have been no executions of terrorists in Israel because Israeli law provides for the death penalty only for wartime treason and genocide. Adolf Eichmann is the only person to have been executed in Israel since the state was founded. There was in 1968, however, and there still is, a policy of preventive internment by which suspected terrorists can be detained for up to three months on the signature of the local military governor. If the suspect has not been brought to trial at the end of the three-month period, the detention can be continued if a review board headed by Israel's chief justice agrees there is cause. In 1968 some Arabs had been detained since the end of the June war and about 1,600 had been taken into custody. Of these, 331 had been sentenced, 700 were awaiting trial, and 600 had been released.

While the Israelis refused to permit UN investigators to enter the occupied territory, they regularly permitted Red Cross teams to make routine inspection of the country's fourteen prisons, including six in occupied territory, and to conduct private interviews with prisoners following Israeli interrogation. Foreign journalists were also given freedom of movement in the occupied territories and permitted to visit prisons.

At that time about 40 residents of the West Bank had been deported to Jordan because of their suspected terrorist connections and 300 houses had been destroyed because their owners had harbored terrorists. Also 2,200 persons were then in prison, about half of whom were serving sentences, 567 were awaiting trial, and another 560 were under administrative detention.

Al-Fatah was unable to produce the kind of terror-counterterror situation in the Israeli-occupied territory they had hoped for after the 1967 war. Even their systematic policy of intimidation against any Arab who cooperated with the Israelis did not always work, although many were murdered toward this end.

Al-Fatah radio called for the murder of Abu Marwan, who had taken part in municipal elections. "Whoever murders Abu Marwan will be a martyr in the Holy War of Islam," the radio broadcast said. In a letter published in *Al-Qads,* an Arab newspaper in Jerusalem, Marwan replied, "In case you come to murder me, there are many Abu Marwans in Jerusalem. To make sure you get the right one my address is . . ."

When Arafat and his cohorts decided that the West Bank was getting too dangerous, they returned to Arab-held land but left cells of local terrorists behind to damage the Israelis as much as they could.

One such group was headed by Abd el-Rahim Jaber. He commanded a group of boys in Jerusalem who were responsible for the Holy City's "Night of Grenades" and for explosions in the Tel Aviv bus station. When Jaber was captured, his second in command, Said Ghazawi, took over. His method of operation was haphazard but effective: he would pick up Arab youths on the street, indoctrinate them in hate and the use of grenades, pick out a target for them, and take off. He was eventually killed by an Israeli patrol near Hebron.

Al-Fatah was not only gaining recruits, it was acquiring competitors. Probably the most important of these was the Popular Front for the Liberation of Palestine. PFLP was formed in October 1967 by a merger of Abtah al-Audah (Heroes of the Return), Munazamat Shabab al-Thar (Youth of Revenge Organization), Jabhat Tharir Filistin (Palestinian Liberation Front), and George Habash's Harakat al-Qawmiyin al-'Arab (Arab Nationalist Movement, or ANM).

Habash, the PFLP's leader, was born in Lod in 1925 of well-to-do Greek

Orthodox parents. Graduated in medicine from American University of Beirut, he plunged almost at once into revolutionary politics. His biography as revised and edited by the PFLP informs us that he was a Schweitzer-like doctor, "running a private clinic with a group of nuns in Amman. This hospital was filled mostly with children and poor old people. Dr. Habash never insisted on being paid, and he bought the drugs for his patients out of his own pocket, then slipped them a roll of notes when they were ready to leave. . . . He spent nothing on himself; a sterilized white coat over old clothes was all he ever wore, and he slept under a crucifix on a cot in his hospital."

Then one day, we are told, Habash closed his clinic and went with the *fedayeen* to "follow the only calling in which he now believed—the pitiless fight for vengeance. It was 1967, and since that day he has given up everything, including his two children and his beautiful young wife, whom he had married five years before."

The only thing wrong with this brief sketch is that it is not true. His clinic was almost certainly a front for his terrorist activities, in which he has engaged since 1959, when he established the ANM with the financial and operational support of the Egyptian government. The ANM was created by the Nasser government for the purpose of carrying out subversive activities against the governments of Jordan, Lebanon, Saudi Arabia, and Kuwait. Originally the group was an extreme nationalist, Pan-Arabic organization, not unlike the Muslim Brotherhood, but after being absorbed into the PFLP it immediately became Maoist.

Habash has said that he accepted money only from "progressive" Arab states and would not touch funds with the "smell of oil on it." The fact is that the Egyptian government paid a subsidy of £2.6 million to the ANM in hard currency. Egypt also assisted the ANM in its propaganda and pledged to extend its support to branches of the group in Lebanon and Kuwait. In 1969 Egypt coerced the Lebanese government into signing the Cairo Agreement, which became the basis for the presence of the PFLP and other terrorist groups in Lebanon. Their establishment there proved a fatal step for that tiny country, which until its near destruction in the recent war had been the most nearly democratic of the Arab countries.

In return for monetary and political support, Habash's organization agreed to let its local cells in all Arab countries serve as funnels for intelligence information to the Egyptian regime and to be at its disposal in other ways. Habash finally fell out with Nasser and, after the founding of the PFLP, became more dependent on Iraq and Libya for support.

The Arab terrorists had not yet succeeded in impressing the Soviets but not because the Russians disapproved of the methods used or were favorable to Israel. It was mainly because the PLO and others seemed to threaten the existence of Arab states with whom the Soviets had aid agreements. Another factor may have been that they distrusted the right-wing background of Arafat and his lieutenants in al-Fatah. Indeed, one Jordanian Communist reported to the Soviets during this period that there was reason to believe al-Fatah was

dominated by Muslim Brotherhood thinking. At a meeting of Arab Communists in Moscow in July 1968, instructions were issued for the Arabs to establish close contacts with the *fedayeen*. This move by the Russians was intended
not only to maintain surveillance over the terrorist groups but also to investigate the possibility of bringing them under Moscow's control.

Habash, who leaned more toward China than toward Russia and whose
group received some training from Chinese instructors, began to have internal
problems in the PFLP in 1968. He was arrested in Syria, perhaps at the
instigation of al-Fatah, and imprisoned in Damascus. Ahmed Jibril, whose
Palestinian Liberation Front had been amalgamated into the PFLP, supported
the Syrians in this move. He expelled the Youth of Revenge from the PFLP,
and the Heroes of the Return walked out in sympathy. The two groups then
expelled Jibril and took over the PFLP again. Some members of the PFLP
went with Jibril, who then set up his own Popular Front for the Liberation
of Palestine—General Command.

Habash was rescued from the Syrians by his followers while being transferred from one prison to another during a threatened coup. Returning to his
headquarters in Amman, he found that one of his deputies, Nayef Hawatmeh,
and another leader of the group, Salah Rafat, had accused him of being a
"fascist demagogue" and were trying to push the PFLP further left. Habash
reacted by quickly rounding up a gang of strong-arm men and sending them
to attack Hawatmeh's crew in the refugee camp they had taken refuge in.

Habash proved to be far more ruthless than either Hawatmeh or Rafat
had imagined. Acting on his orders in April 1969, gunmen shot down Abd
al-Kadari, one of Hawatmeh's followers, in the streets of Amman and kidnapped another one named Muhamed Ibrahim Khalifa, who was tortured for
hours and then thrown into the street to die.

"Khalifa did not fall as a victim of Israeli intelligence or by the bullets
of conquest," a Hawatmeh pamphlet said, "but by the hands of a gang of the
Popular Front, which daily is turning more and more into a fascist front,
including gangs of rascals and ruffians having no trace of patriotic sentiment."

Another pamphlet carried the same message to the Palestinians and their
supporters: "The Popular Front is slaying revolutionary fighters in the streets
of Amman and in fascist prisons. . . . Habash is trying to tear the resistance
movement into pieces from the inside. . . . This fascist gang is sabotaging the
security of the resistance movement and is opening the way for counterrevolutionary forces to intervene in order to destroy the resistance movement."

Hawatmeh renamed his group the Popular Democratic Front for the
Liberation of Palestine (PDFLP) and summoned a conference of the leaders
of Palestinian leftist groups. The Communist party, the Lawyers Association,
the Doctors Association, and others attended and duly denounced the PFLP
for its "fascist methods, stained in blood."

Because Hawatmeh's rebellion followed close on the heels of the Moscow
meeting of Arab Communists at which they received orders to infiltrate the
terrorist groups with the intention of bringing them under Soviet control, it

is not unreasonable to wonder if there was a cause-and-effect relationship between the two events.

The PFLP announced its presence to the world by carrying out the first terrorist hijacking of an airliner in the Middle East. Three terrorists, two Palestinians and one Syrian, seized an El Al 707, bound from Rome to Tel Aviv with forty-eight persons aboard, early on the morning of July 22, 1968, and ordered it to fly to Algiers. When it landed there, the Algerian government announced that it still considered itself at war with Israel, granted the terrorists asylum, and said the plane and Israeli passengers would be held. President Boumedienne apparently changed his mind a little later and said that the thirty-eight passengers would be free to leave but that the Israeli crew and plane would be held. The Israeli government asked Secretary-General U Thant to intervene, and eventually the crew was released.

The next PFLP exploit was the first indiscriminate firing at an airport in a non–Middle Eastern country. On December 26, 1968, two gunmen, Mahmoud Mohammed Issa and Maher Hussein al-Yamani, opened fire on a New York–bound El Al 707 as it prepared to take off from Athens airport. Leo Shanear, an Israeli marine engineer, was shot to death as he sat in his seat on the plane. The two terrorists were arrested and placed on trial in Athens but were freed by another act of terrorism when a Greek airliner to Beirut was hijacked on July 22, 1970.

The Israelis struck back at Beirut, the base of the two terrorists in the Athens attack. Helicopter-borne Israeli commandos raided Beirut International Airport on December 28, 1968, and destroyed eleven Lebanese planes in reprisal. Planes belonging to other international airlines were left intact; only Lebanese planes were hit in the pinpoint raid. Passengers were ordered to disembark from one plane, and after they were safely off, explosives were planted under the wings. There were no casualties, and the Lebanese security guards put up no resistance. The raid did bring expressions of disapproval from various nations, however, including one from the United States.

Another Israeli reprisal, which had occurred several months earlier, produced heavy casualties and had even more effect on the propaganda war waged by the terrorists. A thousand troops supported by tanks and planes moved across the Damia and Allenby bridges to attack the village of Karameh. Their target was a large refugee camp that had become a main *fedayeen* base where Arafat had his headquarters in what had previously been a primary school for girls. Al-Fatah gunmen had taken over complete control of the facility and forced the refugees to cooperate with them.

As the Israelis went into action, the 600-strong *fadayeen* force decided to stand and fight. They were quickly reinforced by 48 Jordanian tanks, 11 artillery batteries, and two brigades of infantry. Fighting in the fortified camp was brisk, with street fighting and hand-to-hand encounters. The Israelis had no difficulty crushing the *fedayeen* but came under heavy fire from the Jordanian forces in the surrounding hills. After occupying the area for about 15 hours, they withdrew but took the precaution of blowing up storehouses and other buildings. They had succeeded in killing 150 terrorists and capturing another 138. The Jordanian losses totaled 100. The Israelis reported 21 dead, 70 wounded, and the loss of some equipment that was left behind. They had clearly won the actual battle in spite of the odds, but they lost the propaganda battle that followed.

Al-Fatah claimed that the fighting had "shattered the myth of Israeli air and technological superiority." An American correspondent who followed the al-Fatah line wrote that the Israeli casualties corresponded to putting out of action about eight thousand Americans in Vietnam in a single day. Atrocity stories concerning innocent refugees who had supposedly been killed in the camp flooded the press. George de Carvalho, writing in the April 5, 1968, issue of *Life* magazine, did not see it that way. He said, "It was proved beyond doubt that Karameh had ceased to be a civilian settlement and had been transformed into one huge terrorist base. There were hardly any civilians in it. The civilian population had evacuated it because the presence of the saboteurs made normal civilian life impossible." Dr. Hisham Sharabi, a Lebanese writer, claimed that "probably no more than three hundred guerrillas" with minor Jordanian support had fought off superior Israeli forces and inflicted heavy losses on it.

The terrorists claimed the Israelis had lost two hundred men plus five tanks and four aircraft. Their own losses they said had been only fifty-nine. "It proved that the Israelis are not supermen," said a jubilant Fatah officer, and Abu Ayed, a Fatah leader, claimed that three hundred Israeli officers and men were tried for cowardliness for refusing to take part in the battle against his valiant fighters.

The Arabs were once again showing their vast capacity to believe their own propaganda, but the story of the false victory was accepted by many outsiders as well and is still being given credit for having had great influence on the growth of terrorism.

"The battle of Karameh was a great deal more significant than the Israelis will admit," Dana Adams Schmidt says in a recent *New York Times* account. It was responsible for a wave of popularity of the *fedayeen* in the Arab world. Al-Fatah's membership reportedly increased from a few thousand at the beginning of 1968 to close to ten thousand in late 1970. The PFLP and other groups grew more slowly, but the PFLP became popular among Palestinians in Lebanon because of its large supply of Chinese and Russian arms, many of which were passed out in the refugee camps during the fighting with the Lebanese army in October 1969.

In addition to the PFLP, 1967 saw the founding of another group. In December al-Sa'iqa, or Vanguard of Popular Revolution, was established by the Syrian Ba'ath party, totally under the control of the Syrian army. Its leaders, such as Zuhayr Mussin and Col. Mustafa Saad el-Din, are officers in the Syrian army and its members are for the most part "camouflaged Syrian regulars."

Mustafa Abd el-Salam, a Syrian regular, was captured by Israeli defense forces in a raid on terrorist bases in Lebanon in September 1972. Under interrogation he admitted he was serving in the group as part of his normal military service. He had first been trained in sabotage at Syrian military schools, he said, and then posted to serve with the terrorists at a higher rate of pay for the remaining two and a half years of his army service.

Al-Sa'iqa has a large number of bases within Syria proper. El-Hamma is four miles west of Damascus, Sahm el-Julan five miles east of the 1973 cease-fire line, and Harna four miles north of Damascus. Muzairib is al-Sa'iqa's main base, while El-Hamma was al-Fatah's main base and headquarters, with Burj Islam north of Latakia being its principal naval base. Ein Saheh, seven miles northwest of Damascus, was the Popular Democratic Front's main base after it broke away from the PFLP in February 1969.

In its continuing overseas terror campaign, the PFLP attacked an El Al jet at Kloten Airport, nine miles west of Zurich, on February 18, 1969. Four Arab guerrillas were waiting behind a snowbank and opened fire with their Russian-made Kalasnikov submachine guns as it taxied for takeoff to Tel Aviv. About fifty slugs hit the cockpit and the first-class compartment, killing the copilot and wounding the pilot. Incendiary bombs were hurled at the plane but missed the wingtip fuel tanks by about three yards and failed to ignite. Hand grenades were also thrown and failed to explode. An Israeli security guard aboard the plane jumped through an emergency hatch after the first burst of fire when the plane stopped, leaped over a fence at the edge of the airport, and rushed toward the Arabs from behind. He killed one of them with a single shot from his 22-caliber Beretta; the other three attackers, one of them a girl, were overpowered by security guards. "If we hadn't stopped him [the Israeli], he would have killed the others as well," one airport guard said.

German-language leaflets found at the site likened the terrorists to Switzerland's legendary hero William Tell and urged "understanding for what we did here today."

In Amman the PFLP issued a communiqué claiming that the attack was in reprisal for "brutality and torture" committed by Israeli authorities against Arab citizens in occupied territory. It also claimed that the plane had been "destroyed," and the PFLP spokesman said in his announcement, "Fly El Al and the Popular Front commandos are at your service."

In June 1969 George Habash agreed to an interview with *Time* magazine and spoke to the Western world for the first time. He was asked the reason for the attacks on El Al planes.

"Frankly, we need the shock value," Habash said, "not for personal publicity but for the whole Palestinian cause. We had to shock both an indifferent world and a demoralized Palestine nation. We must make it clear to our own people and all the world that there can be no political solution short of a return to Palestine."

Asked if Israeli retaliation for the attacks that killed "innocent Arab civilians" bothered him, he said, "No. It is exactly what we want, for we are totally against any peaceful solution that leaves behind an Israel. And this is the only possible peaceful solution in prospect. That means to us 'Stay in your tents forever with no homeland.' Actually Israel helps our cause by retaliating, for it angers the people and diminishes chances for a peaceful solution, which we cannot accept."

Did it worry him that the Middle East crisis might develop into a world war? "Not really," Habash said. "The world has forgotten Palestine. Now it must pay attention to our struggle. No matter what happens to the Arab world or the whole world, we will keep fighting to leave our tents and go home. Whoever opposes our fight will have to fight us. If the world thinks the commando movement is superficial, it is much mistaken. It is the only way open to us to go home."

The PFLP used a front name for their next attack, which took place in Athens, claiming it was the work of the Palestine Popular Struggle Front. An Arab identified as Elias B. Dergarabedian, a Jordanian tailor of Armenian parentage, threw a hand grenade into the downtown El Al office, killing one Greek child and wounding fourteen other persons, including three Americans. A crowd gathered outside the building as Dergarabedian and another Arab were taken away by police. As the pair emerged from the office, the crowd shouted, "Lynch them! Lynch them!" There was no lynching, of course, and both men were set free a few months later as the result of the hijacking of an Olympia airliner on July 22, 1970.

Then came a more vicious attack. Bombs were placed on board a Swissair jet and an Austrian Airline jet by Arab terrorists. The explosion in the Austrian jet blew a hole in the plane but caused no injuries. Miraculously it was able to make an emergency landing at Frankfurt. The fate of the Swissair plane was more tragic.

"Suspect explosion in aft compartment of aircraft," the captain reported and then followed with, "We have fire on board. Immediate landing." A few minutes later he said, "Request police to investigate. We have smoke on board." Then came his final words. "There's nothing we can do. Many thanks." Seconds later the plane plunged, flaming, into woods near Wuerenlingen, twenty miles northwest of Zurich. All forty-seven persons aboard, passengers and crew, died in the crash. That included seven Americans; fifteen Israelis; nine Germans; two Canadians; one citizen each from Belgium, England, Switzerland, Thailand, and Senegal; and nine Swiss crew members. This time the Arab terrorists had spread their terror worldwide.

A communiqué issued in Beirut claimed credit for the destruction of the Swissair plane disaster for the PFLP General Command. It was followed almost immediately by another communiqué from the same group stating it had not planted the bomb and had not issued the first communiqué. Since Hawatmeh's group had been complaining about the excesses of the PFLP and since it is certain that the bombs on the Swissair and Austrian jets had been planted by Habash's people, one must assume that faced with a worldwide outcry of horror, the dedicated physician had decided to transfer the blame for this atrocity to his enemies. Habash had made it quite clear how he felt about the bombing when he announced that attacks would continue on Israeli aircraft: "El Al planes are part of Israel's air force."

Habash was also interested in another angle of the situation. "The PFLP sent its teen-agers on perilous missions to Europe, and its young girls [were] always modishly attired and impeccably polite," wrote Dana Adams Schmidt, because as Habash explained, "We want the world to know that the whole Palestinian community, women and children as well as men, is imbued with revolutionary fervor. And we want it to know that they are modern people and that they are civilized." This was also an effort to improve the world's image of Arabs. Habash did not want them to be thought of "as ignorant savages with knives in their teeth." There is no doubt that during the next few months they did away with that image, replacing it with one of educated terrorists with machine guns under their arms and bombs in their brassieres.

Actually the West's image of the Arab had been more favorable previously than Habash imagined. Many people remembered that officers of the Arab Legion had acted like honorable gentlemen during the 1948 war, often rescuing Jews from Palestinian mobs at risk of their own lives, and older Arabs had offered hospitality to Jews in the face of threatened lynchings by their own people. Habash and his followers succeeded in erasing that favorable impression and proving that there is nothing more savage than an educated man with a personal grievance he considers a cosmic wrong.

The PFLP attacks were not limited to Israeli overseas facilities. On February 16, 1970, bombs were set off near the oxygen reserve of Hadassah Hospital in Jerusalem, killing and injuring many. Five days later a bomb exploded in a Jerusalem supermarket and killed two people and injured nine. An Anglican clergyman of Arab background was implicated in this crime and sentenced to prison in an Israeli court.

Attacks in other countries also continued. On February 10, 1970, Habash gunmen killed one Israeli and wounded eleven other passengers in a grenade assault on a bus at the airport in Munich. Two terrorists burst into the Israeli embassy in Asunción, Paraguay, on May 4, 1970, and murdered the wife of the first secretary and seriously wounded an embassy employee.

When Oriana Fallaci, the Italian journalist who referred to George Habash as an almost Schweitzer-like figure, interviewed him for *Life* magazine, she asked about his medical career. He told her, "Yes, I was a doctor, a pediatrician. I enjoyed that very much, I believed I had the most beautiful job in the world. . . . I loved to care for children. . . ."

On May 22, 1970, Dr. Habash showed that his love for children did not extend to his followers. A group of PFLP guerrillas had crossed from Jordan into Israel and laid an ambush. Their guns remained silent while an Israeli military patrol passed their hiding place. The patrol was a "hard" target, and they were looking for a "soft" one. This soon appeared in the form of a school bus painted bright yellow and carrying children ranging in age from five to eight years from the cooperative farm called Avivim. When the bus came within easy range, about twenty yards, the terrorists opened fire with three 82-mm Russian bazooka rockets, and the vehicle erupted into flames. The driver, two teachers, and seven children were killed instantly and another teacher and child died later. The other twenty on the bus were wounded and lay crying in terror while the Heroes of the Return scurried back across the border to safety in the refugee camps of Jordan.

"If there is anything like a lunatic, radical fringe in the Palestinian resistance movement, it is this splinter group—the PFLP—which has openly admitted responsibility for this most recent atrocity in the Holy Land . . . and so, again, the Arabs have succeeded in demonstrating that they can be their own worst enemies," *America,* the Jesuit magazine, editorialized on June 6, 1970.

Habash was not concerned about what people said about him. His goal was to convince the world that he existed, and his crimes were an existential message carried to the extreme. "We believe that to kill a Jew far from the battleground has more of an effect than killing 100 of them in battle; it attracts more attention. And when we set fire to a store in London, those few flames are worth the burning down of two kibbutzim. Because we force people to ask what is going on and so they get to know our tragic situation. You have to be reminded of our existence."

Fallaci asked what right he and his group had to attack Israeli aircraft and citizens in neutral countries.

"Aside from the fact that these airfields are always located in pro-Zionist countries, I repeat that we have the right to fight our enemy wherever he might be. And as for the non-Israeli passengers, they are on their way to Israel. Since we have no control over the land that was stolen from us and called Israel, it is right that whoever goes to Israel should ask for our permission."

His movement sought not only the destruction of Israel: "We ought to be honest and admit that what we want is a war like the war in Vietnam. We want a Vietnam not just in Palestine but throughout the Arab world."

Following Habash's break with Nayef Hawatmeh, Dr. Wadi Elias Haddad became the PFLP's second in command. Haddad is a far more shadowy figure than Habash, rarely photographed and seldom, if ever, interviewed. From information released by Israeli intelligence, who want him even more than they want Carlos, some facts about his life emerge. He was born to Greek Orthodox parents in the town of Safad but spent his youth in Jerusalem. His father, Elias Nasralla, was a well-known teacher in Palestine at the end of the Ottoman Empire and during the British mandate. Haddad was born in 1930. He studied dentistry at the American University in Beirut at the same time that George Habash was in the school of medicine. Both received their indoctrination in Marxist philosophy from American professors.

Haddad practiced dentistry at the same clinic in Amman at which Habash treated patients. The free medicine they distributed was wrapped in proterrorist leaflets printed on the press in the clinic. From about 1963 onward, the clinic served as a front for their guerrilla activities.

In addition to being second in command, Haddad also serves as Habash's operations officer, which means he is in personal charge of the murder gangs who strike out on PFLP orders. It was he who planned the first hijacking, that of the El Al jet to Algeria in 1968. He also supposedly discovered Leila Khaled and sent her on the hijacking frolic during which she almost blew herself and everyone else up with her careless handling of hand grenades. He is the one who assigned the beautiful Iraqi Katie Thomas to hijack a Japanese jumbo jet. Unluckier than her sister terrorist, Katie did blow herself up. With the assistance of a painter named Muna Saudi, Haddad personally tried to murder David Ben-Gurion during a transit stop at an airport in Denmark.

Haddad established many of the PFLP's liaisons with terrorist groups all over the world. He has conspired with Baader-Meinhof; with the Japanese URA; and with South American, Irish, Scandinavian, and American terrorists. He personally recruited the URA killers who struck at Lod Airport. He has close connections with Qaddafi in Libya, Boumedienne in Algeria, and apparently with Idi Amin in Uganda and is friendly with the leaders of South Yemen and Iraq.

As might be thought, Haddad is a marked man. Not only does Ha Mossad want him, but so do al-Fatah and the Popular Democratic Front. On July 11, 1970, someone almost got him at his apartment on the third floor of the Katarji Building on Muhi Aldin Alhayat Street in Beirut.

A man with an Iranian passport in the name of Ahmad Batzrat arrived in Beirut three months before the attempted assassination. A dark-skinned young man in his early thirties with a moustache and a slender, active figure, Batzrat habitually wore dark glasses and claimed to know no Arabic. An investigation by Lebanese police later revealed that he had come from Europe, traveling via Lufthansa and Air France.

Batzrat rented an apartment on the fifth floor of a building facing the plush Katarji Building. At 2:14 A.M. on July 11, 1970, six Russian-made Katyusha rockets were launched at the Haddad apartment from a distance of about eleven yards. Two of the rockets were duds but the other four exploded in the salon and bedroom, blowing out doors and windows and setting the apartment on fire. Haddad was slightly injured and his wife, Samia, and son, Hani, were burned. All three were taken to the American University Hospital for treatment.

Leila Khaled was visiting the family at the time but escaped unscathed. She later described the incident in her book *My People Shall Live*:

It was July 11, 1970, at 2:15 A.M. and I was sitting in Dr. Wadi Haddad's apartment and we were discussing strategy. His wife and child were asleep in the next room. From out of nowhere a volley of rockets struck the bedroom. Neither of us was hurt. We reached for our guns. Then in the midst of the flames his family burst out of the bedroom screaming and bleeding. The electricity failed.

We panicked momentarily as we tried to extinguish the fire. I grabbed eight-year-old Hani, and ran up and down the stairs shouting "Fire, Fire." Hani was bleeding from the chest and his feet looked squashed. . . . I was anxious, but Hani was absolutely calm and silent. He forced a smile and said to me, "Leila, revolutionaries of the Front ought not to be fearful. You ought to be ashamed to be frightened."

A little shocked by the reminder from the "child revolutionary," Leila rushed outside with him and hailed a cab to take him to a doctor. One driver refused to pick them up and, having recovered courage, Leila spat in his face.

When they managed to get to the American University Hospital, she ran into another problem. The doctor on duty hesitated about offering treatment. Leila drew herself up to her full height, dark eyes flashing scornfully, and threatened loudly, "Yankee doctor, the revolution will make AUB's hospital a hospital for the poor and your kind of doctor will have to be disbarred or sent back to America." In the face of such a prospect, she says, the American apologized and flashed her a "barefaced grin."

A search of Batzrat's apartment by Lebanese police disclosed two suitcases with false bottoms and the rocket assembly with an inscription in English: "Made by Fatah, 1970."

There was reason to believe that Batzrat had not acted alone, that a man named Ahmad Rauf had been his accomplice and that perhaps there were others. Ahmad Rauf had come from West Germany and returned there, as had Batzrat.

Although al-Fatah had been offered the credit, Arafat vehemently denied that he or his organization had been involved, saying that "this criminal operation was a link in the chain of conspiracy woven by the counterrevolution in order to eliminate Palestinian resistance."

The blame or credit for the attempt on Haddad's life has been generally assigned to Ha Mossad because of later Israeli assassinations of Palestinian leaders, but Mossad rockets do not usually misfire. Considering the fact that the attack occurred only a little over a year after Habash and Haddad thugs had liquidated Muhammad Ibrahim Khalifa and Mundhir abd Latif al-Kadari and the further fact that both known suspects had come from Germany, where Palestinian groups were strong among the Arab student population, it would seem that the rocket assembly might better have been inscribed: "Made by the Popular Democratic Front." As of 1977, Haddad was still alive and at large, probably planning future existentialist messages to the world.

One thing that the terrorists seemingly did not plan but that was certainly brought about by their actions was what happened to them and all the other Palestinians in Jordan in 1970. But to examine that properly, we should first look briefly at events that had transpired within the PLO.

Ahmed Shukeiri remained as chairman of the PLO until late in 1967, when he was removed. Yahya Hamuden was elected as interim chairman of the National Council, but al-Fatah took over control of the Executive Council, and early in February 1969 Yasir Arafat was chosen chairman of the PLO during a meeting in Cairo. In addition, the new eleven-man Executive Committee was selected, with four members representing al-Fatah directly and the others favorable to it.

Instead of al-Fatah joining the PLO, the PLO had joined al-Fatah. Included in the deal was the Ba'ath-dominated al-Sai'qa, but the PFLP remained outside because it objected to the distribution of plums in the executive and 105-man council.

Arafat proclaimed that he would "escalate the Palestinian revolution in all parts of occupied Palestine" and added that "the only way of liberating Palestine is by armed struggle." He said he had rejected all political solutions to the problem.

Bankrolled by the rich Arab states and lavishly supplied with Soviet as well as other arms, the PLO seemed to be riding high. Dana Adams Schmidt visited the camp of an al-Fatah *asifa,* or "fighting unit," in Jordan in early 1969. The intensive three-month training course was described to him by the "thoroughly military" training officer, who was perfectly willing to put his men through their paces for reporters and show how they were instructed in the use of weapons, especially the Kalashnikov automatic rifle. The officer thought the Soviet-made weapon was the best all-around weapon in the world and said it was lighter and longer in range than the Uzi, which the Israelis made and used.

The trainees were taught how to deal with paratroopers, helicopters, and tank attacks. Much attention was also given to hand-to-hand combat, and all men learned a few key phrases in Hebrew and how to live off the land if necessary.

As Schmidt watched the young *fedayeen* marching and shouting, he thought he caught a glimpse of what a new Palestinian state might be like. Marching on the double, they chanted:

> To the left, *asifa,*
> To the right, *asifa,*
> At the front, *asifa,*
> At the rear, *asifa.*

Another group jogged by with their leader calling out questions which they answered at the top of their lungs:

> It has been told . . .
> What?
> That we are the *fedayeen* . . .
> What *fedayeen?*
> The *fedayeen* of *asifa* . . .
> What *asifa?*

The *asifa* of the revolution . . .
What revolution?
The revolution of the return . . .
What return?
The return to Gaza, Jaffa, Haifa.

As it turned out, the trainees were only months away from a bloody confrontation with a real army, a full-scale confrontation that George Habash and Wadi Haddad were doing everything in their power to bring about, a confrontation that they could not possibly win.

King Hussein of Jordan had recognized ever since 1966 that the *fedayeen* constituted more of a menace to his country and to his throne than they did to Israel. Hussein was the great-great-grandson of the Grand Sherif Hussein of Mecca who had ridden with Lawrence of Arabia against the Turks. As their part of the spoils of the Turkish empire, the Husseins had received the Kingdom of Iraq for the eldest son, Faisal, and had created the Kingdom of Transjordan for the second son, Abdullah. The most moderate of the Arab rulers, Abdullah had been willing to make peace with Israel in 1948 and was therefore murdered on the orders of the Grand Mufti. When he was shot down on the steps of the El Aksa Mosque in Jerusalem, the assassin also fired at the king's grandson, Hussein, who was then seventeen, but the bullet had ricocheted off a medal on his uniform.

Abdullah had been succeeded by Hussein's father, Talal, who after only a year as king was found to be suffering from severe schizophrenia and was persuaded to give up the throne and retire to a Swiss sanitorium. So at eighteen Hussein became king. He had been a playboy prince; he drank a lot of Scotch, drove fast cars, and chased fast women. He did not change a great deal during the first years of his reign, but following the murder of his cousin King Faisal and of the whole Iraqi royal family by leftist army officers, he seemed to mature. "I have received confirmation of the murder of my cousin, King Faisal of Iraq, and all his royal family," he told reporters. "They are only the last in a caravan of martyrs."

He had been faced with a similar fate a year earlier after his dismissal of leftist Prime Minister Suleiman Nabulsi. Faced with an officers' plot, instead of hiding in the royal palace or fleeing the country, Hussein had driven by himself to the headquarters of one of the regiments supposedly in revolt and appealed in person to the troops. The regiment had reaffirmed its loyalty, and the officers' revolt had been crushed.

As noted earlier, Jordan was the only Arab state to accept the Palestinian refugees as something other than pawns, and the only one to offer them automatic citizenship. But despite the fact that many of them blended quickly into the native population, hundreds of thousands more remained in huge, sprawling refugee camps, camps that were like festering wounds, which soon came under the control of terrorists. Probably over half the population of

Jordan is Palestinian; the rest are Bedouins who between 1968 and 1970 were the king's chief support.

Up to 1968 Hussein had survived eight assassination attempts and countless attempts by Syria, Egypt, and Iraq to overthrow him. Now George Habash and Wadi Haddad, with some reluctant support from Yasir Arafat, were determined that Hussein must go, either by assassination or by rebellion. The PFLP leaders had come to visualize themselves as the real rulers of Jordan, with their followers acting the part of the conquering army.

A group of American scholars went to the Middle East as representatives of American Professors for Peace in the Middle East in July 1968 and were astonished to find that the faculty members of the University of Amman, like the professors at the University of Beirut, were recruiters and propagandizers for the terrorists. The Americans were told that the *fedayeen* were so strong that they could seize power any time they wanted to but the real purpose of the leaders was to force Israel to such extreme retaliation that the other Arab states would start a war against her. That war would end either in victory for Israel, in which case that country would swallow so much more Arab territory that it would be impossible for the Jews to control the Arab population and revolution would result; or it would provoke a world war, in which case the Soviets would see to it that Israel was destroyed no matter what else happened. The American professors went home with somber thoughts about peace in the Middle East.

The terrorists' grip on the East Bank of the Jordan had become so tight and ruthless that tens of thousands of peaceful farmers fled the area. Inside the camps the rule of the *fedayeen* was absolute. Supported by American money and watched over benevolently by UN officials, the terrorists infiltrated the schools and turned them into propaganda centers, set up their own drumhead courts, and executed "spies" and "traitors" at will, and all the while they planned the overthrow of the Jordanian government.

To the proud officers of Hussein's army, most of whom were desert Bedouins with little use for the Palestinians, the presence of the *fedayeen* was a constant irritant. Irritation turned to outright anger when roadblocks were set up in Jordan's cities and along its highways by the terrorists, who took great pleasure in insulting any officer who passed by. Adding fuel to the fire were the house-to-house "collections" being made in Amman and other cities which forced Palestinians and Jordanians alike to contribute to the *fedayeen* cause. No merchant was allowed to open his doors unless he was willing to yield to the terrorist demand for "donations."

On November 4 and 5, 1969, an open break occurred between the terrorists and the army of Jordan. Bedouin troops shelled three refugee camps, killing several *fedayeen* and destroying part of their supplies. The PFLP-held camps were the main target of the attacks because Hussein's officers recognized them as the most fanatical and dangerous of the country's unwelcome guests. To stop the fighting, Hussein and Yasir Arafat met and came to terms under which the terrorists were to police themselves and make their presence less obvious and annoying in Amman and other centers of population. The agreement broke down because the extremists of the PFLP and Popular Democratic Front felt that they were strong enough to confront the government and the army was equally sure they were not.

In June 1970 rioting broke out in the city of Amman. PFLP gunmen murdered the U.S. military attaché, Maj. R. J. Perry, with a burst of automatic fire through the closed door of his home. Hussein moved his troops into the city, as he had done earlier in February, but kept the Third Armored Division on the outskirts.

Then, on June 9, Hussein's motorcade was driving through the crossroad town of Sweileh, twelve miles northeast of the capital, when it came under crossfire from the *fedayeen*. The king's driver slumped at the wheel wounded, but the escorting armored cars opened fire with machine guns and drove the terrorists away.

The PLO in Cairo denied that anyone from its group had tried to kill the king, and Arafat personally congratulated Hussein on his escape. In Amman the fighting went on, and a mob that tried to storm the United States embassy was turned back by Jordanian troops.

In a broadcast from Cairo, al-Fatah charged that the Jordanian action was "a monstrous massacre carried out on American behalf." It urged the destruction of the "reactionary" authorities in Amman and of the U.S. "fortress" in the Arab world.

The PFLP General Command said that the terrorists would negotiate and their terms were that (1) Jordanian forces be withdrawn from the capital, (2) those responsible for the fighting be arrested and tried, and (3) special forces formed by the government to fight guerrillas be disbanded.

The PFLP seized two Amman hotels and held as hostages thirty-two American, British, and West German guests. George Habash ordered the captives brought together at the Intercontinental Hotel, where he harangued them for some time on June 12: "Our code of morals is our revolution. What saves our revolution is very right and very honorable and very noble and very beautiful. . . . We were fully determined that in case they [the Jordanian army] smashed us in the camps we would blow up this building. . . . You are not better than our people. . . ."

Faced with the threat to blow up the hotels and the hostages, Hussein had to give in. Arafat forced the king to include several pro-*fedayeen* politicians in the government. Signing himself "Commander in Chief of the Palestine Revolution," Arafat demanded other concessions, among them the dismissal of Hussein's uncle and strongest supporter, Maj. Gen. Nasser ben Jamil, and the commander of the Third Armored Division, Zaid ben Shaker. The internal security force was also to be disbanded.

Conditions had reached such a state in Jordan that the terrorists, rather than the government, were issuing press credentials to the foreign correspondents, and a flood of stories favorable to the *fedayeen* were pouring out of the country from the typewriters of Western reporters.

Tensions came to a head in September 1970 when first Egypt and then Jordan accepted an American peace initiative calling for a cease-fire along the Suez Canal and the Jordan River and agreed to peace talks under the chairmanship of Dr. Gunnar Jarring of the United Nations. At this point Habash and Haddad put into effect plans made in July to hijack four international airliners, fly them to Jordan, and hold passengers and crews hostage.

Before leaving for a trip to North Korea to obtain more Asian Communist weapons, Habash had said concerning the agreed-on cease-fire, "If a settlement is made with Israel, we will turn the Middle East into a hell." For Jordan, and particularly Amman, that threat was to come true.

In planning their hijacking extravaganza, the PFLP leader and his operations officer had selected New York–bound flights and a weekend target date to ensure that vacationing American civilians would make up as large a proportion of the hostages as possible. The plans had been kept secret from all but a few top leaders of the PFLP, and even the hijackers were not fully informed of the scope of the operation.

Leila Khaled, who had lost her pistol down her pants during her first hijacking, and Patrick Joseph Arguello, a graduate of UCLA, and two others were assigned to hijack El Al Flight 219 at Amsterdam. Arguello, the son of a physician, had been studying for a master's degree in sociology and was the first of many young Westerners who decided to follow their new ideology by offering their aid to the Palestinians. The phenomenon of German, American, and Japanese students in the terrorist ranks was to become more familiar as time went on and terrorism became international. Young Arguello's decision cost him his life.

In *My People Shall Live,* Leila Khaled recounts in her breathless, schoolgirlish way her thoughts as she approached her mission:

> My comrades and I were on our way to Europe to declare international war against the concerted attempts of the superpowers, Zionism, and the Arab states to smash the Arab social revolution and thereby the revolution of the Third World and the oppressed everywhere on this globe. I went to Frankfurt in the full knowledge that we, the Palestinians, the children of despair . . . were carrying the torch of freedom and human liberation on behalf of humanity: if we failed, America would have succeeded in reversing the tide of the world revolution. . . . Our minimum objective was the inscription of the name of Palestine on the memory of mankind and on the mind of every self-respecting libertarian who believes in the right of the subjugated to self-determination.

Leila Khaled and Patrick Arguello met for the first time in front of the air terminal in Stuttgart and compared notes on their mutual assignment, but she did not tell him her real name, only the pseudonym Shadiah. At Amsterdam on September 6, they bordered El Al Flight 219, posing as a young Spanish couple. Leila had a hand grenade in each cup of her bra, and Patrick had a grenade and a pistol. They expected to meet two other comrades on board the plane, but El Al security people had turned them back at the airport.

Like Dr. Habash, Leila loves children and was upset when she saw several board the plane. "I was shocked and secretly lamented that once again I had to face the agonizing problem of what to do to avoid hurting children. I love children and know they are free of guilt."

As the plane took off Leila noticed that Patrick seemed a little nervous, and to improve his morale she told him who she really was. It had the desired effect, and Patrick gave her a victory salute. She noticed a man at the back of the plane staring at them, but when she stared boldly back at him, he "shyly looked the other way."

Patrick drew his pistol and readied his hand grenade while Leila whipped the twin grenades out of her bra and pulled the pins on them before rushing forward toward the first-class section and the cockpit, shouting "Don't move!" at passengers who tried to take cover.

At this point three stewards appeared suddenly in front of her with handguns. She counted six guns aimed at her and Patrick, but undaunted, she forged ahead, knocking down a hostess who pleaded with her in Arabic. She threatened to blow up the plane if anyone fired at them, displaying her two grenades and dropping the safety pins on the floor to convince everyone she meant business. (It is a little difficult to figure out the physical mechanics of this. If she had a grenade in each hand and was holding down the trigger mechanism, she would have had to pull and hold the pins with her teeth and would have had trouble saying anything.)

Patrick was holding the armed stewards and passengers at bay. "Go ahead, I'll protect your back," he told his heroic comrade, and Leila forced the fallen hostess to her feet and made her walk on ahead to the flight deck. They both pounded on the door of the pilot's cabin, but there was no response. Then she heard a shot, and the plane went into a sharp bank, throwing her off balance.

"The firing continued and suddenly I found myself besieged by a pack of wolves, El Al staff as well as passengers." She was knocked down and somehow the grenades were taken from her without exploding. Then she was dragged into the first-class compartment, where she saw that Patrick had also been overpowered.

"The Zionists were acting like mad dogs," she says. "They trampled over every part of our bodies. By that time Patrick was too weak to resist. I was fighting like a caged lion. I fought until I was completely exhausted. Then a vicious thug pounced on me, pulling my hair mercilessly, called me a wicked bitch, a malicious Arab and all sorts of obscene names. I spat contemptuously in his face. I bit his hands. He and others around me beat me incessantly for several minutes."

Then an Israeli guard came from the cockpit, tied Patrick up, and shot him in the back. "Patrick looked at me, gave me a deathly smile, and bid me an eternal goodbye."

She was tied up but not executed, although she was certain it was not because of any humanitarian concern but because "they needed me for display purposes in their human zoo in Israel. I presumed they wanted a witness to testify to their 'bravery'—a prisoner to torture and to extract confessions from."

The plane landed at London airport a short time later, and British police came on board and demanded that she be turned over to them. She says the Israelis became incensed at being deprived of their human prey and "then the Israeli pilot, yes the pilot, came out of his cockpit, lifted me off my seat and gave me a couple of vicious kicks in the bottom."

The British officers cried, "Shame!" and pushed the pilot aside in an attempt to seize her. This resulted in a tug-of-war, the Israelis pulling her feet in one direction and the British tugging at her hands from the other. The British won, and she was thrown over a husky shoulder and carried off the plane.

Remarkably enough, after the harrowing experience she describes, the doctors at the hospital where she was given a general checkup and X-rayed said she was "fit to go."

But Patrick was dead and Leila mourned over him and spoke to him. "Patrick, now you have joined Che in revolutionary love. You are an inspiration for the weak and oppressed. The Palestinians shall build you monuments in their hearts and in their liberated homeland. I long for the hour of liberation under leaders of your stature and selfless dedication."

She asked herself, "What had prompted someone halfway across the world from Palestine to undertake this dangerous mission?" She then provided the answer: "Patrick was a revolutionary Communist. His gallant action was a gesture of international solidarity. A flame of life was extinguished; it lit the world for a moment; it blazed a trail on the road back to Palestine. Arguello lives, so do my people, so does the revolution!"

Then Leila demanded that the Israelis on the plane be arrested for their cowardly attack on herself and her comrade. She was highly indignant that they should have resisted the hijacking, as were her superiors in the PFLP, who later issued a statement saying it was a "gross violation of international law to have armed guards on Israel's air lines."

When the British said the El Al crew would not be arrested, Leila screamed, "Why not? Don't you know they executed my comrade in cold blood?"

"Your colleague was killed in battle," she was told. "The coroner's verdict says his death was lawful homicide."

"Shame on British courts!" she cried. "How could they make a decision on the basis of biased evidence and without even interrogating me? It is the Star Chamber all over again! This time it is directed from Tel Aviv and Washington."

Forty-five minutes after the El Al incident, PFLP hijackers struck again. TWA Flight 741 had taken off from Frankfurt and was over the North Sea when it was seized. "We are being kidnapped," radioed Capt. C. D. Wood, who then set a course for the Middle East. The 707 and its 149 passengers and crew of 10 were at the beginning of an ordeal that was to last for many days.

At the same time a Swissair DC-8 was seized while over France on its way from Zurich to New York. This operation was also headed by a female, and French air controllers were startled to hear a woman's voice come over the plane's frequency. "Our call sign is Haifa One," it said. "We will not answer to any other code." TWA Flight 741 had also been issued a new call signal. It was Gaza One.

Back in Amsterdam the two terrorists who had been kept from boarding the El Al plane to join Leila Khaled had decided to try again. This time they picked Pan American Flight 93, a 747, and found it a much softer target despite the fact that Pan Am had been warned by El Al. A radio message to Capt. Jack Priddy caused him to stop the plane as it was taxiing to take off and go back to look the pair over personally. The two terrorists agreed to let the captain frisk them, but he found nothing.

"They seemed like nice fellas," Priddy said later. "I'm no professional, but I went over their bodies and hand luggage fairly closely."

A short time later, when he was at twenty-eight thousand feet, Captain Priddy felt a revolver against his head and heard one of the "nice fellas" telling him to go to Beirut. It had not been much of a trick for the pair to shove their guns under the seat when it had become obvious they were about to be searched.

The Beirut tower warned the two hijackers that the huge plane could not be landed there. "My brothers, this plane is not like a 707—it requires better facilities," the controller said.

The hijackers paid no attention, insisting that the captain land anyway, and somehow he did set the big bird down. While it was on the ground, it was wired with explosives and then the terrorists ordered that it be flown to Cairo. Lighting the fuses with the plane still in the air, the hijackers told the passengers, "You have eight minutes."

As soon as the plane touched down, the passengers hurried to slide down the emergency evacuation chutes. The crew was disembarking by leaping from the wingtips when the $25 million plane blew up. No charges were brought against the hijackers by the Egyptian government, although *Al-Ahram,* the authoritative Cairo paper, did editorialize that "the attack on international civil aviation does not encourage world feeling of solidarity with the Palestinian cause."

At Dawson Field, an old World War II training base outside of Amman, where the other two hijacked planes had landed, the passengers saw that they were surrounded by a line of tanks and armored personnel carriers. "We didn't know whose side they were on. They just sat there," a TWA passenger said later. They were Centurian tanks and other vehicles of the Royal Jordanian Army, and their Bedouin crews were straining at the bit to move in to the rescue, but King Hussein felt unable to give the orders to let them do so.

The passengers spent the night in total darkness inside the planes sitting on the airstrip, which the terrorists had renamed Revolutionary Field. The next morning the hostages were ordered to hand over their passports and kneel while each was examined. When one woman on the Swissair plane protested, the terrorist in charge snarled, "We have been on our knees for twenty years, so five minutes won't hurt you."

Then began the concentration-camp-like separation of Jew from non-Jew, a tactic the PFLP was to repeat in its Entebbe hijack. The women, the children, and the elderly among the non-Jews were to be transported to hotels in Amman, the hostages were told. The men and Israeli or American Jewish women had to remain in the planes.

"They asked each of us, 'Are you Jewish?' " Nancy Porter, a gentile, told reporters later. "I thought it was going to be the firing squad."

The PFLP denied later that it intended to murder the American Jews and Israelis, saying they were detained only for "further interrogation. Zionism is our enemy, not Jews."

That afternoon 127 passengers, mostly women and children, were bused to three Amman hotels—the Intercontinental, the Philadelphia, and Shepheard's. Almost immediately fighting broke out in the city near the hotels.

"I'm glad I'm not at the airstrip," Sheila Warnock of New York remarked. "But if you ask me, it was safer on the plane."

Things had come to a head in Amman. Hussein could restrain his troops no longer even if he had wanted to. The king's Bedouins, upon whom the safety of his life as well as his kingdom depended, had taken all they were going to from the despised Palestinians. While reviewing his troops just a short while before, Hussein had been startled to see a woman's bra hanging on the gun of one of the tanks. "Do you have a woman on board?" the king asked the tank commander. "We are all women now," the officer had replied.

In another incident at another inspection, each officer had pulled off his *kaffiyeh,* the traditional red-and-white checked headdress of the Jordanian army, and thrown it at the king's feet. Hussein got the message loud and clear. "They are on the razor's edge," he told a correspondent for *Le Figaro.* "They've had enough. They are not accustomed to being so vilified, denigrated, provoked endlessly without being able to react. The situation cannot go on. Every day Jordan sinks a little deeper. There must be peace—or war."

Once earlier he had said, "I will rule Jordan—or I will burn it." The time had come to rule, he decided. He dismissed his cabinet and appointed an army officer, Wasfi Tal, prime minister, but the real appointment was that of Field Marshal Habes Majali, a fifty-seven-year-old Bedouin officer, as commander in chief of the army as well as military governor of Jordan.

Correspondents from various parts of the West were shocked by what followed, as Hussein's desert warriors poured into Amman to come at last to grips with those who had "shamed them before the whole world."

"It was sheer butchery," a *Newsweek* reporter wrote. "There seems to be no doubt that some of the Jordanian troops, particularly the Bedouins, went completely berserk. They shelled houses without apparent reason. They revived an old Bedouin custom of breaking the fingers of some of their prisoners so that the captive would not soon be able to pull a trigger against them."

Foreigners who visited refugee camps were reported to be absolutely disgusted at the carnage wrought by the Bedouins on the Palestinians. To the surprise of the reporters, they discovered the Bedouins were aware that most of the members of the Western press on hand took a favorable view of the Palestinians and warned them to keep their heads down—or else.

"And there seemed to be little doubt that some of the Bedouin troops —who had somehow learned that many of the . . . correspondents among us were pro-*fedayeen*—would have enjoyed shooting the lot of us," the *Newsweek* man wrote.

Arafat and al-Fatah had been more or less dragged into the confrontation by Haddad and Habash. The *fedayeen* could muster about 25,000 men, most of whom were hastily armed militia. Against them was the best trained army in the Arab world, with 56,000 men, 300 Patton and Centurian tanks, 270 armored and scout cars, and 350 armored personnel carriers. Once Hussein had agreed to commit his army, there could be only one outcome.

The presence of the hostages of the hijackings that had helped to precipitate the crisis complicated it, however. The PFLP had issued demands for the freeing of terrorists imprisoned in various countries, including six in Germany; Leila Khaled in Britain; and, at one time, Sirhan Sirhan, the Palestinian murderer of Robert Kennedy. Germany was in almost indecent haste to make a deal with the terrorists, the United Kingdom hesitated, and Israel flatly refused to free any of the several hundred convicted terrorists in its jails. Haddad, who was in direct command while Habash was visiting North Korea, decided to stage another hijacking to obtain more British hostages to put pressure on that government to surrender Khaled. A London-bound BOAC plane was seized shortly after takeoff from Bahrain. The VC-10 plane with 105 passengers and a crew of 10 was ordered by a pair of gunmen to land at Revolutionary Field beside the other two hijacked craft.

The diary of one passenger held on board after most of the hostages were transported to Amman hotels was obtained by the *Los Angeles Times,* and it cast considerable light on the thinking of the terrorists on the scene, if not their leadership in the refugee camps and in Beirut.

The terrorist in charge of the plane in which Peter Ungar was held was a stocky young man in his early thirties—this is almost certainly Bassam Abu Sharif—who said he had been born in Palestine and graduated from the American University in Beirut.

He told the Americans whom he was holding that they would not be released until Israel agreed to give up its imprisoned terrorists, and after that the planes would be destroyed. Asked why they would destroy American planes, he said it was to convince the ruling capitalists in America that support of Israel was going to become expensive. When one passenger pointed out that

99 percent of the American public reacted angrily to hijackings and bombings, the terrorist said that American progressives understood the acts of terror and that many had written to the PFLP expressing their support for terrorism. Some, he claimed, were even fighting beside the *fedayeen*. He told the passengers that America was behind Israel, that Israel was only an American base in the Middle East and would collapse in weeks without American aid.

One of the listeners expressed the feeling that Israel was looked upon as a burden rather than an outpost and that some Americans would be glad if Israel were to disappear one morning.

The PFLP man told his hostages his group did not expect much help from the Arab states or even from the Soviet Union. He admitted, however, that they did get help from China.

Someone asked about the armored vehicles they could see about a half mile away, and the *fedayeen* said they belonged to the Jordanian army. They had exchanged shots with the guerrillas at first, but the army had held its fire when told that both passengers and planes would be blown up if they attacked.

All but about fifty-eight of the prisoners, all males except for several Israeli girls, were eventually sent to Amman hotels. As the fighting grew worse and was going against the terrorists, the hostages were spirited out of the planes and split up into small groups to be hidden in Palestinian refugee camps. Then bombs were placed in the three planes, and on September 12 the three aircraft were blown up.

Of the 414 original hostages, 108 had already left the country and others were awaiting flights out of Jordan. Many of those released were suffering from what psychologists were later to call the hijackee syndrome.

One American woman said, "We have no complaints; we were all treated pretty well."

"Like captives and captors elsewhere, some passengers and commandos developed a genuine liking for each other," *Time* said. "One of the Popular Front men playfully tried on a Jewish boy's *yarmulke* in the hotel lobby, and at least one stewardess showed up wearing a PFLP button pinned to her uniform. Said stewardess Linda Jenson: 'They put so much effort into consoling us that I had no doubt we would get out.' "

"They were both men of high quality and genuinely popular," another passenger said.

"Many of the hostages came away more sympathetic than when they started," *Time* said, and quoted an American teen-ager to make the point. The girl said, "They think the idea of one nation with one religion is prejudiced, and they were kicked out of their homes. They gave us some pamphlets. People said it was propaganda, but I believed that some of it was true."

Psychiatrist David G. Hubbard, director of the Aberrant Behavior Center in Dallas, has said that this attitude of sympathy by hostages toward their captors is not unusual. "It is as common as dirt."

"The hijackers were very kind. We could do anything on the plane, even chat with them," said a twenty-year-old Philippine woman after being released.

The stewardess on the same plane said, "The leader kissed us before we left. I already miss him."

Dr. Hubbard says that the phenomenon is caused by the fact that the hijacker does not use all the force that is available to him. This makes the victims feel grateful. "The fact that he has no right to use the force doesn't come through because people are so damned scared they are not thinking."

Stewardesses have been known to flirt with hijackers, businessmen look at them admiringly, and some passengers announce sudden conversions to whatever cause the hijacker supports. Some hostages have heatedly denounced fellow passengers who complain about the seizure of the plane. Any display of rage toward the captors is felt to be too threatening, so the only option left is "learn to love the hijacker," the psychologists say. Freudians call it "identification with the aggressor," which is a survival mechanism that goes back to childhood.

"It is not a very complex mechanism," says Dr. Hubbard. "You can find it with little boys in the third grade all over the world—the class bully who threatens everyone and suddenly finds everyone following him around worshipping him and doing his bidding. A skyjacker doesn't have to be any smarter than a nine-year-old who knows how to use bluff."

Patricia Hearst would seem to have been a prime example of someone suffering from hijackee syndrome. Unable to cope with the brutality of her treatment, the deprivation of the senses from being kept in a closet, the beatings, and the rapes, she identified with the aggressor and learned to love her captors.

The fighting in Amman, meanwhile, was going in favor of the king's troops. Little by little, the Bedouin-manned tanks, supported by Palestinian-manned artillery for the Jordanian army, pushed their way through the city. House-to-house fighting and the shelling produced considerable civilian casualties, but they were greatly overestimated by the media at the time. *Time* spoke of ten thousand dead, and *Newsweek* told of the slaughter at the refugee camp just outside the city that was named for the Grand Mufti: "About 45,000 Palestinians lived in Al-Husseini before the fighting began, but according to the survivors the camp is now 80 percent destroyed. They admit that it had been a stronghold of the Popular Front. . . . But they cannot believe this justified the army's action in pumping shells into the camp for four days running, without regard for civilians. Said one wounded man: 'The heaviest shelling was on the 23rd. The army destroyed houses indiscriminately. Hundreds were killed that day!' "

Arafat added to the impression of mass slaughter. In a message to ambassadors of other Arab states, he said, "Will you kindly inform your governments that King Hussein, with mature consideration, has drawn up a detailed plan which is bound to end in a bloodbath. I possess irrefutable proof that he intends to liquidate the Palestinian resistance."

Later he became even more dramatic about the alleged genocide. "God is my witness," he wrote in a letter to Arab heads of state. "A massacre has been committed. Thousands of people are under the debris. Bodies have rotted. Hundreds of thousands of people are homeless. Our dead are scattered in the streets. Hunger and thirst are killing our remaining children, women and old men. It is a massacre never before seen in history. A sea of blood and 25,000 killed and injured separate us from the Jordan government." Actually the casualties of the fighting in Amman were probably much closer to the eighteen hundred dead estimated by the Jordanian army than to the twenty-five thousand that Arafat claimed.

Robert Regulary of the *Toronto Daily Star,* who did careful research on the number of casualties, came up with a figure between six thousand and eight thousand. The Israelis, whose intelligence service is excellent, said there were three thousand dead.

While the hostages were being smuggled from hiding place to hiding place and Hussein's army was pounding at the refugee camps and diverting part of its tanks to meet the sudden thrust of a supposed PLA armored column from across the Syrian border, Leila Khaled sat in her London cell writing a letter to her dead comrade Patrick. "Today is day four since we embarked on our immortal journey. Your spirit fills me with hope that the cause we embrace is just and honourable," she wrote. "You wrote history by shedding your blood for others; you united continents by your all-encompassing spirit; you ascended to the realm of Olympian gods by your life-inspiring commitment. You are at once a Lafayette, a Byron, a Norman Bethune, a Che Guevara . . . you are not dead. You live. You will live forever! You are the patron saint of Palestine. In revolution, Leila."

The force that had crossed the Syrian border was made up of five thousand men plus almost three hundred tanks and other armored vehicles. The Syrians insisted it was made up completely of troops of the PLA, the military wing of the Syrian-based PLO. It was noted, however, that many of the tanks had been newly painted with the red and olive-green emblems of the PLA. The advancing column was met by the Jordanians in a classic tank battle near Ramtha Junction. Bearing the black, white, green, and red Hashimite flag and pictures of Hussein, the Jordanian tanks could not have numbered much more than fifty and were older types, which were considered a poor match against the modern T-54 Soviet tanks in the opposing column. During the fighting, it soon became evident that the Centurion and Patton tanks were better suited to desert conditions than the newer PLA equipment. In the 120-degree temperature, the Syrian tanks required daily lubrication and change of air filters, which the Jordanian vehicles could do without.

The Jordanian tactics were also superior. Acting on their king's order to "stand fast and teach the heretic leaders of Syria a lesson in heroism," the Fortieth and Sixtieth Armored Brigades knocked out forty tanks by outthinking and outmaneuvering the enemy. Then the Jordanian air force, mostly

Hawker Hunter fighter bombers equipped with light cannons, rockets, and bombs, came in for support. Aided by the fact that Syrian Defense Minister Hafiz Assad, who reportedly opposed the invasion, kept his MIGs on the ground, the Hawker Hunters knocked out another sixty or seventy tanks. The PLA was sent reeling back toward the Syrian border, harried as they went by armored cars and aircraft. In effect, the civil war in Jordan was over.

"Air power," one *fedayeen* back in the safety of Damascus said. "That's what made the difference."

"See you next time," a PLA officer with the retreating forces told a reporter. "See you next time at the start of World War III."

Hussein's troops had taken as many as ten thousand *fedayeen* prisoners in the refugee camps, including two of Arafat's chief aides. There was a £5,000 reward offered for the heads of Habash, Haddad, and Hawatmeh, whose Popular Democratic Front had fought alongside the PFLP and the PLO. In a final bit of drama, Bedouin troops advancing through the battered New Camp heard shouts from a locked house.

"Help! We are foreign hostages! Help! Help! Don't shoot! We are hostages!"

Breaking down the door, the Jordanians found sixteen of the missing hostages, eight Britons, six Swiss, and two West Germans. Shortly thereafter, the defeated terrorists released thirty-two more, all Americans. Leila Khaled and other terrorists had already been released by the countries that held them, although the Israelis as usual had not released a single one.

"We had reached the point where my people living in Jerusalem under foreign military occupation [the Israelis] were ten times more secure in their homes than people living in Amman, our capital," Hussein told his critics in the Arab world and the West. "They [the terrorists] talked about resisting Israel, but it was not a question of Israel at all. It was a question of a takeover here. . . . There was not a single unit in the army or air force that had not been provoked in terms of their families and homes molested."

It took King Hussein and Prime Minister Wasfi Tal the better part of the next year to complete the destruction of the terrorists in Jordan. The end came in July 1971 when the Jordanian army conducted what was referred to in communiqués as "maneuvers with live ammunition." What they were actually doing was attacking the last *fedayeen* strongholds in the wooded hill country west of Heraah, where some three thousand terrorists had dug in, in bunkers and tunnels. The fighting was brief but bloody; two hundred *fedayeen* were killed and about twenty-three hundred taken prisoner. This last fighting produced the extraordinary sight of some two hundred terrorists wading across the Jordan River with raised hands to surrender to Israeli patrols rather than face the fury of the Bedouins, who took as much pleasure in killing as the *fedayeen* themselves but were more skilled at it.

Jordan had rid itself of terrorists, and Lebanon was to suffer for it. Most of those driven out of the Hashimite kingdom moved into the small Mediterranean country whose delicate balance between Christians and Muslims had maintained fragile peace until the coming of the Palestinians. The first terrorists had arrived in the summer of 1968 when Premier Abdullah Yaffin, under severe pressure from Nasser, had signed a pact with Yasir Arafat that permitted 60 *fedayeen* to set themselves up on Mount Hermon in the southeastern corner of Lebanon. At this time there were 275,000 Palestinians in the country, which had a total population of 2,520,000. A few extra Palestinians hardly seemed important, but they were only the first wedge in a movement that would eventually threaten to utterly destroy Lebanon.

In *The Politics of Palestinian Nationalism*, William B. Quandt listed the names and strengths of terrorist groups in late 1970. The following summary deals with the more important ones:

	ARMED MEN	MAJOR SOURCE OF AID
1. Palestinian National Liberation Movement (al-Fatah)	10,000	Libya, Syria, Kuwait, Saudi Arabia, Algeria, private Palestinians
2. Palestinian Liberation Army	5,000	Arab League through PLO
3. Vanguards of the Popular Liberation War (al-Sa'iqa)	8,000	Syrian Ba'ath party
4. Popular Front for the Liberation of Palestine (PFLP)	3,000	Iraq, Libya, Dhina, Soviets [China, North Korea]
5. Popular Democratic Front for Liberation of Palestine (PDFLP)	1,500	Syria
6. Popular Front for the Liberation of Palestine— General Command (PFLP— GC)	500	Syria, later Libya and Iraq

Late 1970 marked the rise of another, apparently new terrorist group— one that announced its birth in blood.

Prime Minister Wasfi Tal supported King Hussein during the rest of the campaign to rid Jordan of the *fedayeen.* Considered pro-Western, he was that rarity among Arabs, a realist, who realized that eventually some sort of understanding had to be reached with Israel. His realism as much as his part in the liquidation of Jordan's *fedayeen* problem made him a prime target for terrorist hatred. If he had remained in Jordan, surrounded by loyal Bedouin guards, he might not have died, although a previous prime minister had been killed by a terrorist bomb planted in the desk of his Amman office. But Tal accepted an invitation from Egypt's new president, Anwar el-Sadat, to visit that country. (Nasser had died of a heart attack shortly after the September war.) In the lobby of the Sheraton Hotel in Cairo, Tal was shot down by four terrorists, one of whom, in an excess of blood lust, stooped to wash his hands in the red flow from the bullet-riddled body.

The perpetrators of the crime were arrested, and el-Sadat made a great show of shock and of his determination to see justice done. In a telegram to King Hussein, the Egyptian leader expressed "severe condemnation on behalf of myself and the Egyptian people for this crime which took place on Egyptian land." He then promised that "all those guilty will receive punishment. . . . We are extremely grieved that anybody should take advantage of the tolerance and atmosphere of security provided by this country."

If Sadat ever had any intention of punishing the four killers, it was stifled when President Qaddafi of Libya announced that he would not join a proposed federation with Egypt if the murderers of Tal were punished. They were released "on bail" and went scot-free.

The four assassins were from Black September, so named in memory of the defeat inflicted on the terrorists by the Jordanian army during that month. It was at first assumed this was a new terror group, but it has become clear since its first appearance that it is merely a front for al-Fatah, a group designed to carry out missions of such viciousness that the older organization does not want to be associated with it. Al-Fatah even went so far as to issue a statement denouncing the murder of Tal. The assassination, it said, had been inspired by "terrorist, fascist thinking which conflicts with the thinking of the revolution." (A tactic similar to this has been used by the IRA.)

Black September is led by Salah Khalaf, also known as Abu Ayad, who is Arafat's deputy in al-Fatah, and Ali Hassan Salameh, chief of al-Fatah's intelligence unit, Jihaz al-Rasd, and the son of the famous Palestinian leader Sheikh Hassan Salameh, killed in a fight with the Israelis in 1948. It was organized by men seething with rage and bitterness over the defeat in Jordan. It is not clear just how much control the central committee of al-Fatah has over this offshoot, but it is known that al-Fatah supplies it with money, weapons, and recruits.

The knowledgeable London-based Institute for the Study of Conflict has called Black September "adventurist and anarchic, like the murder gangs of Palestine in the 1930s. And like those gangs, [it] has no intricate cell-like infrastructure, but is based on a loose system stitched by political extremism, family and generational comaraderie and strong personalities."

Black September has somewhat changed the pattern of Arab terrorism in that its blows have been aimed more at other Arab countries and the West than at Israel. When it does strike at Israel, it tends to hit at Israel's interests abroad rather than inside her borders. Its contacts with foreign terrorists and countries that support them have been extensive, and its activities abroad have had the support of Palestinians living in the respective areas and of local Communists and other leftists.

A great deal of what we know about Black September came from Muhammed Daoud Audeh, code-named Abu Daoud, who was arrested in February 1973 in the midst of a plot to kidnap the Jordanian cabinet. After some persuasion by the Jordanian intelligence service, Daoud talked quite freely. He told of having been recruited for al-Fatah by Salameh in Kuwait in 1968. He was sent to Cairo, where he took a course in intelligence work for nine weeks during the fall of that year. There were ten other Fatah *fedayeen,* including Salameh, in the same class, and they were trained by Egyptian officers in the use of weapons and the arts of sabotage and espionage.

Following this period of training, Daoud was sent to Jordan, where he set up a guerrilla intelligence network. In May 1969 he was replaced by Salameh, and shortly thereafter, Salameh began to lay the groundwork for a new group within al-Fatah. The Jordan war cut short those plans and wiped out the Jihaz al-Rasd network in Jordan. For two years Daoud and Salameh moved between Beirut and Damascus on various missions for al-Fatah. In July 1972 Salah Khalaf brought Daoud into the plot to kidnap the Jordanian cabinet. Passports were provided from Saudi Arabia and Bahrain, and weapons and money were gathered at the planning center in Baghdad.

During this time, another Black September group unsuccessfully attacked the Israeli embassy in Bangkok, and Saudi and Bahraini passports were found on the terrorists. Khalaf believed that this would jeopardize his operation, so he obtained passports from Oman from a member of the Eritrean Liberation Front in Beirut. Daoud, in trying to cross the border into Jordan, was immediately arrested by Jordanian police because while carrying an Omani passport, he was dressed in Saudi clothes and was being driven in a Lebanese car by a Lebanese chauffeur who was married to a Jordanian. If the plan had succeeded, Black September would have flown the Jordanian ministers to Tunisia and then to Libya, where they expected to be welcomed by Qaddafi.

In his confession, Daoud said that the leaders of Black September were Salah Khalaf, Muhammed Yussif al-Najar, and Ali Hassan Salameh, all al-Fatah men. He also made clear the international connections of the group when he told of his own travels for it. In August 1972 he had gone to Sofia, Bulgaria, to purchase arms and to meet Khalaf, who had stopped there on his way back from Geneva. (It is possible that Khalaf had gone to Geneva to get money from the mysterious Italian millionaire Giangiacomo Feltrinelli, who used Swiss bank accounts to bankroll terrorist groups all over Europe and the Middle East.) It was in Sofia that the decision was made by Khalaf to attack the Israeli team at the Munich Olympics.

There have been attempts to pretend that al-Fatah had nothing to do with Black September. Writer Gerald McKnight interviewed a man who may have been a Black September leader at the American University in Beirut; he asked if Black September was not just a code name for al-Fatah.

"That's not true at all," the man said. "In fact, there has been a lot of fabrication about it. There was an American television interview recently, when Mike Wallace interviewed Abu Daoud, who is in prison in Jordan.

. . . It reported him as saying that Black September and Fatah were one and the same thing, which is simply not true! Another journalist interviewed him afterwards and he denied he had ever said it. Yet people like to believe it is so, and Israeli propaganda keeps plugging the lie down everyone's throats."

The mystery man said Black September was different from the older groups. "Black September goes for the jugular. The method is to hit the enemy hard, wherever he is most vulnerable. It ignores political solutions. Instead, it chooses hijack and other direct forms of attack—not, by any means, methods approved by every Palestinian revolutionary."

Arafat also has denied that Black September is part of al-Fatah. "The CIA has published in more than one American paper a story about my relations with Black September," Arafat told *Time*. "It reached such a point that they assumed in the *Washington Post* that I gave an order to some Palestinians in the embassy [to kill two American diplomats and one Belgian diplomat]. Certainly the CIA knows this is a lie. I did my best. I think that if Nixon had not given in to Golda Meir's blackmail and traded their freedom for that of political prisoners, you would have avoided the tragedy that happened in Khartoum. But he sacrificed his ambassador because he submitted to Israeli blackmail. Why was this declaration made by the CIA in the press? . . . The CIA is plotting against me."

According to Arafat, Black September "is a phenomenon that appeared after the savage massacre in Jordan. . . . We lost twenty-five thousand killed and wounded and eight thousand were jailed. It was, and still is, an overwhelming tragedy for all our people on Jordan's East Bank. This massacre could not help producing such a phenomenon. It is quite evident that Israel and the CIA were the originators of this massacre in Jordan."

One of McKnight's sources, a former CIA man named Miles Copeland, told him that Black September had been formed by thirteen top guerrilla leaders, some from al-Fatah and some from the PFLP and other groups. He said Arafat was not one of the thirteen and only found out about the organization later. Copeland thinks Arafat does not even know who the secret thirteen are. "Black September is like the Provos in Ireland," Copeland says. "I mean they've got away from the world revolution and all that crap. They're centered in on fighting Israel as such."

He also says Black September people on a mission do not know who their comrades are. They know only the name of the man who recruited them and even that is usually not the man's right name. In other words, ". . . each compartment had to be watertight from all the others." He claims that even under torture the Black September people could not reveal any secrets and that the Egyptians found this out when they interrogated the four men who killed Wasfi Tal. The Germans discovered the same thing when they questioned the Black September members they captured in Munich.

Abu Daoud, however, has continued to say that "it is al-Fatah. That's right. Some of the al-Fatah leadership orders them."

Other sources revealed that the team that killed Wasfi Tal was led by

Fakhri al-Amari. Another leader was Mohammed Mustafa Shyein, who was wounded, captured, and executed after the storming of the last terrorist outposts in Jordan in July 1971. Faud Shemali, a Lebanese Christian who died of cancer in Geneva in August 1972, was still another. He left a will advising the terrorists to concentrate on attacks against Israelis held in high esteem by the Israelis themselves, such as scholars, scientists, and athletes.

There is, according to sources contacted by John Laffin, little difference between al-Fatah's intelligence unit, Jihaz al-Rasd, and its special services section—Black September. Muhammed Yussif al-Najar has much influence in the group as has Ali Hassan Salameh.

Even Arafat defers to Salameh. It is he who handles the Black September funds raised by al-Fatah and held in numbered accounts in Switzerland as well as in accounts in Italy and West Germany. Some of the funds are invested in legitimate businesses, and it is estimated the total investment is around £30 million. Additional amounts have been raised by blackmail and hijacking, and still more funds come from European leftists.

Black September will also accept contracts to carry out terrorist actions that have no relationship to the Middle East. An example is the explosion in March 1971 at the Gulf Oil refinery in Rotterdam. This was carried out by a team of Europeans recruited by Black September. It also engages in drug smuggling, which is made easy because diplomatic passports are available to its members from various Arab states. Salameh has two Algerian passports in the names of Abdel Kadir Madani and Ahmed Belkacem. Embassies of Iraq, Egypt, Libya, and South Yemen have all been involved in supporting terrorist and drug ventures of the organization. Guns for terrorist activities are often carried across national borders in the dispatch cases of Arab diplomats.

Qaddafi has offered rewards for the murder of Israelis and has paid out large sums to groups that have carried out particularly violent actions, such as the Munich and Lod Airport massacres. There is reason to believe Qaddafi also paid for the terrible massacre at Rome's airport. He may have ordered it for the purpose of killing as many Americans as possible and to wipe out the Moroccan diplomatic party that was traveling on the American plane.

Black September was estimated at this time to have anywhere from one hundred to four hundred hard-core killers with the option of recruiting extra men or women from al-Fatah when needed. They were heavily bankrolled with money from Arab oil states, blackmail, and drug profits; money from Western sources such as Feltrinelli; and perhaps even funds diverted from those of the World Council of Churches, which has provided financial assistance to "liberation" movements said to be "humanitarian" in character. The murder of Prime Minister Tal was followed on December 15 by an attempt to assassinate the Jordanian ambassador in London, but this effort failed.

On May 8, 1972, Black September struck again. Four terrorists, including 2 women, hijacked a Sabena Airlines plane en route from Vienna to Tel Aviv and forced it to land at Israel's Lod Airport. They demanded the release of 317 Palestinian terrorists being held in Israel. Israel followed its standard policy of not making deals with terrorists. Then Israeli paratroopers disguised as mechanics burst through emergency doors, killed 2 of the male hijackers and wounded 1 of the women. The 2 women were tried, convicted, and sentenced to life in prison.

Other Arab terrorist groups were also active during this period, and they began to hire out their killing. It was hired killers of the Japanese URA contacted by Dr. George Habash who slaughtered American nationals from Puerto Rico at Lod Airport in 1972, and other Americans and Israelis were also being kidnapped and killed by allies of Arab terrorism.

In March of 1971, four American servicemen stationed near Ankara, Turkey, were kidnapped by the Turkish People's Liberation Army, probably at the instigation of the PFLP. The kidnappers demanded the publication of a manifesto attacking American imperialism in Turkey and the payment of 400,000 Turkish lili. Turkish intelligence arrested one of the terrorists and beat the names of the rest out of him. The four Americans were released very quickly after that.

The Israeli consul-general in Istanbul was not so lucky, or Turkish intelligence was not as efficient. He was kidnapped by the Turkish People's Liberation Army, and a demand was made for the release of the previously captured terrorist. The Turkish government refused and the kidnap victim was shot to death.

On February 22, 1972, five terrorists hijacked a Lufthansa jet en route from New Delhi to Athens. They claimed to be members of the Organization for Victims of Zionist Occupation but were actually members of the PFLP. The pilot was forced to fly to Yemen, where the passengers and crew were released. The plane was held for ransom, however, and the German government paid out over $10 million to retrieve it.

On August 5, 1972, Black September members, working with Italian confederates, set fire to an oil-storage facility in Trieste. The resulting blaze caused over a $1 million worth of damage.

On August 16, 1972, 2 British girls vacationing in Rome boarded an El Al 707 jet along with 149 other passengers. The girls had recently met a pair of handsome young Arabs named Adnam Mohamed Hasham and Ahmed Zaid and had allowed themselves to be talked into taking a trip to Tel Aviv by the suave young men. As a "pledge of their love," the Arabs had given the girls a tape recorder, and the girls had packed it in one of their suitcases, which was deposited in the luggage compartment of the El Al craft. That saved the lives of everyone on board. When the pressure bomb in the tape recorder went off, the explosion was contained in the armored baggage compartment. The plane returned to Fiumicino Airport with 4 passengers suffering from minor burns.

The two eighteen-year-old British girls were horrified. Ruth Watkins of Newcastle said, "We gave them our love and what did we get in exchange? We could have died."

"They were so kind," Audrey Walton of Middleborough said. "How could they not have thought that we, too, might have been killed in the blast?"

Their Arab lovers had never intended anything else and were, in fact, preparing to celebrate their demise when they were interrupted by the news that their plan had failed. When police broke into their vacant apartment, they found not only bomb-making equipment and explosives, but a feast of chicken, potato salad, and champagne. They were arrested two days later by Italian police, identified by the girls, and charged with attempted murder. The pair had been traveling on Indian passports provided by cooperative diplomats in Europe.

The monstrous crime that Abu Daoud and Salah Khalaf had discussed in Sofia, Bulgaria, in August 1972 was carried out a little over a month later at the Munich Olympics. Black September had been laying the ground for its operations in Germany for some time. There were about twenty thousand Arab workers and sixteen thousand Arab students in West Germany. Palestinian students numbered around three thousand and the terrorists knew they could depend on them in any operation there. The most militant of the workers belonged to the General Union of Palestine Workers (GUPW), and the students to the General Union of Palestine Students (GUPS). Generally speaking, GUPW follows the Habash-PFLP line; GUPS, once headed by Arafat, supports al-Fatah and Black September.

In charge of operations in Germany was Salah Khalaf. It was he who had planned and carried out the murder of five Jordanians in Hamburg in February 1972, an affair that was covered up by the German police. The Jordanians were believed to have been informers working for Jordanian or Israeli intelligence. It was also Khalaf who arranged for the attacks on oil installations in West Germany and the Netherlands in February and in Trieste in August. These were only the prologue to his most important task, which was to kidnap the Israeli Olympic team.

Eight Black September killers slipped through the night unhindered by security precautions and made their way to the quarters of the Israeli team. The men inside heard a sharp rap on the door. Moshe Weinberg, coach of the wrestlers, opened the door a crack and a voice asked in bad German, "Is this the Israeli team?"

Weinberg leaped back and slammed the door shut, yelling to his teammates to escape. A burst of machine-gun fire cut through the door, and Weinberg fell dead. Boxer Gad Zavary broke a window with his elbow and jumped out.

"I heard the knocking and then a terrible cry," Tavia Sokolsky, weightlifting coach, said later. "But I knew instinctively it was an Arab attack. Then I heard my friends yelling, 'Get out! Escape!' I couldn't open the window, so I broke it and ran out."

Wrestling referee Yosef Gufreund and weight lifter Yosef Romano, both strong men, managed to hold the door shut long enough for several team members and some athletes of other nations to escape. Then they, too, were hit by machine-gun fire. Romano was mortally wounded, and Gufreund was captured. Nine hostages were taken.

The Arabs issued an ultimatum and set a deadline. They wanted the freedom of two hundred Palestinian terrorists being held in Israel, plus the release of Kozo Okamoto, the sole survivor of the Lod massacre team, and the two German anarchists, Ulrike Meinhof and Andreas Baader.

The German authorities were in a quandary. Israel refused to give up any terrorists, and the Black September gunmen refused an alternate offer for Germany to pay a large ransom or for German officials to take the place of the captured Israelis.

A telephone call by Chancellor Willy Brandt to Cairo to ask for the help of President el-Sadat produced nothing but the information that el-Sadat was not available and the statement by Egyptian Premier Azi Sidky, "I cannot preempt a decision of the guerrillas. We do not want to get involved in this."

Brandt was furious. "It was totally unsatisfactory," he said. "The terrorists cannot be allowed to leave."

They not only wanted to leave but wanted to take the hostages with them after their demands were met. "We can't simply ship them off like an airmail package to an uncertain fate," one of Brandt's aides said of the hostages.

After some hesitation, the Germans had come to the right decision, but they blundered in executing the rescue attempt that followed. The terrorists were informed they and their hostages would be flown to a nearby airport in two helicopters and that there would be a plane waiting to carry them to an Arab country. Five sharpshooters were stationed on buildings near the helicopter landing spot with instructions to shoot down the terrorists as they emerged from the helicopters before they could harm the hostages.

The Germans had blundered already. For some reason they had assumed there were only four or five guerrillas. Instead there were eight, and even under the best of conditions, the marksmen would have been hard put to kill all of them before they could retaliate against their captives. Then the sharpshooters compounded the original error with another one. They opened fire before all the terrorists had exited the helicopters and succeeded in killing only two and wounding one. The remaining guerrillas then slaughtered the bound and helpless athletes, surrendering only after three more of their number and a German policeman had been killed.

An Israeli student in Germany expressed the feeling of many of his countrymen. "We have learned to be on guard for this kind of thing almost all the time," Asher Mashia said. "But not here—not with all the nations gathered in peace, with all the talk about sportsmanship and freedom."

All during the negotiations and the massacre that followed, a Russian and a Polish team continued a lively game of volleyball less than a hundred yards from the scene of terror, and many people in the stands cheered the departing helicopters, which they supposed were carrying the terrorists to safety.

The mistakes of the Germans and the insensitivity of some athletes and fans are as nothing, however, compared with the deliberate actions of Muammar Qaddafi, dictator of Libya. Qaddafi runs what the *Toronto Star* has called "the world's one working model of a crazy state."

Born in 1941, the son of a Bedouin shepherd, Qaddafi became the head of one of the world's richest oil states at the age of twenty-nine. He was graduated from Benghazi University with a degree in history in 1963 and from the Libya Military Academy in 1965. He took further military studies in Britain in 1966 and returned home just in time to take part in the coup of September 1969, which overthrew the monarchy. He was appointed to the rank of colonel, promoted shortly thereafter to commander in chief of the armed forces and then to chairman of the Revolutionary Council. Since January 16, 1970, he has been prime minister and minister of defense. A friend of gunmen and terrorists everywhere, he is a bitter enemy of Israel and harbors a venomous hatred for the United States.

Diplomats in Washington and abroad have said that Qaddafi is training, arming, and financing an international terrorist network. Even President Ford said in July 1976 that "we do know that the Libyan government has in many ways done certain things that may have stimulated terrorism."

Although there is no single terrorist conspiracy responsible for acts of terrorism on a worldwide basis, there is a loose network of relationships between various groups that, for lack of a better term, has been called Terror International by an Israeli UN delegate. The groups are as diverse as the apolitical al-Fatah and the Provisional IRA, as anarchistic as Baader-Meinhof, or as purely Maoist as the Tupamaros. They are joined mainly by an anti-imperialist, antiestablishment bias and a determination to replace the few democratic societies left in the world with totalitarian governments.

Qaddafi paid $10 million for the murder of the Israeli athletes at Munich, and he also provided a state funeral for the five terrorists who died in the operation. He did not speak the words, but his actions underscored the sentiment expressed by the guerrilla radio when word came of the massacre: "All glory to the men of Black September. The gold medal you have won in Munich is for the Palestine nation."

A few weeks later when a fresh hijacking, this time of a Lufthansa 727, found the West German government almost pathetically eager to trade the three captured Munich murderers for eleven hostages, it was to Libya that the three flew to be greeted as heroes by Qaddafi.

In addition to serving as paymaster for Black September and the PFLP, Qaddafi has set up his own terrorist strike force under the name of the Special Intelligence Service. Two of its agents tried to kidnap or kill two Egyptian cabinet ministers in March 1976. Another of his murder units was sent to Italy to liquidate one of several former Libyan leaders who had fled the country. A third assassin squad was dispatched to Tunisia to kill that country's prime minister. President el-Sadat of Egypt and President Jaafar Numeiry of the Sudan have both accused Qaddafi of attempting to assassinate them, of sending sabotage teams into their countries, and of trying to overthrow their governments.

According to Maj. Omar Maheishy, a former member of Libya's ruling Revolutionary Command Council who fled to Egypt with his car loaded with files concerning Qaddafi's terrorist campaigns, Libyan diplomats carried the weapons used in the Olympic massacre into the country in their diplomatic bags. Libyan diplomats also carried the weapons into the Sudan that were used on March 1, 1973, by Black September to murder the American ambassador and attaché and the Belgian chargé d'affaires. They are also said to have smuggled into Austria the weapons used by Carlos for the attack on OPEC headquarters.

Qaddafi is determined to obtain nuclear bombs (see Book Five). As of the moment, however, he is generously supplied with the world's most sophisticated weapons. In 1975 he spent $1 billion on armament for his twenty-thousand-man army, which was already overloaded with ultramodern equipment it barely has the ability to use. His army currently has fifteen hundred tanks and more aircraft than his five-thousand-man air force can possibly operate. Money, of course, is no object for a man as rich as Qaddafi. He has turned his country into a gigantic arsenal for Terror International.

Not all of his schemes succeed, however. His most recently aborted plan was to disrupt both the Republican and Democratic national conventions of 1976 with infiltrated terrorists. His idea was to "stun the world and exact revenge against the pro-Zionists in both American parties." Shortly after the Entebbe hijacking plot that he had bankrolled ended in defeat, Qaddafi called in terrorists from Latin America, Turkey, and Iran and tried to persuade them to attack the conventions. But even the most desperate and fanatical of the terrorists were opposed to the plan, from the point of view of both its danger and its counterproductivity. Eventually they were able to convince the dictator to concentrate his efforts elsewhere.

Qaddafi openly admitted aiding terrorists while at the same time denying there were terrorists at a nonaligned-nations summit conference in Colombo, Sri Lanka (formerly Ceylon), in August 1976. To the cheers of the representatives of various military dictatorships and Marxist "people's republics," who are euphemistically referred to as uncommitted nations, Qaddafi said he supports terrorism that is equated with "the struggle of a people for independence, for a just cause. . . . If the struggle of the people of Zimbabwe [Rhodesia] is terrorism, then we support this terrorism. In this case, terrorism has another meaning, another connotation. In this case, terrorism means the struggle of a people for independence, it is the support of a just cause.

"If the Palestinian people who have been expelled from their territory in 1948, if their struggle is terrorism, then we accept this accusation and it is an honor to us because we support oppressed and colonized people for the restoration of their land and independence and sovereignty."

Israel struck back at the nations from which the Black September terrorists had departed on their way to Munich. Israeli planes attacked targets in

Lebanon and Syria, and tank-led troops moved into the portion of Lebanon that had become known as Fatahland. The United Nations condemned the Israeli reprisals but refused to condemn the massacre at Munich.

Israel hinted at that time that it might adopt more direct methods of dealing with terrorists, of hunting them down wherever they might be. The news media noted that there was a precedent in Israeli history for that type of thing, citing the time during the 1950s when the Egyptians had imported former Nazi scientists to develop rocket weapons and Israeli agents mercilessly pursued them, running them down with automobiles and bombing and shooting them during their holidays in Switzerland.

"Listen," one Israeli official was reported as saying, "we would infinitely prefer that other countries control and hunt and expel the terrorists. And we will help them. But you can be sure that what they won't do, we will do. And we will do it anywhere in the world that we must." These were the first hints of the Israeli counterattacks carried out by the Mossad assassin teams calling themselves the Wrath of God.

The United Nations, with only a score or so of democratic nations and a huge majority of military dictatorships and people's republics, continued to ignore the problems of terrorism and hijacking, and time after time Black September and other groups struck at Israel and its interests abroad. They also struck at the interests and nationals of other democratic states.

A letter-bomb campaign began in September 1972 and continued through the next month. A total of sixty-four such bombs was mailed by Black September to Israeli diplomats in London, Ottawa, New York, Montreal, Buenos Aires, and elsewhere. Miraculously there was only one fatality, the agricultural counselor at Israel's London embassy. The bombs are sophisticated devices, some made of plastique that can be rolled out into the shape of a sheet of paper and even written on. They explode when opened and have a lethal range of three feet.

A second letter-bomb campaign was launched in November against Israeli business firms overseas. One exploded as it was being opened by the managing director of a diamond brokerage house in London. Fifty-two such bombs addressed to Jewish firms in Europe were intercepted in Bombay and New Delhi. British authorities intercepted twenty, and Swiss police accounted for five.

On December 28, 1972, four Black September gunmen took over the Israeli embassy in Bangkok and held six hostages for nineteen hours. They demanded the release of thirty-six Arab terrorists from Israeli prisons but were persuaded by the Egyptian ambassador to release their hostages for safe conduct to Egypt. A week later Black September set off a bomb in the offices of the Jewish Agency in Paris.

On March 1, 1973, Black September struck directly at American interests. At Khartoum, a going-away party was being held at the Saudi Arabian embassy to say farewell to American Ambassador George C. Moore. In attendance besides Moore were the American chargé d'affaires, the British and French ambassadors, and the Belgian and Jordanian chargés. The guests had just lined up for official handshaking when a Land Rover eased up to the compound's iron-grilled gate. Eight Black September men armed with machine guns and pistols burst in and forced the diplomats back into the building as they tried to flee. Many, including the French and British ambassadors, managed to escape through the garden, but the two Americans, the Belgian and Jordanian chargés, and the Saudi ambassador were held hostage. The terrorist demands were high. First, they wanted all the terrorists held in Jordanian prisons, including Abu Daoud (who had been singing very loudly ever since the Jordanians caught him). They also wanted all the women terrorists in Israeli jails, the members of the Baader-Meinhof gang, and Sirhan Sirhan. This was at least the second time Sirhan's release had been demanded, although there was never any evidence that he was a member of any such group despite his Palestinian background.

All the countries involved refused to negotiate. The Jordanians said they would not "accept any deal with those criminals." The Israelis again pointed out that they did not make deals with terrorists, and the American government also refused. As one career foreign-service officer said, "If one of us has to die, it is better than all of us being subjected to this kind of terror. Giving in to them is definitely not the answer."

Once convinced they could not win their demands, the Black September killers murdered the two Americans and the Belgian diplomat "ritualistically." They then tried to buy their freedom with the Saudi and Jordanian officials but surrendered when the Sudanese government refused. They asked only that they not be executed on the spot. The Sudanese agreed and kept the agreement.

The president of Sudan, Jaafar Numeiry, said the murderers would be tried. He laid the blame for the murder of the diplomats on al-Fatah, represented in the Sudan by Fawwaz Yassin, who had left for Tripoli on a Libyan airliner only hours before the attack on the Saudi embassy. Detailed plans for the operation were found in Yassin's handwriting on his desk after his hurried flight. The actual attack seems to have been led by Abu Salem, Yassin's deputy, but there is reason to believe that Yasir Arafat himself gave the order for the diplomats' throats to be cut. Both Israeli intelligence and the CIA reported picking up a radio communication and hearing Arafat's easily recognizable voice saying after the deed had been done, "I congratulate you and thank you. Long live Arab Palestine!"

Despite the strongly worded determination of the Sudanese president to try the terrorists, they were, in fact, as is the practice in Arab countries, released shortly thereafter.

King Hussein of Jordan reacted strongly to the Khartoum killings by ordering the execution of Abu Daoud and sixteen other terrorists who had been part of the plot against the Jordanian cabinet. But he let himself be talked out of going through with it. Such an event might have had a salutary effect on the practice of terrorists seizing hostages and demanding the release of other terrorists.

Not only was Daoud not executed, but a few months later King Hussein released Daoud and 763 other Palestinians as a "goodwill gesture." Instead of being executed by his PLO comrades whose secrets he had revealed on television, Daoud went back to work for the PLO, mostly on diplomatic chores, with offices in Baghdad. Later he surfaced again as a commander of a PLO unit during the Lebanese civil war.

In October 1973 Austrian Chancellor Bruno Kreisky closed the Jewish Agency's layover facilities at Schoenau Castle, an action that, according to Israeli Premier Golda Meir, "smudged his country's reputation." As an excuse for his action, Kreisky used the fact that two Arabs had seized four hostages in Austria, but the move seems to have been planned ahead of time by Kreisky in collaboration with Qaddafi. Kreisky has maintained an unusually close relationship with Arab leaders and may have used the closing to win concessions from them. He admitted to "suggesting" to the terrorists that they release the hostages in exchange for shutting down the way station for Jews en route to Israel from Russia. Although a socialist and of Jewish descent, Kreisky is close to anti-Semitic groups in Austria and has gone to extraordinary lengths to break all his links with the Jewish religion. He became angry when referred to as a Jew and snapped, "It's none of your business!" at a Dutch journalist who was brash enough to ask, "Are you a Jew?" He would not, of course, be the first person of Jewish heritage to become anti-Semitic. Kreisky personally arranged for a two-engine private plane to transport the two terrorists to Libya. After landing there, one of the two pilots said, "I was persuaded that the Arabs did not wish us ill and that we were in no danger with them because they are people fighting for a just cause."

War once more came to the Middle East on October 6, 1973. While Israelis were observing Yom Kippur, the holiest of their holy days, they were suddenly attacked by the air forces of Egypt and Syria. All the previous wars had come in the middle of a crisis or had been brought on, at least partly, by terrorist activity. The Yom Kippur War came like a thunderbolt out of a relatively clear sky, and for the first time the Arab armies showed some ability. After scouring away with jets of water the huge sand barrier the Israelis had built up, the Egyptians crossed the Suez Canal on pontoon bridges. Their Russian-supplied rockets gave them an initial success against Israeli armor and air power. SAM-2 and SAM-3 missiles had been seen in the area before, but the new SAM-6 forced the Israelis to pay a heavy price at first.

On the Syrian front the fighting followed a similar pattern, with the attacking Arabs regaining ground in the Golan Heights with a massive tank assault and the Israelis falling back for reinforcement. It was at that bleak moment, according to *Time,* that at 10 P.M. on October 8, the "Israeli commander on the northern front, Major General Yitzhak Hoffi, told his superior: 'I am not sure that we can hold out much longer.' After midnight, Defense Minister Moshe Dayan solemnly warned Premier Golda Meir: 'This is the end of the third temple' [a symbolic reference to the first two temples destroyed by invading Babylonians and Romans]. Mrs. Meir thereupon gave Dayan permission to activate Israel's Doomsday weapons. As each [of thirteen nuclear bombs] was assembled, it was rushed off to waiting air force units. Before any triggers were set, however, the battle on both fronts turned in Israel's favor. The 13 bombs were sent to desert arsenals, where they remain today, still ready for use." The *Time* report goes on to suggest that when the Russians learned of Israel's nuclear potential [through a Soviet Cosmos spy satellite] they dispatched nuclear warheads to Alexandria to be fitted on Scud missiles already based in Egypt. The United States, in turn, says *Time,* "detected the Soviet warheads as the ship carrying them passed through the Bosphorus on October 15 and issued a warning to Moscow by means of a world military alert."

While still falling back in Sinai, Israel launched a counterattack along the Syrian front that soon cleared the Arab army out of the Golan Heights and had Israeli armor within twenty miles of Damascus. Instead of pushing on toward Damascus or destroying the reeling Syrian army, the Israelis turned on the Egyptians. Under General Sharon, troops and armor swept out in a wide flanking movement to the south across the Negev, broke through the Egyptian lines, and crossed the Suez Canal in their rear, trapping the entire Egyptian Third Army and endangering the Second. Only a UN-imposed cease-fire on October 22 saved the Egyptians from a catastrophic defeat.

The postwar period saw no diminishing of the terrorist campaign, but it did witness a certain easing of Egypt's position on the continued existence of Israel and a willingness, under the influence of Henry Kissinger, to negotiate at least a partial settlement. Yasir Arafat and the PLO gave lip service to a plan that might possibly include a Palestinian state on the West Bank and the Gaza Strip. Despite the fact that such a state would hardly have been viable and would undoubtedly have become a staging ground for terrorist attacks on Israel, many Western liberals found it worth discussion. There was only fragmentary support for the idea in Israel, and it is difficult to believe that even Arafat took it seriously. The PFLP, the PDFLP, the PFLP—GC, the Arab Liberation Front (Iraq), and the Popular Struggle Front, a hundred-man group on the Jordan's West Bank, all were against the plan, joining in the Arab Rejection Front.

In spite of the proclaimed "new moderation" of Yasir Arafat and the PLO, 1974 saw some of the most savage and costly—in terms of human life —attacks ever launched against Israel.

On April 11, 1974, three Arab guerrillas crept across the Lebanese border into the small Israeli town of Qiryat Shmonah. There they stormed a residential building and killed eighteen people and wounded sixteen more. "They were even armed with rocket-propelled grenades and they were throwing children from the top floor of the building," an Israeli police officer said after the battle was over. Troops rushed in to the rescue and the terrorists, who belonged to the PFLP—GC, blew themselves up with hand grenades. After the victims of the raid were buried, the Israelis launched retaliatory raids into Lebanon.

Three more terrorists struck on May 15, 1974, attacking first a bus carrying Arab women home from work, killing two and injuring a third. Then they entered an Israeli town called Maalot and killed three more people before seizing a school building in which there were ninety teen-agers. They demanded the release of twenty-three jailed terrorists. When negotiations broke down, the Arabs began to slaughter the children. Israeli security forces rushed the school, killing the terrorists, but the death toll was twenty-nine, including twenty-one teen-agers, and seventy were injured. Israeli aircraft struck back at terrorist bases in Lebanese refugee camps, causing fifty deaths and two hundred injuries. The terrorists were members of the PDFLP, and Hawatmeh announced shortly after the raid that it was designed to destroy the Kissinger peace talks, which he said would "mean the surrender of the Palestinian people."

On July 13, 1974, four Arab terrorists shot their way into an Israeli settlement, killing three women before they themselves were killed. Leaflets were found on their bodies identifying them as members of the PFLP. The leaflets demanded the freedom of one hundred imprisoned terrorists, including Kozo Okamoto, the sole surviving perpetrator of the Lod Airport massacre, whose name crops up on most prisoner release lists.

On June 24, three more Arab terrorists entered Israel and seized hostages in an apartment building in Nahariyya. They murdered four people and wounded eight before they died at the hands of Israeli security forces.

"Any government of Israel will do everything in its power in order to cut off the hands that want to harm a child," Golda Meir had said following the Maalot masacre, and time after time Israeli planes hunted down the terrorists in their nests.

Many American observers, among them newsmen Dana Adams Schmidt and William J. Drummond, have cast doubt on the deterrent value of such raids, but the period that saw the greatest growth in the terrorist organizations and resulted in the most casualties along the Israeli borders was the period when it was Israeli policy not to retaliate. Also John Laffin reports that when he spoke to terrorists or former terrorists, they remembered the Israeli air attacks as the worst part of their careers, particularly terrifying because the Israeli planes "always seemed to know where to find us."

Israel does not view the counterattacks only as a deterrent: they are also revenge. "Thou shalt give life for life, eye for eye, tooth for tooth," says the Book of Exodus. The Koran speaks in much the same way, the Prophet commanding in Sura II, "O believers, prescribed for you is retaliation touching the slain; freeman for freeman, slave for slave, female for female."

In each case Israeli retaliation brought condemnation from the United Nations, which at the same time ignored the original act of terror that provoked the counterattack. Then on October 8, 1974, in its most shameful act since its founding, the UN General Assembly voted by 105 to 4 to invite Yasir

Arafat to address it, and on November 22 it voted overwhelmingly to back the Palestinians' right to "national independence and sovereignty" and awarded the PLO observer status.

The attacks against Israeli citizens continued on into 1975, the deepest penetration taking place early in March. It came during Henry Kissinger's peace campaign to win acceptance by Israel and Egypt of his step-by-step negotiations. Eight terrorists in a rubber raft dropped off by a fishing boat landed near a sewage outlet on the edge of Tel Aviv. Armed with rapid-fire Kalashnikovs and high-explosive charges, their destination was Tel Aviv's Municipality Youth Center, where they hoped to seize a number of children to hold as hostages. That their main objective was the disruption of the peace talks was evident from the words scrawled in English on their raft: *Kissinger's Efforts Will Fail.*

An Israeli policeman spotted the eight gunmen shortly after they entered the city, and he opened fire, aided by an off-duty soldier. The terrorists turned their guns on a crowd of people leaving a movie house. Then they forced their way into the Savoy Hotel, dragging a wounded comrade with them, and took a dozen guests hostage. They made the usual demands for the freedom of imprisoned terrorists, adding this time the name of the Melchite Catholic Archbishop Hilarion Capucci, a Greek national who had been caught smuggling guns for PLO members. The Israelis rushed the hotel; seven of the eight Arabs were killed, but not before they murdered several of the hostages. Three Israeli soldiers and five civilians were dead when the affair was over. The only survivor of the gang was an Arab named Hamid Nedim, and he said they were from al-Fatah. They had been told to say that they came from Egypt "so we could make it less smooth between Israel and Egypt." They had sailed from Lebanon and had been trained in Syria. The attack had been carried out on the personal order of Yasir Arafat, who just five months before had been talking about peace before the United Nations. He apparently launched the raid to block the peace talks and to refurbish his image among Arabs on the West Bank, who were coming more and more to look to King Hussein for help rather than to the PLO.

The Israelis, probably because they thought Arafat was hoping to provoke them into counterattacking, refrained from carrying out retaliation raids against the terrorist bases in Lebanese refugee camps. This caused an attack in the Knesset from Menahem Begin, who, oddly enough, had once used the Savoy Hotel as a hideout when he battled the British and Israeli governments as the leader of the Irgun.

The UN General Assembly, on November 10, 1975, voted seventy-two to thirty-five, with thirty-two abstentions, to brand Zionism as a form of racism. The Israeli delegate observed that it was hard to believe that the United Nations, which "began its life as an anti-Nazi organization, should thirty years later find itself on its way to becoming the world center of anti-Semitism."

An "infamous act," the vote was called by U.S. Ambassador Daniel P. Moynihan, who went on to say, "The General Assembly today grants symbolic amnesty—and more—to the murderers of the six million European Jews. Evil enough in itself, but more ominous by far, is the realization that now presses upon us—the realization that if there were no General Assembly, this could never have happened. In all our postwar history there has not been another issue which has brought forth such unanimity of American opinion."

While protesting in the United Nations against terrorism has been of little use in stopping such actions, the Israelis have found another way of dealing with it. The warning issued following the Munich massacre that Arab assassins would be hunted down and killed was not an idle threat. And so, to deal with the problem, Ha Mossad's "Wrath of God" came into being.

It first struck back at the leaders of terrorist gangs in Beirut on July 8, 1972, just a few weeks after the Lod Airport massacre. Ghassan Kanafani, editor of *Al-Hadaf,* an underground resistance newspaper, and a top PFLP leader, was their target. The PFLP had its headquarters in Beirut, and its offices could not be distinguished from any of the banks or other enterprises in that city. The terrorists had set up shop in Lebanon the way they had in Jordan prior to the 1970–71 war. John Laffin visited the headquarters and wrote in the *Spectator* (August 30, 1975): "To visit these offices, occasionally opulent, is a strange experience. Some have an armed man on the door, but once he is negotiated, the pretty office girls, the filing cabinets, telephone calls, paper-covered desks, and calendars on the walls all lull one into the belief that here is a normal business. But the end product of all the discussion and interoffice memos is violence. . . . I once saw a note, in English, on the desk of a departmental chief in Beirut, 'If we could kill ——, we could terrify the entire Jewish population of New York.' "

So it was at the heart of this bureaucracy of murder that Ha Mossad was striking when it aimed at Kanafani. Asked by a Western correspondent during an interview if death had a meaning for him, Kanafani said, "Of course death means a lot. The important thing is to know why. Self-sacrifice, within the context of revolutionary action, is an expression of the very highest understanding of life, and of the struggle to make life worthy of a human being."

Kanafani's life ended on the morning of July 8, 1972, as Mossad agents watched. Israeli frogmen had swum ashore at night near the city and been met by two Mossad agents resident in Beirut, who guided them to an automobile owned by Kanafani. The next morning Kanafani came out of his house accompanied by his sixteen-year-old niece, Lamees, and got in the car. A radio signal was activated and a bomb exploded.

Kanafani's widow, Anni, a Dane, talked to Gerald McKnight about what had happened. "On the morning of the assassination we all sat longer than usual drinking our Turkish coffee on the balcony. As always Ghassan had many things to talk about. . . . Before leaving for the office, he fixed the electric train for our son, Fayez, and his two cousins. Lamees, Ghassan's niece, was to go downtown with her uncle—she never got there. Two minutes after Ghassan and Lamees had kissed us goodbye there was a dreadful explosion.

"All the windows in the house were blown out. I ran down, only to find the burning remains of our small car. We found Lamees a few metres away; Ghassan wasn't there. I called his name—then I discovered his left leg. I stood paralysed, while Fayez knocked his head against the wall and our daughter Laila cried again and again: 'Baba, Baba. . . .'

"But I still had a small hope that maybe he was only seriously injured. . . . They found him in the alley beside our house and took him away—I had no chance to see him again. . . ."

Anni Kanafani also recalled that the day before, they had all gone to the beach. "We were eight people in the car—it could have happened that day. . . ." She saw Ghassan as a hero, as "one of the Palestinian revolution's great martyrs." She said, "Love of life necessitates violence. Ghassan wasn't a pacifist. He was killed in the class-struggle like Karl Liebknecht, Rosa Luxemburg, Ernst Thälmann, Lumumba, and Che Guevara. As they loved life—so did he. Like them he saw the necessity of revolutionary violence as self-defence against the oppression from the exploiting classes."

Kanafani's successor as editor of *Al-Hadaf* was his friend Bassam Abu Sharif, who had led the hijackers during the Dawson Field extravaganza and had been photographed sitting on the wing of a destroyed plane with his clenched fist raised in triumph. Like so many other leaders Sharif learned his political terrorism at Beirut's American University and has expressed the violent philosophy of the PFLP and Black September. "Why do we do it? Why does Black September exist? What are the reasons for so many young men to take up arms and dash people to death—sometimes to lose their own lives doing it? Do you think Palestinians love to kill? Of course not."

He told Gerald McKnight, "I am committed to killing to save my people. It may take a fifty- to a hundred-year struggle, but even so it is the only solution. There will be no other. Even if a peace is implemented, even if the Israelis surrender the occupied territories, this has to be the outcome. . . . Violence must decide what is and what will be. The bullets I shoot are not the bullets used to exploit and subdue. They are just the opposite. They will remove exploitation inflicted upon me. . . ."

Bassam Abu Sharif had not escaped the notice of Ha Mossad. A book in which a bomb had been planted had blown up in his hands. He had lost the sight in one eye and part of that in the other; his face had been scarred and pitted with shrapnel; four fingers and most of a thumb had been blown off. According to a former CIA man, Sharif had fled in terror following the attack, landing in Britain with a Syrian passport, then going on to Ireland, then to Algeria, and back to London in his efforts to throw off the Mossad men who he was sure were stalking him.

Ha Mossad used terrorist institutions as well as individuals as targets, and on October 3, 1972, they blew up the Palestinian Library in Paris. This was followed by a more important action in Rome the same month. Their target was Wadal Abdul Zuaite, a thirty-eight-year-old Palestinian posing as a translator at the Libyan embassy. Like most diplomats sent out by Qaddafi's government, Zuaite was actually a Black September terrorist with connections to the Italian publisher and terrorist leader Feltrinelli. The Israelis believed that it was Zuaite who had planned to blow up the El Al 707 with a bomb placed in a tape recorder given to two young English girls, plus other terrorist attacks, and they were determined to execute him. On the evening of October 16, two Mossad agents, using specially adapted Beretta long-barreled 22-caliber semiautomatic pistols, opened fire on Zuaite as he was returning to his apartment. Twelve bullets struck the terrorist, and he died instantly. The two agents escaped in a car, which they abandoned shortly thereafter.

Acting for the Black September in Paris, Carlos killed a Syrian journalist, Khader Kano, an Israeli informant, and Ha Mossad retaliated by executing Dr. Mahmoud Hamshari.

Abdul Kheir was Black September's contact with the KGB. Determined to break that contact, Ha Mossad caught up with him on January 23, 1973, in his swank Cyprus hotel suite. A short time after parting from his opposite number in the KGB, the terrorist agent entered his hotel room and flicked on the light switch, triggering a bomb that killed him instantly.

On January 25, Black September murdered a Mossad agent in Madrid and also struck at Ha Mossad in Cyprus when an Israeli businessman was murdered. The killers then attacked the home of the Israeli ambassador and tried to hijack an Israeli plane. Then they killed an El Al guard in Rome. All this was in revenge for the execution of their KGB contact man.

On April 6, 1973, Ha Mossad executed an Iraqi law professor named Basil Koubaissi, the PFLP's top agent in Paris, and over the next three months they also disposed of Black September agents in Paris, Cyprus, Beirut, and Rome.

Another action, one of Ha Mossad's most daring and successful, took place in April 1973. Thirty Israeli commandos, some dressed in mufti, others in the camouflage uniforms favored by *fedayeen,* landed at Dead Man's Beach outside Beirut at one o'clock in the morning. They were led by Mossad agents driving Avis rental cars who drove them and their weapons into the city, where they scattered and began a lightning-quick campaign to "liquidate the terrorists wherever they exist," as Moshe Dayan had phrased it.

The headquarters of the PFLP was blown up by one group. Three file cabinets filled with Black September secret papers were taken and lifted out by helicopter. Two posh apartment houses on fashionable Verdun Street were raided and three Black September supreme leaders were executed—Muhammed Yussif al-Najar, number-two man in al-Fatah and Arafat's long-time associate; Kamal Adwan, director of Black September's operations in Israel; and Kamal Nasser, chief spokesman for the PLO. They also killed fourteen other terrorists or associates, including Najar's wife, who tried to shield her husband with her body.

The Arabs once again had been rocked back on their heels. The Wrath of God had struck them down in their own "state within a state." Angry crowds poured into the streets demanding to know why the Lebanese army and security forces had stood by while Israelis ranged freely through the capital of the country. Saeb Salam, the pro-Palestinian Muslim premier, submitted his resignation in protest over the failure of the army to act. Faced with the shame of this latest defeat, the Arabs blamed the United States for the attack. It seems to be a psychological necessity for Arabs to believe they are being assaulted by forces more powerful than Israel, and the United States has become the scapegoat. Following Egypt's defeat in the Six-Day War, Nasser had made up the story that waves of planes from American and British carriers had actually won the war. Now it was the Americans who had executed terrorist leaders.

"The enemy didn't come from the sea, he came from the U.S. embassy!" mobs shouted at the funerals of the slain terrorists. Yasir Arafat vowed to carry out "terrible reprisals" against the United States and went on to claim that Armin Meyer, former U.S. ambassador to Lebanon, and President Richard Nixon were behind the scheme to wipe out his men. "There is a Zionist-American conspiracy to liquidate the Palestinian people physically," he said.

Golda Meir was pleased by the sensational raid. "We have killed the murderers who were planning to murder again."

Information obtained from the stolen Black September files led to the execution of Mohammed Boudia, the Paris chief Carlos succeeded. The Black September struck back by hiring American "Black Power" gunmen to kill Col. Yosef Allon, the Israeli air attaché in Washington, D.C. Allon was shot from ambush at his home one evening as he returned from a diplomatic party in Georgetown.

Ha Mossad's worst failure, and one that still rankles its officers, was the attempt to kill Ali Hassan Salameh, who helped plan the Munich attack. Salameh's father had been killed during the mandate period when the Hagana blew up his headquarters, killing him and most of his gang. Salameh, who hated the Jews for that, was married to a member of the Husseini family. His wife was a direct descendant of the Grand Mufti and had been raised in the very center of profascist, anti-Semitic beliefs in the Middle East. Because of several blunders and betrayal by a double agent, the Mossad squad thought it had found Salameh in Norway and killed the wrong man, an Arab waiter named Ahmed Bouchiki.

On December 23, 1974, Ha Mossad struck again, this time using cars that appeared to have large boxes in the baggage racks on their roofs. The boxes actually contained rocket launchers, and the cars were parked on streets facing the PLO headquarters located on one of Beirut's busiest boulevards and the PLO research center near the rue Sadat. Triggered by radio signals, the launchers sent salvos of rockets crashing into both buildings, wrecking the headquarters and badly damaging the research center. Five terrorists were wounded in the attack.

During July 1975, Ha Mossad again struck in Beirut, this time under cover of the civil war raging in Lebanon. Two teams of six people each were chosen for the mission, an assassin team and a spotter team to pick out the targets. The assassins, five men and one young woman, went in first, storing their guns and other gear aboard a Bell 205 helicopter of the Israeli air force. Throughout the flight, they kept their faces covered so that even the crew could not get a good look at them. With a second helicopter acting as gunship, they flew in under the radar and landed near Beirut. Mossad agents were waiting with rented cars to drive them to a safe house in the city. A one-word coded message was then sent back to headquarters, and the spotter team went in by motor torpedo boat and rubber dinghies. They, too, were met by resident agents and taken to cover.

A week passed before the spotter team located the target, three Popular Democratic Front leaders, who were followed for another week before the assassination squad was called in. Lying in wait with Berettas until the three leaders came out of an apartment house in the company of another man, they opened fire, killing one and wounding two others.

Meanwhile, the spotters had marked a top PFLP leader for execution. Using "starlight" telescopic sights, the Mossad agents picked him off from a nearby rooftop as he appeared in the window of his apartment. They ended their raid by planting an explosive charge in the basement of a building used by the Popular Democratic Front. The charge was set off on June 29, killing six and wounding thirteen other terrorists.

The latest intelligence on Ali Hassan Salameh came to light in January 1977 during the furor created by the arrest in Paris of Abu Daoud and his abrupt release on a series of specious technicalities. Packed off to Algiers by the French, Daoud was greeted as a hero.

As for the French, there was nothing heroic about their action. Other Western nations were outraged, and Israelis in Tel Aviv bombarded the French embassy with stones and rotten eggs. There were calls for a boycott of French goods and travel to France by congressmen and American Jewish leaders, and President Jimmy Carter said he was "deeply disturbed and very much surprised" by the French action.

As for Daoud, he had entered Paris with a fake Iraqi passport to attend the funeral of Mahmoud Saleh, who was the fourth PLO representative to have been murdered in Paris since the Munich Olympics. Meanwhile, according to intelligence sources, Salameh was said to be lying in a Beirut hospital, more vegetable than human, after being shot up by Israeli agents in cooperation with Lebanese Christians. Other sources say that he was dead. If he is not, he will never have a moment's rest from fear that the Wrath of God will eventually overtake and execute him for his crimes.

Terrorism, spawned in the Middle East, has come to encompass the rest of the world. It is financed by incredibly large sums of money—$90 million a year from Qaddafi alone, plus bonuses for particularly bloody work. In addition to the Libyan money, there is another $265 million a year in oil money from Algeria, Kuwait, Saudi Arabia, and others, plus more millions from donations and extortions from Palestinians as well as money from the West.

Arab money and Arab arms (or rather, Soviet arms supplied by Arabs) and training in their use are available to terrorist groups all over the world. The Arabs have been in the business of exporting terror since the mid-1960s, but their network remains almost impossible for Western intelligence agencies to crack, because of a lack of cooperation among them and restraints placed on them by their own governments. Only Ha Mossad, which operates without restraint, has had any success in its counterattacks against them.

Interpol has been of some help through its information service but has come under attack by pro-Arab forces in the West because of this. It has been particularly under fire in the United States, where Senator James Abourezk of South Dakota (he has been called the senator from the PLO) and others have called for an investigation of the organization. In California, the American Civil Liberties Union and certain members of the state legislature have attacked it. Without information or cooperation, the efforts of intelligence agencies of the West are limited. The terrorists know this and, since their defeats by Ha Mossad, may have decided to transfer more of their operations to softer targets in the rest of the free world.

The preamble to the credo of international terrorism was delivered in P'yongyang, North Korea, by George Habash in 1970. During the symposium on revolutionary strategy organized by the North Korean Workers' Council, he told four hundred wildly cheering delegates, "There are no political or geographical boundaries or moral limits to the operations of the people's camp. . . . In today's world no one is innocent, no one is a neutral."

This theme has been accepted by most terrorist groups. Anyone anywhere in the world is a potential victim. "We teach terror in our classrooms," Habash has said. "The main thing is to have people always expecting terrorism."

There are people everywhere who are willing to help terrorists. Many Arab embassies and consulates serve as safe houses. Help in the form of financial assistance is also forthcoming from the secretariat of the World Council of Churches. Bishops and priests have been known to transport arms, and several European monasteries are considered safe havens, notably one at Cuxa near the Franco-Spanish border. Brussels, Zurich, Milan, and Stockholm as well as Paris and London are hotbeds of terrorist activity.

The actions and inactions of the United Nations and its units, such as UNESCO, are supportive of terrorism. Daud Barakat, accredited to the United Nations from the People's "Democratic" Republic of Yemen, helped to plan many of Black September's most vicious crimes and was among those who coordinated the Munich massacre operation. When Yasir Arafat addressed the General Assembly, congratulatory letters poured into PLO headquarters in Beirut from terrorists all over the world.

The Fourth International, a Trotskyite–New Left worldwide group, preaches terror. Its leading theoretician, Ernest Mandel of the University of Brussels, urges "active participation of our comrades in armed insurrections designed to destroy the established order whether in Ireland or Latin America." The Fourth International maintains particularly close ties with terrorist groups in South America, where it has been instrumental in convincing the guerrillas to switch from rural to urban guerrilla warfare. Its philosophy follows Carlos Marighella's statement, "The urban guerrilla's only reason for existence is to shoot."

On the weekend of October 1–3, 1971, terrorist leaders met at a symposium in Florence, Italy. It was held at a Roman Catholic Jesuit institute, a symbolic setting considering that the Jesuits were the terrorist shock troops of the Counter-Reformation. Jesuit assassins killed Henry of Navarre and William the Silent and nearly succeeded in one of their numerous attempts on the life of Elizabeth I of England. At the 1971 meeting, there were representatives of sixteen groups, including the IRA, Argentina's Ejército Revolucionario del Pueblo (ERP), the People's Revolutionary Army, various Palestinian organizations, and Basque separatists.

The symposium was arranged by the millionaire publisher Feltrinelli, who wanted to establish a working relationship between the IRA and Italian terror groups such as Lotta Continua, which he financed. Feltrinelli's connections with terrorism are still clouded in mystery. There is no question that he was deeply involved with the terrorist underground while living the social life of the chic revolutionary. The Florence meeting made it possible for the groups to make arrangements to exchange ideas, money, weapons, and even assassins.

Feltrinelli was not above murder himself, as evidenced by the fact that the gun used to murder the Bolivian counsul in Hamburg was traced by Interpol to the Italian publisher. The murder was either committed by Feltrinelli or ordered by him. Another killing he was connected with was that of a wealthy Peruvian named Banquero, which occurred in Lima in 1972. Again the gun was traced to Feltrinelli. Evidence of the activities of this dangerous dilettante lies hidden in the police files of a dozen countries. In the end he was killed when a bomb he tried to plant at an electric power station outside Milan exploded prematurely. At his funeral, Regis Debray, another dabbler in revolutionary terror, said that Feltrinelli was killed by the CIA, a charge that is monotonously repeated whenever terrorists accidentally do themselves in.

Up until 1975 Lebanon seemed the most liberal and open country in the Middle East. With a population that was about 55 percent Muslim and 45 percent Christian, it was the only place where a non-Muslim minority was decently tolerated in a Muslim society. It was often called the Switzerland of the Middle East, a neutral island in a sea of turmoil and violence. Beirut was a sophisticated city with good hotels and restaurants, a banking center for the Middle East, and a headquarters for Western corporations.

The happy state of the country, however, was more superficial than real. There had been a cancer gnawing at its vitals ever since leftist leader Kamal Jumblatt had been instrumental in bringing Palestinian terrorists into Lebanon in large numbers. Once in the country, they founded a state within a state from which they could operate freely against Israel and international targets.

The delicate balance of Lebanese democracy had been established by a "national convenant," an unwritten formula that divided power among all the minorities—Christian Maronite, Greek Orthodox, Greek Catholic, Armenian Orthodox, Armenian Catholic, Sunni Muslim, Shiite Muslim, and Druze. The president was always a Maronite Catholic, the premier a Sunni Muslim, the speaker of Parliament a Shiite Muslim, the commander in chief of the armed forces a Maronite, and so on down to minor cabinet posts and lesser officials. The covenant had worked since Lebanon won its freedom in 1943, although there had been a Nasser-inspired civil war in 1958, during which American troops had been landed, and another flare-up in 1968 caused by the Palestinian terrorist presence.

Basically the Left in Lebanon was, and is, Muslim, while the Christians are pro-Western. A large part of the American press has taken the Palestinian side in the crisis, accepting the propaganda that paints Christians as being right-wing or even fascist. *Los Angeles Times* reporter Joe Alex Morris, for instance, constantly refers to Palestinian terrorists as "commandos," a highly inaccurate term because commandos are regular, uniformed troops fighting for an established country. Morris also uses the terms *right-wing* and *extremist right-wing* for Christians and, for some reason not quite clear, refers to the largest Christian party as *Falangist* (perhaps to suggest a connection to the Fascist party in Spain of the same name) rather than the proper spelling *Phalangist.* The press also attacks Pierre Gemayel, founder of the Phalangist party. One story recently in *Newsweek* says that he returned from the Olympics in 1936 so impressed with Hitler that he formed a party based on the Nazis. Another story says his admiration for Mussolini was the reason for his creation of the party. The authoritative *Political Dictionary of the Middle East in the Twentieth Century,* however, refers to the Phalange as a group that seeks "to preserve the liberal, democratic, and Christian character of Lebanon" and to its leader Gemayel as "one of the principal figures to speak out openly against Palestinian guerrilla-terrorists using Lebanon as a base for their raids and to oppose their growth as an independent establishment within Lebanon."

With the help of Kamal Jumblatt and the Cairo Agreement of 1969, the Palestinians have not only become an independent establishment but a state within a state ruled by the gunmen of al-Fatah and the PFLP. So complete was this dominance in southern Lebanon that it became known as Fatahland. The refugee camps and the areas outside them where the Palestinians had congregated were Mao's "sea" in which the terrorist fish swam. Those areas were so totally under the control of terrorists that the Lebanese army and security forces dared not go there. The Palestinian refugees, in effect, had been turned over to the terrorists to be exploited in any way they saw fit. It was this condition, along with Muslim efforts to change the covenant, that led to civil war in the mid-1970s.

The first fighting between Christians and Muslims apparently took place on April 13, 1975, following the murder of a Phalangist leader by terrorists, probably the PFLP. A busload of *fedayeen* invaded a Beirut Christian district and was fired on by Phalangist militia; twenty-seven Palestinians were killed. Other clashes followed in May, June, July, and September, and at times there were as many as twenty thousand gunmen of various groups in action in the capital city. The three-thousand-man security force was totally unable to restore any semblance of order, and the sixteen-thousand-man army was held out of the action in the beginning, when it might have been able to make some headway, because Muslim leaders feared its largely Christian officer corps would interfere on the side of the Phalangists or other Christian groups. The country's plunge into anarchy was stayed briefly by nervous truces, but each one ended when gunmen on one side or the other opened fire again. In the first six months of fighting, in a country containing 2.5 million, more people were killed than in all six years of the "troubles" in Northern Ireland.

Following the first outbreak of hostilities, Arafat maintained that his PLO remained neutral and left the main part of the fighting to local groups. There is reason to doubt this, and, certainly, the PFLP, the Popular Democratic Front, and the PFLP—GC were heavily engaged on the leftist side. If it held back at all, al-Fatah was busy supplying arms to leftist militias.

In the beginning, the leftist forces were far more numerous and better armed than the Christians. Arms were provided to the Left not only by the PLO but by Syria, Libya, Algeria, and Iraq. Egypt and Saudi Arabia may have sent some arms to the Christian side to prevent a complete takeover of the small country by the Left.

Arms are easy to buy anywhere in the Middle East for anyone with money, and both sides seem to have been generously supplied with funds. The Christians received theirs mostly from Lebanese living abroad. The Maronite Christian Phalange Movement and the National Liberals, led by ex-President Camille Chamoun, received money from Egypt and Saudi Arabia as well, at least in the early stages. Qaddafi, according to *Newsweek,* "wrote out a check for $40 million" in August 1975 to be spent on weapons for the leftist forces. Other money was said to come from the Soviet Union, funneled through Communist parties in various Middle Eastern countries, and both Iraq and Syria were generous with funds in the beginning.

Fighting continued through the latter part of 1975 and the early months of 1976, with the Palestinians taking an increasing hand on the side of the Lebanese leftists, and the Christians were slowly forced back. During a particularly vicious phase of the fighting, Beirut's modern hotel skyscrapers became strongholds—the Holiday Inn, the Excelsior, the St. George, and Phoenician Intercontinental becoming the Vimy Ridges and Argonne Forests of this new kind of urban war. The Muslims succeeded in taking most of the skyscrapers and steadily forced the Christians back into the city's Ashrafiyeh area and other Christian strongholds. Water and electricity were cut off in large parts of the city, and the civilian population huddled in homes and apartments, making desperate forays out into streets to find food, a practice that became increasingly dangerous. As al-Fatah became more involved, the Lebanese army, which had not been used as a unit to maintain order, began to divide between the two sides and heavier weapons came into play. Rockets and artillery made the city a slaughterhouse, and tanks appeared on both sides.

When it began to seem that the Left was about to win a total victory, which could have led to wholesale massacre of the defeated Christians, President Suleiman Franjiyeh sent a desperate message to the United States for aid. Secretary Kissinger's answer was to send L. Dean Brown, a "highly regarded Arabist," to attempt to mediate. The choice of Brown, who was on record as saying that "Israel is not a viable state," must have been very encouraging to the Left in Lebanon.

Christian counterattacks cleared the Karantina slum area, which was strategically vital because of its proximity to two bridges that linked Beirut to the Christian north. The last defenders of the Karantina made a stand in a macaroni factory as some three hundred Christian militia men attacked. When two Palestinian prisoners were sent to arrange a surrender, the Muslims killed them and the Christians attacked with a barrage of rocks, grenades, and small arms until resistance ended. The Muslim inhabitants of the area were rounded up, the buildings were burned down, and the whole section bulldozed over. There were unconfirmed rumors that Muslim men were massacred in the Karantina fighting.

The Muslims sought revenge in the capture of a prosperous, thriving Christian town on the coastal highway twelve miles south of Beirut. Fortunately most of the twenty-seven thousand inhabitants had fled before the Muslims began a wholesale slaughter of those who remained. Several thousand trapped civilians fled to the nearby beach, where fishing craft and two gunboats tried to rescue them under heavy fire from the Muslims.

The situation was complicated at this time by an event that seemed certain to bring about a total destruction of the Christian community but which instead meant its temporary salvation. In the last week of January 1976, following a meeting between Yasir Arafat and President Assad of Syria and a public reconciliation between Arafat and Habash (they even embraced for a photograph), the first units of the PLA crossed into Lebanon. As noted before, the PLA is controlled mostly by Syria and staffed by regular Syrian army officers in large part. The Yarmuk Brigade, the shock troops of the PLA, quickly seized control of most of the countryside and drove the Christians back toward the sea. The intervention by Syria raised Lebanon to a position that observers called a potential "confrontation state" on Israel's northern border and "raised grave new doubts about the future course of Middle East peace negotiations." The Syrians avoided a showdown with Israel by keeping their troops north of an imaginary "red line" that the prime minister of the Jewish state had laid down. Assad followed this with a declaration of his intention of enforcing a truce between the two sides that would lead to negotiations.

Like all the other truces, the Syrian truce broke down when the forces of the PLO massacred Syrians and pro-Palestinians in Sidon during early July. Fighting then broke out between the PLA and the extreme Left in Lebanon. The Palestinians, who only a short time before had seemed to be within sight of total victory and who had announced that "we are masters of all strategic points," suddenly found themselves confronted by the forces of a nation that had been their strongest supporter in the Middle East. The reasons for the Syrian change of sides is still not clear, although in March 1976 there were reported signs of a cooling-off between it and the Soviet Union, and Syria probably did not want to risk the confrontation with Israel that might have ensued if Lebanon had come under total control of the Palestinians and their leftist allies.

The Syrian reversal tipped the scale against the far Left. Also aiding the Christians was the fact that both Syria and Israel had begun blocking arms shipments to the Muslims in Lebanon, and Israel had started to ship some small arms to the desperate Christians. Syrian tanks and artillery were now assisting the Christian counterattacks.

That the Muslims had intended to destroy the Christian community totally seems clear from the words of President Assad quoted in a *New Republic* article by John Kimche. "They [Kamal Jumblatt, the Palestinian leaders, and the Muslim Leftist commanders] said to us—let us continue the march for another two weeks. We shall purge the villages and the [Christian] areas. Details were discussed, the names of the mountain villages and the cities in the plan were mentioned."

Instead, Assad proclaimed that the Syrians had moved into Lebanon in order "to protect every oppressed person regardless of his religious denomination, to confront any aggressor or oppressor regardless of his religious claims." He left no doubt that he then considered the aggressors to be the so-called Progressives—Kamal Jumblatt, the Palestinian "revolutionaries," and the Muslim "traders in religion." They were, he said, conspiring against the Arab nation.

Since the Syrians had stayed well clear of the Israeli security zone, south and east of the Hasbani and Litani rivers and the Mount Hermon area that had been known as Fatahland, the Israelis were content. "Matters have developed in such a way today that the Syrians are now the saviors of the Christians, at least for the present," Prime Minister Rabin said.

Habash, Arafat, and Hawatmeh were horrified to discover that Syria had "crossed to the other side," and Arafat and Hawatmeh hurried to Damascus to plead with Assad. They came back with another peace agreement. The agreement broke down before the ink was dry, and on the morning of their return, there were 208 killed in Beirut, a record for one day.

Habash was enraged. He said he had learned the lesson of Chile: "Violence is the only way of settling the contradictions of Lebanese society." He called on the Lebanese to confront the threat presented by the Syrian presence.

Fighting escalated between the Syrians and the Palestinians. The most violent clash was in Tripoli, Lebanon's second city, where al-Fatah terrorists battled with units of the PLA and al-Sa'iqa. Arafat issued a communiqué condemning all acts of "violence by the PLA and Sa'iqa" and sent a cable demanding that the PLA withdraw from the city.

Speaking to a Labour audience in Tel Aviv, Yitzhak Rabin said he had "detected a recent change in Syria's position that could open possibilities for Middle East settlements. Syria is now in a state of war with Fatah and . . . during the past week its forces in Lebanon have killed more Fatah men than the Lebanese had in the past two years." The Syrians had, in fact, he said, "liquidated Fatah terrorists in such cruel ways which, if employed by Israel, would have brought a hue and cry from the world community." The speech was looked on by leftists as proof that Syria was carrying out an American-Israeli scheme to crush the PLO.

By June 1976, one out of every two hundred Lebanese had died in the fighting and another half million, or one out of every six, had fled the country. June saw the murder of the American ambassador and another diplomat by terrorists and the alleged arrest by the PLO of the killers, who purportedly were being held for trial by the Arab League security force that had been called on to replace the Syrians in the country.

In July a force of twenty-three hundred Arab League troops arrived in Lebanon and found themselves as helpless as those who preceded them to solve the problem. There were by then fifteen thousand Syrian troops in the country and the Christians were on the offensive against the Palestinian refugee camps. Equipped with Israeli arms and helped by the Syrians, the Christians were carving out an area that could become a Christian canton in the event of partition. They captured the Jisr Basha refugee camp in East Beirut and then closed in around Tal Zaatar.

Some of the most violent fighting of the war took place at Tal Zaatar, but the Christians slowly got the upper hand after two delegations carrying flags of truce had been shot down by the terrorists. "We did this so that there would be no temptation later in the battle to contemplate surrender. By deceiving the enemy crying wolf, we closed the door on any possibility that our white flag would be honored."

There were thousands of civilians trapped in Tal Zaatar, and they were prisoners of the terrorists as much as they were of the Christians. Two women who managed to escape told reporters that the terrorists were killing anyone who tried to escape and were determined not to surrender. When a Red Cross convoy was permitted through the Christian lines to evacuate the wounded, hundreds of refugees tried to flee with the withdrawing trucks. The terrorists fired on them, shooting down dozens of their own people rather than let them go. Finally, with the arrival of another Red Cross convoy, thousands of desperate, starving refugees streamed out of the camp and fled toward Christian lines under fire from both sides. Tal Zaatar fell shortly afterwards and was bulldozed out of existence by the victorious Christians.

The defeated PLO was in bad shape. Its leadership had been forced to leave Damascus for a safer haven in Baghdad. In Kuwait, the government was cracking down on them, and in Jordan their bank accounts had been frozen.

Arafat was still able to bluster, however. "The battle of Tal Zaatar is a victory for the revolutionary will of the Palestinian revolution." Another leader said, "We have not been weakened. We are healthier than before." A spokesman of the PFLP again accused the United States of inspiring a plot to crush the Palestinian movement, using Syria, Saudi Arabia, and Israel as its tools.

For Israel, the war had been a blessing. It had brought about the clearing of Fatahland and the replacement of Fatah forces with Israeli-armed and -trained Christian forces. The Syrians appeared to be trying to change even the leadership of the PLO. The Fatah Militant Committee was set up in Damascus and demanded a meeting of the PLO council to elect new leadership. "The PLO," said Defense Minister Mustafa Tlas of Syria, "has turned its back on Palestine to get involved in Lebanese politics."

Even some of the PLO leaders seemed to think their popular support was fading in the Arab world. Salah Khalaf said, "Even nine months ago, I had ordinary citizens in Kuwait ask me: 'Do you want to do in Kuwait what you are doing in Lebanon today?' "

The arrival of new Arab League peace troops and a truce that for once seemed to have some chance of success during October 1976 left the situation at least suspended for several weeks, but there can be no doubt that the terrorists had been severely hurt by events in Lebanon.

Writing in the *New Republic,* David Pryce-Jones compared the heyday of PLO power, when Arafat had stood before the United Nations and been cheered, with the situation today:

> Quite why Western journalists and diplomats took Arafat at his word is a mystery best left to some ironizing Gibbon of the future. It was they who projected the false image of Arafat as spokesman for a militant mass, when in fact the two or three million Palestinians are tragically fragmented and bemused by Middle East politics, and permit the PLO to represent them only by default. . . . Perhaps the United Nations cloudbursts of rapture and the ignorant groveling of Westerners had assured Arafat that he really was an independent factor in the Middle East equation. Did not the French foreign minister shake his hand in public? Do not Senators McGovern and Percy—to say nothing of Arafat's representative in the Senate, James Abourezk—still designate him as the recipient of the West Bank? . . . And all this at a time when refugees in Lebanese camps cursed his name. Of the 10,000 men whom the PLO may have had on the rolls, perhaps half are left, frightened and isolated men, to whom the Popular Front is now once more appealing to stand and die.

Shortly after takeoff from Athens on June 27, 1976, the passengers and crew of Air France Flight 139 were surprised to hear the excited voice of a woman coming over the plane's internal communications system. Speaking English with a heavy German accent, she was saying that the plane had been hijacked by the Che Guevara arm of the Gaza Unit of the PFLP.

The speaker was Gabriele Kroecher-Tiedemann, whose last known terrorist episode had been the kidnapping of the OPEC oil ministers in Vienna.

Now wearing a dark wig, she was dressed in a dark blue denim skirt, light blue blouse, blue stockings, and flat-heeled shoes. She had taken a position at the front of the plane, a pistol in one hand and a grenade in the other. Standing next to her was Wilfried Boese, another old comrade of Carlos, who was in charge of the operation. At the rear of the plane were two Arabs, also armed with pistols and grenades, who were later identified as Fayez Abdul Rahim Jaber and Jayel Naji al-Arjam. As founder of the Heroes of the Return, Jaber was an experienced terrorist and was believed to have planned the Rome attack on the Pan American airliner in December 1973.

There seems little doubt that this hijacking was planned by Carlos and Wadi Haddad, and the reason for it, other than the usual ones of trying to free imprisoned terrorists and harassing Israel, may have been to take the world's attention from the worsening situation in Lebanon and to put heart into the badly battered Palestinian forces.

As the plane headed toward an unknown destination Gabriele ordered the 244 passengers to raise their hands above their heads and not move. For the next three hours, the passengers were individually searched in all the intimate parts of their bodies.

At three o'clock that Sunday afternoon the French airbus landed at Libya's Benghazi Airport after circling the field a half-dozen times. Boese, who was described as a "thin, elegantly dressed man," picked up the microphone and told the passengers that the new "captain" of the plane was Bazim el-Nubazi, the leader of the Gaza Unit, and that the plane would not respond to any message that did not address it as "Haifa." While the plane was being refueled by a ground crew that seemed to have been expecting it, the hijackers broke out two boxes of hand grenades and wired them to the emergency doors. Prior to takeoff again, a woman passenger who was six months pregnant and feeling ill was allowed to leave the plane. When the plane was airborne, Boese said, "We're Palestinians. We're going to take you where we please."

The five-hour flight to Uganda's Entebbe Airport was uneventful. One hostage described Gabriele as the toughest of the lot. "She walked up and down the aisles, scratching her wig with one hand, holding a grenade [with the safety pin removed] with the other and ordering everybody to keep quiet." Passengers who wanted to use the toilets had to lift a finger and wait for her to shout her permission. Once when two passengers stood up at the same time, she screamed like a "veritable animal." The hostages took an immediate dislike to her for the way she pushed, threatened, and yelled "Schnell!" ("Hurry!") all the time. "She was a real Nazi," one hostage said.

When the plane landed at Entebbe, it was obvious to the hostages that Ugandan soldiers had been waiting for them. They quickly surrounded the plane and stood staring up at the windows. A few minutes later, the hijackers were joined by four more terrorists carrying submachine guns, rifles, a Beretta pistol, and dynamite. The leader of this new group was Antonio Bouvier, the Ecuadorian national who had taught Carlos guerrilla tactics at Camp Mantanzas and later shared safe houses with him in London.

Nine hours after landing, the 256 hostages were herded into an abandoned terminal lounge and sticks of dynamite were put "all over the plane." Some time later a huge black man in a comic-opera field marshal's uniform, cowboy hat, and Israeli paratroop wings pinned to his tunic made an appearance. "Some of you may know me," he said. "I am Field Marshal Dr. Idi Amin Dada, President of Uganda."

Amin was a disturbing presence to the Israelis. He had defended the Munich massacre in a message to UN Secretary-General Kurt Waldheim: "Germany is the right place where, when Hitler was prime minister and supreme commander, he burnt over six million Jews. This is because Hitler and all German people knew that the Israelis are not a people who are working in the interest of the people of the world, and that is why they burnt the Israelis alive with gas in the soil of Germany."

Now this admirer of Hitler held the fate of more than a hundred Israelis and other Jews in his hands. He had wanted to build a monument to Hitler in his capital and would have done it if the Russians had not objected, reminding him of their own problems with *der Führer*. A vociferous champion of Arab causes ever since he abruptly severed relations with Israel in 1972, Amin has received generous financial aid from Libya, Kuwait, and Algeria.

Amin seemed quite pleased with the situation as he personally "welcomed" the hostages to his country. Blankets and food had been waiting at the airport for the hostages, and Amin walked among them, beaming at the women and patting the children on the head as he assured everyone that he would do what he could to make their stay "as nice as possible." But the hostages knew that he was not their friend. They had seen him meet the plane and embrace the terrorists, and now his own soldiers were guarding them along with the terrorists. Boese even had a Ugandan chauffeur to drive him around the airport and to a nearby town.

The most terrifying moment of the whole affair came when the hijackers began separating the Israelis and Jews from the rest of the passengers. "Israelis to the right," Gabriele commanded. To many of the elderly it was like Germany all over again. Adding to the realism was the little Nazi, threatening and yelling *"Schnell!"*

Then came the demands: the release within two days of forty "freedom fighters" imprisoned in Israel, including Archbishop Capucci and Kozo Okamoto, and thirteen others imprisoned in France, Switzerland, West Germany, and Kenya. The French were pleased to report that one prisoner the hijackers named, Ampara Silva Masmela, a former girlfriend of Carlos, had been released at the end of 1975. This added more weight to the theory that Carlos was logistically involved in the hijacking.

The hijackers warned over Radio Uganda that their hostages would be killed and the airbus blown up unless their imprisoned comrades were delivered to Uganda before the deadline.

On the second day, forty-seven elderly women, children, and sick hostages were released and flown to Paris, a gesture, said the terrorists, that was inspired by the humanitarian pleas of President Amin.

Just two hours before the deadline expired, an urgent message from Jerusalem was relayed to Entebbe. It said that Israel was ready to negotiate for the release of the hostages. For the first time, Israel appeared to have yielded to blackmail, a point that terrorists will not soon forget. Elated by the news, the hijackers extended the deadline another three days and released another hundred hostages.

During all the time they were held in Entebbe, only an eight-year-old boy among the hostages suggested there might be a chance that the Israeli army would rescue them.

At first it seemed that Israel had no other recourse but to capitulate. "If we accept the hijackers' conditions, the Palestinians will escalate their terror and no Israeli leaving the country will be safe," Prime Minister Yitzhak Rabin said to General Mordechai Gur, Israel's chief of staff, "but do we have a military option?"

"At the moment, we don't have a military option," Gur said, and went on to explain that he did not have sufficient intelligence data to offer one.

Nevertheless, troops were alerted and a full round of intensive training was begun in the hope that the necessary intelligence would materialize. The troops were from the Thirty-fifth Airborne Brigade and infantrymen of the Golani Brigade—"the best of the best," one Israeli officer called them. Placed in field command was Lt. Col. Yonatan Netanyahu, an American who was taken to Israel by his parents at the age of two.

Appeals were made by Israel for help in gathering intelligence. French and British security men interviewed the released hostages and obtained considerable vital information concerning the situation at Entebbe. The Pentagon supplied aerial-reconnaissance and satellite photographs of the airport. Black clandestine Israeli agents, either hired by Mossad men in Africa or recruited from among the black Jews who had immigrated to Israel from America several years earlier, were infiltrated into the Entebbe area and the airport itself. Discreet contact was made with the reasonably friendly government of President Jomo Kenyatta of Kenya. Arrangements were made to refuel planes returning from a raid to Entebbe and for medical personnel to stand by at the Nairobi airport to treat the wounded.

Now it was decided there was a military option. The freeing of 147 hostages had left a more manageable number to take out, and intelligence indicated that the terrorists were keeping lax security. The planned assault was practiced repeatedly until the time that would be required on the ground had been shaved down to an incredible fifty-five minutes.

At two o'clock on Saturday afternoon, July 3, nineteen Israeli cabinet ministers, some of whom had walked to the meeting to avoid breaking the religious ban on driving on the Sabbath, assembled in the Tel Aviv cabinet room to be briefed on the raid by Rabin, who strongly supported the military action. An hour and a half later, the vote was a unanimous yes and the meeting ended with a prayer.

Moments later the commandos took off from a desert air base near Sharm al-Sheikh at the mouth of the Gulf of 'Aqaba. The strike aircraft were two propjet Hercules C-130 and two Boeing 707 jets. The Hercules jets were the assault planes; one Boeing was the command plane and the other, which was to remain at Nairobi, the hospital plane.

Heading down the Red Sea with an escort of Phantom jets, which accompanied them as far as possible before turning back, the four planes parted company as they approached the Nairobi landing pattern. The hospital plane landed, and the other three descended sharply for their run to Entebbe. The leading Hercules informed the Entebbe tower that it was an Air France airliner bringing freed terrorists to exchange for hostages. The second Hercules identified itself as an East African Airways flight expected at about that time. Both received permission to land. The 707 command plane circled overhead.

At eleven o'clock, in the pale light of a moonlit night, approximately 150 commandos (the exact number is classified) swarmed down the rear ramps of the giant planes in jeeps and lightweight armored personnel carriers and raced for the old terminal building a half-mile away.

With split-second timing, the Israelis cut down the hijackers and Ugandan soldiers standing outside the building and burst into the area where the hostages were sleeping. Yelling *"Tishkavu!"* ("Lie down!"), they opened fire on the terrorists in the room. One of the first killed was Gabriele. Suddenly Boese came charging into the room with a submachine gun in his hands. He looked wildly about him, his gun swinging into firing position at the huddled hostages.

A hostage, Ilan Hartuv, told what happened next. Just when it seemed that Boese would pull the trigger, he spun on his heels and ran outside, firing into the darkness until he was killed by Israeli bullets. Hartuv believes that Boese's decision was caused by a conversation he had had the night before with Yitzhak David, a survivor of Buchenwald. "This is what your fathers did to me," David told Boese, showing him the concentration-camp number tattooed on his arm. "I've been telling my sons that your generation of Germans is different. How am I going to explain to them what you're doing to us now?"

Three hostages were killed, and Mrs. Dora Bloch, left behind in the hospital, was later murdered on Idi Amin's orders. The rest of the hostages ran to the waiting planes, while the commandos fought briefly with Ugandan soldiers and totally destroyed Amin's air force of a dozen MIGs, to forestall pursuit—an unnecessary effort since no Ugandan pilots know how to fly the Soviet fighter jets. Only fifty minutes elapsed between the landing and the takeoff, and as the freed hostages wept and prayed, one woman kept crying out, *"Ness! Ness!"*—"A miracle! A miracle!"

In Israel, there was wild jubilation mixed with sorrow for the slain hostages and the death of Colonel Netanyahu, the only commando killed in an operation that took the lives of seven terrorists and more than twenty Ugandan soldiers. Antonio Bouvier was the only terrorist to escape the commandos' harsh judgment.

Defeated once again on the field of battle, the Arabs turned to their favorite forum, the United Nations, for help. They demanded condemnation of Israel for the raid, and Kurt Waldheim, whom the *Washington Post* has called the "Afro-Arab bloc's Charlie McCarthy," obligingly denounced Israel, as did various other governments, including Mexico.

Others saw it differently. George F. Will wrote in his syndicated column, "Israelis may be the only people in the East who still understand that it is dangerous to be hated but doubly dangerous to be despised. If Israel's policy of prickly self-respect is contagious, people who say the West will preserve Israel may have things backward."

David Bomberg, president of B'nai B'rith, said that on the two-hundredth birthday of the United States, the Israelis had given a gift to the world. That gift was the Eleventh Commandment: "Thou shalt not bow down to terrorism."

"The basic principle is to fight the terrorist wherever you have a reasonable chance," Prime Minister Rabin said. "You fight them in Zion Square in Jerusalem or you fight them in Entebbe, but you fight. You don't give in."

British Tory politician Rhodes Boyson said that the Israelis had "done more for the rule of law in two days than the United Nations has done in twenty years."

In Kenya one group of villagers offered a $120,000 reward for Idi Amin's head—literally—on a platter.

In the United Nations, the United States and Britain firmly defended Israel, but no other Western nation spoke up. Israeli Ambassador Chaim Herzog refused to accept any guilt. It was not Israel but its enemies who should be accused. "In the dock before us stand the representatives of all those countries who stood and applauded the entry into the hall of the General Assembly of a gun-toting terrorist [Arafat], who, according to the president of Sudan, personally gave the order to execute the American and Belgian diplomats bound hand and foot in the basement of the Saudi Arabian embassy in Khartoum on 1 March, 1973," Herzog said. "Before us stands the rotten, corrupt, brutal, cynical, bloodthirsty monster of international terrorism."

The Security Council condemnation was dropped when it became clear that too many states had decided to abstain for the Arab-African resolution to pass. Defeated the same day, however, for lack of votes was a resolution by the United States and Great Britain to condemn terrorism.

What seemed a major defeat for international terrorism in Lebanon in July appeared in November to have been only one more episode in the history of Middle East terrorism. Arab League intervention had saved the terrorists from catastrophe even more devastating than Tal Zaatar and Entebbe. A Palestinian-Syrian agreement was concluded on October 29 that had major implications for Middle East conflict. Palestinian *fedayeen* were pouring back into Fatahland. They were moving through the Syrian-held Bekaa Valley to staging areas near the Israeli borders from which new terror raids could be launched. The secret agreement between Arafat and Assad would once more turn the terrorists toward Israel.

"This is a significant development," one terrorist leader said. "In conjunction with the Syrian-Egyptian rapprochement and the Cairo summit resolutions, this means that the Arabs are once again prepared to fight the real enemy—Israel."

A spokesman for the PFLP said, "Everybody is sending fighters now, including us."

It would take time for the Arabs to build up a terrorist presence in Fatahland to equal the five thousand they once had there, and Israeli Defense Minister Shimon Peres warned that a "red line" existed some miles north of the Israel-Lebanon border that would bring intervention if crossed by the Palestinians.

Israel had for some time been arming and training Christians along the border area to form a buffer between itself and the terrorists. Weapons up to, and including, tanks and artillery were supplied, and the Christians seemed determined not to permit the area to again become a Fatahland stronghold. Moshe Dayan, however, was calling for stronger measures. "In my opinion there is only one way to close the door before the terrorists come to the southern area of Lebanon. The Israeli government should send a military force into that area."

After eighteen months of brutal fighting, with about forty thousand deaths and fifty-seven failed cease-fire agreements, the Lebanese situation seemed to be right back where it started as 1976 came to a close. By February 1977 a compromise had been worked out among Arafat, Assad, and Lebanese President Elias Sarkis that authorized the Palestinians to concentrate their forces in an area between Nabatiyeh, Tyre, and Sidon, a triangle stretching to within twenty-five miles of Beirut in the north and eight miles from the Israeli border in the south.

Two months later, Palestinian guerrillas had captured several Christian strongholds in south Lebanon on fronts all across the narrow strip north of the Israeli border. Aided by pro-Syrian al-Sa'iqa guerrillas under the leadership of Zuheir Mohsen, Palestinian terrorists captured the town of Deir Mimas, less than two miles from the frontier. Deserted by President Assad once again, Christian leaders pleaded with Arab peacekeepers to save the "life of a sisterly nation." They asked that the 1969 Cairo agreement regulating the presence of armed Palestinians in Lebanon be implemented by force. Camille Chamoun warned that if the Palestinians were allowed to remain in the south, "I don't know what the outcome will be, whether it will degenerate into an all-out war again in Lebanon, or into a war with our neighbors, the Israelis."

Chamoun's warning was emphasized by Zuheir Mohsen, whose strength among the Palestinians was second only to Arafat's. In fact, it was Mohsen who helped Arafat plot the PLO's strategy when the Palestine National Council met in Cairo in mid-March 1977. Interviewed in Cairo at that time, Mohsen outlined the plans for a renewal of terrorist raids into Israel. "We can attack from outside Israel's borders," he said. "Where we find Israeli targets, we will attack them." He saw no immediate hope for renewed Geneva peace negotiations. "Politically, the whole [Middle East] area can do nothing in the coming three years. Egypt, Jordan, and Syria can do nothing but wait, maybe a long time, in order to change the balance of forces in the area. That is the only way to convince the United States to be more serious in trying to create peace."

The Palestinian National Council, which functions as the PLO's "parliament-in-exile," again failed to soften its stand on the basic question of Israel's right to exist. Although the operative word was *moderation*, the council still refused to revoke the portion of its national convenant that calls for the destruction of Israel.

Faruq al-Qaddumi, the PLO's unofficial foreign minister, tried to explain what was meant by moderation: "By moderation, we mean we are ready for peace and working toward that end. We are demonstrating this by saying that we are ready to establish a state on a part of our territory. In the past we said no—[we wanted] all of it, immediately, a democratic state of Palestine. Now we say no, this can be implemented in stages. That's moderation."

The stages, he explained, would begin with a return to the 1967 frontier, then to the borders of 1948; and finally there would be the democratic state of Palestine. The timetable is the essential difference between the moderates and the hard-liners. The rejection front still adheres to the old "everything-right-now" line, while the others are willing to dismantle Israel by stages. There is no disagreement over the ultimate goal. A communiqué issued after the conference even suggested that the new Palestine state would help repatriate Israelis to the countries of their origins. Some non-Zionist Jews would be allowed to remain.

As far as some kind of confederation with Jordan before any future Geneva talks would convene, as Sadat suggested during his talks with Secretary of State Cyrus R. Vance the previous month, Qaddumi explained that a link with Jordan could come only after the Palestinians had established their own independent state on the West Bank of the Jordan River and the Gaza Strip.

In Washington, meanwhile, President Jimmy Carter was contributing to the confusion with a series of gratuitous comments that had both the Arabs and the Israelis in a tizzy. In an off-the cuff greeting to visiting Israeli Prime Minister Rabin, Carter observed that a United States goal in the Middle East is "that Israel might have defensible borders." As used by Israeli officials, *defensible borders* is a code phrase that has come to mean former Arab territories that have been occupied by Israel since the 1967 war.

In the midst of the furor created by this gaffe, Carter explained that his original remarks were "just semantics" and went on to add more semantics in a clarifying statement that suggested Israel should withdraw to the 1967 borders with only "minor alterations" (a favorite Arab code phrase that means the return of all seized lands except for some modifications along the border between the West Bank and Israel where villages were divided by the 1949 armistice lines).

Speaking before the Palestinian National Council, President Sadat flatly rejected Carter's suggestion of "minor" adjustments. "It is not admissible that some should speak of this Israeli notion of secure boundaries," he said. "We should not yield one inch of our land. I repeat for all to hear. We should not yield one inch of our land."

Playing on themes certain to win the approval of the 244 delegates in attendance, Sadat reaffirmed Egypt's support of the PLO as the "sole representative of the Palestinian people." Egypt and the other Arab states, he promised, would not see them out at Geneva. "The Palestinian people are not called upon to give up their rights," he said. "They are not required to make any concessions of any sort. It is not acceptable that Israel, which is the aggressor, should try to keep those people out of the framework of peace. This is rejected by us fully."

A few days later, Carter touched off another controversy when, in response to a question at a town hall meeting in Clinton, Massachusetts, he said, "There has to be a homeland provided for the Palestinian refugees who have suffered for many, many years." In Arab rhetoric, *homeland* signifies that the Palestinians have a legitimate claim to Palestine. "It is a progressive step," Arafat told reporters, "because it means he has finally put his hand on the heart of the problem of the Middle East crisis. If it is true what he said, it helps the whole situation in the area."

That evening Carter shook hands with a PLO official at a United Nations reception. No American president and no senior American diplomat had broken the long-standing policy of no talk or contact with the PLO. When White House and State Department spokesmen hastened to explain that the president's remarks and the handshake should not be interpreted as a change in American policy, Arafat complained that "President Carter has gone back on what he said. This has left a rather bad impression among the members of the Palestine National Council, particularly since it came only twenty-four hours after he declared that Palestinians are entitled to a homeland."

Contributing his own brand of confusion to the situation, Arafat said that some delegates to the council "wanted us to say yes to Geneva while some wanted us to say no. If we say no to Geneva we would close the doors, and if we say yes to Geneva they would know our price. That's why we didn't say yes or no to Geneva."

The council issued a tough but vaguely worded fifteen-point program that gave Arafat and his Executive Committee a mandate to maneuver almost at will in future peace talks with Israel. While the text of the mandate was obscure, most likely to mollify hard-liners like Habash who opposed any peace talks with Israel, it was broad enough to give Arafat virtually a free hand in any international negotiations, including Geneva talks. Although Habash voted against the declaration for peace talks because it indirectly implied recognition of Israel, he pledged to remain with the PLO for the sake of unity.

In Jerusalem Israeli officials were quick to point out that the council's resolutions were extremist and reinforced Israel's refusal to negotiate with the PLO. In a radio address Foreign Minister Yigal Allon said that the council's resolutions provided Israel "with new material to prove our basic thesis that the PLO . . . did not change its attitude. We can use this material as further foundation for our argument that the PLO is not a representative of any faction in the Arab world."

On May 9, 1977, on the day Carter met with Assad in Geneva for a meeting that had been billed as largely a get-acquainted session, Allon announced that in order for Israel to have defensible borders, it must make large areas of occupied Arab lands a permanent part of Israel. There could be no going back to the frontiers that existed before the 1967 war. Permanent new frontiers, he said, must be drawn where Israel can maintain the strength to protect itself from its enemies.

Later that month, Shimon Peres, the Labor party's candidate for prime minister, was defeated by the right-wing Likud party, whose leader was Menahem Begin, the old Irgun terrorist who was perhaps the last man President Carter would have picked to represent Israel at Geneva.

In a way, however, aside from the banking scandal that plunged Rabin from grace, Carter's indiscreet remarks had contributed to Begin's election. There is no question that many Israelis interpreted the new attitude of the United States as increasingly uncooperative if not downright antagonistic. "There was a change in the U.S. administration and our people were not sure what to expect from them," Peres said.

If Israelis were looking for someone to take a hard line in future peace negotiations, they had found the right man in Begin. He lost no time in making his views known. Nor did Carter.

At almost the same time that Begin was being interviewed in Tel Aviv for ABC's *Issues and Answers*, President Carter was telling an audience at the University of Notre Dame that "we expect Israel and her neighbors to continue to be bound by UN resolutions 242 and 338, which they have previously accepted." These resolutions support a peace settlement that guarantees both Israel's right to exist and the return of Arab territories occupied by Israel since its military victory in the 1967 war.

Begin described Carter's proposal as a revival of a plan offered by Secretary of State William P. Rogers in 1969. Begin said that Golda Meir had then characterized the proposal as treasonous for an Israeli leader to accept.

"On this we have a national consensus," he said. "It is not only the point of view of the Likud, but of all the parties except the Communist, to reject unconditionally and under any circumstances that proposal." Israeli withdrawal from the West Bank, he said, would bring every major city and town in Israel into range of conventional artillery. "It is just inconceivable that we would agree to such mortal danger to our mothers and sisters and women and children," he said.

"As far as this so-called Palestinian state is concerned . . . we cannot allow, we cannot afford such a danger. Six million Jews in one generation were killed. We don't want to see our children and women massacred again in our time. It is a matter of our lives." As for the PLO's recognizing Israel's right to exist, Begin said: "We don't ask the so-called PLO to recognize our right to exist. We got our right to exist thirty-seven hundred years ago. Those killers who come to kill our children, we do not ask to recognize our right to exist." Despite his hard line, Begin said he was in favor of reconvening the Geneva conference. "I am ready to lead the Israeli delegation and to speak on behalf of Israel and Zionism."

And so, as matters stood in early spring of 1977, nothing had changed. If anything, the situation was more desperate than ever. The prospect for greater violence was manifest in the strident declarations of the various terror-ist leaders. The caldron of hate, bigotry, envy, and anger was bubbling on the front burner, ready once more to boil over in mindless terror against Israel and free people everywhere. Israel had no choice but to remain vigilant and ready to respond in kind not only against terrorist acts but against attacks from any of its Arab neighbors, as it has done all these years, and will have to continue doing for as long as it wants to remain a free nation.

BOOK THREE

THE PEOPLE'S WAR OF ULRIKE MEINHOF

In the end, when all else had failed, her final weapon was her own life. It is ironic that Ulrike Meinhof, the most famous woman in postwar Germany and a gifted journalist, would have committed suicide on a day when the presses stood still in the Republic. Only one German-language newspaper, the *Neue Zuericher Zeitung,* announced the "ending" of her "consistent way of life," which "had appeared to be destined for something better."

For a brief moment, street battles raged again. Once more Molotov cocktails were thrown at helmeted policemen, evoking memories of the late 1960s, when Ulrike Meinhof had been the archetypal intellectual heroine of the Ausser Parlamentarische Opposition (Extraparliamentary Opposition or APO) student movement. There was rioting in Frankfurt am Main, and bombs exploded in branches of German firms and institutions in Paris, Rome, and Toulouse, but it was only a token protest. Even in the APO capital of West Berlin, where thousands had hit the streets in 1968 following the shooting of Rudi Dutschke, only a few hundred protested the "murder" of Ulrike Meinhof in prison.

Some three thousand mourners turned out for her funeral. Many wore masks or had painted their faces white, and they carried banners reading *Justice Terror* and *Murder in Jail.* Graveside speeches compared her to Rosa Luxemburg, the German Communist revolutionary who was murdered in Berlin by German soldiers in 1919. Meinhof was called "a symbol of hope for the oppressed" and one of Germany's greatest postwar writers. Leaflets described her suicide as "her last combat measure." In a reference to other terrorists in West German jails, the leaflets added, "Ulrike Meinhof is dead. Let's rescue the living."

"Who doesn't resist, dies; who doesn't die, is buried alive." This was what she said about the hunger strike that was to destroy her health and her will to survive. She had been buried alive forty-seven months when she chose death.

Like all ideologically driven revolutionaries, she had waged total war against a society that she considered corrupt and oppressive. At first her lucid prose had illuminated the evils of capitalism in the most prosperous and powerful society in Western Europe. She was greatly admired among politically disillusioned intellectuals who were wrestling with the hedonism of a "materialistic" society. Thousands of students secretly carried her photograph in their pockets.

217

But this New Left movement, like others everywhere in the Western world and Japan, was essentially an idealistic middle-class struggle on behalf of a proletariat that was excluded from its ranks. Its rhetoric was far too sophisticated to appeal to workers, and when it turned to a fiery polemic, the obsessive violence that accompanied it alienated just about everyone. It was a *Volkskrieg* ("people's war") carried out by a handful of fanatics to appease their own hatred.

At the time of Meinhof's death, her own radical formulations had become so convoluted that hardly anyone understood her. The formulations, like her death (whether suicide or murder), were no more mysterious than many another facet in the life of this woman, who had started out to be a nun and became instead her country's most wanted criminal.

Ulrike Marie Meinhof, born on October 7, 1934, in the provincial industrial town of Oldenburg, was six years old when her father, a museum director, died of cancer. Psychiatrists would later try to interpret her transformation in terms of childhood traumas, regarding it as significant that her father's death came shortly after he had experienced severe depressions brought on by his wife's infidelity. "One can conjecture," says Friedrich Hacker, a psychoanalyst who has studied the terrorist mentality, "that there may have been a connection in the mind of the child between her mother's marital indiscretions and her father's death."

A more plausible explanation may be found in the fact that she was the only member of her terrorist gang old enough to have lived through the heyday of the Third Reich. From the paternal clerical side of her family, she received a Christian moral consciousness, and from her mother's side, a drive for social change, evidenced in the refuge this democratically oriented family gave to Communist resistance fighters at a time when the penalty for deviation was the most grievous imaginable. This readiness to subvert the state may have conditioned her to respond decisively in actions she considered right and justifiable.

A pretty little redheaded tomboy, Meinhof had a mercurial personality even as a child, her moods quickly alternating between serious and mischievous. Her mother was an art teacher, and Ulrike attended a Roman Catholic parochial school. For a while she even contemplated becoming a nun, but after her mother's death, she was reared by a foster parent, Professor Renate Riemeck, an idealistic academic who guided her path toward liberal causes. Ulrike compiled outstanding academic records at several schools, completing her studies in Munich, where she studied sociology and philosophy.

It was in the Catholic stronghold of Münster that she first became politically involved. In the 1950s she headed the local committee of the movement opposed to nuclear weaponry. One of the leaders of the ban-the-bomb movement was her mentor Renate Riemeck, who was already playing a leading part in the pacifist Left. Ulrike's brilliant mind and aggressive debating manner brought her to the attention of Klaus Reiner Roehl, the publisher of the magazine *Konkret* in Hamburg, which was just then emerging as the voice of the student Left.

Roehl was to give a new direction to her life. She started to write for the magazine, moved to Hamburg, became editor in chief of *Konkret,* and married Roehl in 1961. A year later she gave birth to twin daughters, Regine and Bettina. In many ways, she was the Gloria Steinem of the German media: a glamorous writer and noted television polemicist. Her columns were some of the best political journalism of the 1960s.

As the star columnist for *Konkret,* which had become West Germany's most popular New Left magazine, Ulrike took passionate issue against all forms of violence. To her amazement, she found that she was suddenly a celebrity. The Roehls were the darlings of the Hamburg literary establishment and were lionized by the journalistic salons.

What was unknown, of course, was that both were secret members of the Communist party. In his memoirs published in 1974, Roehl admitted that *Konkret* was secretly financed by Communist funds to the tune of 1 million marks, which were funneled in devious ways through Prague. The deal had been privately arranged by Klaus and Ulrike in East Berlin, and they kept in contact with their control officers by slipping across the border for periodic visits. Yet there were no strings attached and no hard political line was pursued. In fact, they were free to indulge in all the subcultures of the West German *Schickeria* ("radical chic"). The style was more *Playboy* than *Pravda* —pubic hair and hippy poetry were sprinkled judiciously among weightier fare to lighten the intellectual load. From time to time the editors even criticized their benefactor.

The Roehls lived in a villa in the snobbish Blankenese district. She wore boutique dresses, hobnobbed with the smart set, and was invited to all the elegant parties. The Roehls enjoyed all the bourgeois comforts and luxuries a materialistic society can bestow on those it favors. Outwardly, at least, she seemed happy with her new life.

Then in 1965 a silver clamp was inserted into her brain to ease the pressure from a tumor. Some psychiatrists think that this is another factor that may have triggered her personality change. They see the silver clamp as the main cause for her Jekyll-Hyde transformation.

Exactly when she became disenchanted with her life is impossible to pinpoint. As more nudes, pornography, and crime stories began to fill the pages of *Konkret* to revive its faltering circulation, she gradually turned her attention to the misery of social groups on the periphery—the real victims of the capitalistic system. "She knew she was living a lie," says Renate Riemeck, "cavorting with the rich and yearning to liberate the poor."

Klaus could bridge this disparity with cynicism. "Enjoy capitalism," he would tell her. "Socialism will become difficult." But this kind of fatuous rationalization was impossible for Ulrike, for as the Hamburg weekly *Die Zeit* noted at that time, "Her honesty, also against herself, spoke from every line she wrote."

Klaus considered his status a reward for his efforts. "Okay, I was a Socialist, but I also wanted to eat and drink well, go to the beach, and so on. She would have no part of it." It was about this time, according to Peter Ruhmkorf, a friend of Klaus, that Ulrike learned that her marriage was no match for the "swinging life" of petit-bourgeois playboys and liberated females. The Hamburg scene was typically what Lenin had denounced as "the infantile Left." It was the grotesque spectacle of the new Ruhr rich being titillated by the idea of capitalism's demise. "But with Ulrike," says Ruhmkorf, "action was as decisive as her thoughts were inexorable and radical."

One evening at a gathering in their Blankenese villa, Roehl exhibited a small-caliber pistol, a Landmann-Preetz, to his editors and some visiting student extremists. In his memoirs, he recalls how it was passed from hand to hand "like some newly forged weapon at a gathering of primitive tribal chieftains." One fondled it in his lap, would not let it go, and just wanted to know if "it really shoots? Real bullets? And they can really knock somebody off?" They went out into the garden and fired wildly at bottles and lamp bulbs until the neighbors threatened to call the police. "We were all in the romantic phase of our Viva Maria! world," says Roehl, who was referring to the cinema's two glamorous revolutionary Marias, Jeanne Moreau and Brigitte Bardot.

Ulrike wearied of theoretical chitchat. She longed to liberate the poor, but violence and guns still horrified her. Roehl's teen-age brother, Wolfgang, once took a walk in the woods with Ulrike and suddenly pulled out a pistol and began firing random shots in the air. Ulrike became hysterical, collapsing into a paroxysm of tears. She was on the verge of a nervous breakdown and would not talk to Wolfgang for a full year. Klaus assigns two reasons for this overreaction: her "Christian pacifism" and the "constant terrible head pains" she suffered after her brain operation, which left her with a "panicky fear" of even the tiny noise of a child's toy pistol.

But her hatred of the political system was stronger than her fear of guns and loud noises. The disgust she felt for her way of life became unbearable. In 1968 Ulrike sued her husband for divorce and moved to West Berlin with her two daughters. This marked the start of her tumultuous polical crusade.

Since her school days, the political scene had changed radically. A coalition ruled in Bonn; there was no opposition in parliament. The APO came into being in 1966 and confronted the government with bloody battles. Under the guidance of its chief theorist, Rudi Dutschke, the APO took a radical oppositional stance toward the government. The existing society was pictured as inhuman and decadent.

The antiauthoritarian student movement, which had spread from America, had found a center in the Free University of West Berlin. The movement was combined under the name of the students' party, Sozialistischer Deutscher Studentenbund (SDS), which was also under the leadership of Dutschke. However, not all SDS members endorsed "Red Rudi's" policy of nonaction: "Go into the courts of the bourgeois society, become a part of the courts, but don't become one of the society. If later we who have the right conviction of the new society are enough, we can change the bourgeois society in a revolution from above with the help of our natural confederate, the proletariat."

When the 1968 revolt spread from West Berlin to universities in West Germany, some representatives of the establishment justified the movement by arguing that without the student revolt the College Reform Act would never have been passed. The student revolt in West Germany, as elsewhere in Europe and America at that time, mirrored the revolutionary groups in the Third World. Revolutionary violence against dictatorship and "terror from above" in the Third World served as an example for dissident youth and as a justification of their own violence against a democratic society.

It was an anti-American, anti-Vietnam, anti-imperialism, antiestablishment movement formulated along an orthodox Marxist-Leninist line. The revolutionaries saw themselves as part of a world revolutionary movement to abolish the "power of people over people." Gradually it evolved into an antiauthoritarian formula that formed a link between anarchists and Communists.

An elaborate ideology was evolved by the more radical members that was based on half-baked ingestions of Hegel, Marx, Lenin, Mao, Ho Chi Minh, Vo Nguyen Giap, Bakunin, Carlos Marighella, Régis Debray, Stokely Carmichael, Eldridge Cleaver, Herbert Marcuse, Che Guevara, and Jean-Paul Sartre, who underlined the true meaning of Frantz Fanon's ideology: a guerrilla fighter slays his enemy. In that act of pure violence there is a double act of liberation: the victim has been freed from his false role, and the victor has freed his own spirit for authentic manhood. It is a dialectic concerned solely with life and death. And—most important—death is life. It gives them the necessary rationalization for murder. It is *Burn, baby, burn* German style and studded with the American idioms *cool, high, right on,* and *off the pigs.* Germany, like Japan, its twin in consumer productivity, has a tragic tradition of idealistic philosophy wedded to the death wish. It turned urban guerrillas into Romantic poets of blood and death.

In a brilliant essay in *Encounter* (June 1975), Melvin J. Lasky points out that it was a number of years before Ulrike could transform herself into an urban guerrilla:

> Patty Hearst learned to fondle her machine gun in something under ninety days, but in California everything grows fast, and indeed the precepts of Marxian-Maoist revolution can evidently be learned there in an overnight crash course. Ulrike had to be sure that Hegel (and the True Laws of History) was on her side; and of this she reassured herself by her exegetical study of the writings of Herbert Marcuse, whom she still rereads and recommends to other comrades from her book-lined prison cell. She had to be sure that Late Capitalism with all its Imperialist contradictions was now in its absolutely final and mortal stage; and she took time to read the financial pages on exports, imports, and the movements of capital to convince herself that the end was nigh. She had to be certain that

the organized working-class, with its reformist trade-union leaders, was a lost potential; and that therefore a small remnant of the faithful had to rise up and act on their own, but in the name of oppressed and bewildered masses yearning for authentic freedom.

The word *fascism* rolled easily off the tongues of young APO rebels, who rose against a society that had been halfheartedly patched together by their elders. Ulrike, who was frustrated by the futility of words, was irresistibly attracted to the more militant youths. She devoted herself to the plight of the underprivileged, and wrote a series of articles on children brought up under the terrible conditions of institutions run by the state. The articles were later collected in book form under the title *Bambule.*

Ulrike continued to write for *Konkret,* but her life-style suffered as radical a change as her politics; she went from radical chic to fanatical militant, from high society to the subculture of shabby, hashish-smoking hippie. She created an artificial proletarian way of life, complete with naked light-bulbs in her apartment, although she was receiving $10,000 a year for her articles.

The stage was set on the night of April 2, 1968, when two Frankfurt warehouses were fire-bombed as a protest against the Vietnam War. The four arsonists (Andreas Baader, Gudrun Ensslin, Thorwald Proll, Horst Sohnlein), all APO members, were captured, and Ulrike, at the invitation of Horst Mahler, a young attorney, went to see the prisoners. She was deeply impressed by these young people who had taken the final step in divorcing themselves from society. She caused a sensation by approving their act of political arson: "The progressive aspect of warehouse arson consists not in the destruction but in the criminality of the deed, in the legal violation."

Speaking in court on their reasons for the arson, Gudrun Ensslin said, "I'm not interested in some burned mattresses. I only want to talk about the burned children in Vietnam."

Ulrike was immediately attracted to this young woman. Gudrun was a moralist like herself. She was born on August 15, 1940, the daughter of a Lutheran pastor in Swabia. A gifted student who was educated on a scholarship from a charitable foundation, she studied English and philosophy in West Berlin and passed her teachers' examinations. An early liaison with a student, the son of Will Vesper, a famous Nazi writer, had ended tragically: she bore his child and he later committed suicide.

Gudrun was now Andreas Baader's girl. But who was Baader? Nobody important in the student movement had ever heard of him until the warehouse fire. He came neither from the academic underground (he was expelled from high school at eighteen) nor from a proletarian environment.

Even in the mid-1960s, when leftist students were beginning to go into the streets, Baader's principal preoccupation seemed to be with traffic violations. As a student he was caught riding a motorcylce without a driver's license and registration and was sent to reform school for three weeks. Then in 1964 he was caught in Berlin with a falsified driver's license and was later picked up several times for driving without a license. The result was ten weeks in prison. Baader, as one friend phrased it, "was an idolator of huge cylinder capacities, with an overbearing tendency for showing his ego and making an impression."

He seemed so different from the revolutionary type. He was a happy-go-lucky character who delighted in playing cops-and-robbers games. His friends from those times remember a Baader who loved the brutal and cynical pose; who played "without interruption the early Marlon Brando"; and who, because he was strong, never had to avoid fist fights. Drinking was "in," and "Marlon" Baader could always be found in the same West Berlin pubs. He would always order five double brandies at one time, would gulp them down one right after the other, then raise his hand with five spread fingers and say, "Hit me again."

He looked like a romantic French movie star, but he was tough even as a child. His mother, Anneliese, was unable to give him orders. She recalled the time he had a toothache when he was twelve. "I wanted to give him medication," she said, "and take him to a dentist. But he refused this. He said he wanted to test how much pain he would be able to endure."

The girls called him "Baby," but when he found himself in bed with a new girl, he would turn out the lights because he considered himself too fat. But he was used to having women around him. Born in Munich on May 6, 1943, he was only a year old when his father, a historian, was killed in the last days of the war. He was brought up by three women: his mother, a grandmother, and an aunt. His mother supported the family by doing secretarial work.

Women, particularly sensitive, intelligent older women were irresistibly attracted to him. Ellinor Michel, a painter, was his mistress in his early Berlin days. Although she was still married, she had established herself in nonpolitical Bohemian circles. He moved in with her, and she bore him a daughter. Looking back on her relationship, she credits him with tenderness as well as aggressiveness. The police have been to see Ellinor numerous times, and she always says the same thing: she knows nothing and she finds the whole thing idiotic. She has no idea when it all began. But she remembers Gudrun and the others, with whom she felt ill at ease. "Gudrun and Andy were like Bonnie and Clyde. They saw the film, too. That director should be shot." One day they all disappeared from Ellinor's apartment, and a few days later she read about the Frankfurt fire.

Even while in school, Baader, a classmate recalls, "always had a whole bunch of women, but he never spent any length of time with an individual one. He was searching for a girl who was intellectually his equal."

Although he never finished high school, Baader, according to his Munich principal, Dr. Florian Unerreiter, was an "extremely gifted young man. I supposed at that time that he would go on to become a journalist. He wrote fantastic essays." Baader's only job in that line was a six-month voluntary stint with the *Berliner Zeitung*.

His intellectual equal turned out to be Gudrun Ensslin. Their union was characterized by one gang member was an "explosive constellation." The sparks literally led to the Frankfurt arson. Their two points of view, which were entirely opposite in the beginning, became one in the fulfillment of the "liberating act."

In the opinion of one "fatherly friend," Gudrun, "more than she knew or her intellect admitted, was spiritually dependent on Andreas Baader." In turn he excluded her from his extremely abrasive displays of aggression, which he handed out in generous servings to other female members of the gang, including especially Ulrike Meinhof. Beate Sturm, a gang member who later defected, recalled one incident when Ulrike wanted to discuss the mistakes of individual gang members against the expressed wishes of Baader. He began to rage, "You cunts, your emancipation consists of yelling at your men!" In response, Gudrun very quietly said, "Baby, that you cannot really know." "That was the only moment," says Sturm, "when he really kept his mouth shut."

Women played key roles in the Baader-Meinhof gang. Twelve of the original twenty-two activists were women, and eight of the next twenty members who joined were women. They acted not only as helpers, advisers, and spies but as armed guerrillas, ready to lay their lives on the line alongside the men. Ulrike, Gudrun, and others acted not only as fighters but as organizers, theorists, and strategists. They proved themselves as brave as the men. The fervor with which they adopted women's liberation played an essential part in the gang's concept and activities. To psychoanalyst Hacker, this extreme form of women's lib added up to what he terms the "Patty Hearst syndrome, in which one recognized oneself as a truly emancipated woman only with a gun in hand." Wolfgang Salewski, a Munich criminologist, agrees: "The members . . . are sad, lonely people, feeling an impotent rage against an anonymous state. And the women are more frustrated than the men."

Baader was an anomaly, an anachronism, a square peg in a round hole. There was nothing in his background to suggest an intellectual conversion to revolutionary principles. There was even less to qualify him as a leader of politically motivated liberators. His leadership role becomes understandable only in terms of coincidence. Baader's individual criminal disposition coincided with a central problem of the student movement—that is, the problem of bridging the gap between theory and practice. The New Left's propensities for abstract idealism, for impassioned commitment without action, were finally rejected by a small, hard core of true believers who were ready to begin practicing what they preached.

Sturm describes the dilemma this way: "Here one comes, a student idiot completely removed from practice, who has never done anything at all with his hands for the movement, then one is just simply swept along, as was Ulrike also. The only thing Baader has to explain to her is that action is simply more important than all of her writing. That is enough for her."

Frustrated by the discrepancy between their moral demands and the practice of society, these leftist intellectuals, at least as far as their background was concerned, were inhibited by the society's code of laws, which still subconsciously governed their behavior. On the other hand, Baader could boast that his criminal way of life was an escape from his "class structure." "He transmitted the feeling," says Peter Homann, another gang defector, "that the transgression against social laws was already a revolutionary act by itself."

Action was Baader's personal defense against "the danger of being eaten and digested by the system." His political transformation preceded the criminal transformation of the political leftists he recruited. Homann explains his authority over this group in the following manner: "Of course, most of us had fear which Baader was exactly aware of because he himself had fear. Whenever he accused others of having it, then this was always successful—according to the motto: 'Go ahead and jump if you're not a coward.' Then they always jumped and left all political common sense behind."

Baader's intellectual-in-residence at the time of the Frankfurt arson was his attorney, Horst Mahler, who was busily formulating the group's revolutionary scenario. When two innocent bystanders were killed by rocks in a Munich SDS demonstration, Mahler said, "When I drive off in my car, I can't know beforehand if a tire will go flat." Addressing himself to the idea of the sacrificing of comrades, he was quoted in *Der Spiegel* (February 14, 1968): "This idea adopts bourgeois error, according to which there are only leaders and led, as if not every comrade who is fed up with the bourgeois disorder, who cannot continue what he has done before, cannot decide by himself how he is going to lead his life when he finally succeeds in escaping from the ghetto and pulls down the walls, irrespective of the fact that his lifetime might be shortened."

The statement, which evokes a subjective feeling of repression, is an effective fiction. It offers vicarious experience in terms of Vietnamese, Palestinians, American blacks and Indians, and other oppressed groups caught in basic repressive conditions of life in a world of wealth. Herbert Marcuse has explained this fatalism in a logical and effective way in his essay "Repressive Tolerance." In fact, during the arson trial, Baader referred explicitly to the essay's last sentences, which say that the "suppressed and overpowered minorities" have the "natural right" to employ extralegal means.

All four arsonists were sentenced to three years in prison, but after serving nine months they were freed, pending final sentencing. In November 1969, when they were meant to begin serving their sentences, only Sohnlein turned himself in. The other three had disappeared into the underground. It was during that year and a half between trial and disappearance that the nucleus of the Baader-Meinhof gang was formed.

By then Mahler was also a fugitive. On April 11, 1968, only nine days after the warehouse arson, Mahler bombed the Axel Springer publishing house in Berlin. On that same day, Rudi Dutschke was shot and severely wounded by a young right-wing extremist, who later committed suicide in prison. Upon his recovery, Red Rudi made tracks for England, and when his visa was not extended, he journeyed to Denmark, where he obtained a part-time university post.

Throughout 1968 and 1969, Ulrike continued to write and to lecture at universities on the evils of the establishment. The more violent her words became, the more apprehensive was Klaus Roehl. Although he still wanted her back, as his wife as well as star columnist of *Konkret,* it soon reached the point where she was actually advising readers that the time was ripe for physical violence. Inciting to riot is not part of a radical-chic magazine's format. Then she wrote a savage editorial attacking *Konkret,* which she called an "organ of the Counter-Revolution," and forced Roehl to print it.

In his memoirs, Roehl says that she infiltrated the magazine with conspirators who were to "bore from within" and force a "democratic vote of codetermination." The coup failed because of a passing remark on the telephone by one of the twins as to what "Mutti" was up to these days.

It was perhaps inevitable that Ulrike's first known act of physical violence would be against Roehl. Accompanied by her new comrades, she revisited her old Blankenese villa with the intent of devastating the "once happy home." (Roehl's phrase shows he could still be sentimental about it.) Behaving like vandals, they completely destroyed the furnishings, defaced the walls, and painted a phallus on the front door. In a final act of contempt, they collectively urinated on the old double bed in the master bedroom.

Floating atop the "antiauthoritarian wave" were several separately operating anarchist groups in Berlin, Munich, and Heidelberg: Black Relief, Central Council of the Vagrant Hashish Rebels, Commune I, Commune II, Black Cross, Socialist Patients' Collective, and the Second of June Movement.

By far the most important was Ralf Reinders' Second of June Movement, written "2.6" in the shorthand of Berlin Wall graffiti. Although it started out with less of the Bonnie-and-Clyde panache associated with Baader and Ensslin, with their fast cars and bank jobs, it gradually got caught up in the same violent maelstrom. Reinders, the son of a Dutch prisoner of war who remained in Berlin after World War II, was described by his mother as "the gentlest of my children, a boy who hated all forms of war and violence."

Baader's mother, who refused to believe that her son would actually shoot at policemen, at least tried to address him in his own language. She gave the press a Mao quotation in an open letter to "Andy": "If the consciousness of the masses is not yet awakened and we attack nonetheless, then that is a recklessness. If we stubbornly push the masses into something that they do not want, the inevitable result will be defeat." It was as valuable a piece of advice as he would get from anyone.

Ralf's girlfriend, Ingrid Siepmann, a tall statuesque blond, had her baptism of fire with Baader. Known as the Bank Lady because her air of refinement made her blend naturally with the customers before bank robberies, she stood against the wrong background when she and Reinders tried to hide out in Kreuzberg in 1973. He managed his escape after she was arrested in a shop buying bread. Two years later, when Reinders had a chance to name the prisoners to be released in exchange for Peter Lorenz's safe return, Ingrid was at the top of the list.

Another tall, striking blond member was Angela Luther, a neighbor of the Roehls who grew up in a twenty-room villa in Hamburg and the daughter of an extremely successful Hamburg lawyer. After an early broken marriage to film director Hark Bohn, she became a schoolteacher and gradually slipped into the life of the West Berlin communes. She made headlines even then by stripping to the waist in court to ridicule a judge. It was in 1969 that she met two eloquently passionate advocates of left-wing violence, Heinrich and Georg von Rauch, the sons of a Kiel history professor. She lived with Heinrich for a time, and it may have been when Georg was killed by police that she first decided to devote her life to the revolution. Her beautiful face has graced wanted posters ever since an elegant flat she rented under an assumed name burst into flames on June 15, 1972. Firemen found that it was a bomb factory. She became even more famous in February 1975 when she was identified as the driver of the getaway car during the Lorenz kidnapping.

Two of the von Rauchs' best friends in 1969 were Dieter Kunzelmann and Fritz Teufel, both APO extremists, who tried to attract attention by outrageous behavior designed to shock public morals. They planted a bomb in West Berlin's Fasanenstrasse Synagogue (it was burned down by the Nazis in 1938 and rebuilt after the war) because the people had to get over their *Judenknax* ("thing about the Jews")—that is, their postwar pro-Semitic liberalism. Georg von Rauch declared it was time to "eliminate" political enemies: "We must be clear about this: that in such actions our humanism will be transformed. . . . In such situations we must, I must, simply liquidate human feelings."

Baader's old nemesis, the automobile, caught up with him again on April 4, 1970, when he was arrested in a routine traffic check in Berlin. But he spent only six weeks behind bars. Assuming a leadership role, Ulrike devised a plan to liberate him. Responding to a letter from a bogus publisher, the prison authorities permitted Baader to do "sociological research" in various West Berlin libraries. On May 14, when Baader and his three guards arrived at the Sociology Institute, Ulrike and four comrades (Mahler, Homann, and two women), disguised by wigs, were waiting for him. Under a cover of tear-gas grenades and gunfire, they made their escape, with Ulrike and Baader jumping out of a window and racing off in a stolen silver-gray Alfa Romeo. Left behind were two injured guards and a sixty-two-year-old librarian with a bullet in his liver who subsequently recovered.

Commenting on the incident, Renate Riemeck said that Ulrike had not wanted "to shoot" but had merely tried to "play the necessary role of the extra." Later, in his confession, Homann said that "the entire affair had become a necessity. As one was unable to get free, it was inescapable that one had to join in the next action."

That "next action" lasted for the rest of Ulrike's life. From then on, it was open warfare against the state. The underground was the only place left to her. She dyed her hair and changed her name; and the gang forged passports and identification papers, stole automobiles, worried about roadblocks, secured hideouts and garages, intercepted police radios and set up their own radio communications, established a supply line for weapons and explosives, and plotted bank robberies to secure the wherewithal to carry on the armed struggle.

The cry was raised: "Build up the Red Army!" In the first public declaration after forming the Rote Armee Faktion (Red Army Faction, or RAF), Ulrike asked, "Does any pig truly believe we would talk about the development of class conflicts, or reorganization of the proletariat, without simultaneously arming ourselves?" The term *Red Army* was adopted from the Japanese United Red Army (URA). The Germans had been impressed by the samurai-sword-brandishing Japanese who had hijacked a plane to North Korea on March 31, 1970. In a letter to the Workers party of North Korea, Ulrike explained the name: "The group did not split off from a previously unified movement but was forced to work illegally because of reigning repression—it is not itself a party, but is organizationally, practically, conceptually a necessary component of a Communist party worthy of the name."

Along with the first public declaration on May 22 in the Berlin anarchist paper *Agit-833,* Ulrike wrote:

> Did the pigs really think we would leave Comrade Baader in prison for two or three years? Did they really think we would fight forever with eggs against clubs, with stones against pistols, with Mollies against machine guns? The bullets which struck Rudi finished the dream of peace and nonviolence. Those who don't defend themselves die; those who don't die are buried alive in prisons, in reform schools, in slums of the working districts, in the stone coffins of the new housing developments, in the crowded kindergartens and schools, in the shiny new kitchens and bedrooms with fancy furniture bought on credit. Start armed resistance now! Help build the Red Army!

It was a completely apolitical proclamation, the revolutionary confession of petulant bourgeois children. The trouble was that they meant it. In an interview published in *Der Spiegel* on June 15, 1970, Ulrike said, "We say the person in uniform is a pig, that is, not a human being, and thus we have to settle the matter with him. It is wrong to talk to these people at all, and shooting is taken for granted."

Two weeks after Baader was freed, Meinhof, Ensslin, Baader, Mahler, and Siepmann made their pilgrimage to an al-Fatah training camp, traveling first to Rome, where Ulrike left the twins with revolutionary friends. (A Berlin court had awarded Roehl custody of the girls; with the aid of Interpol, he found them in Rome and brought them back to Hamburg.) The Palestinian military camp was in Jordan. They received training in the use of weapons, explosives, and guerrilla tactics, but the training was cut short by Jordanian troops, who drove the *fedayeen* from their country. By then, however, the Germans had already succeeded in alienating their Palestinian instructors, who remonstrated with them for their drinking and loose morals. When Baader refused to join the others in crawling under barbed wire while machine-gun bullets flew over their heads, the instructor called him a coward. Upon their return to West Germany, there followed a wave of bombing and arson assaults, kidnappings, bank robberies, car thefts, and attempted murder. There were more than eighty bombings and arson assaults in West Berlin alone in 1970.

Commenting on their training period, Mahler wrote in his work on armed conflict, "A fighting group can only come into being through conflict. All attempts to organize, educate, and train a group without the existence of such conflict lead to the most ludicrous results—often with tragic outcome."

On September 29, 1970, three bank robberies were committed simultaneously in West Berlin, involving twelve people using six cars with stolen registrations, for a total haul of 220,000 German marks. A week later all three banks were bombed. There were many arson and bombing assaults, bank robberies, and other crimes assigned to the Baader-Meinhof gang by the press and police.

Ulrike had this to say about the publicity: "Since the end of the training of the first twenty persons there has been no information about our group which came from the group itself. What the RAF does is top secret. The many departments of the police (political police, etc.), the public prosecutor, *Der Spiegel,* and the newspapers of Springer, none of them know anything about our group. The armed fight does not evolve from one headline to another. The political and military strategy of the urban guerrillas extends from our resistance against the fascism in the parliamentary democracy to the erection of the first regular troops of the Red Army for the war of the people. The fight is at the beginning."

The police were probably right when they said that without Ulrike there would be no RAF. It was perhaps equally true that without the praxis of the Tupamaros in Uruguay there would have been no example for the RAF to follow. The purpose of the RAF was not to accomplish "the long march through the institutions of society," as proclaimed by Rudi Dutschke, but to unhinge the state by sudden, strong blows, by "armed propaganda," and by systematic terror.

As the struggle intensified, Ulrike would write, "The strength of the guerrilla is the determination of each of us. . . . We think that the guerrilla is going to spread and gain a footing, that the development of the class struggle will carry through the idea . . . that the idea of the guerrilla developed by Mao, Fidel, Che, Giap, Marighella is a good idea, that no one will ever be able to do away with it."

Carlos Marighella's *Mini-Manual of Guerrilla Warfare* was translated into German and offered in several editions, one under the title *Destroy the Islands of Wealth in the Third World.* His influence over both Meinhof and Mahler in their writing is indisputable.

Marighella defined *terrorism* as "an action usually involving the placement of a bomb or explosive of great destructive power. . . . It is an action the urban guerrilla must execute with the greatest cold-bloodedness." Writing about his own guerrilla campaign in Brazil, he said, "In 1968 we weren't yet a national organization. We were only a revolutionary group in São Paulo with almost no resources, and our ties to the rest of the country were almost nonexistent. . . . We grew as a result of action, only and exclusively as a result of a revolutionary action. . . . We began urban guerrilla warfare in fact, but without publicly saying so . . . our enemies were caught by surprise. . . . The concrete manifestations of the revolutionary were to surge forth in the large cities in Brazil in 1968 and through urban guerrilla warfare and psychological warfare—forerunners of the rural guerrillas in our country."

The hoped-for rural guerrilla never materialized. Instead, he was caught in an onslaught of right-wing counterterror and repression. On November 4, 1969, Marighella was shot and killed by Brazilian police, and within a year most of his group were either dead, jailed, or exiled. By the early 1970s, all Latin American revolutionary strategies of mixing rural and urban guerrilla tactics had failed, including those of the Tupamaros, who were strictly urban guerrillas. In the interim, however, thousands of banks and stores were robbed; businessmen, political leaders, and foreign diplomats were kidnapped, and countless "enemies" were executed. It was a war of nerves that spread fear and confusion throughout the continent. This new form of urban guerrilla warfare seemed to offer great possibilities for revolutionaries in democratic countries, and it was not long before imitators had launched full-scale campaigns.

The most important paragraph in Marighella's writing, the one that everybody has latched onto, offered an alternative tactical objective: "It is necessary to run the political crisis into armed conflict by violent actions that will force the authorities to transform the political situation into a military situation. This will alienate the masses, who from then on will revolt against the army and the police and blame them for the state of affairs."

For a while the Baader-Meinhof theorists found it frustratingly difficult to provoke the Federal Republic, which was still laboring under the shadow of the Third Reich. The rule of law had to be protected for fear of arousing charges of "Gestapo" methods and attitudes. As one Social Democratic minister put it, "We must not be seen putting the jackboot in again."

In a letter to a newspaper, Baader offered his version of Marighella's thesis: "The pigs will stumble around in the dark until they find themselves forced to transform the political situation into a military one." Gudrun Ensslin was more poetic about it: "The system . . . has to be broken, to be turned into a reversed sphere . . . where the pigs themselves are forced to do away with their ideology."

Arrested in October 1970, Horst Mahler continued writing the RAF's manifesto while in prison. Addressing himself to the South American concept during his trial, he had this to say about it: "They accuse me of having, with other comrades, 'formed a closely-knit group, united to fight with all means and especially violence, the social conditions of the Federal Republic following the model of the South American urban guerrilla, and thus to create favorable revolutionary conditions which promise victory.' The accusation rebounds on its authors. They themselves, this gang formed by General Motors, Ford, ARAMCO, General Electric, ITT, Siemens, AEG, Flick, Quandt, BASF, Springer, Unilever, United Fruit, and others—the transnational capital partnerships, the imperialistic monopoly as a whole—are the most monstrous criminal union in history. To destroy this with all necessary and attainable means is a necessity of life for more than three thousand million men."

With a fourteen-year sentence hanging over his head, Mahler had time to concentrate on the merits of revolution. After five years of careful evaluation, he switched to the Maoist Kommunistische Partei Deutschlands (KPD), which believed in violence, but with a long fuse to it. That was why he declined to fly off to freedom when he was named as one of the prisoners to be exchanged for Peter Lorenz. He said something about not deserting the class struggle and remaining "loyal to the Revolution," but it was more likely he was afraid of "political execution" for Maoist heresies.

The problem of arousing the masses, most of whom were living off the fat of the land, proved more difficult in West Germany than in Latin America. In Meinhof's *Urban Guerrillas and Class Conflict,* she was resigned to the fact that "with the realization that the opposition of the West German masses against the reign of capital will not be kindled by the problems of the Third World, but can only develop on problems here, they themselves have ceased to make the problems of the Third World a political objective here." (Years later, in an editorial entitled "The Ugly Germans," *Die Zeit* would observe that "it was Ulrike Meinhof's fatal mistake that she confused Germany in the year 1972 with China in the year 1927. True, German workers will strike for a package of cigarettes, but they will not permit themselves to be forced in this country to bear arms for the liberty of distant nations.")

She reflected on the death of gang members killed by the police, noting that they "died in the battle waged against death in the service of the exploiters. They were murdered so that capital may, undisturbed, murder further and that the people may continue to think nothing can be done about it."

She had something to say about a multitude of problems and activities. On treachery: "Traitors must be barred from the ranks of the revolution. Tolerance of traitors produces new treason. . . . One should not be able to be blackmailed by the fact that they are poor pigs. Capital will make mankind into pigs until we do away with its reign. We are not responsible for the crimes of capital." On bank robbery: "No one claims that bank robbery of itself changes anything. . . . For the revolutionary organization it means first of all a solution of its financial problems. It is logistically correct, since otherwise the financial problem could not be solved at all. It is politically correct because it is an act of dispossession. It is tactically correct because it is a proletarian action." She ended the work with reminiscences on solidarity: "We must avoid unnecessary sacrifices when possible. All men in the ranks of the revolution must care for each other, must lovingly hold together, must help each other."

Strangely enough, there was no solidarity between Baader and Meinhof. They repeatedly fought with each other. The bone of contention was Baader's life-style. His penchant for spacious apartments and big cars infuriated Ulrike. He would occasionally slip off to Paris for weekends of "rest and recreation" and would even dine on caviar for breakfast. Then there was the problem of his high-handed leadership. The members had to discuss their actions and obtain the consent of others; this rule applied to everyone except Baader. Gerhard Mueller, who was with Ulrike when she was finally captured, testified that Ulrike was then considering taking future action without Baader.

The gang, Mueller revealed, had developed a system of code words. The dwellings used by them were called "bag," "barrel," "arbor," "mill," or "bunker." Baader was "Valentin," Ulrike was "Liesel," and Hamburg was "Liesel's City." Berlin was "Dough." It was the duty of every RAF soldier to shoot when threatened with arrest. Attorney Hans-Christian Stroebele, said Mueller, not only brought recipes for explosives back from Jordan but also brought unsure RAF members back into line. Attorney Rupert von Plottnitz, who acted as the gang's psychologist, always appeared on the scene when one of the members seemed on the verge of weakening.

Mueller, it should be pointed out, feared and hated Baader. He felt browbeaten and manipulated, and later when ordered to join in the prison hunger strike, he secretly took vitamin pills. When his lawyers reprimanded him for not having lost enough weight, he wrote a letter to Jean-Paul Sartre to announce that he was finished with "political maniacs like Baader and Ensslin."

Mueller was one of only a handful to turn against their comrades. The most remarkable achievement of the Baader-Meinhof gang was its solidarity. It was on such a high order that it was compared to the cohesiveness of medieval religious sects. The few defectors out of the hundreds involved in operational cells were actually nonideological adventurers who felt rejected by "arrogant and half-crazed bourgeois intellectuals," because they were not included in the theoretical discussions and were assigned only menial tasks. The criminal aspect of terrorism was fine, but the politics bewildered them.

In the beginning, under the banner of "building up the Red Army," the call to action in *Agit–883* had promised the unconditional determination to remove the ruling order—"Of course, they can also be shot." As no immediate vibrations were felt from the Left, the Baader-Meinhof people found themselves forced to make initial attempts at justification, which were followed by others—that is, by attempts to justify their existence. After completing their guerrilla training in Jordan, they had tried to transform their imaginary structures concerning the development of a solid proletarian fighting force into immediate facts. In the "initial logistic phase" of their underground activity, they wanted to create the material promises for their militant actions. At the same time, they wished to undertake political enlightenment, to win new friends and supporters. But as the violence escalated, they no longer had time for political indoctrination and recruitment. They were forced to spend most of their time finding safe houses and escaping from police dragnets. By then some sixteen thousand policemen and soldiers were beating the bushes for them.

The concept of the urban guerrilla announced by Ulrike in April 1971 had expressed the conviction that the time had come for the organization of armed resistance groups in the Federal Republic and in West Berlin. By the summer of 1971 the second phase "of the exemplary attack on the entire apparatus of suppression" had become the order of the day. It cost several lives on both sides and incalculable property damage. Some 2 million German marks were "expropriated" from banks. 'According to the minister of the interior, the radical Left was responsible for 555 acts of terrorism in 1971— a figure that had politicians and policemen asking themselves where they had gone wrong. With the exception of the IRA in Northern Ireland, the Baader-Meinhof guerrillas had been the most successful terrorists in any Western democracy.

The German authorities were faced with a strange dilemma. Because of what had happened under Hitler, they were reluctant to take steps that might be described as "repressive." On the other hand, the very failure of German authority to "stand firm" against Hitler's street gangs had turned out to be extremely costly. This created an emotional ambivalance that was perhaps missing in other more complacent societies.

Under the federal constitution, the police force had been broken up into eleven individual state (Land) forces—this applied even to the counterintelligence organization. (The result was reminiscent of the Dillinger era in the United States before the Federal Bureau of Investigation received interstate jurisdiction.) When a terrorist group crossed state lines, there often was a delay before information was channeled on. But in the spring of 1972, the counterterrorist campaign was centralized under the direction of the Federal Criminal Investigation Department, and public opinion was swinging in favor of a national police force—something that Germans with any sense of history at all strongly resisted.

For a while the government appeared powerless against this small band of determined anarchists. But that came to pass as steel-helmeted policemen with truncheons drawn and automatic weapons at the ready began twisting arms, pulling hair, and dragging away for interrogation anybody who looked sufficiently noncomformist to be a terrorist suspect. New search, arrest, and gun laws were passed giving police greater freedom, and there was a general acceptance by most of the population of daily roadblocks on motorway ramps and border posts, mounted by parliamilitary units using armored cars, machine guns, dogs, and helicopters. They maintained surveillance on the residence, telephone, and mail of thousands of friends, relatives, and acquaintances of gang members. They refused to say how many homes had been searched, how many people had been interrogated, or how many had been arrested.

All of this, contrary to Marighella's teachings, was with the full blessings of the public. Extreme right-wing groups, assisted by the Springer press, had created such a revulsion toward liberals that it bordered on hysteria. Even older liberals were alienated from the young, who were pictured as savages shooting drugs and policemen with equal abandon. The New Left was subjected to so much "Baader-Meinhofization" that it made its legal revolutionary work almost impossible.

That the people would turn against them instead of against the government was not unexpected by Ulrike. "The urban guerrilla has nothing to expect from the public but hostility," she wrote. "The urban guerrilla aims at destroying the ruling system at key points, to destroy the myth of its omnipotence and invulnerability."

"The irrationalism of the anarchists has never achieved anything but an ever stronger reinforcement of the Right," said novelist Günther Grass.

In the editorial "The Ugly Germans," *Die Zeit* pointed out:

> It was the German urban guerrillas who, by virtue of their terrorist activities, caused that situation which made the state react in a manner that made it begin to appear like the distorted image of our society depicted by the terrorists. Ulrike Meinhof wrote from the underground that several dozen fighters would be able to effect a basic change in the political scene, and indeed such a change was effected by the Red Army Faction and its confused followers. Was it really the aim of the bomb-throwers and bank-robbers that the various parties of the Federal Diet limited the liberties of our constitutional state with constitutional amendments and new laws; that police bullets today are released much quicker than ten years ago; that, as in the time of Metternich, following the senseless murder of the poet Kotzebue, denunciations are once again practiced; that young people have degenerated into cowards; and that all our neighboring nations have once more discovered the ugly Germans?

Early in 1972 a campaign to "Save Ulrike Meinhof" was launched by prominent liberals. Writing in *Konkret,* Renate Riemeck pleaded with Ulrike to give herself up. Ulrike was in mortal danger, and besides, the backlash was getting serious: "I don't feel qualified to give you advice, but I do beg you not to keep giving the rightists more ammunition. They are on the march everywhere."

Even Nobel Prize winner Heinrich Böll made an appeal. To reassure her that she would not be shot down like a mad dog if she decided to surrender, Böll asked for an official safe-conduct for Ulrike to protect her—as he phrased it—from the vicious hysteria of sixty million Germans now hunting witches as they once hunted Jews. The analogy did not sit well with the populace.

Indignation over this grotesque comparison nearly destroyed his reputation as a crusading liberal intellectual. Klaus Roehl wanted to sneak her across a border, but he could not find a country that would accept her.

It was all quite pointless. "Successful announcements concerning us," said Ulrike, "can only be: arrested or dead."

On December 17, 1970, a peaceful anti-Spanish demonstration was held in Zurich, Switzerland. Later that evening, a policeman found a plastic sack in a bush and made the following report: "Legal demonstration in connection with the trial of Basques in Burgos, Spain. Participants met at Helvetia Plaza. Found a plastic sack with a Molotov cocktail. Attached was a piece of paper with the following notice: 'Stones of Molotov inside the postal box HB.' "

Two weeks later, Walter Sieger, a seventeen-year-old printer's apprentice, was arrested. A note was found on him: "1 sack of stones, 2 liters of gasoline, possibly 3 liters, ski goggles, scarf soaked with lemon, light battle dress, 1 can of gasoline, rags taken from the business. To bring everything on Thursday 1800 hours, Soz. Room Bunker."

Bunker was the designation for the new Zurich Youth Center. The city had opened the Lindehof Bunker in late October, and it was soon taken over by an anarchist group called Autonomous Republic Bunker (ARB), which immediately proceeded to redesign this meeting place of young people for its goals and aims.

A comparison of the two notes confirmed that they were both written by Sieger, who confessed during interrogation. The demonstration against Spain, he said, had been prepared in the "Socialist Room" of the Bunker. Those present, mostly students and apprentices, received instructions in the manufacture of "Mollies."

Surveillance of the Lindenhof Bunker revealed that the ARB's leading ideologist was a Swiss citizen by the name of André Chanson. When approached by police, Chanson talked gladly and in great detail about "the conditions of armed struggle within a metropolitan city." He received his wisdom from Mahler's *U Street Traffic Regulation,* a handbook on urban guerrilla tactics.

Chanson made inflammatory speeches in the Bunker, speeches that he prepared with great care. In one speech he said, "I believe that the time has come that we try to speak about the concrete conditions in European countries —that is, in Berlin, in Paris, in Amsterdam, but also in Zurich—to find out how the armed struggle which we must take up slowly has to be prepared." In the meantime, two "comrades" stood by his side: Andreas Baader and Claude Meier, a Swiss businessman.

Meier's first contact with the Baader-Meinhof gang was in March 1971 when he was approached by a man and a woman during the "Venedigstrasse Action" in Zurich. They introduced themselves as Rika and Philipp. Their real names were Werner Sauber and Ulrike Edschmidt. Sauber was the son of a Zurich industrialist. As a former student at the Film and Television Academy in West Berlin, he had become acquainted with the RAF's leading members: Meinhof, Ensslin, Baader, Mahler, Holger Meins, and Jan-Carl Raspe. He soon belonged to its most intimate circle.

During the "teach-in" on Venedigstrasse, Rika and Philipp said that they came from the Red Aid in Berlin. This organization surfaced in the spring of 1970 in the Socialist Center, which had been created during the APO uprisings. It was a Good Samaritan organization within the terrorist groups. It provided financial assistance and put on solidarity actions for prisoners. (The German word for *action, Aktion,* is also synonymous with the American term *happening* or *having some action.*)

Werner Sauber and Ulrike Edschmidt talked quite casually with Meier about the occupation of houses in Frankfurt and West Berlin. They described the strategy of the New Left in West Germany and complained that their base of operation was much too small. The answer, of course, was that German and Swiss comrades should work together in the future. However, the visitors kept their distance, giving neither their right names nor their German addresses. Prior to their leaving, they asked Meier for his Zurich telephone number; thus the contact was made.

A few weeks later, at the end of May, Meier received his first call. Rika and Philipp were back in Zurich and a meeting was set up for later that evening. Their request was now somewhat more specific. They talked about weapons and explosives, mentioned that they could be purchased in Italy, and asked Meier to take active part in their acquisition program. To underline their integrity and sincerity, they gave him 3,000 Swiss francs as a down payment toward the future purchase of arms.

Nothing more was heard from them until early in March 1972 when someone called Willi telephoned Meier to say that all hell had broken loose in Germany. The leftist groups had united, but the police were breathing down their necks. There was an urgent need for aid and reinforcement. Following instructions, Meier went to Frankfurt and, with the magazine *Capital* tucked under his arm, proceeded to a certain intersection of Luxemburg Avenue. He paced back and forth until he was approached by a man later identified as Jan-Carl Raspe. A sociologist, Raspe became renowned as the RAF's bomb-assembler.

Raspe addressed Meier very briefly as he walked past. Meier followed him at a distance of a hundred yards. In a side street, both men got into a VW–1300 with Giessen license plates. Raspe listened to police calls while they drove to 36 Raimund Street. Again Meier was asked to follow at a distance of a hundred yards. They entered a two-room apartment that was completely empty except for a telephone on the windowsill. The doorbell rang short-long, short-long. A girl wearing a pageboy entered the room. It was Gudrun Ensslin. She went into the kitchen and made coffee. A little later Andreas Baader and Holger Meins arrived with Ulrike Meinhof and another woman.

Baader was the discussion leader. He gave Meier a lecture on the international network of comrades who thought exactly as they did, particularly the Italians and French. The RAF, Baader said, had taken the leadership of the revolutionary Left in Germany. However, it had an urgent need for weapons and explosives. Ironically, there were weapons lying around uselessly in various depots in Switzerland because of the difficulty of getting them across the border. Meier would have to help. Meanwhile, he was asked to keep himself ready for quick action.

The signal for their next meeting was not long in coming. The code words "Are you coming to have pizza?" were heard on the telephone. The meeting place was a comfortable apartment at Obere Weinsteige 68 in Stuttgart. It was in this apartment that Baader told Meier of his latest bombing plan. Using remote control, ten bombs would simultaneously explode in ten different cities of the Federal Republic. Baader stood up and took Meier into the bathroom. It was his experimental lab for the great undertaking.

Ensconced in a booth at the Lenzhalde coffee house, Baader pronounced the international prospects for the future cooperation of their two countries to an amazed Meier. Through an attorney in Brussels, Baader had established contact with a highly recommended guerrilla organization in Brazil that had strong bases in France and Belgium. No less an individual than George Habash, head of the PFLP, had vouched for the validity of the Brazilian contact. However, suspicious as he was by nature, Baader was determined to test these assertions on the spot. Would Meier fly to Brazil with a Swiss passport? Meier agreed, but his arrest was to abort the mission.

Beginning on May 11, 1972, a series of fifteen bombs exploded in the Federal Republic, not all at the same time, but over a period of a fortnight. The first bombs exploded at the headquarters of the U.S. Fifth Army in Frankfurt, killing one colonel and injuring thirteen soldiers. Bomb attacks on the Augsburg Police Headquarters and the Criminal Investigation Office in Munich caused damages estimated at 100,000 German marks. A bomb attack on the car of Federal Judge Wolfgang Buddenberg severely injured his wife. Thirty-eight people were injured when two bombs exploded in the Springer skyscraper in Hamburg. An American colonel and two soldiers were killed and eight others injured when two bombs exploded within the military compound of the U.S. Army headquarters in Heidelberg.

According to Gerhard Mueller, the Frankfurt bombing attack was conceived by Ensslin and carried out by her, Baader, and Meins. But it came out later at his own trial that Mueller (whose code name was Harry) had picked up the bomb from Dierk Hoff, the gang's Frankfurt bomb-maker (code-named Peach), two hours prior to the explosion and had even paid Hoff. "The explosives were still warm as broth," Hoff testified, "and we had to cool them in the bathtub."

As for the Heidelberg bombing, Mueller said that it was carried out by Angela Luther, Ingrid Moeller, Holger Meins, and Baader. The reason, said Mueller, was because Baader said he wanted "to be taken seriously." But it was later revealed that the gang actually believed that B-52 missions in North Vietnam were controlled by computers in Heidelberg. Three years later, in an exclusive interview, *Der Spiegel* wanted to know whether "you have by now recognized violence against things and human beings . . . doesn't produce solidarity but is repulsive, or do you want to continue it?"

In a jointly drafted reply, they said:

> The question is: Repulsive to whom? In Hanoi our pictures were hung on sidewalk fences, because the bombing in Heidelberg for which the RAF took responsibility has destroyed the computer which had programmed and directed U.S. bombing runs against North Vietnam. American officers and soldiers and politicians felt repulsed because they in Frankfurt and Heidelberg felt reminded of Vietnam, not secure any more, in the rear area. Revolutionary politics these days must be both political and military at the same time. This results from the structure of imperialism: that it must secure its power basis, domestic and foreign, in the metropolis and in the Third World primarily by military means, through military alliances, military intervention, counterguerrilla and "internal security"—enlargement of its power apparatus internally. In the face of imperialism's potential for violence there is no revolutionary politics without solving the question of violence in each phase of revolutionary organizing.

What is truly extraordinary about this response is that the two bombs exploded in the parking lot, at least fifty or sixty yards from the computer building. The explosion rattled a few windows, but it never even scratched the building. This indicates the level of fantasy they lived in. Even Baader's attorney, Klaus Croissant, who claimed to have seen the congratulatory letters from the North Vietnamese, was convinced that the bombs had destroyed the computer center.

A week later, on June 1, Baader, Raspe, and Meins were captured in Frankfurt after a spectacular gun battle during which police used armored cars and television cameramen were on hand to record every moment of the fighting. Meins, who had wanted his bombs "to explode in the conscience of the masses," screamed hysterically as he was dragged from the hideout. Once a student at the Berlin Film Academy, the "eight howls of Holger Meins" became the dramatic highlight of that year's television action-news.

Next to fall into police hands was Gudrun Ensslin. She was arrested in a Hamburg boutique after a clerk spotted a heavy revolver in her handbag and telephoned police.

Finally, on June 15, Ulrike Meinhof's two-year-old revolution came to an end in Hannover. Her capture was symbolic. She was betrayed by Fritz Rodewald, a young left-wing teacher who had taken her into his home, exactly the sort of person who a few months earlier would have protected her at all cost. But Rodewald had been repulsed by the gang's obsessive violence. He became convinced that it was providing reactionary vigilantes with precisely the arguments they needed to destroy the legal New Left movement.

He agonized over his decision for a few days before finally going to a phone booth and calling the local office of the special Baader-Meinhof police unit that had been set up in every city in the Federal Republic. He took a long walk, and by the time he got back home, the police had already carted away his tenants. The lab technicians were still going over the rooms, and Rodewald starred incredulously as the police opened a gift-wrapped ten-pound homemade bomb. There were weapons, boxes of cartridges, false identity papers, smuggled messages from comrades in prison. In Ulrike's purse, they found a "guide" with instructions on the cancellation of safe houses, bomb targets, and the taking of hostages. It had been written by Gudrun Ensslin since her arrest and allegedly smuggled out of her prison cell by Otto Schily, an attorney who had visited her on June 12. To salve his conscience, Rodewald promised himself to donate the reward to Ulrike's defense fund.

As for Ulrike, defeat was hard to take. From the pictures taken of her on that day, the last, in fact, to be released to the press, she was almost unrecognizable. "No one here has touched her," one detective explained, "but her entire face is puffed and swollen because, like some enraged trapped animal, she has been struggling and screaming and weeping for hours." When she refused to look up at the photographer, they pulled her hair and propped up her chin, but she fought with gritted teeth until her strength gave out. "You want to kill me," she cried. She refused coffee and cigarettes, afraid of being poisoned or drugged.

Thus began the final ordeal of Ulrike Meinhof, whom Klaus Roehl would describe as still "more Joan of Arc than red-haired sorceress." Her foster-mother was sorry that her ward ever "put aside her Proust and Kafka to mess about with politics." Feature writers pulled at the heartstrings with musings about "the pretty little girl who used to read Hölderlin and Gottfried Benn and yet loved to dance the boogie-woogie."

> The feeling that one's head is exploding, that the spinal marrow is being pressed into the brain.
> The feeling that the brain is slowly shriveling up like a baked fruit.
> The feeling that one is standing continuously under electric current, as if one were remote-controlled.
> The associations are hacked off, the soul is pissed out of one's body as if it could no longer hold water.
> Guards, visitors, courtyard appear as if made of celluloid . . . headaches . . . flashes.
> The feeling of burning up on the inside, frantic aggressiveness for which there is no escape valve.
> The feeling that one is in a mirrored room that distorts one's image, weaving back and forth.
> The feeling that a whole layer of one's skin is being stripped away.

These surrealistic impressions were recorded by Ulrike Meinhof during the first 231 days of her solitary confinement in the Cologne-Ossendorf Prison. As the sole inmate of the women's psychiatric wing, she was held in a small cell where everything was painted a brilliant white and where glaring neon lights were never extinguished. The only window, high up on the wall, was covered by a fine wire mesh that obscured any view of the sky. The entire wing was virtually soundproofed, acoustically isolating her from all normal sounds of prison life—footsteps, voices, doors clanging shut. She never saw or heard the sound of any other prisoner. She had access to books and newspapers, and there was a radio permanently tuned to one station—"It sounds in the silence, but it cannot relieve it."

Visits from her lawyers, sister, and twin daughters left "nothing behind. Half an hour later one can only reconstruct mechanically whether they took place today or last week." When she learned that guards were recording her conversations—along with descriptions of her gestures, facial expressions, tone of her voice, and even whether she had wept—for a special medical commission that would determine if she was fit for trial, she asked her family not to visit her again.

After eight months in the "silent wing," she was transferred to West Berlin to testify as a defense witness at Mahler's trial. It was a welcome respite, an opportunity to see and hear human beings, but short-lived. Upon completing her testimony, she was returned to the silent wing, a move so shattering that it almost completely unhinged her.

"The shock is as if a sheet of iron had crashed onto one's head," she wrote. "Constant roaring in the ears . . . the feeling that one is moving in slow motion . . . understanding is impossible between prisoners and people who do not know what isolation from noise is . . . obviously when one is there, one would rather be dead."

She noted, "Comparisons, concepts that occur to one under these conditions: Wolf tearing things apart. Space-simulation capsule in which individuals through means of acceleration have their skin pressed flat. Kafka's penal colony. Uninterrupted roller-coaster riding."

When her attorneys charged *Isolationsfolter* ("torture by isolation"), the German police responded that the prisoners were separated and isolated to prevent prison revolts and escapes, as well as the indoctrination of other prisoners. Besides, they pointed out, the prisoners had access to books, newspapers, and radio, plus visits from relatives and attorneys.

"Reading material and the voice in the radio cannot keep the prisoner from incurring physical and psychic damage after prolonged periods of isolation, no more than a daily thimbleful of water could save a prisoner from dying of thirst in the end," Otto Schily countered. "Prison is supposed to prevent the prisoner from escaping or from getting rid of evidence, but it is not permitted to destroy the person. The constitutional state looks good as far as its laws are concerned, but in practice, with regard to penal procedures involving political prisoners, the situation looks different. All political prisoners in

West Germany and West Berlin penal institutions have undergone various periods of isolation. What is significant is the effect of the treatment, not the reasons for it. There can be no excuse for inhuman treatment in a constitutional state."

The government's strategy, Schily and other defense attorneys charged, was to delay the trial until Ulrike and her comrades were sufficiently weakened, physically and mentally, by "barbaric torture." Although few people believed the accusation, it was accidentally confirmed by the minister of justice for the state of Hesse during an interview on Dutch television when he observed, "We must keep the [Baader-Meinhof] prisoners temporarily . . . under isolation in order to make it possible for the prosecution to achieve a proof without any loophole so that it will also stand up in court."

German and foreign scientists warned against the psychic consequences of such isolation. In a detailed analysis, the London *Sunday Times* noted, "The popularity of prolonged solitary as a component of interrogation in depth among secret policemen the world over provides its own grim testimonial. Under conditions less severe than those endured by Meinhof and other members of the group, prisoners have lost their minds, their nerves have been shattered for ever, they have been driven to suicide."

Laboratory studies have proved that even well-paid volunteers on research programs into sensory deprivation have been unable to continue for more than a few days, many for less than a few hours before experiencing sudden, overwhelming surges of panic and weird distortions of feeling similar to those described by Ulrike.

During his visit of prisons in the United States, Charles Dickens was appalled at the practice of isolating hardened criminals. In *American Notes,* he wrote, "I hold this slow and daily tampering with the brain to be immeasurably worse than any torture of the body . . . because its wounds are not upon the surface and it extorts few cries that human ears can hear."

All pleas for mercy fell on deaf ears. German authorities insisted that the prisoners were not being subjected to unusually harsh conditions. However, the defense attorneys produced a letter that gave the lie to this claim. Written by the governor of the Ossendorf Prison to the state's justice department, it stated the facts quite bluntly: "As is well known, remand prisoner Meinhof is in the psychiatric examination section. While remand prisoner [Astrid] Proll . . . can at least take part soundwise in the life of the prison, the prisoner Meinhof is isolated from sound in her cell."

The authorities fell back on the old imperative of "security," which did not explain why everything in Ulrike's cell had to be painted white, with bright lights glaring down on her twenty-four hours a day, and why she had to be shielded from the ordinary sounds of prison life. The matter was submitted to a federal judge, who promptly ruled that "the fear that the defendants can suffer severe psychological or bodily harm . . . is completely unfounded."

But Astrid Proll would give the lie to that too. Prior to Ulrike's capture and incarceration, Proll had spent two periods of three months each in that same cell, under the same conditions but had been separated by a longer period of more lenient confinement. Yet when she came up for trial fifteen months later, the judge had to halt the proceedings until Dr. Jorgen Schmidt-Voigt, an eminent independent specialist, had examined her. His conclusion was that she was incapable of defending herself. Her blood circulation was still deteriorating, leading to insufficient supply of oxygen to the body. In turn, this was affecting her central nervous system, impairing her physical and intellectual responses. His diagnosis was to remove her immediately from prison for treatment. The trial was postponed, and Astrid Proll was sent to an outside clinic to recuperate.

The trial of the group's nucleus (Meinhof, Ensslin, Baader, Raspe, Meins), delayed endlessly by the prosecution, which was compiling a 354-page indictment backed by a 50,000-page record, was finally set for Stuttgart in the summer of 1974. This meant that the prisoners had been held in "investigative detention" for more than two years. But Stuttgart, which never wanted the trial anyway, was a host city for the 1974 soccer World Cup, with six matches to be played in June and July. It was averse to having thousands of happy tourists exposed to obscene radicals protesting the trial, not to mention the possibility of a riot.

Meanwhile, however, a concrete and steel fortress was rising in a sugar-beet field next to Stammheim Prison on the outskirts of Stuttgart. Conceived as a terrorist-proof, bomb-proof building, this $6 million courthouse would be a long way from being finished at the time set for the trial. The burghers of Stuttgart had decided it was too dangerous to hold the trial in the city's regular courthouse. After all, hadn't Meinhof sprung Baader from the Sociology Institute?

Promised that the trial would begin in September, Ulrike was again caught by surprise when it was decided that she would first stand trial in West Berlin on the relatively minor charge of being an accomplice in Baader's escape. The usual practice in West Germany, as in many democratic countries, is to submerge minor charges into the more serious proceedings. Not only had her lawyers been concentrating on the upcoming Stuttgart trial, but she had been mentally preparing herself for it.

Angered and frustrated at the turn of events, her lawyers charged that the switch was designed to test her ability to defend herself after her long detention in the silent wing. Moved to West Berlin's grim Moabit Prison for the trial, she was once again held in complete isolation. Then, shortly before the trial began, three female gang members were brought into the cell block to keep her company, but it was too late. She had already slipped into a profound depressive state.

On the third day of the trial, she suddenly stood up and began crashing her chair on the floor of the dock without saying a word. Ordered removed from the court, she returned to her cell and later in the day met with her attorneys. The next morning she called on all RAF prisoners to begin a hunger strike "in opposition to special treatment and imprisonment in order to destroy all political prisoners."

Fifty-nine RAF prisoners joined in what was to be the third and final hunger strike initiated by Ulrike. The first hunger strike, which had lasted from January 17 to February 16, 1973, was abandoned after water was denied to Baader. The defense attorneys filed a formal complaint with the Constitutional Court regarding prison conditions, but the court ruled against them, saying that the limitations imposed on the remand prisoners were "congruent with the principle of proportionality, that is, of the existing circumstances in this individual situation." In support of their attorneys' complaint, the prisoners began a second hunger strike in May that year which lasted seven weeks.

Throughout this period, from the time of Ulrike's arrest to the start of the third hunger strike, violence in the Federal Republic continued on a regular basis. For example, there were bombing and arson attacks, or attempted attacks, against the *Hamburger Abendblatt,* an evening newspaper associated with Springer Publications; the revenue office in Hamburg; the home of the head of the Pforzheim Provincial Court; the Appeals Court in Berlin-Charlottenburg; the American Club in Berlin-Dahlem; the home of the judge who was sentencing RAF prisoners in Kaiserslautern; the guest house of Axel Springer Publications in Sylt; the home of RAF evaluator Professor Hermann Witter in Homburg-Saar; and the House of German Industry, BDI, in Cologne. None of the above attacks resulted in fatalities.

A successor organization to the Baader-Meinhof gang, the Rote Armee Faktion-Aufbau Organisation (Red Army Faction-Building Organization, or RAF-AO), announced it would launch a rocket attack against the World Cup soccer games planned for Hamburg. Baader's pipeline to the RAF-AO was exposed in February 1974 when his plans for freeing prisoners became known to the public. Among the strategies suggested was the kidnapping of all provincial justice ministers. Then an attack with a twenty-pound bomb on the Ministry of the Interior in Hamburg was foiled only at the very last second.

"Listen here, advice is not worth dirt," Baader was quoted as saying in one of his instruction memos smuggled from his cell. "I have crammed you so full of stuff that you can develop your own tactics." The "boss" was described as coordinating activities inside and outside of the prison by having his attorneys deliver his orders. "The best thing at first is action to spring the prisoners." Even on the telephone, which was monitored by the police, Baader often gave his attorneys hell. "You are a zero," he told one of them. "You can't do a thing right; you're supposed to carry out my instructions exactly as I give them to you." Another time he got extremely angry when an attorney let it slip out that he had already spoken with Ulrike Meinhof.

Whatever Baader lacked in revolutionary theory was probably remedied in prison with extensive reading of leftist literature. He felt himself fortified by it, one of his lawyers observed. "That one [Baader] is able to be human only as a revolutionary. All others who do not forcefully oppose the 'dehumanizing demands of the system' are merely pigs. This is to say that Andreas Baader can only be a 'revolutionary,' whether in hunger strike or giving instructions to rescuers. Even in prison, he is doing battle, as if it were his very last."

There were bank robberies, shoot-outs with police, and numerous arrests and convictions of comrades and sympathizers on charges of "taking part in a criminal association." Then, in June 1974, the Second of June claimed responsibility for the first execution of a traitor in their ranks.

Ulrich Schmücker was judged a "traitor and counterrevolutionary" by a *Volkstribunal* ("People's Court") made up of his former Second of June comrades, and the sentence was death.

On Mother's Day, just three weeks earlier, his mother had traveled from Bad Neuenahr to have coffee and cakes with her son in his tiny Berlin flat because he had telephoned her to say, "Come to Berlin. I'm so lonely."

"He was an idealist," his mother said, when his body was found in a Berlin park with a bullet hole in the forehead. "He wanted to make the world better. He wanted to help other people. He literally gave his shirt away to someone in need on one occasion."

Although Schmücker was only twenty-two when he died and his police file presented him as sensitive and bright, he had been involved with the Second of June Movement from its inception in 1971. His specialty was the preparation of explosives, yet his expertise left something to be desired. Bombs that he placed at the U.S. Army officer's club in Dahlem, and at the Turkish consulate-general in Berlin-Charlottenburg, had failed to explode.

Ordered to blow up the Turkish embassy in Bonn, Schmücker; Inge Viett, a kindergarten teacher; and two others were caught sleeping in a parked Fiat during a routine police check. The car was loaded with bombs, detonators, walkie-talkies, weapons, false license plates, and burglar tools.

Long before his trial started early in 1973, Schmücker had become a stool pigeon, and the tune he sang for antiterrorist investigators made their work a lot easier.

"I'm glad we were caught," he told the court at his trial. "We had a lot of other plans, and that would have made things much worse for me." The reason he had agreed to the Bonn job was "because I was the only one with any knowledge of explosives."

His confession created a sensation as he spelled out the gang's *modus operandi.* As a preface to his disclosures, he told the court, "I have changed my views fundamentally. It has become clear to me that violence only achieves the exact opposite of that intended."

He divulged the names of his comrades, naming Reinders as the head of the gang, and told of their plans to "kidnap representatives of the press, industry, and politics." All had agreed to kill the hostages unless the ultimatum was kept. He said that Inge Viett and two others were responsible for the bombing of the British yacht club in Berlin-Gatow in which a sixty-six-year-old boatman was killed. It was their "answer to the night of Londonderry."

As the gang's liaison with Arab guerrilla groups, Schmücker was able to relate how German terrorists could go into temporary hiding in Lebanon or Iraq for a sum of 3,000 marks (DM). Military training was 10,000 DM per individual; on behalf of his comrades, Schmücker himself had paid 15,000 DM for personal weapons, 5,000 DM for automatic rifles, 15,000 DM for explosives, and 5,000 DM for hand grenades.

After acknowledging the precarious position Schmücker's candor had placed him in, the presiding judge gave him a sentence of two and a half years, with a recommendation for his immediate release and remission of sentence, taking into account the time spent awaiting trial.

Upon his release, Schmücker went into hiding. How he survived during that year remains a mystery. He was last seen in a cheap bed-and-breakfast hotel some eight hours before he was found on a woodland path by American soldiers who could not speak German well enough to understand his dying words.

Two days later a twelve-page handwritten letter was delivered to the German Press Agency in Hamm, Westphalia. The message from Reinders said in part, "In order to bring a balance between the forces of production and the productive relations within the revolutionary movement, we have logically disposed of the case of Ulrich Schmücker. . . . A traitor within the ranks of the Revolution can only find his own certain death." Borrowing a quote from Brecht, he went on, "He must disappear, and totally. For we must get back to our tasks. And since we can't leave him be and we can't take him along, we must therefore execute him."

At the beginning of the third hunger strike on September 13, 1974, Ulrike Meinhof said, "We will fight them with our lives. Better be dead than be reduced to vegetables."

The Federal Diet, as well as the mayors and various state officials and judges, sought to dismiss charges of "imprisonment in order to destroy" and "torture by isolation" as "simply untrue." They attempted to explain that neither hunger strikes nor the threat of thirst strikes were meant to serve the amelioration of supposedly wretched prison conditions but were in reality "part of a planned struggle against the constitutional state with the ultimate goal of forcing release from rightfully incurred imprisonment contrary to legal stipulations, or to at least raise a doubt regarding the constitutionality of the responsible institutions in the mind of the public, to cause them to fall into disrespect, and to shake their very foundations."

The entire panel of defense attorneys came under suspicion of having illegally aided and abetted their clients in continuing their conspiracy by passing correspondence back and forth between cells and the underground that called for new terrorist acts and by coordinating the hunger strike between the various prisons.

Attorney Hans-Christian Stroebele circulated a letter in which the "Dear Comrades" were informed that Baader had developed "great plans for Info-Central" and that "further instructions and information will arrive soon." There was also a "plan with details" for "the concrete schooling of the group" and for the "cataloguing of analyses" . . . all "from Schwalmstadt," then Baader's prison.

An internal evaluation by the Federal Criminal Investigation Department concluded, "The suspected defense attorneys play a 'key role' in the continuing work of the Baader-Meinhof gang while in prison. Only with their help can the continuity of the RAF and the organizational cohesion of its members be maintained. The suspected defense attorneys, some of whom are working as legal RAF members and must be looked upon as such, are at this time the greatest security risk in view of the possible liberation of the Baader-Meinhof prisoners."

The defense attorneys were not dissuaded from their commitment by official criticism or censure. Seven of them, including Eberhard Becker, Joerg Lang, and Klaus Croissant, camped for four days on air mattresses and in robes in front of the federal court in Karslruhe in protest of "solitary torture." Placards bore signs like *BGH* [Federal Criminal Justice Department] *Equals Brown Gangster Clique* [Hitler's Brown Shirts] and *No Legal Means Is Effective Against Torture.*

Attorney Frank Niepel declared: "The fight against an unjust power structure may also be conducted with illegal means if the use of legal means does not achieve results." Croissant laid it right on the line: "If one defends revolutionaries, one must also defend revolution. After all, an attorney for industry does represent capitalism and its power structure."

The director of the prison where Klaus Junschke, Manfred Grashof, and Wolfgang Grundmann went on their hunger strikes claimed to have evidence that "all of the hunger strikes are authorized by the highest levels which direct everything." The attorneys were said to be the strategists because "all those people involved are acting only according to the direction received from their attorneys."

Stroebele dismissed the charge as senseless. It would be "simply idiotic to believe that any lawyer would be able, for example, through eloquence to convince individuals that some of them should go on a hunger strike or to keep them from so doing once they had decided to go through with it." Such activities were completely out of the scope of a "defense counsel's duties." Attorney Kurt Groenewold admitted that "the question of a hunger strike was discussed in greatest detail between attorneys and prisoners." However, "the final decision was made by the prisoners themselves."

"Political prisoners have come to perceive the hunger strike as the most extreme measure in their struggle against isolation," Otto Schily said. "Their alternatives: unlimited hunger strike or suspension of isolation—risking their lives during a hunger strike or gradual deterioration up to the point of a final destruction of personality in isolation. It is their decision, not that of their attorneys. It is not the attorneys who have the means for ending hunger strikes, but rather those who have the power to suspend isolation. Experience has proved that it is possible to suspend isolation without lessening security. Most political prisoners held in Berlin's penal institutions are no longer in isolation, without a noticeable change in the prevailing security situation having taken place. The arrogation of power by anonymous security agencies endangers the constitutional state as much as the neglect of the human rights of militant political prisoners. Injury to the human rights of those who are subject to the power of the state poisons the constitutional state, replaces law by the right of the fist."

The motto of those on hunger strikes was "Strength from Weakness." It became evident to the authorities that the prisoners were willing to go all the way this time. Dr. Helmut Henck, the physician at Stammheim Prison, believed that "once the point of view is prevalent that it is magnificent to die, if such a view is constantly inculcated, then they will gladly die, in the same way some of them will set themselves on fire."

"I think we shall not break off the hunger strike this time," Baader wrote in a cell treatise. "That means that this time someone will be destroyed."

"Certain of our types will get theirs at this time," Holger Meins wrote to a fellow prisoner. At the time that he wrote this, Meins was in the worst shape of anybody and the most likely prospect to fulfill his own prophecy.

Writing about forced feeding, which was instituted on the fourth week of the hunger strike, Meins described what it was like to be subjected to this torturous procedure:

Five to six green ones, probably police or attendants, two to three first-aid assistants, one doctor. The green ones grab, push, pull me onto an operating chair. It is more like an operating table with all kinds of gadgets, turntablelike, etc., and collapsible into an armchair with head, footrests, and armrests. The tying down: two handcuffs around the ankles, one approximately thirty-centimeter-wide belt across my hips, left arm with two wide leather pieces with four straps from the wrists to the elbows, right arm to wrist and elbow, once across chest. From behind a green one or a first-aid assistant takes my head with both hands and presses it tight against the headrest. If I resist actively with my head, another man on each side is added, holding onto my hair and beard and across my neck. In this manner the entire body is fairly fixated. If the necessity arises, another will hold onto my knees or my shoulders. Movement only possible muscularly and within the body. This week they pulled the belt straps very tight so that, for example, the blood was kept from circulating in my hands. They turned blue, etc.

Forced feeding: A red stomach hose is used, thus not a probe. The latter has the approximate width of the middle finger. The hose is oiled but hardly ever enters without automatic retching as it, the hose, is only approximately one to two millimeters thinner than my esophagus. The retching can only be prevented if one voluntarily swallows and remains generally very quiet. Even with slight excitement, the introduction of the hose leads to immediate retching and nausea. Then to cramplike chain reaction with increasing force and intensity that grip the entire body, which struggles against the hose. The more forceful and the longer, the more terrible. A steady retching, vomiting accompanied by waves of cramps.

On October 31, 1974, Holger Meins wrote a letter to his friend Manfred Grashof setting forth the reasons for his dedication to the revolution. It is a letter that could have been written by any of his comrades, for it expresses the reformer's fanatical zeal for a cause that is more fantasy than reality:

> Either human being or pig. The only thing that matters is the struggle—now, today, tomorrow—whether we eat or not. What is important is what you make out of it. A leap forward to become better, to learn from experience. The point is that one has to learn from all of this. Everything else is dirt. The struggle will continue. Every new fight, every action, every skirmish, brings with it new unknown experiences, and that is the evolution of the struggle. It can only evolve in this manner—the subjective side of the dialectic of revolution and counterrevolution. What is decisive is to understand how to learn.
>
> Through the struggle, for the struggle; from the victories, but even more from the mistakes, from the knockdowns, from the defeats. That is the law of Marxism.
>
> To fight, to be defeated, once more to fight, to be defeated again, to fight anew and so on and on to the final victory. That is the logic of the people says the old man.
>
> Man is nothing but matter, as is everything else. The whole human being, body and consciousness, is material matter, and what makes a human being what he is; his freedom is that his consciousness rules over matter, over itself and over external nature and, above all, over one's own existence. The one side of Engels, crystal clear; the guerrilla, however, materializes himself in the struggle, in the revolutionary action, and that means without an end; that is, fight to the death, and, of course, collectively.
>
> That is no concern for matter but one for politics. Of practice. As you say, concern is always today, tomorrow, and onward. Yesterday has been. Criterion also but above all concern. Whatever is now rests first of all with you. The HS [Hit Song] has a long way to go yet before it ends.
>
> And the fight will never end.
>
> But there is, of course, a point to be made. If you know that with every pig victory, the concrete intention to commit murder becomes more concrete and you then decide to pull out, to have more safety for yourself, and by this action give victory to the pigs—that is, you desert us—then you are the pig that splits and withdraws in order to survive yourself. Then you just keep your mouth shut. Don't say something like the *Practiced Slogan:* "Long live the RAF. Death to the system of the pigs." When you no longer hunger with us, then you should have the guts—it would be more honest, if you still know the meaning of honor—to say "I live. Down with the RAF. Victory to the system of the pigs."

Either pig or human being
Either survival at any price or fight to the death
Either problems or solutions
In between there is nothing

Victory or death say our types everywhere, and that is the language of the guerrilla even in the tiny dimension here, because with life it is the same as with dying. Human beings, meaning us, who refuse to give up the struggle, they either win or they die, instead of losing and of dying.

Pretty sad to have to write you something like that. Of course, I don't know how that is either, when one dies or when they kill one. Where should I know it from? In a moment of truth one morning it penetrated my skull as the very first thought: So it is going to be that way. Certainly had not known it yet and then right in front of the barrel aimed right between the eyes—well, anyway, that was it. In any case, on the right side.

I'll tell you this, man: Everyone dies anyway. What matters is how, and how you lived. It's simple. Fighting the pigs as a human being for the liberation of man, as a revolutionary, fighting to the last, loving life, disdaining death. That's my idea of serving the people and the RAF.

Nine days later Holger Meins was dead. The six-feet-tall Meins had wasted away to eighty-six pounds. The official response was to publish an outright lie: "Neither his attorneys nor Holger Meins himself ever requested a physician of his choice." While, in fact, a request filed on October 14 with the Senate Criminal Investigating Committee was denied for all members of the RAF's nucleus on grounds that "there was no evidence to prove that the physicians in the respective penal institutions neglected their duties or were unable to cope with their tasks."

Yet a few days later the West German Senate had evidence that the prison physician at Wittlich could not "cope with his tasks." In a statement to the court, the physician declared himself "unable" to accomplish the forced feeding of Holger Meins in the customary complication-free manner—that is, the introduction of a tube of only four to five millimeters in diameter into the nose, a procedure for which, according to the judges, "a specialist is not required."

Instead Meins was being force-fed with a tube twelve millimeters in diameter that was pushed through the esophagus, which was only slightly wider than the tube—a dangerous procedure that could lead to cramping and injuries to the mucous membranes—not to mention that it was prohibited by law because it subjected the individual to avoidable suffering.

It was not until October 22 that the Senate Criminal Investigation Committee rendered its final decision to have Meins fed with a nasal tube because "technical difficulties should not prevent the execution of legally approved stipulations." An outside specialist who was called in to examine Meins found that a nose probe was impractical because of the "crookedness of his nose" and a "penny-sized perforation of the nasal septum." Meins continued to be fed through the mouth, but now, at least, it was with a five-millimeter probe.

No one knew why the physician had used such a thick hose. It was also not explained why he had failed to notice the physical deterioration of the prisoner. As required by law, he and the prison director should have sought the assistance of the Senate to have Meins transferred to the intensive-care unit of a hospital.

Instead he called off all artificial feeding for Saturday, November 9, and left that Friday for an extended weekend without providing for a physician to take his place. When Meins's attorney, Siegfried Haag, arrived at the prison around noon on Saturday, the authorities, for security reasons, refused to allow Haag to visit Meins in his cell. The supposedly dangerous Meins was taken to the visitor's area on a stretcher. Meins asked for a cigarette, but he was so weak that Haag had to place it between his lips. Around four o'clock, just moments after Haag had left, prison officials decided to call for medical assistance. When the doctor arrived at 5:15 P.M., Meins was already dead.

The official cause of death was listed as cardiac arrest, which was disputed by the defense attorneys. However, a post-mortem examination indicated that he had died of consumption, literally a wasting away.

There were numerous other cases of mistreatment, but there were no other fatalities, largely because of more rigorous inspection by the secretary of state. When Ronald Augustin hovered near death in the Hannover prison, he was transported by helicopter to the prison hospital in Lingen (so that he could get into a "real hospital," said Secretary of State Bartsch), then back to Hannover to the school of medicine, and then again into a "real hospital." The physicians at Lingen promptly took away Augustin's drinking water, because "we always do this." Water was only supplied with salt for washing. He remained without water for three and a half days—until, in fact, the county court at Osnabrück forbade further water deprivation. "These measures had not been discussed with us," says Bartsch. "There is no one here in the house who would not have screamed bloody murder had he found out about it." Deprivation of drinking water, especially in conjunction with a hunger strike, can cause irreparable damage. Kidney functions can fail completely after three or four days. Yet water deprivation was used from time to time as a means of breaking a hunger strike. Previous results had demonstrated that thirst becomes far more painful as time progresses. The guards at the Straubing prison called water deprivation the "therapeutic measure of the house."

There were cases of outright deception by prison officials. Klaus Junschke and Wolfgang Grundmann were described as "hale and hearty" by the prison director at Zweibrücken. They were supposedly receiving a ration of 2,450 calories and 2.2 quarts of liquid every two days. Junschke, said the prison director, "even aided us enthusiastically by inserting the small hose himself and holding onto the end."

But Dr. Johannes Jacobs, an independent physician, found that story to be "grotesque." "Considering their nutritional condition, the prisoners could not have received more than a third of the rations indicated on the record," raged Jacobs. "If you take someone who is completely emaciated, their statement just cannot be true. This is totally absurd."

The day after Holger Meins died, four young people carrying bouquets of flowers—Ralf Reinders; Angela Luther; Inge Viett, who had escaped from prison; and Fritz Teufel—called at the home of Günter von Drenkmann, who was celebrating his sixty-fourth birthday and who, as the president of the West Berlin's appeals court, had never ruled on any proceedings involving the Baader-Meinhof gang. He opened the door, and all four shot him at point-blank range, killing him instantly and destroying at the same time their first opportunity to create something far more important than revenge, something that had been missing from the very beginning of their revolution—a heroic legend of martyrdom.

There was more violence, with rioting in some cities, but the sympathizers were getting fewer in number all the time. An arson attack against the German consulate in Florence was committed by an Italian group called Commandos Holger Meins of the Armed Resistance Groups. Seven fires were set in official buildings and private domiciles in Göttingen. An arson attack on the bus depot of the federal communications system caused 800,000 DM worth of damages. A pipe bomb exploded near the home of a Hamburg judge, and six people were injured when a bomb exploded in a locker at the Bremen railroad station.

Finally, on February 5, 1975, after nearly five months on the hunger strike she had initiated, Ulrike Meinhof decreed that it was time for the strikers to start accepting food and water in their cells. "Our lives are now our only weapon," she said. "It fell to me to try to persuade you to eat again. To live. I act, not at the state's orders, certainly not to help solve a problem for the authorities, but to save lives. Not for a moment could I accept that the life of a terrorist is more expendable than the life of a politician."

To many sympathizers, this decision appeared to be the better part of valor in view of the unwavering attitude of the state. By then she, along with Baader, Raspe, and Ensslin, had been transferred to the Stuttgart-Stammheim Prison to await the opening of their trial, set for the latter part of May. Meanwhile, in her absence, the West Berlin court had sentenced her to eight years in prison for her part in Baader's escape from the Sociology Institute.

At a low point in December 1974, Klaus Croissant had flown to Paris and persuaded Jean-Paul Sartre to visit Baader in his Stammheim cell. One of the most revered contemporary philosophers of intellectual militants, Sartre was allowed an hour of private conversation—Sartre spoke for fifteen minutes, Baader for fifteen minutes, and the court-appointed interpreter for thirty minutes. Later at a press conference, with Daniel Cohn-Bendit acting as interpreter, Sartre said there were "many lines in Baader's face. Every time he spoke, one was able to see more lines. He has the face of a tortured human being." Addressing himself to the prison's conditions, he spoke about torture: "This is not a torture like the Nazis. It is a different form of torture. A torture which is meant to bring on psychic disturbances; that is what happens when the human being is completely cut off from everything." As for the reasons behind the torture, he said the attempt was made to destroy "the psychic and intellectual capabilities of a human being," either "in order to render him incapable of defense while in prison . . . in order that he would become insane . . . or in order that he would die as it has been witnessed here."

As for the conditions themselves, "Baader and the others live in a white cell. In this cell they hear nothing except three times daily the steps of the guard who brings the food. For twenty-four hours around the clock, the light is left on. At 11:00 P.M. Baader's light is shut off. However, in the cells of the other prisoners it remains on."

These conditions would change as the trial date drew nearer. Soon authorities would proudly point to the extra cell given to Ensslin just for her extensive library. Her own cell covered more than twenty square yards. The lights were now extinguished at 10:00 P.M. in the winter and 11:00 P.M. in the summer. Day after day Ensslin, Meinhof, Raspe, and Baader held a supervised "meeting of the minds" session that could last up to four hours. And their attorneys came almost daily.

As before with Ulrike in West Berlin, it was too little, too late. Irreparable damage had been done to all four prisoners. There had been a brief moment of hope during the Lorenz kidnapping. The message from the five released prisoners after they had arrived in Aden was heartening: "We greet our comrades in Germany who are outside prison and those who are in prison. We shall devote our energy to making a day as lovely as today break for them soon too. We shall conquer."

Their dream of imminent liberation to some Arab country was soon dispelled by the Second of June's disastrous siege of the West Germany embassy in Stockholm, which had been staged to obtain the release of twenty-six prisoners, including Baader, Meinhof, Ensslin, and Raspe.

The words of Chancellor Helmut Schmidt before the Bundestag must have been a bitter pill for them to swallow. "We didn't make it easy on ourselves yesterday," Schmidt admitted to applause from all sides of the chamber, "but today I am convinced that we fulfilled our duty correctly." Referring to Baader and Meinhof by name as "terrorists," he said, "Among the twenty-six names was the hard core of the criminal Baader-Meinhof association, at whose door numerous murders, attempted murders, bombings, and bank raids are to be laid. Those responsible for these had, until the Stockholm crime, at least nine dead and more than a hundred injured, some seriously, on their conscience. A release of these criminals, some of whom are still awaiting their trial, would have meant an inconceivable shattering of security for us all and our state."

Schmidt promised that his government would pursue fugitive criminals around the world. He said "international cooperation was required to combat the horrible epidemic of international terrorism." He saw no comparisons between the Stockholm attack and the Lorenz kidnapping, for in the latter case, they had had no hope of saving Lorenz's life because they did not know where his captors were holding him. The government had been forced to deal with criminals who were negotiating from the "darkness of anonymity." Reminding his audience of his "get tough" warning to terrorists after the Lorenz kidnapping, Schmidt said the decision to reject the Stockholm raiders' demands should serve notice that the country's political parties were ready to meet new challenges with the same determination. "A constitutional state can meet its obligations only if its citizens can entrust it to enforce the law. Terrorists may not take for themselves decisions over the freedom and lives of others." There was no "patent recipe" for combating terrorism, he said. "Whoever wants reliable protection from it must be inwardly prepared to go the limit of what a free constitutional state allows and requires."

Two weeks later Schmidt said it was time to start thinking about a national police force. "Violence and terror helped to bring about the end of the first German democracy," he said. "At that time, too, many citizens, though for different reasons, no longer regarded the Weimar Republic as their state. God knows, the situation today is very different."

As the trial date drew closer, there were some who questioned the possibility that the accused would receive a fair trial. There were so many factors to take into consideration. To begin with, there was the fortified monster of a courthouse, an invincible alcazar of steel, concrete, and bullet-proof glass, surrounded by a high wooden wall that blocked out any view of the inside of the grounds and that was itself enclosed within a nine-foot-high barbed-wire fence studded with Spanish riders. Steel nets were strung over the prison yard to prevent any helicopter rescue attempt, and the court building was covered by a steel-reinforced net made of synthethic material to protect against remote-controlled model airplanes carrying bombs. Listening devices were sown in the ground and scores of closed-circuit television cameras constantly surveyed the entire area. The whole complex was lit up by fifty-four searchlights, and even the surrounding beet fields were drenched in the light of twenty-three double neon searchlights.

The street circling the entire area was secured by five hundred policemen in tanks, patrol cars, and motorcycles and on foot. Others manned antiaircraft guns. Even this was not enough for Police Inspector Reinhod Mikuteit, who felt he had to balance a "lack of personnel" with an "optimum use of technology," which included the following purchases, among others: eight hundred submachine guns; two hundred 9-mm Walther pistols; precision tooled guns for sharpshooters; bullet-proof vests; and so-called brighteners of residual light, which are capable of increasing even the blinking of the stars eighty thousand times, in case it became completely dark in Stuttgart-Stammheim.

There were three ways to reach the courtroom. The public entrance was through steel revolving doors and steel turnstile checkpoints where all personal belongings were impounded and returned on leaving, with searches conducted by hand and electronically. All visitors were constantly under observation from an overhead bullet-proof control tower, which was in contact with armed guards in the gangway. The prisoners were brought handcuffed to their guards from the eighth floor of the prison to the ground floor and transported the remaining 150 yards in an armored car. In front and behind them were mounted police, and to the right and left of them were twin rows of uniformed men with submachine guns. At the rear of the courthouse, they were searched again prior to their entering the courtroom. The third entrance was reserved for the judges and prosecuting attorneys, who passed through without physical inspections. As an added precaution, the courtroom offered a completely free visual field to the dozen sharpshooters positioned above the main entrance in the galleries. The five judges, prosecutors, defendants, and witnesses sat behind bullet-proof glass security screens.

The defense lawyers and defendants charged that such massive security precautions constituted "a preordained guilty verdict, in glass and reinforced concrete." Sympathizers were quick to point out that prominent ex-Nazis had been tried in far less oppressive surroundings. Not since the Nuremberg war-crimes trials had the search for truth involved such extreme security measures. "Is it merely a reflex to an extraordinarily great security risk," *Der Spiegel* asked, "or is it already prejudice that has turned into concrete? Can a legal system which has to more or less imprison itself for the duration of the trial find in any other way than against the defendants who have caused all of these measures? . . . In addition, with special regard to this trial, laws were changed and judges were selected. All of this may be politically correct and may even have been necessary. Only the question remains, Which value between fiction and farce remains to the legal belief in the innocence of the defendants, which supposedly every man has up to the very day of judgment?"

It was estimated that the trial would last from one to two years and cost approximately 15 million marks, not including the security forces. The four defendants were charged with five murders, fifty-four attempted murders, six bombings, and a series of bank robberies, arsons, and thefts. The 354-page indictment covered a catalog of crimes encompassing the entire Federal Republic for a time span from mid-August 1970 up to spring of 1972.

Before and after the gang's imprisonment, the Baader-Meinhof syndrome remained on everybody's mind as if the continuation of the constitutional state depended on their capture and conviction. Sixty million Germans stood ready to help in the apprehension of the guerrillas whose "people's war" was as ridiculous and irrational as the government's hysterical response to it. It was typical of the Baader-Meinhof syndrome that the government seemed to be instituting a political high-treason trial rather than a criminal trial. Nothing in the country's postwar history has caused more political sparks and tension between the political parties. Debates concerning violent extremism usually ended in trivial semantic quarrels: Should one say *group* or *gang?*

The Christian Social Union (CSU) press service managed to include in one sentence "anarchist attorneys, prisoner co-ops, and pseudointellectual auxiliary troops in the mass media of socialistic academicians and literati." The chairman of the ruling Social Democratic party (SDP) responded by charging that the head of the CSU was "mentally a terrorist." Others charged that the coalition in Bonn had conjured up a *Zeitgeist* that "provokes ridiculing of the state."

It was time for a closing of the ranks when the Second of June struck at Stockholm. "We'll have to give it to them this time," Schmidt said, as if he had been waiting for this moment. From then on the parties tried to outdo each other in security politics: "Carry the fight to terrorism . . . spend millions for constitutional protection and federal criminal investigation services . . . change the Criminal Procedures Act . . . call this minimal consensus prepared for the voters 'solidarity of democrats.' "

They went on to overreach themselves by leaps and bounds, all of which cost money. Between 1969 and 1974, expenditures for police doubled, from 2.5 billion to 5.1 billion marks; the budget for the Federal Criminal Investigation Department grew sixfold. Millions more were spent for sophisticated equipment. As one Hamburg police official noted, "Today things are given to one almost free. What our office tried to get some time ago, the terrorists are getting for us now. It's like the terrorists were trying to make it easier for us."

A quasi-national police was set up when the Criminal Investigation Department was given federal authority over counterterrorist activities. It would decide "the identity of the target person of an undercover search" and could expect that its "requests, advice, and suggestions" would be "carried out" by the police departments of the various provinces. It was another step toward carrying protection "to the very limits" of the constitutional state. It was once again the "restoration of the mold of yesteryear," as one police director phrased it. "The process of a police force that felt itself close to the citizen" had been sidetracked by terrorism and probably "gone into a regressive phase."

Professors of jurisprudence warned that a legislative drift toward the past seemed to have infiltrated Bonn's parliament. The decrees of the Bundestag in the spring of 1975 that were aimed directly at the Stammheim trial fundamentally changed the structure of the Criminal Procedures Act:

- No defendant may have more than three defense attorneys of his own choice; each defense attorney may defend only one defendant in the same trial.
- A defense attorney may be excluded from participation in a trial if he is under strong suspicion that he is a participant in the criminal act of his client.
- No defense attorney will be allowed to give explanations during every stage of the proceedings, but only after each individual piece of evidence has been presented.
- It is permitted to proceed with a trial even during the absence of a defendant if said defendant has been excluded because of "behavior contrary to the

rules" or if the defendant has rendered "himself incapable of participating in the trial."

The "Lex Baader-Meinhof" was criticized by a left-wing SDP youth group as undemocratic and "inquisitional." Jurgen Baumann, an eminent criminal law professor, warned that "one is too quick in signing away fundamental positions within the constitutional law in order to meet short-term or momentary threats to the constitutional state."

By the time the trial date had arrived, defense attorneys Eberhard Becker, Jörg Lang, and Siegfried Haag, because of legal actions instituted against them by the state, had disappeared into the underground. Attorneys Croissant, Stroebele, and Groenewold had been excluded on suspicion of complicity in criminal activities, and Heinrich Hannover, Ulrike's attorney, had decided to retire from the case. The only confidential attorneys left to defend them were Ruppert von Plottnitz and Otto Schily. Less than a month before the trial started, the court appointed defense attorneys for all four accused, with whom they never even exchanged a single word. The court would later deny the defendants' petition to exclude the compulsory attorneys. Baader's response: "Those are supposed to keep their mouth shut."

Several legal experts considered the reasons for exclusion insubstantial. The liberal *Süddeutsche Zeitung* suggested that the exclusions were a cover-up for the fact that some of the evidence for the prosecution had been obtained by illegal means.

It was a physical impossibility for the new attorneys to prepare themselves for the trial. Just to get through the basic material alone would have required a daily reading of two thousand pages. The prosecution had had three years to prepare itself. Hundreds of criminologists had polished each minute piece of evidence until it fitted perfectly in a circumstantial chain that placed the responsibility for a series of bank robberies, bombings, and murders committed in the Federal Republic between 1970 and 1972 on the four defendants. The only flaw was that there was no direct evidence against any of them. They had not confessed to any of the crimes, and there were no eyewitnesses. Of the 996 witnesses ready to testify for the prosecution, none had been there when shots were fired and bombs exploded. The 80 expert witnesses, with a thousand documents to interpret the meaning of all evidence for the court, were in the service of the Federal Criminal Investigation Department or that of provisional criminal divisions, which meant they were tied to directions and were therefore not independent, as required by trial law. They could be excluded on motions by defense attorneys.

Finally, there was the selection of the presiding judge, or "chairman," and his four assistant judges. There are no jury trials in the Federal Republic. The law stipulates that a judge must be selected according to the court's assignment schedule. This constitutional imperative was designed to prevent the *ad hoc* choice of a judge to influence the result of a trial. Fortunately for the state, the chairman's position in Stuttgart was vacant early in 1974. By switching the trial to Stuttgart, the state got to choose the man it wanted for the job. Instead of having to be stuck with an old-timer from a provincial superior court, the state picked Theodor Prinzing, who at forty-nine was described by his colleagues as a "hardy chap" and physical-fitness enthusiast, a man whose "sense of duty is not anything negative" but who possessed "a sharp intelligence and a witty cleverness." In the opinion of Stuttgart officials, Prinzing was selected because "he had never lost a verdict while holding the chairmanship in Karlsruhe." As for the assisting judges, the Stuttgart officials concurred: "You can rest assured that we paid close attention during the assignment of these positions that only judges would be considered who would be able to cope with the extraordinary demands of this case." As a result, the court turned out to be a perfectly legal *ad hoc* committee.

On the opening day of the trial, the defense's first move was to try to get Croissant, Stroebele, and Groenewold reinstated, but to no avail. Otto Schily argued that their exclusion was part of an organized official attempt to "suppress the defense." To exclude three lawyers who had become thoroughly versed in the evidence "not merely weakens the defense, it destroys it and makes it impossible." When Prinzing objected, Schily pointed out that if that kind of exclusion were allowed "we might as well replace the chairman of this court by a Bundeswehr general and his judges by military officers." Making an effort to remain calm, Prinzing replied that Schily was "clearly overstating it." Quick-witted, glib, and not averse to a little histrionics at times, Schily retorted, "Why don't we just close up shop?" and with elaborate disgust sat down.

On June 11 Baader's new confidential attorney, Hans-Heinz Heldmann, asked the court for a ten-day recess to give him an opportunity to familiarize himself with the material. A self-described "radical democrat," Heldmann was a board director of the Humanistic Union and had an international reputation, having on two occasions during the late 1960s defended political criminals in Teheran at the request of Amnesty International. He had defended student activists as well as Palestinians threatened with expulsion, foreign Communists persecuted in the Federal Republic as well as Arabs looking for asylum.

Heldmann explained that it was because Andreas Baader was obviously not adequately defended that he had accepted him as a client when asked by Schily and Croissant, two colleagues who "always act in the best interests of their clients and are absolutely sincere." Baader, said Heldmann, had been without an attorney of his choice because "the concerted action of the authorities removed his defense attorneys." Prinzing, who was the only one of the five judges who spoke or moved, observed that Baader had had enough time to look for replacements.

Baader shook his head. "What sheer nonsense," he said.

After deliberation for ninety minutes with the judicial panel, Prinzing ruled that the proceedings must go on without delay. Heldmann then petitioned the court to free the four defendants from handcuffs when they were transported in and out of the court. It was inhumane and damaged the honor of the court, he said, to chain the defendants "like wild animals." The prosecutor countered that the handcuffs were essential for "security reasons" and referred to reported plots by comrades to free the prisoners, without venturing to explain how that could be accomplished at Stammheim. Heldmann mentioned his Persian experiences: "Not even a military tribunal required the handcuffing of prisoners." After lengthy deliberation, Prinzing granted the petition, which was a first for the defense.

The following are brief excerpts from the trial transcript:

Trial day number 26, August 19, 1975

Chairman:	Defendants are standing. What is that supposed to mean?
Raspe:	That we want to be excluded by you.
Chairman:	Mr. Heldmann, sir, we wish to have no more confusion here. I would like to speak with the defendants for a moment. Do you have the wish to be excluded, or. . . .
Baader:	Exactly, yes.
Chairman:	As you know, it is the duty of the defendants and the court to make sure that the defendants are present.
Baader:	Yes, what is that supposed to mean?
Chairman:	You are supposed to be seated and take part in the proceedings.

[*The defendants remained standing.*]

Baader:	No, we shall not continue to take part in these proceedings. Have us excluded.
Chairman:	If you continue to stand around in this manner and are not willing to. . . .
Baader:	Well, what do you want then? That we begin to scream or something? Why don't you quit these silly. . . .
Chairman:	You are supposed to be seated and take part in these proceedings quietly.
Baader:	We shall not take part in these proceedings.
Chairman:	Mr. Baader, you have declared that. You refuse to be seated.
Raspe:	Are you trying to make sure that we disturb these proceedings formally, or what else is this supposed to mean?
Chairman:	Mr. Raspe declares the same thing. I have to exclude both of you. . . .
Meinhof and Ensslin:	Exclude us also.
Chairman:	Mrs. Ensslin, Mrs. Meinhof, the same thing. I have to point out to you that what you are doing now is a disturbance of the main trial. If you continue to do this, you will have to be excluded.
Baader:	Well, I hope so. Well, go ahead, you old monkey.
Chairman:	Are all of the participants of the same mind?
Ensslin:	Yes.

Chairman:	Therefore you refuse to remain here?
Baader:	Yes, and what now?
Chairman:	The Senate has decreed the defendants will be excluded.

Trial day number 27, August 20, 1975
[*The defendants rise and begin packing up their things.*]

Chairman:	Mr. Baader, please sit down.
Baader:	We want to go now.
Chairman:	You want to go now? Is it your wish to go once again? You once again wish to repeat the same act as yesterday?
Baader:	You're the one who wants this act.
Chairman:	You would like to be excluded again? This is no reason to exclude you, because you want this. Mr. Schily, sir. . . .
Schily:	If I understand you correctly, standing up is already considered a disturbance.
Chairman:	No, not exactly. Therefore, I say you have the word now. You may continue.
Baader:	What do you really want? Do you want once again this treacherously arranged act like yesterday? Do you want to have this again?
Chairman:	I would like to inform you legally that the exclusion of defendants is an extremely serious matter. It has to be based on certain premises. It is not simply a matter of the defendants standing there and declaring, "We now want to leave the courtroom." No court is able to decree exclusion in such a case.
Baader:	I cannot understand at all why you are getting so excited, because you have interrupted me at least fifty times during these last three months. Therefore, what is this supposed to mean?
Chairman:	Mr. Baader, you are at this moment not permitted to speak, but your attorney Schily is. However, you may remain standing if you wish to do that.
Baader:	I conclude therefore the following: Exclude us now and don't try as you did yesterday to possibly provoke us.
Chairman:	And I conclude that you cannot be excluded from this trial on the basis of behavior as you show it now. In that case the legal premises for such a serious measure are lacking.
Raspe:	Are you trying to provoke us?
Baader:	One can also, of course, look at this in another way. One is able to clearly point out that you are really the archetype of. . . .
Chairman:	Mr. Schily, sir, you have the word.
Baader:	. . . of a fascist.

Chairman:	Please eradicate that word.
Baader:	That is really ridiculous.
Chairman:	Mr. Schily, sir, you have the word.
Baader:	Well, what do you want? You want to force us to remain here? I conclude once again as I did yesterday: You are a fascist old asshole. Is that enough?
Raspe:	Let us repeat it.
Ensslin:	You fascist pig.
Chairman:	The defendants know that on the basis of their present behavior they must be excluded. Are you willing, and I ask you once more, to be seated, to follow the trial, or do you wish to behave in the same manner that you are behaving at this moment?
Baader:	We do not wish to change our behavior. We want to be excluded, damn it.
Chairman:	Do the other defendants go along with this declaration?
Raspe:	Yes, of course.
Meinhof:	Yes, you fascist pig.
Chairman:	The defendants will be, according to a decree by the Senate, excluded from these proceedings for the rest of the week.

The controversy over prison conditions and the fitness of the defendants to stand trial finally came to a head when four professors of medicine unanimously agreed that they were able to stand trial "only on a limited basis" and above all were "in need of treatment." Since the court had appointed the four medical experts, it could not very well dismiss them as sympathizers.

Without equivocation, the defendants were described as being in miserable condition. Baader's ears were humming. Meinhof had problems of forgetfulness, articulation, concentration, and perception; feelings of weakness; inability to work; and headaches. Raspe had acute headaches and a prevailing feeling of hunger. Ensslin's blood pressure had become reduced to a dangerous degree. All four had experienced considerable weight loss: Baader, approximately forty-six pounds; Raspe, forty pounds; and the two women, each twenty-eight pounds. Their muscle substance was atrophying, their concentration was poor, and problems of vertigo were increasing.

Wildred Rasch, chief of forensic psychiatry at the Free University of Berlin, said that "the state of health of each of the defendants can become worse; however, that stage of development cannot be predicted." The diagnosis was "psychophysical exhaustion," but this would not negate, the doctor explained, the "aggressive stance and verbal outbreaks" sometimes exhibited by the defendants in the course of the trial.

The hunger strike was not the primary cause of their "extremely poor state of health." The "lack of proper nutrition resulting from the often repeated hunger strike," Rasch said, had to be "taken into consideration" along with the "unusual prison conditions within a modern prison system," to which they had been exposed. Although they were allowed to listen to the radio and to receive visitors, the "relationships of the defendants are strictly channeled, the accused are kept from normal or quasi-normal interactions, they live outside of the informal internal structure of the prison through which prisoners experience a certain psychic support."

For the first time, medical opinion from a neutral source had confirmed what the defense lawyers had maintained for years. The prison conditions had been injurious to their health to the point of endangering their lives. The basic solution was to relax the prison conditions. That was part of the therapy suggested by the experts. "The restoration of the unimpeded ability to stand trial could not be attained through the use of medications by themselves." They suggested "stimulation and physical exercise, possibly in the open," and characterized "the suspension of social isolation" as "desirable from a medical point of view."

The doctors agreed that the defendants could take part in the three weekly court proceedings for periods of two to four hours each and were able to follow the proceedings and to defend themselves. Visibly irritated by this new development, Prinzing took only three minutes to report the medical findings before postponing the trial for a week.

When the court reconvened a week later, Prinzing declared that the trial would go on without the defendants.

Otto Schily jumped to his feet. "Are you not ashamed of yourself?" he shouted.

Heldmann called it a "terrible perversion of justice."

The court's rationale was that the defendants were responsible for their condition, which had been induced in a premeditated and illegal manner. Prinzing turned the medical findings around. Basing his argument on trial logistics, he claimed that with nine to twelve weekly trial hours, the trial would not be concluded in a reasonable amount of time. In view of the extensive material to be covered, the "incapability of standing trial would also extend to those whose ability to stand trial was reduced to such a degree that the proper conduct of a major trial could not be performed." By isolating the defendants from the court, the court in a very real sense was isolating itself as well.

In the face of overwhelming criticism, Prinzing reversed himself. By this time, however, the court's impartiality was no longer a reality. A climate of animosity existed between the court and the defense. The provocative behavior of the defendants and their ideology-prone attorneys, who refused to play traditional roles, had become the main issue. This same attitude was reflected in the trials of other Baader-Meinhof defendants, in which the severe penalties gave rise to the question of whether the court was evaluating the evidence or the behavior of the defendants. Fritz Teufel, the RAF's political buffoon, had uttered a classic line when ordered by the court to stand up: "If it serves in finding the truth."

Whether West German courts were constitutionally capable of finding the truth was something Ulrike Marie Meinhof would never really know. No doubt she had strong negative opinions on the subject that would not have been disputed by most Germans. Nobody in the Federal Republic seemed to doubt the outcome of the trial. Unless they were "liberated," died, or went mad, the four defendants would surely be found guilty and given life imprisonment.

Had she committed suicide, as one defense attorney suggested, "only as a result of a clear-cut and matter-of-fact decision to bring an end to the conditions of imprisonment"? What about her global "war of liberation" directed at the "computer-guided commando centers of U.S. imperialism" and her vision of the Federal Republic as a "fascist power" whose "counterrevolutionary" policies aided in the increase on all continents of "exploitation, hunger, and misery?" Was life worth living only as long as she could fight for the "damned of this earth," even if the struggle had to be conducted from behind prison walls?

She had maintained her "revolutionary identity" in prison as long as possible. Until physical searches of the attorneys by prison officials had stopped them from smuggling out her messages, she had tried to motivate her comrades to engage in new "daily militant actions" and had prepared attempts to free prisoners. She had worked to promote friendship and cooperation among RAF prisoners and had helped to restructure the Stammheim trial into a political forum.

It is possible that she gradually began to realize the futility of it all. The public had become bored with the trial, and even the most passionate appeals fell on deaf ears. Guerrilla actions had come pretty much to a standstill in the Federal Republic. Ralf Reinders was in prison, and the ranks of the Second of June Movement had been decimated by relentless undercover police investigations.

What horrors awaited her after Stammheim? A lifetime of isolation, of "uninterrupted roller-coaster riding?" What effect had Otto Schily's words when he charged in court that "not only the verdict has already been programmed but also the execution. The isolation tract in which the defendants are supposed to spend their entire life has been completed at the Bruchsal penal institution, according to information I am supplying this court"? Schily went on to describe torture cells in a "dead tract" of "cells insulated with styrofoam and other sound-proofing material," equipped with steel-concrete walls six inches in thickness and with "hidden cameras."

"This is as if one were building the gallows in front of the court building prior to the beginning of a trial," Schily concluded. The Stuttgart ministry of justice denied the allegation, but whom would the prisoners believe?

Add to all of this Baader's ugly disposition and Meinhof's own deteriorating mental and physical condition, and her suicide begins to make some sense. After her death police found fragments of messages from Baader to "G and U" (Gudrun and Ulrike) in which he called them "terribly disoriented pigs" who had "become in the meantime a burden." In another message to

THE PEOPLE'S WAR OF ULRIKE MEINHOF

Ulrike, Baader said, "Now then, keep your mouth shut until you have changed something, or otherwise go to the devil." Morning after morning, according to prison officials, Baader tore up the manuscript pages she had typed the night before, saying, "All of this is crap."

Saturday, May 8, 1976, appeared to be a routine day. In the morning and early afternoon, the four prisoners met in a corner of their own floor; their discussion was about "identity and consciousness." Ulrike skipped the "exercise period" because, as Ensslin recalled, "it was too hot for her." Instead she worked at her typewriter most of the day and on into the evening. Shortly before the light bulbs were collected by a female prison official at ten o'clock, Gudrun and Ulrike visited from one cell to another and "had a good time," according to Ensslin.

What happened next was reconstructed by prison officials. Working in complete darkness, she pulled her bed away from the outside wall, upended it against the opposite wall to allow her more room, pulled the mattress to a place below the cell window, and placed a chair on top of it. She tore a blue and white prison towel into strips and fashioned a rope, knotting it tightly around her neck before climbing on the chair and fastening it to one of the vertical window bars. When the duty officer unlocked the cell door on Sunday morning, she was dead, her body kneeling on the chair, which had slipped to the side.

There was no farewell note, but for those who looked more closely at the constitutional state, there was no question that her death, like her life, marked the end of an era for the people of West Germany. They were the ones who were paying the real price of terrorism.

BOOK FOUR

A TERRIBLE BEAUTY

Starting at midafternoon, bombs aimed only at civilian targets began going off in the heart of Belfast. Thirteen persons died in 20 explosions in an hour and a half, and 130 more were rushed to hospitals, among them more than 20 children and 2 72-year-old women. Three bus stations, 2 railroad stations, a bar, and a number of stores were hit. In one bus station 4 civilians and 2 soldiers were killed. One of the women who died had her head blown off. Two women were killed in a cooperative supermarket on Belfast's western outskirts. The IRA has specialized in bombing cooperatives because they claim the management is a Protestant monopoly. The Provisional IRA claimed credit for this day's work.

McGurk's Bar, a favorite gathering place of IRA sympathizers, was pulverized when a large gelignite bomb exploded. The bar was packed with customers and 14 of them were killed, including 3 women and 2 children. A British major supervising the rescue work was shot in the head by an IRA sniper.

Catholics have been burned out of their homes but so have Protestants living in Catholic areas. In August 1971, some 338 homes on Farringdon and two adjoining streets were burned after the residents were warned anonymously to get out by August 15. The IRA didn't wait for the date of the evacuation order. The

A man armed with a Sterling submachine gun stepped from a car and blazed away at 2 uniformed postmen on their way to work. The pair never saw their killer who pumped at least 20 rounds into their backs and kept on firing even after they fell to the ground dead. Then he turned the gun on a small group of men standing nearby and another man fell wounded. All of the victims were Catholics.

A 100-pound bomb exploded in a Belfast Roman Catholic enclave as members of the Provo IRA were loading it into a car. Six were killed, and 18 injured. At least 3 of the dead were IRA men, and all were Catholics. The same day shooting broke out between 2 groups of Protestants and Catholics who had been taunting each other by singing Republican and Loyalist songs. Five persons were wounded, including 3 girls and an elderly woman.

Rosaleen McNearn, 22, went shopping for a trousseau with her 21-year-old sister Jennifer in downtown Belfast. They stopped for coffee at the Abercorn Restaurant, filled as usual on a Saturday afternoon at 4:30 with women and children. A bomb went off, killing 2 and injuring 136. The injuries were so ghastly that 8 operating rooms at the Royal Victoria Hospital were in constant use for 6 hours. One surgeon operated late into the eve-

street went up in flames on August 9, the day internment began. Later, 2 Catholic priests began to rebuild the houses in an attempt to reconcile the warring tribes and bring the Protestants back. They had little help with the work, and no one has offered to move back into the finished houses.

They march silently behind the coffin, men and women wearing dark sunglasses and dark-green berets, as they accompany fallen comrades to the grave. They goose-step to drown out the jeers of Protestant onlookers. The dead will be buried in a special IRA plot in Milltown Cemetery, where tombstones bear the inscription "Murdered by the British Army."

"They're on three sides of us," a middle-aged Protestant said. "The Catholics have all the guns. We've only rocks and petrol bombs, really nothing to defend ourselves with. That's why men like myself join the B-Specials."

ning and then collapsed on learning that his own 21-year-old daughter had been one of the 2 killed outright. Rosaleen lost both legs, an arm, and an eye. Her sister lost both legs.

"The fears, the tensions, the hatreds are beyond belief," Father Columb O'Donnell says. "I asked a lad in the first grade the other day what he wanted to be when he grew up. 'An IRA man,' says he, 'so I can shoot British soldiers.' What's to become of us all when violence is an everyday way of life?"

"We want the army out. We'll stone them out and burn them and murder them and tar and feather them. They're Gestapo. They're pigs. There's no bacon in England because all the pigs are here. We'll give the bastards cheap haircuts. We'll melt them down into rubber bullets. We'll gelignitate them. Have you no ears? We'll gelignitate the limey bastards," said an eight-year-old boy.

From the ninth floor of the Europa Hotel, the red-bricked city of Belfast resembles an abandoned New England mill town, one devastated by some terrible force that has left it crippled beyond repair. Thousands of bombs, both explosive and incendiary, along with ages of decay and neglect, have reduced much of the city to little more than rubble.

The Europa itself, which is protected by a wire fence and security guards, has been bombed twenty-eight times since it opened its doors in 1971. It is the only decent hotel left in the besieged city. Its proximity to the Great Victoria Street Railway Station has placed it in even greater jeopardy, for the station is a popular target of the Irish Republican Army. One explosion in the station, which injured seventy, shattered every window in one entire side of the hotel. Another time two women were able to conceal enough dynamite under maternity smocks to obliterate one of the hotel's two remaining elevators.

Being searched is a way of life in Belfast. Every time you enter a shop or commercial building, someone waves an electronic sensing device at you, moving it from your head to your toes and from shoulder to shoulder, giving it a sign-of-the-cross flourish, a mechanical blessing to ward off violence. Wire mesh and steel bars are ubiquitous, and as night falls in the shopping areas, there is the loud clatter, very much like the rattle of machine-gun fire, of iron curtains being dropped over display windows. People do not walk; they scurry.

It is at street level that the ugliness becomes oppressive. At least from the height of the ninth floor, one can gaze beyond the stunted skyline to the emerald hills that ring the valley, a truly lovely setting for a city. Unfortunately, natural beauty has little to do with the reality of life in Belfast today.

As for man-made beauty, there is none in evidence. Vandalism picks up where bombs and decay leave off. There is hardly an inch of space that has not been marred by vandals. The aerosol-paint business must be Northern Ireland's second-largest growth industry. The first is the artificial-limbs industry.

British soldiers in battle gear, with automatic weapons at the ready, are also ubiquitous. Fifteen thousand strong, they ride in jeeps, tanks, and weapon carriers and huddle behind barriers in barricaded streets, their presence creating the eerie sensation that one is always on the edge of sudden violence.

"Since the trouble started up again in 1969," says Jim Campbell, a reporter with the *Belfast Sunday News,* "I find that I'm drinking twice as much as I did before. We sort of live the kind of life people did during the blitz in London. You see all this good hail-fellow-well-met comradeship that existed then. People tend to be very happy and gay and drink a lot and tell jokes and laugh; otherwise I think they'd cry. You have to laugh or it gets on top of you." He paused and shook his head. "Eight hundred years of laughs. Some of us are getting a wee cynical."

The problem in Belfast, like the problem of Ireland itself, is rooted in antiquity. The city was not planned and built by local people but by transplanted Scotchmen, a British fifth column that now numbers a million Protestants, giving them a dominance of two to one over Catholics in the six counties of Northern Ireland, known as Ulster, which remained a part of Britain when the twenty-six Catholic-dominated counties in the south achieved independence in 1921 and later became the Republic of Ireland.

Much of the violence since 1970, the year the IRA split into two hostile wings—the Official IRA, which is Marxist, and the Provisional IRA, or "Provos," which is nationalist—has been over the Provos's struggle to oust England from Irish soil. Their goal is reunification of the thirty-two counties. On the other side, the Protestants are dedicated to preserving partition—the "border," as they call it—and remaining under British protection.

Since there are several Protestant denominations and since the once all-powerful Loyalist party has been fragmented into various competitive Unionist enclaves, the most enduring single influence in Ulster today is the Orange Order, the nexus of Protestant purity.

"Here, in Northern Ireland," says Campbell, "it doesn't matter what a man believes, it doesn't matter how intelligent or how professional he is; all he has to say to be elected by the Loyalist people is the right phrase, the right slogan—'Not an inch! No surrender! Ireland will never be united! The hell with the pope!' If you come out with these slogans, the Loyalist people will elect you time and time again, even though you kick them in the teeth, even though you betray them after the election. As long as you wave the flag and beat the Orange drum, they will elect you."

The hottest topic of conversation in recent years, both in the north and south, has been about England being on the verge of pulling out. The result, most concede, would be a bloodbath on the scale of America's Civil War. "Well, they have been here for eight hundred years," says a Provo leader. "Eight hundred years is a long period of history, but they have to go sometime. The reasons for their going are getting more urgent all the time. Yes, I do indeed think they're going to leave."

In most places in the world today, the "now" is all important and the consideration of historical events is played down or ignored entirely. Not so in Ireland. On that lovely green jewel of an island, history is everything. People talk about historical figures as though they were contemporaries.

Strongbow . . . William of Orange . . . King Billy . . . Wolfe Tone? What is it all about? Why are men in the last quarter of the twentieth century killing each other over what happened in centuries past? It has been said that the only happy country is one without a history. Ireland is bent low with the weight of its history. There is a Chinese curse that says, "May you live in interesting times," and the Irish, God bless them, have lived in interesting times throughout their long and bloody past.

"Even the moderate Catholics, who don't like the rioting, who want to see the place pull itself up, still share to some extent the same basic beliefs," said a Catholic community center director. "They can be talking all sweetness and light and soon as you scratch them it comes out—'four hundred and fifty years of repression,' 'three hundred years of repression.' 'Ireland a nation once again.' The whole thing is stored up in the back of their minds."

Do the Irish really live in the past? In the election year of 1932, campaign posters appeared on the walls of Dublin buildings proclaiming, "Remember 1170." That was the year Strongbow and his Normans came to Ireland.

The country is gone mad. Instead of countin' their beads, now they're countin' bullets; their Hail Marys and their paternosters are burstin' bombs and the rattle of machine guns; petrol is their holy water; their mass is a burnin' buildin'; their De profundis is "The Soldiers' Song"; an' their creed is, I believe in the gun almighty, maker of heaven and earth—an' it's all for the glory o'God an' the honor o'Ireland.
                                    —*Sean O'Casey,* Shadow of a Gunman

Wrap the green flag round me, boys,
To die were far more sweet
With Erin's noble emblem, boys,
To be my winding sheet.

On Easter Sunday, 1916, there were almost 200,000 Irishmen, all volunteers, fighting in Flanders for the British. At the same time some 1,500 rebels were moving into Dublin to begin the six days of violence that would come to be known as the Easter Rising.

Two years before, it had seemed that the home rule the Irish had been agitating for since the 1860s was about to be achieved by peaceful means. The Liberal government of Herbert Henry Asquith was dependent on the eighty-odd votes of the Irish Nationalist party to maintain itself in office, and the Liberal party had been committed to home rule since William Gladstone's time. The main basis for optimism, however, was in the recent passage of a parliamentary reform bill that had stripped the House of Lords of its right to veto bills passed in Commons. Time after time during Gladstone's day home-rule bills passed Commons by good majorities only to be thrown out on the second or third reading by the Tory-dominated Lords. By the simple expedient of threatening to order the king to create a whole new horde of Liberal lords to change the makeup of the upper house, the Liberals had forced that chamber to agree to give up all its power but that of delaying legislation.

Asquith and John Redmond, who had succeeded Charles Parnell as the leading Irish spokesman for home rule, went ahead with their plans for a free united Ireland as though unaware that trouble was brewing in Ulster. Orange outrage at the prospect of being submerged in a Catholic free state was the overriding problem both in Ulster and among the Unionists in England. It was the rock upon which the dream of Irish peace and unification was to founder once again.

Redmond was no wild-eyed revolutionary. He was not in fact even a Republican. His vision for Ireland was a dual monarchy on the order of the Austro-Hungarian empire. Asquith and the Liberals were more than willing to meet him halfway in that kind of demand.

In Ulster the old mottoes of the Orange Order were being shouted loud and clear: Home Rule Is Rome Rule! and No Popery! Volunteers were being formed into units and being armed, as Protestants sang defiantly, "The crown o' the causeway on road or street, and the population under our feet!"

Asquith and his fellow Liberals continued to proceed as though there was no opposition in Ireland to a thirty-two county state. The home-rule bill that was presented to Commons contained no mention of a separate Ulster. They were well aware, of course, that there were people in the north who would prefer death to Catholic rule, but they hoped that some kind of a compromise might be reached at the last moment. In order not to lose the support of Redmond and his eighty stalwarts in the House of Commons, they had to act as though there were no roadblocks.

But roadblocks there were, and they became more dangerous to ignore when they were found to be manned by a hundred thousand Ulster Volunteers armed with smuggled German weapons and shouting, "Free us or fight us!"

The prospect of civil war led to the formation of another volunteer force in the south, which the home-rulers called their National Army. It too was equipped with smuggled German arms, but not as well as the Ulstermen.

The Conservatives, still bitter over the Parliament Act of 1911, which had destroyed their stronghold in the House of Lords, took up the cause of Ulster with a vengeance. They accused the Liberals of trying to turn the Protestants over to the rule of Rome. Sir Edward Carson, although born in the south of Ireland and a member of Parliament for Dublin University, was a fanatic Protestant and placed himself at the head of Ulster forces that were ready to resist home rule even if it meant fighting England for the right to remain part of the British Empire. It seemed unlikely to the Liberal ministers that many Englishmen were willing to fight to compel Ulstermen to become Irish.

In the Belfast suburb of Balmoral, the Ulster Volunteers displayed and saluted a Union Jack measuring forty-eight feet by twenty-five, which they called "the biggest flag ever made in the world." They also drilled with rifles under the orders of former officers of the militia and were promised machine guns, an ambulance corps, and transport to fight a modern war.

Part of the Liberal government, including First Lord of the Admiralty Winston Churchill, who supported home rule, were nonetheless unwilling to order British troops to fight to coerce Protestants into a united Ireland.

At this point the government became concerned over the safety of arms stored in Ulster at small military posts. If the Ulster Volunteers were to seize heavy weapons and ammunition, they would probably be unstoppable. It was decided to dispatch fresh troops to protect the military supplies and to be in position if it became necessary to fight. Since it was believed that the Great Northern Railroad of Ulster would refuse to carry the troops, they were to be sent by sea. At the Admiralty, Churchill decided to dispatch the third battle squadron of older battleships to Lamlash. If necessary, they could be moved quickly to Belfast to support the troops.

Mild as these measures were, a howl went up from the Tories that the government was planning to massacre the loyal subjects of Ulster in the interest of the rebellious subjects in the south. Then an event occurred that shook the government to its foundations. At the instigation of the War Office, the commanders in Ulster called together the officers of the British troops stationed there. Churchill wrote of it in *The World Crisis:* "These military measures, limited though they were, and the possible consequences that might follow them, produced the greatest distress among the officers of the Army, and when on 20th March the Commander-in-Chief in Ireland and other Generals made sensational appeals to gatherings of officers at the Curragh to discharge their constitutional duty in all circumstances, they encountered very general refusals."

The government accused the Conservatives (quite rightly) of urging mutiny on the military. The Conservatives replied with a move to vote censure of the government. While the debate on this was going on, Sir Edward Carson left the House just in time to catch the night mail train to Belfast. It was feared that he might at any moment proclaim a provisional government of Ireland. Since it was Carson who had recruited and armed the Ulster Volunteers, the

British cabinet considered charging Carson with treason, but Redmond and other Nationalist leaders urged against it.

Faced with dissension in the military and mounting opposition in the country, the government was forced to amend the home-rule bill to permit the counties of Ulster to opt out of the Free State on a county-by-county vote. By majority vote they could decide to remain outside the Irish Free State for a period of five years. After they had seen how the new government worked, there would be another vote. It was the Liberals' hope that by then Ulster would be willing to enter the Free State.

The amendments pleased no one. The Nationalists felt betrayed, and from Ulster there was more defiance. "Give us a clean cut or come fight us!" was Carson's cry. It was a tense situation. All Nationalist Ireland objected to the exclusion of Ulster, especially since it would leave large Catholic populations under Protestant rule, and the moderates under Redmond were being undermined by the more militant Sinn Fein Republican movement. Ulster refused to accept anything but final exclusion. Passions on both sides rose higher and higher, and no matter what the British government did, it was wrong.

In the midst of all this fury, the assassination of the Archduke Franz Ferdinand of Austria at Sarajevo did not even rate a headline in most British papers. Bismarck had once warned that the great European war would someday come out of "some damn stupid thing in the Balkans," but in that beautiful spring of 1914, no one thought that this would be the stupid thing.

Partition seemed inevitable if there was to be any home-rule bill at all, and the discussion was revolving around which counties should be included and which should not. Churchill has described how the Asquith cabinet became aware that they were faced with something that overshadowed the possibility of civil war:

> The Cabinet on Friday afternoon sat long resolving the Irish problem. The Buckingham Palace Conference had broken down. The disagreements and antagonisms seemed as fierce and as hopeless as ever, yet the margin in dispute, upon which such fateful issues hung, was inconceivably petty. The discussion turned principally upon the boundaries of Fermanagh and Tyrone. To this pass had the Irish factions in their insensate warfare been able to drive their respective British champions. Upon the disposition of these clusters of humble parishes turned at that moment the political future of Great Britain. The North would not agree to this, and the South would not agree to that. Both the leaders wished to settle; both dragged their followers forward to the utmost point they dared. Neither seemed able to give an inch. . . . Failure to settle . . . meant something very like civil war and the plunge into depths of which no one could make any measure. And so, turning this way and that in search of an exit from the deadlock, the Cabinet toiled around the muddy byways of Fermanagh and Tyrone.

The discussion proved fruitless and the meeting was about to break up when Sir Edward Grey, the foreign secretary, rose and began to read the text of the Austrian note to Serbia. Even Churchill's nimble mind was so stultified by the endless haggling over Ulster that it was several minutes before he realized the import of what he was now hearing. Then it began to become clear that this was an ultimatum that Serbia could not agree to and remain an independent state. Behind Austria stood Germany, and behind Serbia, Russia and France. England had unofficial commitments to France.

"The parishes of Fermanagh and Tyrone faded back into the mists and squalls of Ireland, and a strange light began immediately, but by perceptible gradations, to fall and grow upon the map of Europe."

Shortly afterward Churchill was back at the Admiralty making dispositions of the British fleet to meet what he saw as the imminent threat of war. In the next few days it became certain as first Russia and Germany and then France was drawn into the quarrel between Austria and Serbia. England had given assurance to the French that the German fleet would not be permitted to come through the straits of Dover and attack French ports. England was still not committed to war, but the movement of German troops toward the Belgian border made it clear that she soon would be.

In the face of a world war, both factions in Ireland offered aid to Great Britain. From F. E. Smith, the Ulster leader, a message came to Churchill. "I have spoken to my friends of whom you know and I have no doubt that on the facts as we understand them—and more particularly on the assumption (which we understand to be certain) that Germany contemplates a violation of Belgian neutrality—the Government can rely upon the support of the Unionist party in whatever manner that support can be most effectively given."

The Nationalists were not far behind. John Redmond rose in the House of Commons to offer the help of the Catholic south. "Irish Catholics," he declared, "are ready to fight beside their Protestant brethren of the north in the cause of Belgian and European freedom."

Never had goodwill on both sides come about more quickly. As Sir George Trevelyan put it, ". . . there was a detente, which with luck or good handling might have led to a solution of the Irish question. But Ireland seldom had luck and seldom had good handling. The War Office, under the control of Lord Kitchener, 'thwarted, ignored and snubbed' Redmond's generous offer of Irish recruiting. Meanwhile the Home Rule Bill was put on the Statute Book accompanied by the provision that it should not come into force till a year after the end of the War."

Despite the fact that Kitchener was less than gracious about it, thousands of Irishmen flocked to the colors as they had in every war that Great Britain had ever fought, and Protestants and Catholics fought side by side in the mud of Flanders and the heat of Gallipoli.

Back in Ireland, the Nationalist cause had been seriously hurt by the fact of partition. Redmond and his colleagues had lost face by their failure to win a united Ireland. Into the vacuum moved the Sinn Fein, a political organization that had existed since the turn of the century but had previously had little support in the country. Another organization, the Irish Republican Brotherhood (IRB), composed of the residue of the Nationalist volunteers raised in response to the Ulster Volunteers, received arms from Germany and from the United States, and for the first time since Wolfe Tone's day there was talk of taking advantage of England's troubles to win total freedom for a united Ireland.

Sir Roger Casement, a former imperial civil servant, journeyed first to America and then to Germany, where he attempted to convince Irish prisoners of war to desert to the German side and to obtain more arms for revolution in Ireland. He was unsuccessful in swaying the Irish troops, but he did get a promise of arms from the German government.

Many of the leaders of the IRB and Nationalist volunteers were hesitant to resort to arms, because they thought the prospects of success were minimal. Among these was Eoin MacNeill, the IRB chief of staff. He was of the opinion that an uprising was hopeless unless the British government tried to introduce conscription into Ireland. (There were thousands of Irish volunteers in the British army, but the idea of being forced to serve was repugnant in the extreme in the Catholic south.) Other leaders in the IRB decided to proceed behind MacNeill's back. The outbreak of World War I had vastly reduced the strength of the IRB because so many of its members had joined the British army. There remained a total of perhaps twelve thousand men, some of them unarmed, upon which to draw in an attempt to seize power. They were joined by the leftist James Connolly and the Irish citizens army, the tiny Hibernian Rifles, which was the military wing of the Ancient Order of Hibernians. As soon as the German arms obtained by Casement reached Kerry, the word to rise would go out. It was hoped that after the seizure of strategic points in Dublin and elsewhere, the whole countryside would turn out, even if armed only with knives and forks.

MacNeill was shown a document, probably forged, purporting to show that the British intended to arrest all Nationalist leaders. This, along with the news that the German ship *Aud* had sailed from Lübeck on April 9, convinced the reluctant leader to go along with his subordinates' plans.

The *Aud* never docked in Ireland. It was seized at sea by British destroyers and escorted into Cork Harbor, where it was scuttled by its captain. Casement tried to slip into Ireland from the U–19 and was captured. On hearing the news, MacNeill changed his mind and sent out orders that the rebellion was not to take place. The more extremist elements ignored the orders.

"The Military Council decided to strike. The Rising would be a failure, the Volunteers slaughtered and the Military Council shot, but Ireland desperately needed a glorious failure to awake the latent revolutionary tradition," J. Bowyer Bell wrote in *The Secret Army*.

"Don't let the soldiers shoot me, no.
Don't let the soldiers shoot me, no," a
2½-year-old chants to himself.

"Burn, burn, burn the soldiers
Burn, burn, burn the soldiers
Burn, burn, burn the bastards
Early in the morning," goes a Catholic
children's song.

It was a bad time for a Rising. Ireland was in the middle of an economic boom brought on partly by the war. Agriculture was in better condition than at any other time in living memory, with the war driving up prices. Ireland was growing rich on the necessities of its warring oppressor. Consequently, there was really very little support for the rebellion in the beginning. It was only later that British reaction was to produce any genuine sympathy.

British intelligence had reported the possibility of a rebellion to Dublin Castle, but the officials there deemed it impossible under the circumstances. A Rising without any support from the population and with no hope of success seemed totally illogical to the British. It was this very lack of logic that made the Easter Rebellion as nearly successful as it was. The British in Dublin were taken completely by surprise and the twenty-four hundred troops in the city were hard put to contain the situation until reinforcements could be brought in.

It began on April 24, 1916, when groups of armed men in gray-green uniforms seized the General Post Office, the City Hall, the Law Courts, and St. Stephen's Green. An attempt to take the almost defenseless Dublin Castle failed only because the Irish panicked after killing the sentries and withdrew in confusion. Shortly after noon, Padraic Pearse, the poet and rebel, appeared at the front of the General Post Office and read a flowery Proclamation of the Republic to a few disinterested idlers. The Irish flag was run up over the building as preparations were made to defend it. The rebels made no effort to advance farther. They simply settled in at various strong points and waited to be surrounded and wiped out. It was a strange revolution, aimed only at creating martyrs.

Scattered between the post office, City Hall, St. Stephen's Green, and Boland's Bakery were about a thousand Irish rebels. In moving to support the surprised troops, the Royal Irish Rifles were ambushed and suffered casualties, and a sortie by a company of lancers was broken up by IRB gunmen firing from barricades. But the British troops recovered quickly, and reinforcements came pouring in. They moved into Trinity College and the Sherbourne Hotel overlooking St. Stephen's Green, splitting the rebel forces in the city. Artillery and machine guns were brought up, and the buildings where the Irish were barricaded came under heavy fire from them and from the gunboat *Helga* anchored in the River Liffey.

The Irish dug in and held out. There was bitter house-to-house fighting, but by Wednesday only a few outposts had actually fallen. A column of

Sherwood Foresters attempting to storm the barricades defending the Lower Mount Street Bridge were beaten back. Instead of waiting for artillery support or calling for gunfire from the *Helga* to smash the defenses, they went in again and again and suffered the heaviest casualties on either side in the rebellion. After five hours the position was finally taken at a cost to the British of almost 250 killed and wounded.

The Irish position was most precarious. Fires set off by artillery in several parts of the city were spreading. Firemen tried to hold the conflagrations in check but could not extinguish them because of the constant firing. By Thursday the fires were out of control and the Rising had been taken firmly in hand by the British. Individual units of rebels were besieged and dealt with separately. They had no communication with each other and just held on as long as they could. Connolly was wounded twice and another leader killed. The group in the post office had to get out of the flaming ruin and into a house on Moore Street. At noon on Saturday, realizing that what had been a hopeless cause from the beginning was now a lost one, Pearse sent Elizabeth O'Farrell, a member of Cumann na mBann (the Republican women's auxiliary), with a white flag and a note saying, "The Commandant General of the Irish Republican Army wishes to treat with the Commandant General of the British forces in Ireland."

There was still little or no support among the people of Ireland for the rebellion. Defeated Republicans being marched off by British troops were hissed by Dublin crowds. The church, the press, and political leaders of the country all expressed shock and horror at the mad actions of the rebels.

Again British leadership failed. Pearse and fourteen leaders of the Rising were shot, and Eamon de Valera, who had been the last to give up, was saved only by the fact that he had been born in the United States and held an American passport. Casement was taken to London, tried for treason, and hanged.

"The execution of the rebel leaders, though perfectly in accordance with the law, revolted many loyal Irishmen," one historian observed. "The old Nationalist party, from this time onward, began to lose its hold, and Sinn Fein was well launched on its career to ultimate power in Southern Ireland."

> I write it out in verse—
> MacDonagh and MacBride
> And Connolly and Pearse
> Now and in time to be
> Whenever green is worn,
> Are changed, changed utterly:
> A terrible beauty is born.
> —*W. B. Yeats,* "Easter 1916"

The end of the Easter Rebellion of 1916 did not mark the end of Ireland's efforts. The Rising was a failure in terms of actual accomplishment, but it proved a definite success in the area of legend-making. By executing the leaders, the British reversed public opinion, and a movement that had almost no popular support was suddenly transformed into a national cause.

"In Ireland the shift from shock and horror to admiration had begun early in May," said Bowyer Bell. "Songs on Easter Week were heard. Poems were written. All the rites which turn a dead rebel into an eternal Irish martyr were performed."

When the 1918 Parliament met at Westminster, instead of the usual eighty Nationalists from Ireland taking their seats, there were only seven, which left seventy-three empty chairs representing the seats won by Sinn Fein members who refused to take part in the alien parliament.

Sinn Fein was almost the sole creation of Arthur Griffith, a mild, studious compositor in Dublin who had spent several years reading his way through the Kildare Street library's section on revolutionary movements in Europe, with particular emphasis on the separatist movement in Hungary in the nineteenth century. What emerged from all this reading was the unlikely idea that the solution to Ireland's problem was a dual monarchy on the order of the Austro-Hungarian empire, a concept almost identical to Redmond's. He came to the conclusion that all Irish rebels of the past had failed because they had not put first things first. They had concentrated on the destruction of the established government before they planned something to take its place. He proposed that the Irish set up their own parliament, their own court system, their own tax-collecting system, and their own police. The government imposed from England would remain but be ignored by the people.

In effect, however, Sinn Fein was not a pacific organization. The alien government did not go away, and the leadership of Sinn Fein were men who had been involved in the Easter Rising. Eamon de Valera, the American-born son of a Spaniard and an Irishwoman, was its political leader, and Michael Collins, a former post office clerk, was its moving spirit. Its so-called police was the Irish Republican Army (IRA), which had replaced the IRB as the paramilitary wing of the organization. By 1919 the movement was definitely turning to terrorism to accomplish its purposes, shooting civilians who insisted on using English courts and ambushing the British-maintained Royal Irish Constabulary (RIC).

Michael Collins directed the campaign of guerrilla warfare and assassination on a bicycle. Constantly on the move through Dublin, planning jail escapes, supervising the construction of bombs in a factory beneath a bicycle shop, or plotting to murder the viceroy, Lord French. He was the most wanted man in Ireland but looked so innocent and cheerful that he was constantly passed through military patrols without their ever suspecting he was the master assassin they were searching for.

The first violence was directed against the RIC. Between May and December of 1919, eighteen men were murdered and several isolated police posts were attacked and others evacuated. By the end of the year the situation had grown so serious that the RIC had to depend on thirty thousand troops to maintain a semblance of order.

It was possible to commit murder in broad daylight with a dozen witnesses on hand, all of whom proved blind when questioned by police. Through fear and intimidation or through dedication to the cause no one in Ireland would testify against IRA gunmen. In this situation, where the ordinary processes of justice had broken down, counterterror became the answer to terror.

It led to the formation of an auxiliary force for the RIC raised from among war veterans in England. Because insufficient police uniforms were available, the new recruits wore black leather jackets over their old khaki uniforms and were soon dubbed the Black and Tans by the Irish. Ill-trained and as violent as the IRA themselves, the Black and Tans were to fight a war of extermination against the rebels. (Some Black and Tans later joined the British Palestine Police and fought against rioting Arabs and Jews.)

On November 21, Bloody Sunday, Collins's killers conducted a mass extermination of British agents and civil servants, murdering fourteen undercover men and two RIC members. Three IRA men were arrested and shot "while attempting to escape," and the Black and Tans fired into a crowd of football fans in which IRA gunmen had hidden, killing twelve and wounding sixty.

No thought on either side was given to protecting innocent citizens, whether men, women, or children. The Black and Tans burned three towns in County Clare on the assumption that they were harboring IRA men. Three men, possibly IRA gunmen or perhaps just civilians defending their homes, were killed in the raids. Police officials and the courts were either unwilling or unable to restrain the auxiliaries. It was only when those accused of crimes were turned over to the regular army, which disliked their methods, that they were ever tried or sent to prison.

Ambushing of small patrols on isolated roads was another IRA tactic, and there were never any survivors, whether it was military personnel or the police. Those who were captured were shot out of hand. So, however, were many IRA men after being taken. "Shot while trying to escape" became a standard phrase in such cases.

The IRA executed informers, whether men or women, and it was not above torture either. Although many of the stories were probably propaganda, there were several authenticated cases. One Black and Tan was thrown into a boiler and boiled to death at Tralee.

One of the most savage IRA massacres took place in Kilmichael, County Cork. An IRA brigade under Tom Barry, the Cork commanding officer, ambushed a patrol of nineteen Black and Tans, killing several outright and wounding the rest. Then the wounded were massacred in cold blood. Only one, who was thought to be so badly wounded that he could not survive, lived to tell the tale.

There was no restraining the Black and Tans, even if anyone had tried, after that affair. They literally burned down the city of Cork. No distinction was made between the property of Protestant or Catholic, Republican or Loyalist. The killers had come from Cork, so all of Cork must suffer. The damage was estimated at £3 million, but luckily the Black and Tans contented themselves with arson, and the citizens of the city escaped with their lives.

Oddly enough, in the midst of all this killing and burning, home rule, for which the Irish had striven for hundreds of years, had quietly gone into effect. At the time no one seemed to have even stopped to think about it.

It was at this time that de Valera returned from the United States. Although sentenced to life imprisonment, he had been released in the general amnesty of 1917. In the latter part of that year, the Sinn Fein members who had refused to take their seats at Westminster elected him president of the Irish Republic. Rearrested by the British the following year on suspicion of rebellion, he escaped with the help of the Sinn Fein and went to the United States, where he succeeded in raising $5 million to support the revolutionary movement. No sooner had he arrived in Ireland than he was captured by a party of British troops searching for arms. At the time he had with him most of the "state papers" of the Irish Republic.

There was a price on his head, and de Valera spent a very uncomfortable night expecting to be again imprisoned or shot the next morning. Instead he was released on orders from London. Prime Minister Lloyd George, a clever and devious Welshman, was now beginning to think in terms of negotiation and wanted Irish leaders at large with whom he could talk.

De Valera was forced, however, to leave behind the Republic's state papers, which proved to be not so much incriminating as an interesting comment on the problems of a government on the run. As summed up by John Collier in *Just the Other Day:*

> The Minister of Finance complained that the Minister of Labour was never to be found in his office; the Minister of Labour wrote long minutes on every subject but those connected with his office—chiefly elaborate and impracticable schemes for propaganda abroad; the President devised formulae asserting his absolute authority over the Cabinet and Parliament; Parliament was hampered by the necessity of meeting in relays—it was inexpedient to bring together more than fifty illegal legislators at a time; one document did credit the statesmanlike forethought of the President, when he criticized a project for persuading farmers to refuse payment of British income-tax. The original plan was, the farmers should burn all papers sent to them, but Mr. de Valera pointed out that it would be better that returns of income should be made, and that non-cooperation should be delayed until the time came for payment . . . and the statements of income would form a basis for taxation when the Republic came into its own.

Both sides were tiring of the struggle. The IRA was disintegrating in areas where martial law had been proclaimed, and by January 1921, in eight counties in the south and west, the troops were harrying the guerrillas relentlessly, cutting off their supplies, money, and ammunition. The peasants were tired of having their food, cottages, and barns taken over and used to feed and quarter the illegal army. They began to withhold help on the theory that they were as likely to be shot by Black and Tans for aiding the gunmen as they were to be shot by the IRA for failing to. Irish Unionists in the south were tired of having their houses burned by the IRA in reprisal against the British, and army and police casualty lists were growing. In the first seven months of 1921, 240 policemen and 94 soldiers were killed and 428 policemen and 10 soldiers were wounded. IRA casualties, while smaller, were in proportion.

A month after his mysterious release, de Valera received a letter from the prime minister proposing that a peace conference be held. Unable to crush the IRA without massacring the Irish, Lloyd George had decided to negotiate.

A new Home Rule Bill had been passed in 1920, and on June 7, 1921, the Stormont parliament in Ulster had taken advantage of the built-in escape hatch to declare itself out of the Free State. Sir James Craig, who had been willing to start a civil war against the British in 1914 to prevent union with Catholic Ireland, became its first prime minister. The southern parliament, the Dail, was declared open in Dublin some days later, but it was a party to which nobody came. Out of 128 members, only 4 showed up. They went home, and there were no more meetings of the southern parliament.

Lloyd George was not discouraged. With the help of Winston Churchill, who had been made chairman of a cabinet committee on Irish affairs, he continued his behind-the-scenes maneuverings to settle the matter. Since partition was now the main stumbling block, he worked to bring the two sides together. Lord Fitzalan, a Catholic, was appointed viceroy, and the Dail was permitted to meet openly, which eliminated its having to meet in small groups lest the whole Irish government be captured in the middle of a debate. Craig and de Valera were brought together through "strange and circuitous negotiations." Although nothing came of that meeting and Ulster remained adamant, a truce was declared shortly thereafter and peace negotiations were begun. De Valera went to London to meet with Lloyd George, but again the negotiations were unsuccessful. De Valera treated the prime minister to a long harangue on the wrongs against Ireland. Asked later what had happened, Lloyd George said de Valera had spoken steadily for three days about Ireland and had not even gotten up to the Norman Conquest yet.

A new meeting was arranged, and by some means, Arthur Griffith and Michael Collins prevailed upon de Valera to stay at home while they headed the Sinn Fein delegation. It is not clear if this was subterfuge on their part or a deliberate move by de Valera to avoid accepting what he must have known was inevitable, a peace that did not meet all of his demands.

A boy not more than six was hefting bricks at paratroopers. Not strong enough to throw them very far, his bricks were falling far short of the soldiers, but he shook his fist and yelled at them, "We've had fifty years of this and we're standin' for no more!"

"Mother o'God, Mother o'God, have pity on the pair of us. Oh Blessed Virgin, where were you when me darlin' son was riddled with bullets, where were you when me darlin' son was riddled with bullets! Sacred Heart o' the crucified Jesus, take away our hearts o' stone and give us hearts o' flesh. Take away this mudtherin' hate and give us Thine own eternal love."

—*Sean O'Casey*, Juno and the Paycock

On December 5, after two months of fruitless discussion, Lloyd George made what was in effect an offer that could not be refused: Either make peace or go to war. He apparently convinced the Sinn Fein people that he meant it, and on December 6, 1921, Griffith and Collins signed a treaty that established the Irish Free State but recognized the partition of the six counties of Ulster.

Nobody was pleased with the treaty. The Ulster Unionists screamed they had been betrayed, while they actually had gotten most of what they wanted. De Valera and many others of Sinn Fein felt they had been sold out. Some more extremist elements wanted to arrest Griffith and Collins for treason. It is interesting to note that de Valera prevented this. Despite the uproar, the Dail accepted the treaty by sixty-four votes to fifty-seven. Calling the treaty a humiliating compromise, de Valera resigned the presidency, and Griffith was elected in his place. A provisional government was set up under the leadership of Collins, and a committee was appointed to draft a constitution for the new state.

The treaty gave the Irish Free State the status of a British dominion, but it also required that members of the new parliament take an oath of allegiance to the king. Ireland would have its own army but would depend on the British navy for defense at sea. Ulster was to have the choice of joining the Free State or remaining under British rule. If it chose the latter, a commission would be set up to determine the border between it and the Free State.

The uproar in Ireland over the treaty was nothing compared to that in England when the terms became known. Lloyd George and Churchill became the most reviled men in Britain. Both were soon ousted from office.

The immediate clamor was not as great in Ireland as in England, but the effects were more lasting. The oath of allegiance was a sore point, and many members elected to the Dail refused to take office because of it. Partition, however, was the real issue, the one that would rankle from then on.

Then something occurred that still haunts people today, even those in Ireland who are most anxious to have the British out. British troops were suddenly evacuated; Dublin Castle was "surrendered," and hundreds of Irish prisoners were released from jail. The result was chaos and civil war.

The IRA split between treatyites and antitreatyites widened over the next few months, and the vacuum caused by the sudden British withdrawal was filled by all sorts of struggling groups. One group of irregulars led by Rory O'Connor seized the Four Courts in Dublin, and O'Connor proclaimed himself head of a Republican government of all Ireland.

On July 10, 1922, there was rioting in Belfast, with 161 Catholic homes burned and fifteen persons killed. The Protestants, fearing that the border would disappear and they would be absorbed into an all-Catholic Ireland, fought in the streets with Catholics. Craig announced that Ulster was a "rock of granite" and the Ulster Volunteer Force was revived with a hundred thousand men sworn to uphold Protestant rule. There were also ugly incidents along the border in Armagh and Tyrone.

Those Republicans in favor of the treaty had won a majority in the Dail, and Griffith and Collins moved quickly to organize a viable government. A ministry of defense was established, and an army chief of staff chosen. Men were recruited from the IRA and other segments of the population for a new army and a new police force. In the meantime, the radical elements of the IRA were said to be "one step from declaring a military dictatorship."

In an attempt to bring about a reconciliation in Dublin between the two feuding factions, it was arranged that the provisional government of the Free State would exchange arms with the IRA so that the British could not blame the Free State for the invasion of the north, where sectarian fighting had already caused many Protestant and Catholic deaths. The scheme fell through because fighting broke out between the IRA and the government before any organized attack against Ulster could be launched.

The government moved in response to IRA bank raids and seizure of buildings in Dublin, as well as other tactics considered illegal and undemocratic. Troops using artillery left behind by the British attacked the IRA stronghold at the Four Courts, reducing it to a flaming wreck and forcing the surrender of the IRA gunmen and most of the leadership. Other IRA strongholds in Dublin were likewise reduced. Cathal Brugha, who was de Valera's chief of staff, agreed to surrender after holding out to the last minute in the Hamman Hotel, but was shot and killed when he came out with a pistol in his hand.

The IRA outnumbered the Free State army by four or five to one, but the army had artillery, armored cars, and more machine guns. The army also seemed to have had a better basic training in the kind of military operations that followed. For only the second time in its history, the IRA resorted to stand-up-and-fight tactics, which proved as disastrous against the Free State as against the British. Driven out of Dublin, the IRA attempted to set up a defensive line to the south. This was attacked by Free State forces, and in a number of set-piece battles, the IRA was badly beaten.

The IRA then turned to assassination, its most reliable tactic. Harry Boland, an old-time IRA man, was shot and killed in his hotel room in Skerries. Michael Collins, director of the revolution and founder of the Free State, was ambushed and murdered in County Cork two weeks later. Since

Griffith had died shortly before of a heart attack, the leadership of the state passed into the hands of William Cosgrave and Kevin O'Higgins. They felt they had the answer to the continuing guerrilla tactics as they had to open civil war. A systematic program of executing captured IRA men for making war against the state was instigated. Legislation was enacted setting up military courts, and on November 17, 1922, four IRA men were shot. Even an old friend of many of those in power, Erskine Childers, was shot when a pistol was found in his possession. The spectacle of former IRA men hunting down and killing present IRA men must have caused anguished consternation to the families of Ireland's revolutionary martyrs.

The IRA murdered a senator who had voted for the Murder Bill, as they labeled it, and wounded another one. The government replied by executing four IRA leaders, Rory O'Connor, Liam Mellows, Joseph McKelvey, and Richard Barrett. The war went on with some three hundred casualties a month and over ten thousand IRA men rounded up and imprisoned. Former IRA men proved not only more ruthless, but far more effective enemies of the Republicans than the British had been.

Finally, with the leadership largely wiped out after seventy-seven executions and the majority of volunteers in prison, the IRA asked for terms. The Free State would not offer terms; it insisted on unconditional surrender. IRA leaders decided to keep their weapons and disperse. Eamon de Valera sent out a message to IRA forces still in the field, addressing them as "Soldiers of the Republic, Legion of the Rearguard," and said, "The Republic can no longer be defended successfully by your arms. Further sacrifice of life would now be vain and continuance of the struggle in arms unwise in the national interest and prejudicial to the future of our case."

The fighting did not end at once, of course. There were more assassinations and more executions, and even occasional fire fights, but the IRA discovered that a government that had the support of the people could not be overthrown by force. Later they were to have better luck through the ballot box, but the totally doctrinaire and fanatic among them were to reject that solution even when it seemed to be working.

The party founded by William Cosgrave came to be called Fine Gael. He was the first *taoiseach* (Gaelic for "prime minister") of the republic and the father of the present one.

De Valera, who had been imprisoned for eleven months during the fighting, this time by his own country, again became head of Sinn Fein upon his release. Since Sinn Fein followed a policy of nonparticipation in the Dail, de Valera led a dissident faction of Sinn Fein, the Fianna Fail, in 1927, and reentered the Dail. The Fianna Fail party, which was in opposition to Fine Gael at this writing, has been in power for much of the Republic's existence. Both parties are centrist, with Fine Gael tending a little more toward the liberal side but with Fianna Fail being somewhat softer on the IRA. Neither, however, has been sympathetic to IRA extremists.

The first justice minister, Kevin O'Higgins, expressed the attitude of most of Ireland when he said, "We will not have two governments in this country, and we will not have two armies in this country. If people have a creed to preach, a message to expound, they can go before their fellow citizens and preach and expound it. But let the appeal be to the mind, to reason rather than to physical fear. They cannot have it both ways. They cannot have the platform and the bomb."

As badly beaten as they were, the IRA did not just disappear but began to plan for fresh campaigns based on the expressed principle that it would "reconstruct and build up an invisible machine that may be used more on terrorist lines amongst the civil population than as a fighting force in the field."

When de Valera came into power, he proved as willing as the other leaders to move against the IRA. Acting on the idea that "the first duty of democracy is to protect itself," he smashed the Blueshirt Movement, a quasi-fascist group, and several IRA power grabs during the 1930s.

De Valera had campaigned on a platform of abolishing the oath of allegiance to the crown and of withholding the "land annuities," the monies Ireland owed Britain for the land it had bought from absentee landowners to sell to the peasants. A new constitution was drawn up in 1937 which provided for a president and a Dail and Senate. It also replaced the name *Ireland* with the Gaelic *Eire*. After World War II further steps were taken that removed Eire from the British Commonwealth of Nations.

> Out of Ireland have we come
> Great hatred, little room
> Maimed us at the start.
> I carry from my mother's womb
> A fanatic heart.
> —*W. B. Yeats*

De Valera's steadily increasing prestige and power and the growth of Fianna Fail over the years led to a decline in the credibility and influence of the IRA. There was much bitterness in the ranks against their old comrade. The IRA had been weakened by internal strife, but its basic organization was still in existence. It was only a matter of time until eager young recruits would join with loyal older members to try to win by force what de Valera was trying to accomplish by reason and diplomacy, the removal of partition and the joining together of all thirty-two counties into one Republic of Eire.

The IRA carried out two campaigns between 1939 and 1962. The first extended from 1939 to 1945 and was aimed mainly at England; the second was directed mostly at the border with Ulster and lasted from 1956 until 1962. Neither accomplished much beyond upholding the Irish claim against British squatters in the north and adding a few more mayhems to the long list already preserved in legend and song. The wartime campaign included an attempt to gain Nazi help, the harboring of German spies, and the successful delivery of arms by U-boat. These were countered by effective and ruthless measures instituted by the de Valera government. The entry of the United States into the war shut off the flow of money from those Americans "who support violence at a distance and who can sleep on the wounds of others," as Liam Cosgrave recently phrased it.

Among the Irish people there was very little support for the IRA's World War II campaign, perhaps because of the attempted Nazi alliance when tens of thousands of Irishmen, Protestant and Catholic, were serving in the British armed forces. And de Valera's police were so efficient that the IRA came closer to being wiped out than at any other time in its history. So many of its leaders were hunted down that some volunteers became convinced their own chief of staff was a traitor; they spent weeks torturing Stephen Hayes in the hope of making him confess. Although handcuffed and suffering from the constant ill-treatment, Hayes managed to escape and stagger into a police station, after which the whole tragic affair became general knowledge, adding to the IRA's already mounting problems. By 1944 the IRA was in such a sad state of affairs that its Belfast leader had to flee the city and join the Magnet Dance Band in Derry as a banjo player. The chief of staff in Dublin was captured, tried, and hanged, breaking the organization's last link of continuity.

It took from 1945 until the early 1950s to get the IRA moving again and to realign its goals with Sinn Fein. The border campaign of 1956–62 did not end as disastrously as the wartime campaign, but it had little or no support in either the south or the north.

During the last years of the border campaign even the most persistent of the IRA men were becoming discouraged. Many of the best fighters had drifted away from the battle units; others had given up on Ireland entirely and emigrated to America and England. Even worse was the fact that support among Republican sympathizers was evaporating. No longer was it possible to find a safe house in every town or village.

Ruairi O Bradaigh, the current president of Provisional Sinn Fein, was chief of staff of the IRA during part of the border campaign. In an interview with this writer, O Bradaigh put it this way: "The difference is between the door being on the latch, the teapot on the table, and the caddy beside it, everything there together and people retired to bed. In other words, if you've to run in off the street, you can get in and bolt the door behind you, make yourself a drop of tea, and there's a bed upstairs if you want to get to it. Now at the other end of that stick is where those people bolt that door and you've to break it down. Then you're lost. It's as simple as that. A small group doesn't hold a mass of people at the point of a gun. This is what happened here at the end of the civil war. The Republicans found themselves having to break down doors. Now when that came, they had lost, and in the civil war the Republicans had the largest army ever they had; they had more weapons than ever they had and more training than ever they had, more material, more money than ever they had; but they hadn't the support of the people, and all the guns in the world were no good. And this is the reality of it. If the people turn against you, you're lost. If there's no water for the fish to swim in, then that's it; the fish will die, be it long or short."

Since that is the way it was in the border campaign, the IRA leadership decided to call off the fighting and settle down to getting ready for the next round by recruiting men, storing up arms, and collecting funds.

An official proclamation, written largely by O Bradaigh, was issued on February 26, 1962, calling off hostilities:

> To the Irish People:
> The leadership of the Resistance Movement has ordered the termination of the Campaign of Resistance to British Occupation Launched on December 12, 1956. Instructions issued to Volunteers of the Active Service Units and of local Units in the occupied area have now been carried out. All arms and other material have been dumped and all full-time active service Volunteers have been withdrawn.
> The decision to end the Resistance Campaign has been taken in view of the general situation. Foremost among the factors motivating this course of action has been the attitude of the general public whose minds have been deliberately distracted from the supreme issue facing the Irish people—the unity and freedom of Ireland.

The battle was over but so that no one would think the IRA was finished, O Bradaigh added another paragraph:

> The Irish Resistance Movement renews its pledge of eternal hostility to the British Forces of Occupation in Ireland. It calls on the Irish people for increased support and looks forward with confidence—in cooperation for the final and victorious phase of the struggle for the full freedom of Ireland.

The results of the campaign had been minor, and the casualties had pretty well matched them. Eight IRA men had been killed, as had two members of Saor Ulandh, an IRA breakaway group. Two Republican civilian supports had also died. Six Royal Ulster Constabulary (RUC) men had been killed and thirty-two wounded.

When asked about the low number of casualties, O Bradaigh laughed and said, "Ah, we were very gentlemanly in those days—ah, it was another time altogether, nothing like the present."

O Bradaigh's background was Republican on both sides of the family. His father was with the IRA during the Black and Tan period and carried eight British bullets in his body to the end of his days. His mother was a supporter of the cause and a student of Irish history.

"Certain things stand out," O Bradaigh says of his childhood. "I remember my father bringing me to the funeral of a hunger-striker in 1940. It passed through Longford, and I found it very difficult to understand because I knew that the British had been gone out of this part of Ireland since 1921, so why had a man to die of hunger strike south of the border? And it became a very vivid image for me to see the funeral arriving, troops slowing down, the guard of honor marching through the town, to see the flags—the businesses were closed, flags at half-mast—the wreaths, the huge Easter lilies and that type of thing.

"People would say, 'Well, these men died on hunger strike, they committed suicide.' Even though I was a child I knew it wasn't just like that. I remember the same year Burns and McCormick were hanged in Birmingham, and they were from near to us at home, forty miles away, and before we went to school that morning, my father, when the church clock struck nine, said to my sister and myself, 'Kneel down. Pray. There's two Irishmen being hanged in England.'

"Certain things are just there; a very strong acquaintance with Irish ballads and all that type of thing. I remember the 1938 commemoration of 1898. My father was chairman of that. He was also chairman of the local Easter commemoration committee. All this atmosphere was there."

After his father died, ten-year-old Ruairi still had his mother to ask about things that puzzled him, like why a detective sergeant with the Special Branch had been killed by the IRA. "Well, there must have been very good reasons because men don't risk their lives unless there's some good reason. He must have been very active against the IRA."

When he wanted to know why the IRA raided banks, she told him, "Well, it's an act of war."

"I don't know why I was so hung up with all this moral justification. Of course, I was at this developing stage, from ten on, that these things were important to me, while she had been in the Cumann na mBann."

Almost as soon as he entered college in 1950, he joined Sinn Fein, and six months later he went into the IRA itself. This was at the time of the arms raids that were part of the buildup to the border campaign.

"The activities then were just sporadic raids until a definite campaign emerged in 1956. I organized a unit at home in County Longford, and I was pretty active with the Dublin unit, and in 1954 I went down to Roscommon, where I live now, as a teacher and from then to 1956, for two years, I was very much involved in political work and also in training. I was the training officer."

Recruiting became easy once the campaign started in the north, and the organization of the IRA was the same as it is today. "It was, and is, a military force, subject to military discipline. To join is voluntary; to leave is voluntary. After that, the volunteer end stops. You do what you're told. There's no oath, you take a promise; you promise your word of honor. It's organized in sections and companies, which means the company is of platoon size, battalions and brigades. You only get brigades somewhere like Belfast, where there's a big population. It's the usual military staff—the commander and his adjutants, the administration officer, quartermaster, training officer, intelligence, finance, transport—that type of thing.

"Policy is decided by the Ard Fheis at its annual convention, which is composed of delegates from the different units, represented according to strength. That's the supreme authority, that convention. In wartime the convention doesn't meet because it's not consistent with security. They decide policy, they deal with the resolutions sent in from the units, they elect a twelve-man Executive. When the convention breaks up, the Executive meets and elects its own chairman and secretary before electing an Army Council of seven, the names of which are kept secret from the convention delegates.

"Besides electing the Army Council, the Executive has two functions: it can advise but it can't bind, and if it believes there's something going wrong, it can call an extraordinary convention, which would put the existing Army Council out of office and restore all power to the convention. It's a safeguard similar to the bicameral system.

"The Army Council is the supreme army authority between conventions. It elects its own chairman and secretary and appoints a chief of staff. The chief of staff then names his adjutant general, quartermaster general, the heads of the various departments, and they are ratified by the Army Council. So the Army Council has to meet at least once a month and in practice meets a lot oftener, but the chief of staff has to report to it, which gives you a collective leadership. The chief of staff is really the servant of the Army Council. He's just one voice. He may or may not be a member of it. If he's not a member, he attends as an eighth person, but he doesn't have any vote. If he's a member, he just has one vote, the same as anybody else."

In 1955 O Bradaigh was elected to the Executive by the Ard Fheis. "That summer I was in charge of an operation in England. There was a raid on a military barracks there called Arborfield." He and his men raided the base, tied up a number of British soldiers, and escaped with two lorries loaded with weapons. One lorry was stopped by two unarmed constables, and that part of the stolen arms were recaptured. The rest were supposedly shipped to Ireland.

"I had been very much involved all those summers [from 1950 to 1956] in training camps and that kind of thing. In 1956, then, after the convention, I emerged as a member of the Army Council. I was just about twenty-four at that time, which made me the youngest on it. That summer and autumn we decided to go ahead from the sporadic raids to an all-out campaign, which took place in December, and I was involved in it in South Fermanagh, and after some weeks a few of us were arrested by the police on the Republic side of the border. We got six months for not answering questions as to our movements, a purely technical charge. So there was a reaction here in the south, a development to the action taken against us. The government fell, and there was a general election, and Sinn Fein contested that election, and I was one of the four people elected to the parliament. There was a change in government and Mr. de Valera's government came back in very strong and after three or four months, they opened the internment camps, although there hadn't been any trouble this side of the border."

Sinn Fein received 65,640 votes, giving the IRA in the south something to cheer about after they had lost the battle in the north. The incarcerated O Bradaigh was elected to the Dail, but he refused to serve even after he was released from prison. After the violence simmered down, de Valera released most of those who had been interned. When this resulted in new violence, de

Valera promptly did an about-face and had the IRA leadership rearrested. O Bradaigh felt the government reacted that way because it was composed of IRA men of an older generation, who were nearly at the end of their days, fading away. "If there was any difficulty, if anyone rocked the boat, you just put them in jail. That was simply it. So that's what they did."

He did not agree with those who felt the campaign had been a waste of time and effort. "Another link was added to the chain of resistance. It's like listing a squatter's right. If you don't dispute the other fellow's claim every so often, you'll become like Wales or Scotland or some of those places. You see, you just fade out. So to actually make good your claim is important."

There was also the advantage of gaining experience, which he thought important because it helped to prepare the IRA for its terrorist activities.

Mairin de Burca, a leader of the Official Sinn Fein, also remembers the campaign but feels it was totally worthless: "At that time it [the IRA] was purely Nationalistic, fairly right-wing, and its purpose at that stage, the purpose of the political end of the movement was purely to sort of maintain the organization's existence between military campaigns. It had no other real function. It issued statements from time to time, and it got out its newspaper; but mainly the emphasis in those days was on the military organization. When I joined it, the campaign of the 1950s was just about to begin. Then when the military campaign stopped in 1962, the leadership of both the political and military sections of the movement decided to analyze thoroughly the whole previous fifty years of history, the reasons for the failure of the various campaigns, the reasons why the Irish people, though in the main mildly sympathetic, were still not supportive of the government and its aims and objectives, and to see if anything could be done to rectify that position."

Seamus Costello, who took part in the border campaign as head of one of the IRA's columns and who has since broken away and formed his own Irish Republican Socialist party, agreed with the decision to call off the military campaign. "It was the only logical decision under the circumstances because there was no popular support for armed resistance at that time. There hadn't been any degree of popular support for armed resistance for a few years before that, and a guerrilla movement can't function without popular support."

"There's no life here," a Catholic housewife told a reporter. "The fellow next door, Barney Watt, was shot dead . . . it was those bloody soldiers. I couldn't live with them, not ever again, not those Protestants over there. We'll never forget. We'll never forgive all the things they did to us."

"The trouble has always come from the far side of the road," a Protestant housewife said, gesturing toward the Catholic area. "The Kincaid lad was one of those shot dead last June, and my husband carried him through our door. It was awful. I don't see how the two sides could ever live together again. All my dreams of good times are in the past, not in the future."

"The Catholics feel persecuted, and the Protestants fear the overthrow of the state of Ulster," said the Reverend Eric Gallagher, Chairman of the Irish Council of Churches. "The result is that we both act like we're under siege."

They didn't kick me,
Or break my arm.
But what they did
Does me more harm.
For they shot and killed
My brother, Sean.
        —*Poem by an eight-year-old*
            Belfast pupil

"By the time a child finishes primary school in Belfast, his attitudes are fixed and he sees Catholics or Protestants as a natural enemy, the people who are going to burn them out and shoot and kill them," says a psychiatrist who has studied them. "My feeling is that not much can be done with a child after this age."

The period following the border campaign was one of considerable optimism both in Eire and in Ulster. Events seemed to be moving in the direction of an eventual peaceful settlement of the Irish question. Middle-class Catholics in Ulster were becoming more numerous and appeared to be "establishing an easier relationship" with Protestants, who for their part seemed more tolerant of Catholicism, although nothing had been done about restrictions on voting, gerrymandering, and discrimination in jobs and housing.

Captain Terence O'Neill, Unionist prime minister of the Stormont government, was moving gradually—too gradually, as it turned out—to redress many of the wrongs that fell heaviest on working-class Catholics. He was also moving to establish closer relationships with the government of Eire, where attitudes also were changing. Fianna Fail had placed the issue of partition on the shelf. Eamon de Valera felt that any reunion of the two sections of the country should be left to time, that improvement of conditions in the Republic would eventually make it attractive enough for the people of Ulster to give up the border on their own initiative.

The conciliatory attitude in the south made it possible for Captain O'Neill to invite Sean Lemass, the Fine Gael prime minister, to Belfast when Lemass briefly replaced de Valera. This was followed within a few weeks by an O'Neill visit to Dublin.

These visits, viewed approvingly by London and by many people in both the north and south, stirred up the extremists on both sides of the issue. Some members of the Dail wondered aloud whether these meetings might be leading to *de jure* recognition of Stormont's right to exist as the government of the Six Counties; at the Stormont, there was muttering about the meetings being an erosion of the constitutional guarantees of separation from the twenty-six counties of the Catholic south.

The British position was fairly well summed up by Foreign Secretary Patrick Gordon Walker when he was asked whether he agreed that the maintenance of partition no longer served British or Irish national interests and whether he would favor a clear pronouncement that Britain had no desire to maintain the partition of Ireland.

"First of all," Gordon Walker said, "I reject the suggestion that the British government is maintaining partition, and I feel certain that any problems in this connection are best settled by the Irish people themselves. The recent meeting of Mr. Lemass and Captain O'Neill was welcomed by everybody and must be regarded as an encouraging step in the right direction. It is by such contacts that real progress can be made. For seven hundred years Britain has made the mistake of trying unsuccessfully to run the affairs of Ireland, and that mistake must not be repeated."

In addition to the problem of the border, there was a series of problems in Ulster itself that led to the return of the "troubles" to Ireland. Discrimination against Catholics was very real in jobs, housing, and, to some extent, voting. Working-class Catholics, like blacks in America, were often the last hired and the first fired. This situation was aggravated by the fact that unemployment in Ulster was much higher than in the rest of the United Kingdom or in the Republic of Eire. Housing was often under the control of city and county officials, as it was in the United Kingdom, and in those areas where Protestants were in control, Catholics were discriminated against. Where voting was concerned, there was one man, one vote in national elections—that is, in voting for the twelve members elected to the British House of Commons at Westminster. Election of the fifty-two members to the Stormont House of Commons was also by universal suffrage. The upper house, or Senate, consists of two ex officio members and twenty-four elected by the House of Commons, by a proportional representative system. It was in the Stormont election that gerrymandering had been resorted to by the Protestant majority to keep down the number of Catholic representatives. Voting in local elections was done on a system that was abandoned in the rest of Britain in 1949. It was based on real estate. Those who owned property or paid rent were allowed to vote; those who did not were not. This meant that other adults living in the house, such as children who were of age, could not vote in city or village elections. If a person owned two pieces of property (for example, a home and a business in another area), he had two votes. This system discriminated against the poor, the larger proportion of whom were Catholics.

It is possible, even probable, that discrimination in housing, voting, and, to some extent, jobs might have been eased considerably by the O'Neill government without violence if it had not been for the rise of two demagogic figures on the Irish scene. Many Protestants were certainly willing to go at least as far as doing away with the voting inequities, and the leaders of the dominant Unionist party seemed to be moving in that direction, but they were moving too slowly to suit the Catholics and too fast for some of their constituents. The man who first realized the depth of Protestant discontent with the liberalizing trend and took advantage of it was the Reverend Ian Paisley.

A tall, burly man with a commanding presence and a voice that projects and resounds like a Shakespearean actor's, Paisley was ordained by his father, the Reverend J. Kyle Paisley, in 1946. His father had been a breakaway minister of the Presbyterian church and Ian followed in his footsteps by founding the Free Presbyterian Church of Ulster. He received his doctorate of divinity from the Bob Jones University of South Carolina, a small fundamentalist college with a student body of three thousand. In the early days of his ministry he preached in a World War II Quonset hut but later moved to the Ravenhill Road Mission Hall in a working-class suburb of Belfast. His first years as founder and moderator of the Free Church were spent in run-of-the-mill antipopery tirades that earned him a considerable following among the more bigoted Protestant working people.

"In Britain the press and television tended to present him with good-humored contempt as an anachronistic demagogue who had somehow strayed from the seventeenth into the twentieth century," Iain Hamilton says in *The Irish Tangle*. "His potential as a populist rabble-rouser was acknowledged in passing, but any suggestion that this ranting preacher possessed possibly the shrewdest political intelligence in Northern Ireland would have been greeted with derision."

Hamilton is not alone in his assessment of Paisley's cleverness. "Paisley is a very shrewd man in two fields. He's a religious fanatic who belongs to the seventeenth century, but he uses very good twentieth century ways of collecting money," says Belfast reporter Jim Campbell. "Maybe he believes all he says, but it's certainly pure bigotry to talk in the twentieth century about the pope trying to take over the world and working hand-in-hand with Communists."

Of Paisley's top assistant, Clifford Smyth, Campbell says, "He's a carbon-copy of Paisley, but more so. I mean, he really believes that the world is going to be taken over by a sort of conspiracy between the Kremlin and the Vatican, and that Communism is only the tool of the Pope."

Paisley found a target much closer to home than "Old Red Socks," as he refers to the pope, when he took dead aim at Capt. Terence O'Neill and his hands-across-the-border campaign.

"I tell you, friends, the prophets foresaw exactly what is happening in Ulster now, the last dying struggles of O'Neillism," Paisley said during his campaign against reform. "I call down the curse of God on the traitor Capt. Terence O'Neill!"

He held a large family Bible in his hand as he spoke, opening it every now and then to read a few lines. "Praise the Lord, brethren and sisters," he would conclude and grin mischievously at the congregation, "I don't read anything here about praising Old Red Socks."

Murray Sayle of the London *Sunday Times* says Paisley is a master orator. "He is the only speaker I have heard who comes close to Fidel Castro. Their techniques are oddly similar, probably as old as the art of oratory itself, an almost schoolmasterly exposition broken by asides, savage humor, endless repetition of key phrases, picturesque abuse, and above all a total absorption in the changing moods of the audience."

Paisley's rise to importance almost paralleled that of another demagogic figure, one created more by the media than by her own doing, and one at the opposite extreme from Paisley. Bernadette Devlin was, and still is, as far to the Left as Paisley is to the Right. Paisley took advantage of the fears and prejudices of the Protestant majority to advance his political career, and Devlin took advantage of the very real grievances of the Catholics to advance her leftist totalitarian beliefs. She was partly a creation of the media, which used phrases like "Maid of Bogside" (apparently a comparison to Joan of Arc, the Maid of Orleans) to describe her and greatly exaggerated her importance. She shares with Paisley, however, a major portion of the blame for the polarization of opinion on both sides that has led to so much bloodshed in Ireland.

"The pope," says Ian Paisley, "is the enemy!"

"It's a class war," says Bernadette Devlin, "not a religious war!"

After her election to Westminster by a coalition of Republicans and leftists in 1969, Miss Devlin said, "We'll have a three-sided civil war: the Protestant bigots, the papist bigots, and us in the middle."

The Northern Ireland Civil Rights Association (NICRA) also played an important role in the events leading up to the "troubles" in Ulster. Views differ as to how it was formed, who made up its membership, and its purpose for coming into being. The Institute for the Study of Conflict says that NICRA was founded on February 1, 1967, by nonpolitical liberals and its purpose was to coordinate the activities of numerous local associations working to improve the lot of Catholics. Almost at once, however, the International Socialists— a revolutionary Marxist organization based in London—was "attracted by the potential cover such a liberal movement could provide for revolutionary activity and began to infiltrate the organization through its associate body People's Democracy founded in 1968 at Queen's University, Belfast." People's Democracy, of course, was Bernadette Devlin's base of power and was more Trotskyite than orthodox Marxist.

Public opinion in America, influenced by television and press coverage, was convinced NICRA was basically like the Southern Christian Leadership Conference of Martin Luther King, Jr., or the Urban League. This is the image that its spokesmen try to maintain to this day.

"NICRA was formed in 1967 by a very divergent group of people, ranging from members of the Unionist party, mainly trade unionists involved in the Belfast Trade Council particularly; people involved in the community; work community associations; tenant associations; Socialists; Communists; members of the Labour party; Republicans—the lot," Margaret Willard, an organizer of NICRA, told this writer. "Basically the organization was formed to bring about a level of democracy similar to that that exists in the rest of Britain because this area has always been denied democratic rights and civil rights, ranging from issues of the vote to internment without charge or trial.

In the early NICRA, our main work was fighting the Special Powers Act, the act which was allowing internment without charge or trial, which countervenes both the Universal Declaration of Human Rights and the European Commission on Human Rights.

"The responsible agent for all the situation even though the Unionist party was initially the agent that was carrying out the discrimination, because this was how the Unionist party maintained its power in the north of Ireland—political patronage and discrimination, religious discrimination, discrimination in housing, employment, opportunity, and so on—but overall the British government is responsible and always has been responsible."

Others active in the founding of NICRA tell different stories. Seamus Costello says that NICRA came into being while the IRA was still a unified organization: "The formation of the Northern Ireland Civil Rights Association came about as a direct result of the decision made by the Republican movement at that time. It was they who decided actually to start a civil rights association, and they did this through the Belfast Wolfe Tone Society. This was the agency through which the Northern Ireland Civil Rights Association was organized. The initial meetings were convened by them, and the association was set up by them. Republicans took a very active part in the formation of it, along with people who weren't in the Republican movement, and there were members of the Communist party involved; there were Nationalists involved; there were liberals involved; but the principal driving force behind the formation of it was the IRA."

Mairin de Burca says that NICRA was an effort to get in touch with people it had never bothered with before and to try to mobilize their support: "So the way we decided to take them into consideration was first to contact them. You see, up to this time the movement had no contact whatever with the Protestant population, because it never found it necessary to have such contact. Now we wanted to have contact of some kind, however low a level, and to try and build up some sort of trust and mutual activity between the two groups. The second thing was to form a civil rights organization that would stop the discrimination being practiced against the Irish minority in the north."

Sammy Smyth, one of the founders of the Ulster Defense Association (UDA), a Protestant paramilitary organization, gave his version of the founding of NICRA and its membership. After European revolutionaries failed in their attempt to take over the government of France, Smyth said, they looked around for someplace else to promote trouble and zeroed in on Northern Ireland because it had all the ingredients necessary to foment discontent that could be stirred into rebellion. "So the Northern Ireland Civil Rights Association was born. Now, three peculiar things immediately come to mind. Nationalists never, if they can possibly avoid it, call Ulster 'Northern Ireland.' They always call it 'Six Counties.' The second was that they had no Protestants. They'll tell you they had one or two Protestants, but I think you'll agree with me that if you have a population of ten thousand white people and you have three black people in it, you wouldn't call it a multiracial society. So the Northern Ireland Civil Rights Association could not call itself a nonsectarian organization. It *is* sectarian. The third point is that it's not a civil rights association. It is, in fact, a political organization whose aim has always been to destroy the government of Northern Ireland, any government of Northern Ireland. That was its aim. That is a political aim. It's not interested in civil rights.

"So the revolutionaries came over, and they decided to use all these ingredients in creating the Northern Ireland Civil Rights Association, and then the IRA joined in with them. They used us as a vehicle to start off their campaign. They would go in the streets and march; and because they were identified as Roman Catholic, as Nationalists, no support was available from the Protestants, which is a pity in one way and a tragedy, because if it had been a pure civil rights organization, the Protestants would have joined it, and who knows, they might have had a different society altogether today. Because at that time the world was in a change, the old values were starting to go, and the ordinary grass roots, the ordinary working people, were demanding a bigger say and a bigger share of the national cake. But this didn't happen simply because the Northern Ireland Civil Rights Association was sectarian—it was Roman Catholic, it was Nationalist, it wanted to destroy Northern Ireland. Therefore, no Protestant could support it.

"The revolutionaries set it up, supplied it with money, and the Communists have always been in that organization right from the start. I knew one of the girls from when she was a wee girl of about seventeen. She has always been a Communist all her life; she's always been involved in a Northern Ireland civil rights association. The Communists have always had a strong say in it, along with the international revolutionaries.

"So that got off the ground, as I say, and thus started the sequence of events that led to the destruction of Stormont and eventually to the situation as we have it now. The propaganda campaign they launched came at the right time for them. The Free State backed them, supported them in their propaganda throughout the world. The world perhaps was looking for something. Vietnam had been going on and was a bit boring, so they wanted something new. Here it was right on their doorstep as far as the United Kingdom was concerned, as far as the European press was concerned, and all of a sudden you find that for almost two and a half years, the Roman Catholics and the Nationalists and the revolutionaries could do no wrong. No matter what they did, they were hailed as saints. The Protestants, people like me, who had went to school in their bare feet—I worked as a laborer when I could get work— were suddenly labeled as jackboot Nazis. And I know what it is to starve. Many a time I had no meal on any particular day of the week, maybe three or four meals a week. In fact, we had free dinners in the local Roman Catholic parochial hall—that's the wee hall attached to the chapel—and we had our free dinners in there along with the Roman Catholic children, you know. But I was a jackboot Nazi."

NICRA did go into the streets with its demands, which were met at first by suspicion and then by violence. Paisley demagoguery stirred up all the old hatreds, and leaders such as Home Affairs Minister William Craig found it difficult to resist "playing the Orange card," the popular term used to describe the appeal to bigotry in Ulster. Captain O'Neill, however, was moving slowly toward granting most of the demands. His movement must have seemed glacial to the Catholics, but to many of his supporters in the Unionist party and to the oligarchic Orange Order it seemed like a disastrous avalanche hurtling down on them.

In Ulster there had always been the old and defiant custom of celebrating previous bloody clashes between Protestants and Catholics with taunting parades through areas where the opposition lived. The anniversary of William of Orange's victory at the Battle of the Boyne on July 12, 1690, was the excuse for tens of thousands of Protestants to parade. The men dressed in black suits and bowler hats with Orange Order ribbons draped across their chests. The women wore dresses made of Union Jacks and tall hats that matched, and they all marched to the sound of skirling bagpipes and huge Lambeg drums while thousands of Union Jacks and Red Hand of Ulster banners floated overhead. Easter was the Catholic's day. They celebrated the Easter Rising with tricolors, Easter lilies, and the singing of "The Soldier's Song." Unless the parades can be flaunted in front of the other side, they are considered less than successful.

NICRA marches had somewhat the same spirit to them. They were intended to provoke violence, and they almost invariably did. On August 24, 1968, the first march of three thousand NICRA members from Coalisland to Dungannon was peaceful, but it was one of the few that was. A march to Derry was planned next but was banned by William Craig. It was held anyway and led to a confrontation with the RUC during which some marchers were clubbed in full sight of the ever-watchful cameras of television. Viewers in Britain were shocked to discover that such things could go on in parts of the United Kingdom, and there were demands in Westminster that reforms be carried out.

Strangely enough, in spite of all the agitation from Paisley and other Protestant extremists, reforms were passed by the Stormont, and this has been largely lost sight of in the escalation of violence that followed. The *Irish Times,* published in Dublin, hailed the progress that had been made in its annual review of 1969:

> Now we enter a new period of history and of rapid change. Who would have believed this time last year, when we had what could be described as a Protestant Democracy and a Catholic Democracy, that Unionism would be in such a crisis, that the B Specials would be disarmed and [were] being phased out, that the RUC would have become a civilian service, that Unionism's local power

would be threatened by the new Housing Authority, that the Special Powers Act would be on the way out, that not alone one-man, one-vote but votes at 18 had been granted, that new electoral boundaries were being drawn, that an Ombudsman had been appointed, legislation against religious hatred enacted, new economic investment and new millions had been provided?

We are in danger of having a progressive State for a neighbor with all its challenge. . . .

In twelve months the Civil Rights movement had obtained more than all other movements, armed and constitutional, had achieved in fifty years.

Since most of the demands of protesting Catholics were being met, why didn't peace result in Ireland? There were three reasons. The first was that before the reforms were brought into effect the violence had escalated so rapidly that it had developed a momentum of its own. The second was that the reforms had so alienated the Protestant community that the leaders who had instituted them had lost most of their power base. The third, and perhaps basic, reason was that civil rights reform had not been the real reason for the demonstrations in the first place.

O Bradaigh gets right to the heart of it. "Well, supposing even the full civil rights program was implemented—so what? That's not what we were in business for. That's only a step up the road. The fact of the matter is that in our analysis of things, full civil rights are impossible under the status quo." In other words, the civil rights movement was only one step toward the ending of partition and the establishment of a thirty-two-county Ireland, which is the IRA's nonnegotiable goal.

Bernadette Devlin also made it clear that to her and People's Democracy the civil rights movement was only a tactic to promote the overthrow of both the governments of Ulster and Eire: "I don't want to 'rejoin' the Irish Republic, I want a thirty-two-county republic."

In July 1969, she said, "The Civil Rights Association is becoming radicalized too, you know. It's got groups in all the big towns who are getting set for action. . . . We'll have to start initiating—things like Free Derry, rent strikes, squatting, workers' control of the factories. . . . What matters is that the true conditions be exposed so that a united movement—a socialist movement—can be built up."

A representative of Devlin's People's Democracy on the Executive of NICRA said on February 13, 1970, "The only long-term solution is a workers' republic. . . . We do intend to push the Civil Rights Association to the Left."

Another IRA leader, Tomas MacGiolla, went even further: "Our objective is the reconquest of Ireland, from the ground landlords, the river barons, the speculators, the cartels and monopolies; and the struggle against them will now be intensified. If need be we must be prepared to win back our country farm by farm, river by river, mine by mine, shop by shop, and factory by factory."

Five members of Ireland's most popular showband were driving back from a gig when they were flagged down by UVF men in what appeared to be battle dress. Thinking it a routine security check, the musicians got out of the car as ordered. They were lined up against a hedge while two of the Protestant extremists began to attach a bomb to the van. The bomb exploded, and when the band members tried to flee, four were shot down. Three died, one was seriously wounded, and the fifth escaped to alert police. The bodies of two UVF men were beside the van, and police theorized they were attempting a "proxy" bombing by attaching a bomb to the van and forcing one musician to drive it to a spot where it would be exploded, by holding his buddies hostage. The plan backfired and with two of them dead, the other terrorists panicked and killed the band members.

A red minibus carrying twelve workers home from a textile factory in South Armagh was flagged down by a group of masked men. Asked if they were Catholic, the two people who said they were were allowed to leave. The Protestants who remained were fired on with automatic weapons. Ten were killed instantly, and the eleventh, sheltered by bodies piled around him, was severely wounded.

Christmas shoppers scattered as a car sped around a Belfast corner and opened fire on a British patrol with submachine-gun fire. Margaret McCorry, twenty, was hit in the head and died instantly. Twenty bombs were set off the same day. The IRA had boasted it would "wreck Belfast by Christmas," and this was December twentieth.

After all, what business is it of the British if we Irish want to slaughter each other? They were glad to have us slaughter their enemies when they needed us.
—George Bernard Shaw

The Bogside is a big, sprawling slum area of Londonderry, called Derry by Catholics, where approximately twenty-five thousand of them live in dilapidated old Victorian houses and flats. It was the scene of many of the most violent clashes between Catholics and Protestants, Catholics and police, and ultimately Catholics and the British army. Bernadette Devlin was on hand during many of the riots to harangue the Catholics, while Paisley and his aides performed the same function for the Protestants.

In late April 1969, the disturbances had been particularly intense in Belfast and Londonderry, and during one flare-up the RUC used batons, water cannons, and tear gas against mobs of Catholics throwing rocks and fire bombs. Devlin was there and she talked about it later in a speech to the House of Commons. She had helped collect stones to be thrown at police, she said, and "I organized the civilians in that area to make sure they wasted not one solitary stone in anger."

After several acts of sabotage had been committed against power and water facilities in Belfast, the government of Ulster asked for help from the British troops for the first time. The IRA was blamed for the attacks but declined to take credit. Five hundred of the more than thirty-five hundred troops who were then permanently stationed in Ireland were assigned to guard the key public-utilities installations at this time, but none was as yet committed to the streets. Those not on utility guard stayed in their barracks.

Prime Minister James Chichester-Clark's weak leadership may have precipitated the rioting of the summer of 1969, which was the real beginning of the troubles that have plagued Ulster ever since. Advised by high police officials to call off the Orange Day parade, the prime minister failed to act and bowler-hatted Orangemen waving Union Jacks poured into Belfast and Londonderry, some from as far away as Scotland and Canada.

The two previous years the marchers had been carefully controlled by police on the orders of then Prime Minister O'Neill, but this time they were allowed to move too close to the Bogside. They were attacked by Catholic mobs and the "balloon went up."

Riots ensued, and after two outbreaks of violence in the next month, both Catholic and Protestant moderates called on Chichester-Clark to ban sectarian demonstrations, including the annual parade to celebrate the end of the Catholic siege of Londonderry on August 12, 1689. He chose to disregard their request, and busloads of Orangemen roared into Londonderry bedecked with their customary sashes, bowler hats, and banners with the portrait of William of Orange.

When the parade reached the Bogside, Catholic youths began pelting the bands and the jig-dancing "Prods" with rocks from behind the shelter of police barriers. The rocks were picked up by marchers and thrown back. The battle was on. As the melee got worse, the RUC moved in behind shields in a series of baton charges and began driving the Catholics back into the Bogside. By late afternoon the place was a fortress. Hundreds of people built barricades while others laid nail-studded boards across roads to stop the armored cars of the police. It was obvious from the start that this was going to be no ordinary riot.

Tricolor flags appeared on the barricades, and Catholics armed with rocks, nail bombs, and Molotov cocktails defied the police to enter their "no-go" area. It bordered on insurrection, and Bernadette Devlin was there, dressed in jeans and boots and shouting, "Anyone who is not doing anything, get behind the barricades and help strengthen it! The rest of you, we need more rocks! We're in this together!"

When the RUC tried to move in, they were driven back with hails of large stones and fire bombs. As the bombs exploded they set men afire, and charge after charge with billy clubs and shields resulted in retreat. The fighting went on for days and spread to other areas.

"This is the worst fighting since this state was set up fifty years ago," Michael Farrel, a NICRA leader said. "I can see no end to it, only bloodshed and war coming."

The insurgents had stated that it was their intention to create chaos so that British troops would be forced to intervene and with them would come direct rule from Westminster. Bernadette Devlin made it clear when she declared that the "ultimate solution" she and her followers wanted was for the British to abolish the Ulster government and "rule directly from Westminster on a temporary basis while working out an acceptable form of government."

Chichester-Clark took the one last step open to him before calling for British troops. He announced "with reluctance" that the police reserves would be mobilized. Until then there had been approximately a thousand men of the Ulster Special Constabulary, or B Specials, on active duty. This mobilization would bring another ten thousand into the streets and would serve more as an irritant to the Catholics than a calming measure, because of the Protestant makeup of the B Special units.

The RUC used tear gas in Londonderry, which, according to some sources, was the first time it had ever been used against civilians in the history of Great Britain. It failed to clear the rioters from the Bogside barricades and enabled the RUC to gain only 150 square yards of the area.

"We will never give in now, never," one woman said as fire bombs were being made on an assembly-line basis and homemade gas masks were passed out. The Molotov cocktails were a new and more dangerous kind suggested by the Defense Committee. In addition to the half-bottle of gasoline, they contained sugar and detergent, which would stick to the skin of the police and to the sides of buildings and vehicles.

Chichester-Clark appealed for peace over television, asking for an end to "hooligan irresponsibility," which he blamed on "anarchists and others." Violence would not bring reform, he warned, and called upon the rioters to cease resistance to police, saying "peace, not vengeance" was their aim.

Sean Keenan of the Provisional IRA talked to this writer about the riot: "I was involved in civil rights. I always took part in their marches and protests, but in 1969 after some terrible incidents by the RUC when they batoned and used water cannon and boots or any other cudgel, in Derry then we set up what was known as the Derry Citizens Defense Committee, DCDC. This committee was set up to provide a defense for the people.

"There was always trouble during an Orange demonstration, and the Orange demonstration was due to take place on the twelfth of August. That's one of their big days in Derry. We set up this committee because we had seen the RUC coming into districts, smashing doors, breaking windows, batoning people. Every time there was a protest march, looking for civil rights, it usually ended up in the Bogside area. The protesters would get involved in a fight with the RUC, stones would be thrown, batons were used, water cannon were used against them, but eventually the RUC would drive them back into the Bogside. Then late at night when most people had dispersed, then they would come into the Bogside and overrun it and do all sorts of depredation.

"We decided to set up this committee, coming up to the twelfth of August, and I was elected chairman of this committee, which was representative of people in all walks of life. It wasn't just Republicans who were involved in the Defense Committee. We had people from different political parties. They were there from the Labour party, they were from the Nationalist party, they were Independents.

"On the eleventh of August, I came to Dublin to ask Jack Lynch for help because we realized what was going to happen. I didn't see Jack Lynch, but I told his secretary that the whole thing was going to blow up on the following day and that we expected them to provide protection or else to give us what was necessary to protect the people. He told me that they of Fianna Fail considered the people of Derry and the people of Belfast to be as Irish as the people of Dublin or Cork or Kerry or any other part of Ireland. He then referred me to the proper department, and they said this was a decision that would have to be taken at the highest level. Needless to say, they didn't give us anything, and on the following day, as we had forecast, all hell broke loose. The RUC invaded the Bogside with heavy armored lorries; they were followed by the B Specials and by a strong, militant Unionist group. They came down to the Bogside; they smashed the windows there. Look, they were all working together and a battle ensued then."

That was when Keenan's Defense Committee went into action, but they had nothing for the defense. Not knowing what else to do, they erected barricades. The fight lasted a long time, and the RUC seemed to be winning. Then something happened.

"Petrol bombs were used against them and a few direct hits were made and the RUC were through. We then strengthened the barricades, but for the next forty-eight hours the RUC poured CS gas into the Bogside steadily. Unceasingly, they fired canister after canister of CS gas into the Bogside. People in the area did not know what was going to happen. Children, old people, were all suffering from the effects of the CS gas.

"On the night of the thirteenth, Jack Lynch appeared on the television screens and said that they would not stand idly by and allow this to happen, but they did stand idly by. It was so bad in Derry that I rang up the chairman of the Civil Rights Committee in Northern Ireland, and I asked him to bring the people out in protest all over the Six Counties to take the pressure off Derry. The people came out, but in Belfast they suffered greatly for that, because on the night of the fourteenth, five hundred homes burned to the ground and nine people were shot dead. It was the same in other areas but not quite so bad. There was a man shot dead in Armagh by the name of James Gallagher. So here then we had a widespread protest against the brutalities.

"The people fought back and eventually they devised means of defense. Correspondents were coming to Derry from all the English papers and wanting to know who drew up these plans. Nobody drew up the plans of defense except for the barricades, but as the fighting went on, new plans were thought of and devised even by the young men themselves. The RUC made several attempts to invade the Bogside but—there's a high block of flats there at the entrance to the Bogside, high-rise flats—the young men went up atop the high-rise flats and they were kept well provided with petrol bombs. Every time the RUC made a foray, they were driven back by the petrol bombs. But, as I say, this grew out of the Troubles itself. Then the British army came in, and they said they came in to protect the people. They did not come in to protect the people; they came in to protect the RUC who were beaten to a standstill."

The fighting had reached a critical stage on August 13, when a well-organized strike force of Catholics poured out of the Bogside and advanced on the gasworks, generating plants, and a public housing office with the intention of destroying them. The mob was turned back from the power plant but seized the gasworks and were planning to set it afire when Jack Hume, a Catholic member of Parliament who was later active as a leader of the Social Democratic Labour party, arrived and managed to talk them out of it.

The first five deaths of the many that were to follow took place on August 14. In Belfast, opposing Catholic and Protestant mobs charged and counter-charged each other across a no-man's-land between the Catholic Falls Road and the Protestant Shankill Road, a historical battleground. Other pitched battles were fought along Crumlin Road and throughout the Ardoyne district. Rooftop sniping and street gunfire broke out during the night as the IRA went into action and armed Protestants occupied high ground around the local Catholic church and returned the fire. A total of twenty-nine persons were shot and five killed during the fire fights. Eighty-nine civilians and sixteen police were injured by other means.

Prime Minister Chichester-Clark, faced with the reality of escalating violence and a three-thousand-man police force that could be supported only by the unreliable B Special reserves, finally made the decision he had been putting off. He ordered the chief constable of the RUC to request British troops. Having been standing by in their barracks for several days, the troops were ready and moved out at once.

The news that the troops had been committed was greeted with joy in the Catholic areas. "Things will never be the same in Ulster again," a riot leader said, and those manning the Bogside barricades began to sing "We Have Overcome."

Within an hour heavily armed troops of the Prince of Wales Regiment arrived on the scene and moved toward the barricades through rock-strewn, glass-littered streets. They were met by Catholic women bringing "tea for the lads" and wild cheering.

"We have an impartial force now in the area!" Paddy Dougherty shouted after speaking to the officer in command. "We've won a magnificent victory!"

Bernadette Devlin popped out from behind the barricades to speak to British officers. She told them the residents of the area were glad to see the troops but reminded them that the "Bogside is ours."

Unlike the Catholics who had greeted the troops so joyfully, the IRA saw the intervention in a different light: "The military intervention was a crafty maneuver by Stormont to manipulate troops to allow the police and the B Specials to terrorize other Catholic areas. The police kept one step ahead of the troops in attacking our people."

Emergency powers were invoked on August 16, and a roundup of IRA members started with Special Branch detectives arresting twenty-five leaders under the Special Powers Act.

The arrival of British troops in Londonderry cooled things momentarily, but the fighting in Belfast, where the troops had not yet arrived, flared up even worse. Seven hundred of the RUC's three thousand men had been injured, some from having been set afire by gasoline bombs, and the rest were exhausted. No policeman, however well intentioned, could have contained the fighting that raged in Belfast. Armed gangs of IRA and Protestant militants roared through each other's areas, spraying anyone in sight with machine-gun and rifle fire. Snipers firing from rooftops pinned down police in many areas. As a last resort, armored cars were sent in with revolving machine guns to take out the rooftop snipers. Catholics charged that this indiscriminate firing was aimed at them, and they have continued ever since to view it this way. By the weekend, two hundred persons had been wounded and another eight killed by gunfire.

By late August, thousands of Catholics and Protestants had been forced out of their homes and 168 houses were destroyed by fire. More Catholic than Protestant residences had gone up in flames and each side blamed the other.

"The Protestants were there all right," a Catholic woman said. "About eleven o'clock it started. A crowd of dozens of them, boys and men, and women too; they're just as bad as the men, shouting, 'Fenian bastards, get out or we'll burn ye out!' One of our men ran and got the military to chase them, but they came back again, and it was about two o'clock some said they heard the shots."

"It started when they came up here screaming like Comanches," a Protestant said."It was like the battle of the Little Big Horn, it was."

Asked why more Catholic houses had been burned if the Catholics started it, the man replied, "They did it themselves. To make it more black."

"The Protestant majority of Northern Ireland is at war with the hierarchy of the Catholic Church," Ian Paisley announced not unhappily.

"There's going to be a civil war," Bernadette Devlin rejoined, "Catholic bigots against Protestant bigots with us in the middle."

Gen. Sir Ian Freeland, the British commander in Northern Ireland, issued orders that weapons hitherto kept in their homes by B Specials would now be handed over to the custody of the army and would be issued only at his discretion if and when the constabulary duties required them. "It is a great worry here in Northern Ireland," he said, "because there are so many weapons about on both sides of the community."

Sammy Smyth said of what happened, "You had the situation where the British army were brought in. They were brought in to defend the Roman Catholic areas, which in my opinion were not under attack. Now they were received with cups of tea and what have you, and in Belfast we laughed because we knew it was only a matter of time before they would do the dirty on the British army—start shittin' 'em! Anyone with a grain of sense could have told the British army, but because of the very effective world propaganda the

British army came over and were quite convinced that the Loyalists were jackboot Nazis. They believed this. The British army, the ordinary soldiers and the officers, actually believed this as well."

He said that when the relationship between the army and the people deteriorated in Londonderry, the battle started up again in the Bogside, and as it became clear the Catholics were losing, a priest was sent to Belfast to create a diversion to take the pressure off Londonderry.

Smyth continued, "The first attack in Belfast came from the bottom of Percy Street, and they fired into the Protestant district up Percy Street and I was there. I was on my way home, actually, when the shots were fired up my street. That was the first confrontation, but we then attacked the Roman Catholic areas because we were under attack. It's been said that we attacked those areas first; this is incorrect. I was there. We were attacked, and we attacked back. I'm saying 'we' but these were individuals, there was no regular corps at that particular time.

"The army also moved into Belfast. They laid themselves around the predominantly Roman Catholic areas, and they faced the Protestants. The IRA would move out of those areas in their cars. They'd throw petrol bombs, they'd shoot all around them, and then they'd go back into their areas. And they did this through the ranks of the British army. Now imagine a situation like that with the British army, maybe three or four of a patrol, standing on a street corner. A car flies through them, throws a few nail bombs, within vision and hearing as it scooted round the districts, fired through a lot of Protestant windows, then went back in through the patrol into the Catholic area. Multiply that by a hundred, and this is what was happening all over Belfast. Obviously this situation was intolerable.

"This was happening in Louisa Street, so we got fed up, and one night we waited on them. They came flying through, threw a few bombs, fired a few shots, and we were ready, so we went after them. We had no guns at the time; we were prepared to take them unarmed."

Smyth and his friends got as far as the entrance to a Catholic area before they were stopped by an army patrol.

"What are you stopping us for?" they demanded.

"You're not allowed to go in there."

"Well, then, you fuckin' well stop those bastards coming into our areas."

"Our orders are to protect the Roman Catholic people," the patrol told Smyth's angry group and warned they would shoot if any of them went into the street leading to the Catholic area.

The Protestants held a meeting and went to see a Colonel Eccles. They told him, "You'll have to stop the IRA." The colonel told them clearly and unequivocally, "My job is to protect the Roman Catholics. My job is to do nothing to antagonize the Roman Catholics."

"The colonel said that was his orders. Now that particular regiment stood with their backs to the Roman Catholic areas, and do you know how many soldiers they lost shot in the back? They lost seven soldiers shot in the back. Again, this is *fact*. Seven young fellows shot in the back from the people they were defending."

A car bomb exploded in a crowded street in a Catholic district at rush hour, injuring thirty persons. Troops arriving at the scene were fired on by IRA snipers. A mob led by IRA men dragged a city worker from his truck and beat him to death. It was later learned he had nothing to do with the bombing and was there to deliver a load of materials to board up damaged buildings. A Protestant, he was responding to a call by Catholic community workers. A priest who spoke at the funeral, attended by both Catholics and Protestants, said he wouldn't reveal the names of of the leaders of the mob because "they will suffer enough."

"They got buckshot right in the face— right in the face, the bastards," said a Protestant man. "My friend got a bullet right through his neck," added an eighteen-year-old. "They were sniping from the top of the Clonard Monastery. That's the Church of the Holy Redeemer. They had the permission of the pope."

Fred Proctor, a Belfast Protestant and city councillor, denounced the violence on both sides in a newspaper interview. Four days later there was a knock on his door and a gunman pumped six shots into him. Now he hobbles around on crutches, pelvis held together by steel pins.

The situation in Ulster was complicated by internal conflict within the IRA that finally resulted in the creation of two distinct factions who were at war not only with the Protestants and the British but with each other as well. There had always been a leftist trend in the IRA as well as the traditional Catholic nationalist view. Some of its heroes—Connolly, Mellows, O'Donnell, Ryan, Gilmore, and others—were men of the far Left, so it is not surprising that after the period of soul-searching that followed the failure of the border campaign, there should have been a swing leftward among the leadership. Nor is it surprising that there would be others in the organization of a more traditionalist turn who would fight that swing to the end.

The shift to the Left had led to the expulsion of many old-timers. In 1966, 250 members were expelled, including many well-known figures. In their place younger men, most of whom were Marxist, were joining both Sinn Fein and the IRA. The traditionalists were becoming more and more disenchanted and felt that without action the IRA would become merely another adjunct of the Communist party. They did not do anything about the situation, however, until it came to a showdown on the always touchy subject of abstention from constitutional political activity. Their refusal to recognize either government in Ireland as valid was a basic tenet that the traditionalists refused to give up. They never actively took part in elections and refused to take their seats if elected.

The stronger Marxist faction of the organization had decided this policy was self-defeating and were eager to plunge into political action. Sinn Fein headed by Tomas MacGiolla and the Army Council, headed by Chief of Staff

Cathal Goulding, wanted a complete shift away from abstention and sporadic violence into political action and agitation. They desired to make common cause with other leftist groups in the north and disassociate themselves from the old antipartition emphasis of the IRA. In December 1969 the Army Convention met in Dublin against a background of increasing turbulence in Ulster. It voted thirty-nine to twelve for de facto recognition of both Irish governments and the Westminster Parliament, an action that would leave the way open for Sinn Fein to contest elections in all three bodies.

The traditionalists immediately withdrew and issued a statement setting forth their views: "We declare our allegiance to the thirty-two-county republic proclaimed at Easter 1916, established by the first Dail Eireann in 1919, overthrown by force of arms in 1922 and suppressed to this day by the existing British-imposed six-county and twenty-six-county partition states."

The Provos also attacked the Official's view that the correct tactics should be political and criticized their failure to resort to guns in sufficient force in the north. In the beleaguered Catholic areas of Belfast and Londonderry, they said, IRA stood for "I Ran Away."

"We call on the Irish people at home and in exile for increased support towards defending our people in the north and the eventual achievement of the full political, social, economic, and cultural freedom of Ireland."

Although it was thought that the break was only temporary, the Provos immediately began contacting Republicans all over Ireland, drumming up support for a return to the old ways.

The break became final in January 1970 during Sinn Fein's Ard Fheis. The question of abstention was again raised by those who felt that the IRA should not "be diverted into the parlimentary blind alleys of Westminster, Stormont, and Leinster House."

Abandonment of abstention was voted on Sunday night, January 11, and failed by nineteen votes of getting the two-thirds majority required by the constitution of Sinn Fein. Prior to the vote, Tom Maguire, the last surviving member of the old Dail Eirann, said that the "convention had neither the right nor the authority to pass a resolution ending abstention" and indicated that if it did so, the traditionalists would walk out for good. A vote supporting the policy of the IRA leadership passed by a simple majority, and 80 of the 257 delegates walked out and met in a nearby hall hired ahead of time for the purpose. There they formed a Provisional Army Council and a caretaker Executive of Sinn Fein.

The caretaker Executive later made it clear that the action had been taken not only because of the abstention issue but also because of the leadership's support of extreme socialism leading to totalitarian dictatorship, the failure to protect the people of the north the previous August, and the expulsion of older members and their replacement by people interested "in a more radical form of movement."

A new paper, *An Phoblacht,* was started. Ruairi O Bradaigh became president of Provisional Sinn Fein and serving on the Executive were his brother Sean, John Joe McGirl, Sean MacStiofain, Eamon Thomas, P. Mulcahy, Charlie McGlade, Joe Clarke, and Larry Grogan.

Garret FitzGerald, foreign minister of the Republic of Ireland, spoke to this writer concerning the problems that beset Ulster and the part played by the two wings of the IRA: "The underlying problem is one of fear. The northern Protestants have a double fear. They are a minority. They can see themselves as a racial minority of Irishmen with extra loyalties, some of them to Britain, in the island of Ireland; and they have seen themselves historically in a dominant position, a part of a dominant group—certainly the Church of Ireland ones can. Presbyterians were in a somewhat different position because one day they were also in a subordinate position like the Catholics—of a dominant group but a minority with the advent of universal suffrage and Catholic emancipation and all the rest. They found themselves threatened, threatened with being a part of a whole new Ireland, eventually an independent Ireland, and that fear of domination by the majority group combined with the fact that they associate the majority group with the authoritarianism of the seventeenth-century Catholic Church and all the myths and traditions built around that intensified their fear. So their fear was not simply a simple intercommunity or racial fear but intensified by this particular fear of authoritarian Catholicism as they imagined it. It was that sense of fear that made them not want to be part of a single island of Ireland, because they had this sense of separateness and identity without necessarily denying their Irishness, which many of them would accept.

"The problem was compounded by the decision to divide Ireland, which, however well meaning, maybe had other motives behind it too, but the effect was to put this fear-ridden minority into a local majority position where they were able to work out their fears on a minority created within the area, which they proceeded to do, because to them the minority became part of the threat. It was the threat of the Roman Catholic Republic looming up to the south of them with twice as big a population and, as they see it, having more and more children than them. And what they saw was the 'Catholic Fifth Column' in Northern Ireland, who didn't accept the state, who were never allowed to accept the state or were never encouraged to, and were therefore seen as a threat to the state. So the fears they had as a minority on the island of Ireland were given an opportunity to work themselves out and were intensified, in a sense, by partition, in that they saw a dual threat, externally and internally, and so they moved to protect their position by discrimination in housing, in employment, and in politics.

"It is that that has created the basic situation which the Civil Rights movement was designed to overcome, and did largely resolve, but unfortunately in the resolution there were inevitably forces of repression that came up against the Civil Rights movement. This led to violence, and the British army, at the request of the Catholics, was brought in to protect the minority from the violence of those in authority in Northern Ireland, and that created a situation the IRA was able to exploit because the British army was actively present the way they hadn't been previously.

"So they came in to protect the Catholics. Their presence gave the IRA a chance to revive and so the Provisional IRA broke away as a nationalist anti-Communist wing of the IRA, rejecting Marxist philosophy of the post-1962 IRA, which had taken up a Communist-type position that they must unite the working class in order to destroy capitalism and therefore they were to unite Catholics and Protestants, not merely in the tradition of Wolfe Tone and Davis, eighteenth and early nineteenth century, but in the tradition of Karl Marx also. This sophisticated Marxist Republican tradition was rejected by these people who were the anti-Communist, extreme nationalist, authoritarian wing of the IRA, and they broke away and formed the Provisional IRA, moving in to exploit the situation. They are, in effect, a far-Right group with a certain amount of Socialist jargon to cover up the fact that basically they're extreme nationalist.

"It is the IRA tradition, although it had been subsumed into a Marxist-type Republicanism; there were enough of the old guard, militant Roman Catholic–orientated Republicans, in the sense they would be anti-Communist for traditional reasons, many of them indeed practicing Catholics and not too happy with the way the IRA was going anyway, and they suddenly saw a chance of breaking away and of reestablishing the IRA in what they saw as its role in the war against the British army.

"They therefore escaped from the constraints of not merely the post-1962 Marxist IRA, but effectively the whole IRA since 1922 had imposed on themselves the constraint of never starting trouble in Belfast. After 1922 the IRA had always avoided entering Belfast because they knew, the older generation knew, if you start something in Belfast, you start sectarian warfare and pogroms, and Catholics will suffer. But these people broke away from that tradition in order to take up cudgels against the British army, regardless of the consequences to the Catholics in Northern Ireland."

Mairin de Burca offered the Official IRA view of the split: "The change in IRA policy, the soul-searching that followed the border campaign, was not an overnight thing. It took about three years really, and the results of the deliberations were that the movement became socialist. The political organization became, in fact, a political organization, not just a supportive organization for the military wing. It initiated activities of its own of a political nature. Although we had always contested elections, it had always been on an abstentious basis, and it was now proposed to contest elections on a nonabstentious basis, to take serious part in the political activities, not just of the north but of the south, the whole country. This was resisted by the old guard of the movement, who went along with the traditional idea that Sinn Fein was simply there to support the military organization whenever a campaign was pending or in process. This came to a head in 1969 as a result of the Civil Rights Association activities in the north and because in 1969 it looked as if abstention was going to be defeated finally as political principle or policy of the moment.

In any case, the movement was split. On the one hand, you had the old guard who wished the movement to continue as it was and who were very anti-Left; they were mainly devout Catholics and Nationalists who saw Ireland in terms of Irish-speaking Catholic Republicans and not at all left-wing. And on the other hand, you had the new element brought in by the years of planning and investigation and what have you."

Mairin de Burca did not agree that the Official IRA is a Communist organization. "I don't think we've progressed that far, but we are progressing." Most members are Marxist, but it is still possible to find some non-Marxists. They are not interested in establishing a society like that of the Soviet Union in Ireland. As she points out, "Russia is not actually a Communist society." What would be desirable from the Official IRA point of view would be a dictatorship of the proletariat in all of Ireland. Asked to name a present-day society that fits their vision for Ireland, Cuba was the best she could do. "The closest I think we can come to any particular country would be Cuba, but even there, there are differences of degree. Cuba has a very high illiteracy rate. We don't have that problem. Cuba had a very, very vicious and brutal totalitarian regime, Batista. We don't have that problem yet. But on the other hand, we have what Cuba had, which is a very powerful imperialistic neighbor. Cuba had America, we have Britain, who would do their damnedest to see that their nearest neighbor did not go Left. Cuba was to a great extent a Catholic country; we are a Catholic country. But the Irish revolution when it comes— and it will come—will be totally unique."

O Bradaigh naturally sees things differently. He agrees that after the border campaign there was a period of self-examination by the IRA with the adoption of some socialist ideas, but he seemed to view the shift to the Left as more the result of infiltration from outside the IRA: "A number of people then emerged who had been in either the Irish Communist party, which was known as the Workers' party then and has since been renamed the Communist party, or the Connally Association in England, which is an Irish section of the British Communist party. And one or two of these people arrived on the scene as technicians and were taken in, and one of them was named as director of education and so on. And there seemed to be no definition of what the ultimate objective was. There were a couple of things emerging, anyone could see that. First, the IRA was being progressively disarmed and run down as a military force; and second, Sinn Fein was being brought more into the realm of ordinary constitutional politics, and I mean in the sense of the status quo, participating in the existing political setup in the system, becoming part of it while saying it wanted to change it, and moving closer all the time to the official Communist party, working together for political objectives, and finally, the forming of a formal alliance to be called the National Liberation Front. As it was coming to a head, the northern troubles broke.

"The split in the movement was there all the time. What brought it into the open in dramatic fashion was the absolute escalation of violence that took place. It was obvious to the most simplistic observer that the troubles had started with the police banning of a march and battering the marchers with batons. It escalated then—that was in October [1968]. In November, Paisley's people took over the center of Belfast and attacked a civil rights march with sticks and cudgels. In January, there was the People's Democracy march from Belfast to Derry, which was ambushed and attacked and so on, and it ended up with mob violence, and the police sat in their tenders and watched it. It went from that to the police invasion of the Bogside. Then in April, following Bernadette Devlin's election, the police again invaded the Bogside in Derry, beat up people, and a man died as a result. Anyone could see that the escalation was there, the violence was getting greater and greater, and the next time round there would be shooting.

"There had been some shooting because the police were armed, and in some situations they had drawn their revolvers and fired them. It was at this time that there was a meeting of the Army Council, and I asked what was being done to meet the escalation situation, that it was obvious it was getting rougher every time and it was obvious there was going to be shooting and what was being done to defend the people. I asked about street committees and picket duty—this was the language of the 1920s. I asked about defense committees having caches of arms in every area, even though they were only sporting rifles. But Goulding stood up and said, 'It is not our job to be a Catholic defense force, and when the time comes, we'll put it up to the official forces, the army, and the RUC to defend the people.' "

O Bradaigh felt that because of their commitment to Marxism the leadership of the IRA was wearing ideological blinders. They were following a book that had been written for other countries and other situations. He spoke of an old-time IRA man who was in his eighties and lived down in the country but had been able to see the problem more clearly than the leadership as represented by Goulding and MacGiolla: " 'The civil rights now has just brought this along very nicely and the election of Bernadette Devlin did no harm either,' he told me, 'but I tell you, you'd best be watching out, you need to be getting a few guns together and keeping them piled up because this thing is going to boil over and you don't want to be caught out.' "

Aside from the issues of the resort to arms and abstention from regular politics, O Bradaigh said there were other differences between his organization and the Officials. "Let's get down deeper into first causes, if you like. Now their line, the official Communist line, is that anyone who doesn't agree with them is a fascist—the slogans for the masses and the great woolly theoretical stuff for people who read or try to think.

"What we want to see is—and we would agree with their analysis to a great extent on colonialism and all that type of thing—but when it comes to solutions, we want to see a socialist federal Ireland. We want to see power broken up at the center and brought down to the provinces and to the people. We don't want a unitary state."

They want to set up four provincial parliaments, self-governing communities, and the devolution of power right down the line to local areas. This would accomplish three things, the first of which would be a solution to the problem of Ulster. With the British gone from the north, one parliament would be established for the nine northern counties (three that are now in the Republic were once considered part of the province of Ulster). This would supposedly give the Protestants a majority of 58 percent to 42 percent in that area. Each of the other provinces would set up a parliament, and all would be under a federal system but would have control over their own affairs in everything except foreign affairs, defense, and national finance. The system would be somewhat similar to that of Switzerland, with its cantons and communes, and would give the maximum amount of self-government, allowing the ordinary citizen to have the maximum amount of say over his own affairs. There would be considerable socialization of big business—industries, banking, and insurance—and an upper limit would be imposed on the amount of land one corporation or individual could own.

This was quite different, O Bradaigh felt, from the totalitarian state the Officials wanted, with all authority concentrated in one place, Dublin, and the individual left without control over his rights.

Mairin de Burca and Seamus Costello, among others, have said that the Provos have no philosophy but that of the gun. Professor Neil F. Keatings of Trinity College, Dublin, seems to agree with them: "I don't think the Provos are socialist. To my mind, the socialist coloring, or the nonnationalist side of their program, is something they've just had to cook up in order to answer the questions that they haven't thought about. I think it's a botch-up; I don't think it's a coherent philosophy. I don't think any of this has a great meaning for the supporters of the movement." Neither does he think the Provos are fascist as the Officials claim: "I would think that they're right-wing in so far as they place a mystical emphasis on the nation, but that, I think, is really as far as it goes. I think essentially their position is holding themselves on this very narrow path of achieving statehood for the whole of Ireland without bothering terribly much as to what sort of state it would be."

"Most of us came here four or five months ago and we never knew or cared whether a man in the unit was Protestant or Catholic," said Charles Ritchie, a twenty-eight-year-old career soldier, "but here that's the first thing that people ask you. I tell them that I'm Christian. They don't seem to know what that means."

Three British sergeants drinking in a pub were approached by two girls named Pat and Jean, who lured them away to an apartment with the promise of a party. There they were forced by IRA gunmen to lie face down on a bed and were then riddled with bullets from a pistol and submachine gun. A fourth soldier escaped with only a shattered jaw by jumping out a window. The girls were members of the Cumann na mBann.

Three British soldiers died and a fourth was seriously injured when twelve to fifteen Irish Republican Army gunmen attacked an observation post in the border province of Armagh. The fifth soldier was uninjured after thirty-five minutes of rifle and machine-gun fire poured into the post.

At 3:00 P.M. the troops go on "lollipop" patrol, keeping peace between Catholic and Protestant children on the way home. Kids throw stones and epithets and teen-age snipers shoot at them. One man was killed. "What can you do?" a soldier asks. "You can't shoot kids, but I know a couple of 'em I'd like to ship though."

In Catholic neighborhoods, housewives pound cricket bats on the sidewalks to warn the IRA of approaching police or military patrols. Catholics paint the sides of houses and other buildings white so patrolling troops will be clearly outlined for IRA snipers. The army resprays the walls with black or purple paint. "The loser may be the side that runs out of paint first," joked a British officer.

To the glorious, pious, and immortal memory of King William the Third, who saved us from Rogues and Roguery, Slaves and Slavery, Knaves and Knavery, Popes and Popery, from brass money and wooden shoes; and whoever denies this toast may he be slammed, crammed, and jammed into the muzzle of the gun of Athlone and the gun fired into the Pope's belly, and the Pope into the Devil's belly, and the Devil into Hell, and the door locked and the key in an Orangeman's pocket; and may we never lack a brisk Protestant boy to kick the arse of a Papist.

—*Orange Order toast*

The increasing demands of the Catholic civil rights movement and the demagoguery of Ian Paisley and others created a climate in Ulster that led to the foundation of militant Protestant groups that were in a way mirror images of the IRA. There had been Protestant extremists all the way back to the formation of Ulster and the riots of the 1920s, and while the Orange Order does not officially endorse violence, it is the spiritual home of a great many Neanderthal types who do.

A new line of Protestant vigilante and terrorist organizations that have ominous implications for the future of Ireland began to emerge in 1966 when the Ulster Volunteer Force (UVF) was founded. Stating that they were opposed to equality for Catholic Nationalists as well as the Communist-Left coalition of Sinn Fein and other revolutionary groups in the north, the UVF announced its arrival on the scene by murdering two young men in Belfast simply because they were Catholics.

At that early point in the escalation of violence, the so-called Malvern Street murders almost touched off the same sort of bloody events that came later. Only the fact that the RUC moved quickly to arrest the perpetrators, who were tried and sentenced to long prison terms, prevented the Catholic retaliation. Prime Minister Terence O'Neill followed through by banning the group shortly thereafter. As a result, the UVF faded for a while, but as the Troubles increased, it reformed and beefed up its membership until it was estimated by the Institute for the Study of Conflict that in 1971 it consisted of over five thousand armed and drilled men.

If Paisley was not directly involved in the founding of the UVF, his rhetoric was undeniably of the type that inflamed the passions and prejudices of the members of the UVF and other paramilitary organizations. "The love which the ecumenicists bleat about is full of dissimulation," Paisley argues against Protestants associating with Catholics. "They breathe charity to the Antichrist and his worshippers and hate to the true Christ and his worshippers —the so-called love which cleaves to evil, evil teachers, evil systems, evil doctrines, and evil associations is a bastard charity and the offspring of hell itself."

"Not an Inch!" was Paisley's theme. "We will show these compromising, pussyfooting, fence-sitting Unionists that there are still Protestants in this country not prepared to compromise."

In about as close to a deliberate provocation to violence as he ever came, Paisley called upon the Protestants of Londonderry, who were busy making fire bombs to destroy the homes of their neighbors in Catholic districts, to resist actively the IRA, which he said was about to take over the city.

"Now there may be attacks on the Bogside by Roman Catholics pretending to be Protestants," he said. "If there are, you'll know they were by Catholics because I've told you about it."

On April 28, 1969, Terence O'Neill resigned as prime minister of Northern Ireland over the failure of his moderate policies. He was succeeded by James Chichester-Clark, another man of moderate views. Several months after O'Neill resigned, Ian Paisley was elected to Stormont from O'Neill's former constituency in Bannside, County Antrim, and proclaimed triumphantly, "This is a day of thanksgiving. Last year at this time I was in prison clothes and Terence O'Neill was in parliament. Today I'm in parliament and in Terence O'Neill's seat. It's a miracle."

According to Jim Campbell, "There are five Protestant paramilitary organizations; the two big ones are the UVF and the UDA, and they fluctuate in power. One time the UVF is in the ascendancy, a couple of months later it's the UDA."

The Ulster Defense Association (UDA) was the larger and perhaps at one time had as many as eighty thousand members, some of its leaders claimed. They paraded through the heart of Belfast wearing old army uniforms, commando jackets, boots, forage caps, and black hoods.

"It would have frightened you," Campbell said. "I stood on the street and watched them. Thousands of masked men in military uniforms marching through the streets in perfect military ranks, and the police and the army just standing watching them. They did it several times. Every time they wanted to threaten the government, they staged one of these marches."

Protestant terrorism was a response to Catholic terrorism and also a cause for the escalation of it. Mob violence by both Catholics and Protestants had been endemic in Ulster for generations, but in the 1966–69 period it became a way of life. The IRA was involved but so were the Loyalist groups.

Through the early 1970s Protestant terrorism grew until it was as great a force to be reckoned with as the IRA. By the summer of 1973, the UDA and the more violent UVF were the main perpetrators of crimes against Catholics and against the state that they claimed to be defending. "From January to August of that year, 69 people died in sectarian murders and 40 of them were Catholics; during June and July Loyalist extremists planted 36 bombs, killing 3 people and injuring 70," D. L. Price wrote in a study.

In mid-June of 1973 still another Protestant terror gang made its appearance. The Ulster Freedom Fighters (UFF) introduced itself to the troubled area with a "death list" containing the names of Social Democratic Labour party leaders who were taking part in the new power-sharing Executive that had been set up by the Sunningdale conference.

Like the UVF, the UFF made some pretense of being a political organization, but the RUC said both groups had large numbers of common criminals as members. Ulster police estimated that over 75 percent of their membership consisted of criminals from the Belfast dockyards. Some were already well known to the police, and it was thought that their only motive for joining such groups was as a cover for their criminal activities or out of a craving for violence. There were other elements in the UVF, however, who were able to exert influence over local chapters, such as that in East Antrim which stated it would give up "active service" (terrorism) and concentrate its efforts on "community activities." The reason given for this move was the success of "loyalist" candidates in the Assembly and local government elections.

There may have been other reasons for the change as suggested by Jim Campbell. "The position of the UVF is in a state of continual flux. There are elements within it that are pretty progressive—I'm speaking comparatively here. At the moment it's controlled by a moderate group. Two months ago it was controlled by an extreme right-wing group which carried out a series of sectarian assassinations and bombings. Because of this the police arrested most of the leaders and outlawed the UVF. In reaction to this, the men who have taken over have been more moderate and sensible, politically minded."

After it was outlawed by the O'Neill government in 1966, the UVF reemerged in 1970 during a period of attempted reconciliation by Merlyn Rees, the secretary of state for Northern Ireland. It was legalized and remained so for about two years. It was told, says Campbell, that it appeared to be more politically orientated, "so we will make you a legal organization in the hope that you will work on a political front." For a short time it did, but within the organization were people who saw the political orientation of the UVF as dangerous. They thought it was being taken over by the Left, so they took control of it and the militants became powerful, took over command, and started shooting, killing, and bombing again until finally the UVF was outlawed again by the British government.

Like the IRA, Protestant terror groups killed not only the opposition but often their own members. Tommy Herron, former vice-chairman of the UDA, was shot to death by gunmen from his own organization amid allegations of racketeering and extortion in his East Belfast section.

Protestants claim they act in self-defense or in defense of their coreligionists, and this was precisely the claim made in the beginning of the violence by the IRA. There has been little Loyalist activity aimed at police or the army in Ulster and consequently security forces have been less active in hunting down Protestant terrorists, leading to accusations of partiality on their part.

On May 17, 1974, terror struck in the Republic of Eire. Three cars loaded with explosives blew up in the busiest areas of Dublin and another went off in Monaghan, killing 28 people and injuring 150 more. The RUC reported that the cars had all been stolen in Protestant districts of Belfast, and a hitherto little-known Protestant gang called the Red Hand Commandos claimed responsibility for the deaths.

Writer John Laffin has suggested that these car bombs may not have been the work of any Protestant group. He reasons, "The heart of world terrorism is Tripoli, Libya. Qaddafi underwrites and directs much terrorism and provides the final haven for those terrorists too hot to be taken in elsewhere. Most foreign terror groups, including the IRA, have a permanent representative in Tripoli. The IRA man arranges for arms, ammunition, and explosives and periodically the Libyans give him instructions about how the IRA should operate in Eire, Ulster, and Britain. The car bombs which exploded in Dublin with so much destruction last year were probably the result of Libyan advice or influence."

Mairin de Burca thinks Laffin could possibly be right. "The Provisionals initiated a military campaign in the north, which was perfectly compatible with their strategy, you see. If a military campaign doesn't succeed, then there's a period of lull while you reorganize and then there's another military campaign. And so they carried it out, but this time the campaign was different than it had been. If it had been the usual kind of campaign, well, I suppose a few soldiers would have been killed, but this time they became far more sophisticated—if that is the word one is looking for—and more ruthless. They adopted, for instance, some pretty risky tactics. They adopted the car bomb for one thing. Daithi O'Connell, who is now in prison, one of their top leadership, took the credit, accepted the credit—he called it *credit,* I would say *blame*—for having introduced the whole element of civilian casualties.

"I was in the movement during the whole 1950s campaign and I don't think there was a civilian casualty in six years. If there was, it was absolutely, utterly an accident. Quite frankly, knowing the people of that day, I believe that they would have died themselves rather than endanger one innocent civilian. But all that has changed and they are responsible for an appalling number of civilian casualties through indiscriminate bombing of civilian targets, not only in Ireland but in England."

Others have also noticed the change both in type and viciousness of the violence in Ireland. Benjamin Briscoe, a member of the Dail, is the son of Robert Briscoe, onetime Lord Mayor of Dublin and probably the only Jewish member of the IRA during the 1916–20 period. Comparing the level of violence during his father's time with that going on today, Briscoe said, "I want to tell you one thing. When we were fighting for our independence here from 1916 to 1921, there were only two civilian targets destroyed. One was the General Post Office, where the fighting broke out, and the other was the Custom House, which was set on fire because all the documents of the British administration were housed in it. Just two civilian targets. They didn't shoot innocent people; they didn't kidnap people or take hostages.

"These people are psychopaths; these are people who have no conscience. They act like Palestinian terrorists. In his writings, Dr. Habash states that there's no quarter shown. If you're in the business of terrorism, you must show no mercy whatsoever, and that's the kind of training these people get."

There can be no doubt of the change in the level and type of violence in use in Ireland. Is it possible the new violence is an import as are most of the weapons?

Whoever was responsible for the car bombs in Dublin and Monaghan, the fact is that the UDA, the UVF, and the UFF exist and have been matching the IRA kill for kill in recent years. The largest of these groups, the UDA, does not consider itself a terrorist organization—but then neither do the IRA, the PLO, the Baader-Meinhof gang, or any other terrorist group.

"Let me make it clear that we do not consider ourselves a terrorist organization," Sammy Smyth said. "We are purely a defensive organization, and in fact, that is a weakness rather than a strength. Had we been an offensive or terrorist organization, we probably would have been more effective, but because we are a defensive organization it has left us weak in terms of motivation."

Smyth's reasoning is that the UDA had to be formed because the rioting and the violence that accompanied NICRA marches had forced the government to give in to Catholics so much that the Protestants were endangered. He blamed much of the government's weakness on media propaganda, particularly the television coverage of the rioting.

"The Unionists melted under the fiery effect of propaganda, so what happened? First of all, you had the USC, the Ulster Special Constabulary [B Specials] disbanded, and then the Royal Ulster Constabulary were disarmed. Why were the USC necessary? They were a localized police force, reservists who knew everything about their local area, which meant they knew every IRA man and every IRA sympathizer. You've got to remember that the state has always been under constant attack since the day it was set up in 1920. In the early years, 1920 to 1927, the IRA were fairly active; after that, they were sporadic. Maybe every five to seven years they would come out and blow up a few phone boxes and shoot a few policemen and what have you. The USC was created because the members were localized, because they knew their area and the people in them. They did not saturate any area except during periods of IRA activity; during periods of quietude they met only about once a month to keep up their shooting. Then when the IRA had an upsurge, the numbers were increased and the USC would put up roadblocks in different parts of the province.

"The RUC were very effectively organized before the army came in. They could close off the province in ten minutes. Before the two states were set up, the Royal Irish Constabulary was the police force for the whole of Ireland, and basically it carried on into each of the respective forces. So if the RIC were in Dublin, they joined the Gardai there; if they were in Northern Ireland, they joined the RUC."

Smyth claimed that with the RUC disarmed and the B Specials disbanded, the Protestants felt threatened and could expect no help or sympathy from the British troops.

"So we said, 'We can't let those bastards come in and shoot us up every night.' So we went and got wood and put up wooden barriers. These wooden barriers went up from seven o'clock at night until seven o'clock the next morning. We manned them at two-hour intervals so everybody could get some sleep. The first night we put them up, the army came flying around in their jeeps and knocked them hell for leather. So we got uptight about it, and we went to the army and said, 'What the hell are you doing?' 'You're not allowed to block the Queen's highway.' 'All right, are you going to block it then and stop those IRA cars from coming through?'

"There were a number of vigilante groups which sprang up all over different parts of Belfast, and we called a meeting of the groups. Sammy Boyle, Hardin Smith, and myself went to these other areas, and we called a big meeting to take place. At that meeting over a thousand men attended, representatives of the vigilante groups from all the front-line areas, and from that the Ulster Defense Association came into being. I was appointed the coordinator and the organizer, and I became the first and only public organizer that the Ulster Defense Association ever had, and also their spokesman.

"For the next eight months, I went round the whole of Northern Ireland, speaking at meetings, explaining the position about the front-line areas, pointing out that if the front-line areas were left to fall to the IRA, then you'd have the domino theory, that the next area would become the front line and so on. At the end of the eight months, we stopped organizing and concentrated on disciplinary methods, on formation, drill, training, and what have you."

The Orange Order was not involved in the UDA, Smyth said, nor was the UDA in any way a political group. "We were a spontaneous emergence of front-line people. The RUC were disarmed and demoralized, so we had to be ready to protect the Protestants. This was grass roots. The middle class deserted their traditional role of leadership and left us without leaders. It is predominantly a working-class organization. Not Communist, not radical, not anything. We simply defend our areas. We are not a political body."

Once organized, the UDA began to show their power to the hitherto disdainful authorities and politicians. They organized a march through Belfast.

"Now when we held that march of eighty thousand people, all of a sudden the politicians became very conscious that the UDA existed. Prior to that, they didn't want to know such a lot of rabble, the scum of the earth, as it were. All of a sudden here was a force that could be used, so the politicians tried to move in. So they were told politely to 'bugger off! Don't want to know ye!'

"Then the internationalists, the Commies, tried to move in. 'Oh, here's a terrific force! What we could do with eighty thousand men! We could turn not only Northern Ireland, but the whole of Ireland into a revolutionary state!' So one by one we picked out the Communists as they infiltrated, and we removed them, we executed them, because we were not a political organization.

"We allowed no political infiltration of any kind. The biggest weakness, if you could call it that, was the fact that we were defensive. The IRA, the Provos, the IRSP, all are very successful because they have an aim and an objective; that is, the destruction of Northern Ireland. That is their primary objective. The second objective for IRA Officials is the creation of a thirty-two-county socialist republic; the second objective of the Provos is the creation of a thirty-two-county Ireland; the second objective of the IRSP is the creation of a revolutionary state; but their primary objective is the destruction of Northern Ireland. Now when an organization has an objective, it has motivation, it has a reason for people to hold together, to cling together, to fight together, to stand together, but when you have a defensive organization which only becomes operative when it's under attack, the motivation is not there when you're not under attack, so it means the membership of the UDA goes up and down like a Yo-Yo. When we're under attack, the membership swells; when we're not under attack, it falls away and you have only your hardcore group of five thousand dedicated men.

"Within that core group, you have a very, very small select elite group. This numbers twenty-five. Now, they are in fact unknown to the leadership of the UDA. Their job, as they see it, and they were formed for this specific purpose, is to execute anyone who would destroy the UDA, execute anyone who poses a threat to the cohesion of the UDA."

If anyone doubted that the UDA was a fanatical organization, this revelation of what amounted to a murder squad in their midst certainly should erase that doubt.

"This elite group is very important. They're the ones who execute the political motivators, who in fact execute anyone who will pose a positive threat to the structure and the coherence and the cohesion of the Ulster Defense Association. If they thought I was opposed, I would be dead tomorrow. In fact, they have protected me on a number of occasions because I happen to think the way they think.

"They don't hold kangaroos; they just execute. They make the decision. They don't do it spontaneously; they watch someone over a long period of time because a person may react to a given situation only for a wee while, but as time goes on then he may hang back, change his position. In other words, they may not have all the facts, so they don't act spontaneously. They watch someone, and then if they find out that in their opinion he is acting or working in such a way that he threatens the unity of the UDA, then they will remove him."

Their jurisdiction was restricted, however. It did not extend to ordinary discipline such as someone wanting to leave the UDA or going out on his own to shoot or bomb the enemy. In the first instance, a member of the hard core of five thousand isn't permitted to leave—once he's in, that's it, but it would be up to the leadership to decide what measures to take if someone should leave. It would also be up to the leadership to deal with unauthorized action.

"The twenty-five wouldn't worry about that. That is not threatening to the unity of the UDA. It may bring a bit of bad publicity, but if it was aimed at the enemy, they wouldn't worry about it. The overt leadership would worry about it because it involves discipline.

"There are times when something happens in a particular area that might seem irrelevant to the leadership but which could be of supreme importance to the unit in that area. Say one of their men was shot or a Protestant house was burned out in a Roman Catholic district, and the locals know if they don't act, there will be more of the same type of thing. To show the opposition they'd better stop such activity, it may be imperative to bump one of them off or plant a bomb. In such a case, the local unit wouldn't have time to get permission from the central leadership. Such decisions have to be made instantaneously and carried out even at considerable risk to the participants. The discretion for such decisions exists because the UDA is not a formalized army and leeway has to be allowed."

Aside from the five thousand hard-core members, support fluctuates, a condition Smyth says the IRA does not have to worry about.

"They have the support of the Roman Catholic people as a whole, both working class and middle class. And I know this. I worked with both, and I know the strength of Sinn Fein. Because this image of a united Ireland some-how coming about has grasped the imagination and the heart and soul of the Roman Catholic people. I'm not saying they agree with everything the Provisionals or Officials do, but the support at the end of the day is always there, which means that the IRA can often go ahead, step out in front of the Nationalist people knowing that hardy comes to hardy; they can still pull those Roman Catholic people with them. The UDA cannot do that and has never been able to do that. The UDA must never take more than a very short step in front of the people that give it support. The minute they step forward and leave the people behind, those people will express their dissatisfaction with the UDA very forcibly."

Money is also hard to come by. Protestants, Smyth says, are peculiar. Except for times of stress, money is difficult to raise. "So what we did for a while was obviously get money from other sources. We got money from Canada, from America, and Australia, all collected. None from international revolutionary movements which we would have nothing to do with. The Canadians have been very good to us; the Yanks not so much. The Australians have been very helpful, and all that money went to buy arms and guns and what have you."

As to the actual action taken against the IRA, it was mostly forays into the Catholic districts and other guerrilla tactics, up to and including assassination. "If you read about the assassinations, you'd think everybody was a saint in Northern Ireland, that the only people killed were saints, but the vast number of assassinations were, in fact, IRA personnel or people involved with the IRA."

The terrible fear the Protestants have of being swallowed up in a predominantly Catholic nation comes through strongly whenever mention is made of anything regarding the border. Nothing else seems to matter quite as much.

"That border must remain sacrosanct. That's it! No argument, no discussion, no compromise! The border must remain. That is the motivating factor of the Loyalist population. And, of course, the motivating factor of the Roman Catholic population is that the border must be done away with, so it's the irresistible force against the immovable object. But that's it."

The reason the Unionist party has had the support of the Protestant population is because they were the only ones who guaranteed the border. The Loyalist working-class people had no one else to elect, and therefore no matter what else the politicians did or said, as long as they guaranteed the border, they were returned. "If you're a politician belonging to the Unionist party," Smyth said, "you don't have to do constituency. You don't have to do anything except promise that the border will be there. I *dare* not *not* vote for you, because if I don't, the enemy—the SDLP, the Alliance party, the UPNA—will get big votes, the Loyalist politician will get only wee small votes, and Westminster is going to think the people want what the Alliance or the SDLP or the UPNA want. So the Loyalist knows he has to vote for the bloody Unionists.

"So the border is the pivot; it's the linchpin of the whole problem in Northern Ireland, and until people realize that, they do nothing but talk a lot of nonsense. If only America, England, and the rest of the world understood that, they would understand the problem a lot more clearly than they do."

The spokesman for any organization naturally presents its aims and motives in the best light possible, defends its mode of operation, and claims only the highest devotion and selfless dedication of its members, and Sammy Smyth was no exception. The UDA, however, is not precisely as he painted it. The infamous "Romper Room" incident shows very clearly the viciousness of some of its adherents. "Romper Room" was originally the name of a children's program shown on Northern Ireland television, and the term had been adopted to describe the torture rooms said to be used by paramilitary organizations on both sides.

The brutal murder of Ann Ogilvy shocked even the Loyalist community in Belfast. Her crime was that she was a Catholic who fell in love with a married UDA member. On the evening of July 23, 1974, Ann Ogilvy and her small daughter were forced into a car by a group of UDA women. She apparently was so convinced of the power of the gang that she made no attempt to get away and even when the police stopped the car and offered her assistance, she made no complaint. The women took her to a "romper room" on Hunter Street, left the little girl in the hallway, and hustled the mother inside, where she submitted to being hooded and having her hands tied behind her. When the first blow was struck, she collapsed on the floor and passively accepted the beating and torture until she died. During the hours of savagery that ensued, the women took time out occasionally to have a smoke and listen to the child pounding on the door, screaming hysterically for her mother. After they had beat her to death, they threw the body out a window and went off to a discotheque for a drink.

The battered body was discovered six days later, and the RUC arrested eleven women and a man for the crime. After a sensational trial, Henrietta P. Cowan, eighteen, and Christine K. Smith, seventeen, were sentenced to fifteen years in prison; Elizabeth Douglas, forty-one, commander of the branch in Sandy Row, was given ten years; two women received three years; and seven others were given eighteen months.

In passing sentence, the judge took the opportunity to condemn the UDA itself as a vicious, brutalizing organization: "What appears before me today under the name of the UDA is gang law, a vicious and brutalizing organization of persons who take the law into their own hands by kangaroo courts, intimidation, and terrorization of the neighborhood. This is not an association of decent, hard-working and respectable people that is represented before me as defense counsel said. The fiendish behavior brought to light in the case has brought disgrace on on the name of women. And these are the representatives of the UDA in Sandy Row."

He expressed a hope that the ordinary, decent citizens of Sandy Row would recognize the evil among them and drive out those associated with it. But there were people present in the courtroom who disagreed with his evaluation of the UDA. One man was carried from the place cursing, kicking and fighting as the judge passed sentence. And as the women left the dock, some shouted "Up the UDA!" and "No surrender!" and waved to friends in the public gallery.

And if ever ye ride in Ireland,
  The jest may yet be said,
There is the lane of broken hearts,
  And the land of broken heads.
—*G. K. Chesterton,* Ballad of the White Horse

From the moment of the founding of the Free State, the IRA has refused to recognize the legitimacy of its government or that of the partitioned state in the north. Sean Keenan is an IRA man whose life bridges the span of years between that time and now. "I was born in Derry in 1915. I was sort of born into a Republican family. My father had been active all his life and served many terms of imprisonment for his Republican principles. We grew up on the Bogside, where most of the troubles took place during the civil rights campaign, and there certainly is a great deal of unrest there still."

His father worked in the shipyards in Derry until he lost his job when the yard closed down after the partition. After that he worked at many jobs, and although the family was never well off, they never wanted for a meal or shoes to wear to school.

Sean left school at fourteen and became an apprentice bartender. In later years he worked in one of Ulster's legal betting offices. Today he is manager of Sinn Fein's Dublin office. Like his father before him, he became deeply involved in Republicanism, and he, too, spent many years in prison and internment.

"I was first arrested in 1935 for the terrible crime of carrying a tricolor at an election rally. It was a crime and probably still is under the Special Powers Act. This flag portrayed a thirty-two-county republic, which the Unionists did not subscribe to, so therefore they banned the tricolor or any other emblem representing a tricolor."

Twenty years old at the time of his arrest, Keenan received a summons to appear in court, refused to appear, and was sentenced to three months in jail. His refusal, of course, was based on the IRA contention that the present governments in Ireland are illegal. Keenan explained the reasoning behind this: "After the elections in 1918, when the people of Ireland by an overwhelming majority voted to be an independent sovereign republic, they had 80 percent of the people of *all* Ireland taking part in the election and they elected a Republican government. But Britain refused to allow the government to function, although it did function for a little while before it was suppressed."

Protestants also voted for that republic. "There were Protestant candidates, and Republican Sinn Fein contested every seat, and they had about 77 percent of the vote for a free, independent Ireland. We believe that was the last legal government in Ireland because since that time we have never had free elections. Yes, we have elections in the twenty-six counties and we have elections in the six counties of Ireland—there are two parliaments in Ireland, both set up by a British act of Parliament, not by the wish or will of the Irish people. So our attitude was adopted at that time, nonrecognition of the courts, and Republicans have followed that attitude, that principle, even to the present day."

Another measure they used to deny the legality of the government, and to interfere with the functioning of the northern parliament, was the refusal to attend its sessions. Keenan says, "Back in 1935 and 1936, Republicans were contesting elections on the abstention policy. If elected, they refused to take their seats in the northern parliament. They just refused to give any recognition to a partition parliament."

O Bradaigh further elaborated on this traditional attitude: "It goes back to this particular nuance, to the whole attitude of why don't we sit in parliament, why don't we look for permanence of the place where we collect money, and so on. And there is the question of recognition of the courts and the basis that 'what I have done, I am entitled to do, and I refuse to plead. I refuse to say guilty or not guilty.' It's a moral stance."

In various periods of extensive IRA activity, the governments of both Ulster and Eire have resorted to arbitrary methods of justice, usually in the form of internment without trial or the Special Courts.

In an interview with this writer, Desmond O'Malley, former Eire minister for justice, explained the government's view on the Special Courts: "As far as I'm concerned, our laws are by no means repressive in any normal meaning of that word. Those who are affected by them describe them as that, which I suppose is a normal enough thing, and their fellow travelers and front organizations here describe them as that. But internment hasn't been used in this country in recent years, and we enacted legislation at the end of 1972 which proved very successful. It enabled people against whom specific charges could not be brought to be dealt with by being charged with membership in an illegal organization. Of course, they are members, and this can be proved by the sworn evidence of a chief superintendent or higher officer of the Gardai. If they wish to deny membership, they can do so, and that's the end of it."

If a member of the IRA denies his membership falsely, O'Malley said, he is not prosecuted for perjury. "It's almost impossible to prove perjury. In effect, if they deny it, whether on oath or not, it has been the practice of the court since 1972 not to convict. Any of them that make any attempt to defend themselves, or deny, even by an unsworn statement, are acquitted of membership. I think it's fair to say that there has never been a conviction of anybody who shouldn't be convicted, but by doing this we have avoided the difficulties that would undoubtedly be created by internment, and nobody had ever seriously complained about it being unfair or unjust because it's not."

The defect of this procedure is that in not recognizing the court or the government it represents, IRA members, as well as Sinn Feiners, must refuse to plead, which means they are then tried and convicted. O'Malley suggested that this law might be useful against the Mafia in America.

"The problem we were faced with in the early seventies was to some extent influenced by what the United States did in relation to the Mafia in the late twenties and early thirties, and that was that they couldn't prove, because of intimidation and other factors, the actual crimes that these people were committing, but they got them very successfully on income tax charges. Now this, of course, is quite a different thing, but the way I approached it was that way. I said to myself, how did the U.S. overcome the not dissimilar problems of proof of crime against people who were clearly violent, serious criminals, and without interning them. I began sort of reading a bit and thinking a bit about it, and I discovered that the way they got a lot of them was, in fact, not to prove they committed a particular crime, but to get them on a semitechnical charge."

Considering the people against whom the law was being used, O'Malley felt it was perfectly fair and had also been very successful. "Everybody now involved in the IRA can no longer regard himself as being immune from prosecution. Some of the senior people before were getting minor, junior people to carry out the crimes. They were getting away with it because they weren't directly involved, and it was almost impossible to prove conspiracy against them. Now these people, if they can't be convicted of anything else, at least can be convicted of membership in an illegal organization, of which of course they are in fact members."

One particularly beneficial effect, he thought, was that IRA members who committed acts of terror in the north could no longer flee south of the border. Because of the Special Courts, the Republic no longer served as a sanctuary.

"Even if they can't be extradited or can't be tried for crimes they committed in the north, they can at least be charged with membership in an illegal organization, and as a result you don't get any movement to a great extent down here now."

But how could a law possibly work that accepted even an unsworn statement of innocence from a known terrorist? Anyone charged could simply deny belonging to the IRA and get off scot-free.

"That's not the way they do it," O'Malley said. "If you stand up in court and say, either on oath or otherwise, 'I am not a member,' then you are taking part in the proceedings and you are recognizing the court. And they don't recognize the courts here."

O'Malley felt that the Offences Against the State Act, which was passed in 1972, was also working very well. Under it, a suspect could be held for forty-eight hours without being charged, and wiretaps were legal if a warrant was signed by the minister of justice authorizing it. These laws, in conjunction with the Special Courts, were designed to stop terrorism.

As the first to be sent to prison by the Special Courts, O Bradaigh naturally does not view the laws in the same light. "What they have done is a refinement of the internment procedure. Under the internment procedure, the police send up peoples' names to the minister of the state, and he, going on police advice, orders that so-and-so be taken from the community and put in an internment camp, held there at his pleasure. Now a refinement of that is to have a court in which there is no jury. The next thing you do is you abolish the evidence. You just accuse or arraign the prisoner. So the book of evidence against me was one sentence. Chief Superintendent Fleming said, 'I believe he, on such a date, was a member of the IRA.' That's the evidence. That can get you up to two years. So instead of the police sending your name up to the minister and you being taken from the community and put into internment, the police arrest you, bring you to court, tell the court what they would have said to the minister in the internment procedure, and the court says under the law, 'Yes, that's okay,' and you get a stated period in prison.''

On the whole, though, O Bradaigh preferred imprisonment to internment. "I would say that imprisonment was far more acceptable than internment, because in prison you have a definite period to serve and you have the privacy of your cell. Internment is indefinite; it could go on forever. There's no card on your door saying you'll be out after so many years, and the human mind finds that pretty hard to grasp."

After he had served his first term in prison during the border campaign, O Bradaigh had been interned. "When the six months expired, the internment camp had been opened, so they simply took us at the gate and threw us into the internment camp. I was there for a year and three months, from July of 1957 to September of 1958, when I escaped.

"The conditions were very primitive. When people are herded on top of each other, they get on each other's nerves. You could do nothing in private. Even if you wrote a letter, you would find that everyone in the place was looking over your shoulder. Even when you went to the toilet, you were under observation. You could never get away from people in this sort of concentration camp, whereas in prison you could retire to your cell and lick your wounds. I found it had a very great effect on men, on their minds and nervous systems. I discovered from experience that you can take two men—if A serves three years of a four-year sentence, while B spends a similar period in internment, A will emerge in far better shape than B."

The IRA has used hunger strikes to press their demands for special treatment in prison, and O Bradaigh explained their reasons for such demands. "It's based on a moral attitude. You are not a criminal prisoner; you're a political prisoner. You're not in prison because you've done something for personal gain or personal spite or spleen but because you're serving a particular cause which is above and beyond yourself, and that, as such, you're entitled to the dignity of prisoner-of-war status and should not be degraded to criminal or convict level. If you decide on this particular way of protest to get political-prisoner status, or in the case of the Price sisters [sentenced to long terms in England for bombings] and their comrades, you want to be transferred to prisons back home to serve your sentence, well, that's it—you state your terms. Then you do the only thing you can do, the only effective way you can fight from within prison walls. Or if you go further and say, 'I believe my imprisonment is unjust, the people who hold me have no moral right to hold me.' If it's the British in the north of Ireland, they have no right to exercise jurisdiction there. 'I'm going to fight from inside, and the people will fight on the outside in support of me.' "

Sean Keenan, now over sixty, has spent almost a third of his adult life in prison and internment camps because of his Republicanism. A small, dark Irishman with an indomitable will, his attitude toward the courts of Ulster and Eire are typical of the IRA. He was asked what would happen to a member who did not follow the rule of not recognizing the court. Suppose an IRA man were to plead in court, would he be thrown out of the organization?

"Yes, if he's a member. You have to abide by the rules. The regulations are there for everyone. You go into it with your eyes open, and you *believe* in it. If you don't believe in it, then there's no place for you in the Republican cause."

After his arrest in 1935, he refused to appear in court and was sentenced to nine months in Londonderry Prison. "It was very primitive, very old," he said, "an eighteenth-century prison." He has had many experiences with prisons and internment since then: "I was arrested on many occasions after that. No matter what happened, I would be picked up and questioned, interrogated. Interrogation then was not as bad as it is today; they hadn't got to what they now call interrogation in depth. You would get a kick in the backside or a punch in the face or something like that, but nothing compared to the torture which goes on today.

"Shortly after the outbreak of war, I was arrested on St. Patrick's Day of 1940, and I was held until November of 1945 without any charge or trial. You were held on detention for three or four weeks, then eventually they would come along and give you an internment order, which stated that you had acted, or were about to act, in a manner prejudicial to the peace and good order of the area. It seemed as if someone looked into a crystal ball and said that you were about to act in a manner prejudicial to the peace."

Asked if he had been doing anything illegal prior to his arrest, Keenan's reply was that he was active in the Republican movement. "It didn't really matter what I was doing. If I had been doing something wrong, then they could have taken me to court. No charge was prepared against me, nor did I have a trial. Many people at that time were arrested because they were active in an Irish-language movement, like the Gaelic League. There were people arrested and interned because they were active in an athletic association such as the GAA [Gaelic Athletic Association], which caters solely to Irish games—hurling, football, handball.

"I, first of all, was taken to Derry jail. I was kept there from March until September and was then taken to a prison ship on Strangford Lough called the *Al-Rawdah*. There the food was bad and there was very little exercise. There were times when the sea would be so rough we'd be cut off entirely from land, when we could not get bread, we could not get potatoes, could not get milk. This happened on many occasions. That lasted until March of 1941, at which time we were brought to Belfast Prison and stayed there the rest of the internment. Conditions hadn't improved very much. We made many protests against conditions, against food, against facilities for education and visits, and sometime in 1942 there was an improvement in that we were allowed to exercise a little longer each day. There was a slight improvement in the food, but conditions were still primitive."

The internees were all released when the war was over, some having been detained for as long as seven years, which was the maximum they could be held at that time.

Sean sometimes had no visitors for months. His father and two brothers had been interned at the same time, his mother and only sister had died shortly before his arrest, and his youngest brother had been sent down to the south of Ireland to friends so that he would not also be arrested. His father served two years for distributing an underground Republican newspaper and died not long afterward.

"Neither my brothers nor myself were allowed out for his funeral, which was unheard of. All kinds of people can get parole for funerals, but we were refused parole. My father died in a hospital next door to the prison and was buried in Derry, and none of us got to go to the funeral. He fell into ill health with the terrible imprisonment and other things. Conditions were very, very bad."

Released from prison in 1945, Keenan was married in 1946. Things were quiet for a few years, Republicanism was at a low ebb after all the internment, but eventually things started to build up again. Getting married did not interfere with Keenan's politics, because his wife had also been interned.

"My wife and her sister. On the night that I was arrested for internment, St. Patrick's night, we were holding a meeting in Derry to devise ways to raise money for the families of the men in jails. My wife and her sister were there, and everybody was arrested. Some were released the next morning, but before releasing them, they raided everyone's house that was present at the meeting. And during the raid on my wife's home, they found a paper called *Irish Freedom*, which was published in England and was not barred there. But it was barred in the north of Ireland, and they were both sentenced to nine months for that paper. They served their nine months in Armagh Jail. They were then released, and a few months later they were again picked up by the RUC and interned for the duration of the war without any charge."

The Republican movement revived, and Keenan was again involved in reorganizing and building it up. He thinks it is the only future for Ireland and that all British solutions have failed completely.

"It's a good thing to have a wife who really believes in what you are doing and understands. If I had not been involved, she would have been, but my wife spent most of her time raising the family. I did a job and in my spare time helped the Republican movement. So in 1956 another campaign was launched against British occupation of Ireland, and I was arrested in December of the year and was held until 1961 without charge or trial. This was all served in Belfast Jail.

"It's an awful place. It's a very old building. The cells were very small, damp, and very cold, with a small window set with little panes of glass and bars over it. The prisoners could see daylight but very little else. There was no running water in the cells, and while the men could use toilets when on exercise or association periods, they had to use chamber pots when locked up.

"At one stage, prisoners who had been sentenced for ordinary crimes would come to the door every morning when the warden would open up and you would slop out. That was after you were in a cell for eighteen hours a day. The smell was bloody bad.

"And the high gray walls. All you could see when you'd be on exercise was the sky.

"People got all sorts of complaints and diseases. I saw young men, strong in mind and in body, be driven insane. I saw strong men die. At least they had reached a stage where recovery was just not on and they were released to die.

"If a person developed a toothache, it would eventually be taken care of, but he might have to wait up to six months or longer. The doctor was part of the prison establishment and made no bones about it, left no doubt about which side he was on. No matter what a prisoner was suffering from, he usually got two aspirin, which was about the extent of the medicine prescribed.

"Internment in the north of Ireland is a way of life. Now since the state was set up in 1920, there has been internment in every decade. Internment in the twenties, thirties, forties, fifties, sixties, and now into the mid-seventies, we still have internment, imprisonment without charge. And as long as Britain continues to hold the north, it will have a repetition of this."

A point of contention has recently arisen over the special status accorded political prisoners. When Merlyn Rees was British secretary of state for Northern Ireland (he was replaced in 1976), he favored doing away with special treatment for IRA internees, implying that they were living in a country-club atmosphere.

Keenan argued against this. "Republicans, be they sentenced or unsentenced, claim the right of political prisoners. They fought hard for this, and in 1972 quite a number of men in Belfast prison who had been sentenced to terms in prison went on hunger strike, a long, suffering hunger strike, for political treatment. They did not want to wear prison clothes; they did not want to be identified as criminals. Whitelaw, when he was secretary of state, granted political status to Republicans, and now Rees has threatened—indeed, has made up his mind—to withdraw political status for political prisoners.

"That doesn't mean imprisonment is any easier. It means that men can wear their own clothes, that men can study as they will—but he does not provide facilities for our study—that men can do handicrafts such as woodwork, leather work, and the painting or decorating of handkerchiefs. This is all it means. Perhaps to get a visit more than the ordinary criminal. And to be separated from the ordinary criminals."

Keenan, of course, continued his involvement in Republicanism all through the 1960s and on into the early 1970s when he was once again "lifted" for his activities.

"In August of 1971 the British army made a roundup all over the Six

Counties. I was at home, I had just been fifteen minutes at home on the ninth of August when the British army arrived, and I was taken out and thrown into a Saracen tank. I was taken to British army barracks at Everington, and we were identified by the Special Branch of the RUC, who just gave a nod. 'That's the right one, that's the right one.' We were held there five or six hours before being taken to an interrogation center, where we were kept for seventeen hours before we even were given a cup of tea."

Keenan was questioned but not mistreated. "I don't know why I wasn't. It probably was that I had been arrested so many times and they knew they couldn't get any information from me. Perhaps they decided it was only a waste of time anyhow. 'Your name'—which they knew already—I gave. 'Your address,' which I gave. 'Your religion,' which I refused to give. I didn't see what that had to do with it, although they knew I was Catholic. Then 'What rank do you hold in the IRA?' I said, 'I am answering no more questions.' Now they sat there talking away, but I refused to answer. As I say, perhaps they thought, 'This fella has gone through it before; it's only a waste of time.' So I was taken back to the hut."

Later they were taken by helicopter to the prison ship *Maidstone*, which was anchored in Belfast Lough. "When we got there, we realized that some of the men were missing. We were all handcuffed together, taken off of the helicopter, but some men were missing. These men had been taken away for what they call interrogation in depth. They went through hell. A hood was placed over their head, they were made to stand at what they called the search position—legs wide apart, fingertips just touching the wall. And if they felt tired, or moved, they were beaten and told to get back in the same position. They were deprived of sleep, they were deprived of food, they were beaten with batons on every part of the body.

"Then they would try to lie down after a period of this and there were noises, loud buzzing noises, and they didn't know where it was coming from. Some of them thought they were being driven mad. Those men suffered this for seven or eight days. Eventually we all came together again. I got statements from some of the men, not only from Derry but other areas, who had gone through this. Some of them were trussed up. They were tied legs up behind their back, arms behind their back, and trussed up like a chicken and pulled up to the roof of the hut and left hanging there. Some of them had their teeth pried open with knives. I got statements from each of them. I was spokesman for the men there.

"I had a visit from John Hume [a SDLP leader] after a few days, and I passed these statements to him unnoticed. He did not use them himself, but he handed them over to reporters from the London *Times* which published them. This was the first notification the people had that this sort of torture went on. This went on, on a very large scale."

From the prison ship, Keenan was again taken to the Belfast jail and a month later was moved to a prison camp called Long Kesh where he once more became spokesman for the men.

"I examined the men who were brought in after arrest and interrogation and some of them were black and blue; their bodies were just a mass of bruises, cuts, faces swollen so you could hardly see the eyes were there. I was horrified myself at the sight of some of those men. The conditions at Long Kesh were the worst I had ever seen. The place was designed to destroy men in body and spirit. The huts in the camp were built on the runway of an old airport with no drainage, which caused flooding when it rained. The huts themselves were leaky and drafty and terribly overcrowded. The British soldiers turned us out of our beds at all times of the night. We would be driven out to the wires outside and made to stand there for hours while they searched the huts. This happened in the rain and snow, men driven out barefoot and in night clothes."

Some months after this interview, and five years after Keenan's ordeal, the European Commission of Human Rights found the United Kingdom guilty of the inhuman treatment of prisoners in Northern Ireland under Article 3 of the Human Rights Convention. The violations occurred between August 1971 and December 1971, in various holding centers throughout the Six Counties. The prisoners were subjected to the so-called five-techniques method of psychological and physical deprivation. Yet in spite of these findings, the British government has managed to protect the identity of those responsible for the torturing. None has been disciplined, much less prosecuted; indeed, several have been promoted and are still on active service within the RUC and the British army. The RUC officer in charge of the Palace Barracks, a British detention center just outside Belfast where the most vicious and systematic brutality was administered, has since been promoted to superintendent and is currently one of the senior staff officers on the RUC's Belfast headquarters.

Keenan's wife died of heart trouble in 1970, and while he was in Long Kesh, he received word of another tragedy. "I was in bed asleep when one of the boys woke me up and said, 'We have bad news for you, Sean. Your son Colin was shot dead.' Colin was eighteen when he died on the fourteenth of March in 1972. There had been a great deal of shooting in Derry on that particular night. Collin and another lad were in a neighbor's house having a cup of tea, and they came out after the shooting had died down to see what happened, and two shots rang out, fired by the British army, and the two boys fell dead. So I got out for the funeral and returned to Long Kesh. Six or seven weeks after that, I was released."

Once more out of internment, Keenan tried to play a part in putting an end to British interference in Ireland by traveling to the United States as a kind of roving ambassador, to raise money for the support of the families of internees. The British and Protestants maintain that the money raised in the United States is used primarily for the purchase of arms.

"Upon my return from the States, I learned that my other two sons had been arrested. Sean was interned; Seamus was tortured after arrest and admitted a crime which I'm sure he had nothing to do with rather than go through with the torture. He is now serving eight years, and Sean was released after two and a half years. My daughter Nora's husband was also sent to Long Kesh, and he suffered a great deal. He was beaten into unconsciousness by warders on several occasions. It was while Nora was in the hospital having her baby that Colin was taken into the same hospital dead. While I was out of Long Kesh for Colin's funeral, I also attended the christening of my grandchild. Two weeks later the baby was dead. His death was caused by the CS gas the British poured into the Bogside. The mothers suffered from it, and it was passed on to the children. There was another lad at Long Kesh at the same time, and his child, which was just a few weeks old, died the night before my grandson."

Despite his many years of imprisonment and personal tragedies, Sean Keenan remains an optimist. "I believe we're on the verge of victory. I'm more convinced of that today than ever before. I say this because first of all we see one of the greatest fascists, the man that's more responsible than anybody else for what happened in the early days of the civil rights movement, William Craig, who now acts the moderate. Craig has realized that the moment of truth has arrived. Craig sees that the British are intent on pulling out. Now that is one point. Then not too long ago Fianna Fail did a somersault and called for a British declaration of intent to leave. England itself is growing steadily tired. The majority of British people want the troops out. Desertion from the British army was never higher. So these are all signs. I never was more convinced that freedom is now within our grasp. We are on the brink of freedom!"

Whatever one thinks of men like Sean Keenan and their cause, there is a basic contradiction in the IRA attitude toward internment. They claim to be in a state of war with Britain and refer to themselves as soldiers doing battle in rebellion, not as terrorists. Soldiers taken prisoner by the enemy are not tried in courts; they are simply taken to prisoner of war or internment camps and held until hostilities cease. Rebels against a government, on the other hand, are tried and, if convicted, sent to prison. Internment, which ended early in 1976, would seem to fit the IRA tradition.

IRA men do not accept either prison or internment passively. Escape if possible is the policy of the organization. After the escape of nineteen men from Portlaoise Prison in Eire, a Gardai officer related how other prisoners had escaped by dressing as priests, changing cells with those due to be released, and digging tunnels under the walls. The most dramatic escape, however, was made by helicopter in 1973. A man with an American accent identified himself as a film-maker named Paul Leonard, hired a helicopter, and when aloft ordered the pilot to set the craft down in an open field where two IRA gunmen came aboard. The pilot was then forced to fly in over Mountjoy Prison and land in the courtyard. Seamus Twomey, the Provos chief of staff in Belfast, and his two top aides, Kevin Mallon and Joe O'Hagan, were waiting. They dashed to the helicopter, which quickly lifted into the air and flew to an abandoned racecourse, where two cars were waiting for them. The pilot was freed, unhurt but suffering from shock. The entire operation had taken only half an hour.

Police in Strabane said an anonymous caller telephoned to say a bomb was planted in a store at Abercorn Square and was timed to explode in twenty minutes. Police rushed to the scene, but the bomb, planted in a car parked at the curb, exploded only seven minutes after the call. It killed six-month-old Alan Jack sitting in his perambulator and wounded his mother and three other adults.

The bodies of three young Scots of the Royal Highland Fusiliers were found beside a lonely road near Belfast. They had all been shot in the back of the head at close range. Joseph McCraig, eighteen, his brother John, seventeen, and Dougald McCaughey, twenty-three, were in civilian clothes and apparently accepted a ride with the wrong people. Both factions of the IRA denied being involved.

Harry Gray, a seventy-one-year-old Protestant, was fatally wounded while sitting in his favorite White Horse pub in Belfast's mixed Springfield Road area. He was at the bar when three gunmen entered. One aimed a Thompson submachine gun at the patrons and ordered them to line up against the wall while the other planted a bomb. Gray was hard of hearing and advanced on the armed man, but it was unclear whether he wanted him to repeat what he had said or meant to grapple with him. The gunman shot Gray in the stomach, and he died on the way to the hospital.

Rosaleen Gavin, eight, was on an errand for her mother when she was hit by a bullet fired by terrorists at an army post.

A large, fiercely moustached British soldier was standing sentry duty in downtown Belfast when a diminutive old lady marched up to him, hit him sharply on the shin with her umbrella, and said, "You should be ashamed for what your army did at Drogheda!" The massacre of Drogheda took place in 1647.

Following the terrible rioting of 1969 and the split in the IRA, both the Officials and the Provisionals, with different objectives and methods, began their separate campaigns to force the British to assume direct rule and subsequently to withdraw in favor of a thirty-two-county Ireland. After some initial terrorist acts, the Official IRA settled into a Marxist-type program that they hoped would eventually bring about a revolution in both north and south, while the Provisionals began a campaign to bomb and shoot Ulster into the Republic.

The leadership of Provisional Sinn Fein rested in the hands of Ruairi O Bradaigh, its president, and Daithi O'Connell, its vice-president, who took over from Sean MacStiofain when he resigned his membership after his failure to carry through a hunger strike while in jail.

The military leadership was assumed by Seamus Twomey following his escape from Mountjoy. Twomey is considered the IRA's number one "hawk" and is credited with the invention of that particularly irresponsible weapon, the car bomb (some say this was O'Connell's invention). Once a clerk, Twomey is a devout Catholic who has been married for twenty-eight years and is the father of six children.

Sean MacStiofain is English-born and served three years in the RAF. His mother was Irish, and he adopted the Celtic version of his English name, John Stephenson, after serving time in prison in 1953 for taking part in an IRA arms raid. He is one of those who was close to Cyprus terrorists while in jail and says he learned from them that "successful guerrilla warfare is possible in a small country." Up until the time of his resignation he was a fervent nationalist and hoped to impose Gaelic on Ireland as its sole language after an IRA victory. He was considered one of the IRA's most active proponents of violence. "I have always accepted the inevitability of force," he says. "I could never see any way to achieve Ireland's freedom otherwise."

Daithi O'Connell, who is married, was very much in the news following the publication of Maria McGuire's book *To Take Arms,* which relates the details of their gun-buying odyssey to Europe as well as what she had to say about their love affair. The arms deal fell through, but had it been successful, it would have provided the IRA with a sizable amount of Czechoslovakian arms. The group lost $200,000 on the deal, but O'Connell was apparently cleared by the leadership of any fault in the fiasco.

The Provisional IRA membership is estimated at thirteen hundred, but not all members are active in Ulster. Its leadership is generally quartered in Dublin, where Sinn Fein has offices in Kevin Street.

Cathal Goulding is the Official IRA chief of staff. Other military leaders are Sean Garland and Liam Macmillan; Seamus Costello was one of their number until he broke away in December 1974 to form his Irish Republican Socialist party (IRSP). The political leadership of Official Sinn Fein lies with President Tomas MacGiolla, Secretary Mairin de Burca, Tony Heffernan, Sean Kenny (American organizer and owner of the *United Irishman,* organ of the Officials), and Malachy McGurran (organizer of the Republican Clubs movement in Ulster, which is a front for the Officials). Membership in the Officials is estimated at around a thousand.

The year 1970 was one of escalating violence, during which many lives were lost in shootings and bombings. It also saw more intercommunity rioting between Catholic and Protestant mobs. The Catholic population in the Bogside and various Belfast neighborhoods barricaded themselves in and set up "no-go" areas, into which the police and, in theory, the army were forbidden to enter. The army set up "peace" lines of barbed wire and sometimes barricades between the two tribal groups. As the Troubles continued, it became necessary to heighten these barriers in an effort to break both sides of the habit of sniping at each other from the upper floors of buildings or lobbing fire bombs over the top.

Rioting flared up all through winter and early spring, with British troops forced to go into action to defend police stations and to keep rival gangs apart. Prime Minister Chichester-Clark flew to London for emergency talks with British Home Secretary James Callaghan on the deteriorating situation. The

IRA was trying to stir up trouble between the Catholic population and the British army. Most active in this campaign was Maire Drumm, Provisional Sinn Fein vice-president in Belfast, who specialized in rabble-rousing speeches urging Catholics "to send the British soldiers home in their coffins."

The IRA made its first open threats against the military: "If a civilian is killed by security forces in Northern Ireland, we will shoot a British soldier. As from now, our official policy is to hit back against British troops. If necessary we will kidnap a number of them, and if any civilians are shot by British, we will do the same."

General Sir Ian Freeland warned that anyone manufacturing or carrying a gasoline bomb could be jailed for ten years or shot dead in the street if he persisted after one warning.

Despite the defiance of the Catholics behind their barricades, the military sent "snatch squads" into the Bogside to make arrests of known terrorists. In one such raid on March 29, sixteen men and five women were arrested and taken away over the resistance of a mob.

In June, Prime Minister Jack Lynch of Eire fired three of his ministers in quick succession when it was revealed the three and at least one army officer had become involved in a plot to smuggle Czechoslovakian arms to the IRA in Northern Ireland. Lynch, whose hand may have been forced by opposition leaders who found out about the plot, announced that the weapons were to have been brought in under the guise of a regular military shipment. Following this announcement, twenty-five hundred British troops swept through the border areas of Ulster searching for arms.

Also in June, Bernadette Devlin's appeal failed and she began her six-month jail term in Armagh's women's prison. Catholic mobs began hurling bricks and gasoline bombs at British troops and police when news of her imprisonment spread. Troops used tear gas in Belfast as Catholic and Protestant mobs clashed in the Ardoyne area. A thousand extra troops were rushed to the Bogside in Londonderry to disperse mobs throwing rocks and gasoline bombs.

As rioting continued, Prime Minister Edward Heath announced that more troops were being sent to reinforce those already in Ulster. Chichester-Clark closed the pubs at 8:00 P.M., two hours early, and a curfew was placed on civilian traffic in riot areas, with a warning that it would be enforced.

British troops carrying out searches of the homes of known IRA sympathizers a week later came on large supplies of bombs, guns, and ammunition. By then five more people had died in the renewed rioting, raising the toll for the period to twelve. Dozens of families in both Catholic and Protestant areas had to be evacuated as mobs set fire to shops and homes. Armored cars and army lorries rolled through the streets carrying women and children from "front-line" areas, while Catholics rioted over demands that Devlin, who had been jailed for inciting similar riots the year before, be freed, and Protestant mobs rioted in return.

Chichester-Clark said, "In the activities of the gunmen, and the carefully planned incendiarism, there is clear evidence that there are people involved who want to destroy Northern Ireland." He appealed to Protestants to avoid counterdemonstrations, because they would be "playing into the hands of those who are attempting to overthrow the state."

Fighting continued on through July 4, and British troops fought their way through heavy sniper fire to put down rioting in a fifty-block area of Belfast. Seventeen soldiers were wounded, and five civilians were killed, one of whom was a sniper. There were still some women and priests in the Catholic districts trying to prevent bloodshed, but when a number of women joined arms to form a human barrier to keep the mob from attacking the troops, a group of young thugs commandeered a bus and drove it right through the women, injuring several.

The troops were given orders to shoot at "identifiable targets," meaning anyone throwing gasoline bombs or the flash of sniper weapons. A total curfew was declared at 10:30 P.M., and helicopters used loudspeakers to warn the crowd from overhead, "Go to your homes! Go to you homes or you will be arrested!" Most of the older people drifted away, but gangs of youths continued the rioting. Fifteen hundred troops swept through the area under heavy sniper fire, and the army had to send sharpshooters to the roofs of taller buildings.

As a shaky peace was established the next day, three thousand Catholic women marched through the lines of troops to bring food to those manning the barricades in the Falls Road district. They said their men would stay away, and they did. In Dublin, Prime Minister Lynch issued a statement calling for the disarming of all those illegally armed in Belfast. More to the point, considering what had happened in 1969, Lynch denounced as "highly irresponsible" the fact that Protestants were permitted to hold their Orange Day and Prentice Boy parades on July 12 and August 12, respectively.

Conor Cruise O'Brien, Labourite member of the Irish Republic Dail, while touring Belfast's Falls Road area, blamed the behavior of the troops on the fact that the Labour government had been replaced by a Conservative one in London.

Paddy Devlin, who represented the Catholic district in the provincial parliament, said he planned a stiff protest because "the tactics employed by the military were abominable and out of all proportion to what was needed."

Since July 12 fell on a Sunday, the Orange Day parade was held on Monday, July 13. More than a hundred thousand Protestants marched, and to almost everyone's surprise, it was peaceful, mainly because the route was lined with almost twelve thousand troops and helicopters patrolled overhead. Protestant women in Union Jack–printed dresses and carrying umbrellas of the same material danced alongside the line of march while Catholics glowered from the sidelines.

The parade ended outside of town in Finegby Field, where speeches were made paying tribute to "Good King Billy" under banners bearing his portrait or replicas of the Red Hand of Ulster. Some of the speakers denounced

Chichester-Clark and condemned Catholic "treachery."

Sporadic fire-bombing, sniping, and rioting continued through the fall of 1970, with British troops increasingly becoming the targets of both IRA gunmen and rioting Catholics. Deaths rose to 175 in 1971, and the IRA constantly called for increased attacks on the military. "They have acted in a most brutal and bullying manner," a Provo spokesman said. "They've carried out arms raids, searched our homes without warrants, broken and entered them while their owners were out, even ordered families out on the streets in order to commandeer their homes. They've slept in our beds and pilfered ornaments." IRA violence, he said, was in reprisal for British raids. The raids had turned up 500 pounds of explosives, 185 grenades and gasoline bombs, 10 machine guns, 82 rifles, 106 pistols, and 50,000 rounds of ammunition.

Riots in February 1971, set off when a five-year-old Catholic girl was accidentally run over by a British armored car, caused seven deaths and a score of injuries. That same month the IRA held public funerals for two of its gunmen, Bernard Watt and James Saunders, killed in gun battles with British troops. Provos dressed in khaki combat jackets and black berets marched behind the coffins to Milltown Cemetery, where a massive stone memorial to thirty-six IRA martyrs stands. The coffins were draped in the green, white, and orange flag of the Irish Republic and a volley of pistol shots was fired over the graves. During the procession, heavy security by British troops prevented open clashes with Protestants, but at one point when the cortege came to a brief halt, a Protestant youth darted out of the crowd, yanked open the door of the hearse, and made off with one of the Irish tricolors covering the coffins.

In March, Chichester-Clark's government fell. It had been under constant attack by former Home Minister William Craig and Paisley and was replaced by another Unionist regime under Brian Faulkner. Faulkner attempted to bring Catholics into the government but met with rejections from both Protestants and Catholics. Catholic leaders had begun to boycott the Stormont.

August 1971 saw four nights of guerrilla warfare in Belfast that left twenty-five persons dead, including three British soldiers. It sent five thousand Catholics streaming across the border into the Republic and forced fifteen hundred Protestants to flee their homes. Property worth millions of dollars was destroyed, and five hundred homes and fifty factories were burned to the ground.

The rioting was set off when British troops, mistaking a backfire for gunfire, killed the driver of a delivery truck. A few days before the flash point, Faulkner had flown to London for a secret meeting with Prime Minister Heath, who had agreed to invoke the Special Powers Act. At dawn of the day on which detention went into effect, British troops began rounding up some three hundred IRA suspects.

"We are acting," Faulkner said, "not to suppress freedom but to allow the overwhelming mass of our people to enjoy freedom from fear of the gunman, of the nightly explosion, of kangaroo courts and all the apparatus of terrorism." Also banned for the first time in Londonderry was the Apprentice Boys parade.

Detention was a subject upon which the Catholics of Ulster could focus all their rage. "There is one issue on which virtually every Catholic, moderate and extremist, antipartition and propartition is united," a Catholic lawyer said. "And it is an almost psychopathic revulsion toward internment."

The rioting that followed the introduction of internment was the worst to that date, spreading to previously untouched areas. Snipers killed several uninvolved people, including a Catholic priest who was administering the last rites to a man he thought was dying. Belfast's Farrington Gardens, a "mixed" district, was attacked by IRA-led mobs. Protestant homes were burned not only by Catholics but by their owners to keep them from falling into Catholic hands.

The indefatigable Bernadette Devlin, released from prison, was at it again. She organized four hundred Catholic women who marched out of the Bogside past British troops chanting, "Oh, we hate the British soldiers, yes we do, yes we do," and lifted the hats of the soldiers as they went by.

The rioting had lifted Devlin's political stock despite the fact that she was unmarried and pregnant by a man she refused to name. A Catholic priest said, "If she were the whore of Babylon, we'd elect her now."

IRA leaders claimed a victory and stated that their strategy was to bring down the Faulkner government and force a return to direct rule by London for the first time in fifty years. Prime Minister Lynch of the Republic condemned the Ulster government for resorting to internment, although he had threatened to use it himself against the IRA the year before.

Ivan Cooper, the only Protestant M.P. among the opposition in the Starmont was quoted as saying, "In this country, moderate is spelled c–o–w–a–r–d. We have too much religion and not enough Christianity."

Marie Drumm, or "Grandmother Venom," as the British soldiers called her, led a club-swinging mob of IRA women into a meeting being held by Catholic and Protestant women working for peace. The meeting hall was wrecked, and the women scattered.

Lynch met with Faulkner and Heath at Chequers and discussed ways to bring peace to Ulster. The meeting was unprecedented in that it brought the Irish government in tripartite discussions over the fate of Ulster. Britain's Home Secretary Reginald Maulding also invited representatives of Ulster's Catholic community to a round-table conference to consider reforms that would give the Catholics "an active, permanent, and guaranteed role in the life and public affairs of the province."

"The British are six months late," a Catholic observer said. "They've always been six months late in Ireland."

Bernadette Devlin was stumping the riot and potential riot areas proclaiming that she had "no intention of discussing anything with Maudling until every last man who is at present interned has been released."

She was denounced by moderate Catholics. "We are on the verge of the most appalling bloodshed," said Oliver Napier, vice-chairman of the nonsectarian Alliance party, "and you are not prepared to get around a table and discuss issues on which many lives may depend. You are steering straight toward civil war."

Bernadette was not the only one. Paisley spoke to a wildly cheering crowd of twenty thousand Protestants and announced the formation of a "civil defense corps." Waving his Bible, he called for "lead bullets, not rubber ones," referring to the rubber bullets fired at rioters by British troops.

It was estimated during that bloody summer of 1971 that there were some 102,000 weapons, ranging from shotguns to automatic rifles and machine guns, in private hands. In fact, about the only people who were not armed were the RUC.

"No night passes without sporadic bombings and snipings, no day without bomb scares," wrote *Time* correspondent Curtis Prendergast. "On downtown streets there are almost as many armored cars as city buses. Steel mesh is going up over more and more shop windows. Guards at government offices keep street doors locked and check callers in and out like jailers."

In December 1971, the IRA swept through Belfast and the surrounding countryside on murder sprees. Senator John Barnhill, a member of the upper house of parliament, was shot down in his home, and a bomb thrown into his house destroyed it. Seven raids were made on the homes of well-to-do Protestants, most of them magistrates or city councillors, in Belfast's Malone Road district. Two houses were wrecked by bombs, the wife of a city councillor was wounded by gunfire, a UDF sergeant was seriously wounded, and the husband of Edith Tagger, Ulster's only woman senator, was pistol-whipped.

The New Year, 1972, was welcomed in Belfast by eight bomb blasts. A few days before, the forty-third British soldier to die that year had been felled by a sniper. Except for bomb blasts, however, New Year's Day was quieter that year than usual because there were thirty fewer pubs to celebrate in. The IRA had made sure of that in a campaign that led some to wonder whether the IRA was in cahoots with the Temperance League.

"This is not just another glorious phase in Irish history," Sean MacStiofain, then chief of staff of the IRA, said. "We must win. We can't afford to lose. We will keep the campaign going regardless of the cost to ourselves, regardless of the cost to anyone else."

As 1971 came to an end the Ulster police thought they saw attrition beginning to tell on the IRA. Many of the best and most experienced men had been killed or interned. The new recruits, according to the RUC, included many who "would never have been allowed into the old IRA. They're letting in criminals, drinkers, hooligans, and psychopaths."

Ruairi O Bradaigh denies this, pointing out that every army since the beginning of time has probably contained a certain proportion of undesirables, but the IRA had fewer, rather than more, such people because of its careful screening of volunteers.

Catholic Bishop William McFeely denounced "the callous men who are now prepared to plunge this whole country into anarchy and strife. We must be on our guard against the untold evil that unthinking words and actions could do to this country."

The church was not united against the terrorists, however. Father Michael Connolly of Tipperary proclaimed that the terrorism "is not just a war, but a holy war against pagans and people who have no respect for human dignity."

Protestants were expressing fear that they were about to be abandoned by the British. Billy Hull, chairman of the Loyalist Association of Workers, said Ulster might be abandoned by "perfidious Albion" and might share the fate of Czechoslovakia. "If we're sold down the drain, there wouldn't be civil war. There would be armed rebellion against the government of Britain."

The Provisional IRA has said that it resorted to violence to protect the Catholic population of the north and to win their eventual freedom. Both O Bradaigh and Sean Keenan repeatedly told this writer that they had been forced to go to the aid of the Catholics under attack by Protestants, the RUC, and the British army. Others, including members of the Official IRA and Paddy Devlin, a leader of the predominantly Catholic SDLP, disagree. They blame the Provisional IRA for most of the violence in the north and believe they have done the Catholic cause more harm than good. On some occasions, the Officials have accused the Provisionals of being little more than racketeers. "The Provisionals are beginning to look more like the Mafia than Irish republicans," one release said.

Eolas, the Official Sinn Fein international newsletter, said, "Nothing could be more contrary to the revolutionary strategy of the Republican movement than the indiscriminate bombing and burning campaigns of certain elements. It is completely sectarian in that most targets are Protestant-owned, and seems designed especially to alienate the Protestant people from this struggle for justice of their fellow Catholics."

Another Official publication, the *Ballymurphy News,* called on the Provos to end their terror campaign: "We make the following appeal to all the ranks of the Provos, from those who supply the materials to those who make up and deliver the bombs: end the bombing war against the Irish people."

Mairin de Burca, who believes in a Marxist revolution when the time is ripe but does not believe in pointless violence, was bitter over the Provo terrorism when she spoke to this writer. "They had a military campaign of sorts in the thirties; they had a military campaign during the war in the forties; I lived through and worked through a military campaign in the fifties. None of them had a hope of succeeding and nobody cared that they had no hope of succeeding. It was the tradition that was followed. When it was over and the movement was at a pretty low ebb, you set to, you organized, you worked, you brought people together, you sold your paper, you made collections, and when you got yourself worked back up to the same position, you had another military campaign. You were carrying on a glorious tradition."

She agreed with those who said the Provos were waging a sectarian campaign: "People are being killed purely because of their religion. A leaflet we are getting out points out that while people are engaged in sectarian attack, social and economic deprivation exists and is being ignored. 'Sectarianism Kills Workers,' our posters say, and the Provos are out in the north tearing them down off the walls."

She rejects the Provos' claim of having a social program: "I mean, they say they're socialists, but you don't go by what people say; you look at the things they do. And if you look at the things they've done over the past years, if you can find for me one action which could possibly be construed as socialist, then I will admit that they're a socialist organization—one action. They've blown up cooperatives; they've blown up libraries; they've blown up labor exchanges, where people get their unemployment benefits; they've blown up factories where hundreds of people were employed. Now honestly, you cannot go by what people *say;* you can only judge them by what they *do!* A socialist organization does not throw people out of work; they don't blow up things which ordinary people depend on both for the necessities of life and for the little luxuries, like a book out of the bloody library. There isn't a library in the north left standing because the Provos blew them up. Places where people had to go to get their money when they were on the dole were blown up, involving all sorts of problems and people going for weeks without any labor-exchange money."

That the whole campaign of terror had been self-defeating seemed obvious to her. "They have set the unification of Ireland and the establishment of any kind of socialist state back probably out of our lifetime. And they have, to my mind, absolutely degraded and distorted the word *republican.* In Ireland the word *republican* up until a few years ago was a respected word; now it has been totally discredited. I would hesitate in public to describe myself as a Republican because of what they've done."

Bloody Sunday, January 30, 1972, in Londonderry started with a march by NICRA that obstensibly was intended to protest internment. It did not matter that all marches had at long last been banned—Orange Day, Apprentice Day, Easter parades had finally been outlawed by the government. NICRA, at least still partly controlled by the IRA, decided to ignore the ban. The procession of about ten thousand people moved down William Street toward the Bogside singing while British troops stood watching. Bernadette had just started to address the crowd when two to three hundred young men began to assault the British troops who had closed the main business street and stood behind barbed-wire barricades. Stones, bottles, and nail bombs rained on the soldiers, who responded at first with gas grenades and rubber bullets and then with water cannons that sprayed the crowd with purple dye.

Saracen armored cars loaded with paratroopers arrived to reinforce the troops, and they waded into the attacking mob with clubs, rounding up forty-three of the attackers. Suddenly, other soldiers opened fire. Bullets whistled down the long stretch of Rossville Street toward the largest part of the crowd gathered around a lorry being used as a speaker's platform. The shooting lasted eighteen minutes and left thirteen Catholics dead and seventeen others wounded.

A British army spokesman insisted that the troops had come under fire first by "a total of two hundred rounds of ammunition fired indiscriminately in the general direction of the soldiers." The troops had fired, he said, only at "identifiable targets," that is, gunmen and terrorists of the IRA. Four of the dead men were on the army's wanted list, it was claimed, but no weapons were found on the bodies. Nor were any soldiers killed or wounded by bullets.

The IRA has admitted that their gunmen were present but claim they did not open fire until after the troops did. This is possible, of course, but it is also possible that the IRA took advantage of the confrontation to stage the kind of bloodletting they hoped would set all of Ireland afire. The troops under a hail of rocks and bottles had panicked as expected and fired into the crowd.

Paddy Devlin indicated to this writer that he thought the army had overreacted. "The military foolishly enough descended on the Catholic areas far too heavily. And the Provos kept throwing stones, and the next thing that happened was they pushed little fellows in with Derringers and they fired a few shots at the military; the military retaliated and fired shots right into the crowd. Well, you use a modern rifle in a crowd, you're killing about six and the war is on."

Almost literally, the war was on. Provo-led mobs burned the British embassy in Dublin, and Bernadette Devlin warned, "Nobody shot at the paratroops, but somebody will shortly."

Oliver Napier said, "Sooner or later, the IRA has been saying, British troops would put the boot in good and hard. People have been expecting this. Sunday in Derry has fitted the piece of the jigsaw in. My personal view is that the risk of civil war here has never been greater."

There is no question that Bloody Sunday did much to divide Ulster even more. "I wish it had been thirteen hundred of the bastards," a Protestant worker said.

Again in defiance of the law, NICRA led twenty thousand Catholics into Newry in tribute to the "Derry 13." By some miracle there was no bloodshed, so a new tactic was adopted. They declared a "D-day" in which they hoped to bring the state to a standstill by a combination of sit-ins, picketing, and postal and telephone disruption. The tactic failed, but NICRA promised more. "Today is only a token," said Miriam Daly, an economics lecturer at Belfast's Queen's University. "We're just beginning."

Information leaked to the press by those close to Prime Minister Heath suggested that as a concession to the Catholics the internment policy might be relaxed, that while Stormont would be retained, Catholics might be guaranteed certain key cabinet posts, and that massive economic aid for the province might be forthcoming.

Prime Minister Lynch, who had constantly wavered between statesmanship and demagoguery during the troubles, chose to introduce the subject of the border again. "Derry was a watershed. It showed that the IRA is not the problem; the division of the country is the problem. The IRA would become irrelevant in the context of a united Ireland."

That brought an ominous response from Ulster. William Craig replied that any menace to the border would mean "civil war within hours."

IRA terrorism escalated through February and March. Bombings and shootings increased steadily in Ulster and spread to England. From January 1 to April 3, 325 bombs rocked Northern Ireland cities an average of more than three a day. Then in the last week of March, misleading phone calls from IRA sources sent scores of pedestrians in downtown Belfast fleeing from the threatened street into Donegal Street. Then when the frightened shoppers were all gathered there, a hundred-pound gelignite bomb exploded right in their midst instead of the place designated in the phone calls, killing 6 people and injuring 146.

In the rubble the wounded were screaming and crying. An aged woman lay against a wall where she had been thrown, staring in disbelief at the bloody stumps of her feet. A young girl whose legs had been partially sheared off lay sobbing in the arms of a British paratrooper who cried out in anger, "I've served in Aden and for months in Ulster, but I've never seen things as bad as this."

In the Bogside, a sniper firing from a pub killed a British soldier, the fiftieth to die since the troops had come to Ulster. A bomb exploded in the Catholic Craggan Estate as Protestant militants struck back and wounded twenty-six persons. Belfast's Great Victoria Railway Station was nearly wrecked by a bomb that also broke windows and damaged rooms in the nearby Europa Hotel.

As the funeral procession for one of the victims of the Donegal Street bombing moved down a Belfast street, another explosion went off nearby and one of the woman mourners cried, "They won't even let us bury our dead in peace."

On the other side of the barricades, William Craig was staging a rally attended by fifty thousand Protestants, many of them members of his Vanguard party. The former home minister had moved into a position where he was the principal spokesman of the right wing.

"We have an organization that covers every part of this land. It must be used to build up dossiers on the men and women who are enemies of this country, because one day, ladies and gentlemen, if the politicians fail, it would be our job to liquidate the enemy."

Craig and Paisley had played key roles in the fall of both the O'Neill and Chichester-Clark governments, and Craig was now head of a loosely knit group of right-wing Protestant organizations, ranging from the Orange Order through the "Tartan" teen-age gangs, to ex-members of the B Specials and the paramilitaries.

"We Protestants have the power to make government in this country impossible," Craig said prophetically.

"People are tired, they want to be done with this mess," a Protestant pub owner said. "If it's all to wind up in a shoot-out anyway, they want to get it over with. There's no middle ground anymore. And when Bill Craig says, 'Let's get the guns out,' they'll listen to him."

Joe McIlroy was barman at Kelly's Tavern in Ballymurphy housing estate where dozens of fans had gathered to watch a soccer match between England and West Germany on color television. Joe won a beer on a bet with a customer and put it under the counter, saying, "I'll drink it in a minute. It will be safe there, out of reach of certain long-armed gentlemen." Suddenly a bomb exploded in a car parked outside and the blast ripped out the door and windows of the bar. Panic reigned for a few minutes as men blundered around yelling or lay wounded where they had fallen. Joe picked himself up off the floor and said, "Come on now, lads. It's not all that bad, we could all be dead." Three minutes later he was killed by a high velocity bullet fired by a terrorist outside the building.

"We've no Catholic friends," said a twenty-year-old Protestant man. "Individually a Catholic can be all right, but as a group they're dangerous. I'd never turn my back on a Catholic."

"After they planted the bomb, the owner of the shop ran outside after them but did not try to tackle them," a police spokesman said. "One of the terrorists turned and shot him down. As the man's wife rushed to his aid and knelt by his side, the gunman deliberately shot her in the back."

A fifty-pound gelignite bomb was tossed through the window of a furniture store crowded with Christmas shoppers, killing four. Among the dead were two-year-old Tracy Munn and seven-month-old Colin Nichol, killed as his mother pushed him along in his carriage. This occurred in the Shankill Road district where Protestants live and was blamed on the IRA.

"The kids play at riots," says psychiatrist Morris Fraser. "They use tomato sauce for blood one day, then they see real blood the next. Fantasy and reality exist side by side. Some of these kids can't tell the difference."

There was only one card left for the British government to play and reluctantly Prime Minister Heath played it. Commons met on March 24, 1972, and looking pale and tense, Heath rose to deliver his message. He was proroguing Stormont and imposing direct rule from Westminster.

Most Catholics greeted the move with pleasure. "We have lost the feel of jackboot Unionism," said Gerry Fitt of the SDLP.

Bernadette Devlin for once had nothing to say. "She slumped like the dormouse in *Alice* on the Labour benches, and merely watched the proceedings through her spaniel hair," *Time* correspondent Honor Balfour reported.

The IRA declared a cease-fire following the imposition of direct rule, but by July 1972, the hawks of the organization, led by Seamus Twomey, succeeded in breaking it. Twenty-four Protestant families had previously been forced by IRA gunfire to leave their homes on the edge of a Catholic district, and the army eventually agreed to let Catholic families move into the houses. When the Protestants protested, it was decided to delay the move until after July 12 and the Orange Day marches that were being planned despite the ban against them. The IRA refused to wait, loaded the furniture of sixteen families into trucks, and, accompanied by a mob of a thousand Catholics, advanced into the formerly Protestant neighborhood, where the army had set up barricades. As the mob and trucks came closer, the army opened fire with rubber bullets and water cannon.

"That's it!" Twomey, who was personally leading the operation, shouted. "The truce has been violated!"

Fighting broke out in Belfast almost at once. Sniper bullets and gelignite bombs broke the silence people had barely gotten used to. Six unarmed Catholics were killed as Protestant paramilitaries went into action. A man who ran to get a priest for the dying was killed along with the priest and a thirteen-year-old girl.

William Whitelaw, secretary of state for Northern Ireland, replied to those in the House of Commons who praised his peace efforts, "I deserve none of those things because I am not succeeding." He said he would continue to carry on, however, and fresh troops were sent in to bring the total in Northern Ireland to seventeen thousand.

Following an IRA action that has come to be known as Bloody Friday, when bombs killed 9 people and wounded 130 in Belfast, Operation Motorman was put into effect by the British army. For once something went off well in Northern Ireland with a minimum of bloodshed. Whitelaw issued a warning before the operation began that his forces "would be involved in substantial activity and citizens could best protect themselves by staying off the streets." Then army units moved into Catholic no-go areas in Belfast and Londonderry that the IRA had sworn to defend to the death. The IRA gunmen looked at the Centurian tanks that were knocking down the barricades, at the armored cars, and at the thirteen thousand troops coming behind them and decided to run away to "fight again some other day."

Following this successful takeover of the Bogside and Belfast, Whitelaw offered an olive branch to the Catholics. He would hold a plebiscite to determine if Ulster should become part of the Republic of Ireland or should remain as a part of Great Britain. He also released 14 members of the Official IRA from internment at Long Kesh and promised other releases (there were still 267 interned) if terrorism decreased.

That November a preliminary document known as a green paper was issued in London. Under it, Northern Ireland was to remain part of Great Britain as long as a majority of its citizens wanted it to, but it would have to be on Britain's terms. Westminster would retain control of security forces; the Catholic minority must have more say in any future Ulster government, preferably through a regional assembly, molded perhaps along the lines of the Greater London Council. In addition, any future administration must recognize the province's "position within Ireland as a whole," which might be accomplished by setting up joint bodies with Eire to discuss economic and security problems.

The government at Dublin responded by announcing a referendum on whether the Irish constitution should continue to grant a "special position" within the Republic to the Roman Catholic Church.

The year 1973 saw the introduction of hopeful new initiatives. A plebiscite was held in March and out of a possible 1,030,084 voters, 591,820 elected to remain in the United Kingdom and 6,463 voted to join the Republic of Eire. (Most Catholics boycotted the voting.) Following this a broad agreement was reached in favor of newly developed institutions centered on a unicameral legislature with seventy-eight elected members. There were also provisions for consultation on an all-Ireland basis.

The so-called power-sharing administration, or Executive, was intended to bring together Catholic and Protestant leaders. It was outlined in the white paper of new constitutional proposals that was enacted by the British Parliament on July 18, 1973. The Northern Ireland Constitutional Act confirmed the status of Ulster as part of the United Kingdom for as long as a majority of its people wished it. It abolished the old Stormont parliament and set up in its place a Northern Ireland Assembly and a power-sharing Executive, which would, it was hoped, reflect both Protestant and Catholic opinions. The members of the Assembly were to be elected by a single transferable vote method of proportional representation, as in the Republic. The same system would be used to elect the area's twelve members of Parliament.

The white paper met with a mixed reception in Ireland. There were indications that a large percentage of the voters would vote for representatives who opposed power-sharing; and the two right-wing parties, the Democratic Union party (DUP), led by Paisley, and the Vanguard Unionist Progressive party (VUPP), led by Craig, expressed opposition to the plan.

The Alliance party, nonsectarian and composed mostly of businessmen and middle-class voters, and the moderate Catholic Social Democratic Labour party agreed to work within the Executive. The Unionist party endorsed the proposal with reservations.

An election was held in which eighteen-year-olds voted for the first time and the Unionist party emerged as the strongest, winning over half the seats. The SDLP won nineteen of the seventy-eight members; the Alliance party took eight. Of the Unionist representatives, it was discovered that twenty-two favored Faulkner's limited support for power-sharing and thirteen were hostile to it. Paisley's DUP won eight seats and Craig's VUPP won seven. Faulkner then proceeded to form a power-sharing Executive with the SDLP and the Alliance party. Headed by Faulkner and SDLP leader Fitt, the Executive consisted of four SDLP members, six Unionist, and one Alliance member.

The white paper had proposed also the setting up of a Council of Ireland, which would move toward the development of north-south relations. On December 6–9, 1973, a triparty conference was held at the Civil Service College at Sunningdale in England. The British delegation was headed by Prime Minister Heath and the Eire delegation by the new Prime Minister Liam

Cosgrave. All eleven members of the Northern Ireland Executive also attended. Amidst a great deal of goodwill and even good fellowship, it was agreed that the Council of Ireland would contain only representatives from the two sections of the country. A consultative assembly made up of thirty members of the Irish Dail and thirty members of the Northern Ireland Assembly was proposed.

This was not by any stretch of the imagination a union of the two Irelands. In fact, in order to help improve the chances for success of the new Executive, it was suggested that the Irish parliament should recognize that Ulster would remain a part of the United Kingdom for as long as the majority of its population wished. This was done by the Dail in March 1974. But as early as December 10, 1973, Protestant extremists had sworn they would wreck power-sharing. On January 4, 1974, the Ulster Unionist Council, the policy-making body of the Unionist party, rejected the Sunningdale proposals by a vote of 427 to 374. Faulkner then resigned his party leadership and proposed submitting the matter to a referendum of the electorate.

Craig and Paisley, however, were determined to wreck power-sharing and especially the Sunningdale agreement. There was violence when the new Assembly met in Belfast on January 22, and Paisley, who had threatened a day of "blood, sweat, and tears," was in the middle of it. Shouting right-wingers upset furniture, seized the four-foot silver mace that was the symbol of the parliament, and spat in Faulkner's face. The police finally had to be called to restore order and carry out some of the members. This was followed the next day by Harry West and the official Unionists walking out, and then Craig's and Paisley's people did the same. The Alliance, the SDLP, and Faulkner's branch of the Unionist party carried on, but the chances for success had now faded.

The British general election on February 8, 1974, was disastrous for the hopes of peace in Ireland. Although it brought in a Labour government headed by Harold Wilson that continued to support the Conservative government's initiatives in Ireland, it also sent West, Craig, and Paisley to the Westminster Parliament along with seven like-minded men. A single seat in Parliament was won by Northern Ireland moderates.

The Northern Ireland Assembly and the power-sharing Executive lasted for three more months before they were brought down by a general strike of the Ulster Worker's Council, a newly formed labor organization headed for the most part by extreme Loyalists. Despite attempts by the Trade Unions Council, the regular British labor group, to break the strike, it crippled Ulster. Merlyn Rees, the new Northern Ireland secretary of state, declared a state of emergency and moved troops in to restore some services, but in spite of all efforts, the power-sharing Executive collapsed.

The British Labour government salvaged some of the ideas embodied in the power-sharing and Sunningdale proposals with a new white paper in July 1974 that proposed organizing elections to a constitutional convention that, like the old Assembly, would have seventy-eight members. It would be the task of this convention to work up plans that would eventually be submitted to

Parliament on the founding of a new government. Effectively that is where the situation remains to this day.

There was a sharp drop in violence in 1974 from the previous year, but as in 1973 there also were bombings in England and in the Irish Republic. Adding to the toll of those killed in Protestant and Catholic feuding were those slain in the feuds between IRA Officials and the breakaway IRSP and between Official and Provisional IRA. There were also feuds between the various militant Protestant organizations.

The violence had leveled off some, however, and was mostly concentrated in the countryside rather than in Belfast and Londonderry. South Armagh, a mainly Catholic area, became the favorite killing ground as the IRA struck against the outnumbered Protestants, producing such an atmosphere of terror that even the British army seemed reluctant to challenge the territory called Free Armagh. But after the minibus massacre in which the Provos killed ten Protestant working men and blamed it on a group they called the Republican Action Force, which had allegedly broken away from the main group, British troops were moved into South Armagh in large numbers.

IRA terror had not been confined to Ireland. It struck in England as early as 1972 when a bomb planted by an IRA terrorist exploded at the Aldershot army base, killing seven and wounding five. A letter- and fire-bomb campaign was launched in August 1973 in London, Birmingham, and Manchester. By September 28, more than forty bombs had exploded, leaving twenty-nine people injured. Letter bombs were discovered at the British embassy in Paris on August 28 and in Lisbon on September 17. Another letter bomb sent to the British embassy in Zaire wounded a British official on September 17, and other such devices turned up at British offices in Gibraltar and Brussels.

A bomb set by IRA members injured two men and a woman in King's Cross and Euston railway stations in England. At London's Heathrow Airport a bomb injured three persons and damaged fifty cars. The Tower of London was bombed on July 17, 1974, killing one person and injuring forty-one.

Birmingham also suffered from the hatreds in Ulster. When an IRA lieutenant by the name of James McDade accidentally blew himself up while setting a bomb at the Coventry telephone exchange, the English IRA wanted to give him a hero's funeral. The home secretary would not permit it, so six members of the IRA decided to avenge McDade's death and at the same time give him a suitable memorial. They planted bombs in two pubs in Birmingham and phoned in a warning only seven minutes before the explosions were to occur. The caller worded the warning so vaguely, saying only, "A bomb is planted at the Rotunda and at the tax office," that it was almost useless.

The Rotunda was a seventeen-story building, and the police had barely begun their search when the first bomb went off in the Mulberry Bush, a tavern located in the basement that was a favorite hangout of teen-agers and off-duty railwaymen. Eight people were killed at the bar and 2 in the street outside. Less than two minutes later, another bar, called the Tavern In Town, was wrecked by a blast. This was frequented by salesgirls from nearby stores and again 8 young people were killed outright; 2 others died shortly afterward. Dug from the debris, 120 others were rushed to hospitals by taxi drivers from the railroad station close by.

The Provisional IRA, in a somewhat ambiguous statement, said the bombings had not been ordered by the leadership in Dublin, but a check was being made to see if any Republicans in England were involved. When eight men from Belfast were arrested and charged with the crime, police discovered they were members of an IRA "sleeper" unit composed of Irishmen long resident in Birmingham who had been called into action after most men of another cell in the city had been rounded up and arrested. The leader of the group, "Big Mick" Murray, had recently spent a month in Dublin. He was not involved in the actual bombing, but he threatened those arrested for the crime with death if they talked.

Shortly after the Birmingham bombings, the Provisionals declared a truce with the British army. Effective December 23, 1974, it was originally scheduled to last for eleven days. This was extended to twenty-five and then, because of public reaction when it was ended, was brought back into effect in February 1975 with no time limit set. But the truce did not end the sectarian killings and bombings in Ulster.

The reasons for the truce seemed to stem from traditional IRA practices. Many of the leaders, particularly Daithi O'Connell, felt that the campaign was bogging down and the members were becoming tired and discouraged. After considering many grandiose but impractical schemes, such as kidnapping Prince Charles, the leadership decided on the truce, which would give them a chance to regroup. The ending of internment in early 1976 and the release of all those still held seems to have added new impetus to the terrorism that continues to afflict Ireland.

By November of 1976, terrorist acts in Ulster had taken the lives of nearly fifteen hundred people, and some twenty thousand had been maimed by bombs and stray bullets; hundreds more were punished by traditional knee-capping (ritualistically shot in the knee) and tar-and-feathering. While these casualties do not match the tens of thousands killed in Lebanon, they form a legacy of horror that has adversely affected not only the adults but the children of the community as well.

One hundred of those who met untimely deaths were under eighteen and forty were of school age. The youngest victim was Alan Jack from Strabane, who was six months old when a bomb blew his pram to bits. Angela Gallagher was seven months old when a sniper's bullet struck her. Michelle O'Connor was three when killed by a bomb planted in her father's car. Eileen Kelly was six when Provo gunmen burst into her home November 5, 1975, and killed her with bullets meant for her father, an Official IRA sympathizer.

Some of the terrorists themselves are scarcely more than children and seem to get younger all the time. A thirteen-year-old was arrested for carrying a rifle and a RUC officer said, "Compared to some we have caught, she's a veteran. There's more than three hundred teen-agers in Ulster jails convicted of crimes ranging from murder and armed robbery to the possession of explosives. Many more would be there, but they blew themselves up."

One RUC report stated, "Many young people have been procured by adults to engage in vicious acts of violence."

Everyone talks about being concerned for the children and some people actually try to do something to combat the terrible atmosphere of poverty and violence youngsters have to live and grow up in. It is not easy, and the results are discouraging, and at times tragic, because of the virulent regional hatreds.

The British army has tried to establish contacts and work with the youth of Ulster. "We have tried several schemes before, and we have several going at the moment," a British officer said. "We don't relish publicity because in the past our projects ended up being bombed out of existence."

One thirty-four-year-old British sergeant named Nick White quit the army and married an Ulster girl. Wanting to do something to bring the young people of both sides together, he set up a disco in the no-man's-land between Catholic and Protestant areas, and for a while teen-agers of both religions gathered to play records and dance. Then gunmen from one side or the other waylaid White and left his bullet-riddled body as a warning to other would-be peacemakers.

The death of three children killed by the out-of-control car of an IRA gunmen who had been shot by a British soldier has resulted in the People for Peace movement. Betty Williams was driving home when she saw the accident, in which Anne Maguire and her children were pinned against a school railing by the dead man's car. Mrs. Maguire was seriously injured; her daughter Joanne, eight, and her two sons, John, three, and Andrew, six weeks, were crushed to death.

"When I saw on television that the children were dead, I just couldn't take any more," Mrs. Williams said. "I was sitting with my sister and a friend, all of us apathetic—like so many others—behind our venetian blinds. I said, 'I'm going out and I'm going to knock on people's doors in Andersontown to see how many people feel just as we do!' "

The three young women walked through the IRA stronghold of Andersontown, going from door to door with their notepads, and soon had hundreds of signatures on a peace petition. "I was like Pied Piper," Mrs. Williams said later. "I ended up with a hundred women doing the same as me that night."

She was joined by Mairead Corrigan, an aunt of the three dead Maguire children, and they, along with ten thousand Protestant and Catholic women, held a rally the next Sunday at the place where the children had been killed. The following Saturday, twenty thousand women showed up, carrying homemade banners giving the names of their streets and demanding peace.

Corrigan invaded the strongly Loyalist Shankill Road district and was embraced by Protestant women. "I went there to meet some of the Protestant women who have been organizing from their end," she said. "Do you know, that was the first time I had been there in seven years."

Both the IRA and the Protestant extremists recognize the menace of this snowballing peace movement and have done everything in their power short of killing the leaders to stop it. Paisley's *Protestant Telegraph* denounced the women's peace efforts as "spurious" and "priest-inspired." Bernadette Devlin, now Mrs. McAliskey, appeared once again in America to attack the peace movement, denouncing the women who she said advocated peace-at-any-price and defending the IRA's methods. Even Sean MacStiofain, in retirement since his failure to carry out a hunger strike while in prison, was trotted out to denounce the peace marchers.

The lives of Williams and Corrigan have been threatened by terrorists and their sympathizers. *Death to Betty Williams* was scrawled on a roadway near her home, and one gang of hoodlums tried to set fire to her house. She and Corrigan have received obscene letters and been branded as "touts" (informers).

Things began to go wrong. The peace-march organizers were attacked by mobs led by members of the IRA women's auxiliary, the Cumann na mBann. Betty Williams and Mairead Corrigan were forced to take shelter in a nearby Catholic church while the mob howled outside.

It was believed that the attack was ordered by Maire Drumm, who personally led previous attacks on other groups seeking peace. Drumm was proud of her activities as an IRA organizer in Northern Ireland. She told the English journalist Gerald McKnight several years ago, "I have done three jail sentences for recruiting for the IRA. . . . I have probably been responsible for a number of boys being killed. And I've felt very bad about them. . . . I feel regret that we've lost those boys, . . . but it was their cause as much as mine. . . . But I've got to be perfectly honest . . . I don't care how many British soldiers die. I have no compassion in the world for them."

It was the British troops who nicknamed her Grandma Venom, and the title fit because even in a nation of strong haters she stood out. In the end the violence she preached so vehemently caught up with her. On October 28, 1976, as she was recovering from eye surgery in Belfast's Mater Hospital, three Protestant members of the UFF burst into her room and shot her to death. The Provos said they knew the identity of one of the gunmen and issued this statement: "Maire Drumm will be avenged. She was a patriot and a courageous woman."

The cycle of death and violence goes on.

But the Sergeant foiled their daring plan, he spied them thro' the door;
Then the Sten guns and the rifles, a hail of death did pour;
And when the awful night was past, two men were cold as stone;
There was one from near the Border and one from Garryowen.

No more he'll hear the seagull cry o'er the murmuring Shannon tide,
For he fell beneath the Northern sky, brave Halon at his side,
He had gone to join the gallant band of Plunkett, Pearse and Tone,
A martyr for old Ireland, Sean Sabhat of Garryowen.

—*From* They Kept Faith

Although a great deal of the money that buys the murder weapons comes from America, there are also many links between Irish terrorists and terrorists in other parts of the world. Information supplied this writer by the British Foreign and Commonwealth Office detailed an international web that supports terrorists in Ireland and England and works toward the overthrow of all open societies.

Oddly enough, the Provisional IRA, which is usually considered traditionalist and even rightist, has more contacts with international leftist groups than does the orthodox-Communist Official IRA.

From the first contacts with Nicos Sampson, the Cypriot murder master, in British prisons during the 1950s, those who became Provos have steadily widened their outside connections, especially among Trotskyite and Marxist groups. They have been aided in this by People's Democracy, founded by Michael Farrell and Bernadette Devlin. While Devlin carefully conceals her connection with international terrorists during her American visits, where she is referred to in the press as the "Irish Firebrand," Farrell is more direct.

In his recent book, *Northern Ireland: The Orange State,* Farrell frankly outlined what he hopes will result from the Ulster conflict: "The stakes are high in the Northern conflict. A successful struggle in the North could not only defeat the Loyalists and unite Ireland but it could topple the Southern regime as well and complete the anti-imperialist revolution in the country. And a revolution in Ireland could have incalculable consequences in an ailing Britain, and indeed, during the present crisis of Western capitalism, throughout Europe."

In other words, Farrell hopes victory for the IRA in Ulster will eventually result in totalitarian regimes in all of Europe. There are others in Europe and the Arab world who share that dream and are working with the Irish terrorists to achieve it.

According to the British Foreign Office, "New Left activity in Ireland first became evident when People's Democracy, originally a left-wing student civil rights group set up in 1968 at Queen's University, Belfast, by Bernadette Devlin and others, fell under the influence of the Marxist 'Young Socialist Alliance' and the London-based International Socialists in 1969. Michael Farrell, the PD leader, came to regard this organization as being in the mainstream of world revolutionary and student protest movements."

The British International Marxist Group also worked to stimulate the interest of foreign revolutionary groups in Ireland through its contacts with the Trotskyite Fourth International. A branch of the Revolutionary Marxist Group was established in Ireland; and Gary Lawless, chief Irish expert of the International Marxist Group (IMG), visited Trotskyite organizations in Europe. Ernest Mandel, the head of the Fourth International, visited Dublin to confer with Irish terrorists.

Lawless worked to integrate the Provisionals into a worldwide union of terrorists, saying that the IRA bombing campaign had "tremendous" possibilities for the whole revolutionary movement. Then Peter Graham, a young Irish teacher who had been sent to Dublin to set up Irish branches of the IMG, was found murdered, and it was revealed that he had been engaged in gunrunning on behalf of the Provisionals and European Trotskyites.

Provisional leaders were also active on the Continent. Sean O Bradaigh, Ruairi's brother and publicity director of Sinn Fein, and others traveled through Belgium, Germany, Italy, Switzerland, and France, drumming up support, funds, and weapons in mid-1972. O Bradaigh spoke of these moves in the Provo journal *An Phoblacht:* "The Republican Movement has shown that it is not just an insular inward-looking movement, but that it is spreading its wings worldwide in its efforts to achieve justice and freedom for the Irish people. It has shown that it is aware that international support can shorten the struggle for freedom."

There was an indication that these international contacts were paying off in hardware when in March 1974 the columnist Jack Anderson revealed that intelligence reports indicated the IRA had obtained from Arab sources Soviet shoulder-fired missiles for shooting down British helicopters. According to Anderson, thirty-pound Strella SA–7 missiles were "originally smuggled into Belgium in Libyan diplomatic pouches." British intelligence reported there was "firm evidence that Arab terrorists are working with the Irish Republican Army and are part of the bombing campaign which has plagued London in recent months."

In May and June of 1975 a group representing not only the Provisional Sinn Fein but also People's Democracy and the IRSP toured Belgium, Holland, Germany, and Switzerland. It was part of the Action in Europe campaign, designed "to breach the web of misrepresentation and gross distortion woven by English propagandists around the Irish questions." The touring group found that "there is considerable support for the cause of Irish freedom throughout Europe," according to *An Phoblacht.*

That support had apparently been building for some time because British intelligence as early as January 1975 had told correspondents of the *London Daily Mirror* that "terrorist groups throughout the world are organizing the deliveries of weapons and explosives to the IRA." The latest big shipment, according to the paper, had been through what the Special Branch called the French Connection and had arrived in Ireland from Quimper in Brittany, on the northwest coast of France. The weapons had been carried in a French fishing boat, transshipped into an Irish fishing boat someplace off Cork, and then landed. The weapons supply line was being run by Breton separatist Catholics. That there had been a close relationship between the IRA and Breton terrorists for some time had been generally known, and several Breton leaders who had collaborated with the Nazis during World War II had long been refugees in Ireland.

This shipment had been organized by Jean Materot of the extremist Front de Libération du Québec (FLQ), a Canadian separatist group. The weapons had come from Montreal through the French port of Le Havre, but they had been shipped to Canada by Arab terrorists in Syria and Libya, who had obtained them from Communist suppliers in Czechoslovakia and East Germany.

The secret police in Czechoslovakia (the Soviet invasion of which had been supported by the IRA in 1968) have organized weapon shipments to Ireland by a more direct route across Europe. They have funneled SKS automatic rifles and RPG rocket launchers to the IRA. The exact route of shipment is not known, but it is known that the arms pass through West Germany with the aid of fringe members of the Baader-Meinhof gang and are stored at Versailles, outside Paris, until enough have accumulated to make a shipment; then they are taken to Quimper or the tiny fishing port of Benodet. From there Breton fishermen carry them to Ireland. The British have estimated that a thousand weapons a month have been arriving in Ireland through this route.

There is some evidence that that the Soviet Union is directly involved in the supplying of these weapons to the Provisional IRA. During question time in the House of Commons, ministers have denied that Soviet submarines have been operating in British territorial waters, despite claims that photographic evidence shows them on the surface of an Irish sea lough in daylight. Reports that Russian subs have been firing disarmed torpedo casings loaded with AK47 assault rifles, SKS carbines, and RGP–7 rockets ashore in Ulster seem farfetched because it would be far easier to transship the weapons into Irish fishing boats at sea than to use the torpedo method. The Soviet's motive for direct aid is the usual one: any terrorist activity or revolutionary movement against capitalism anywhere in the world ultimately benefits the Soviet Union.

Richard Behal, a member of the Provisional Sinn Fein Executive, is said to be the chief liaison man with European terrorist groups. He appeared with Ruairi O Bradaigh at the conference in Trieste and was also present at a press conference on July 9, 1974; in May 1975, he attended a conference with Sean Keenan in Milan.

There are indications of solidarity between the IRA Provos and the anarchist Lotta Continua, and in 1971 Seamus Costello attended a secret meeting organized by the Italian publisher and terrorist Feltrinelli at a Jesuit institute in Florence.

Lotta Continua cooperated with People's Democracy in the making of a film. Fulvio Grimaldi, a journalist and one of the Italian group's leaders, has addressed People's Democracy meetings in Ulster. He also tried to pass off surplus bullets as evidence of British violence on Bloody Sunday to the Wiggery tribunal that was investigating the incident. The bullets were found to have been fired into sand.

Dolours Price, now serving a life sentence in Ulster for her terrorist activities, led a group of People's Democracy delegates to Italy to confer with Lotta Continua leaders. Both People's Democracy and the Provos were represented along with the Popular Democratic Front for the Liberation of Palestine at Lotta Continua's first national congress in January 1975. In May of 1975, Sean Keenan and Richard Behal conferred with Lotta Continua, the Maoist II Manifesto group, and other extreme leftist organizations during an Italian visit.

The West German–Irish Solidarity Committee was set up by Baader-Meinhof supporters and others in 1972 and is now the most active of all West European groups that support terrorism in Ireland. Until the end of 1974 it had supported the Official IRA but changed its allegiance because of the lack of terrorist activity by the Officials. It arranged a joint IRSP–People's Democracy–Provo tour of Europe in May and June 1975. People's Democracy issued a statement concerning this: "Their [the West German–Irish Solidarity Committee] work of gathering support for the revolutionary struggle in Ireland may prove to be of immense help in view of the critical situation facing the anti-Unionist working class in the Six Counties and the effect it could have on Ireland as a whole."

The French Committee for the Liberation of the Irish People was founded early in 1972. It has held demonstrations in Paris and is dominated by the Trotskyite Ligue Communiste, although it also has connections with the Communist party of Brittany.

In July 1974, Ruairi O Bradaigh and Richard Behal reportedly established contacts with Carlos's group of the PFLP at a meeting in Trieste. What, if anything, has developed in the way of cooperation between the Provos and Carlos is not known at this time.

The Basque Euzkadi Ta Azkatasuna (ETA) has probably been the most active of the European groups in cooperating with the IRA. José Echebarrieta, an ETA leader, is reported to have made two secret visits to Ireland in 1972. In her book *To Take Arms,* Maria McGuire says that Basque leaders supplied MacStiofain with fifty revolvers in exchange for training in the use of explosives. The IRA allegedly provided the explosives used by the ETA in the murder of the Spanish prime minister, Adm. Luis Carreras Blanco.

The Official IRA, although it follows the Stalinist line fairly closely, has been far less violent in recent years than the Provos, and this has detracted support from foreign terrorist groups. Mairin de Burca, Official Sinn Fein secretary, has warned of the danger of "becoming identified in international affairs with small groups of people with handfuls of gelignite." She has also opposed campaigning for the release of convicted foreign terrorists. On a visit to Germany, she openly disagreed with representatives of the League Against Imperialism who tried to win her support for the release of imprisoned Baader-Meinhof leaders.

Bernadette Devlin feels differently about international ties: "We see ourselves as an integral part of the working-class international movement and see the necessity ultimately of being part of that international struggle, not simply in terms of everybody struggling in their own country but building links with international organizations."

Through the years, the IRA, People's Democracy, NICRA, and IRSP have expressed support for Palestinian aims. Qaddafi has expressed his support with arms, money, and intelligence. Sean Ryan and Louis Maguire, both members of the Irish-Arab Society, which arranges exchange visits between Ireland and the Arab world, visited Tripoli as government guests while Libyan agents went to Dublin and made plans for Irish "teachers" to work in Libya. One such teacher, Eddie O'Donnell, has been in Libya since 1972, working supposedly as an educational adviser to the government. Qaddafi expressed open support for IRA terror in June 1972: "At present we support the revolutionaries of Ireland who oppose Britain and who are motivated by nationalism and religion. The Libyan Arab Republic has stood by the revolutionaries of Ireland. . . . There are arms and there is support for the revolutionaries of Ireland."

Proof of Libyan arms for Ireland was found in March 1973 when an Irish gunboat halted and searched the Cypriot coaster *Claudia* as she approached the Eire coast. On board was Joe Cahill, former commander of the Belfast Provos, and a large consignment of arms. The owner of the vessel, a West German arms smuggler named Günther Leinhauser, admitted he brought the guns from Libya: "I went to Tripoli to fix the deal with Joe Cahill." For a while Qaddafi even toyed with the idea of supplying arms to the Protestant militants in Ulster. He believes that anything that keeps the revolutionary pot boiling is worth doing.

In the final analysis, the greatest source of money and arms is America. Money is raised in Irish bars and clubs all over the United States, donated mostly by conservative Catholics who close their eyes to the IRA's contacts with leftist revolutionary groups.

"The ascendancy of the terrorist, particularly the IRA, is to a significant degree made possible by large subsidies from Irish-Americans in the United States," the *New Republic* noted on October 18, 1975. "The full extent of the assistance is unknown. But the files of the Foreign Agents' Registration Office in Washington, D.C., suggest that the aid must be very large. One of the major fund-raising groups, NorAid [the Irish Northern Aid Committee], officially declared that it had remitted $823,000 to Ireland between 1971 and 1973. Between January 1974 and 1975 it declared an additional $213,000. One of the two chief recipients of their money was Joe Cahill, known as the Provisional 'quartermaster' until his arrest in 1973 by the Irish navy while in the process of running guns into Ireland."

The money collected by NorAid is supposedly given for relief purposes, but Joe Cahill does run a war chest for terrorists, not a social welfare service for widows and families of interned members. As the *New Republic* pointed out, the amounts of money officially reported is only the surface of a vast collection ring of funds. Nor does the report list the contributions of weapons and explosives, which is extensive.

A British army spokesman has said that 75 percent of the arms captured or used in Northern Ireland are of American design. More than half of them have been shipped directly from the United States. Hundreds of Armalite rifles stolen from American armories have shown up in Ulster, and the British army in recent years has captured 3,740 rifles and pistols, 180 machine guns, and 725,000 rounds of ammunition, mostly of American origin.

An IRA official said recently that "you cannot buy arms in large quantities on the European continent. Authorities are tipped off after most large purchases. It is much easier to get arms from the United States; the States is our major supply line."

British authorities have estimated that since 1969 more than $2 million raised in the United States supposedly for relief purposes has actually gone for the purpose of arms.

American politicians have for generations made their careers by sticking their fingers into the boiling caldron of Ireland, hoping to snatch political advantage out of other people's misery without burning their own hands. Senator Edward Kennedy has been a consummate practitioner of this art. Sometimes his brinksmanship has frightened even the IRA, especially his demand for the overnight withdrawal of British troops. The Irish want the British to leave, it is true, but as a phased withdrawal. The extent of Kennedy's involvement in Irish affairs was revealed in Maria McGuire's book *To Take Arms,* when she spoke of Joe Cahill having been barred from the United States as a criminal. "We did ensure, though, that when Provisionals flew to the United States they should not encounter the same difficulties. We knew that Edward Kennedy would be quite ready to play Ireland for all it was worth— if he was going to use us, we might as well use him—and we enlisted the help of the prominent Civil Rights lawyer Paul O'Dwyer. Whenever there seemed to be any difficulty over obtaining a visa for a member of the Provisionals intending to go to the United States to raise funds, we would phone an official of one of the New York Irish-American Associations, Jack MacCarthy; MacCarthy would contact O'Dwyer; a phone call from Kennedy's office to the American Embassy in Dublin would result and all difficulties would magically disappear."

Kennedy also helped people who were accused of smuggling arms to Ireland. The U.S. Department of Justice, up until December 1, 1975, had prosecuted some two dozen persons for gunrunning, and at least two grand juries were at work on other cases. In the case of the so-called Fort Worth Five, defended by the firm of O'Dwyer and Bernstein, Senator Kennedy constantly intervened. Jailed for contempt of court because of their refusal to testify after being granted immunity, the group was defended, in addition to O'Dwyer, by his American Committee for Ulster Justice and the Center for Constitutional Rights, all acting free of charge "for the cause." Kennedy kept up a barrage of appeals on their behalf. After failing to influence the Justice Department to release the men, he appealed to the U.S. Supreme Court to approve bail for them. His constant machinations and the work of defense committees eventually resulted in the freeing of the five and forced the Justice Department to drop the case.

Kennedy is not the only American politician who plays the Green Card with the same cynical skill that Randolph Churchill in the 1880s played the Orange Card in Ulster. Senator Abraham Ribicoff joined Kennedy in his game, as did numerous congressmen from the East Coast who have large Irish constituencies in their districts. The *Philadelphia Inquirer* condemned the Kennedy-Ribicoff resolution on Ireland in August 1975 as "a mild example of an old American political custom of playing politics with the Irish question." The *Christian Science Monitor* criticized Kennedy for "a totally unwarranted intrusion into British internal affairs."

Representatives of the Republic of Ireland have constantly pleaded with the American Irish to stop supplying arms and money to terrorists. Foreign Minister Garret FitzGerald made several trips here to press that point. Prime Minister Liam Cosgrave of Eire told a joint session of Congress on St. Patrick's Day, 1976, that Americans contributing such money "are helping to kill or maim Irish men and women of every religious persuasion. They are clearly and directly postponing any possible hope of realizing the traditional aim of Irish nationalism, . . . the establishment of harmony and a sense of common identity among Protestant, Catholic, and dissenters in Ireland." Such contributors, he said, are "people who support violence at a distance and who can sleep easy on the wounds of others."

Some English people outside government have also interfered in Ireland on the side of violence. The best-known and most bizarre case was that by Rose Dugdale, whose adventures in Ireland provided more comedy relief than tragedy.

"I have really reached a point of despair," a Catholic housewife says. "The other night when a bomb went off nearby, I just rose up off my chair and screamed. I would have gone completely berserk if my husband had not held me down. We would get out and never come back if we could find someplace to live away from this city, even if we have to abandon our home and our furniture."

Ross McWhirter, founder of the Guinness Book of Records, put up a reward of $102,000 for the capture of persons conducting a campaign of bombing in London. He said at that time the reward could make him a target for assassination. It did. He was shot down from ambush as he opened the door of his house to greet his wife and stood outlined against the lights inside.

"My parents didn't bring me up to be biased or to hate and I wouldn't bring my son Darren up that way. He can pick his own friends. But my father wouldn't let me marry a Catholic and I'd never let my son marry one."

"People outside Belfast don't realize that Catholic and Protestant here can go through life without meeting each other," notes a Belfast psychiatrist. "They're completely divided in schools, neighborhoods, and jobs. The atmosphere of hostility is ever present."

Born in March 1941 into a family of wealth and position, Bridget Rose Dugdale grew up on a six-hundred-acre estate in the fashionable countryside of Devon, with riding lessons and a French governess to teach her to curtsy when guests entered the room. She was devoted to her father, Col. Eric Dugdale, who headed a successful Lloyd's insurance syndicate, but it was her mother who fiercely dominated her life. An intelligent and rather formidable woman, Caroline Dugdale was determined that her daughter would have a proper upbringing, marry well, and settle comfortably into an aristocratic life-style.

Although forbidden to speak to village children, Rose was described by a cousin, Betty Turner, as "a most attractive girl, a child full of vitality, happy, . . . full of laughter, a great giggler."

She attended Miss Ironside's, an exclusive academy for ladies in Chelsea, and went on from there to finishing schools in France, Germany, and Switzerland. She returned home in 1958 to "do the London season" just to please her mother. She would later say of that period, "I did it very reluctantly, refusing to take part in anything more than I had to. As a debutante I was out on the social register and invited to parties and balls which I hated. . . . God! . . . when I think of the money that was wasted on the whole business. Each dress I wore was tailor-made by Worth, and my coming-out ball was one of those pornographic affairs which cost about what sixty old-age pensioners received in six months."

That fall, contrary to her mother's wishes, she matriculated at Oxford's St. Anne's College to study philosophy, economics, and politics. The white organdy dresses and satin slippers were replaced by what was to become the new Dugdale uniform—baggy men's trousers, shirts, and "sensible" shoes. Since she had inherited her mother's jutting jawline and was rather strongly built, it may be that this new attire was more suited to her personality.

After completing her undergraduate studies, she was given an assistant-ship at Mount Holyoke College in Massachusetts, where she earned a master's degree in philosophy. Throughout this period, her behavior was more conservative than radical. She rode around in her specially imported MG sportscar and wrote pleasant little pieces for the college magazine, but she was aggressive enough to interview President John F. Kennedy and Martin Luther King, Jr.

Returning to England in 1964, she traded her MG for a red Lotus Elan, and through her former Oxford tutor wangled a job with the United Nations in New York, which she held for only a brief period. Back in England again, she was given a post at the Ministry of Overseas development, where she specialized in trade prospects for developing countries.

Friends believe that it was this job that saw the beginning of the real radicalization of Rose. But this employment did not last long either. She enrolled at Bedford College, London University, to begin her studies for a doctorate of philosophy, which she successfully obtained; she was appointed to a year's lectureship in economics in the sociology department. In 1968 she volunteered to join a group of students visiting Cuba under the auspices of the French Vietnam Solidarity Campaign. By then she was already fascinated by the writings of Karl Marx and particularly by what he had to say about the plight of the Irish under British rule in Ireland. That was the year that student radicalism came into full bloom: students were hurling mollies at tanks in Prague, cobblestones at the gendarmes in Paris, and feces at Mayor Daley's Democratic Convention in Chicago.

In Cuba, meanwhile, Rose became fascinated by Fidel Castro's magnetism and his rapport with the masses. She too was learning to relate to peasants. Peter Ayrton, who went on the trip with Rose, was quite impressed by her behavior: "I think that what always amazed me was her outgoing nature. . . . This is extremely rare for someone to say, with that background she has in terms of speaking to anyone, in terms of speaking to people in pubs, speaking to people in the street; she obviously has a certain obstacle in that she has a certain education and that she talks with a kind of posh accent. But that has never kind of stopped people being able to immediately relate to Rose as kind of human.

"I can tell of one example. When we were in Cuba there was a dance, a dance organized in some small village in the country. And at that dance young people had been invited, and we were all dancing together and the older people had not been invited, because I think it was felt like that we wouldn't get on too well. I think actually Rose saw these old people who were looking in from the outside, totally kind of amazed, and she insisted that they be brought in, and the Cubans there said, 'OK, they can come in,' and these old peasants came in, and she immediately proceeded to dance with them, and she didn't even speak Spanish, but she kind of related for the whole evening. . . . But she had absolutely no problem of getting on with people from totally different backgrounds and spoke a totally different language and everything."

Upon her return from Cuba, she began seriously looking for local causes to embrace. She became active on the civil rights front and even took part in the occupation of the London School of Economics. She conversed with anarchists of the Angry Brigade, Trotskyites, and Marxists and stood bail for Black Power demonstrators; but although she seemed to be terribly active on the militant scene, she joined nothing. She moved to Tottenham High Road and founded, at her own expense, the Tottenham branch of the Claimants Union.

"If she had a creed it was a form of 'direct action,' " Tom Mangold wrote in *Encounter,* "a species of libertarian anarchism. She threw herself into a campaign to 'help the poor and deprived.' She tried to get free school milk for children, bought and distributed free coal for pensioners, assisted squatters, and interrupted local council meetings by shouting down councillors on behalf of her 'clients.' She stood bail and paid the legal costs of neighbours and tenants in trouble."

By now she had become "incomprehensibly militant" to her parents. The social value of Oxford for a graduate of Miss Ironside's had been dubious enough, to say the least, but this new posture was totally beyond comprehension. In 1971 her father endowed her with a personal fortune of £80,000, and a year later she met the man who was to involve her in the politics of revolution.

Wally Heaton was a forty-year-old petty crook with impeccable working-class credentials. The son of a Leeds millhand, Wally joined the Irish Guards at sixteen, later became a shop steward at a bottle company, and once led an unsuccessful "work-in" after the closing of the plant. He was a big drinker, with a gift of gab and a police record of twelve convictions for offenses ranging from traffic violations to robbery. But his only failing, in Rose's eyes, was his wife and two daughters.

There are friends in North London who discount the love match and maintain that "Wally knew a meal-ticket when he saw one," but Wally's wife, Audrey, was bitter about it in any case: "She [Rose] was really scruffy, she dressed very erratically, she was dirty, her hair was unkempt. She'd sit on a chair with her legs up, with a cigarette dangling from her mouth. Her fingers were black with nicotine, and well, . . . her language was obscene at times, but you know, she had that nice accent with it. It just wasn't natural.

"They'd come up here [to the flat] and talk to each other and ignore me. One night, I was sort of uptight about it, and I threw a cup of coffee over Wally. I was really mad; they were sitting toasting each other with their cups of coffee, speaking in Gaelic. I couldn't understand it. And they used to leave me right out of the conversation. I used to tell them to get out, but they completely ignored me. There was nothing I could do about it. . . .

"Well, I found them together in bed. I became rather hysterical you know. . . . It was a shock. He'd had affairs all his married life, but I'd never come that close to it. Well, I smashed up the room, and she just lay there, and, you know, as if it were quite natural. I told her to get out. She got out of bed and she left, and later I found a note just inside the front door that Rose had put for Wally. Naturally I opened it, and it read: 'Dear Wally, it was beautiful. I'll see you soon. Comrade Rose.' "

Rose's reaction was to buy off Audrey. She informed her father that she wanted to sell her shares in the Dugdale Trust and then handed Audrey £25,000 in cash and a further donation to Wally of £10,000. The first thing that happened to the £25,000, which was deposited in a joint account requiring Wally's signature, was that Wally bought himself a big Mercedes-Benz and a whole new wardrobe. His sartorial elegance contrasted sharply with the masculine dishabille of his paramour.

Colonel Dugdale took it upon himself to remind his daughter of a "simple motto" he had learned in the army: "Money lost—little lost; honour lost—much lost; heart lost—all lost. . . . I can only hope that you keep your honour and your heart." He also reminded Rose that the standard of living for the poor had "improved beyond all measure" and wondered why "someone of your acute intelligence does not notice this" and went on to say that "three or four" Dugdales had died in wars for their country and that the others had provided employment "at a fair wage and under decent conditions of service." In closing, he said he would "never slam the door. Although you have had all the money that I have to give, you will always find a welcome if you return."

Five weeks later, Rose replied:

Dear Daddy,

I hope that you won't shelter under such sanctimony as accusations that I have cut all love between us away. As one of the boys across the water said to me the other day, I will die fighting the oppressor but I will give my life for the poor people. So let's not have any more about the self-sacrifices of our ancestors who died while ordering the men out over the trenches to death for nothing but the well-being of a handful of rich men who own the world; there will always be a place for you amongst the brave men who are prepared to shoot in the back those commanders. The jolliest time for Lloyd's was the last war, was it not? When Guardsman Heaton takes your money, it is for the taking. You can't take your accumulated theft with you of course, though you can be a man who refuses to dishonour himself and family whilst mothers with children are thrown on to the streets which their ancestors built.

Love,
Rose

During this period, Rose and Wally became "deeply committed" to the Irish Republican cause. They spoke Gaelic and did some heavy Irish drinking in North London pubs between trips to Londonderry and Belfast, where they allegedly met with IRA gunmen. They both took part in a civil rights march in Londonderry, but their only encounter with the law at this time came when they refused to identify themselves at a checkpoint and were detained for a few hours by British soldiers.

When the money ran out, Wally introduced Rose to Ginger Mann, a reject from London's criminal underworld. According to Ginger, Rose "wanted me to set up a firm, a criminal firm which would be, you know, pretty sophisticated for doing big robberies and to steal arms, ammunition, explosives. This sort of thing, you know. First of all, we was to look around for the things and then plan to rob. Anything that would bring money for the IRA cause, you know.

"Well, in the beginning I thought it was a laugh, really. But after a while I began to get a bit worried because I thought to myself, what I am doing, actually, is sitting with these two people and others, and conspiring to commit treason, and it's not only that I am not that kind of animal, but I wouldn't do it, I wouldn't do it anyway. You know there's a lot of bird [prison] involved with treason. . . .

"They were, I suppose, you could call them really fanatics, especially Rose. Rose was very, very fanatical. Although what she was up to, or what she was trying to get, was bent or political bent; she was still straight, you know. Her background made her straight. Yet I could never trust Rose Dugdale at all in any way, and I was surprised really at the tie-up with Wally. . . . It didn't seem . . . you know . . . it didn't seem sort of natural."

As it turned out, it was Ginger who could not be trusted. While Rose and Wally, along with three accomplices, were appropriating some £80,000 worth of paintings and antiques from Colonel Dugdale's Devon estate, Ginger Mann was squealing to the Special Branch.

The highlight of the trial was Rose's cross-examination of her father, who appeared as a prosecution witness. "There is a massive battle between us which nothing will remove but the disappearance of one of us," she told him. "I love you, Daddy, and if there were any danger threatening you, I would stand between you and that danger. But I hate everything you stand for."

Curiously enough, her defense was more in line with that of Patricia Hearst than that of Angela Davis. She pleaded not guilty on the grounds that her associates had forced her to cooperate in the burglary. The trial lasted through the summer of 1973, and on October 22, she was found guilty of burglary and Wally was found guilty only of handling stolen goods. Yet Wally got six years in prison and Rose was given a two-year suspended sentence. Before sentencing was pronounced, Wally had warned the judge, "You cannot imprison Rose and me, because we don't exist. But we are everywhere— invincible, incorruptible, and indestructible." But with six years in the "bird" staring him in the face, he reminded the court of the enormity of its error: "Not since Christ has there been a greater travesty of justice."

Rose expressed her displeasure at the discrepancy in their sentences, describing it as "class justice," and the judge pleasantly told her that he doubted she would do this sort of thing again. "You have turned me from a recalcitrant intellectual into a freedom fighter," she replied. "I cannot think of a finer title."

With Wally in prison, Rose moved permanently to Ireland, settling in Donegal, where she became actively involved with an IRA unit of Young Turks in the border town of Strabane. It was here that she became romantically involved with Eddie Gallagher.

Until he met Rose Dugdale, the single greatest tragedy in the life of Eddie Gallagher was the death of his mother when he was fourteen. Her death left a void in his life he could not seem to fill. Following his mother's death, there was an immediately discernible difference in Eddie's attitude toward his father and their small hill farm home near Ballybofey in Donegal, a few miles from the border of Northern Ireland. His school work suffered, and he became a loner. He began drifting in and out of small jobs, and there are suggestions that he first met Rose in North London, where he worked as a tunneler. Almost certainly it was there that Eddie received his first on-site lectures in republicanism, for he returned home a convert to the cause. He joined the local Provisional Sinn Fein and became active in all their activities. It was only a small step from joining Sinn Fein to becoming directly involved in the IRA, which exploited his intimate knowledge of the border countryside in the booby-trap raids of the early 1970s.

When Rose arrived in Donegal in late 1973, they soon found each other. There was a six-year difference in their ages, and it has been suggested by friends that Eddie found some consolation in the older woman for his lost mother. Even in her sensible shoes, the five-foot-six Rose towered over her diminutive lover. Their "honeymoon" was spent studying the geography around Strabane for what would turn out to be one of the most bizarre episodes in IRA history. The IRA has since filed a disclaimer, but there is persuasive evidence that Rose Dugdale and Eddie Gallagher were part of an active-service unit that was cleared by the Army Council to commit certain assigned acts of local terrorism.

On January 22, 1974, a tall, blue-eyed, fair-haired woman calling herself Stephanie Grant registered at a small hotel in a remote part of County Donegal. She was accompanied by two men, and all three identified themselves as journalists interested in hiring a helicopter to visit Tory Island just across the water.

Two days later the woman, later identified as Rose Dugdale, and three men were picked up by a helicopter that landed behind the hotel. Moments after takeoff one of the men pulled out a pistol and ordered the pilot to fly to a nearby monastery. Rose, who was sitting next to the pilot, unfolded a map and proceeded to give instructions. Thus began the IRA's first air raid.

After landing on a jetty near the monastery, the men ran to an old cowshed to fetch five ten-gallon milk churns, each packed with one hundred pounds of explosives, but because of the helicopter's cramped space, only four could be loaded on the chopper. Even four turned out to be too much weight and two churns had to be jettisoned in Mulroy Bay, leaving the air raiders with only two milk churns for their attack on the Strabane police station.

Nerves were getting taut, however, and someone prematurely lit one of the fuses, which had to be pulled out to prevent it from exploding inside the helicopter. Now fuseless, it too was jettisoned, dropping harmlessly into a river. With one milk churn left, they made their run on the police station, the "bomb" dropping into a nearby rose garden without exploding.

Major Richard Earle of the First Battalion of the Royal Fusiliers was an eyewitness to the air raid: "I think the effect generally was good for morale because it's always satisfactory to see one's enemy making a fool of himself. There was some useful discussion in barracks on this new military weapon— the AGMIC—the air-to-ground milk churn, and some unfavorable comparison between this attack and others which we've been subjected to in the past, such as Dunkirk and Tobruk."

Prior to the raid, Seamus Twomey had been quoted in the *Daily Express* to the effect that the IRA would one day soon be making use of air power. Curiously enough, the IRA never claimed credit for the raid, nor expressed further opinion on its projected plans for utilizing air power. Eddie's role in the episode was never delineated.

Already wanted by British authorities on charges of arms smuggling, the RUC now circulated throughout the province a mugshot of a rather masculine-looking Rose on a "Have You Seen This Woman" poster. Her days were numbered, but she still had one fabulous caper left to play.

On the evening of April 15, 1974, Rose and three armed men invaded the hundred-room mansion of Sir Alfred Beit in Blessington, in the country-side near Dublin. Identifying herself as Vanessa Kelly and affecting a thick Irish brogue, Rose and her gang quickly tied up Sir Alfred and his wife and proceeded to make off with nineteen paintings valued at $20.4 million. The collection included a Goya, a Frans Hals, a Vermeer, a Gainsborough, and three paintings by Rubens. The world's biggest art robbery was carried out in a matter of minutes.

A ransom letter demanded that Home Secretary Roy Jenkins grant the request of the Price sisters, Dolours and Marion, for a transfer from British to Ulster prisons, plus a payment of £500,000 for the return of the collection. The Price sisters were serving life terms in London's Broxton Prison for car bombings that killed 1 person and injured 238 others.

If the burglary was approved by the IRA, someone forgot to tell Daithi O'Connell about it. He was said to be furious over the raid because it was taking the headlines from an imminent hunger strike by the Price sisters. Besides, the police roadblocks all over Ireland were a bloody nuisance. O'Connell had been around too long to think that the British government would negotiate over nineteen inanimate art objects, however valuable.

In an interview, O'Connelll expressed the IRA's position on Rose Dugdale: "Well, Dr. Dugdale was not a member of the Republican movement. She was known to personnel in the movement. She had been to Derry way back in the days of the civil rights and so forth. From what one knows, she was a very dedicated person, one with deep convictions. . . . However, it is a known fact that the IRA was not involved in procuring any of those paintings."

A week later the police swooped down on a rented cottage in a rural area of County Cork and took Rose and the nineteen paintings into custody. At first it looked like Rose was getting the best of a plea bargain: she pleaded guilty to receiving stolen property and the other charges were dropped. This time, however, the judge could not be accused of class discrimination, for she drew nine years. "I stand in absolute condemnation of the government of Ireland," she told the court, "which, trading on the victories of our armies in the north, is wheeling and dealing with a government of murderers, assassins, and torturers in London."

In November she was tried for the helicopter "bombing raid" over Strabane and received another nine years, to run concurrently with her earlier sentence. The others were given six years.

One month later Rose gave birth to a baby boy in Limerick Prison. A former inmate, Teresa Colbert,* recalled that night: "The maternity unit was a triple cell at the end of the corridor. We could hear Rose screaming. There was a sixteen-year-old girl in the cell beside her. Everyone seemed to think Dr. Dugdale should have been transferred to a hospital, but the Department of

---

*Quotes from Peter Ayrton, Audrey Heaton, Ginger Mann, Major Richard Earle, and Teresa Colbert were tape-recorded by Tom Mangold for a BBC-1 documentary, *Midweek,* which he later incorporated in an article in *Encounter,* a literary magazine edited by Melvin J. Lasky.

Justice turned this down for security reasons. Rose apologized afterwards for all the noise and confusion. It was rough, but everything went off okay in the end."

She named the baby Ruairi, and Eddie Gallagher admitted he was the father. His friends do not doubt his deep passion for her—the Special Branch called Eddie and his associates Rose's Heroes—nor her attachment for him. "A curious factor of the recent renaissance of the IRA as a fighting force," Peter Dunn wrote in the *Sunday Times,* "has been the number of middle-class English women intellectuals with a boundless fascination for small, earthy Irishmen in revolutionary donkey jackets."

Eddie tried three times to spring her from Limerick. The first time was in February 1975, when she was still caring for the baby in her cell. Under a death threat, a regular visitor was forced to smuggle in a hacksaw blade. She managed to saw through three bars, patching the cuts with toothpaste, before she was caught at it. The second attempt came in April with bomb threats that failed after police discovered three bombs in downtown hotels.

The third attempt was the most desperate. Six weeks before Eddie and nineteen-year-old Marian Coyle kidnapped Dr. Tiede Herrema, the chief executive of the Dutch-owned Ferenka steel plant in Limerick, a letter was found on a woman visiting Limerick prison. It was from Eddie, and it told Rose to be "ready" to leave at a moment's notice. Somebody would be kidnapped to secure her release, and they would soon be together again.

Advised of Eddie's intentions, the Special Branch placed him under surveillance instead of arresting him. This is curious, since Eddie was an escaped convict and there were wanted posters out on him. Eddie regularly visited the family in Navan that was caring for his and Rose's son, Ruairi, but after the letter was intercepted, he made no further visits. Yet the Special Branch had him under surveillance almost right up to the very last minute. Gallagher and Coyle were seen drinking in The Hurler's, a Limerick pub, about a mile from Dr. Herrema's home, the night before the abduction. The reason for the Special Branch's reluctance to pull him in, one source suggested, was that they were waiting for Eddie to pull the "big one" so they could act with full public backing and secure at least a thirty-year sentence for him. Which they did, of course, but in the meantime they put Dr. Herrema and his family through a five-week personal hell that was completely unnecessary.

The Irish government refused to release Rose Dugdale; Marian Coyle's lover, Kevin Mallon, who had been recaptured after his helicopter escape from Mountjoy with Twomey; and another prisoner, James Hyland, whom the press considered to have been a token gesture of kidnappers' republicanism since Hyland had no apparent connection with either one of them. Both Eddie and Marian were publicly disowned by the Provo's Army Council for their unauthorized stunt, which severely damaged the IRA's support in the Republic. There were indications that the leadership was gradually losing control of its rank and file. Recent bombings in London were said to be the work of restless young renegades trying to force the older leaders to abandon their cease-fire policy.

O Bradaigh addressed himself to these various problems: "All this talk about the young people being impatient with the leadership is one of those facile, simplistic explanations that aren't always right. The Gallagher thing was a purely personal matter. He was involved with this Dugdale woman. Gallagher and two other ex-members of the movement went and did something for private gain [robbed a bank prior to the kidnapping], and then the other two left the country, but he stayed behind because he wanted to get his woman out, and eventually he linked up with the Coyle girl who was involved or felt herself involved with Mallon. Hyland was named because they wanted sympathy and support in his home area, which is where it all happened. So then they made their demands, but it wasn't political motivation; it was strictly personal motivation.

"As for Dr. Dugdale, I have never met her. Insofar as she feels that she wants to better the human condition, I think that's very praiseworthy. So far as she's prepared to turn her back on riches and position, I think that's praiseworthy, too. But I do feel that people like that who are in revolt against their upbringing and perhaps feel a bit guilty about their comfortable situation in life . . . well, that's all very welcome, but I think that people who are the direct product of the situation—Marian Coyle comes from Derry—I think that's a lot better to build on than Dr. Dugdale.

"Dr. Dugdale was associated with various unauthorized acts, but I understand she helped some of our people get out of England when they were in a tight corner, and when she had to leave England herself, we could hardly say, 'We don't want to know you.' But you've got to have discipline. We wouldn't last very long without it.

"As for the leadership losing control of its rank and file—my goodness, the leadership was never in better control than it is right now. The bombings in London—well, if you focused sufficiently on things beginning in early 1975, you'd realize that these were ordered by a central command in retaliation for breaches of the cease-fire by the other side. There were certain terms and articles to the truce which was accepted by both sides, but if the British don't adhere to their end of it, well, you've got to make sure they don't continue making mistakes. When you see the British saturating areas, kicking in doors, abusing people, well, we say, 'What kind of blooming truce is this?' People want to know where it's leading to. It can't remain static. They've had their conventions, and it hasn't worked. They can prolong it if they like, but we feel that they've got to face up to the situation now, that they're going to have to declare themselves out of this situation; they can't just go on without a policy any longer. They're going to have to face up to the whole Irish situation, the total Irish situation, decide what their long-term policy towards the whole of Ireland is going to be. And we know what we want it to be."

"Every Protestant I know is convinced civil war will come and they have made arrangements to get their wives and young children out if it happens," says Colin Baker, UPI reporter and native of Ulster. "They all say the men and older boys will stay and fight."

I found a big stone
To throw at a soldier.
I'm going to get a gun
When I'm a little older.
                    —*Eight-year-old Belfast pupil*

"I can't stand the trouble any more. It sickens me, listening about it, talking about it. When I saw the picture of the girl who was tarred and feathered, I vomited. I'm sick to the heart. I hate it," said a thirteen-year-old Protestant girl. "I hate people being called Protestants and Catholics. God created everyone."

"I'm only nine years old,
My father's son.
When I grow up,
I'll buy a gun
And shoot those British soldiers."
                    —*Belfast schoolboy*

"Here I am, the last livin' person in Ireland, and I can't remember if I'm Catholic or Protestant."
            —*Caption under Oliphant cartoon showing a little man with a gun*
                                          sitting in a graveyard

The big question facing Ireland, for both the north and the south, is, What would happen if the British pulled out and left the resolution of Ireland's troubles to Irishmen?

Would civil war break out, as it has in so many other colonies Britain was forced to abandon? "That depends on whether it's an immediate or phased withdrawal," Mairin de Burca said. She felt that during a phased pullout, the saner Protestant leadership would come to cooperate with the Catholics. "They would see the disaster of a civil war for all concerned." But wouldn't the Protestants fight to protect the border? "In a phased withdrawal, you'd have time to negotiate. The position of the British at the moment is that they want out, and the only bar to that is the warring Irish."

Conor Cruise O'Brien sees the solutions in Ireland as "alternate routes to the graveyard. The presence of British soldiers in Belfast is not bringing peace to hate-ridden streets, but for the moment it is probably preventing a massacre. Even if the British were to withdraw, the Irish would probably continue murdering one another without foreign assistance; killing seems to have moved into a self-delighting phase."

"Much depends on the attitude of the British," says Seamus Costello. "If they want to promote a civil war here, they can do it quite easily. The key factor is the weapons which are currently in the possession of the Ulster Defense Regiment, the RUC, and the RUC Reserve. If the British decide to withdraw militarily from Ireland and leave the weapons in the control of these forces, why then that's a recipe for civil war. On the other hand, if they disarm and disband these forces before they leave, the potential for civil war is vastly reduced. There will still be some conflict, but the scale of it will be minimal."

Paddy Devlin thinks the British would like to get out because of the economic burden: "Four hundred million pounds every year they have to pour into Ulster to maintain social services. I would say they want to withdraw but they can't because first of all they can't leave this kind of situation behind them.

"There's always the possibility of a civil war. That's why we're putting so much into trying to get it switched off. See, some of the leaders are fuckin' idiots! A bunch of fuckin' kamikaze pilots, except the Japanese didn't recruit them. These guys, they think politics are about hitting one another and the one who delivers the most blows wins."

Once a member of the IRA, Devlin quit because of its devotion to violence. "I'm opposed to attempts to free Ulster over the heads of the majority of the people. Nothing moves until the people move. It can't be that I'm such an idiot that I think I can impose my solution on the other million and a half people here. You don't use arms, you don't use force in a democracy."

Jim Campbell says the British want to leave but can't. "You've got the poor embarrassed British, who've got as much out of the country as they can; now they're embarrassed by it because it's sort of a seventeenth-century reactionary corner of Britain where they're fighting about religion when the rest of the civilized world has given it up. The only way to settle it is obviously by the two of them clashing, but when that happens, there's going to be an awful lot of innocent people killed. Everybody wants to do what they can to stop civil war.

"It's a complete vicious circle. I mean, everybody keeps saying to me, 'Do you think we're going toward civil war?' Well, quite often I do think we're drifting toward civil war. We've got a head-on confrontation situation—irreconcilable aims. Two views, and we're not like the British. We won't compromise over anything. Other countries can say, 'Well, let's wheel and deal a wee bit. We'll compromise.' But we haven't compromised for eight hundred years."

He doesn't think there would be Russian intervention in case of an Irish civil war, nor does he think the Provos would emerge as the most powerful force on the Catholic side.

"We won't know until there is a civil war, but I don't think the Provisionals would emerge as the powerful force. Remember, in the Spanish civil war, on the leftist progressive side, we had various different shades. They were all Republican but you had anarchists, you had Communists, you had trade unionists. On the other side, you had various different shades of nationalists. It would be the same here if there was a civil war tomorrow. All the Republican elements would unite, and on the other side all the Loyalists elements, who are fighting each other at the moment, would also unite. Who would emerge as the powerful force on either side, I don't know; but it's very possible that the Officials would because they've got the best international connections. They would be bringing in support from other groups. Then again, what is a civil war? It could become a shooting-style civil war, or, as I think more likely, it could deteriorate into a guerrilla situation.

"If you look at a map of Northern Ireland, the two most densely populated areas are Down and Antrim, with Belfast in the center. Once you go into Armagh, Derry, Fermanagh, Tyrone, you find that if the Catholics aren't in the majority, they're certainly not a small minority, so I think if we develop into that kind of civil-war situation where we were having set-piece battles as they did in Spain, Belfast would itself very quickly be surrounded. And you'd have Republicans from the south coming across the border and things like that. The slaughter might not be all one way."

Garret FitzGerald thinks the IRA could provoke a civil war in the north and drag the Republic into it. When asked what the army of the Republic would or could do, he seemed uncertain. "The question of what action a nation might or might not take is hypothetical, and I've got no government answers; but it is self-evident from the figures—East Ulster has 700,000 Protestants and 20,000 Catholics. Those 700,000 Protestants include the greater part of 14,000 legally armed men in the RUC and RUC Reserve, plus most of the greater part of the paramilitaries, which number between 20,000 and 30,000. With the Catholics as hostages in ghettos throughout the area and above all in Belfast, and with our own armies numbering at their best 13,000 men. . . ."

The impression he left was that with the best of intentions it would be extremely difficult for the Republic's troops, most of which are garrison troops stationed throughout the country, to control a situation that sixteen thousand better-armed and -trained British troops had failed to contain. "If the British army left before the situation is resolved, it would create a vacuum in which there would be no force present capable of protecting the twenty thousand Catholics in East Ulster."

Ruairi O Bradaigh feels that the government of Eire does not really want the British to withdraw, "because they have a comfortable constituency as they are now. They're in power now; the others will be in next time around. Don't rock the boat. They pay lip service to this idea of a completely free Ireland. The political situation in Northern Ireland has become very radicalized. They want to seal it off. If they could build a Great Wall of China around that border and let the English and Irish Protestants and Catholics die up there, as long as they're all right here, that's the important thing."

The Provos want the British to go but even they do not want it to happen overnight, because they feel it would almost certainly lead to civil war, which they do not want.

"They always say, 'If England left in the morning' or 'If England went under present circumstances.' We have never asked for that. We've asked for a planned, phased, and orderly withdrawal—that Britain declare her intentions of going and that there's a time scale and all the rest of political arrangement. Everything else can be negotiated."

The Protestants would be ready to talk, O Bradaigh thinks, if they knew that the British were going. Smyth, Paisley, and Craig would be forced into a position of negotiation. "The point is, if and when Britain sends them the message that she's ultimately going to get out, what are they going to do? They have to come to terms with the remainder of the population in the Six Countries, without which they cannot govern even an independent Northern Ireland."

O Bradaigh sees the present situation as a form of blackmail: "The Ulster Loyalists worked out what their minimum conditions were and then proceeded to exact them from Britain at the point of a gun, and the gun wasn't pointed at Britain so much as at their Catholic neighbors, . . . they would slaughter the Catholic population unless Britain agreed to the particular political arrangements they wanted. If Britain takes a decision in principle to get out over a period of years and communicates that in whatever manner gets the message through to the Loyalists, well, then the whole ball game changes."

If Britain were to go, O Bradaigh believes, the quarrel with the English would be at an end and Ireland would be no menace at England's rear. "Does England believe that we're going to pursue this thing beyond the grave? Once we're in control of our own affairs, isn't that it? I mean, do we want to carry on for vengeance? Haven't we had just enough of that? And don't we want to see our children grow up and not go through this type of thing?

"We have always said that we seek an honorable accommodation with the British, followed by, or linked with, an honorable accommodation with the Loyalists. That's the way it's got to be, and there's no other way, but the accommodation with the British has got to come first or the two have to come together. We want the British on the peace lines, in the barracks, and we want a gradually phased, orderly pullout. I think it's fair to say that the attitude of Republicans is to prepare for any eventuality. But we don't want a civil war. When all is said and done, the British can be gone a thousand times, Garrett FitzGerald and all of us in the movement can be long in our graves, but the people in this country will one day have to live together. And that's the truth of it."

That was not the kind of truth that Sammy Smyth's UDA was contemplating in the event of a British withdrawal, phased or otherwise. "You'd have to have a civil war because I couldn't afford not to have a civil war," Smyth said. "With one-third of the population Roman Catholic, which is not a minority, and two-thirds Protestants, how are we going to work together? The issue still remains: Does the border still exist? Let's assume the border remains. You still have this aspiration toward a United Ireland. So eventually the third of the population are going to become 51 percent. Don't forget, the Roman Catholic population is increasing all the time and the Protestant population is declining. Assuming democratic institutions evolve, they could vote Northern Ireland into the Republic of Ireland in a few years.

"Therefore, the only way I can insure that this situation never arises is, in fact, to put the Roman Catholics out of Northern Ireland. Obviously, some will not go without a fight. They will have to be killed. Since my aim is never to have a United Ireland, I can't afford to have any Nationalists at all in my independent state. Killing them will inevitably involve the twenty-six counties since a lot of their volunteers would come up to fight on their side, so you'd have a full-scale conflict.

"This is why a civil war is inevitable. The moment Britain makes its intentions known, we'd say, 'Fair enough. Get out overnight. We're not going to tolerate a slow withdrawal.' That's to the other side's advantage. We're operating with a clearly defined strategic plan which I drew up for this contingency. I first drew it up in March of 1971, and the committee of twenty-five, of which I'm a member, updated it every six months until recently; we're now continually updating it."

The UDA would strike quickly, even to taking arms away from the British army as they were leaving. "I'm not saying they're going to hand them over, we'd probably have a fight. And we'd take them out of police stations with no buts about it. But speed is essential. It would be something like the Israeli Six-Day War. We have an overall strategic plan to take over the whole of the province, all the points of communication, TV, radio, roadways, railroads, fuel and supply lines—in other words, everything that's necessary to keep people on the move, to prevent the enemy from using them.

"It's not a question of whether we could win or not, but we could make a hell of a hole. In other words, there may be a lot of us slaughtered but we'd slaughter a hell of a lot of them. Who would win, you wouldn't know."

Asked what would happen to Protestant political leaders like Paisley and Craig, he said with chilling calm, "Oh, I'd bump them all off. It would be an opportunity to pay them back for all the things they've done. We'd no longer need them. Take it from me, as far as I'm concerned, the politicians will be the first to go. Look at it this way: If I'm going to die in the streets of Ulster, I'm bloody well not going to die so Paisley and Craig can strut around after it's all over. So my first tactic will be, once we know a civil war is in the offing, to eliminate all the politicians of every stripe on both sides. It's as simple as that. Fair enough, if a compromise is going to be reached after I'm dead, I prefer it to be another breed, or a younger generation, who can build a new place, but certainly not those bastards.

"An important point to remember is that the Ulster Protestant is not standing with his back to the wall; he's standing with his back to a precipice. I'm standing with my back to a precipice. I can only go forward."

It was suggested that the IRA might win a civil war because of its superior training in guerrilla tactics. "I will not fight a civil war on guerrilla tactics. I would follow Hussein's example in Jordan. He wasn't prepared to fight the PLO on guerrilla tactics. What he did was surround the areas where they were and proceed to reduce it to rubble so there was nowhere to hide, and he solved his problem in a couple of days. Obviously I would have to do the same. We would have to demolish the Roman Catholic areas so there was nowhere to hide. We'll wipe out the IRA and the Officials overnight. Then I'm quite prepared to burn the city down. No buts about it. You know, the price of survival. With my back to the precipice, I'd have to be completely ruthless.

"As far as the rural areas are concerned, we have a force, the UVF proper, and I emphasize the word proper. You have two UVFs. The urban UVF don't deserve the name. They're just a bunch of gangsters—a few among them belonged to the original vigilante group—but the others are a pure replica of the Mafia. There is no real honesty among them. We'd get them to shape up or we'd just shoot them. In a situation like that you can't afford division. But the country UVF would in fact very effectively control the rural areas.

"Then we'd be faced with the Republic of Ireland. What we do there is to devastate the Republic so it takes them fifty years to get a grin back on their faces and they're too busy licking their own wounds to worry about what's happening in Northern Ireland.

"If we win—naturally, we've taken that fact into account—we would have mass immigration into Northern Ireland. We'd get a lot of Scotch Protestants and English Protestants and any other Protestants that wanted to come back into Northern Ireland. For the obvious reasons—to replace the people who were killed in the conflict and to get the Protestant population breeding again, plus the fact that we're going to need a permanent army for the future. Also, and this hasn't been agreed upon yet, we might enlarge the territory.

"For the first ten years, we're going to need some form of dictatorship. That's too strong a word; Ulster men won't tolerate a dictatorship, but at the same time you're going to need one government, and when you have one government, you have a dictatorship no matter what you call it. The Roman Catholics think we're a bunch of patsies, but they have another think coming. It's not totally unreal that we could take all of Ireland and make it a Protestant country."

From all indications, it appears that war is almost inevitable if the British leave Ulster. Conor Cruise O'Brien has said that in the event that war breaks out, the Republic's army would not be capable of doing more than securing a single border town. During the Londonderry fighting in 1969, before the British intervened to protect the Catholics, the Republic had considered going in but found that its army only had ammunition for forty-eight hours' fighting. Granted that Eire is spending more on its army, civil war could destroy that small island beyond repair.

Even a unification of the thirty-two counties could destroy the economics of both countries. The Republic is not in a position to pump £400–500 million a year into Ulster's economy. It is possible that American aid could replace British aid or that even after withdrawal the British would continue to carry at least part of the burden. It has been suggested that a reunion should be stretched out over a period of a dozen years, with a British garrison left behind to reassure the Protestants and an Irish garrision to protect the Catholics.

UN forces are also a possibility, but the record of UN peace-keeping in the rest of the world is such that it would probably only aggravate the situation. An Anglo-Irish peace force would seem preferable, but hardly ideal.

What form would an Irish civil war take if it came about? Barring the success of Sammy Smyth's operation, it would almost certainly be a Beirut-type situation, and as in Beirut, the casualties in Belfast would soar into the tens of thousands. There would be intervention from outside forces. Communist terrorists of all stripes would probably become involved on the Catholic side, and no doubt Arab arms and money would be available. The Soviet Union could conceivably provide arms and and money for the Communist side. There is also a chance that the IRA Provisionals and Officials would fight it out to decide who would control the Catholics. Soldiers of fortune would undoubtedly be enlisted on both sides. Scottish, Canadian, and Australian aid would be available for the Protestants. Americans of Irish descent who would be willing to help a clearly nationalist Catholic campaign might hesitate to join one that had come under the domination and control of the Communists.

However the fighting develops, Sammy Smyth will not be leading the Protestant troops in his carefully planned blitz. Not long after this interview, Sammy Smyth received the traditional "knock" of Belfast. He was staying at his sister's house at the time, and when he answered the door, two gunmen pumped bullets into him. He died instantly. Police speculation is that he was killed by UDA gunmen. His fate is symbolic of that of all those who plan the violence in Ireland. Like Maire Drumm, he died in the violence he helped to create. There is always the chance that Ireland itself will die the same way.

BOOK FIVE

APOCALYPSE

Political terrorism is a by-product of the Industrial Revolution, a disorder created by the destruction of the ancient patterns of life. A society that had been largely agrarian was thrust suddenly into a world of machines and factories, of labor and capital. The resulting displacement of populations, the deterioration of the environment, and the disruption of an entire way of life fed the fires already ignited by political repressions and the writings of intellectuals who inspired the violent deeds that have been with us ever since.

Although terrorism's philosophical underpinnings antedate the last two centuries (organized and irregular warfare are almost as old as the human race), religious and economic anarchism are the true antecedents of modern political terrorism.

For example, the Cathari, or Albigensians, and other gnostic heresies held that the universe was totally corrupt, unreal, and without meaning: only the world of the spirit was important, and all authority of a temporal nature was denied. Accused of immorality, devil worship, blood sacrifice, and heresy, they were persecuted by the Catholics. St. Dominic, the founder of the Dominican Brothers, preached the destruction of Cathari by terror. The wholesale massacre of both heretics and Christians was excused on the theory that "God will know His own."

The Anabaptists believed they belonged to the Community of Saints. They denied the rule of church and state, considering them unnecessary, since they were in direct contact with God. Authority was evil because it stood between man and the divine light within him. The existing society had to be destroyed so that the new order could be established, with its laws revealed by the inner light of the prophet or leader. This was the first time that anarchical philosophy embraced the total leadership of an inspired individual.

Plague, economic disaster, heavy taxation, and religious strife added to the misery of the people of Switzerland, Germany, and the Low Countries. This allowed Jan Mathys and his disciple John of Leiden to arouse the Anabaptists to a fever pitch. The city of Münster was sacked, and all records of contracts and debts were destroyed and all books and manuscripts were burned. They established a communal state, seizing food, clothing, all worldly goods, and placed them in a common store.

After Mathys was killed leading a sortie, John of Leiden instituted a reign of terror accompanied by polygamy and sexual excess. When Münster was retaken in 1535, John of Leiden was tortured to death. The Anabaptist revolt had many features later found in anarchistic movements: belief in the healing properties of violent destruction, the importance of violence as an end in itself, and the belief in the dream of building an entirely new social order on the ruins of the old. As in the cases of the Albigensians and the Peasants' Revolt, Anabaptist terror led not to the desired end but to the destruction of their society, the death of their leaders, and the eradication of their movement by counterterror of unbelievable fury.

The Inquisition and the Dominican order were instruments of organized terror, but the Jesuits provided the closest parallel to today's concept of terrorist groups. Founded by Ignatius Loyola in 1533, the Society of Jesus was called by Loyola "the little battalion of Jesus." Organized to combat the Reformation and to propagate the Roman Catholic faith among the heathen, it grew into one of the largest and best-organized groups of terrorists in history. The Jesuits were the shock troops of the Counter Reformation. Their casuistical principles and the nature of their secret society caused them to be damned and feared by both Protestants and Catholics.

Their belief in the "sovereignty of the people" and "tyrannicide" was anarchical in theory and action. God had vested sovereignty in the people, who voluntarily delegated it to the monarch. The people were free to reassert their prerogatives and depose the monarch whenever he failed to govern in accordance with their wishes. In the Jesuits' judgment, this failure occurred when the sovereign either adopted Protestantism or seemed likely to do so. Under the casuistical principle that the end justifies the means, killing a ruler who had turned away from the church was a sacred duty—not a crime.

Whenever the society deemed it necessary to eliminate a king, prince, or other important personage, the Jesuit assassin was prepared in a ceremony called the Blessing of the Dagger. Next to the Dark Chamber where Jesuit novices were initiated was a small room called the Cell of Meditation. A painting was placed in the center of an altar, covered with a veil and surrounded by torches and lamps of a scarlet color. A casket covered with hieroglyphics and bearing a representation of a lamb (symbolic of Christ) on its lid was placed on a table. The brother chosen for the "deed of blood" came here to receive his instructions. When he opened the casket, he found a dagger wrapped in a linen cloth. An officer of the order removed the dagger, kissed it, sprinkled it with holy water, and then handed it to a deacon, who attached it to a rosary and hung it around the neck of the chosen one, informing him that he was the elect of God and telling him the name of his victim.

Then a prayer was offered for his success: "And Thou, invincible and terrible God, who didst resolve to inspire our elect and thy servant with the project of exterminating [the name of the victim], a tyrant and heretic, strengthen him, and render the consecration of our brother perfect by the successful execution of the great work. Increase, O God, his strength a hundredfold, so that he may accomplish the noble undertaking, and protect him with the powerful and divine armor of thine elect and saints. Pour on his head the daring courage which despises all fear, and fortify his body in danger and in the face of death itself."

The veil was then removed from the painting and the elect beheld a portrait of Jacques Clément, the young Dominican monk who had assassinated Henry III of France, surrounded by a host of angels carrying him to celestial glory. The implication was clear; the current elect would also be wafted to the side of a grateful God once his mission was accomplished.

A crown, symbolic of the heavenly crown he was about to win, was placed on his head. "Deign, O Lord of Hosts, to bestow a propitious glance on the servant thou has chosen as thine arm, and for the execution of the high decree of thine eternal justice. Amen."

The technique was not unlike that employed by the Old Man of the Mountain, who used to drug some of his young assassins into a deep sleep and transport them to his secret pleasure garden, persuading them when they awoke that he had brought them to Paradise itself. Drugged again, they would awake in the everyday world, now forever convinced that their master could reward them with eternal Paradise after death if they did his bidding while they were alive. How far removed is all this from today's URA? Kozo Okamoto, the sole surviving terrorist of the Lod Airport massacre, wanted to commit suicide because "we soldiers after we die want to become the three stars of Orion. The revolution will go on, and there will be many stars."

The Jesuits' powers grew quickly and their terroristic methods caused such fear that they came into conflict with civil and religious authorities in most countries where they operated. The Jesuits were driven from France in 1594, from England in 1579, from Venice in 1607, from Spain in 1767, and from Naples in 1768. They were finally suppressed by Pope Clement XIV in 1773 and not revived until they had turned away from terrorist tactics.

Gradually the concept of anarchy moved from the religious realm to the economic. Nineteenth-century pamphleteers exemplified the shift in their demands for social justice. One wrote, "Magistrates, provosts, beadles, mayors —nearly all live by robbery . . . they all batten on the poor . . . the stronger robs the weaker." Another said, "I would like to strangle the nobles and the clergy, every one of them. . . . Good working men make the wheaten bread but they never chew it; no, all they get is the sifting from the corn, and from good wine they get nothing but the dregs and from good clothing nothing but the chaff. Everything that is tasty and good goes to the nobles and the clergy."

This school of anarchism, which differed from Pierre Proudhon's peaceful "philosophic anarchism," relied on terror to achieve its purposes. It grew out of the socialist movement of the nineteenth century, but in 1872 the International Workingmen's Association expelled the anarchists led by Mikhail Bakunin from the International.

Since that time, socialism and anarchism have tended to diverge sharply, although both are strongly anticapitalist. Many anarchists took part in the trade-union movement, becoming loyal members of unions with a syndicalist program—syndicalism rejects the Marxian concept of the proletarian dictatorship and envisions a stateless society in which production will be conducted only to satisfy the needs of the community, which will be administered by a national federation of self-governing workers. Although nonviolent, syndicalists regard the struggles of unions primarily as skirmishes in which workers gain experience in class warfare until the day they can create a more equitable society.

Bakunin's followers accepted the terrorist policy of assassination, which they called "propaganda of the deed." Yet despite the popular view that has unjustly identified all anarchism with violence, it is fair to say that most anarchists have not advocated terrorism. However, this view has been enforced by such assassinations as those of French President Marie François Sadi Carnot in 1894, King Humbert I of Italy in 1900, United States President William McKinley in 1901, and King George of Greece in 1913, all committed by anarchists.

There were countless other assassination attempts on crowned heads, with quite a few successes, but not all by any means were carried out by anarchists. Russian Czar Alexander II was killed by a bomb thrown under his sled. In the Balkans, the terror was nationalistic, a reaction to Turkish rule. The Internal Macedonian Revolutionary Organization began operating against the Turks in 1894 but gradually became pro-Bulgarian and anti-Serbian. In Serbia, the Uyedinyenye Ili Smrt (Black Hand Society), composed of army officers, raided the palace and murdered King Alexander I Obrenovich and his queen with their cavalry sabers.

It was the leader of the Black Hand Society, Col. Dragutin Dimitrijević, who plotted the assassination of Archduke Franz Ferdinand at Sarajevo. As in so many acts of terror, the victim was of liberal tendencies, a friend of minority peoples in the Austrian empire, who would have introduced reforms for their benefits. (Czar Alexander II freed twenty-three million serfs before he was assassinated.) The Serbian government got wind of the plot and tried to close its borders, but the Black Hand had sent a dozen young terrorists to Sarajevo. Two failed with bombs that same day before the third succeeded with a pistol. The killing of the archduke and duchess triggered World War I. Whether the war would have taken place at a later time, as most historians believe, is beside the point. The fact is that one terrorist act ignited a certain set of circumstances which resulted in twenty million deaths.

Between 1918 and 1922, there were 367 political murders in Germany —22 by left-wing groups and 345 by right-wing groups. The courts failed to enforce the law against either groups. Political terrorism was an important weapon in Hitler's rise to power, and he continued to use it after he gained power.

In Yugoslavia, the Hrvatski Ustashi (Croatian Uproar), at the urging of Hitler, assassinated King Alexander and the French foreign minister. After the German invasion of Yugoslavia, the Uproar, headed by Ante Pavelić, formed a government and began the systematic extermination of a half-million Serbs.

Many Uproar leaders escaped punishment after the war by settling in Western nations.

Political terrorism continued in Russia even after the Revolution. Several Soviet officials were murdered by terrorists. Dora Kaplan attempted to assassinate Lenin and the German ambassador, Count von Mirbach. Sergei Kirov, a member of the Politburo who was close to Stalin, was killed in 1934, and the purge trials that followed were judicial assassinations. The mass government terror of the Stalin regime was unprecedented. Lenin, Trotsky, and the other Russian disciples of Marx were revolutionaries, not terrorists. They concentrated their efforts on organizing the people rather than on individual terror. The key to their success was that they succeeded in persuading the masses to fight at their side.

There was something romantic about the Russian czar-killers of the late nineteenth century. Unlike the propaganda-conscious terrorist groups of today, who shy away from the word *terrorist,* the members of the Terrorist Brigade were proud of the label. They brought the word *terrorist* into common political usage. They believed that political murder "shakes the whole system to its foundations," but the assassination of Czar Alexander II only meant greater repression. Then the assassination of the czar's uncle, Duke Sergei, followed by the execution of the responsible terrorist led to the October Revolution and its savage repression. The brigade disintegrated in 1908 when it learned that its leader was a member of the secret police.

The Terrorist Brigade was immortalized by Albert Camus in his play *The Just Assassin.* It is the story of a young revolutionary who is chosen to kill the head of the secret police. The plan calls for him to throw a bomb into the target's carriage, but as the carriage draws closer, the terrorist can see that the police official is holding two small children on his lap. Bomb in hand, he turns and runs away, having decided that the deed must be done another day. Agreeing with his decision, his comrades say, "Even in destruction, there's a right way and a wrong way—and there are limits."

There are academicians today who point to this example when they want to show that terrorism has undergone a radical transformation in recent years. Their thesis is that terrorists used to operate under a code of honor, that their murders were strategic and for a cause.

"Until about the middle of the twentieth century, terrorism was most often a modernist version of the older politics of assassination—the killing of particular people thought to be guilty of particular acts," Michael Waltzer wrote in the *New Republic* on August 30, 1975. "Since that time terrorism has most often taken the form of random murder, its victims unknown in advance and, even from the standpoint of the terrorists, innocent of any crime. The change is of deep moral and political significance, though it has hardly been discussed. It represents the breakdown of a *political code* worked out in the late 19th century and roughly analogous to the laws of war, developed at the same time."

The code made a distinction between combatants and noncombatants.

"In former times," says Waltzer, "children, passers-by and sometimes even policemen were thought to be uninvolved in the political struggle, innocent people whom the terrorist had no right to kill. He did not even claim a right to terrorize them; in fact his activity was misnamed—a minor triumph for the forces of order. But today's terrorists earn their title. They have emptied out the category of innocent people; they claim a right to kill anyone; they seek to terrorize whole populations."

Examples to the contrary would fill another book. Bombings during the nineteenth century killed hundreds of "innocent" people. Two incidents come immediately to mind: the Haymarket and Wall Street bombings. The following sentiment was expressed by French poet Laurent Tailhade: "Qu'importe les victimes si le geste est beau?" ("What do the victims matter if the gesture is fine?")

The best description of a terrorist can be found in Sergei Nechayev's *Revolutionary Catechism:*

> The revolutionary is a dedicated man. He has no personal inclinations, no business affairs, no property, and no name. Everything in his life is subordinated towards a single exclusive attachment, a single thought, and a single passion—the revolution. . . . He has torn himself away from the bonds which tie him to the social order and to the cultivated world, with all its laws, moralities, and customs. . . . The revolutionary despises public opinion . . . morality is everything which contributes to the triumph of the revolution. Immoral and criminal is everything that stands in his way. . . . Night and day he must have but one thought, one aim—merciless destruction . . . he must be ready to destroy himself and destroy with his own hands everyone who stands in his way.

Anarchists who advocate violence, whether Anabaptists or Baader-Meinhof gang members, have spilled a great deal of blood, innocent or otherwise. They preach terrorism for its own sake, the destruction of the old system and the building of the new. "We are not in the least afraid of ruins," said Spanish anarchist leader Buenaventura Durutti. "We are going to inherit the earth. There is not the slightest doubt about it. . . . We carry a new world, here in our hearts."

The words are representative of the ideal of anarchism and symbolic of the reality. In the end it was the Fascist who built on the ruins of Spain and the people were subjected to dictatorship.

Anarchist philosophic beliefs and anarchist violent actions are separated by a chasm. The philosophy teaches that man is naturally good and made evil only by laws and governments, that given a stateless condition his reason and primitive sense of right and wrong would assert themselves, permitting all to live peacefully and cooperatively in bliss.

The contradictions of idealism and coercion have caused splits within all anarchical movements. It is perhaps the reason why such movements have never made a successful revolution. Their political theories are based on the false assumption that love and violence are synonymous.

Terrorism also has failed as a tactic because it is ineffective against a ruthless tyranny or strong democracy. Unlike organized revolution, it has never overthrown or even seriously threatened a totalitarian state. What limited success it has achieved has been against parliamentary monarchies and weak democracies. Only in countries like Spain in 1936 and the Weimar Republic has it been possible for unaided terrorism to achieve results commensurate with the effort expended.

The strategy of terrorism is to generate fear, to employ that weapon in a special and complicated sort of way. Terrorism is an illusionist's trick. The power of the terrorist is unreal. Revolution, like war, has been described as the strategy of the strong, while terrorism, being the work of a small elite, is the strategy of the weak. Terrorism is a weapon used by those who lack strength to act directly. The strategy is to achieve its goal not through its acts but through the enemy's response to them. For terrorism is merely the first step in a revolutionary struggle. It is a psychological assault intended to produce a psychological result. It can be fear, frustration, anger, helplessness. Whatever the reaction, the idea is to provoke the government into embarking on a course of action the terrorist desires. In other words, the terrorist is in the peculiar position of having to undertake actions he does not desire, such as hijackings and the murder of innocent people, in order to provoke one he does desire—for example, a brutal police repression. The objective is to reveal the hidden weakness, evil, or corruption of the existing government—to unmask the beast, as it were. In revealing the real face behind the mask, the terrorist hopes to enlist the support of the people, which is the next step toward achieving conditions propitious for revolutionary guerrilla warfare.

The terrorist has been compared to a magician who tricks his mark into watching his right hand while his left hand, unnoticed, makes the switch. The strategy of deliberately killing the innocent is a risky one. The act may appear particularly horrifying to the public because it seems so pointless. The reaction could turn the terrorists into enemies of the people as well as of the government. Che Guevara was opposed to terrorism for precisely this reason. He argued that it hinders "contact with the masses and makes impossible unification for action that will be necessary at a critical moment." In his treatise on guerrilla warfare, he dealt with terrorism in a single paragraph.

On the other hand, Carlos Marighella had much to say about it in his *Mini-Manual of the Urban Guerrilla:* "Terrorism is an arm the revolutionary can never relinquish. Bank assaults, ambushes, desertions, diverting of arms, the rescue of prisoners, executions, kidnapping, sabotage, terrorism and the war of nerves are all cases to point. . . . The government has no alternative except to intensify repression." The aim, he says, is to escalate the situation so that people "will refuse to collaborate with the authorities and the general sentiment is that the government is unjust." The idea is to show that the capitalist state depends for its continued existence upon the use of violence and its own terror. This is the conventional wisdom of a wide spectrum of terrorist groups—IRA, FLQ, ERP, RAF, ETA, URA, ALN, MIR, FAR, PLO, PFLP, PDFLP, ALF, ELF, TPLA—a veritable alphabet soup of terror, not to mention the separatist movements active all over the globe.

The most successful terrorism is that practiced by governments to sustain their power. Yet even a mild form of repression can boomerang in a colonialist situation, as happened in Ireland and Israel. Great Britain defeated itself, as France did in Algeria. A motley band of Algerian nationalists calling themselves the National Liberation Front (or, by its French initials, FLN) was able to persuade a mixed indigenous population, with no history of its own, to think of itself as the citizenry of a separate nation. The FLN's strategy was to pressure the French into reacting in a way that would demonstrate the unreality of the French claim that there was no distinct Algerian nation, that it was genuinely a part of France. French reaction to random violence was to treat all persons of non-European origin as suspects, even to transferring army units of Muslim Algerian troops into mainland France and replacing them in Algeria by European troops, thereby signaling the end of Algérie Français. When people began to feel excluded from the existing community, their sympathies went to the FLN, which was able to shift from terrorism to organized guerrilla warfare.

The terrorist tactics used in colonial countries seldom succeed against an indigenous government, which is far more reluctant to relinquish its hold than a colonial power with a country of its own to which it can withdraw. The Israelis, who are fighting on home ground, with their backs to the sea, have no place to which to retreat. In Uruguay, once the model democracy of Latin America, the terror of the Tupamaros not only failed but led directly to a repressive military dictatorship.

Despite their inherent weakness, terrorists nonetheless have scored many political successes in the last few decades. They have caused enough damage to intimidate and blackmail powerful governments. Technology—jet travel, satellite communication, lightweight bazookas, plastic bombs, compact automatic weapons—has enabled them to invade the political arena and to express their ideological goals on a more organized level than in the past. Also, world opinion is on their side. Imperialism is now regarded as immoral, even by the United Nations. The colonial empires are dissolving so quickly that it is almost impossible to keep count. This is in part the result of costly wars in Indochina, Indonesia, and Algeria and in part of centrifugal pressures from dissident ethnic minorities. The breakup of large heterogeneous countries into smaller national units has been accelerated by terrorism carried out in the name of oppressed ethnic minorities seeking self-rule.

The United Nations had 51 members in 1945; by 1960 there were 82; there are now 138 and another 20 nations are not members. Indications are that there may be 200 or even 300 politically independent nations in the world by the end of the century.

Brian Jenkins wrote in a Rand Corporation report:

The resultant international system is likely to resemble the political complexity of Renaissance Italy, in which major kingdoms, minor principalities, tiny states, independent city republics, Papal territories, and bands of *condottieri* engaged in incessant, but low-level, warfare with one another. Medieval Europe, and India in the seventeenth and eighteenth centuries also come to mind. . . . The world that emerges is an unstable collection of nations, mini-states, autonomous ethnic substates, governments in exile, national liberation fronts, guerrilla groups aspiring to international recognition and legitimacy via violence, and a collection of ephemeral but disruptive terrorist organizations, some of which are linked together in vague alliances, some perhaps the protégés of foreign states. It is a world in which the acronyms of various self-proclaimed revolutionary fronts may take their place in international forums alongside the names of countries. It is a world of formal peace between nations—free of open warfare except, perhaps, for brief periods—but of a higher level of political violence, of increased internal insecurity.

Although most terrorists identify with Mao and Castro, few have the patience to go into the mountains for decades if necessary to wage their revolution. Mao developed the modern theory of guerrilla fighting. He formulated a series of relationships that differed from existing military strategies and earlier Marxist theories of revolution. Contrary to the Marxists, his emphasis was on military power. Political power depends on military power; or, as Mao put it, "political power grows out of the barrel of a gun." Although his forces were initially inferior, Mao reasoned that the superior political motivation of his guerrillas, strengthened by the political support of the Chinese peasants, made it possible for them to survive military reverses. The strategy was to wage a protracted military campaign that would eventually wear down the enemy.

By politicizing and mobilizing people who would be mere bystanders in a conventional conflict, Mao introduced a relationship between military action and propaganda. The effect that any violent action has on the people watching may even exceed the importance of the conflict itself. Terrorism is that principle applied on the grandest scale.

Terrorism, as noted earlier, is theater. Because of the technological advancement in world communications, the violence is directed at an international audience. The dramatics are staged to evoke sympathy for a cause that the audience may not have been aware of until that moment. The Palestinians, unable to goad Israel into self-defeating reaction, directed their attacks elsewhere, the strategy being to achieve the greatest shock value possible without completely alienating the audience. But what is too much? Was Munich too much? Rome? Lod? Athens? Were Palestinian goals damaged by these atrocities? Apparently not. There is sufficient evidence, from the United Nations to the Israeli cabinet, that a new Palestinian state is closer to realization today than ever before. It is also plausible that the IRA will one day drive England from Ulster with equally shocking violence. There is nothing like success to fire the imagination of fanatics. Dismayed at the welcome accorded Arafat by the United Nations, left-wing journalist Paul Johnson wrote that "step by step, almost imperceptibly, without anyone being aware that a fatal watershed has been crossed, mankind has descended into the age of terror."

How many people had heard of the Fighters for Free Croatia or of their cause until they hijacked a TWA 727 jetliner in New York and persuaded five major newspapers *(New York Times, Los Angeles Times, Chicago Tribune, Washington Post, International Herald Tribune)* to publish their propaganda messages, which accused the Yugoslavian government of suppressing its Croatian minority?

Their thirty-hour hopscotching odyssey to Paris with fifty hostages ended once they received proof that their communiqués had been printed according to their instructions. Photocopies of the published statements were transmitted to Paris and rushed to de Gaulle Airport. Acting on orders from the hijackers, an escort plane had made low swoops over London and Paris to drop thousands of pink leaflets calling for the independence of Croatia. TWA had similar leaflets dropped by helicopters and private planes over New York, Chicago, and Montreal.

On the first leg of their odyssey, the hijackers had directed authorities in New York to a locker at Grand Central Station, where the police found the communiqués along with a bomb in a pressure cooker. One policeman was killed and three were injured when they tried to disarm it at a firing range. The hijackers warned that unless the texts of their manifestos were published as ordered, another bomb would be detonated in a "highly busy location" somewhere in the United States. The four American newspapers complied as well as they could according to their press runs—the request came late on Friday night (September 10, 1976), but the *Herald Tribune* failed to comply, because its Saturday edition had already been printed.

In the text of their eight-page statement, the hijackers said, "We decided to undertake this particular action for many reasons ... our goal was to present an accurate picture of the brutal oppression taking place in Yugoslavia." But they were under no illusions:

> We expect all peace-loving forces in the world to describe us as terrorists, criminals, and murderers. From the time of Caesar, through Hitler, Stalin, Franco, and Salazar, as well as with numerous other colonial and neocolonial governments, those fighting for national liberation have always been described in such terms.
>
> Recently, a UN diplomat expressed this idea, stating that today only a small number of diplomats had never been imprisoned or convicted of terrorism or criminal acts. One man's terrorist is another man's patriot, depending solely on one's national and political objectives and suitability.
>
> The point to be made here, obviously, is not to conclusively define *terrorism,* an impossible and unnecessary task, but, rather, to explain the ultimate

necessity for our extreme decision and to ask others to judge this decision objectively and unemotionally.

We must remember that today's "terrorists" are often tomorrow's policymakers, having participated in the formation of a new, independent state. Such was the position of the supporters of the Declaration of Independence, after the American colonies were freed from British subjugation. Thus, the unsuccessful continue to be "terrorists" but, upon success, are courted by all governments. With this reality reappearing dependably from one day to the next, all ethical and moral revulsion felt for so-called terrorist acts is necessarily irrational.

They quoted Sean McBride, winner of the Nobel Peace Prize: "If oppression amounts to genocide, . . . people are entitled to fight back. The framers of the Universal Declaration of Human Rights recognized that; in the declaration they point out that unless human rights are protected under the rule of law, people will be driven to the use of violence."

The hijackers told the pilot they knew the penalty for air piracy but that they were "ready to die if their demands were not respected." The penalty is a minimum of twenty years in prison. If death results from the piracy, the penalty can be death or life imprisonment. After confirming publication of their statements, the terrorists surrendered. The bombs they had smuggled through airport security were fakes. "That's show biz," said one of them. Before leaving Paris in the custody of the FBI, they expressed satisfaction in having accomplished their aim: publicity for their cause. "We are proud of what we did," said their leader.

Considering that the threat was phony except for one small bomb in a pressure cooker, it was indeed a remarkable accomplishment. Once again terrorists had demonstrated the power of terror.

"No editor wants to be blackmailed, but they put a gun to our heads," said Benjamin C. Bradlee, executive editor of the *Washington Post.* "We thought there were lives at stake. We didn't really have much of a choice."

"At that point it wasn't a very difficult decision," said William F. Thomas, editor of the *Los Angeles Times.* "The murder coming on the heels of their demands added weight to their threats."

With this in mind, is it stretching the bounds of imagination to wonder what will happen when we confront, as we surely will, perhaps a lot sooner than any of us realizes, the ultimate blackmail—the terrorist threat to detonate a nuclear bomb?

Whether by design or coincidence, Carlos and Hans-Joachim Klein were in Belgrade at the time of the Croatian hijacking. In Algiers earlier that month, American and West German intelligence agents had identified the two terrorists, along with three associates, as they boarded a plane for Yugoslavia. Both Washington and Bonn alerted Belgrade authorities, and France and Austria requested their immediate arrest. Although Yugoslav officials initially confirmed the identification, all five terrorists were allowed to board a jet for

Baghdad, where they once again disappeared into that Arab world Carlos knows so well.

The United States lodged a formal protest. State Department spokesman Frederick Z. Brown disclosed the letter of protest and said the department had supplied enough details of Carlos's whereabouts for Yugoslav officials to have apprehended him, had they wished. "Yugoslav authorities allowed him to slip through their fingers," Brown angrily complained. Other diplomats speculated that Carlos had slipped through the net with help from Communist friends. The Yugoslavs, they said, wanted to curry favor with those Third World nations that support Carlos's activities. Belgrade's response was that the whole episode was a case of mistaken identity.

A few days later, a Cairo newspaper, *Al-Akhbar,* reported that Carlos was back in Western Europe, hiding in an Arab embassy, and that he had a small nuclear bomb in his possession that he apparently intended to use in a terrorist operation.

This chilling disclosure, buried in the middle of a UPI story, was generally ignored by the press. Yet West German authorities had reason to ponder its chilling aspect. Hidden in the files of the *Verfassungsschutz* (Federal Office for the Protection of the Constitution) was a secret investigative report concerning the relationship between Dr. Klaus Robert Traube, a brilliant nuclear physicist, and Hans-Joachim Klein. Four months before the OPEC raid in Vienna, Klein and Traube had vacationed together for ten days in Yugoslavia. Traube, who admits to having joined the Communist youth movement after the war, first made contact with younger radicals through Inge Hornischer, a Frankfurt attorney who handled his divorce. As a teen-ager, Klein had worked as a messenger for Fraulein Hornischer, whose radical clientele included Wilfried Boese, the terrorist picked by Carlos to lead the Entebbe hijacking.

When informed of the background of some of his friends, Traube argued that his relations with them were innocent. Nevertheless, his employer, Interatom, which manufactures nuclear reactors, argued that it had no alternative but to fire him. Interatom's fears were that West Germany's controversial nuclear energy program would suffer if the investigation were leaked to the press, which occurred a year later.

The importance of this incident goes far beyond the innocence or guilt of Dr. Traube. It goes to the very heart of the threat inherent in this nuclear age. The possibility of nuclear terror is something that is now recognized by most governments. Some years ago, when this danger was still being minimized by the Atomic Energy Commission (AEC), Russian diplomat Dmitri N. Kolesnik brought it up in the United Nations during a debate on terrorism: "Robin Hood was armed with bows and arrows, but modern terrorists prefer to have rifles and bombs, and tomorrow it's quite possible they will have death-carrying germs or maybe stolen atomic bombs. And with the help of these bombs, they can blackmail any government."

After years of controversy between maverick nuclear scientists and the

AEC, it is now the conclusion of most nuclear experts that given a sufficient amount of special nuclear material, one or more terrorists without advanced scientific and technical skills could make a simple, but devastating, atomic bomb.

Back in 1971 the city of Orlando, Florida, was subjected to nuclear blackmail. In testimony before Senator John O. Pastore's Senate committee, an AEC witness said, "What happened was this. We were notified one evening late that Orlando had been threatened, and this came through the FBI. Orlando had been, through a series of notes, threatened by a hydrogen bomb. The notes suggested that if the police department wanted to know where the material came from, all they had to do was to call the AEC because that material was from its shipments. We immediately instituted actions to find out what had happened with respect to the shipment of materials . . . and we notified the FBI the following day that we found nothing in the system that was missing."

The Orlando police demanded evidence and, in return, received a drawing of the device with a note that said, "Just to clear any doubts you may have about us having a hydrogen bomb, there is a drawing of it with this letter. You will need an expert in nuclear weapons to tell you if it is genuine, but believe me, it is."

The sketch was rushed to McCoy Air Force Base, where an armaments officer indicated that "it would probably work." The police were directed to deliver $1 million in cash to a vacant lot, and subsequently a fourteen-year-old science student was taken into custody and confessed. AEC experts refused to say for certain that the design would not work.

Four years later a twenty-year-old college student was asked to design a homemade atomic bomb for the Nova television science series. A chemistry major at Massachusetts Institute of Technology (M.I.T.) with no previous knowledge of nuclear engineering, the student spent five weeks on the project. He read books at the M.I.T. science library and made one trip to Washington to study the unclassified papers from the Manhattan Project. "I was really quite surprised at how easy the bomb was to design," the student said. "I estimated that it would cost about $10,000 to actually build, weigh about eight hundred pounds, and require about fifteen pounds of plutonium."

His twenty-eight-page report was submitted to nuclear-weapons experts; but they refused to comment, because to do so might violate their security clearance. The report was sent to Dr. Jan Prawitz, a nuclear physicist at the Swedish Ministry of Defense. "There is a fair chance that it would not go off," Prawitz said, "but there is also a chance that it would." The bomb would have the destructive force of two million pounds of TNT and could kill a hundred thousand people.

A year later, a Princeton University student, John Aristotle Phillips, designed a nuclear bomb that measured only two feet in diameter and weighed 125 pounds. Compact enough to fit in the trunk of a car, it would have half the power of the atomic bomb that destroyed Hiroshima.

Phillips spent five months on his report. His physics adviser merely directed him to books that are available to anyone. The books told him all he had to know except for one missing link: how to arrange the explosives to achieve a supercritical mass. That information is still classified. "I made a conceptual guess," Phillips said. "I had a flash and it turned out to be right. It was profoundly simple once I saw it, and someone else with determination could see it too." That was the point of the experiment. "Any determined terrorist with a basic understanding of physics could do what I did," he said. "I wanted to draw attention to the issue of safeguarding nuclear materials." To make Phillips's bomb work, a terrorist would need to steal only twenty-one pounds of plutonium, an amount roughly the size of a softball.

The Achilles heel in both the civilian and military nuclear programs has always been the "safeguards" on special nuclear materials. Without highly enriched uranium-235 or plutonium, which is a natural by-product of conventional nuclear reactors using uranium, the bomb assembly would obviously be useless. The "Nova" documentary also showed that plutonium was not all that difficult to acquire. Terrorists could hijack trucks or planes carrying it between nuclear installations all over the world, or lab technicians could steal small amounts over a period of time by falsifying a plant's plutonium inventory. The government calls this MUF—materials unaccounted for. The AEC concedes that it is impossible to balance the books on nuclear material, which means it is impossible to tell whether material has been stolen, embezzled, or simply lost in the system while being machined, sintered, or compacted into pellets.

One of the most celebrated MUF cases took place at Westinghouse's fuel-fabrication plant at Apollo, Pennsylvania, in 1965. A check of the inventory revealed that over a six-year period some 207 pounds of highly enriched weapons-grade uranium had disappeared. The AEC closed the plant down and began a full-scale search for the material. Fifty-nine pounds were recovered: 13 pounds turned up in air filters at the plant, and another 15 pounds were found at a mountain burial pit, eight miles from the plant, but the rest was never found.

The Apollo loss jolted the AEC into taking a harder look at its material-accountability system and on March 10, 1967, it issued a 121-page report on safeguarding nuclear material. A key paragraph says, "Safeguard programs should also be designed in recognition of the problem of terrorist or criminal groups clandestinely acquiring nuclear weapons or material useful therein. . . . It should be recognized that political and social restraints would not influence terrorist, insurrectionist, or criminal groups."

In trying to explain the Apollo MUF to this writer, Ralph G. Page, deputy director of the Office of Nuclear Material Safety and Safeguards at the Nuclear Regulatory Commission [NRC] said that Westinghouse's "problem was that they allowed their scrap material to accumulate and they kept assuming that the material was in the scrap pile, and when they processed the scrap, it was not; they had overestimated the quantity of material in the scrap. We now require that scrap be processed essentially on a continuing basis. The regulations say that no scrap can remain on inventory longer than six months. We also have sharpened up our management controls. We require that a management audit be performed at least on an annual basis, that there be an audit of the measurement system on a continuing basis, that there be shipper-receiver measurement comparisons made so that we compare the shipper's stated quantity of material and the receiver's stated quantity of material. This comes to NRC. If there is a variance, then an investigation is initiated to determine why there is a difference between what the shipper and receiver showed. We do look at the system of accounting for material in each material balance area. We require that books for the plant at large be kept, but we also require that each of the custodians for each material-balance area keep separate records, and of course, we make comparisons between the records and the plant, and this provides a separation of functions so that a theft of material would be likely detected."

In other words, Westinghouse lost enriched uranium-235 scrap worth millions, and that was all the explanation the NRC required. This is the kind of irresponsible management that only aggravates the problem. While doing research at the Ministry of Defense Library in London, this writer came across a reference sheet from the House of Commons Library Research Division that offered another explanation for the Apollo MUF: "Nearly fifteen years ago an American plant lost 207 lb of nuclear fuel, enough for many bombs. After a few months only 59 lb were recovered and the USAEC is said to believe that the rest was 'diverted' to China or Israel." We know that China has since joined the "nuclear club," and we now believe that Israel readied thirteen atomic bombs before the tide turned in its favor during the Yom Kippur War of 1973.

What would be the value of weapons-grade uranium and plutonium on the black market? As early as 1969, AEC Commissioner Clarence E. Larson was worrying that "once special nuclear material is successfully stolen in small, possibly economically acceptable quantities, a supply-stimulated market for such materials is bound to develop. . . . As the market grows, the number of thefts can be expected to grow. . . . I fear such growth would be extremely rapid once it begins. Such a theft would quickly lead to serious economic burdens to the industry and a threat to national security."

Charles Thornton lasted a year and a half as director of nuclear materials safeguards. Described by a colleague as "a great undiplomatic breath of fresh air who rattled everybody," Thornton was too outspoken a critic to please the AEC. Interviewed by writer John McPhee, Thornton lived up to his description. Said Thornton, "All the guys who tell you that American industry is experienced in protecting its vital materials—that's a crock. Mankind has never handled as dangerous a commodity as plutonium. We have never developed the skill. . . .

"The aggregate MUF from the three diffusion plants alone is expressible in tons. No one knows where it is. None of it may have been stolen, but the balances don't close. You could divert from any plant in the world, in substantial amounts, and never be detected. In a diffusion plant, take any pipe and freeze out the material that is passing through. Set up a diversionary pipe. Cool it with liquid air, and get it into a bottle. Coca-Cola trucks go in and out of the restricted areas there all the time. All sorts of people.

"The statistical thief learns the sensitivity of the system and operates within it and is never detected. Scenarios to get stuff out of the cascades are as varied as the ingenuity of individuals. Put a saddle valve into a pipe. Cool the pipe with methyl chloride. Take a saltshaker each day in your lunch bucket. Take a hundred grams a day. A kilogram every ten days. Or hit the shipping point. Or doctor the record of sampling bottles. That would not be my choice, though. Fully enriched uranium in a conversion plant—a pale yellow fluid—could be put in a hot-water bottle under your shirt.

"The AEC can say officially that quantities of MUF are not dangerous. This is not so. Tons have been lost. They can say they have impregnable barriers, sensitive modern instruments. Not that impregnable, not that sensitive. They can say, 'The numbers are not good, but we don't know how to do any better.' If you admit that this industry is not controllable, then you shut down. You wait until it is controllable and then start up.

"The incremental capital for an adequate safeguards system would not destroy the industry if it were designed in. It's late in the history of the world to go into the safeguards business."

There is nothing new about white-collar crime. Employees steal anywhere from $20 to $30 billion from their employers every year. As late as August of 1976, the NRC was conceding that its security system was not strong enough to repel an attack by as few as three armed terrorists and that there were still weaknesses in the accounting system.

In a letter to the House Energy and Environment Subcommittee, NRC Chairman Marcus A. Rowden said that an investigation of fifteen fuel-fabricating plants revealed weaknesses in all their security systems. Many of the problems were corrected quickly, but a second checkup later showed that seven of the plants still could not meet test standards. The NRC criteria called for plant defenses able to defeat "an external threat comprised at a minimum of three well-armed, well-trained persons who might possess inside knowledge or assistance." The problems involved guards who openly indicated that they would be reluctant to engage an attacking force, in part because of fears of legal liability. Other problems included guard forces judged too small, poor control of access to nuclear materials, inadequate searching of persons leaving a plant, and failure of plant security systems to have adequate radio and other links to local law enforcement.

Rowden said that Army Special Forces experts were working with the commission to analyze the vulnerability of truck convoys that move substantial quantities of nuclear material. New regulations and training for drivers and guards were instituted as a result. Convoy procedures were generally found to be adequate, but they were not always properly carried out. For example, drivers would maintain prescribed intervals between trucks while on the road, and guards would be properly armed, but they all would gather and have lunch together in the middle of the trip, thereby making themselves vulnerable to attack. Of course, Rowden added, the convoy operations have been improved. "There is room for improvement," he said of the security problem generally, but "we think that we're coming down to a state where the industry will be beyond criticism."

This was not the first time the AEC had promised to upgrade the industry. A 1970 study by the Institute of Nuclear Materials Management, a professional society of nuclear experts who became concerned about the adequacy of the AEC's safeguards, singled out transportation as the weakest link in the security chain. "Potential mechanisms for diversion include the hijacking of trucks and aircraft and thefts from traffic terminals," the report stated. "To these cogent concerns there had been no statement or assurance by our Government that preplanned and debugged mechanisms exist that would provide an adequate response to these threats." The report emphasized that this country's trucking routes were an utterly unsafe way to ship nuclear material. In an appendix, the institute pointed out that theft from truck hijacking amounted to well over $1 billion per year. "The transportation industry is infiltrated by organized crime and must be adjudged incapable of providing reasonable protection for valuable or strategic cargo." In its own study of 735 Mafia members, the AEC found that significant numbers were associated with trucking either as union officials or as owners of trucking firms.

The AEC has been tinkering with safeguards for a long time without satisfying its critics. An earlier General Accounting Office (GAO) report (November 1973) had given it a pretty stiff jolt. However, the agency's track record seems to indicate that it relies too heavily on the good intentions of the industry it is mandated to supervise. Yet time and again investigations have pointed out that private companies have frequently and flagrantly ignored the AEC's comparatively mild regulations. The following examples are taken from the report:

> We believe that Licensee A's security system was significantly limited in its capability to prevent, detect, and immediately respond to possible S.N.M. [special nuclear material] diversions or diversion attempts. The security personnel consisted of a part-time security officer and four guards. . . . Each guard on duty carried a .38-caliber revolver. The weapons qualification scores, however, showed that none of the guards had met A.E.C.'s requirements. . . . The watchclock tapes which recorded the guard patrols indicated that the guard on duty did not vary the time or route of his patrol. When he was not making watchclock checks, the guard was located in a small guard post. . . . The guard could not observe about 80 percent of the general plant area from his post. . . . The fence could be easily disassembled because the nuts, bolts, gate hinge pins, and fenceposts were not secured by welding or peening. . . . One of the storage areas— which housed both S.N.M. scrap and S.N.M. of high strategic importance—was a prefabricated steel structure. . . . We tested the impediment value of the panels

with an adjustable-jawed wrench. Within 1 minute we were able to remove five metal screws from one of the panels. At this point the only impediment to entry was a small rivet which, in our opinion, could have been forced manually. . . . We also tested the impediment value of the sheet-steel panels by cutting a sample of the panel. Within 30 seconds we were able to make a 19-inch cut with an ordinary pair of tin cutters. . . . The garage-type door could be opened with little effort because its lock had been broken and the door could be opened without activating the alarm. . . . The other storage area, which provided limited protection, was smaller and constructed of cinder block. . . . On the side of the building facing the perimeter fence were two unalarmed vents leading inside. This side of the building, which was about 16 feet from the perimeter fence, was not visible from the guard post and, according to a licensee official, was inspected only once a month. One of the vents was located about 2 feet from the ground, measured about 18 by 30 inches, and was secured on the outside by louvers and an ordinary window screen. . . . The licensee's manager for safeguards and accountability concurred that with little effort the louvers could be pulled out by hand and that the inside screen could be manually forced, providing access to the building interior. The other vent was . . . secured on the outside by louvers and on the inside by a piece of thin sheet steel fastened to the cinder blocks by four bolts. . . . Again the licensee's safeguards and accountability manager concurred that this vent could easily be pulled out without tools and that the sheet steel could be forced manually. Portable S.N.M. was readily accessible within the cinder block warehouse. . . .

The integrity of the front wall [at Licensee B's plant] was impaired in that none of the windows were laminated, sealed, locked, or alarmed; windows (frames and glass) were nonexistent at two openings; one of the doors was open with a broken seal attached; and none of the doors were alarmed. The rear of the building was windowless, did not have protective fencing, was not visible from the guard station, and was not routinely patrolled by the guard. During our tour around the building, we observed a screen covered with plasterboard which was used to secure an opening. . . . The screen was held in place by three toggle bolts. Within 15 seconds and using no tools, one person was able to remove the bottom toggle and open the screen to about a 45′ angle. . . . The opening led directly into an S.N.M. storage room which was locked but not alarmed and which contained significant quantities of S.N.M. stored in easily portable half-gallon containers. The opening was cemented and sealed within 1 hour after our tour. . . . We tested the accounting controls by comparing seal numbers provided by the guard lieutenant with those on the doors and gates and found that only 5 of the 10 were correct. . . .

Licensee C had established liaison with local law enforcement authorities and had developed an informal plan intended to provide assistance in the event of an emergency. The licensee's arrangements called for hourly communication checks to the local police. If the police failed to receive the call at the designated time, they were to contact the licensee by radio or telephone and, if contact could not be made, were to respond by dispatching a squad car. In a test of the effectiveness of this arrangement, we found that the local police attempted to call the licensee within 15 minutes after the licensee failed to call at the appointed time; the squad car which was dispatched, however, went to the wrong facility 14 miles away.

NRC is not the only one having problems accounting for nuclear material. Its twin on the military side, the Energy Research and Development Administration (ERDA)—in 1975 the AEC itself underwent fission, losing its licensing authority over the unclassified nuclear power industry to NRC and its military or classified programs to ERDA—was also in trouble in 1976. A GAO report charged that "tens of tons" of special nuclear materials were unaccounted for. "Because enriched uranium is traditionally measured in terms of kilograms and plutonium in terms of grams, the fact that the cumulative MUF amounts to tens of tons indicates the magnitude of the problem," the report said. The tens-of-tons figure was arrived at by totaling the GAO's accounts of how much material was missing from each nuclear facility. In analyzing ERDA's security, the GAO found that "serious deficiencies in both the material accountability and the physical security systems were found. . . . The evidence raises serious questions as to the ability of ERDA's facilities to detect and prevent a theft of bomb quantities of special nuclear materials."

ERDA's response was to call the report inaccurate. A spokesman said, "There is no nuclear material outside the processing system that we aren't totally aware of. You have to understand there may be sixty miles of piping in a uranium processing plant, and there could be a lot of material stuck in those pipes."

The army, however, has had considerable trouble keeping its weapons out of the hands of terrorists and criminals. The Baader-Meinhof gang supplied its terrorist friends with weapons and explosives stolen from U.S. Army depots in West Germany. A report by the army's Physical Security Review Board in 1975 said that "organized criminal elements" have already taken advantage of lax security to steal thousands of American military weapons and explosives in the United States and abroad. Some of these arms were sold to criminals and terrorists for "huge profits," indicating that a precedent has already been established that might lead to the theft of nuclear materials on a wholesale level.

In terms of the human element, Congress heard testimony in 1974 to the effect that thirty-six hundred persons with access to nuclear weapons had been removed from their jobs in a year's time. Some were considered security risks because of alleged drug abuse, mental illness, alcoholism, or problems of discipline. One, a top AEC national security officer, was a compulsive gambler who had borrowed $239,000 from his fellow employees at the AEC in a period of eight years, of which he failed to repay over $170,000. The fact that he had access to atomic secrets at the same time his superiors were unaware of his weakness made him a prime target for blackmail.

One of the most ouspoken critics of AEC safeguard policies has been Dr.

Theodore B. Taylor, a theoretical physicist who was a conceptual designer of nuclear bombs at Los Alamos from 1949 to 1956. Among his many designs were Davy Crockett, then the lightest and smallest fission bomb ever made, weighing less than fifty pounds, and the Super Oralloy Bomb, the largest-yield fission bomb that has ever been exploded anywhere.

In a series of interviews with John McPhee, published in *The New Yorker* and later in a book, *The Curve of Binding Energy,* Taylor takes the readers step by step through the process by which it would be relatively easy to steal nuclear materials and fashion a bomb with the aid of readily available printed matter.

The AEC maintains a public reading room at 1717 H Street in Washington, D.C., which makes information available that includes diagrams of all nuclear plants, location and capacities of the vaults, voluminous correspondence about future plans and present shipments. The Atomic Energy Act, as amended in 1954, for example, gives the public the right to know about bomb designs, fission fractions, plutonium metallurgy, yields, systems, performances, critical-mass determinations, computer codes, hydrodynamics, nuclear-reaction cross sections—not exactly a blueprint for the ordinary bomb-maker, but with the proper expertise, the formula is suddenly as crackable as the *Times* Sunday crossword puzzle is with a dictionary. To eliminate the tedium of note taking, the agency provides the researcher with a Xerox machine.

At a nominal cost, the AEC will sell the aspiring researcher *The Los Alamos Primer,* declassified in 1964, which contains the mathematical fundamentals of fission bombs; also at a nominal cost, the Office of Technical Services of the U.S. Department of Commerce offers a book entitled *Manhattan District History, Project Y, the Los Alamos Project,* declassified in 1961, which contains the supersecret technical description of the problems that came up during the building of the first atomic bombs. A legal notice on its inside front cover says, in part, "Neither the United States, nor the Commission, nor any person acting on behalf of the Commission . . . assumes any liabilities with respect to the use of, or for damage resulting from the use of, any information, apparatus, method or process disclosed in this report." It contains an extensive bibliography of works that provide information that was once so secret that mere possession was considered treasonable.

When AEC officials are confronted with questions about the risks of nuclear terrorism, they are quick to point out that many of their problems began with the 1954 revision of the Atomic Energy Act of 1946. When President Dwight Eisenhower introduced his program called Atoms for Peace in 1953, the idea was for the United States to share the atom with all the world for the benefit of mankind, for the development of emerging nations, for the making of what was described as "meterless power." In order to promote the peacetime development of atomic energy, Congress loosened up controls on nuclear materials so that private industry would be able to participate in making and processing nuclear fuel. Although the AEC would police the nuclear industry and write regulations for the handling of nuclear materials,

American corporations would make, transport, and process nuclear fuels on a massive scale all over the world.

There were critics who pointed to the potential evil inherent in a system that automatically produced weapon-grade plutonium-239 as a natural by-product in nuclear reactors using uranium. During World War II, the AEC built big "production reactors" at Hanford, Washington, to fission uranium for the express purpose of producing plutonium-239, because, for one thing, it takes two to three times less plutonium-239 than uranium-235 to create a nuclear explosion. The extraction of plutonium nitrate in a water solution was a long slow process, but eventually it was that plutonium which destroyed Nagasaki.

That is not the case today, however. Utility companies have been stock-piling plutonium since 1972 when the Nuclear Fuel Services reprocessing plant in West Valley, New York, was shut down for repairs because radioactive leaks were contaminating workers and the environment. Another recycling plant, General Electric's Midwest Fuel Recovery Plant at Morris, Illinois, may not start operations until 1978. That leaves the Allied General plant in Barnwell, South Carolina. It was scheduled to open in 1977, but construction has since been halted by President Carter.

A typical nuclear power plant contains in its "furnace" more than 150 tons of uranium fuel rods enriched to 2 or 3 percent in U-235. As it occurs in nature, uranium consists of 1 part of uranium-235 to every 139 parts of a heavier species of atom, uranium-238, but since natural uranium cannot be used in modern light water nuclear electric-generating plants, it has to be processed to upgrade the percentage of U-235. During the operation of the plant, plutonium is produced in a nuclear core, converted from some of the U-238. This makes a nuclear plant both a fuel burner and a fuel producer. Once a year, some of the fuel rods in the core are discharged, and after a suitable "cooling time" they can be chemically processed to separate out small quantities of plutonium. A high-power plant will produce about five hundred pounds of plutonium in a single year. In the recycling process, the bundles of spent fuel rods are chopped into small pieces to expose the nuclear material they contain and then dissolved in acid so that the reusable uranium and plutonium can be separated out for purification and eventual shipment to fuel-fabrication facilities.

Already private industry owns as much, if not more, plutonium than exists in all the bombs of NATO. With the predictable proliferation of nuclear reactors on a worldwide basis, it is estimated by Dr. Taylor that the power companies will produce a cumulative total of twenty million pounds of plutonium in the last quarter of this century. Considering that the triggering quantity of plutonium in a nuclear device is only ten pounds, the prospects are horrible to contemplate.

Although plutonium is the most toxic substance known to man—a pound could kill nine billion people—it is not radioactive once it is separated from the spent fuel rods. You could carry plutonium oxide in a paper bag and hold it next to your heart or brain without danger, but you cannot breathe it. An invisible speck of plutonium dust taken into the lungs will kill anyone in a matter of hours, or at most a few days.

The power of plutonium as a fissionable material is even more awesome than its toxicity. Taylor told McPhee that one of the most astonishing realizations he had ever experienced in physics had to do with binding energy. When the Fat Man bomb exploded over Nagasaki, the amount of matter that changed into energy and destroyed the city was one gram—a third the weight of a penny. A number of pounds of plutonium were in the bomb, but the amount that actually released its binding energy and created the fireball was only one gram. E (twenty kilotons) equals M (one gram) times the square of the speed of light.

Taylor then went on to describe what happens when an implosion bomb detonates: "The temperature in the core builds up to several hundred million degrees in one hundred-millionth of a second. That is many times the temperature in the center of the sun. It's a temperature high enough to strip the electrons off any but the heaviest elements. All you're left with is the bare nucleus in a sea of electrons. (In a hydrogen bomb, the temperature can be five times as high. It strips off electrons even from uranium—almost all ninety-two electrons gone! It's incredible.) In an implosion, pressures at the center build up to a hundred million atmospheres, and with these pressures the core begins to expand at speeds of—let's see, 2 times 10^8 centimeters per second—about 5 million miles an hour. Meanwhile, neutrons are multiplying, with a whole new generation every hundred-millionth of a second. (At the center of an efficient thermonuclear explosion you have so many neutrons that they actually form a gas with the density of a metal.) Plutonium and uranium split unevenly. It is rare that they split into two equal parts, and in the explosion their fragments become every element below them. Anything you can name is there—molybdenum, barium, iodine, cesium, strontium, antimony, hydrogen, tin, copper, carbon, iron, silver, and gold. I am trying to describe the beginning of the explosion—something twelve inches across expanding faster than anything else that happens in the universe, unless there are other people who make bombs."

In a statement to the House Subcommittee on Energy and the Environment, Dr. Taylor warned that "information and nonnuclear materials needed to make fission explosives are now widely distributed and available to the general public. Dozens of nations have or could acquire the skills and facilities required to design and build reliable, lightweight and efficient fission explosives. Crude, inefficient, and statistically variable yield, but nonetheless highly destructive fission explosives that could be transported by automobile could be designed and built by small groups of people, conceivably by individuals working alone, if they somehow managed to acquire the needed quantities of special nuclear materials. Under some conditions this could be done in an ordinary home workshop, using equipment and materials that are commercially easily available worldwide. Such devices, if exploded in especially densely populated areas, such as the financial district of New York City, could kill more than a hundred thousand people.

"Plutonium, highly enriched uranium, or U-233 of the isotopic compositions used or produced in all types of power reactors could be used as core materials for fission explosives. Metallic, oxide, and some other chemical forms of these could be used."

All one would need to make a crude bomb would be nine pounds of pure plutonium-239 shaped into grapefruit size; or seventeen pounds of plutonium produced by reactor plants; or twenty-two pounds of plutonium oxide for fuel pellets; or thirteen pounds of uranium-233 produced by fissionable thorium-232 in a high-temperature helium-gas-cooled model of the breeder reactor; or thirty-seven pounds of the highly enriched uranium used to fuel nuclear submarines and to power the high-temperature gas-cooled reactor plant at Fort St. Vrain, near Denver.

Taylor estimates that one person would need only a few weeks to complete the project. Anyone with a fairly good grade in an introductory course in reactor engineering or reactor theory, even at the undergraduate level, could pull it off without too much trouble. To achieve the most powerful explosion, the bomb-maker would need to convert plutonium into a metal, but the techniques for this, says Taylor, are in some respects no more difficult than refining heroin in an illicit laboratory.

As for the actual manufacture of the bomb, the trick is to devise a means of assembling nuclear material rapidly and holding it together so that it can produce a chain reaction. For example, suppose the bomb-maker has fifty pieces of plutonium metal each the size of a domino spread out on a table. Assembling ten of these pieces in a square will produce no effect, but with each new layer it begins to approach the point of "criticality"—that is, the point at which a chain reaction starts to take off. At that point, adding just one more piece produces an "overcritical assembly" and a chain reaction of atom splitting is set loose. However, no explosion would result, because the chain reaction would shut itself off by the mechanism of heat pushing the pieces apart into a noncritical array, disassembling the chain.

The key to creating an explosion is to bring a sufficient amount of properly shaped fissionable material into an exceedingly rapid assembly and to hold it together for an infinitesimal fraction of a second. This was done in the Hiroshima bomb by using a gun-barrel type of device plugged at both ends, with a mass of U-235 at one end and a projectile of the same material at the other. To detonate the bomb, the U-235 projectile was hurled by conventional explosives down the barrel and into the mass at the other end, forming an overcritical assembly: the density of the combined masses of U-235 suddenly increased enough so that the fast-moving neutrons triggered a chain reaction and the bomb exploded. The result was an explosion equal to twenty-eight million pounds of TNT.

The Nagasaki bomb used the more efficient implosion technique. An implosion is simply an inwardly focused compression wave. A hollow sphere of plutonium was enclosed by shaped explosive charges. When the TNT was detonated, it sent much of its force inward, crushing the plutonium into a solid ball, a "supercritical" mass that transformed the core itself into a multimillion-degree inferno of unimaginably compressed gas. The result was even more devastating than the Hiroshima blast. With the proper plastic explosives and some plutonium fashioned into the proper shape, a skilled amateur might well produce an awesome weapon. There are literally tens of thousands of people with training and experience in nuclear engineering in all the developed countries and in some of the underdeveloped ones.

Taylor is so convinced that it will happen that to him it is only a question of time. "Is it worse, or better, if it happens sooner, or later?" he said to McPhee during the 1973 interview. "Someone, somewhere, stealing material and making a bomb. I think it is better sooner than later. I would not be surprised if it happened tomorrow, and I would not be surprised if it didn't. I would rather have it happen tomorrow than ten years from now, when so much more material will be floating around. I've sometimes found myself actually wishing it would happen—perhaps an unusual group of people, ten years ahead of their time, who would sort of jump the gun on everybody else before a large number of organizations could be ready and poised to do the same thing. If it happened just once, the lid would be slammed shut. As shut as possible, anyway. In another ten or fifteen years, it will be too late. If I were to read it in the papers tomorrow, I'd be frightened and alarmed, but if it aborted and very few people got hurt, I'd be, in a sense, happy."

Taylor's critics at the AEC have pounced on this comment, and Taylor has since modified it. In an interview with this author, Taylor rephrased it: "Sometimes I thought that an *abortive* attempt to steal the material would serve as a warning before the material is dispersed all over the place. This was also in the context of three years ago, when the extent to which the United States would seem to be really willing to move was too slow. It's moving better now in terms of serious talk about the future.

"From a technical and economic point of view, I think it is possible to safeguard special nuclear material at a level we can live with. From an institutional and political point of view, it remains to be seen whether the problem can and will be put under control.

"The idea that it's fairly easy to make a bomb, that the safeguards were very inadequate from anybody's point of view, that amounts of plutonium and highly enriched uranium were in the process of proliferating, all these things were known to the AEC, to many people in the industry in 1966 and 1967. You might argue they should have known in the early 1950s, but I think people then were stuck on the myth that a bomb requires a Manhattan Project, and it tended to make people not worry about it.

"Some years ago if you talked to a nuclear-facility manager about the state of the safeguards for plutonium in his facility and asked, 'Couldn't some armed people come in here and steal it?' he'd say, 'Well, sure, we couldn't stop them if they were a heavily armed group, but who in the world would want that? What would they do with it? It took your whole Manhattan Project. . . .' That's one of the reasons why there was no physical security to speak of until the late 1960s, and then people started getting concerned about this, partly because terrorism began to be more internationally visible, and more bizarre and destructive."

Taylor says his anxiety over safeguards is "just as great today, and it may be greater. The reason for that is the rate of expansion of nuclear power plants abroad. Countries like Iran, Egypt, Brazil, Argentina—some thirty additional countries have announced intentions to acquire large nuclear power plants within the next ten years. In terms of the institutional and political aspect of it, I must say I'm less optimistic about the future. Just the sheer numbers of countries involved and their different forms of government magnifies the problem."

David M. Rosenbaum, a physicist and former AEC consultant, has been a vocal critic of nuclear safeguards since the AEC commissioned him to study the problem in early 1974. The AEC was merely reacting to Taylor's criticism, which it viewed more as a nuisance than a contribution. They hoped that Rosenbaum's findings would work as a counterbalance to get the old nuclear business, which it regarded as too fragile to be shared with a hostile public, back in good graces.

When it discovered that Rosenbaum, one of their own, had handed them an even hotter report, they decided to pigeonhole it. The AEC never had much of a taste for adverse publicity. Through the years it had suppressed numerous unfavorable studies and dissenting views and might have succeeded once again if Senator Abraham Ribicoff had not gotten wind of it.

Ribicoff not only forced information out of the AEC but printed it in the *Congressional Record* after a speech on the Senate floor. "As serious as the safeguards problem is today . . . it will magnify manyfold unless we come to grips with it now," Ribicoff said in disclosing the Rosenbaum report. Pointing out that it only took twenty pounds of plutonium to make a nuclear bomb, Ribicoff said many times that amount would be available in the United States if the industry proceeded with its plans to move toward a "plutonium economy." The current generation of light-water reactors would produce 60,000 pounds of plutonium a year by 1980, he said, and the breeder reactor would produce 600,000 pounds of plutonium annually by the year 2000. "The basic message of the report is that we must design effective nuclear safeguards before it is too late."

In an interview with this writer, Rosenbaum said that Taylor's criticism was accurate but understated. "It was worse than Taylor realized, because he didn't have the entrance to all the places we did," Rosenbaum said. "And he didn't have the knowledge of how the system actually worked that we had in our team. It was far easier to get at plutonium or highly enriched uranium than Taylor realized.

"There are essentially three holes in the safeguards system. One is the licensed civilian nuclear sector, which comes under the NRC. That is an institutional arrangement. Another is someone acquiring the materials or indeed a bomb itself from United States government facilities, which are not licensed. They include the National Laboratories, Oak Ridge, Portsmouth, Livermore, Paducah, Sandia, Savannah River, Hanford, and lots of other places, many of which handle weapons—design, inspect, and do various other things with nuclear weapons. This includes the transportation of weapons by ERDA when they are turned over to the military. ERDA facilities have enormous amounts of highly enriched uranium and plutonium. In fact, they produce all the weapons-grade plutonium for the military program, which is a different mix of isotopes than civilian plutonium. In addition, there are all the installations of the United States government—army, air force, navy—in this country and all around the world, the depots where nuclear weapons are assembled and disassembled and checked and rechecked, all of it vulnerable to theft and well-organized raids. Thirdly, there are the facilities of all the other countries of the world that have nuclear reactors and weapons, many of whom have holes in their systems far greater than ours.

"Nuclear weapons or plutonium stolen anywhere in the world can be smuggled into this country without any problem. The borders of this country are essentially open. Hundreds of thousand of illegal Mexican farmhands come across the Rio Grande every year. Tons and tons of drugs are smuggled in every week. The best sensor system we have are hills: when small planes crash into them, we know they came across. Thousands of yachts and small boats sail into marinas every day of the year and nobody pays any attention to them. So smuggling nuclear weapons or material into this country presents no problem. So if you're worried about the nation's welfare, it's not just a question of tightening up the civilian licensed sector. ERDA safeguards are in worse shape than those of NRC, and so are the safeguards of the rest of the world. Even if the government closed our own nuclear industry, we would still have the safeguards problems of the rest of the world."

It is fair to say that retired Maj. Gen. Edward B. Giller does not agree with Rosenbaum. As deputy assistant administrator for national security in ERDA's Division of Safeguards and Security, Giller is well versed on the subject of safeguards. In an interview with this writer, Giller said that it was the Munich massacre that turned ERDA's thinking around.

"I decided that was for real and we'd better do something," he said, "and we started on it that day by writing a letter to Defense saying, 'We're going to review completely all of AEC's facilities and we're going to upgrade them. We suggest you review your own,' on which they started. That's when physical security became *the* issue, the special thing to do, and that's about the time the Taylor articles came out. So he was criticizing about the time we were changing everything.

"You can say we were a little slow in recognizing it, we should have seen it five years ago instead of three. But terrorism, you know, this senseless kind of terrorism—you always have crazy individuals—but this mass terrorism demonstrated at Munich was a new thing.

"We studied what we should do in physical security and how much money it was going to cost and what was our rationale for doing it. You don't just run out and build five fences because you suddenly think of five fences. There's got to be some rationale for how many fences, separated by how many yards—how many television cameras, motion detectors, and all the gadgetry that goes with protection. What sort of communication system and transportation, the special trucks—a thousand things. You don't just say, 'Fellows, order all of them and put them everywhere,' because you don't even know if you're putting them together right.

"So during this period of time, there was an attempt to figure out what our problems were and how best to tackle them, where best to put the money we had. You know, you don't walk up to the bank and say, 'I've just got a new problem, cash my check.' You've got to figure out what it is you want, where you want it in the system and then your money comes, months later, and by the time you actually do it a year passes. But we had decided we were going to move, in which direction, and we were after the money; in fact, we were doing things with the money we already had. But NRC was trying to figure out what regulations should they force on industry, and to keep away from the business of changing the rules every week. Over a period of eight or nine months in there, NRC people were trying to decide, 'Gee, what should we really make industry do? What's our rationale for it? And does that fit with what the government side of the house is doing so we don't get the two of them out of step.'

"It was during this period of discussion and disagreement on how to proceed that the Taylor articles came out. Then Rosenbaum and his group came along and they examined the system which we'd already examined. We knew there were holes. They wrote some scenarios on how you can break through the system. You can write a dozen more. I mean you can write a hundred scenarios. They wrote five or ten—I don't remember—but their scenarios were known to the people here. We knew where the holes were. So they said, 'Gee, look at this story. You go this way, that way, this way, and see what you get.' We knew that! I mean, it's not news to us that you could break through the system under a certain set of assumptions. So I don't think Rosenbaum got anything new. What he did was put a lot of noise into the system, like a lot of public attention, which, I admit, most of what it did was to put heat under the AEC maybe to move faster, not because they'd discovered something new, but because it had become an issue."

Asked about the outlook for the future as far as the terrorist threat was concerned, Giller said, "The threat's the same. I mean, the reasons for doing things are the same. The problem of physical security being equivalent everywhere—it is recognized internationally that there are weak links in the chain of security, recognized by the International Atomic Energy Agency, the United States—and as far as I know, the fifty or sixty countries I've talked to have problems that have to be dealt with. So there's no problem with the question.

"Not as fast as the United States, but not reluctantly either, every one of these nations is upgrading its physical security by a considerable degree. So I'm convinced that the international scene is girding itself very rapidly to essentially the same level as the United States. They have to do it differently; their laws are different sometimes, but the issue is whether international organizations like IAEA [International Atomic Energy Agency] shall have some role. As you probably know, up to this time, many of the sovereign nations have not wanted IAEA to be in the physical security role in the same way as they're in the material accountability role because most physical security comes under the police power of the state and no state wants a bunch of other people mucking around in that business."

At least fifty countries will have nuclear power plants by 1985. Some of these countries will have as many as 200 reactors. This means that tens of tons of plutonium and enriched uranium will really be brought out into the open, traveling routinely by truck, rail, air, and ship, moving from point to point in the nuclear fuel cycle and from country to country, going in and out of busy harbors and airports in the Middle East, Europe, Africa, southern Asia, South America, Canada, not to mention the United States, which has 60 power plants presently in operation and another 60 now under construction, plus 150 more on the drawing board. Plutonium in its various forms—metal, nitrate, or oxide —will travel in shipments of fifty or so kilograms, a tempting target for terrorists with the necessary expertise to build a bomb.

Even more awesome a prospect is the next generation of nuclear reactors called the "fast breeders." Incredibly efficient (they use 60 percent to 70 percent of the energy in their fuel as opposed to 1 percent to 2 percent in today's fission reactors), they would extend nuclear fuel supplies for centuries. However, they make more plutonium than they use up. Once they get into operation, weapons-grade plutonium will multiply geometrically.

Little is publicly known about the efforts in other countries with nuclear power programs to develop and implement their own safeguards to protect against nuclear theft. Yet terrorist organizations are even more a threat in several of these countries than in the United States. As Rosenbaum pointed out, the risks of nuclear theft affect the whole world. Material stolen in one country can be used in another. International safeguards are analogous to a simple chain, and the problem is finding the weak link. Outside of a few preliminary technical efforts, there has been almost no serious discussion of this problem at the international level. The time that national political and industrial leaders have to deal with the problem is rapidly running out. So far leadership has been woefully lacking.

Responsibility for international safeguarding lies with the IAEA, which has its headquarters in Vienna. Established in 1957, largely as a response to President Eisenhower's Atoms for Peace proposals, the IAEA is the international watchdog on safeguards, sending its nuclear auditors to check on member nations to prevent (or at least discourage) clandestine diversion of plutonium or enriched uranium from peaceful uses to military ones. It performs this task only when invited to monitor agreements between nuclear and nonnuclear countries. It later became the quasi-police agent of the Nuclear Non-Proliferation Treaty (NPT), which went into effect in 1970. The NPT was a compact between nuclear powers, which were thereby committed to end their arms race and work toward nuclear disarmament, and the nonnuclear powers, which, in exchange for forgoing acquisition of nuclear weapons, could look forward to reaping the benefits of the peaceful uses of nuclear energy. Yet only three of the nuclear powers—the United States, Russia, and Britain—have ratified the treaty; France, China, and India have not even signed, and they give no indication that they will.

Unfortunately, the nonnuclear countries refusing to sign or ratify the NPT are exactly the ones that should be prevented from having nuclear weapons. Some of the countries that are presently capable, or will soon acquire the capability, of making nuclear weapons include Pakistan, Libya, Iran, Iraq, Egypt, Turkey, Saudi Arabia, Israel, Brazil, Argentina, Chile, Cuba, Spain, Greece, Portugal, Algeria, South Korea, Taiwan, and a number of African states, including South Africa. This is not to say that NPT members could be prevented from diverting plutonium if they decided to join the nuclear club. India did it by building its own small chemical-reprocessing plant to extract plutonium from the spent fuel of its research reactor supplied by Canada.

"The IAEA safeguard and inspection procedures amount to little more than accounting methods for verifying the efficiency of national or regional inspection systems," says Senator Ribicoff, whose Senate committee has been delving into the pitfalls of nuclear power. "The agency is heavily dependent on the goodwill and cooperation of nations whose nuclear facilities it inspects and audits."

A week later, as if to confirm that fact, the CIA reported that without IAEA detection, Argentina had recently removed fifty kilograms of plutonium waste from its Atucha nuclear station—enough for five bombs.

Six nations have the bomb today, and by 1985, more than twenty countries could have their own nuclear weapons. As one leading arms-control authority put it, "India is not the sixth member of the nuclear club but rather the first of twenty potential new members."

By early 1976 the mad rush toward nuclear chaos was on in full swing. The peaceful technology was providing not only the means but also the cover for countries determined to make their own bombs. Some of them, unfortunately, were not only unstable but also harbored hijackers and terrorist political organizations.

President Qaddafi of Libya was providing his own hair-raising scenario. "The nuclear monopoly is about to be broken," he boasted. "Soon the atom will have no secrets for anybody. Some years ago we could hardly procure a fighter squadron. Tomorrow we will be able to buy an atom bomb and all its parts." Back in 1969, he sent his top aide, Abdul Salem Jalloud, to China to buy such a bomb, but the Chinese declined his offer, which was said to be in the billions. Having failed in China, Qaddafi has since offered a lavish reward to any terrorist who will bring him nuclear weapons. In June 1975, he signed an agreement that will provide him with a number of nuclear reactors, which in turn will supply him with the precious plutonium he so desires. Meanwhile, he has seized six thousand square miles of territory from Chad, his neighbor to the south, an area where it is believed there may be rich uranium deposits.

Atomic weapons in the hands of Qaddafi would mean they were also in the hands of Carlos, Wadi Haddad, George Habash, the Japanese Red Army, or any other terror groups willing to follow the dictates of the mad Libyan dictator.

According to a member of South Africa's Atomic Energy Board, its nuclear program is "more advanced than that of India. Our technology and science have advanced sufficiently for us to produce it [the bomb] if we have to."

Turkey has announced its intentions of building its own nuclear weapons, and Israel's President Ephraim Katzir stated at the end of 1974 that his country "has the potential" to make nuclear weapons "and if need be, we will do it." However, the CIA estimates that Israel already has a stockpile of ten to twenty nuclear weapons "ready and available for use." Israel is not an NPT member.

Israel's interest in acquiring nuclear bombs dates back to its birth. Chaim Weizmann, a chemist of international repute, encouraged nuclear scientists to produce low-grade uranium from phosphate in the Negev, and they came up with an efficient technique for producing heavy water. In an exchange with France for these processes in 1953, Israeli scientists were permitted to study France's nuclear program and participate in its Sahara tests. Then in 1955, under the Atoms for Peace Program, Israel purchased its first research reactor from the United States and established the Nahal Soreq Research Center just south of Tel Aviv. Two years later the French sold Israel a twenty-five megawatt reactor; they also helped with the design of the Dimona Atomic Research Community in the Negev. Comparable in size to the Savannah River center in South Carolina, Dimona is important militarily because it is a heavy water reactor which can produce weapons-grade plutonium from natural or unenriched uranium. For years Ben-Gurion, Shimon Peres, Golda Meir, Yigal Allon, Levi Eshkol, Moshe Dayan, and other Israeli leaders argued over the merits of building a plant to separate plutonium, without arriving at a decision.

However, the decision was made for them during the Six-Day War by Dayan, who secretly ordered the plant's construction. Dayan was convinced that a nuclear capability was essential to the survival of Israel. "Israel has no choice," he told *Time*. "With our manpower we cannot physically, financially, or economically go on acquiring more and more tanks and more and more planes. Before long you will have all of us maintaining and oiling the tanks."

According to the *New York Times,* Washington has been "conducting its Middle East policy on the assumption that Israel either possesses an atomic bomb or has component parts available for quick assembly."

The Israeli government has officially denied this, but it has maintained top security at Dimona. It is protected not only by Israeli troops but by highly sophisticated electronic systems and radar screens; all aircraft are barred from flying over the area. An Israeli Mirage III was shot down when it inadvertently flew over Dimona during the Six-Day War, and when a Libyan airliner strayed off course toward the forbidden area in 1973, Israeli fighters shot it down after warnings to turn back were ignored, causing the death of 108 passengers.

Even a congressional mission headed by Senator Ribicoff was refused permission to visit Dimona. The group went to Israel in November 1976 to study "how supervision and control both here and in Egypt can ensure that atomic energy will be for peaceful uses only," Ribicoff said before he was told of the ban. The senators were there because the promise of Nixon and Kissinger in 1973 to sell nuclear reactors to Israel, Egypt, and Iran still awaited the Senate's approval of safeguard measures before the agreements could be ratified.

A spokesman for Rabin said the request to visit Dimona was refused "on principle," not for security reasons. Senator John H. Glenn felt the group had more important things to worry about than Dimona. "I'm more concerned that we get some kind of nuclear agreement not only with Israel but with all of her neighbors to see that this is a nuclear-free zone. This is an area fraught with very high tensions, and the danger of war. It would be a tragedy if we someday see a mushroom cloud—atomic clouds—over Tel Aviv or Jerusalem or Cairo."

For several years, following the deterioration of its relationship with France, Israel has refused to give details on its uranium purchases, beyond saying that the ore has always been available on the open market. Aside from the possibility that some of the missing uranium from the Apollo plant may have been diverted to Israel, as noted earlier in this chapter, Israel also has been accused of receiving the two hundred metric tons of natural uranium which mysteriously disappeared from a West German freighter in 1968. The ship, which was bound from Antwerp, Belgium, to Genoa, Italy, was said to have vanished in the Mediterranean. A year later it reappeared with a new name, a new registry, a new crew, but no uranium.

The incident remained shrouded in mystery for nine years. It came to light in April 1977, when Paul L. Leventhal, a former counsel to the U.S. Senate Operations Committee, mentioned it during a speech at a conference of nuclear power opponents in Salzburg, Austria. "It is assumed that it [the uranium] was unloaded in Israel," he said. "The main point is not the country that got it, but that nuclear material could be stolen."

When Israeli officials denied the story, Haakon Wiker, formerly Norway's chief prosecutor, disclosed that the source was an Israeli Mossad agent, Dan Aerbel, who had volunteered the information to Norwegian police in 1973 after being held with four other Mossad agents for the killing of an Arab waiter, Ahmed Bouchiki, whom they had mistaken for Ali Hassan Salameh, a Black September terrorist who had helped plan the Munich massacre.

Aerbel, who was pardoned after serving twelve months, told a Tel Aviv newspaper that the Norwegians were "full of fantasy." It is doubtful that the full story will ever come out, but if it is true that the cargo was diverted to Israel, it should be noted that two hundred tons is enough natural uranium to operate the Dimona reactor for more than ten years and produce thirty nuclear weapons.

The Shah of Iran, who has embarked on a $27 billion nuclear program, was quoted in a French magazine to the effect that Iran would be one of the next countries to join the nuclear club. Few doubt this prediction. Twenty percent of M.I.T.'s total number of graduate students in its nuclear engineering department are Iranians, and more than 250 other Iranian students are enrolled at nuclear engineering departments around the United States.

In an editorial, "The Great Iranian Uranium Connection," M.I.T.'s official student newspaper, the *Tech,* noted M.I.T.'s refusal to entertain "discussion of the issues—nuclear proliferation, M.I.T.'s obligation to society, M.I.T.'s obligation to its own educational standards"—and presented a moral argument in "Selling M.I.T.: Bombs for the Shah": "A resounding 'No!' from the community to the Institute's plans to train nuclear engineers for the Shah could, if M.I.T. is as influential in the scientific world as M.I.T. likes to keep telling itself it is, be a leading factor in forcing deeper consideration of the issues involved everywhere. In the meantime, M.I.T. can try to think of other, less reprehensible ways to make ends meet which will not involve the moral abdication implied by this plan."

The Science Action Coordinating Committee (SACC), in an academic leaflet, *Issues Raised by M.I.T. Training of Iranian Students in Nuclear Engineering,* charged that the institute had been preparing in secret a deal that was only disclosed by the *Tech* and presented the administration's "excuses" for its action: "It wasn't M.I.T.'s idea anyway so we have no responsibility for our actions. . . . There is nothing sinister about providing a fanatic absolute dictator with uranium and engineers. . . . They [the Iranians] are in desperate need for nuclear power despite being the second largest oil producers in the world."

Then SACC proceeded to rebut each of the institute's defenses: "The cause for alarm, of course, is the possibility of Iran using the materials and knowledge available to build nuclear arms. . . . Politically, the situation is ominous: Iran is under absolute dictatorship of the Shah. . . . No government in the world is more repressive, less principled, than that of the Shah, who has admitted on U.S. TV to unquestioned use of immediate execution to quench internal dissent. . . . As the second largest oil-exporting nation Iran is rapidly becoming a world power, and the Shah is very happy with his position . . . working full-time to prepare for his rise."

The Shah, who came to power in 1953 through one of the better-known CIA coups, is a self-admitted dictator with a will to re-create the Persian Empire of his ancestors. The thirty thousand to forty thousand political prisoners (including Gholam Hussein Sa'edi, Iran's greatest modern playwright) in Iranian prisons are proof enough of Iran's repressive regime. The Shah himself stated on CBS television's *Sixty Minutes* that he had executed two prominent writers, Khosrow Golsorklti and Iaramat Daneshian, and confirmed the deaths of six more victims.

In trying to get at the motivation for M.I.T.'s interest in advancing Iran's nuclear technology, the independent student newspaper *Thursday* charged that the "Shah of Iran has offered M.I.T. a $2 million bribe to be made to the Compton Lecturer," a reference to the institute's prestigious annual faculty lectures. In a column entitled "Venom," Scott Batterman speculated, "With Iran trying to buy the Nuke E. department, I've heard rumbles through the corridors about the possibility of a competitive bid entered by Saudi Arabia, while Spain is interested in picking up some good Chem. E. tools."

As a signatory to the NPT, the Shah has the right to process his own nuclear wastes, giving him the means to separate his own plutonium, but the Shah, of course, has pledged on his honor not to use the plutonium to make nuclear bombs. The Shah's government has also pledged on its honor not to torture its critics. Meanwhile, Westinghouse and General Electric will make a shah's ransom, thanks to an agreement "in principle" between the United States and Iran to let American firms build half of the $27 billion project.

Saudi Arabia, with the world's largest oil reserve, has committed $50 billion over the next five years to a nuclear-power program that will make it independent of oil as an energy source. "We think oil is too valuable," said Prince Mohammed al-Faisal, second son of the late King Faisal. "It should not be used for energy. It should be used as a raw material—meaning as feedstock for petrochemicals."

Brazil, the most powerful nation in Latin America and one of the most repressive, made a quantum leap toward membership in the nuclear club in 1975, when it became the first country in history to buy the "complete fuel cycle" needed for nuclear-weapons development. The $4.8 billion deal with West Germany includes eight nuclear power stations, a reprocessing plant to separate the plutonium from the spent fuel, and a facility for enriching their vast native supply of uranium—another means of achieving weapons-grade material.

The so-called London Group of nuclear exporting countries (United States, Canada, France, Britain, West Germany, Russia, and Japan) are locked in feverish competition for the billions in profits that can be reaped in the nuclear market. The group is currently being enlarged to include some other potential nuclear exporters, such as Sweden, the Netherlands, East Germany, Italy, Belgium, and Czechoslovakia. West Germany has plans to sell enrichment and reprocessing plants to Iran, and France has contracts to sell reprocessing plants to Pakistan and South Korea.

Because of the tight reins held by Congress, the United States has never exported such technology, but the nuclear industry, backed first by Nixon and then Ford, wants a free hand to compete in the world market. Dixie Lee Ray, a former AEC chairman, expressed the industry's thinking when she remarked, "I'm worried about our industry losing potential nuclear contracts because we require more rigid conditions than the IAEA or other countries."

Five days before the 1976 election, President Ford announced a shift in his nuclear policy. Earlier in the campaign, Jimmy Carter had suggested a voluntary moratorium by all nations on the sale or purchase of nuclear enrichment and reprocessing plants. Carter specifically criticized Ford for not having done more to persuade France and Germany to halt sales of this technology to Pakistan, Brazil, and Iran. Carter's appeal came at a time when the Ford administration already was under mounting congressional pressure to tighten nuclear export controls reached at a series of secret meetings with the London Group in 1975. But Ford and Kissinger had refused to cut off reactor fuel supplies to U.S. allies who sold this dangerous technology, particularly to the less stable nations of the developing world.

So five days before the election Ford said, "I have concluded that the reprocessing and recycling of plutonium should not proceed unless there is sound reason to conclude that the world community can effectively overcome the associated risk of proliferation." Coming when it did, the Ford proposal sounded more like political rhetoric than viable nuclear policy, as his successor, President Carter, would discover in the months ahead.

Brazil and West Germany lost no time in expressing their displeasure over the new president's plans to interfere in the private matter of two sovereign governments. "It is a *fait accompli*," said Brazil's minister of planning. "We signed the agreement. The agreement had the approval of the International Atomic Energy Agency—it received a favorable vote from all the big powers, including the United States. That is all we have to say about it." The Bonn government said it would ignore Carter's statement. "It is a signed treaty that we are looking forward to fulfill," said West German Ambassador Horst Roding.

Carter's plutonium policy, announced at the White House press briefing in April 1977, immediately ran into a storm of opposition, not only from the rest of the world's nuclear powers, but also from the American nuclear establishment, which charged that by turning away from plutonium reprocessing and the breeder reactor, Carter had placed a "mortagage on our energy future."

"There is no dilemma today more difficult to address than that connected with the use of atomic power," Carter told reporters. "Many countries see atomic power as their only real opportunity to deal with dwindling supplies of oil, the increasing price of oil, and the ultimate exhaustion of both oil and natural gas." On the basis of intelligence reports, Carter said, "several nations are on the verge" of being able to produce nuclear weapons from plutonium produced in peaceful nuclear systems. "The United States is deeply concerned about the consequences of the uncontrolled spread of this nuclear weapons capability. We can't arrest it immediately and unilaterally. We have no authority over other countries. But we believe these risks would be vastly increased by the further spread of reprocessing capabilities of the spent nuclear fuel from which explosives can be derived."

Carter went on to say that "we are not trying to impose our will on those nations like Japan, France, Britain, and Germany, which already have reprocessing plants in operation. They have a special need that we don't have in that their supplies of petroleum products are not available."

"Persuasion," an administration official explained at a later briefing, "is different from imposition because it takes longer." Supplies of slightly enriched uranium, the kind used in conventional reactors, would be available in amounts adequate for the needs of foreign countries that rejected plutonium technology. Foreign critics suggested that Carter was less interested in stopping the proliferation of atomic weapons than in making the United States a sort of uranium OPEC. The implication was that the United States was planning to use its power as the major supplier of enriched uranium as a stick to beat countries that exported technology back into line.

Carter's policy was rejected by an international conference on nuclear energy attended by delegates from forty-one nations, including the U.S.S.R. and the United States. It was opposed by the IAEA and the London Group. The Soviet Union issued a policy paper that completely ignored Carter's proposals. The Soviet paper asserted that both reprocessing and the use of plutonium will continue to grow in the world and that it should be encouraged. The only stipulation was that safeguards should be under IAEA control.

By the time Carter arrived in London for the economic summit the first week in May, he knew the exact dimension of the "dilemma" his policy had created in the international economic community. The showdown that had been predicted never took place. Instead the problem was turned over to a special group that would study it for more than a year before reaching final conclusions. In a brief talk with newsmen after the summit, Carter acknowledged that the issue of nuclear nonproliferation "was the most divisive and the most difficult question that we addressed. It was a subject that they have always agreed previously not to discuss because nations have their own autonomy and sensitivities. I think it is very significant to get the group to support publicly a study of this question. We suggested the study, and after the long debate, all the other leaders felt it was a good idea."

Carter promised to follow through. "We have about twelve or fifteen nations referred to as threshold countries," he said. "Those are ones that have not yet acknowledged that they have explosive nuclear capability. But we think they either do or will very shortly. How to deal with those countries—if we supply them with nuclear fuel as Canada did India, what should we do if they create an explosion? So it is one that they have avoided, apparently, in years gone by, but it will be addressed this year . . . the entire problem will be addressed in a very frank fashion."

The IAEA inspection system is totally inadequate against a country determined to build atomic weapons. The agency has few inspectors and no

physical control over the nuclear materials of its member countries. The IAEA
has been described as "a burglar alarm, but not a lock." Even so, any controls
are better than none, but what can be done about the forty-one countries that
have not ratified the NPT? They include Argentina, Brazil, Chile, Belgium,
Egypt, Saudi Arabia, Libya, Algeria, West Germany, Israel, Italy, Japan, the
Netherlands, Pakistan, South Africa, Spain, Portugal, and Switzerland. Even
the nations that are now party to the treaty have the option to reconsider their
situation and withdraw at any time, after giving the requisite three months'
notice.

Interviewed in Vienna by this writer, IAEA Inspector-General Rudolf
Rometsch talked about international safeguards. He referred to the provisions
of the original Atomic Energy Act which required that all cooperation agreements contain a safeguards clause.

"At the beginning this safeguards clause meant that inspectors from the
United States would go into the receiving country to inspect the nuclear facility
receiving imports from the United States to make sure it would not be used
to make bombs or to further any military purpose.

"Later on, all these safeguards requirements contained in the bilateral
agreements between the United States and the receiving country were transferred to the IAEA. In the beginning, of course, the United States was the only
nation capable of exporting nuclear material and equipment, which made it
possible for it to impose safeguards as a condition of supply. But by the late
1960s there was a real breakthrough in the development of nuclear energy and
other suppliers came into the picture. Quite a number of states started building
nuclear power reactors, some with and some without the help of the United
States, and they began producing nuclear equipment for themselves and for
export, so that the pure safeguards system based as a condition of supply no
longer worked as before. A number of politicians, having foreseen this, had
started negotiations for a nonproliferation treaty, which creates an entirely
different basis for safeguards; namely, when a state joins that treaty it accepts
the responsibility not to make or transfer nuclear weapons.

"One of the problems is that the nuclear weapons states themselves,
including the United States, are not doing their part to make the whole system
more acceptable. That has been mentioned all over the place, and it is for them
to fulfill their part of the NPT as stated in Article Six, which calls for them
to negotiate in good faith to stop the nuclear arms race. That would improve
the political atmosphere around the NPT and would make it more effective,
because the NPT is mainly effective as a political instrument. Any piece of
paper of that type—international treaty—has as much worth as the political
will to keep up that compromise."

The provisional Strategic Arms Limitation Agreement concluded in
November 1974 at Vladivostok by Ford and Brezhnev allowed both superpowers to expand their strategic nuclear forces over the next ten years, which was
contrary to their NPT commitment to move toward nuclear disarmament.

Asked if mankind had opened a Pandora's Box, Rometsch said, "It is true that it becomes progressively more difficult to control, from every aspect of it, but I wouldn't call it a Pandora's Box. But it is true that this technology is now rather widely distributed all over the world and nobody can say, 'Let's stop it and put it back in the box.' That time is over, so I'm trying to be realistic and say, 'What can we do in that case?' I personally consider it essential to keep that kind of technology under a certain amount of internationally understood regulations and safeguards."

The IAEA safeguards are quite different from those of the NRC. Its charter is to set up a program for detecting diversion of nuclear material that could be used in a military program. It has no direct responsibility for physical security.

"We have no control at all over the kind of security safeguards that would protect material against terrorist groups. That function is the responsibility of the police of the various sovereign states."

Talk of terrorists, plutonium, and Dr. Taylor annoys Rometsch: "I don't understand why he sees the danger, risks, only there, only around the bloody plutonium. If you are not interested in an isolated field, but in the overall situation of society in relation to its technology, then you have to listen to Taylor, of course, to judge what he says, but you have also to listen to others if you think he is not competent to cross fields. And that, I think, is not sufficiently done. By his picking out and magnifying one problem, one distorts the real danger. Of course, life is dangerous.

"Taylor has a very strong feeling and puts his finger on it and that has certainly helped to reestimate certain risks which might have been, to a certain extent, underestimated. But now you come into the wonderful psychological problem that you have the feeling—I have the feeling—that it has been over-dramatized. On the other hand, I would consider it totally wrong to minimize the problem, because it implies the same danger as overdramatizing. What I consider so much more important in modern society is to evaluate the problem, give it the right weight, and take the correct action. That is very easily said, but what is the right weight and what is the correct action? In the end it will be like this nasty event with the murder of the Turkish ambassador here in Vienna. All the security didn't help him. There will happen certain nasty events, and I don't want it. Totally don't want it!

"Total security you cannot establish. Even when you overdramatize and make a Chinese wall around every gram of plutonium, you cannot completely exclude certain risks. So you have to treat it like you do other parts of society; you have to find that equilibrium which gives you a sufficient and a reasonable protection."

"The IAEA was only set up to stop countries from stealing their own plutonium to make bombs," says Rosenbaum. "That's quite an impossible feat to start out with. There are no regulations at all under IAEA to stop outside groups from stealing it. As for the countries who want to divert plutonium into a weapons program, the IAEA would in no way deter them. They can easily beat the system. Even if the IAEA found something suspicious, it is not allowed by the bilateral treaty to report to anybody anyway. Eventually, after six months or so, it might get up to the IAEA board of directors and in another six months to the UN General Assembly or Security Council. But, in fact, in its entire history the IAEA has never reported anything suspicious done by any country—which is a little strange in itself. The system is based on faith. Well, if the countries are behaving in good faith, then you don't need the IAEA, and if they are not, there's nothing the IAEA can do about it. The problems are intrinsic in the system."

One of the "certain risks" Rometsch mentioned is that by 1985 there will be enough plutonium generated by nuclear reactors in Third World nations to produce three thousand atomic bombs per year. The danger of nuclear war between small nations grows with each new reactor that goes unchecked. Given the combination of insecurity and nationalism that is rampant in the Third World, and given the bad example set by the United States and Russia in failing to achieve genuine arms reduction, it is inevitable that nuclear proliferation will continue at a terrifying rate. As David E. Lilienthal, who served as the first chairman of the AEC, told a Senate committee, "If a great number of countries come to have an arsenal of nuclear weapons, then I'm glad I'm not a young man and I'm sorry for my grandchildren."

"Equally important," says Senator Ribicoff, "is the need to reach agreement on minimum physical security standards to reduce to an absolute minimum the risk of nuclear theft and sabotage by terrorist and criminal groups."

The problem of safeguards, even at an elementary level, seems insurmountable. As late as May 1977, after all the years of criticism and promised improvements, the GAO was still complaining that the United States lacked the ability to detect and respond quickly to a nuclear theft. Literally "thousands of kilograms" of uranium and plutonium were unaccounted for at commercial facilities. "Although these quantities do not necessarily denote lost or stolen materials," the report said, "the fact that it is missing greatly detracts from the integrity of the safeguards system."

The GAO's report was reinforced by Fred C. Ikle, formerly director of the Arms Control and Disarmament Agency under Presidents Nixon and Ford, who charged that shipments of weapons-grade uranium and plutonium often moved unguarded and unmonitored in international commerce. "We sometimes lose track of these things for months before their arrival is certified to the International Atomic Energy Agency in Vienna," he said in an interview. In fact, ERDA has been working for the past two years to determine exactly where all the tons of uranium and plutonium shipped abroad since the 1950s have gone. "Their statistics were in dreadful shape. They had to go back through a lot of old ledgers that were inadequately kept. It was a lot of work, and they kept discovering errors, things that wouldn't total up."

Ikle estimated that as many as 150 shipments of weapons-grade materials moved in international traffic each year. Ideally, he said, armed guards would accompany airborne shipments and, at each landing along the way, report to a global operations center, located perhaps at IAEA headquarters in Vienna.

"This way we'd know hour by hour where a shipment is. Has it arrived at Shannon Airport or hasn't it? Is it in transit to Dakar on the way to South Africa or is it still in Paris? You want to detect a diversion of a shipment within two hours, not a month later. Time makes a lot of difference if you want to chase material before it gets fabricated into a weapon."

If terrorists have demonstrated anything, it is that both nuclear fuel and nuclear weapons stockpiles are vulnerable to raids by dedicated and disciplined groups. It may well be that impatient, unskilled, or lazy terrorists could decide to bypass the civilian safeguards system and go directly to the military for their weapons. By stealing one or more of America's thirty-one thousand nuclear weapons, they would solve all of their problems. Why bother constructing a crude bomb that would probably kill fewer than a hundred thousand persons outright when the government has such sophisticated bombs scattered at home, at sea, in Europe, and in Asia.

The nuclear arsenal is divided into two types of weapons: strategic and tactical. The difference between the two is one of distance. Tactical nuclear weapons have a shorter range but are sometimes more powerful than strategic weapons. As of mid-1976, the United States had 9,500 strategic nuclear weapons on multiple-warhead-carrying delivery vehicles (1,054 land-based Minuteman and Titan missiles, 656 Polaris-Poseidon missiles on 41 ballistic missile submarines, and nearly 500 SAC bombers) and was producing them at the rate of 3 per day until the total reached 21,000, the limit set by the Vladivostok Agreement.

As for tactical nuclear weapons, 22,000 of them have been widely dispersed by the armed forces. In Europe alone, the United States and its NATO allies have 2,250 aircraft, missile launchers, and nuclear cannons that can deliver 7,000 nuclear bombs having a combined nuclear capability equivalent to an estimated 460 megatons (or 460 million tons of TNT), which is a force roughly 35,000 times greater than that of the bomb that destroyed Hiroshima. There are about 1,700 tactical nuclear weapons deployed in South Korea, the Philippines, Guam, and Midway; some 7,000 strategic and tactical nuclear weapons at sea on 284 ships and submarines. The navy can deliver up to 12,000 tactical nuclear weapons in bombs, depth charges, torpedoes, and missiles.

The remaining fifteen thousand or so nuclear weapons are kept in the United States, at Minuteman and Titan missile sites, at SAC bomber bases, and in the custody of armed-forces units. The seven army divisions on active duty in the United States have the full spectrum of tactical nuclear weapons.

"The risk of war with the Soviet Union has long been regarded as the primary threat to the security of the United States," Barry Schneider, a research staff associate at the Center for Defense Information, wrote in the *Bulletin of the Atomic Scientists.* "In hopes of averting such a catastrophe, thousands of man-years have been spent by analysts exploring how such a war is likely to erupt.

"The research and contingency plans designed to control escalation of crises and limited wars, to prevent accidental war or unauthorized attacks, and to deter a surprise attack may be ignoring a likelier danger to Americans—the nuclear terrorist.

"A half-dozen terrorists with a homemade or hijacked nuclear weapon could cause thousands of deaths in a city like New York. One of the hundreds of U.S. nuclear bombs in the one-megaton range, if exploded on Manhattan Island, would inflict casualties exceeding the combined totals of the war dead from the American Revolution, the War of 1812, the Mexican War, the U.S. Civil War, the Spanish-American War, World War I, World War II, the Korean War, and the Vietnam War. Nearly 1½ million people would perish in such an event.

"More than 50 major terrorist groups are reported to exist worldwide. Urban guerrilla activities, Olympic murders, airplane hijacking, terror bombings, and airport massacres are all well known.

"How safe are nuclear weapons from theft by terrorist groups? Not very, according to the few indicators available in this highly classified area. U.S. Army Special Forces exercises have shown that nuclear weapons storage areas can be penetrated successfully without detection despite guards, fences, and sensors. Their example could obviously be accomplished by a daring and well-organized terrorist organization.

"The United States, its allies, and the Soviet Union have now deployed thousands of nuclear weapons across the world, each in an effort to bolster its own national security. In doing so, these governments have made their societies more vulnerable to the nuclear terrorists."

There are critics who suggest that thefts of military nuclear weapons may well have occurred already. They are dubious of the accounting system, asking such questions as this one: Why, at any given time, does the military think it still has all the bombs it thought it had? Even if the military knew that a few of its bombs were missing, would the world be told about it?

"Fission energy is safe only if a number of critical devices work as they should, if a number of people in key positions follow all their instructions, if there is no sabotage, no hijacking of the transports, if no reactor fuel processing plant or reprocessing plant or repository in the world is situated in a region of riots or guerrilla activity, and no revolution or war—even a conventional one—takes place in these regions. The enormous quantities of extremely dangerous material must not get into the hands of dangerous people or desperadoes. No acts of God can be permitted."

The above statement by Dr. Hannes Alfven, Nobel laureate in physics, offers a lot of potential "ifs." Since 1968 there have been 175 cases of threatened violence and assorted small bombings and arsons at nuclear facilities, but no group has yet launched a serious attack against a nuclear plant or attempted to hijack a truck carrying fissionable material in this country.

There was the Carlos–Puig Antich bombing attack at the Fessenheim nuclear plant in 1975. Two years earlier, guerrillas armed with machine guns and hand grenades attacked a nuclear plant just north of Buenos Aires, over-powered the guards, stole weapons, painted slogans on the walls, but made no attempt to steal nuclear material or damage the reactor itself. In 1974 Italian police arrested several persons in connection with a plot to use stolen radioac-tive waste to poison the water systems of several large Italian cities. Police also arrested an engineer at the research center from which the material was stolen and charged him with conspiracy in the plot.

The danger from radioactive waste is another problem awaiting solution by the NRC. At nuclear-reactor sites in the United States, spent fuel rods are currently being housed in "cooling" ponds that are usually located in concrete or corrugated-steel buildings next to the reactor core. Since 1972, when recy-cling for private industry was stopped in the United States, a backlog of spent-fuel assemblies has been piling up at power plants. A GAO inspection in 1974 revealed that at most plants the spent-fuel pond was "more accessible and vulnerable to sabotage than is the reactor core. The highly radioactive fuel does not have the same degree of physical protection as that provided . . . by the reactor vessel." It recommended additional security "as soon as possible," but to date no changes have been made in NRC regulations pertaining to spent-fuel security.

"A takeover, particularly of a nuclear power plant near a large metro-politan area," the GAO said, "could threaten public health and safety if ra-dioactive materials were released to the environment as a result of sabo-tage."

How vulnerable are nuclear reactors to sabotage? "Licensee and AEC officials agreed," says the GAO, "that a security system at a licensed nuclear plant could not prevent a takeover for sabotage by a small number—as few perhaps as two or three—of armed individuals." Other government-funded studies, notably those done by Sandia and Mitre research firms, confirmed the GAO findings that a skilled, well-armed team of saboteurs could overwhelm the defenses of most nuclear plants. The current system is designed to repel an attack by two aggressors armed with pistols and to delay an attack by forces of up to ten persons until local police arrive with reinforcements. Considering the sophisticated weaponry employed by terrorists in worldwide activities, critics call these assumptions naïve.

NRC officials are well aware that plant security systems are not designed to withstand a Munich-type raid. "Several people with high explosives who really know how to use them can probably go through a nuclear plant like butter," one NRC high official conceded.

At some plants a lone saboteur could walk right in without being chal-lenged. John Darcy and Joseph Shapiro, two former security guards at Metro-politan Edison Company's nuclear power plants near Harrisburg, Pennsyl-vania, were fired because they charged that competing guard companies at the plant played "tricks" to discredit one another, which included unhooking gates to the plant and giving out three hundred unauthorized keys to the facility; that guards were insufficiently trained; that security records were falsified; that firearm tests for guards were rigged; that electronic security devices did not work; and that unauthorized people could walk in and out of the plant without much trouble. In a prepared statement released by Ralph Nader, they said, in part, "We certainly do not regard our experience at Three Mile Island as an isolated problem. If lax security exists at Three Mile Island, it probably exists at other plants."

Once inside the plant, the saboteur would not have to penetrate all the physical barriers between himself and the fission material churning within the reactor. By disabling the primary and emergency cooling systems to the reactor core, he could in effect allow the reactor to do most of the destructive work.

Basically, a light-water nuclear reactor is hardly more complicated than a fire. It operates pretty much like the combustion chamber of a coal or oil furnace. Water pumped through the reactor picks up heat generated by nuclear reactions and is piped out to power a turbogenerator. This generator produces electricity in the same way it would if fired in a coal or oil furnace. Except, of course, that the core of a nuclear reactor is a silent, flameless source of heat produced by atomic reactions inside uranium fuel pellets, each the size of a marble, which are loaded into rods half an inch in diameter and thirteen feet long. The pellets, about ten million of them, can produce heat for a full year without replacement. As atoms inside the fuel pellets split, they shoot off particles called neutrons. These neutron "bullets" crack into other atoms nearby, splitting them and causing more neutrons to be "fired," bringing about a heat-producing chain reaction. The rods, some forty thousand of them, in spaced bundles with control rods inserted among them to increase or decrease the atomic fire, are then submerged in water in a steel tank shaped like a giant drug capsule. The water slows the neutrons emitted by the uranium atoms in the fuel bundles, increasing the likelihood of their entering and fissioning other uranium atoms. It also cools the fuel bundles, for the reactor must be cooled. Even with the control rods fully inserted and the chain reaction shut off, it would heat up and destroy itself without water. The uranium, with a melting point of about five thousand degrees, would melt, taking fuel rods and reactor vessel with it. A nuclear reactor is a fire, but with a significant difference: except by disassembly or slow decay, it cannot be extinguished.

Obviously, a saboteur with the foresight to check out the reactor's docket prior to his attack would strike at the coolant system. Since the disaster that nuclear engineers most fear is one involving a loss of coolant, much of the effort —and the expense—of reactor design has been devoted to its prevention or containment. Safety systems stress redundancy: emergency core-cooling systems, backup electrical generators to power emergency pumps, heat exchangers, decontamination sprays, primary and secondary containment structures of steel or concrete or both. Yet, even though the core is surrounded by a thick steel pressure vessel, radioactive gases from a core melt could gush out through a ruptured pipe. But these gases would then be trapped inside yet another defense system—a massive reinforced-concrete structure built to withstand the pressure of a nuclear accident. And there are additional safeguards within this structure to remove heat and radioactivity from the trapped air. Could everything ever fail?

In March 1975, a workman in the control room of the Brown Ferry nuclear complex in Alabama lifted a candle to the ceiling to check an air leak and accidentally set ablaze the insulation around some cables that controlled the reactor's emergency cooling system. The emergency pumps and fans were disconnected. If the regular cooling system had failed at the same time, something like the following could have happened:

> At the nuclear power reactor at Indian Point, twenty-four miles north of downtown Manhattan, three operators are making checks of the dials on the long instrument panel. Everything seems normal. A small power surge occurs, with an accompanying increase of pressure and temperature inside the reactor. The operators ignore the surge because the many control rods are supposed to compensate automatically for any power variances within the reactor.

> A few minutes later the scram alarm sounds. The No. 2 Cooling Line has ruptured; the cooling water, which stabilizes the reactor's temperature, is now gushing out from the heart of the reactor. The operators rush to activate the emergency core cooling system as the temperature inside the reactor climbs from 650 degrees at 30 degrees per second. The emergency cooling core system is turned on but the flow of water is blocked by steam back-pressure. The water that does reach the core is immediately vaporized and forms a protective shield so that other cooling water cannot reach it. There is no way to prevent what follows.

> The reactor temperature continues to rise until it reaches 5,400 degrees, forty-five minutes after the cooling line ruptured. The reactor core, a 180-ton molten object, begins to sink. Everything in its way either melts or vaporizes. Water remaining in the réactor explodes as it is trapped within core pockets. Zircoloy, used as a protective bond to keep the reactor from losing its poisonous fuel, undergoes a series of chemical explosions.

> About eight hours after the accident began, the core has melted through all its [steel and concrete] containment barriers. The twenty percent of its deadly radioactive poisons which are gaseous are immediately released into the air. Large quantities of the liquid and solid radioactive fuel are spewed into the air as a result of steam and zircoloy explosions. The dreaded accident has occurred. Radioactivity the equivalent of 300 Hiroshima bombs has been released into the atmosphere and a ten-mile per hour northerly wind is blowing it toward New York City.*

This imagined horror story is subject to a number of gruesome endings. People living within a forty-mile radius would have to be immediately evacu-

---

*From an article by Richard H. Sandler and Peter Gruenstein in the November 1973 issue of the *Progressive*.

ated for an indefinite exile. A forty-mile radius drawn around the Indian Point reactor would take in eighteen million people. Within ten hours after the accident began, an invisible radioactive cloud would cover the entire area, exposing those caught behind to a dose of up to one thousand RADs (units of radiation exposure), and within a few weeks most of them would die an agonizing death from radiation poisoning. The rest would die of cancer within fifteen years, and tens of thousands of children born generations later would be seriously deformed. It is impossible to estimate how many lives would be lost, but property damage would run into the hundreds of billions.

Meanwhile, back at the reactor, the core would be a huge radioactive molten blob eating its way into the earth; scientists call this the China syndrome. It may not reach China, but it would take years for it to cool. Once it reached groundwater, it would react explosively, forming clouds of radioactive steam that could escape through cracks in the reactor building or create explosive geysers in the ground.

The NRC places its faith in the laws of probability. In a $3 million study that NRC sponsored, Dr. Norman Rasmussen of M.I.T., a spokesman for nuclear power, estimated that the chance of a meltdown accident is about one in every seventeen thousand years of a reactor's life. That is one in seventeen years if a thousand reactors are operating, but there is nothing in that kind of statistical juggling that says the catastrophe must come at the end of the predicted period. It could just as well come at the beginning.

Rasmussen did not speculate on the probability of sabotage, because he felt there was no way to quantify this risk. Yet the danger is real enough for ERDA to have doubled its budget allotment for precautionary antiterrorist measures. In response to charges by critics that NRC officials are more interested in promoting the growth of the nuclear industry than in making it safe, Rasmussen said that saboteurs have dozens of other installations to chose from, and if they are determined to wreak havoc, they will find these more accessible than nuclear sites.

"In human, moral terms," Dr. Barry Commoner wrote in *The Poverty of Power*, "it seems to me there is no valid comparison between the risks of personally tragic individual events like auto accidents and the risk of operating a device which has the acknowledged design capability—however improbable —of killing tens of thousands of people at once."

It is Commoner's explicit assumption that the Rasmussen report was to give nuclear power the appearance of nearly absolute safety rather than to estimate forthrightly its degree of danger. Estimates of extreme catastrophe in the report are hedged with comparisons favorable to reactor safety almost to the point of absurdity. The report's implied conclusion is that nuclear power is safer than any other risk to which mortal man exposes himself. To this Commoner responds, "It should be noted as well that the extremely small probability relates only to whether or not the accident will occur, and not to the consequences. However improbable, when an accident does happen, it is likely to be highly destructive."

Edward Teller, the designer of the hydrogen bomb and a proponent of nuclear power, is very much aware of the real danger inherent in a reactor catastrophe. He described it this way: "In principle, nuclear reactors are dangerous. . . . They are not dangerous because they may blow up. The explosion of a nuclear reactor is not likely to be as violent as the explosion of a chemical plant. But a powerful nuclear reactor which has functioned for some time has radioactivity stored in it greatly in excess of that released from a powerful nuclear bomb. There is one difference, and this difference makes the nuclear bomb look like a relatively safe instrument: in the case of an atmospheric nuclear explosion, the radioactivity extends into the stratosphere. . . . The gently sweeping nuclear reactor can put its radioactive poison under a stable inversion layer and concentrate it into a few thousand square miles in a truly deadly fashion."

Except to emphasize the impregnability of nuclear power plants, a questionable assumption to say the least, the Rasmussen report ignores sabotage except to note in passing that "the worst consequences associated with acts of sabotage at reactors are not expected to lead to consequences more severe than the maximum consequences predicted by the study."

The "maximum consequences," assuming the "worst" nuclear plant accident that could happen, would result, says Rasmussen, in 3,300 early deaths, 45,000 cancer fatalities, 5,100 genetic defects, $6 billion in property damages,* and the total abandonment of 290 square miles of land. That's assuming, of course, the orderly evacuation of 18 million people in less than ten hours. Estimates by critics have placed the deaths from such a meltdown anywhere from 100,000 to 5 million.

If nuclear power, as Rasmussen's report concludes, is safer than any other risk to which mortal man exposes himself, why is it that private insurance companies, or combinations of companies, have refused to provide the power companies with the amount of insurance they want? Congress had to pass the Price-Anderson Act, which authorizes the government to insure owners of nuclear power plants against claims resulting from nuclear disaster. First passed in 1957 and renewed in 1965, the act insures the companies against claims up to $560 million. Currently, insurance companies will provide only $110 million in coverage for each reactor, and it does not offer coverage of nuclear hazards in homeowners' insurance policies. Each reactor owner pays $225,000 to $450,000 a year for his $110 million policy but only $90,000 for his $560 million government policy.

It may well be that anyone who thinks that New York City could be evacuated in ten hours should not be making reliability predictions. The good people of New York may not even get ten hours to battle their way through the most monumental traffic jam in history. Nuclear critic David Comey has another scenario for a meltdown. If the core coagulated to "drop into water

*A 1957 AEC study estimated maximum damages at $7 billion, and a 1965 revision raised it to $17 billion. What would the figures be if adjusted for the post-1965 years of inflation?

collected below the reactor vessel," it would set off "a phenomenon known as a steam explosion. A tremendous release of energy would drive the molten core straight upward like a cannon projectile—right through the top of the pressure vessel and then through the containment dome—with an exit velocity of about 350 miles per hour. The entire contents of the reactor core (160 tons of radioactive uranium and plutonium) would then come down, . . . giving off radioactive gases. As far as I know, that would be the worst conceivable accident. . . . This is where things get gruesome because people would get radiation sickness and begin dying."

The fallout would be equal to a thousand Hiroshima-sized atom bombs. M.I.T. professor Henry W. Kendall, a leading critic of nuclear power, says, "The uncontrolled release of even 5 or 10 percent of this inventory could bring instantaneous death to persons up to 60 to 100 miles from a large fission-power reactor. Persons hundreds of miles distant could suffer radiation sickness, genetic damage, and increased incidence of many diseases, including cancer."

High-level radiation poisoning causes excrutiating deaths. Symptoms include dysentery, the turning of the bowels to water, fever, nausea, vomiting, prostration, stupor, and hysteria. The hair falls out, and radiation burns reduce the number of white cells. Finally there is delirium and death.

"We nuclear people have made a Faustian bargain with society," says nuclear scientiest Alvin Weinberg. "On the one hand, we offer . . . an inexhaustible source of energy. . . . But the price that we demand of society for this magical energy source is both a vigilance and longevity of our social institutions that we are quite unaccustomed to. . . . In a sense, we have established a military priesthood which guards against inadvertent use of nuclear weapons. . . . Peaceful nuclear energy probably will make demands of the same sort on our society. . . . The society must then make the choice, and this is a choice that we nuclear people cannot dictate."

The moment when society still had a choice, one based on the myth that nuclear power is the key to economic development, has long since passed. But do the benefits of nuclear power, in fact, justify the risk in any society?

"Apart from the difficulties of disposal and possible accident, nuclear power represents a kind of thermodynamic overkill," says Barry Commoner. "In a power plant, the basic task of the energy source is to boil water to produce the steam that drives the generator. If this task is to be accomplished with thermodynamic efficiency, it will require temperatures in the range one to two thousand degrees F. At such temperatures, fossil fuels produce chemicals (such as sulfur dioxide and nitrogen oxide) that cause pollution problems. The pollutants and the cost of controlling them constitute the unavoidable price that is paid to achieve the necessary thermodynamic linkage between the energy source and the energy-required task.

"In a nuclear reactor, the price is much higher, for the extreme energy of the ionizing radiation of the nuclear reaction is well beyond the range appropriate to the task of generating steam. Expressed in terms that are equivalent to the temperature scale, the energy associated with the nuclear-fission process is in the range of a million degrees. All the difficulties and dangers that are due to the radiation associated with a nuclear reactor are, in this thermodynamic sense, unnecessary, since the task of generating steam can be achieved by the much lower energies of ordinary fuels. The use of nuclear radiation for the relatively mild task of producing steam violates the familiar caution against attacking a fly with a cannon. The task of killing the fly is likely to be accomplished, but at the cost of considerable unnecessary damage."

To compound the tragedy, the introduction of nuclear power in the Middle East by Nixon and Kissinger has put a hair-trigger on the Doomsday machine that could set off the nuclear holocaust of World War III. Nixon's "triumphal" tour of the area following the October 1973 war, when he promised nuclear power plants to Arab countries, may turn out to be one of the costliest diplomatic maneuvers in history, one born of political expediency. The specter of nuclear war in the Middle East now will haunt diplomats searching for the settlement formula that has eluded them for three decades. There might have been some justification for the Nixon-Kissinger move if there had been some overwhelming need for nuclear power in the world's richest oil region, but that was hardly the case. The ominous possibility of nuclear conflict in that tinderbox seemingly dawned on Kissinger when he said in Milwaukee in 1975, "Political inhibitions are crumbling. Nuclear catastrophe—whether by plan or mistake, accident, theft, or blackmail—is no longer implausible."

Yes, anything is now plausible. Disaster scenarios are limitless. Terrorists could detonate a nuclear bomb in Israel, provoking it into massive nuclear retaliation, which in turn could bring retaliation from the Russians, a move that could get the United States to retaliate against them. The terrorists could detonate a bomb in an Arab state, and the end results would be about the same. The tragic fact is that a terrorist act could be so designed as to produce a belief in one nation that it has been attacked by another and to maneuver the two superpowers into a nuclear-showdown position from which they could not peacefully disengage.

Or the terrorists could strike directly at the United States with a threat to destroy one or more cities with nuclear weapons. How do you ransom a city? Do you empty the national treasury by extending unlimited assistance to Third World nations? Do you release all "political" prisoners? Do you dissolve the government? Do you lynch the president in the Rose Garden at high noon? Do you destroy Israel? What is sufficient value to save a city? Five cities? One million or ten million people?

"The world at the turn of the century will be dominated by proliferation of nuclear weapons," says David Rosenbaum. "Terrorist groups armed with nuclear weapons could become a greater threat than that of worldwide nuclear war. The whole strategy of deterrence becomes meaningless when you have no base against which to retaliate. How do you strike at a shadow? The sad truth is that we've opened a Pandora's Box and there is no way to return to a world safe from nuclear disaster at the hands of terrorists. This fact, even more than hunger and material shortages, may dictate the political realities of the last quarter of this century. 'Atoms for Peace' may turn out to be one of the most unfortunate ideas of our times."

The *raison d'être* of terrorism is that it sets in motion forces calling always for more extreme measures. The success of one terrorist group would inevitably lead to worldwide nuclear terror campaigns by other groups bent on destroying the two dozen or so open societies left in the world. These democratic governments, swinging widely in all directions like blinded Goliaths, would be forced to destroy basic freedoms with draconian martial laws that would be welcomed by the frightened populaces.

Liberties once lost, as Rousseau observed, are seldom regained. Therein lies the greatest danger of terrorism. Repression becomes popular in an atmosphere of terror. In order to appear competent, rather than bungling and helpless, governments would increase the level of alarm to justify more draconian measures.

As chairman of the Research Council of the Center for Strategic and International Studies in Washington, Walter Laqueur has devoted considerable time to the study of terrorism. In the November 1976 issue of *Harper's,* he wrote:

> If any lesson can be drawn from the experience of several decades of terrorism, it is the uncomfortable and indeed shocking conclusion that the more the injustice and repression, the less terrorism there is. In other words, terrorism succeeds only against nonterrorists, namely, groups of governments which refrain from responding to indiscriminate murder with equally indiscriminate repression. Terrorism continues in Ulster not because the terrorists are invincible but because the British government treats the violent men of both sides decently, unlike the Brazilians or Iranians, Russians or Yugoslavs. A professor of law in testimony to a Congressional committee said recently that he was not sure whether deterrence against terrorism worked. He could not have been more mistaken: the problem, alas, is not whether terrorism can be stamped out; even fifth-rate dictatorships have managed to achieve this. The real issue is, of course, the price that has to be paid to eradicate terrorism.

Nuclear terrorism is the wave of the future. There is no easy solution for stopping it. Terrorism feeds upon itself. It is self-breeding, and even the resolution of the injustices terrorists claim to be fighting to right would not necessarily alleviate the situation. The only societies that would survive are those highly disciplined totalitarian states where the act and its punishment would disappear without a ripple in the all-pervasive calm.

Even if given a choice, a terrified people would prefer controlled Marxist terror to uncontrolled anarchist violence. In a nuclear Orwellian society, terrorists and citizens alike would learn to love the state and would eventually discover that they had never existed.

INDEX

Aaiun, el-, 21
Abdesselam, Belaid, 9, 10, 14, 15–16, 17, 18
Abdullah, King of Jordan, 124, 127, 162
Abourezk, James, 196, 203
Abtah al-Audah. *See* Heroes of the Return
Abu Sherif, Bassam, 61–62
Abu-Su'ud family, 128
Acosta, Valentin Hernández, 16–17
Acre, Palestine, 89, 90
Aden, South Yemen, 4, 20, 34, 35, 36, 69, 92, 116
Adwan, Kamal, 132, 193
Aerbel, Dan, 407–8
Africa, 4, 79, 405. *See also names of countries*
Agit-833 (anarchist paper), 228, 232
Air France, 30
　hijacking to Entebbe, 51, 62, 159, 169, 184, 203–8
Ajax (cruiser), 85
Al-Ahram (newspaper), 168
Al-Akhbar, 105, 388
Alami (el-Alami), Musa Bey, 89, 118
Alami, Zuhair al-, 132
Al-Anwar (newspaper), 141
Aleppo, Syria, 69
Alexander I Obrenovich, King of Serbia, 380
Alexander II, Czar of Russia, 380, 381
al-Fatah, 123, 127, 128, 137, 139–45, 151–52, 153–54, 175
　Arab support for, 138–39, 155, 190
　Baader-Meinhof gang and, 228–29
　Black September and, 176, 177–79, 186
　founding of, 131–32
　Haddad and, 159, 160
　Hussein and, 164, 170
　naming of, 132
　after 1967 war, 148–49, 150
　PLO dominated by, 161
　Syrian war on, 202–3
　training of, 134–35
　See also Arafat, Yasir; *fedayeen*
Alfven, Dr. Hannes, 416
Algeria, 126, 205, 384, 405, 412
　Arab terrorists and, 134–35, 153, 159, 175, 195
　extradition of Carlos and, 19–20
　Jews driven from, 115
　OPEC raid and, 16, 19, 20, 21
Algiers, Algeria, 15, 16, 17, 18, 19, 54, 58, 61, 92, 153, 195, 386
Al-Hadaf (underground newspaper), 191, 192
Al-Husseini, Jordan, 172
al-Jihad al-Maudaddas (the Holy Struggle), 128
Al-Kuwait, 132
Allen, Major, 107
Allied General nuclear reprocessing plant, Barnwell, S.C., 397
Allon, Yigal, 40, 110–11, 212, 406
Allon, Yosef, 194
Al-Qads (newspaper), 150

Al-Rawdah (prison ship), 327
Altalena (ship), 109–11
Alush, Naji, 140
Amari, Fakhri al-, 179
America (magazine), 158
American Committee for Ulster Justice, 357
American Emergency Committee for Zionist Affairs, 81
American Professors for Peace in the Middle East, 163
Amin, Idi, 159, 205, 206, 207, 208
Amman, Jordan, 103, 152, 155, 158, 163, 164, 169–71, 172
Amnesty International, 257
Amouzegar, Jamshid, 14, 17, 19, 20
Amsterdam, Netherlands, 38, 165
Anderson, Jack, 353
Angry Brigade, 360
An Phoblacht (journal), 307, 353
Antich, Puig, 42, 416–17
APO, 220, 222, 236
Arab Development Society, 118
Arab Executive, 73, 74, 79
Arab Front of the Liberation of Palestine, 134
Arab Higher Committee, 85, 89, 92, 94, 97, 101, 102
Arab League, 21, 91, 96, 103, 135, 175, 202, 203, 208
Arab League Council, 135
Arab Legion, 94, 99, 108–9, 113, 124, 126, 147, 157
Arab Liberation Army (ALA), 89, 94, 96–97, 101, 127
Arab Liberation Front (ALF), 139, 188
Arab National Committee, 101, 103, 120
Arab Nationalist Movement (ANM), 134, 150, 151
Arab Palestinian Fedayeen, 134
Arab Rejection Front, 4, 8, 18, 20, 61, 188
Arabs, 69, 353
　British promises to, 69, 79, 88
　historical link to Palestine of, 68
　origin of fighting with Jews and, 70–75
　UN approval of partition of Palestine and, 91–101, 104
　UNSCOP and, 85, 88
　World War II and, 77, 78–79
　worship of violence by, 120–23
　See also Arab states; Arab terrorist groups; Palestinian refugees; Palestinian terrorist groups; *names of countries*
Arab states, 8, 20–21, 76–77, 92, 127, 423
　border attacks by on Israel, 124–45 *passim*
　economic pressures on Israel and, 122
　fighting after partition and, 94, 96–97, 101
　Jews driven from, 114–17
　Jordanian crackdown on terrorists and, 172–74
　1948 war and, 102, 103, 105, 108–13
　1964 Cairo summit and, 135
　1967 war and, 145–47

425

oppressiveness of, 120, 121
Palestinian refugees and, 101–5, 113–14, 117–20
support of terrorist groups by, 125, 127–45 *passim,* 151, 154–55, 159, 161, 173, 175, 177, 179, 183–84, 190, 195–96, 353, 355–56, 374
UNSCOP and, 86, 88–89
See also names of countries
Arab terrorist groups, 74, 76, 93–97, 103, 105–6, 124, 144, 180. *See also* Palestinian terrorist groups
Arafat, Jamal, 128, 131
Arafat, Yasir, 8, 13, 20–21, 57, 137–45 *passim,* 175, 188, 189–90, 194, 196, 203, 208, 211, 386
Algerian rebels and, 134–35
-Assad agreement, 209
background of, 127–31, 151
Black September and, 178, 186
as chairman of PLO, 161
founding of al-Fatah and, 131–32
Hussein and, 163, 164, 170, 172–73
Lebanon civil war and, 199, 200, 201, 202
after 1967 war, 148–49
training of, 130, 131, 144
See also al-Fatah
Arche, L' (magazine), 39, 58
Ard Fheis, 288–89, 306, 307, 311
Aref, Ari, 58
Argentina, 197, 401, 405, 412
Argentinian People's Liberation Army, 57
Arguello, Patrick Joseph, 165–67, 173
Arjam, Jayel Naji al-, 204
Arlosoroff, Dr. Chaim, 110
Armageddon in the Middle East (Schmidt), 97
Armagh Jail, 328, 335
Arms Control and Disarmament Agency, 414
Arm of the Arab Revolution, The, 8–9, 21, 54
Armstrong, Angela, 46–49, 54–56
Asia, 4, 61. *See also names of countries*
Asmar, Fouz el-, 114
Asquith, Herbert Henry, 271, 273
Assad, Hafiz, 144, 174, 200, 201, 209, 212
Assad, Sheikh, 135
Asunción, Paraguay, 157
Athens airport, 63, 153
Atomic Energy Act, 396, 412
Atomic Energy Commission (AEC), 388–404, 417, 421n
atomic weapons and terrorists, 387–425
Atoms for Peace Program, 396, 404, 406
Aud (ship), 275
Audeh, Muhammed Daoud (Abu Daoud), 176–77, 178, 186–87, 195
Augustin, Ronald, 250
Aurore, L' (newspaper), 39, 59
Australia, 85, 90, 321, 374
Austria, 3, 89, 187
Carlos and, 19, 20, 184, 387
negotiations for OPEC hostages and, 8, 9–14
World War I and, 273, 274
See also Vienna, Austria
Austrian Airlines, 156
Autonomous Republic Bunker (ARB), 235
Ayed, Abu, 154
Ayrton, Peter, 360, 365n

Azam Pasha, 91
Azm, Khaled al-, 118
Azzawi, Riyadh al-, 9–13, 14

Baader, Andreas, 9, 25, 39, 182, 236–38, 242, 251–52
background of, 222–24
hunger strikes by, 243, 247
as leader, 224, 232, 245–46, 262–63
prison escape of, 227, 228, 242, 251
Second of June movement and, 226
terrorist activities of, 222, 225, 229, 237–38
training of, 228–29
trial of, 242, 253–63
Baader, Anneliese, 223, 226
Baader-Meinhof gang, 4, 7, 9, 22, 24, 32, 39, 41, 54, 159, 186, 224–25, 232–44, 245–63, 354, 355, 395
cohesiveness of, 232
founding of, 225, 228
hunger strikes by, 243, 246–51, 260
naming of, 39
training of, 228–30, 232
trial of, 242, 253–63
Bagdikian, Ben H., 117–18
Baghdad, Iraq, 16, 17–18, 34, 35, 37, 41, 61, 177, 202, 388
Bahrain, 177
Baker, Colin, 368
Baku, U.S.S.R., 23
Bakunin, Mikhail, 221, 379, 380
Balfour, Arthur, 69
Balfour, Honor, 344
Balfour Declaration, 69, 70, 88, 137
Balkan countries, 77, 273, 380. *See also names of countries*
Ballymurphy News (newsletter), 340
Bambule (Meinhof), 222
Bangkok, Thailand, 185
Banna, Hassan al-, 128–29
Banquero, 197
Barakat, Daud, 196
Bar Kochba, Simon, 68
Barnhill, John, 339
Barrett, Richard, 287
Bartsch (West German official), 250
Basque Euzkadi Ta Azkatasuna (ETA), 355
Basque separatists, 22, 42, 235, 355
Bassim, 31
Batista, Fulgencio, 310
Batterman, Scott, 409
Batzrat, Ahmad, 159, 160
Baumann, Jurgen, 256
Baybars I, 123
BDI (House of German Industry), Cologne, 243
Becker, Eberhard, 246, 256
Be'er Tuveyah, Palestine, 82
Begin, Menahem, 80–81, 83, 87–88, 90–91, 190
Ben-Gurion and, 110, 111
on Deir Yassin, 99
as Israeli prime minister, 212–13
Behal, Richard, 354, 355
Beirut, Lebanon, 18, 20, 21, 25, 26, 29–30, 31, 32, 33, 34, 35, 36, 37, 39, 40, 49, 50, 62, 103, 132, 133, 159, 168, 191–92, 193, 194
Beirut International Airport, 153

Beir Zeit, Palestine, 94
Beit, Sir Alfred, 365
Belfast, Northern Ireland, 291, 300, 307, 315, 370
  bombings in, 267–69, 343
  disturbances in, 299, 302, 303, 304, 305, 309, 311, 313, 319, 334, 335–39, 345, 347, 351, 374
Belfast Prison, 327–29, 330
Belfast Sunday News (newspaper), 269
Belfast Trade Council, 294
Belfast Wolfe Tone Society, 295
Belgium, 237, 274, 353, 409, 412
Belgrade, Yugoslavia, 387, 388
Bell, J. Bowyer, 63, 275, 278
Ben-Bella, Muhammad, 134, 135
Benghazi, Libya, 35, 204
Ben-Gurion, David, 77, 81, 82, 83, 95, 107–8, 109–13, 159, 406
Ben-Nathan, Asher, 59
Berlin, Germany. *See* East Berlin; West Berlin
Berlin-Dahlem, Germany, 243
Berliner Zeitung (newspaper), 223
Bernadotte, Count Folke, 112–13
Betancourt, Rómulo, 23
Betar, 74, 80
Bevin, Ernest, 103
Bidault, Georges, 109
Biltmore Program, 81
Birmingham, England, 348–49
Black and Tans, 279–80, 281, 287
Black Cross, 226
Black Hand, 134
Black Hand Society, 380
Black June, 112
Black Legions, 79
Black Power, 360
Black Relief, 226
Black September group, 21, 33, 63, 112, 192, 193, 194
  al-Fatah and, 176, 177–79, 186
  attack at Munich Olympic Village and, 32, 177, 178, 179, 181–82, 183, 184, 185, 196, 408
  letter bombs of, 185
  naming of, 176
Bloch, Mrs. Dora, 207
Blood Oath League, 30
Blueshirt Movement, 285
BOAC, 93, 170
Boese, Wilfried, 39–40, 42, 50–51, 53, 61, 62, 204, 205, 207, 388
Bohn, Hark, 227
Boland, Harry, 283
Böll, Heinrich, 234
Bomberg, David, 208
Bonn, West Germany, 33, 62
Bouchiki, Ahmed, 194, 408
Boudia, Mohammed, 25, 26, 30, 32, 33, 194
Boumedienne, Houari, 20, 32, 134, 153, 159
Bouteflika, Abdelaziz, 17, 19
Bouvier, Antonio Dages, 23, 25–26, 49, 50, 60, 61, 62, 204, 207
Boyle, Sammy, 318
Boyson, Rhodes, 208
Bradlee, Benjamin C., 387
Brandt, Willy, 182

Brazil, 230, 237, 401, 405, 409, 410, 412
Breton separatists, 22, 353, 354
Brezhnev, Leonid, 412
Bridmead, A. J., 101–2
Briscoe, Benjamin, 317
Briscoe, Robert, 317
British International Marxist Group, 352
Brotherhood Volunteer Battalions, 128
Brown, Eddie, 95–96
Brown, Frederick Z., 388
Brown, L. Dean, 200
Brown Ferry nuclear complex, Ala., 419
Broxton Prison, London, 365
Brugha, Cathal, 283
Buddenberg, Wolfgang, 237
Bulletin of the Atomic Scientists (journal), 415–16
Bunche, Dr. Ralph, 85
Burgos, Spain, 355
Burj Islam, Syria, 155

Cahill, Joe, 356, 357
Cairo, Egypt, 35, 79, 92, 94, 103, 106, 128, 135, 143, 144, 147, 168, 176, 177
Cairo Agreement, 151, 198, 209
Callaghan, James, 334
Campbell, Jim, 269, 293, 314–16, 369–70
Camp Mantanzas, Cuba, 23, 25, 204
Canaan, Hamid, 149
Canada, 85, 89, 321, 353, 374, 409, 411
Capucci, Hilarion, 190, 205
Caracas, Venezuela, 22, 49, 53
Carey, Grizelda, 8, 9
Carlos. *See* Ramírez Sánchez, Ilich (Carlos)
Carmichael, Stokely, 221
Carnot, Marie François Sadi, 380
Carreras Blanco, Luis, 355
Carson, Sir Edward, 272–73
Carter, Jimmy, 195, 210–11, 212, 397, 410–11
Carvalho, George de, 154
Casement, Sir Roger, 275, 277
Castro, Fidel, 19, 23, 293, 360, 385
Catholics, 378–79
  in Northern Ireland, 267–374 *passim*
Center for Constitutional Rights, 347
Center for Defense Information, 415
Central Council of the Vagrant Hashish Rebels, 226
Central Intelligence Agency (CIA), 49–50, 54, 142, 178, 186, 192, 197, 405, 406, 408
Chad, 406
Chamoun, Camille, 199, 209
Chanson, André, 235
Charles de Gaulle Airport, Paris, 45, 50, 386
Chemical Warfare Defense Establishment, 44
Chicago, Ill., 386
Chicago Tribune (newspaper), 386
Chichester-Clark, James, 300, 301, 303, 314, 334, 335–36, 337, 343
Childers, Erskine, 284
Chile, 22, 62, 405, 412
China, 22, 27, 139, 152, 154, 171, 175, 391, 405, 406
Christians, 68, 114, 174, 377–79
  in Lebanon, 197–203, 209
  in Palestine, 104
  See also Catholics; Protestants

Christian Science Monitor (newspaper), 358
Churchill, Randolph, 357
Churchill, Winston, 76, 77, 79, 80, 272, 273, 274, 281, 282
Claimants Union, 360
Clarke, Cenon. *See* Ramírez Sánchez, Ilich (Carlos)
Clarke, Joe, 308
Claudia (ship), 356
Cleaver, Eldridge, 221
Cohen, Joshua, 112
Cohn-Bendit, Daniel, 39, 251
Colbert, Teresa, 365–66
Collins, Michael, 278, 281–82, 283
Cologne, West Germany, 243
Cologne-Ossendorf Prison, 240
Colombia, 17, 60
Colombian Center, 60
Colombian Trades Union, 45
Comey, David, 422
Commando Boudia cell, 33, 38
Commentary (periodical), 104
Commoner, Dr. Barry, 420–21, 422–23
Commune I, 226
Commune II, 226
Conference of Arab Refugees at Homs (1957), 119
Congressional Record, 401
Connally Association, 310
Connolly, James, 275, 306
Connolly, Michael, 340
Cooper, Ivan, 338
Copeland, Miles, 178
Copenhagen, Denmark, 39
Corrigan, Mairead, 350, 351
Corsican separatists, 22
Cosgrave, Liam, 284, 286, 346–47, 358
Costello, Seamus, 290, 295, 312, 334, 354, 368
Council of Ireland, 346–47
County Cork, Ireland, 279–80, 282, 283, 365
County Donegal, Ireland, 364
Cowan, Henrietta P., 322
Coyle, Marian, 366, 367
Craig, Sir James, 281
Craig, William, 297, 332, 337, 343–44, 346, 347, 370, 372
Croatia, 380–81, 386–87
Croatian Uproar (Hrvatski Ustashi), 380–81
Crocker, Sir John, 97
Croissant, Klaus, 9, 238, 246, 251, 256, 257
Cuba, 23, 57, 310, 359, 360, 405. *See also* Dirección General de Inteligencia (DGI)
Cumann na mBann, 277, 312, 351
Cunningham, Sir Alan, 82, 89
Curve of Binding Energy, The (Taylor), 396
Cyprus, 84, 85, 193, 334
Czechoslovakia, 85, 89, 119, 126, 334, 335, 339, 354, 409

Dail Eirann, 281, 282, 283, 284, 285, 289, 307, 317, 336, 347
Daily Express (newspaper), 364
Daley, Richard, 360
Dalmau, Angel, 57
Daly, Miriam, 342

Damascus, Syria, 18, 39, 94, 103, 143, 152, 188, 202
Damascus Protocol, 69
Dan, Palestine, 96
Daneshian, Iaramat, 409
Darcy, John, 417–18
David, Yitzhak, 207
Dayan, Moshe, 146, 147, 149, 187–88, 193, 209, 406
Day of the Jackal, The (Forsyth), 4
Debray, Régis, 197, 221
de Burca, Mairin, 290, 295, 309–10, 312, 316–17, 334, 340, 355, 368
Declaration of World War by the Red Army and the PFLP (film), 31
de Gaulle, Charles, 134
Deir Yassin, Palestine, slaughter at, 97–99, 101, 104, 105, 106, 109, 112
Del Mar, Norman, 46
Dergarabedian, Elias B., 156
Derry. *See* Londonderry, Northern Ireland
Derry Citizens Defense Committee, 301–2
Der Spiegel (newspaper), 225, 228, 229, 237, 254
Destroy the Islands of Wealth in the Third World (Marighella), 230
de Valera, Eamon, 277, 278, 279, 281, 283, 284, 285, 289–90, 291
Devlin, Bernadette, 294, 298, 299, 300, 301, 303, 304, 311, 335, 338–39, 344, 351, 352, 355
Devlin, Paddy, 336, 340, 342, 369
Diaspora, 68, 70
Die Zeit (weekly newspaper), 219, 231, 234
Dimitrijević, Dragutin, 380
Dimons Atomic Research Community, Negev, Israel, 406, 407, 408
Din, Mustafa Saad el-, 154
Dirección General de Inteligencia (DGI), 22, 23, 57
Direction de la Surveillance de Territoire (DST), 50–54, 55–56, 58, 60
Dome of the Rock, 68, 70
Donatini, Jean, 50, 52–53
Dougherty, Paddy, 303
Douglas, Elizabeth, 322
Dous, Raymond, 50, 52, 53
Doxi, Michael Archamides, 59
Drenkmann, Günter von, 251
Drogheda, Lord, 46
Drugstore, Le, Paris, 4, 38, 51
Drumm, Mairie, 335, 338, 351, 374
Drummond, William J., 189
Dublin, Ireland, 27, 275–78, 281, 283, 286, 291, 297, 307, 316, 317, 323, 334, 336, 342, 352, 356
Dugdale, Caroline, 359
Dugdale, Eric, 358, 360, 361–63
Dugdale, Rose, 358–67
Dugdale, Ruairi, 365–66
Dulles, John Foster, 127
Dunn, Peter, 366
DuPont, Hector Hugo. *See* Ramírez Sánchez, Ilich (Carlos)
Durutti, Buenaventura, 382
Düsseldorf, Germany, 36, 37, 39
Dutschke, Rudi, 220, 225–26, 229

Earle, Richard, 364, 365*n*
East Berlin, Germany, 25, 35
Easter Rising (1916), 271, 275–78, 297, 307
East Germany, 119, 354, 409
Echebarrieta, José, 355
Edschmidt, Ulrike, 235, 236
Egypt, 8, 20, 21, 51, 73, 74, 113, 120, 124, 163
    blockade of Suez and Gulf of 'Aqaba, 123
    concentration camps in, 131
    Jews driven from, 115–16
    1967 war and, 145–47
    1970 cease-fire and, 165
    nuclear weapons and, 401, 405, 407, 412
    Soviets and, 124, 125, 126, 145–46
    -Syria mutual-defense pact, 126, 145
    terrorist groups and, 106, 124, 125, 128–29,
        138, 141–42, 143, 168, 177, 178, 179, 183,
        211
    during World War II, 79, 106
    Yom Kippur War and, 187–88
Eichmann, Adolf, 78, 79, 149
"eight howls of Holger Meins," 238
Ein el-Hilwe, Lebanon, 140
Ein Saheh, Syria, 155
Einsatz Kommandos (SWAT team), 7
Eisenhower, Dwight, 396, 404
Ejército Revolucionario del Pueblo (ERP), 197
El Al Airlines, 4, 30, 31, 40, 153, 155, 156–57,
        159, 165–67, 168, 180, 193
El Alamein, 79
El-Hamma, Syria, 155
Elliott, Lady, of Harewood, 46
Encounter (periodical), 221, 360
Energy Research and Development Adminis-
    tration (ERDA), 395, 402, 414, 420
Ensslin, Gudrun, 25, 223, 224, 232, 236, 251,
        252
    arrested, 238, 239
    Second of June Movement and, 226
    terrorist activities of, 222, 237
    training of, 228–29
    trial of, 242, 253–63
Entebbe, Uganda, 51, 61, 62, 169, 184, 203–8,
        388
Eolas (newsletter), 340
Eritrean Liberation Front, 22, 177
Eshkol, Levi, 146, 406
Eshmawy, Saleh, 130, 131
Ethiopia, 91
Europe, 4, 32, 33, 34, 37, 38, 61, 92, 133, 415
    Black Legions in, 79
    Irish problem and, 334, 353
    Jewish paramilitary forces in, 74
    Nazi atrocities in, 77, 79, 81
    See also Eastern Europe; Western Europe;
        names of countries
European Commission on Human Rights, 331
Exodus (ship), 85–86

Faglin, Amihai, 90–91, 110, 111
Faisal, Ibn Abdul-Aziz, 21, 162, 409
Faisal, Mohammed al-, 409
Fa'iz, 148
Fallaci, Oriana, 157, 158
Fanon, Franz, 140, 221
Farouk, King, 106, 116, 129
Farrel, Michael, 300, 352

Fasanenstrasse Synagogue, 227
Fatherland Front, 112
Faulkner, Brian, 337–38, 346, 347
fedayeen, 121, 124, 141, 145, 148, 151–52, 153–
        54, 161, 162, 163, 164, 170, 171, 174, 175,
        198, 229. *See also* al-Fatah
Fedayeen (periodical), 143
Federal Bureau of Investigation (FBI), 387,
        389
Feltrinelli, Giangiacomo, 177, 179, 193, 197,
        354
Ferdinand, Archduke Franz, 273, 280
Fessenheim nuclear power plant, West Ger-
    many, 42, 416–17
Figaro, Le (newspaper), 169
Fighters for Free Croatia, 386–87
Filastinuna Nida el-Hyal (magazine), 132, 139,
        140
Fitt, Gerry, 344, 346
Fitzalan, Lord, 281
FitzGerald, Garret, 308–9, 358, 370, 371
Fiumicino Airport, Rome, 180
Flag Is Born, A (Hecht), 109
Fleming, Chief Superintendent, 326
Florence, Italy, 197, 354
Ford, Gerald, 183, 409–10, 412, 414
Ford Foundation, 118
Fort Worth Five, 357
Fourth International, 196–97, 352
France, 4, 13, 17, 36, 37, 51, 92, 126, 206, 237,
        353
    Algeria and, 126, 134, 384
    attitude toward terrorism in, 51–52, 57–58,
        195, 205
    Balfour Declaration and, 70
    Carlos and, 19–20, 22, 38, 62, 387
    1948 Arab-Israeli war and, 109
    1956 Suez war and, 126–27
    nuclear weapons and, 405, 406, 407, 409,
        410, 411
    World War I and, 274
    See also Direction de la Surveillance de Ter-
        ritoire (DST)
Franco, Francisco, 43
Franjiyeh, Suleiman, 200
Franjyeh, Hamid, 88
Frankfurt, West Germany, 41, 42, 58, 61, 167,
        222, 236, 237, 238
Fraser, Morris, 344
Freeland, Sir Ian, 304, 335
Free Officers, 106, 121, 129
French, Lord, 278
French Committee for the Liberation of the
    Irish People, 355
French Territory of the Afars and Issas, 58
Friedman-Yellin, Nathan, 99, 112, 113
Front de Libération du Québec (FLQ), 353
Front de Libération Nationale (FLN), 115
Furaya, Yutaka, 36, 37, 38–39

Gabon, 7
Gaelic Athletic Association (GAA), 327
Gaelic League, 327
Gaitan, Jorge Eliecer, 22
Galili, Israel, 83
Gallagher, Angela, 349
Gallagher, Eddie, 363–67

Gallagher, James, 302
Garland, Sean, 334
Gavin, Rosaleen, 333
Gaza Strip, 188, 210
    attacks against Israel from, 124, 125, 142, 145
    Palestinian refugees in, 117, 127, 128, 133
Gebhard, Glenn. See Ramírez Sánchez, Ilich (Carlos)
Gemayel, Pierre, 198
General Command of Palestinian Self-Organization, 134
General Electric, 409
    Midwest Fuel Recovery Plant, Morris, Ill., 397
General Union of Palestinian Students (GUPS), 132, 181
General Union of Palestine Workers (GUPW), 181
Genesis 1948 (Kurzman), 93
Geneva, Switzerland, 58, 177, 210–11, 212, 213
Genscher, Hans Dietrich, 39
George, King of Greece, 380
Germany, 74, 85, 89, 170, 353, 377
    during Nazi reign, 73, 77, 78, 79, 81, 89, 106, 116, 137, 198, 205, 227, 233, 285, 286, 380
    Northern Ireland and, 275
    World War I and, 274
    See also East Germany; Weimar Republic; West Germany; names of cities
Ghannam, Fahad el-, 13
Ghazawi, Said, 150
Ghouri, Emile al-, 89, 92, 105
Giap, Vo Nguyen, 221
Giller, Edward B., 402–4
Gilmore (IRA member), 306
Giscard d'Estaing, Valéry, 57–58
Gladstone, William, 271
Glenn, John H., 407
Glubb Pasha, 99, 126
Golan Heights, 124, 145, 147, 187, 188
Goldfoot, Stanley, 113
Golsorklti, Khosrow, 409
Gonzales Duque, Luis, 57
Goulding, Cathal, 307, 311, 334
Graham, Peter, 352–53
Grand Mufti of Jerusalem. See Husseini, Haj Amin el-
Grashof, Manfred, 246, 248
Gray, Harry, 333
Great Britain, 92, 107, 126, 131, 135, 146, 170, 384
    Arab-Jewish conflict in Palestine and, 71–84, 93–107, 279
    Carlos and, 20, 52
    conflicting promises to Jews and Arabs by, 69–70, 88
    Conservative party of, 76, 272, 336, 347
    Easter Rising and, 271, 275–78
    Entebbe and, 206, 208
    IRA letter bombs in, 348–49
    Irish home rule and, 271–74, 280, 281
    Irish Nationalist party of, 271, 273, 274, 277, 278
    Jewish civil disobedience policy against, 81–91
    Labour party of, 81, 96, 336, 344, 347–48

    Liberal party of, 271, 272, 273
    1939 White Paper and, 75–76, 79, 81
    Northern Ireland and, 269–70, 280–82, 283, 285, 287, 291–92, 294, 297, 299–301, 303–74 passim
    nuclear weapons and, 405, 409, 411
    Palestinian refugees and, 117
    police in, 17, 60, 167
    Suez Canal and, 271, 272, 273
    withdrawal of from Northern Ireland, consequences of, 368–74
    withdrawal of from Palestine, 107, 108
    World War I and, 271, 274
    See also names of cities
Great Victoria Street Railway Station, Belfast, 268, 343
Greece and Greeks, 68, 79, 405
Grey, Sir Edward, 274
Griffith, Arthur, 278, 281–82, 283, 284
Grigori Ordshonikidse (ship), 34
Groenewold, Kurt, 246, 256, 257
Grogan, Larry, 308
Grossman, Meir, 77
Gruenstein, Peter, 419n
Grundmann, Wolfgang, 246, 250
Guam, 415
Guatemala, 85, 89
Guevara, Che, 143, 221, 383
Gufreund, Yosef, 181–82
Gulf of 'Aqaba, 123, 127, 146, 207
Gulf Oil refinery, Rotterdam, 179
Gur, Mordechai, 206
Gurney, Sir Henry, 88

Haag, Siegfried, 250, 256
Habash, Dr. George, 4, 18, 19, 20, 25, 26, 30, 33, 49, 54, 134, 150, 151–59 passim, 162, 163, 164, 174, 180, 196, 201, 211, 237, 317, 406
Hacker, Friedrich, 218
Haddad, Hani, 159
Haddad, Samia, 159
Haddad, Wadi, 25, 54, 61, 158–60, 162, 163, 174, 204, 406
Hadibi, Hassan al-, 129–30, 131
Hagana, 74, 77–78, 81, 83, 84
    Irgun confrontation with, 109–12
    after partition vote, 93, 95, 99, 101, 104, 105, 106, 107
    UNSCOP and, 85–86
Hague, Netherlands, 38–39, 51, 58
Haifa, Palestine, 80, 81, 99–100, 101–4, 120
Haiti, 91
Hama, Syria, 69
Hamady, Dr. Sania, 120
Hamburg, West Germany, 237, 238, 243
Hamburger Abendlatt, (newspaper), 243
Hamshari, Dr. Mahmoud, 32, 54, 193
Hamuden, Yahya, 160–61
Hannover, Heinrich, 256
Hannover, West Germany, 238
Haram al-Sharif, 70
Harazallah, Khader, 14
Harna, Syria, 155
Harper's (magazine), 424
Hartug, Palestine, 93
Hartuv, Ilan, 207

Hasham, Adnam Mohamed, 180
Hashomer (Watchmen), 74
Hassan, Khalid al- (Abu Said), 132
Hassan Saeed al-Khafari, Ala, 6, 7, 10, 13, 16
Hawatmeh, Nayef, 18–19, 139, 152, 156, 158, 174, 189, 201
Hayes, Stephen, 286
Haymarket bombing, 382
Hearst, Patricia, 172, 221
Heath, Edward, 335, 337, 338, 342, 344–46
Heath, Kingsley, 72
Heathrow Airport, London, 41, 50, 348
Heaton, Audrey, 361, 365n
Heaton, Wally, 360–63
Hebron, Palestine, 73, 93–94, 108–9, 142, 150
Heffernan, Tony, 334
Hegel, George Wilhelm, 221
Heidelberg, West Germany, 226, 237–38
Heldmann, Hans-Heinz, 257–58, 261
Helga (gunboat), 276, 277
Heller, Edith, 3, 5, 9
Henck, Dr. Helmut, 247
Henderson, Loy, 91
Heroes of the Return, 144, 150, 152, 158, 204
Herranz, Jean, 50, 51, 52–53
Herrema, Dr. Tiede, 366
Herron, Tommy, 316
Herut, 80–81
Herzl, Theodor, 68
Herzog, Chaim, 208
Hidakas, Yoko, 36
Higher Arab Committee, 127
Hijazi, Mahmud Bakr, 142
Hilldring, Gen. John, 91
Hillegaart, Dr. Heinz, 41–42
Himmler, Heinrich, 78, 79
Hipodikon, Hector. See Ramírez Sánchez, Ilich (Carlos)
Hiroshima, Japan, 400
Histadrut, 107
Hitler, Adolf, 70, 73, 75, 76, 77, 78, 79, 81, 114, 116, 127, 198, 205, 233, 380
Ho Chi Minh, 221
Hoff, Dierk, 237
Hoffi, Yitzhak, 187
Homann, Peter, 225, 227
Homs, Syria, 69, 119
Hornischer, Inge, 388
Hrvatski Ustashi (Croatian Uproar), 380–81
Hubbard, David G., 171–72
Hulagu, 123
Hull, Billy, 340
Human Rights Convention, 331
Humbert I, King of Italy, 380
Hume, John (Jack), 303, 330
Hussein, Grand Sherif, 162
Hussein, King of Jordan, 21, 133, 142–43, 146, 162–64, 168–69, 172–74, 186–87, 190, 372
Hussein, Sharif, 69
Hussein, Talal, 162
Husseini, Abd el-Kader el-, 94–97, 105, 127, 128
Husseini, Haj Amin el- (Grand Mufti of Jerusalem), 71, 72, 73, 74, 79–80, 82, 84, 87, 88, 89, 96, 106, 124, 162, 194
    Arafat and, 128
    death of, 127

evacuation of Arabs from Palestine and, 101, 104, 105
    partition of Palestine and, 92, 94
    during World War II, 78–79, 116
Husseini, Jamal el-, 82, 89, 92
Hyland, James, 366, 367

Ibrahim Abu-Dia Unit, 144
Ikle, Fred C., 414–15
Ilah, Prince Abd al-, 121
India, 79, 85, 90, 92, 119, 138, 142, 405, 411
Indian Point nuclear power reactor, N.Y., 419–20
Indochina, 27, 384
Indonesia, 79, 384
Institute for Palestinian Studies, Beirut, 104
Institute for the Study of Conflict, 176, 294, 314
Institute of Nuclear Materials Management, 393
Interatom, 388
Internal Macedonian Revolutionary Organization, 380
International Atomic Energy Agency (IAEA), 403, 404–5, 410, 411–15
International Herald Tribune (newspaper), 386
International Marxist Group (IMG), 352–53
International Socialists, 294, 352
International Workingmen's Association, 379
Interpol, 196, 197, 228
Iran, 7, 14, 19, 85, 90, 184, 401, 405, 407, 408–9, 410
Iran, Shah of, 3, 19, 40, 408–9
Iraq, 9–10, 15, 67, 78, 80, 94, 105, 116, 120, 124, 139, 146–47, 151, 159, 162, 163, 175, 179, 188, 245, 405
Ireland, Republic of, 267–374 passim, 384
    creation of, 269, 271–73, 280, 281–82
    Fianna Fail of, 284, 285, 291, 302, 332
    Fine Gael of, 284, 291
    NICRA and, 296
    1937 constitution of, 285
    Special Courts of, 324–26, 327
    See also Dail Eirann; Irish Republican Army; Northern Ireland
Irgun Zevai Leumi, 74, 75, 77, 78, 80–84, 86, 87–88, 89, 90–91, 94, 97–99, 107, 109–12, 112–13, 190
Irish-Arab Society, 355
Irish Freedom (newspaper), 328
Irish Republican Army, 22, 176, 197, 233, 267–372 passim, 385
    air raids by, 364, 365
    founding of, 278
    Official, 269, 306–7, 309–12, 319, 320, 333, 334, 340, 345, 348, 352, 355, 369, 374
    prison escapes by, 332, 366
    Provisional, 26, 269, 270, 301, 306–7, 309, 310–12, 316, 319, 320, 332, 333, 337, 340–42, 348, 349, 351–73 passim
    See also Sinn Fein Republican movement
Irish Republican Brotherhood (IRB), 275, 276, 278
Irish Republican Socialist party, 290, 334, 348, 353, 355
Irish Tangle, The (Hamilton), 293
Irish Times, Dublin (newspaper), 297–98

Islam, 68, 70, 122–23, 127, 129, 137. *See also* Koran; Muslims
Islamic Liberation party, 133
Ismailis, 121–23
Ismirli, Yousef, 6
Israel and Israelis, 4, 6, 8, 26, 30, 32, 54, 58, 67–213, 384, 385
  Arab goal of destroying, 117, 119, 133, 135, 137, 138, 156, 163, 178
  attitude of toward terrorism, 20, 62, 149–50, 170, 179–80, 185, 186, 206
  Black September and, 176, 178, 179–80
  border attacks on, 124–45 *passim*
  branded rascist by UN, 121, 137, 190–91
  cease-fire lines and, 67, 124, 127, 210–11, 212
  Egypt's blockade of Suez and, 123
  Entebbe raid and, 206–8
  Jewish historical link to, 67–68
  Jewish refugees absorbed by, 114, 116–17
  Jordanian war on terrorists and, 174
  Knesset of, 113, 190
  Likud party of, 212
  Mapai party of, 81
  National Religious party of, 146
  1948 war and, 108–13, 157
  1967 war and, 145–48, 406, 407
  1973 war and, 187–88, 391, 423
  nuclear capability of, 188, 391, 405, 406–8, 412
  origins of name of, 67, 108
  police of, 31, 36, 50
  proclaimed a state, 107–8, 137
  reprisals for terrorist attacks on, 124, 125, 143, 145, 153–56, 184–85, 189, 191–95
  UN approval of Palestinian partition, 91–92
  U.S. recognizes, 107–8
  See also Jewish terrorist groups; Jews; Mossad L'Tafkidim Meyubadim, Ha; Palestine (before May 13, 1948)
Israeli National Water Carrier, 141
Issa, Mohammed, 153
Issues and Answers (ABC-TV), 212
Issues Raised by M.I.T. Training of Iranian Students in Nuclear Engineering (leaflet), 408
Italy, 32, 179, 197, 236, 237, 353, 354
  Balfour Declaration and, 70
  nuclear weapons and, 409, 412, 417
  police of, 181
  terrorist activities in, 183
  World War II and, 77, 78
  See also names of cities

Jabber, Mihdi el-, 59
Jaber, Abd el-Rahim, 150
Jaber, Fayez Abdul Rahim, 204
Jabhat Tharir Filistin. *See* Palestinian Liberation Front
Jabotinsky, Vladimir, 74–75, 80
Jack, Alan, 349
Jacobs, Dr. Johannes, 250–51
Jacobson, Eddie, 92
Ja'far, 121
Jaffa, Palestine, 70, 72, 80, 81, 94, 104
Jalloud, Abdul Salem, 18, 406
Janda, Josef, 3, 5, 6, 7

Japan, 26–32, 33–39, 58, 159, 180, 221, 228, 406, 409, 411, 412. *See also names of cities*
Japan Air Lines, 31, 34–35
Japanese United Red Army (URA), 22, 26–32, 33–39, 58, 159, 180, 228, 406
Jamil, Nasser ben, 164
Jarring, Dr. Gunnar, 165
Jarum el-Sheik, Sinai, 131
Java, 79
Jedid, General, 144
Jenkins, Brian, 384–85
Jenkins, Roy, 365
Jenson, Linda, 171
Jerusalem, Israel, 93, 97, 98, 105, 128, 135
  British leave, 107
  fighting in, 70–73
  as holy city to Jews and Muslims, 68, 70–71, 124
  1948 war and, 113
  Palestinian partition and, 90, 92, 93, 104, 106
  terrorism in, 80, 83, 95, 96, 104, 150, 157
Jessup, Philip, 108
Jewish Agency
  in Austria, 187
  in Palestine, 74, 76, 78, 81, 82, 83, 84, 95, 107, 108, 110
  in Paris, 185
Jewish Executive, 82
Jewish Foundation Fund, 95
Jewish terrorist groups, 74–113 *passim*
  Ben-Gurion and, 82, 83, 107, 109–11, 112–13
  See also Hagana; Irgun Zevai Leumi; Mossad L'Tafkidim Meyabadim, Ha; Stern Gang
Jewish Workers Council, 102
Jews, 33, 58
  Arab evacuation and, 101–5
  driven from Arab states, 114–17
  First Temple of, 68
  historical link of, to Israel, 67–68
  immigration of to Palestine, 69, 73, 74, 75–76, 77–78, 82, 84, 85, 86–87, 88, 90
  Nazi Germany and, 73, 77–78, 79, 81, 114
  Second Temple of, 68, 70
  separated from non-Jews on hijacked planes, 169, 205
  violence following partition vote and, 92–100, 104
  See also Israel and Israelis; Palestine
Jibril, Ahmed, 18, 139, 144, 152
Jiménez, Marcos Pérez, 23
Johnson, Herschel, 91, 92
Johnson, Paul, 385
Jordan, 20, 21, 25, 32, 88, 105, 126, 151, 210, 228
  attacks against Israel from, 124, 125, 141, 142, 143, 145, 157–58
  crackdown of on terrorists, 143, 160, 169–70, 172–74, 176, 177, 178, 179, 186, 202, 229
  Israeli reprisal attack on, 153–54
  1967 war and, 146, 147
  Palestinian refugees in, 114, 117, 119, 133, 162–63
  PLO covenant and, 137
  terrorists dominate, 161–64, 168–69

Jordan River, West Bank of, 140, 148, 149–50, 188, 210, 212
Jumblatt, Kamal, 197, 198, 201
Junschke, Klaus, 246, 250
Just Assassin (Camus), 381
Just the Other Day (Collier), 280

Kadari, Abd al-, 152, 160
Kailani, Mohammed Rasul el-, 143
Kanafani, Anni, 191–92
Kanafani, Fayez, 191–92
Kanafani, Ghassan, 191–92
Kanafani, Laina, 192
Kanafani, Lamees, 191–92
Kano, Khader, 32, 193
Kapital, Das (Marx), 54
Kaplan, Dora, 381
Karameh, Jordan, 153–54
Kastel, Palestine, 97
Kato, Yoshitaka, 29
Katzir, Ephraim, 406
Kauwakji, Fauzi ed-Din el-, 89, 94, 96, 127
Keatings, Neil F., 312
Keenan, Sean, 301–3, 323–24, 327–32, 340, 354
    family of, 328, 331–32
Kelly, Eileen, 349
Kendall, Henry W., 422
Kennedy, Edward, 357, 358
Kennedy, Robert, 170
Kenny, Sean, 334
Kenya, 88, 206, 208
Kenyatta, Jomo, 206
Kfar Darom, Palestine, 106
Kfar Etzio, Palestine, 93–94, 95–96, 104
Kfar Szold, Palestine, 96
KGB, 21, 22, 23, 24, 25, 32, 57, 193
Khalaf, Salah, 21, 132, 143, 176, 177, 181, 203
Khaled (member of OPEC raiding team), 7, 17, 18, 19
Khaled, Leila, 31, 103, 159–60, 165–67, 168, 170, 173, 174
Khalid, King of Saudi Arabia, 19
Khalifa, Muhamed Ibrahim, 152, 160
Khan, Aga, 123
Khan, Mangu, 123
Khartoum, Sudan, 8, 32, 178, 185–86
Khatib, Ubayd Allal al-, 123
Kheir, Abdul, 193
Khrushchev, Nikita, 22
Khuri, Twfik, 132
Kilani, Rashid Ali al-, 78
Kilmichael, County Cork, Ireland, 279–80
Kimche, John, 201
Kimchi, 84
Kirov, Sergei, 381
Kissinger, Henry, 40, 63, 188, 189, 190, 200, 406, 410, 423
Kitchener, Lord, 274
Klein, Hans-Joachim, 7, 9, 11, 14–15, 20, 39–40, 54, 61, 387, 388
Kloten Airport, Switzerland, 155
Knash, Suleiman al-, 121
Kolesnik, Dmitri N., 388
Konkret (magazine), 219, 222, 226, 234
Koran, 114, 116, 189
Kotov, Yuri, 25, 32

Koubaissi, Basil, 54, 193
Krabbe, Hanna Elisa, 40, 42
Kraft, Joseph, 113
Kreisky, Bruno, 11–12, 14, 187
Kroecher-Tiedemann, Gabriele, 14, 40
    Entebbe and, 61, 62, 203–5, 207
    on flight from Vienna, 15, 16
    raid at OPEC conference and, 4, 5–6, 10, 54, 61, 203
    terrorist background of, 4
Kuhlmann, Brigitte, 39, 42, 51
Kunzelmann, Dieter, 227
Kurzman, Dan, 93
Kuwait, 6, 36, 63, 131, 133, 141, 151, 175, 177, 195, 202, 203, 205

Laffin, John, 120, 143, 179, 189, 191, 316
Lang, Joerg, 246, 256
Lang-Gons, West Germany, 40
Laqueur, Walter, 424
Lara, Maria Teresa, 19, 47, 48, 55, 57, 58
Larra Zamora, Pedro, 57
Larson, Clarence E., 391
Lasky, Melvin J., 221, 365*n*
Latif, Adil Abd, 105
Latrun, Palestine, 83
Lawless, Gary, 352
Lawrence, T. E., 69, 162
League Against Imperialism, 355
League of Nations, 70, 73, 76–77, 88
Lebanon, 8, 20, 25, 26, 88, 92, 151
    al-Fatah and, 132, 141, 174–75, 198, 208–9
    civil war in, 187, 194, 198–203
    Israeli reprisal attacks on, 153, 185, 189
    until 1975, 197–98
    Palestinian refugees and, 64, 117, 119
    Phalangist party of, 198–99
    police of, 36, 49, 50, 160
    as terrorist base, 151, 174, 197, 198, 244
    URA and, 27, 29, 33
    See also names of cities
Leila, Omar Abu-, 148
Leinhauser, Günther, 356
Leleu, Jean-Mariel, 57
Lemass, Sean, 291, 292
Lenin, Nikolai, 6, 23, 221, 381
Leonard, Paul, 332
Leonardo da Vinci Airport, Rome, 62–63, 179
Leopolder, Kurt, 7
Leventhal, Paul L., 407
Liberia, 91
Libya, 6, 9, 13, 16, 18, 20, 52, 205
    Jews driven from, 115
    Northern Ireland and, 355–56
    nuclear weapons and, 405–6, 407, 412
    terrorist groups and, 139, 151, 159, 175, 177, 179, 183–84, 316
Life (magazine), 154, 157
Lilienthal, David E., 414
Limerick Prison, 365–66
Lindehof Bunker, Zurich, 235
Lingen prison, 250
Lloyd George, David, 280, 281–82
Lod, Palestine, 81, 93
Lod International Airport, Tel Aviv, terrorist massacre at, 30–31, 34, 35, 37, 159, 179, 180, 189, 379

Lohamei Herut Yisrael (Fighters for the Freedom of Israel). *See* Stern Gang
London, England, 41, 50, 57, 185, 196, 294, 366–67, 386
  Carlos in, 24, 25–26, 32, 33, 42–46, 58, 61, 62, 204
  police of, 32, 46, 59–60, 61, 167
London Daily Mirror (newspaper), 353
Londonderry, Northern Ireland, 299–304, 305, 307, 311, 314, 323, 332, 334, 335, 338, 343, 345
  Bloody Sunday (1972), 341–43, 354, 373
Londonderry Prison, 327
London *Economist* (newspaper), 102
London *Evening Standard* (newspaper), 103
London *Guardian* (newspaper), 59
London Jewish *Chronicle* (newspaper), 46
London *Observer* (newspaper), 22
London School of Economics, 26, 60
London *Sunday Times* (newspaper), 241, 293, 366
London *Times* (newspaper), 330
Long Kesh prison camp, 330–31, 332, 345
Lorenz, Peter, 4, 40, 41, 227, 252, 253
Los Alamos, 396
Los Alamos Primer (AEC), 396
Los Angeles Times (newspaper), 113, 119, 170, 198, 386, 387
Lotta Continua, 197, 354
Loyalist Association of Workers, 340
Lufthansa Airlines, 63, 180, 183
Luther, Angela, 227, 237, 251
Lynch, Jack, 302, 335, 336, 338, 342–43

Maalot, Israel, 189
McAliskey, Bernadette. *See* Devlin, Bernadette
McBride, Sean, 387
MacCarthy, Jack, 357
McCaughey, Dougald, 333
McCoy Air Force Base, 389
McCraig, Joseph and John, 333
McDade, James, 348
McFeely, William, 339–40
MacGiolla, Tomas, 298, 306, 311, 334
McGirl, John Joe, 308
McGlade, Charlie, 308
McGuire, Maria, 334, 355, 357
McGurk's Bar, Belfast, 267–68
McGurran, Malachy, 334
Machado, Gustavo, 22
McIlroy, Joe, 344
McKelvey, Joseph, 284
McKinley, William, 380
McKnight, Gerald, 177–78, 191, 192, 351
McMahon, Sir Henry, 69, 79, 88
MacMillan, Gen. Sir Gordon, 96–97, 112
Macmillan, Liam, 334
McNearn, Rosaleen, 267–68
MacNeill, Eoin, 275
McPhee, John, 391, 396, 398, 400
MacStiofain, Sean, 308, 333, 334, 339, 351, 355
McWhirter, Ross, 358
Madrid, Spain, 32, 34, 61
Maghribi, Bashir el-, 143
Maguire, Anne, and family, 350
Maguire, Louis, 355

Maguire, Maureen, 153–54, 213
Maguire, Tom, 307
Maheishy, Omar, 184
Maheu, René, 121
Mahler, Horst, 25, 222, 225, 228–29, 230–31, 235, 236, 240
Maidstone (ship), 330
Majali, Habes, 169
Mallon, Kevin, 332, 366, 367
Malta, 73
Malvern Street murders, Belfast, 313–14
Mandel, Ernest, 196, 352
Mangold, Tom, 360, 365*n*
Manhattan District History, Project Y, the Alamos Project, 396
Manhattan Project, 389, 400, 401
Mann, Ginger, 362–63, 365*n*
Mao Tse-tung and Maoism, 22, 27, 28, 39, 60, 151, 221, 385
Marcuse, Herbert, 221, 225
Marighella, Carlos, 197, 221, 229–30, 234, 383
Marino Muller, Edgar José, 53
Marshall, Gen. George, 108
Martínez Torres, Carlos Andres. *See* Ramírez Sánchez, Ilich (Carlos)
Marwan, Abu, 150
Mashia, Asher, 182
Marxism, 27, 39, 47, 54, 118, 134, 158, 221, 269, 359, 360, 380, 385
  IRA and, 294, 306, 309, 310, 311, 333, 340, 352
Mashma, Mohammed, 144
Massachusetts Institute of Technology (M.I.T.), 389, 408, 409, 420, 422
Materot, Jean, 353
Maulding, Reginald, 338
Mauritania, 21
Mauritius, 86
Mecca, Saudi Arabia, 68
Medina, Saudi Arabia, 68
Meier, Claude, 32, 235–36
Meinhof, Ulrike, 24, 39, 40, 41, 56, 182, 224, 233–42 *passim*
  arrested, 238–39
  background of, 218–22
  brain surgery of, 219, 220
  disagreements with Baader and, 224, 232, 262–63
  death of, 217–18, 262–63
  hunger strike by, 245, 251
  in prison, 240–42, 245, 252
  radicalization of, 222, 226, 227–28
  revolutionary writings of, 231–32
  training of, 228–29
  trials of, 242, 253–63
Meins, Holger, 236, 237, 238, 247–50
Meir, Golda, 178, 187–88, 194, 212, 406
Mellows, Liam, 284, 306
Melville, Albert, 107
Menezes, Certania, 57
Metropolitan Edison Company, Harrisburg, Pa., nuclear power plant, 417–18
Mexico, 208
Meyer, Armin, 194
Meyer-Lindenberg, Herman, 42
Michel, Ellinor, 223
Michelsen, Alphonso Lopez, 60

Michener, James A., 119–20
Middle East, 4, 8, 14, 16, 24, 32, 55, 61, 63, 67–213, 423
  Deir Yassin's significance to, 99
  history of, to twentieth century, 67–68
  OPEC raid's effects on, 20–21
  origin of fighting in, 70–75
  URA and, 27, 28, 29
  See also Arabs; Arab states; Arab terrorists; Jewish terrorists; Jews; Palestinian refugees; Palestinian terrorists; *names of countries*
Midway Island, 415
Midweek (BBC), 365*n*
Miesau, West Germany, 39, 58
Mikuteit, Reinhod, 253
Mini-Manual of Guerrilla Warfare (Marighella), 229–30, 383
Minute (magazine), 39, 59
MIR, 57
Mirbach, Count von, 381
Mitre research firm, 417
Moabit Prison, West Berlin, 242
Moeller, Ingrid, 237
Mohammad, Prophet, 68, 70, 114, 123
Mohammed Boudia Commandos, 41
Mohsen, Zuheir, 209–10
Mollet, Guy, 126
Montevideo, Uruguay, 62
Montreal, Quebec, 62, 386
Moore, George C., 185
Mori, Tsuneo, 28–29
Morocco, 20–21, 115, 179
Morris, Joe Alex, 113, 198
Moscow, U.S.S.R., 34, 152
Mossad L'Tafkidim Meyubadim, Ha (Institution for Special Tasks), 7, 21, 25, 32, 36, 62, 148, 159, 160, 191–96, 206, 207–8
Moukarbel, Michel Wahab, 33, 38, 39, 40, 49–50, 50–53, 58, 60
Mountjoy Prison, 332, 333, 366
Mount Scopus, Palestine, 105–6
Moyne, Lord, 79–80, 112
Moynihan, Daniel P., 190–91
Mueller, Gerhard, 232, 237
Mulcahy, P., 308
Muller Bernal, Adolfo José. *See* Ramírez Sánchez, Ilich (Carlos)
Munich, West Germany, 226, 237
  Olympic Village attack in, 32, 177, 178, 179, 181–83, 184, 185, 194, 196, 205, 402, 403, 408
Munn, Tracy, 344
Münster, West Germany, 377
Murray, "Big Mick," 349
Musah, Ahmed, 141
Muslim Brotherhood, 106, 123, 126, 127, 128–31, 133, 152
Muslims, 68, 70, 71–72, 79, 104, 114–15, 174, 197–203. *See also* Islam; Koran
Mussin, Zuhayr, 154
Mussolini, Benito, 78, 198
Muzairib, Syria, 155
My People Shall Live (Khaled), 159–60, 165

Nabhani, Sheikh Taqi el-Din el-, 133
Nabulsi, Suleiman, 162

Nacional, El (newspaper), 22
Nader, Ralph, 418
Nagasaki, Japan, 397, 398, 399–400
Nagata, Hiroko, 28–29
Naguib, Gen. Mohammed, 129–31
Nahal Soreq Research Center, 406
Najar, Mohammed Abdel, 105, 106
Najar, Yussif al- (Abu Yussif), 132, 177, 179, 193
Napier, Oliver, 339, 342
Nashashibi family, 84
Nasralla, Elias, 158
Nasser, Gamal Abdel, 106, 116–17, 119, 123, 126, 127, 134, 139, 194
  death of, 176
  1967 war and, 145–47
  "Palestinian state" and, 133, 135
  terrorism and, 124, 125, 128, 129–31, 133, 135, 143, 144, 151, 175, 198
Nasser, Kamal, 193
Nasser, Walid Arab, 143
Natanya, Palestine, 82
National Council of Jews in Palestine, 80
National Front of the Liberation of Palestine, 134
National Liberation Front, 139, 384
National Liberation Organization, 130
NATO, 397, 415
Nedim, Hamid, 190
Netanyahu, Yonatan, 206, 207
Netherlands, 38–39, 85, 89, 353, 409, 412
Neue Zuericher Zeitung (newspaper), 119, 217
New Republic (magazine), 201, 203, 356, 381
Newsweek (magazine), 169–70, 172, 198, 199
New York City, 386–87, 421–22
New Yorker, The (magazine), 396
New York Times (newspaper), 63, 132, 154, 386, 406–7
New Zionist Organization, 75
Nicosia, Cyprus, 32
Niepel, Frank, 246
Nigeria, 16
Nimri, Kamal, 148
1948 Arab-Israeli war, 102, 103, 105, 108–13, 123, 157
1967 Arab-Israeli war, 70, 115, 119, 145–48, 194, 210, 212, 406, 407
1973 Arab-Israeli war, 52, 187–88, 391, 423
Nishikawa, Yun, 34–39
Nixon, Richard, 178, 407, 409, 414, 423
Nochodka, U.S.S.R., 34
Nokrashy Pasha, 129, 130
NorAid (Irish Northern Aid Committee), 356
Northern Ireland, 233, 267–374
  Alliance party of, 321, 339, 346, 347
  British help sought by, 299–300, 303, 308–9
  B Specials of, 301, 302, 317–18, 363, 366
  Democratic Union party (DUP) of, 346
  direct rule imposed on, 344–46
  European aid for, 335, 339, 353–55, 357
  future of, 368–74
  inhuman treatment in prisons of, 331
  Irish home rule and, 271–74, 280, 281–82
  Loyalists of, 269–70, 315, 316, 321, 322, 347, 352, 369, 371
  1969 riots and, 299–307, 310
  1970 violence in, 334–37

1971 violence in, 337–39
1972 violence in, 339–46
1973 plebiscite in, 346
Social Democratic Labour party of, 303, 315, 321, 330, 340, 346, 347
Unionists in, 314, 321, 337, 346, 347
UPNA of, 321
Vanguard Unionist Progressive party (VUPP) of, 346
See also Ireland, Republic of; Irish Republican Army; names of cities
Northern Ireland Assembly, 346, 347
Northern Ireland Civil Rights Association (NICRA), 294–97, 298, 300, 302, 309, 317, 341–42, 355
Northern Ireland Constitutional Act, 346
Northern Ireland Executive, 346, 347
Northern Ireland: The Orange State (Farrell), 352
North Korea, 175, 196, 228
Norway, 407–8
Nubazi, Bazim el-, 204
Nuclear Fuel Services reprocessing plant, West Valley, N.Y., 397
Nuclear Non-Proliferation Treaty (NPT), 405, 406, 409, 412
Nuclear Regulatory Commission (NRC), 390–91, 392, 395, 402, 403, 413, 417, 420
nuclear weapons and terrorists, 387–425
Numeiry, Jaafar, 183, 186

O Bradaigh, Ruairi, 286–90, 298, 307–8, 310–12, 324, 325–27, 333, 339, 340, 354, 355, 367, 370–71
O Bradaigh, Sean, 308, 353
O'Brien, Conor Cruise, 336, 368, 373
O'Connell, Daithi, 316, 333, 334, 349
O'Connor, Michelle, 349
O'Connor, Rory, 283, 284, 306
Odessa, U.S.S.R., 23
O'Donnell, Father Columb, 268, 306
O'Dwyer, Paul, 357
O'Farrell, Elizabeth, 277
Ogilvy, Ann, 322
O'Hagan, John, 332
O'Higgins, Kevin, 284–85
Ohnesorge, Benno, 40
Okamoto, Kozo, 30–31, 32, 182, 189, 205, 379
Okamoto, Takeshi, 31
Okudaira, Tsuyoshi, 29–31
Old Man of the Mountain and his Assassins, 121–23, 379
Olympia airlines, 156
O'Malley, Desmond, 324–25
Oman, 177
Omar
  caliphate of, 68
  Covenant of, 114–15
  Mosque of, 124
O'Neill, Terence, 291, 292, 293, 297, 300, 314, 315, 343
Operation Hilton, 64
Operation Magic Carpet, 116
Organization for Shattering Settlement Programs, 120
Organization for Victims of Zionist Occupation, 180

Organization of Petroleum Exporting Countries (OPEC), 10
  negotiations to free members of, 8, 9–14, 18–19
  results and aftermath of raid of, 20–21
  Vienna conference, raid at, 3–8, 16, 39, 54, 58, 61, 184, 203
Organization of the Sons of Occupied Territories, 35
Orlando, Fla., 389
Orly Airport, Paris, 4, 36, 40–41, 51
Otaola, Angela, 43–46, 49, 54, 58, 59–60, 61

Page, Ralph G., 390–91
Paisley, Ian, 292–94, 297, 299, 304, 311, 313, 314, 337, 339, 343, 346, 347, 350–51, 370, 372
Paisley, J. Kyle, 293
Pakistan, 138, 142, 405, 409, 410, 412
Palace Barracks, Northern Ireland, 331
Palestine, 61, 384
  as British mandate, 70–92
  British withdrawal from, 107
  history of, to World War I, 67–68
  Jewish immigration into. See Jews, immigration into Palestine
  origin of Arab-Israeli fighting in, 70–75
  partition of, 84, 86, 87, 88, 89–101
  See also Arabs; Israel and Israelis (as of May 13, 1948), Jews; Palestinian refugees
Palestine (newspaper), 105
Palestine Arab party, 89
Palestine Emergency Regulations, 88
Palestine Liberation Army (PLA), 142, 173–74, 175
Palestine Liberation Organization (PLO), 13, 20–21, 128, 144, 151, 175, 187, 188, 194, 211, 212, 213
  covenant of, 135–38
  Cuba and, 57
  Executive Committee of, 138–39, 161, 211
  founding of, 135–39
  Jordan and, 21, 164, 173, 174
  Lebanon civil war and, 199, 200, 202, 203
  1969 changes in, 160–61
  UN and, 190
Palestine National Council, 1977 meeting of, 209–10, 211, 212
Palestine Popular Struggle Front, 156
Palestinian Alumni Federation, 130
Palestinian Liberation Front, 134, 144, 150, 152
Palestinian Library, Paris, 192
Palestinian Military Organization, 134
Palestinian National Congress, 135, 139, 143, 144
Palestinian Post (newspaper), 80, 95
Palestinian Rebels Front of Mohammed Abu Sakhila, 134
Palestinian refugees, 20, 25, 26, 32, 61, 64, 113–14, 117–20, 124, 355
  as issue in Middle East, 101, 113
  Jordan's crackdown on terrorists and, 170, 172, 173
  number of, 113–14, 117
  reasons for evacuating, 101–5
  See also Palestinian terrorist groups

Palestinian Revolutionary Movement, 134
Palestinians, The (Smith), 104–5
Palestinian state, 8, 16, 20, 133, 135, 145, 155, 161, 188, 190, 210, 211, 212–13, 385
Palestinian Student Federation, 130
Palestinian terrorist groups, 7, 8, 22, 113, 114, 119, 133–34, 385
  backing from Arab states for, 125, 127–45 *passim,* 151, 154, 155, 159, 161, 173, 175, 177, 179, 183–84, 190, 195–96, 199
  hijacking by, 153, 156, 159, 165–72, 173, 174, 179–80, 203–8
  motivation of, 62–64
  in 1970, numbers and support for, 175
  rise of, 127–45, 148–64, 175–86, 188
  See also Arab terrorist groups; *names of groups*
Palmah, 74, 81, 82, 111
Palme, Olof, 41
Palomares Duque, Lema, 53, 57, 58
Pan American Airlines, 168, 204
Paris, France, 19, 26, 30, 32, 33, 36–37, 40, 41, 42, 45, 47, 49, 51–52, 54–55, 57, 59, 62, 185, 192, 193, 195, 196, 386
Parliament Act of 1911, 272
Parnell, Charles, 271
Pastore, John O., 389
Patria (ship), 86
Pavelić, Ante, 380
Pearse, Padraic, 276, 277
People for Peace movement, 350–51
People's Democracy, 294, 298, 311, 352, 353, 354, 355
Peres, Shimon, 212, 406
Perry, R. J., 164
Peru, 85, 89
Philadelphia Inquirer (newspaper), 358
Philippines, 91, 415
Phillips, John Aristotle, 389–90
Pinochet, Augusto, 22, 62
Pinsker, Leon, 68
Plottnitz, Rupert von, 232, 256
Po'ale Zion, 107
Poland, 74, 80, 107, 119
Polisarios, 21
Political Dictionary of the Middle East in the Twentieth Century, 198
Politics of Palestinian Nationalism (Quandt), 175
Pollak, Manfred, 15–19
Poniatowski, Michel, 22, 57, 58
Popular Democratic Front for the Liberation of Palestine (PDFLP), 139, 152, 155, 159, 164, 174, 175, 188, 189, 195, 198, 354
Popular Front for the Liberation of Palestine (PFLP), 4, 18, 25, 26, 32, 50, 54, 61, 139, 151–59 *passim,* 161, 178, 180, 183, 188, 191, 195, 198, 203, 209, 355
  founding of, 134
  hijackings by, 153, 156, 159, 165–72, 173, 174
  Hussein and, 163–64, 170, 172, 174
  Lebanon civil war and, 199
  in 1970, 175
  Orly Airport attack and, 40–41
  Second of June movement and, 40
  URA and, 27, 30, 31, 36

Popular Front for the Liberation of Palestine— General Command, 139, 152, 156, 164, 175, 188
Porras, Carlos, 24
Porter, Nancy, 169
Portlaoise Prison, Ireland, 332
Portugal, 405, 412
Poverty of Power, The (Commoner), 420
Prawitz, Dr. Jan, 389
Prendergast, Curtis, 339
Price, D. L., 315
Price, Dolours, 326, 354, 365
Price, Marion, 326, 365
Price-Anderson Act, 421
Priddy, Jack, 168
Prinzing, Theodor, 257–61
Proctor, Fred, 306
Progressive (magazine), 419n
Proll, Astrid, 241–42
Proll, Thorwald, 222
Protestants, 378
  in Northern Ireland, 267–374 *passim*
  Orange Order and Orange Parade and, 269–70, 271, 297, 300, 301, 313, 318, 336, 345, 357
Protestant Telegraph (newspaper), 350–51
Protocols of the Learned Elders of Zion, The, 70
Proudhon, Pierre, 379
Provisional Irish Republican Army. *See* Irish Republican Army, Provisional
Pryce-Jones, David, 203
P'yongyang, North Korea, 31, 196

Qaddafi, Muammar, 13, 14, 18, 20, 32, 33, 54, 115, 116, 159, 177, 179, 183–84, 187, 192, 199, 355, 405–6
Qaddumi, Faruq el- (Abu Lutuf), 132, 210
Qassem, Abd-ul-Karim, 121, 133
Qiryat Shmonah, Israel, 188

Raanan, Mordechai, 97–99
Rabat, Morocco, 20, 35
Rabin, Yitzhak, 202, 206, 208, 210, 212, 407
Rafa, Palestine, 84
Rafat, Salah, 152
Rahman, Ibad el-, 132, 133
Ramdan, Sa'id, 133
Ramírez, Doña Elba Sánchez (Carlos' mother), 17, 24, 26, 45
Ramírez Navas, Dr. José Altagracia (Carlos' father), 22–24, 26
Ramírez Sánchez, Ilich (Carlos), 3–62, 159, 194, 204, 355
  background and training of, 22–25, 53, 61
  Bouvier and, 25–26, 49, 60–61, 62
  Entebbe and, 204, 205
  Furaya and, 38–39
  identity and aliases of, 17, 26, 30, 32, 46, 58, 62
  as international terrorist, 4, 17, 22, 32–33, 46, 57, 58–59, 62, 193
  negotiations with Austrian government and, 8, 9–14
  nuclear weapons and, 386–87, 406, 416–17
  Paris activities of, 22, 30, 32, 38–39, 40, 41, 42, 46–59 *passim*

raid at OPEC conference and, 4, 5, 7, 21, 61, 184
Reinders and, 40–42
terrorist reputation of, 4, 13, 17
Western European governments and, 17, 19–20, 62, 387
women as "helpers" for, 23, 26, 33, 42–61
Ramírez Sánchez, Lenin (Carlos' brother), 23
Ramírez Sánchez, Vladimir (Carlos' brother), 23
Ramla, Palestine, 72, 73
Rand Corporation, 384–85
Rasch, Wildred, 260
Rasd, Jihaz al-, 176, 177, 179
Rasmussen, Dr. Norman, 420, 421
Raspe, Jan-Carl, 236, 238, 242, 251, 252, 253–63
Rauf, Ahmad, 160
Rawenduzy, Dr. Wiriya, 14–17
Ray, Dixie Lee, 409–10
Raziel, David, 75, 80
Red Army Faction. See Baader-Meinhof gang
Red Cross, 150, 202
Red Hand, 134
Red Hand Commandos, 316
Redmond, John, 271, 273, 274, 275
Red Star, 39
Rees, Merlyn, 315, 329, 347
Regulary, Robert, 173
Reinders, Ralf, 40, 41, 42, 226–27, 244, 245, 251, 262
Rengo Sekigun. See United Red Army
Research Council of the Center for Strategic and International Studies in Washington, 424
Reuter's, 38, 41
Revolutionary Catechism (Nechayev), 382
Revolutionary Marxist Group, 352
"Revolutionary Studies" (pamphlet), 138
Reyes Herrera, Ernesto, 57
Reynier, Dr. Jacques de, 96
Rhodesia, 184
Ribicoff, Abraham, 358, 401, 405, 407, 414
Riemeck, Renate, 218, 227, 228, 234
Ritchie, Charles, 312
Rodewald, Fritz, 238–39
Roding, Horst, 410
Rodriguez Sainz, Paul, 57
Roehl, Bettina, 219
Roehl, Klaus Reiner, 218–20, 226, 227, 228, 235, 239
Roehl, Regine, 219, 228
Roehl, Wolfgang, 220
Rogers, William P., 212
Romano, Yosef, 181–82
Romans, Palestine and, 67–68, 70
Rome, Italy, 30, 31–32, 42, 62–63, 153, 179, 192, 193, 204
Romero, Maria, 43, 45, 54, 57, 60–61
Rometsch, Rudolf, 412–14
Rommel, Erwin, 78, 79, 106
Rosenbaum, David A., 401–2, 403, 404, 413, 423–24
Rote Armee Faktion. See Baader-Meinhof gang
Rote Armee Faktion-Aufbau Organisation (RAF-AO), 243

Rothschild, Lord Lionel Walter, 69
Rotterdam, Netherlands, 179
Rowden, Marcus A., 392–93
Royal Irish Constabulary (RIC), 278–79, 318
Royal Irish Rifles, 276
Royal Jordanian Army, 168, 169–70, 171, 172–74
Royal Ulster Constabulary (RUC), 287, 297, 300–304, 311, 314–18, 322, 328, 330, 331, 339, 340, 349–50, 368, 370
Ruhmkorf, Peter, 220
Ryan (IRA member), 306
Ryan, Sean, 355

Sabena Airlines, 179
Sabri, Dr. Ismail, 131
Sacred Fighters, 94–97, 109, 128
Sadat, Anwar el-, 8, 20, 116, 175–76, 182, 183, 210, 211
Sadat, Gihane el-, 58
Sa'edi, Gholam Hussein, 409
Sahara, Spanish, 21
Sahm el-Julan, Syria, 155
Said, Nuri, 121
Sa'iqa, al-, 139, 154–55, 175, 201, 209
Saladin, 123
Salam, Mustafa Abd el-, 154–55
Salam, Saeb, 194
Salameh, Ali Hassan, 176, 177, 179, 194, 195, 408
Salameh, Sheikh Ali Hassan, 176, 194
Salazar, Albaida, 57, 58
Saleh, Mahmoud, 195
Salem, Abu, 186
Salewski, Wolfgang, 224
Sampson, Nicos, 352
Sanchez, Nancy, 46–49, 52, 53, 55, 57
Sandia research firm, 417
Sandler, Richard H., 419n
Sandstrom, Emil, 85
Saor Ulandh, 287
Sarkis, Elias, 209
Sartre, Jean-Paul, 6, 221, 232, 251–52
Sauber, Werner, 235–36
Saudi, Muna, 159
Saudi Arabia, 6, 7, 13, 19, 20, 21, 68, 124, 135, 138, 151, 175, 177, 186, 195, 405, 408, 412
Saunders, James, 337
Saunders, Major, 72
Schaz, Ulrike, 57
Schily, Otto, 239, 240–41, 246–47, 256, 257, 259, 261, 262
Schmidt, Dana Adams, 97, 132, 154, 157, 161, 189
Schmidt, Helmut, 25, 41, 252–53, 255
Schmidt-Voigt, Dr. Jorgen, 242
Schmücker, Ulrich, 244–45
Schneider, Barry, 415–16
Schoenau transit camp, Russia, 11
Science Action Coordinating Committee (SACC), 408
Scotland, 374
Scotland Yard, 54
Season in Hell, A (Rimbaud), 31
Second of June movement, 4, 40, 41–42, 51, 226, 244, 252, 255, 262
Secret Army, The (Bell), 275

Secrets of the Assassination of the Royal Family of Iraq (Hanzal), 121
Senard, Count Jacques, 38
Serbia, 274, 380
Seventh Asian Games, Teheran, 36
Shaker, Zaid ben, 164
Shaltiel, David, 98–99
Shanear, Leo, 153
Shapiro, Joseph, 417–18
Sharabi, Hisham, 148, 154
Sharif, Bassam Abu, 170, 192
Sharm al-Sheikh, 146, 147, 207
Sharon, Gen., 188
Sharon area, Palestine, 104
Shaw Commission, 73
Shawi, Dr. Mahmoud, 131
Shell Oil refinery, Singapore, 36
Shemali, Faud, 179
Sherif, Kamel Isma'il el-, 133
Shieb, Israel, 112
Shigenobu, Fusako, 26–30, 32, 33–39 *passim*
Shiite Islam, 121
Shukeiri, Ahmed, 135, 137, 142, 144, 146, 160
Shyein, Mohammed Mustafa, 179
Sidky, Azi, 182
Sieff, J. Edward, 33, 46
Sieger, Walter, 235
Siepmann, Ingrid, 25, 226–27, 228–29
Silva Masmela, Ampara, 38, 54, 58, 59, 205
Simferopol, Russia, 23
Simonov, Col. Victor, 23
Singapore, 36
Sinn Fein Republican movement, 273, 275, 277, 278, 279, 281–82, 284, 286, 289, 290, 306, 307, 309, 310, 320, 323, 324, 353
    caretaker Executive of, 307, 315, 354
    Official, 334, 355
    Provisional Army Council of, 307–8, 333–34, 335, 353, 363, 364, 366
Sirhan, Sirhan, 170, 186
Six-Day War. *See* 1967 Arab-Israeli war
Sixty Minutes (CBS-TV), 409
Smith, Christine K., 322
Smith, Colin, 104–5, 113
Smith, F. E., 274
Smith, Hardin, 318
Smyth, Clifford, 293
Smyth, Sammy, 295, 304–5, 317–21, 322, 370, 371–74
Socialist Patients' Collective, 226
Sofia, Bulgaria, 177, 181
Sohaily, Mohammed Ali el-, 13
Sohnlein, Horst, 222, 225
Sokolsky, Tavia, 181
Solzhenitsyn, Alexander, 20
Somali, 51
Soustelle, Jacques, 58
Sout el-Asifa ("The Voice of the Storm"), 143
South Africa, 405, 406, 412
South America, 4, 22, 27, 32, 61, 92, 159, 184, 230–31. *See also names of countries*
South Armagh, Northern Ireland, 348
South Korea, 405, 409, 415
South Yemen, 25, 35, 139, 159, 179
Soviet Union. *See* U.S.S.R.
Sozialistischer Deutscher Studentenbund (SDS), 220–21, 225

Spain, 42, 44, 51, 60, 383, 405, 412. *See also* Basque separatists
Special Night Squads, 75
Spectator (periodical), 191
Springer Publications, 225, 231, 234, 237, 243
Sri Lanka, 184
Stalin, Josef, 381
Stammheim prison, Stuttgart, 9, 242–63 *passim*
Stavsky, Abraham, 110, 111
Stebbens, Henry C., 103
Stephenson, John, 334
Stern, Abraham, 78, 79
Stern Gang, 75, 78, 84, 86, 89, 94, 97–99, 107, 112–13
Stockholm, Sweden, 39, 41, 42, 252, 253, 255
Stockwell, Maj. Gen. Hugh, 99, 103, 104, 120
Stolnitzky, Bezael, 110, 111
Stone, I. F., 105, 114
Strategic Arms Limitation Agreement (1974), 412
Straubing prison, 250
Strictly Illegal (Mardor), 86
Strike Terror (Yaari), 127
Stroebele, Hans-Christian, 232, 245, 246, 256, 257
Struma (ship), 78
Studer, William, 52
Sturm, Beate, 224
Stuttgart, West Germany, Baader-Meinhof trial in, 242, 253–63
Sudan, 183, 184, 186
Süddeutsche Zeitung (newspaper), 256
Suez Canal, 8, 59, 129–30
    blockade of, 123
    nationalization of, 126
    1967 war and, 147
    Yom Kippur War and, 187, 188
Suez War of 1956, 125–27
Sufis, 123, 129
Sunni branch of Islam, 122–23
Sunningdale conference, December 1973, 346–47
Supreme Muslim Council, 71
Sweden, 37, 41–42, 85, 89, 409
Swissair, 156, 168, 169
Switzerland, 38, 179, 235–37, 353, 377, 412
Sylt, Germany, 243
Syria, 18, 20, 69, 78, 88, 92, 94, 105, 121, 152, 185
    attacks against Israel from, 124, 125, 143, 145
    Ba'ath party of, 140, 144, 154, 161, 175
    -Egypt mutual-defense pact, 126, 145
    Hussein and, 163, 173–74
    Jews driven from, 116
    Lebanon civil war and, 200–203
    1967 war and, 145, 147
    1973 war and, 187–88
    Palestinian agreement and, 208
    Palestinian refugees and, 117
    terrorists supported by, 139, 141, 143, 144, 154–55, 175, 190
    See also names of cities
Syrkin, Marie, 104

Tagger, Edith, 339
Tailhade, Laurent, 382

Taiwan, 405
Taketomo, Takahashi, 33, 36, 37
Tal, Wasfi, 169, 174, 175–76, 178
Tal Zaatar, Lebanon, 202, 208
Tashkent, Russia, 23
Taylor, Dr. Theodore B., 395–96, 397, 398–401, 403, 413
Tech (M.I.T. newspaper), 408
Teheran, Iran, 36, 257
Tel Aviv, Israel (after May 13, 1948), 80, 82, 90, 110–11, 125, 153, 155, 190, 195
Tel Aviv, Palestine (before May 13, 1948), 30, 59
Teller, Edward, 421
Terror International, 183–84
terrorism, history of, 377–82
Terrorist Brigade, 381
Teufel, Fritz, 227, 251, 261
Thant, U, 146, 153
Third World, 9, 23, 119, 137, 221, 231, 414
Thomas, Eamon, 308
Thomas, Katie, 159
Thomas, William F., 387
Thornton, Charles, 391
Thursday (student newspaper), 409
Tichler, Anton, 3, 4–6, 10, 16
Time (magazine), 147, 155–56, 171, 172, 178, 187–88, 339, 344, 406
Tirat Zvi, Palestine, 96
Tlas, Mustafa, 203
Tohira, Kuzuo, 38
Tokyo, Japan, 28, 37
Toronto Daily Star (newspaper), 173, 183
To Take Arms (McGuire), 334, 355, 357
Tower of London, bombing of, 348
Tradal, Ramon, 52
Trade Unions Council, 347
Transjordan, 71, 74–75, 86, 162
Transjordanian Arab Legion, 84
Transnational Terror (Bell), 63
Trans World Airlines, 167–69, 386
Traube, Dr. Klaus Robert, 388
Trevelyan, George, 274
Trial and Error (Weizmann), 75
Tripoli, Libya, 13, 17–18, 61, 115, 201, 316, 355
Trotsky, Leon, and Trotskyites, 7, 294, 352, 353, 360, 381
Trotskyite Ligue Communiste, 355
Truman, Harry S, 92, 108
Tunis, Tunisia, 35
Tunisia, 115, 177, 183
Tupamaros, 22, 230, 384
Turkey, 58, 69, 184, 380, 405, 406
Turkish People's Liberation Army, 180
Turkish Popular Liberation Front, 22
Turner, Betty, 359
Twomey, Seamus, 332, 333–34, 344, 345, 364, 366

Uganda, 51, 61, 62, 159, 169, 184, 203–8, 388
Ulrike Meinhof–Puig Antich group, 42
Ulster, Ireland. See Northern Ireland
Ulster Defense Association (UDA), 295, 314–15, 316, 317, 318–22, 371–72, 374
"Romper Room" incident, 322
Ulster Defense Regiment, 368
Ulster Freedom Fighters (UFF), 315, 317
Ulster Unionist Council, 347

Ulster Volunteer Force (UVF), 313–14, 315–16, 317, 373
Ulster Volunteers, 272, 275
Unerreiter, Dr. Florian, 223
Ungar, Peter, 170
United Irishman (Official IRA paper), 334
United Nations (UN), 101, 108, 123, 124, 135, 144, 145, 150, 185, 189, 208, 385, 386
approves partition of Palestine, 91–92, 103, 104
General Assembly of, 57, 137, 189–91, 196, 203, 208
membership of, 384
1967 Arab-Israeli war and, 145–46
nuclear power and terrorism and, 388
Palestinian refugees and, 114, 118, 119
Security Council of, 20, 124, 208
truces in Arab-Israeli fighting and, 112, 113, 147–48, 165, 188
UNESCO, 121, 196
UN Relief and Works Agency (UNRWA), 113, 114, 117–18, 120, 127
UN Special Committee on Palestine (UNSCOP), 84–92
United States, 67, 95, 126, 135, 146, 153, 170–71, 183, 185–86, 190–91, 194, 196, 198, 203, 238, 324–25, 386
Entebbe and, 206, 208
1967 Arab-Israeli war and, 148
1977 Middle East peace efforts, 210–12
Northern Ireland and, 275, 280, 286, 294, 321, 331, 351, 352, 356–58, 373, 374
nuclear energy controls and, 388–404
Palestinian refugees and, 117–18
Qaddafi and, 184
recognizes Israel, 107
State Department of, 91, 92, 107, 108, 388
Suez War and, 127
terrorists of, 159
UN vote on partition of Palestine and, 91–92, 96
See also Central Intelligence Agency; Federal Bureau of Investigation
U.S. Army Physical Security Review Board, 395
U.S. Army Special Forces, 392–93, 416
U.S. Department of Justice, 357
U.S. General Accounting Office (GAO), 393–95, 414, 417
U.S. Supreme Court, 357
United Tokyo-Yokohama Struggle Council Against the U.S.-Japan Security Treaty, 26
Universal Declaration of Human Rights, 387
Urabi, Yussuf, 144
Urban Guerrillas and Class Conflict (Meinhof), 231
Urdaneta Urbina, Luis Angel, 53
Uruguay, 62, 85, 89, 384
Uruguayan Tupamaros, 22, 230, 284
U.S.S.R., 22, 32, 54, 67, 70, 74, 80, 92, 127, 138, 201
Balfour Declaration and, 70
Egypt and, 124–25, 126, 145–46
1967 Arab-Israeli war and, 145–46, 147–48
nuclear weapons and, 405, 409, 411, 414, 416
OPEC raid and, 21
Palestinian refugees and, 118

terrorism in, 380–81
terrorist groups supported by, 23, 139, 148, 151–52, 154, 161, 175, 196, 199, 353, 354
World War I and Russia, 274
Yom Kippur War and, 188
See also KGB; Marxism; names of cities
U Street Traffic Regulation (Mahler), 235
Uyedinyenye Ili Smrt (Black Hand Society), 380
Uyl, Joop den, 38

Vance, Cyrus R., 210
Vanguard of Popular Revolution, 139, 154–55, 175, 201, 209
Venezuela, 4, 11, 16–17, 22, 23, 47, 49, 54, 57
Vesper, Will, 222
Vienna, Austria, 3–8, 15–19, 38, 61, 404
Vietnam, 119, 158, 221, 222, 237
Viett, Inge, 244, 251
Villiers sur Marne, France, 33
von Rauch, Georg, 227
von Rauch, Heinrich, 227
Voyages pour les Jeunes, 57
VZ58, 37

Waldheim, Kurt, 205, 208
Walker, Patrick Gordon, 291–92
Wallace, Mike, 177
Wall Street bombing, 382
Walton, Audrey, 180–81
Waltzer, Michael, 381–82
Warnock, Sheila, 169
Washington Post (newspaper), 178, 208, 386, 387
Watkins, Ruth, 180
Watt, Bernard, 337
Wauchope, Sir Arthur, 74
Wazir, Khalil el- (Abu Jihah), 131–32, 134, 143, 144
Weinberg, Alvin, 422
Weinberg, Moshe, 181
Weingarten, Mordechai, 106, 107
Weingarten, Yehudit, 106–7
Weinrich, Johannes, 39–40
Weizmann, Chaim, 74, 75, 77, 84, 108
Wessel, Ulrich, 41–42
West, Harry, 347
West Berlin, 4, 25, 35, 220–21, 225, 227, 229, 235, 240, 241, 242
Western Europe
  airport security in, 41, 45
  Carlos and, 17, 19–20, 62, 387
  DST warning to, 50
  KGB in, 25
West German-Irish Solidarity Committee, 355
West Germany, 32, 33, 353, 354, 395, 409
  attitude toward terrorism in, 41, 42, 182, 183, 233–34, 252–53
  Carlos and, 19, 20, 50, 62, 178, 179, 180, 386, 388
  Christian Social Union (CSU) of, 255, 256
  Criminal Procedures Act of, 255–56
  Federal Criminal Investigation Department of, 246, 255, 256
  Munich Olympics in. See Black September, attack at Munich Olympic Village
  nuclear weapons and, 410, 411, 412
  Palestinian supporters in, 133, 141, 159, 181
  police of, 17, 39, 51
  Senate Criminal Investigative Committee of, 249–50
  Socialist Democratic party (SDP) of, 255
  terrorist groups of, 4, 39–41, 217–63. See also Baader-Meinhof gang
  URA and, 34
  See also Germany; West Berlin
Westinghouse Corporation, 409
  Apollo, Pa., fuel plant, 390–31, 407–8
White, Nick, 350
Whitelaw, William, 345
Wiker, Haakon, 407
Will, George F., 208
Willard, Margaret, 294–95
Williams, Betty, 350, 351
Wilson, Evan M., 145
Wilson, Harold, 347
Wingate, Orde Charles, 75
Witter, Hermann, 243
Wood, C. D., 167–68
Woodhams, Barry, 42–46, 59–60
World Federation of Democratic Youth, 60
World Union of Zionist Revisionists, 75
World War I, 69, 74, 271, 273, 274, 380
World War II, 75, 77–81, 106, 107, 112, 116, 126, 137, 285–86, 353, 397

Yaffin, Abdullah, 175
Yamamoto, Mariko, 36–37
Yamamoto, Tunichi, 28–29
Yamani, Sheik Ahmed Zaki, 6–7, 8, 13–14, 16–20 passim, 58
Yamani, Maher Hussein al-, 153
Yassın, Fawwaz, 186
Yemen, 116, 146, 180, 196
Yizernitzky, Yitzhak, 112
Yom Kippur
  1973 Arab-Israeli war starting on, 52, 187–88, 391
  Wailing Wall incident on, 71–72
Young Egypt party, 106, 115
Young Socialist Alliance, 352
Young Turks, 363
Youth of Revenge Organization, 150, 152
Yugoslavia, 79, 85, 380, 386–88
Yusef, raid at OPEC and, 4, 6, 7, 161
Yussef, Abu, 95

Zaid, Ahmed, 180
Zavary, Gad, 181
Zengakuren, 26
Zetler, Yehoshua, 98, 112
Zionist Congress, 74, 75, 81
  First, 68
  Twenty-first, 77
Zionist Executive, 74, 75, 107, 108
Zionist Federation of Great Britain, 33
Zionists, 68, 69, 71, 78, 79, 110, 137, 213
  Jewish immigration rate and, 73, 76, 78
  Jewish State party, 77
  revisionists, 74–75, 80, 110
  Stern Gang and, 79–80, 81–82
  UNSCOP and, 85
  UN vote on partition and, 91–92
Zuaite, Wadal Abdul, 192–93
Zurich, Switzerland, 38, 58, 168, 235–36
Zwaiter, Wadal Adel, 32